To my wonderful family and gre

K. D.

To Gordon Schloming,
who stands firmly, feels fully,
and lives in the spirit

B. P.

Contents

Preface

This study is the first book produced by the Russian Littoral Project, sponsored jointly by the University of Maryland at College Park and the Johns Hopkins University's School of Advanced International Studies, and directed by Drs. Dawisha and Parrott.

Both the book and the project emerged from the authors' conviction that the transformation of the former Soviet republics into independent states demands a thorough study of the determinants of the domestic and foreign policies of these new countries. The book and the project attempt to lay the basic groundwork for future study of these issues.

This book is an outgrowth of a November 1992 report written for the U.S. Department of State by Drs. Dawisha and Parrott. Of course, the views contained in the book do not necessarily reflect the views of that department.

The authors wish to acknowledge the superb research assistance of Griffin Hathaway, Petr Lunak, Stephen Guenther, Ibrahim Arafat, and Michael Cully. Florence Rotz spent untold hours assisting in the preparation of the manuscript. For their generosity in reading and commenting on various parts of the manuscript, or in providing materials, the authors would like to thank Muriel Atkin, Bohdan Bociurkiw, Oleg Bukharin, Patricia Carley, Adeed Dawisha, Richard Dobson, Raymond Garthoff, Steven Grant, John Hardt, Dale Herspring, James Millar, Peter Murrell, Ilya Prizel, and Steve Sestanovich. The errors in the book are our own, but we know there are fewer for their assistance.

Karen Dawisha also wishes to thank the U.S. Institute of Peace and the John D. and Catherine T. MacArthur Foundation for individual research awards prior to 1992 that allowed her to begin the collection and analysis of data for the book.

Russian Littoral Project

The objective of the Russian Littoral Project is to foster an exchange of research and information in fields of study pertaining to the international politics of Eurasia. The interaction between the internal affairs and foreign policies of the new states is to be studied in a series of workshops in Washington, D.C., between May 1993 and April 1995. Scholars are invited from the new states, North America, and Europe to present papers at the workshops.

The workshops focus on the following determinants of foreign policy, which correspond to the chapters of this book, for the geographic areas of Russia, the Western newly independent states (NIS), and the Southern NIS: history, ethnicity and national identity, religion, political culture and civil society, economics, foreign policy priorities and institutions, military issues, and the nuclear factor. A series of volumes containing the papers presented at each workshop will be published by M. E. Sharpe beginning in 1994.

The authors wish to acknowledge the generous and timely contributions of the project's Coordinating Committee. The members have provided invaluable advice and expertise on earlier versions of the manuscript and on the project.

The Coordinating Committee members are: Dr. Adeed Dawisha (George Mason University); Dr. Bartek Kaminski (University of Maryland); Dr. Catherine Kelleher (The Brookings Institution); Ms. Judith Kipper (The Brookings Institution); Dr. Nancy Lubin (Carnegie Mellon University); Dr. Michael Mandelbaum (The School of Advanced International Studies); Dr. James Millar (The George Washington University); Dr. Peter Murrell (University of Maryland); Dr. Martha Brill Olcott (Colgate University); Dr. Ilya Prizel (The School of Advanced International Studies); Dr. George Quester (University of Maryland); Dr. Alvin Z. Rubinstein (University of Pennsylvania); Dr. Blair Ruble (The Kennan Institute); Dr. S. Frederick Starr (Oberlin College); Dr. Roman Szporluk (Harvard University); and Dr. Vladimir Tismaneanu (University of Maryland).

The authors also wish to acknowledge the excellent work of the executive director of the Russian Littoral Project, Janine Ludlam, who kept the project on course during the writing of this book.

Drs. Dawisha and Parrott are grateful for the support of the John D. and Catherine T. MacArthur Foundation, the Friedrich Ebert Stiftung, the Pew Charitable Trusts, and the National Endowment for the Humanities, and especially wish to thank Kennette Benedict, Dieter Dettke, and Kevin Quigley, for without their generosity, the Russian Littoral Project would not have been possible.

Finally, the authors are grateful to President William Kirwan, Dean Irwin Goldstein, Associate Dean Stewart Edelstein, Director of the Office of International Affairs Marcus Franda, and Department of Government and Politics Chair Jonathan Wilkenfeld at the University of

Maryland at College Park; President William C. Richardson, Provost Joseph Cooper, Vice-Provost for Academic Planning and Budget Stephen M. McClain at the Johns Hopkins University; and Dean George Packard and Associate Dean Stephen Szabo at The School of Advanced International Studies, who have all provided invaluable and continuing support for the Russian Littoral Project.

Michael Holdsworth at Cambridge University Press in Cambridge was a constant encouragement and promoted the idea of the book from the beginning. Richard Hollick, Sophia Prybylski, Cary Groner, and Patricia Woodruff at Cambridge University Press's New York offices worked diligently to get the book out in a timely fashion.

Maps

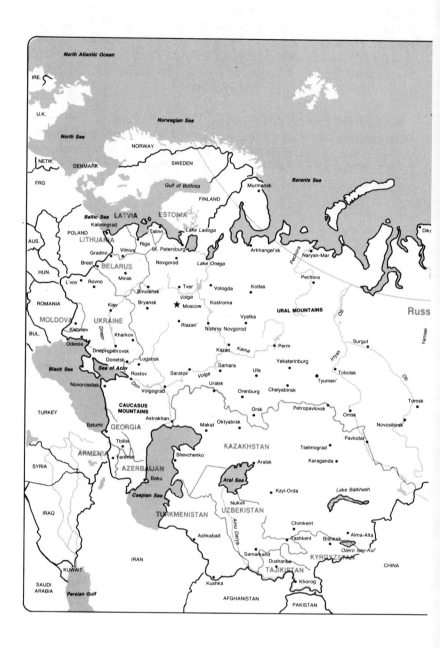

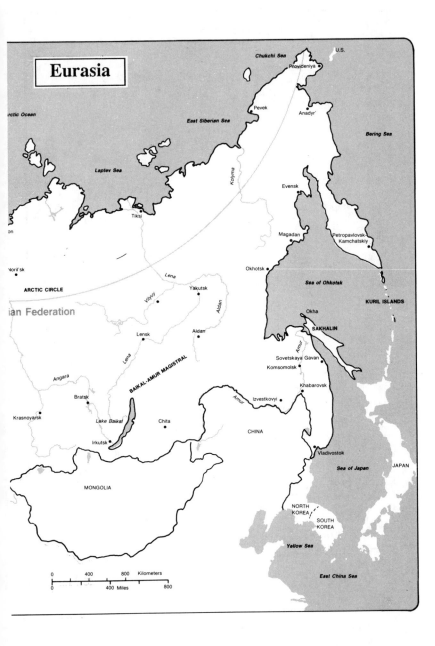

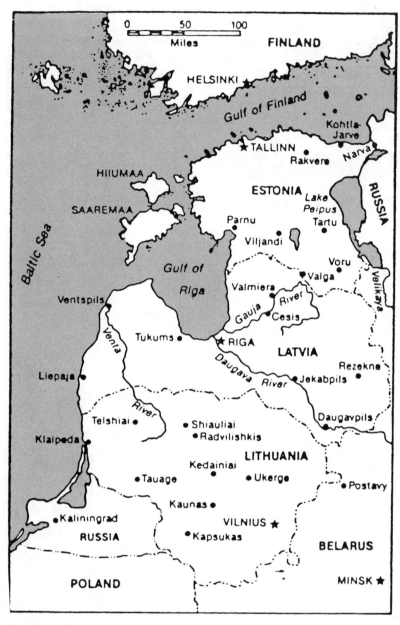

Estonia, Latvia, and Lithuania
Copyright 1993 Congressional Quarterly Inc.
Used by permission of the publisher.

Belarus, Ukraine, and Moldova
Copyright 1993 Congressional Quarterly Inc.
Used by permission of the publisher.

Administrative

Divisions of Russia

ts and their centers

⊙ Kray

○ Autonomous okrug
  or autonomous oblast

0	500

kilometers

0	500

miles

2168 1-93 STATE (INR/GE)

Chukchi
Sea

WRANGEL
ISLAND

Bering
Sea

East Siberian
Sea

Chukotka

Anadyr

SEVERNAYA
ZEMLYA

NEW
SIBERIAN
ISLANDS

Laptev
Sea

Koryakia

o Palana

Taymyria

Kamchatka
Oblast

o Dudinka

Magadan

Yakutia

Petropavlovsk-
Kamchatskiy

I   A

Evenkia

Yakutsk o

Sea of
Okhotsk

Tura o

Occupied by the Soviet Union
in 1945, administered by
Russia, claimed by Japan

Sakhalin
Oblast

Krasnoyarsk

Amur
Oblast

Yuzhno- o
Sakhalinsk

Birobijan Khabarovsk

in dispute

Blagoveshchensk

Birobidzhan

...assia

Ust'-Orda

Buryatia

Lake
Baikal

Chita

...akan

Ust'-Ordynskiy o

Primorskiy
(Maritime)
Kray

Irkutsk o

Ulan-Ude

Aginskoye o
Aga

in
dispute

CHINA

Sea of
Japan

Tuva o Kyzyl

MONGOLIA

Vladivostok

Names: Names of republics and autonomous okrugs and oblasts are provisional names approved for use by
the U.S. Board on Geographic Names (BGN). Names of some oblasts are not yet accepted or recognized by the BGN.
Oblasts and krays are named only when the name differs from that of its administrative center.

N. KOREA

JAPAN

The New States of Central Asia

Kazakhstan   Kyrgyzstan
Tajikistan   Turkmenistan
Uzbekistan

Produced by the Office of The Geographer, Bureau of Intelligence and Research, US Department of State

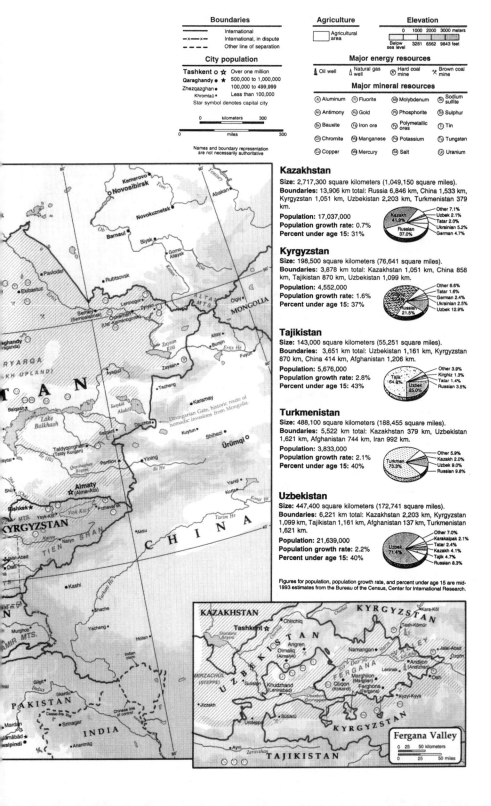

Boundaries

——————	International
—x——x—	International, in dispute
— — — —	Other line of separation

City population

Tashkent o ☆	Over one million
Qaraghandy ● ★	500,000 to 1,000,000
Zhezqazghan ●	100,000 to 499,999
Khromtaū ●	Less than 100,000

Star symbol denotes capital city

0   kilometers   300

0   miles   300

Names and boundary representation
are not necessarily authoritative

Agriculture

☐ Agricultural area

Elevation

0	1000	2000	3000 meters
Below sea level	3281	6562	9843 feet

Major energy resources

⬛ Oil well	⬛ Natural gas well	⊗ Hard coal mine	⤫ Brown coal mine

Major mineral resources

(A) Aluminum	(Fl) Fluorite	(Mo) Molybdenum	(So) Sodium sulfite
(Ab) Antimony	(Au) Gold	(Ph) Phosphorite	(S) Sulphur
(Bâ) Bauxite	(Fe) Iron ore	(Po) Polymetallic ores	(Tn) Tin
(Cr) Chromite	(Mn) Manganese	(Pt) Potassium	(Tu) Tungsten
(Cu) Copper	(Me) Mercury	(Sa) Salt	(U) Uranium

Kazakhstan

Size: 2,717,300 square kilometers (1,049,150 square miles).
Boundaries: 13,906 km total: Russia 6,846 km, China 1,533 km, Kyrgyzstan 1,051 km, Uzbekistan 2,203 km, Turkmenistan 379 km.
Population: 17,037,000
Population growth rate: 0.7%
Percent under age 15: 31%

Kazakh 41.9%
Russian 37.0%
Other 7.1%
Uzbek 2.1%
Tatar 2.0%
Ukrainian 5.2%
German 4.7%

Kyrgyzstan

Size: 198,500 square kilometers (76,641 square miles).
Boundaries: 3,878 km total: Kazakhstan 1,051 km, China 858 km, Tajikistan 870 km, Uzbekistan 1,099 km.
Population: 4,552,000
Population growth rate: 1.6%
Percent under age 15: 37%

Russian 21.5%
Other 6.6%
Tatar 1.6%
German 2.4%
Ukrainian 2.5%
Uzbek 12.9%

Tajikistan

Size: 143,000 square kilometers (55,251 square miles).
Boundaries: 3,651 km total: Uzbekistan 1,161 km, Kyrgyzstan 870 km, China 414 km, Afghanistan 1,206 km.
Population: 5,676,000
Population growth rate: 2.8%
Percent under age 15: 43%

Tajik 64.9%
Uzbek 25.0%
Other 3.9%
Kirghiz 1.3%
Tatar 1.4%
Russian 3.5%

Turkmenistan

Size: 488,100 square kilometers (188,455 square miles).
Boundaries: 5,522 km total: Kazakhstan 379 km, Uzbekistan 1,621 km, Afghanistan 744 km, Iran 992 km.
Population: 3,833,000
Population growth rate: 2.1%
Percent under age 15: 40%

Turkmen 73.3%
Other 5.9%
Kazakh 2.0%
Uzbek 9.0%
Russian 9.8%

Uzbekistan

Size: 447,400 square kilometers (172,741 square miles).
Boundaries: 6,221 km total: Kazakhstan 2,203 km, Kyrgyzstan 1,099 km, Tajikistan 1,161 km, Afghanistan 137 km, Turkmenistan 1,621 km.
Population: 21,639,000
Population growth rate: 2.2%
Percent under age 15: 40%

Uzbek 71.4%
Other 7.0%
Karakalpak 2.1%
Tatar 2.4%
Kazakh 4.1%
Tajik 4.7%
Russian 8.3%

Figures for population, population growth rate, and percent under age 15 are mid-1993 estimates from the Bureau of the Census, Center for International Research.

Fergana Valley

0   25   50 kilometers

0   25   50 miles

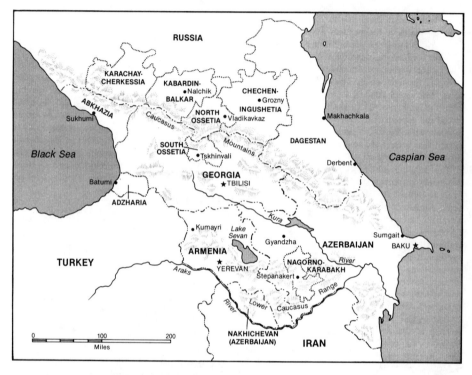

The Caucasus and North Caucasus
Copyright 1993 Congressional Quarterly Inc. Used by permission of the publisher.

Introduction

The Soviet Union's disintegration into fifteen states is a development whose vast ramifications may lead future historians to treat it as the most important event of the twentieth century. For the first four or five decades of its existence the USSR was the self-styled exemplar of a noncapitalist form of sociopolitical organization and an inspiration to revolutionary groups in the industrial and underdeveloped worlds. After making a decisive contribution to the defeat of Nazi Germany in World War II, the Soviet Union sought leadership of the anti-Western bloc of socialist and prosocialist countries that emerged from the political tumult and anticolonial movements unleashed by the war. Despite the failure of the USSR's subsequent efforts to shift the global correlation of forces decisively in its favor, its military might and capacity for internal repression helped maintain a harsh but fixed constellation of political alignments among the states of Eurasia and among the peoples of the Soviet Union itself.

The collapse of the Soviet Empire has created historic opportunities and historic dangers. On the one hand, the abandonment of Marxism-Leninism and the democratization of politics within Russia, Ukraine, and other newly independent states of the former USSR have improved the possibility of global cooperation transcending the enmities of the Cold War. On the other hand, acute instability within the new states, and growing tensions among them, have created a serious risk of interstate military clashes and widespread civil war in the heart of Eurasia. Even if such a dire eventuality is avoided, the political implosion of the Soviet system has undermined the international alliances originally designed to counter Soviet expansionism and has created a major risk of sociopolitical instability extending far beyond former Soviet territories into the adjacent countries of Europe, the Middle East, and Asia.

Because it is bound to be protracted, the post-Soviet upheaval in Eurasia will shape America's foreign policy agenda for many years to come. Even the wave of decolonization between the Second World War

1

and 1960 did not witness such a sudden emergence of so many strategically located new states encompassing so much territory, so many
competing nationalities, and such an accumulation of economic, ecological, and psychological scars. Nor has history ever known the collapse
of a nuclear-armed state, let alone one with the world's largest military-
industrial and nuclear-weapons complex. The West no longer faces the
familiar Soviet strategic threat, but Western interests are challenged by
a situation that is more diffuse, amorphous, and infinitely more difficult
to gauge. The momentous upheaval in the former USSR thus poses a
challenge that is both political and intellectual.

Contemporary analysts must devise new assumptions and research
methodologies that take account of at least five profound shifts in Eurasia's political dynamics. First, the collapse of the Soviet system has
inaugurated what is likely to be an extended period of state-building
that has few parallels in the twentieth century. Only the collapse of the
Habsburg Empire following World War I and the turbulent replacement
of the Russian Empire with the Soviet state offer partial analogies. In
neither case, however, had the country that collapsed played so central
a role in determining the international political order and balance of
power as did the Soviet Union following World War II. For closer
analogies one must turn to the era of European state-building during
the sixteenth and seventeenth centuries.[1] Nor is the contemporary state-
building process confined only to the non-Russian countries that have
emerged from the wreckage of the USSR. In Russia, too, an effort is
under way to construct a fundamentally new state. This process requires
an analytical approach radically different from those applicable to the
collective and individual dynamics of established state systems.

The central importance of state-building is closely linked to a second
change in the international political landscape. Many former Soviet
regions and nationalities that once seemed of marginal significance for
an understanding of international relations have become critically important for charting the geopolitical transformation of Eurasia. This
unfamiliar circumstance, which already has kindled new public and
professional interest in the work of Western specialists on the non-
Russian components of the former USSR, poses a major challenge for
scholars of all stripes, but perhaps especially for the large group of
Russianists who have traditionally dominated the study of Soviet affairs.
To be sure, students of Eurasian developments can scarcely ignore
Russia, which remains vitally important and is undergoing a profound
sociopolitical crisis; but any serious study of the international politics
of Eurasia must now examine the interaction among developments in
Russia and developments in the other newly independent states.

Third, in each of the new states the government's long-standing totalitarian dominance of society has been destroyed, and foreign relations and domestic affairs have become inextricably intertwined. Even in those successor states where authoritarian regimes have been established, government policies are being buffeted by powerful socioeconomic forces that have become a fundamental determinant of external relations and have clouded the customary distinction between domestic and foreign policy. The new governments' political weakness or inexperience has often hampered their ability to generate a coherent conception of the national interest and to pursue that conception in the face of domestic opposition groups. Moreover, many issues that were internal matters in the Soviet era now belong to the realm of foreign policy but remain in the hands of the old "domestic" bureaucracies. Indeed, the web of human, institutional, and economic connections linking many of the new countries to one another is so complex, and the political agendas facing the national leaders so novel, that choices having major foreign policy consequences may sometimes be decided without giving serious attention to their foreign policy implications.

A fourth fundamental change is that in the new states the lines of influence between domestic and foreign affairs now run in both directions. Students of international politics sometimes assume the nation-state as a given and explain international events as a consequence of the character of particular states or of the "anarchic" international environment in which these states exist.[2] In the tremendously fluid post-Soviet environment, however, the new states' foreign relations are likely to have a telling effect on the political arrangements that crystallize within the new states themselves. This observation extends well beyond the proposition that material aid from the Western democracies and Japan may facilitate peaceful transitions in the former Soviet republics. It implies that the ability or inability of the leaders of the new states to manage their relations with other countries will have a critical long-term impact on the institutionalization of domestic political relationships. If the international environment appears to warrant the maintenance of powerful military and police bureaucracies and invites attacks on the domestic political opposition as a tool of foreign enemies, the domestic order will be pushed in an authoritarian direction. If the external environment provides a convincing basis for arguing that internal differences do not endanger the new state's existence and that powerful coercive institutions are unnecessary, the chances for the creation of a liberal domestic order will be enhanced.

Finally, the former USSR has been transformed from a secretive regime about which useful data were sometimes impossible to acquire into a group of countries releasing masses of information too large for scholars to evaluate in a timely fashion. Whereas Western analysts of the USSR previously adopted narrow scholarly specialties in an effort to sift nuggets of information from mountains of low-grade ore, they now find themselves pushed to specialize by the very wealth of the information sources that have become available. The field of post-Soviet studies will be in flux for many years to come, and deeper Western understanding of trends in Eurasia will depend on detailed research in archival and other specialized sources. However, the extraordinary fluidity of developments in the former Soviet republics has created a pressing need for efforts to synthesize specialized knowledge, even though that knowledge remains far from complete, in order to gain a better sense of the complex interactions among various political, social, and economic trends. Such syntheses can enable Western observers to identify important concatenations of events and reduce the chances that we will once more be caught off-guard by massive changes in the Eurasian political landscape.

The purpose of this book is to provide a broad overview of the relations among the post-Soviet states and neighboring countries and to analyze some of the key variables that will shape those relations during the coming years. Focusing on the interaction between the internal affairs and foreign relations of the newly independent states, the book examines the impact of (1) the historical legacies of the new states; (2) the resurgence of ethnicity and debates over national identity; (3) the revival of religion; (4) political culture and the emergence of new sociopolitical groups; (5) economic determinants of the new states' foreign policies; (6) national attempts to recast foreign policy priorities and institutions; (7) developments within the post-Soviet armed forces and steps to create separate national military establishments; and (8) trends and debates concerning the future of nuclear weapons. Each of these variables is taken up in a separate chapter of the book and is examined first with respect to Russia, then with respect to the western belt of new states extending from Estonia to Ukraine, and finally with respect to the southern tier of new states extending from Georgia to Kyrgyzstan.[3]

The aim of the book is also to clarify the international impact of these major factors, not to attempt a comprehensive history or a definitive explanation of all the events transpiring in Eurasia. The book concentrates primarily on the post-Soviet states and devotes less attention to the policies of established countries in neighboring regions, even though the responses of neighboring countries to the collapse of the USSR will do much to shape Eurasia's future political geography. The coverage of specific post-Soviet states also varies substantially. Readers, for example, will find fuller discussion of large new states such as Russia and Ukraine than of small new states such as Moldova and Georgia. In part this distribution of coverage reflects our judgments about the relative importance of various political actors.

The forces that destroyed the USSR and are shaping the behavior of the newly independent states have deep roots in tsarist as well as Soviet history. In the following chapters we examine these forces topically and in considerable detail. The analysis in those chapters, however, assumes a general understanding of the functioning and evolution of the tsarist and Soviet systems. Hence we begin with an overview intended to provide nonspecialist readers with essential background information and to clarify for specialists the vantage point from which we approach our subject. In order to put later findings in context, the remainder of this chapter sketches the evolution of the nexus between state power, nationalism, and foreign relations in the tsarist and Soviet eras.

The Tsarist Experience

The history of the tsarist empire is a chronicle of the tsarist elite's efforts to balance the requirements for the development of international power against the domestic prerequisites for the maintenance of autocratic rule. Geared to the twin purposes of strengthening the empire's position in the international arena and supporting the nobility's privileges at home, the tsarist state dominated society virtually up to the revolution of 1917. Members of the small noble class were expected to serve in the armed forces and civilian governmental apparatus; in exchange the tsar gave them promotion within the official table of ranks, land, and, until 1861, serfs. Although the state periodically accelerated the development of key sectors of industry and commerce, particularly those essential for the generation of military power, its stability rested on the political inertness of the bulk of the population. This inertness was maintained not only by political coercion but by a high level of illiteracy, which impeded the dissemination of subversive political ideas and, despite several popular uprisings in the seventeenth and eighteenth centuries, helped ensure popular acceptance of the claim that the tsar ruled by divine right.

Together with the preeminent importance of the state apparatus as a channel of upward mobility, the tsarist government's insistence on keeping all political initiative in its hands also constituted a major obstacle to the emergence of independent social and economic groups. By the second half of the nineteenth century a tiny but active intelligentsia had coalesced and begun to champion notions of society's interests that clashed with the official tsarist ideology. Although this development constituted one step toward the creation of a civil society, a deep cultural gulf separated the intelligentsia from the peasantry, which bore the political and economic imprint of centuries of bondage long after the abolition of serfdom in 1861.[4] For example, during the 1870s the intelligentsia's effort to promote political reform in the countryside was met with peasant incomprehension and hostility. Sizable urban social classes opposed to the state's political tutelage began to develop only late in the nineteenth century. Although the autocracy needed to foster and tap the economic energies of these classes in order not to fall behind in the quickening international race for military power, it treated them with a political ambivalence that demonstrated its inability to govern a dynamic society effectively.[5]

The tsarist state's relations with the outside world were a complex mixture of defensive and aggressive behavior. In the course of its history Russia was repeatedly exposed to the risk of occupation and dismemberment at the hands of foreign enemies, including the Mongols, the Ottoman Turks, Poland, Sweden, France, and Germany. The history of recurrent military conflict helps explain the tsarist polity's autocratic character and its preoccupation with the accumulation of military power. But these characteristics were based as well on the driving ambitions of such monarchs as Ivan the Terrible, Peter the Great, and Catherine the Great. They were also rooted in the pre-nineteenth-century practice of distributing large quantities of captured peasants and land to individual nobles as rewards for military service, and in the ideology of Russian imperial expansion that gained currency by the nineteenth century. Although the Russian sense of military and political vulnerability was generated partly by the country's objective circumstances, the fact remains that the internal dynamics of the tsarist system contributed to a vast geographical extension of the empire between the fifteenth and the late nineteenth centuries.[6]

This expansion transformed tsarist Russia from a country with a large measure of ethnic homogeneity into a multiethnic empire. Before the nineteenth century, tsarist annexation of non-Russian territories was primarily a function of *realpolitik*. These "borderlands" served as sources of tribute and as buffers in Russia's relations with other great powers, particularly the great powers of Europe. The tsarist polity was not a nation-state, and the tsar's legitimacy was undergirded by dynastic loyalty and religious tradition rather than by a modern form of Russian ethno-nationalism.[7] Although the inhabitants of some non-Russian regions were subjected to pressures to restructure their local institutions along Russian lines and to convert to the Orthodox faith, in a number of cases St. Petersburg tolerated the existence of distinctive local political institutions, and for the most part it did not demand the cultural russification of its non-Russian subjects.[8] The tsar's noble servitors, for instance, included large numbers of Baltic Germans and other non-

Russians, and until well into the nineteenth century many tsarist aristocrats had a poorer command of the Russian language than of German or French.[9] Combined with tsarism's relative openness to the cooptation of non-Russian elites, Russia's colonization of contiguous territories rather than separate continents blurred the understanding of the tsarist political elite – and the understanding of later students of imperialism – that Russia was involved in an imperialistic enterprise.[10]

During tsarist Russia's last century, however, the dynamics of imperial domination underwent a dramatic change. The rise of modern nationalism elsewhere in Europe and the gradual modernization of tsarist society awakened national feelings among the Great Russians.[11] The same phenomenon occurred in several non-Russian portions of the empire, particularly in western regions such as the Polish and Ukrainian provinces. Intensifying Russian and non-Russian nationalist sentiments thus fed off one another – not least because of the large numbers of Russian settlers who continued to migrate from Central Russia into the various border regions. As noted below, Russian nationalism itself posed a significant political challenge to the dynastic claims of divine right that had customarily been invoked to legitimize tsarist rule. Nonetheless, the proliferation of nationalist movements inside the empire helped persuade tsarist officials that a policy of russification was an essential means of cementing together the empire's diverse social components.

The ruling elite's concern with the political cohesion of the empire was linked to broader developments in international politics. Foreshadowed by the French Revolution, a wave of nationalist movements during the mid-nineteenth century created new states in Italy and Germany, threatened the existence of Europe's multinational empires, and affected the foreign relations of all the great powers. For example, the tsarist government's military suppression of the rebellion that broke out in its Polish provinces during 1830 contributed to Russia's estrangement from the British and French constitutional monarchies and its closer alignment with the conservative Habsburg and Prussian polities.[12] Later in the century, the stirrings of nationalism among the Russian empire's Ukrainian and Baltic populations threatened to make the western borderlands susceptible to separatist movements inspired from abroad, especially from Imperial Germany. Urged on by an increasingly nationalist Russian public, the tsarist authorities therefore launched a policy of cultural and linguistic russification that was particularly harsh in the western provinces. The spread of heterodox thinking, the emergence of nationalist intellectuals, the expansion of popular education, and the growth of publishing all combined to make Russia's hold on the borderlands a problem not just of administrative and military subordination but of political control in a broader cultural sense.

Due to the spread of modern nationalism, the exertion of such control had become a matter of vital consequence for tsarist foreign policy.

Tsarist efforts to cope with these novel challenges came to an end in 1917. The tsarist autocracy's collapse was caused, inter alia, by the gradual erosion of belief in the regime's legitimacy not only among persons with advanced education but among the mass of poorly educated workers and peasants; by the autocracy's inability to cope with the unprecedented political and economic demands of mobilizing the country for total war; and by the emotional impact of millions of battlefield deaths and widespread human suffering. Not least among the causes of the regime's collapse were errors of political and military leadership that cost the tsar and his ministers the substantial popular support they had previously derived from Russian nationalism. Once primarily a source of political support for the regime, conservative Russian nationalists now joined Russian liberals in condemning the autocracy for the nation's suffering and defeats on the battlefields of World War I.[13] Although tsarist officials had employed Russian nationalism and russification to buttress the empire against centrifugal forces, they never fully managed to neutralize the populist current that identified the Russian people, rather than the monarch, as the ultimate source of political authority. Under the acute strain of protracted war, state-sponsored Russian nationalism escaped the autocracy's control and contributed to its destruction.

From Lenin to Stalin

It is particularly ironic that the Bolsheviks, who proclaimed themselves opponents of all forms of nationalism and prophesied its early disappearance, ultimately became the bearers of a new form of state-sponsored Russian nationalism. Although more decisive political action by the liberal provisional government that succeeded the tsarist regime might have discredited Lenin and his colleagues as pro-German collaborators working to bring about Russia's military defeat, the provisional government lost this crucial political opportunity early in the fall of 1917.[14] Once the Bolsheviks seized power and civil war broke out, an unusual combination of circumstances enabled them to present themselves as defenders both of Russia and of the empire's non-Russian minorities. Western and Japanese intervention in support of the White forces allowed the Bolsheviks to depict themselves to Russians as defenders of the Russian fatherland against foreign invasion; this factor was particularly important to the Bolsheviks' success in recruiting large numbers of former tsarist officers into the newly organized Red Army.

At the same time, the commitment of the principal White leaders to the restoration of the Russian empire allowed the Bolsheviks to win the support of many non-Russians with the promise of full civil rights, including the right of national self-determination, for all the empire's nationalities.

The Bolshevik commitment to the concept of self-determination was shaped more by calculations of power than by considerations of principle. In the European borderlands, vigorous anti-Bolshevik resistance and Western political pressure led to the establishment of Poland, Finland, Estonia, Latvia, and Lithuania as independent states. However, the outcome was quite different in former tsarist territories that had less diplomatic salience or whose fate was more difficult for the West to influence. In Ukraine and the Caucasus the Bolshevik government disregarded its prior declarations and dispatched the Red Army to conquer national regimes that had declared their independence during the Civil War.[15] Nonetheless, in the decisive phases of the Civil War the promise of self-determination was effective in mobilizing non-Russian groups and contributed substantially to the defeat of the Whites. Due to the exhaustion of most of the Western powers during World War I and their preoccupation with working out a postwar settlement in Central and Eastern Europe, the postwar foreign intervention on behalf of the Whites was not sufficiently powerful to overcome the political factors working in favor of the Bolsheviks.[16]

Despite its strong admixture of political expediency, the Bolshevik attitude toward nationality problems had a more positive side in the 1920s. During most of that decade the Communist Party leadership attempted to chart a course that curbed Russian chauvinism and treated non-Russian national groups more fairly than had been the case in the late tsarist era. The key features of the policy were the stress on the indigenization, or *korenizatsiya*, of personnel in the political-administrative apparatus of the non-Russian regions; a significant measure of autonomy in the institutional division of powers between Moscow and the regions; greater latitude for the use of indigenous languages in non-Russian regions; and a relatively lenient policy toward the development of distinctive national cultures.[17] Because most of the non-Russian nationalities consisted of an unusually high proportion of peasants, the pro-peasant New Economic Policy introduced by Lenin during the same period effectively worked in favor of the non-Russian population. Underlying the regime's whole approach during the 1920s was the expectation that more evenhanded economic treatment and greater concessions to the cultural needs of non-Russians would gradually win their unqualified loyalty to the Soviet state.[18] Had this policy been maintained, it is conceivable "that the Soviet Union coulα have continued to evolve as a viable multinational state in which friction among the various nationalities would have been minimal."[19]

The adoption of a relatively accommodating policy toward the non-Russians also meshed with Bolshevik foreign policy. During the 1920s Lenin and other party spokesmen condemned the tsarist treatment of non-Russian ethnic groups as a blatant example of imperialist exploitation that, they claimed, had been brought to an end by the advent of the world's first socialist regime. The Bolsheviks' more forthcoming policy toward the non-Russian nationalities tied in with Lenin's foreign policy strategy of exploiting national sentiments among the victims of Western colonialism as a means of weakening the major capitalist states. Vigorously condemning Western imperialism, Bolshevik spokesmen pointed to the improved fortunes of the non-Russian peoples inside the USSR and urged the emerging national elites of Western colonies and dependencies to align themselves with the USSR.[20] In addition to its impact in Asia and Africa, this stratagem had some effect in Eastern Europe, where several governments were pursuing policies highly inimical to the national minorities within their borders. The Bolsheviks' relatively benign policy toward Soviet Ukrainians and Belarusians, for example, exerted a strong pull on the Ukrainian and Belarusian minorities living under the harsh treatment of the new Polish state created at the end of World War I.[21] The regime's moderate treatment of Soviet Azerbaijanis had a similar impact on the Azerbaijani population of Iran.[22] One mark of the success of the USSR's "anti-imperialist" line is that in later decades observers of many political persuasions came to regard imperialism as a form of behavior peculiar to developed capitalist regimes rather than a historical characteristic of most major powers, Soviet Russia included.

Of all the Bolsheviks' early decisions about the handling of ethnic relations inside the new socialist state, the most fateful may have been the decision to give a formal political expression to the territorial identity of major ethnic groups. The result was the creation of a series of "national republics," ultimately numbering fifteen, within the federal governmental structure of the USSR. Viewed historically, this step was not entirely surprising, in that many of the non-Russian minorities had resided in specific homelands both before and after their incorporation into the tsarist empire. The decision was also consistent with the strand of Bolshevik doctrine that identified territoriality as a key feature of nationhood.[23] Perhaps most important, the creation of national republics appealed to Lenin and some other Bolshevik leaders as a way of defusing potential national opposition to the fledgling Soviet state when it sought to consolidate its power after the Civil War.[24]

Despite these political benefits, the decision to establish national republics also entailed nettlesome problems. In the first place, it was difficult to square with the Marxist claim that national differences would gradually disappear under socialism. Although the grant of national statehood, even if more nominal than real, might be seen as an indication of the Soviet regime's determination to treat major non-Russian nationalities fairly, it also lent an aura of permanence to ethnic differences. Furthermore, by establishing republican governmental structures that were identified with individual national groups – Russians, Ukrainians, Georgians, Armenians, and so forth – Moscow gave the principal ethnic groups an institutional focus for their national identity and reduced their inclination to regard all of the USSR, in equal measure, as their homeland. During the 1920s the centralization of the Communist Party apparatus served to check any separatist impulses within the federal state structure, but the long-term influence of the institutionalization of ethnicity on the evolution of various national identities proved far more difficult to control.[25] The establishment of the national republics created an administrative basis not only for tensions between Russians and the titular nationalities of the non-Russian republics, but also for tensions between the titular nationalities and the members of other non-Russian minorities in each national republic, even the minorities whose historical roots in the republic warranted describing them as indigenous.[26]

The consolidation of Stalin's personal dictatorship in the late 1920s and early 1930s brought brutal changes to Soviet nationalities policy. Notwithstanding his Georgian origins, Stalin made a chauvinistic brand of Russian nationalism a central part of the totalitarian system's political scaffolding. Although the Soviet state nominally remained "internationalist," from the 1930s onward, Soviet ideology was increasingly permeated with Russian nationalist traditions and values carefully selected to buttress the power of the state. The measured administrative and cultural autonomy granted to the non-Russian republics during the 1920s was obliterated by a wave of mass terror that intensified political centralization, led to the establishment of carbon-copy administrative institutions in every republic, and produced widespread cultural uniformity.[27]

Moreover, in a perverse turn, Moscow now required that the internal passports of all citizens specify their ethnic identity, and that this nationality entry be determined strictly according to the nationality entries in parents' passports, regardless of the individual's personal wishes and cultural characteristics.[28] Although the Stalinist regime continued the original Bolshevik policy of recruiting and training non-Russian political and technical elites, the slightest hint of political nonconformity was sufficient basis for arrest, and tens of thousands of non-Russian party officials and intellectuals were executed on fabricated charges of participating in "bourgeois nationalist" conspiracies against the socialist state.[29] Meanwhile Stalin's introduction of central economic planning and crash industrialization after 1927 wrought special devastation on those national groups, such as the Ukrainians and the Kazakhs, that were engaged primarily in agriculture.[30] Although Stalin's economic policy promoted the industrial growth of most regions, it also forged a highly specialized division of labor that curtailed each republic's foreign economic relations and increased its dependency on the rest of the Soviet economy.

These draconian measures meshed with the Stalinist approach to foreign affairs. Relying on stringent censorship and massive propaganda, the Stalinist regime sought to present a monolithic facade both to the outside world and to the Soviet populace. The aim was to mask the internal conflicts and turmoil caused by the drive for social transformation and thus prevent the exploitation of these weaknesses by foreign governments or domestic political opponents. Stalin and his lieutenants were profoundly suspicious of any economic or social contacts – especially contacts based on a shared ethnic heritage – between Soviet citizens and foreigners. By the mid-1930s the Stalinist drive for economic autarky, which far exceeded similar tendencies in the crisis-ridden economies of Europe and America, was paralleled by the imposition of an unprecedented level of cultural autarky. While it cut off all but a trickle of authorized foreign contact for Russians and non-Russians alike, the regime went to special lengths to prevent any interchange between several non-Russian nationalities and their ethnic kinsmen living outside the USSR.[31] Distrustful of foreign political allies whom he could not control, Stalin abandoned the Soviet courtship of anti-imperialist national movements in most of the Western colonies. He did, however, seek to exploit ethnic unrest among certain foreign ethnic groups having counterparts inside the USSR, particularly the Turkic tribes in the Chinese territory of Sinkiang. During the 1930s and 1940s Stalin attempted, with considerable though transitory success, to turn portions of Sinkiang into a Soviet protectorate.[32]

To judge by their behavior, Stalin and his minions regarded the USSR's non-Russian borderlands not only as a geographic buffer against foreign invasion but also as a major potential source of strategic vulnerability. At the end of the 1930s the Soviet conspiracy with Nazi Germany to carve up Poland, the Soviet military attack on Finland, and the forcible incorporation of the Baltic States were all intended in part to give greater geographic depth to the USSR's defenses against the dangers of impending world war.[33] Earlier in the decade the regime had already begun the mass relocation of ethnic groups that it suspected of complicity with one or another potential military opponent of the USSR.[34] Soviet territorial expansion into Poland and the Baltics was accompanied by large-scale deportations and executions of the indigenous national elites in order to crush all potential resistance and strengthen Moscow's political control over the conquered territories. Given the brutality of the Stalinist regime in the period preceding the Nazi attack on the USSR, it is understandable that significant numbers of non-Russians initially welcomed the Nazis as liberators and that some non-Russians fought against the Soviet army during the remainder of the war, although the participation of some of the partisans in anti-Jewish atrocities cannot be condoned.[35] When the Soviet forces drove the Nazi armies out of the western borderlands, anti-Soviet guerrilla activity continued, especially in the Ukrainian and Baltic regions, and Moscow resorted to new waves of indiscriminate deportations and executions to buttress its dictatorial control.[36]

As the glow of the Allied victory over Germany and Japan gave way to the Cold War with the United States, Stalin took steps to tighten his grip on all of Moscow's dependencies, both in Eastern Europe and within the USSR itself. Although distinguished by an exceptional level of economic exploitation, Moscow's repressive political policies toward its East European satellites were paralleled by almost equally repressive policies directed against the non-Russian Soviet republics.[37] In the late 1940s Stalin and his backers carried xenophobia and state-sponsored Russian nationalism to heights unprecedented even during the late 1930s. Moscow-directed purge trials were staged in several of the East European satellites, while purges of "bourgeois nationalists" were carried out in several Soviet republics and an anti-Semitic campaign against "rootless cosmopolitans" reached a hysterical pitch.[38] Unofficial reports indicate that on the eve of his death in 1953 Stalin was contemplating a mass deportation of Soviet Jews from their areas of residence to distant northern and eastern provinces of the USSR.[39]

The Post-Stalin Era

During the three post-Stalin decades presided over first by Nikita Khrushchev and then by Leonid Brezhnev, the Soviet regime abandoned mass terror and sought a less draconian formula for managing relations among the country's nationalities. Although major variations in policy occurred under the two leaders, some broad trends are nevertheless visible. Stalin's successors abandoned the most xenophobic and chauvinist elements of his policy toward the non-Russians and allowed a limited devolution of authority from Moscow to the national republics.

Khrushchev's attempt to restore the regime's moral authority and strengthen his own political position by denouncing Stalin's purges of the party led to public acknowledgment of some of the wrongs that had been inflicted on particular minorities during the Stalin era. Within definite limits, the post-Stalin thaw offered non-Russian intellectuals and cultural figures a margin of freedom to pursue a partial rectification of the Stalinist distortions of non-Russian cultures and national histories.[40]

Having eschewed the use of the secret police to inflict mass terror, Stalin's successors attempted to strengthen their other instruments of control over the non-Russian republics. The party chiefs increased the small number of hand-picked non-Slavs selected for membership in the party Politburo, the country's highest policy-making body. At the same time, however, they systematized the party's administrative controls over the non-Russian regions. This policy involved making regional party appointments that yoked together party secretaries from different ethnic backgrounds – one party secretary of the region's "titular" nationality, usually posted from a previous position within the region in question, and another secretary of Russian or Slavic origin, usually posted from a previous position in the central party bureaucracy in Moscow. In addition, the senior party chiefs excluded non-Russians from the core of the Soviet political apparatus – the central party Secretariat in Moscow – and ensured that the responsibility for overseeing cadre appointments in non-Russian areas remained in the hands of ethnic Russians.[41] The aim was to ensure that the party officials in any given region would have an effective working knowledge of local conditions but would remain responsive to Moscow's bidding.

By the mid-1960s the course of events persuaded some unorthodox political activists that their needs and grievances could not be satisfied by working within the existing political system. This outlook was precipitated by Khrushchev's attempts during the late 1950s to accelerate the "merging" of Soviet nationalities as part of his campaign for the building of full Communism; by the harsh offensive that Khrushchev simultaneously launched against religious believers of many confessions and nationalities; and by some intellectuals' fear that the Brezhnev clique, having deposed Khrushchev, would not only bring the process of de-Stalinization to a complete halt but rehabilitate Stalin and his cultural policies. Thanks to this combination of circumstances, an organized dissent movement came into existence.[42] For the first time since the 1920s, clearly identifiable spokesmen openly challenged the party's claim to speak for the various elements of Soviet society, including its non-Russian components.

In response, the Brezhnev leadership adopted a policy of graduated coercion intended to suppress dissenters while reducing their opportunities to establish ties with other strata of the population. Thus KGB warnings, political trials, and harsh imprisonment of activists were combined with a tempering of Khrushchev's aggressive campaigns for ethnic merging and for the eradication of religion. Not least important, the steady improvement of the standard of living between the mid-1960s and mid-1970s and the continuing policy of elite cooptation in all the republics gave the non-Russian elites and most ordinary citizens a tangible stake in the existing political order.[43] Although this mix of policies did not prevent all the currents of nationalist dissent from acquiring mass support – Lithuania being the most notable example – it did obstruct the formation of ties between active dissenters and the mass of the population in most of the major nationalities.[44]

A further result of the altered post-Stalin environment was that the non-Russian segments of the party apparatus began to advocate policies that, in limited measure, reflected the interests of the national territories over which they presided. In the 1950s, Khrushchev's decision to transfer substantial economic authority to regional economic councils produced autarkic regional behavior with significant nationalist overtones, which in turn helped stimulate the recentralization of planning authority in Moscow. Attempts under Khrushchev to downgrade the teaching of non-Russian languages also met resistance from a few assertive republican party secretaries.[45] These economic and educational controversies led to the removal of most of the officials involved, but regional party officials continued to show a marginal receptivity to local nationalist sentiments, either because they were genuinely sympathetic to these sentiments or because effective governance required a partial accommodation with the views of the local population.[46] During the post-Khrushchev era Moscow's control over developments in the non-Russian republics weakened substantially. The Brezhnev Politburo's commitment to the policy of "trust in cadres" slowed personnel turnover within the republican party and governmental apparatuses, sharply reduced the number of republican party officials seconded from the central party apparatus in Moscow, and significantly increased the share of republican officials selected directly from the region they were appointed to oversee.[47] Moreover, around the end of the 1960s the long-term overall migration of ethnic Russians from the Russian heartland to the non-Russian periphery came to an end, as the number of Russians leaving several of the non-Russian republics exceeded the number of new Russian arrivals.[48] Reinforced by demographic trends among many of the non-Russian nationalities, this shift gradually increased the share of non-Russians in the population of a number of the non-Russian republics and reduced the relative weight of the ethnic group that, taken as a whole, constituted one of Moscow's principal instruments for shaping developments in the non-Russian regions. Concern about the cumulative political effect of these trends was probably one of Moscow's motives for upgrading the role of the KGB in the governance of the non-Russian republics after the mid-1970s.[49]

In the post-Stalin years the linkages between Soviet foreign relations and domestic nationality policy underwent subtle changes that seemed of little immediate consequence but had major effects over the long term. Under Khrushchev, Soviet diplomats and propagandists vigorously courted the emerging countries and anticolonial movements of the Third World by showcasing the socioeconomic advances of the non-Russian republics.[50] Khrushchev's emphasis on building ties with the countries in the "zone of peace" was intended to seize the geopolitical initiative by making inroads into the colonies and dependencies of the Soviet Union's capitalist rivals. By the late 1970s, however, the USSR's increasingly tarnished international image, its loss of economic dynamism, and the gradual fading of anti-Western sentiment in the Third World deprived this tactic of effectiveness.

During the same period, the potential for undesirable feedback from the international arena to the Soviet empire slowly increased. The party leadership showed deep apprehension about the potential impact of Marxist revisionism not only on Moscow's East European client states but on the stability of the Soviet Union itself. In 1956 the crisis in Poland and the Hungarian revolt elicited public demonstrations of support in the Baltic republics, and the Czechoslovakian reform movement of 1968 awakened hopes for basic political reform among Russian and non-Russian dissenters, particularly in Ukraine.[51] In both instances the Soviet leadership's decision to intervene militarily was prompted in part by the fear that the spillover from Eastern Europe would destabilize the internal Soviet order.[52] The military suppression of the Prague Spring had the additional purpose of demonstrating to the Western powers that the only path to closer Western relations with Eastern Europe led through Moscow, and the recognition of this reality was one of the factors that produced the limited East-West detente of the 1970s.[53] Meanwhile the deepening Sino-Soviet conflict, which played a major role in the Soviet decision to seek a rapprochement with the West, led Moscow and Beijing into a propaganda war in which each side attempted to foment unrest among disaffected minorities in the territories of the other.[54]

In the 1970s, however, external influences more subtle than Chinese propaganda or the threatened collapse of East European Communist regimes began to affect national relations inside the USSR. The Brezhnev leadership's formula for detente with the West included a commitment to continued struggle against "bourgeois ideology" and the rejection of "outside interference" in Soviet domestic affairs. This was different from the Western understanding of detente, and as a result Soviet treatment of dissenters became an issue in relations with the Western democracies. The Soviet signature in 1975 of the Final Act of the Conference on Security and Cooperation in Europe (CSCE) constituted a particularly important step toward the linkage of arms control and East-West trade with the Soviet handling of human-rights matters.[55] Despite the USSR's repeated rejection of Western representations on this topic, the Helsinki Accords became a source of inspiration for human-rights advocates throughout the Soviet bloc. Soviet dissenters increasingly addressed their appeals to the United Nations and other Western agencies, and such human-rights organizations as Helsinki Watch and Amnesty International turned their attention to Soviet domestic affairs. This new strategy reflected most dissenters' conviction that the party leadership would never undertake meaningful domestic reforms, and, to a lesser extent, the dissenters' growing discouragement about the receptivity of ordinary Soviet citizens to the ideas of the dissent movement.

In the long run, however, this turn of events produced a basic change in the capacity of Soviet dissenters to affect the thinking of the Soviet populace. Though the appeal to external audiences reflected the inability of dissenters to communicate directly with rank-and-file citizens, it actually became the key to transcending the domestic obstacles to unfettered political communication. Thanks to the smuggling of privately circulated (*samizdat*) writings to the West and the transmission of their contents back into the USSR via Western radio broadcasts, the ideas of national dissenters gradually became accessible to large numbers of Soviet citizens who were not necessarily prepared to challenge the party-state apparatus but were nevertheless becoming more receptive to the charges leveled against the regime by its critics.[56] Coupled with the Brezhnev oligarchy's sustained push to reduce income differentials between white-collar and blue-collar workers, the sharp slowdown in the growth of Soviet GNP and consumption in the late 1970s contributed to a deepening disillusionment among white-collar workers and professionals.[57] No doubt this disillusionment was sharpened by the rank corruption spreading through the party's upper echelons under the cover of "trust in cadres."[58]

From Soviet Reform to Soviet Collapse

Mikhail Gorbachev's selection as general secretary of the Communist Party of the Soviet Union in March 1985 paved the way for a dramatic new phase of Moscow's relations with major foreign powers and with the components of both the Soviet "external" and "internal" empires. During his first year as party chief, Gorbachev launched a public drive to revitalize the Soviet system by tightening discipline, purging the party apparatus of dead wood, and attacking corruption. As part of this campaign, he and his political supporters sought to reestablish Moscow's power over the regional party machines that had become deeply entrenched in the national republics during the past two decades. Although Gorbachev succeeded in renovating the party elite, he also discovered that replacing indigenous cadres with Russians dispatched from Moscow could produce explosive results. In December 1986, for instance, Moscow's decision to install an ethnic Russian as party chief of Kazakhstan in place of Dinmohamed Kunayev, an ethnic Kazakh and a staunch supporter of Brezhnev for the better part of two decades, sparked riots in Almaty, the republican capital. Even if these riots were fanned by Kunayev and his local backers, they showed that efforts to tighten Moscow's control over the borderlands could provoke a strong backlash among non-Russians. The episode also suggested that ideologically orthodox non-Russian apparatchiks could wrap themselves in the mantle of national rights when it was politically expedient to do so. As shown in later chapters, several regional party leaders who learned this lesson outlasted Gorbachev and ultimately emerged in the guise of "national democrats."

Around 1987 Gorbachev swung toward a new political strategy that emphasized political liberalization rather than the tightening of authoritarian controls. In essence, his strategy was to encourage greatly expanded public participation in political life in order to generate the power needed to ram through basic reforms of the institutional structures inherited from the Stalin era. Toward this end, Gorbachev engineered a sweeping relaxation of censorship and enlisted the artistic and professional intelligentsia, whose numbers had been dramatically increased by the expansion of higher education since the early 1960s, to serve as a spearhead of reform.[59] He also maneuvered to introduce an element of electoral competition into the selection of state and party officials, and he launched a de-Stalinization campaign that, unlike Khrushchev's, located the origins of Stalinism in the institutional flaws of the early Soviet system rather than in Stalin's character. Over the objections of other Politburo members, Gorbachev encouraged the establishment of "informals," organizations created through spontaneous social action that lay outside the administrative control of the party and governmental bureaucracies. With these steps, Gorbachev set in motion a historic shift in the relationship between society and the state in the Eurasian heartland. Although some precedent for the shift could be found in the growth of liberal groups in the twilight of the tsarist era, that tendency had rested on a far more fragile social base than did the liberal trend of the mid-1980s.

Among the informal groups that drew encouragement from Gorbachev's radical new policies were several inclusive national fronts first established in the Baltics and then imitated in other republics. During the initial stage of Gorbachev's campaign for liberalization, he and the national fronts made common cause against the entrenched bureaucrats of the regional party-state machines. Thanks partly to widespread support from the emerging informal sector, Gorbachev was able to push through a political reform calling for the creation of a semidemocratic parliament with real legislative power and members selected partly through competitive elections.[60] In 1988 and 1989 most of the social movements and parties emerging in the western borderlands and in Russia itself were favorably disposed toward Gorbachev and his campaign to restrict the power of the party apparatus.

However, the de-Stalinization campaign's shocking revelations of the extermination of millions of persons, Russian and non-Russian alike, estranged the liberal members of virtually all national groups from the idea that the Communist polity could be reformed. Almost overnight, Gorbachev's public image shifted from that of a radical reformer to being the representative of a doomed system. In the words of one analyst, "rampant glasnost effectively transformed the Soviet Union into a criminal state."[61] Gorbachev argued repeatedly that the non-Russian republics had a vital economic stake in the preservation of the Soviet state. However, even if this argument contained a substantial element of truth, it sounded hollow in view of the worsening economic conditions that began to make the Brezhnev years, ridiculed by Gorbachev as the "era of stagnation," look favorable by comparison. Faced with increasing political polarization, Gorbachev began to search for conservative counterweights with which to check the centrifugal forces threatening to pull the Soviet system apart. In contrast, Boris Yeltsin, who had made himself the champion of liberal Russian nationalism, advanced a program challenging the authority of Gorbachev and the federal government on the grounds of national self-determination for Russia and the other Soviet nationalities.

Radical Russian democrats and non-Russian nationalists thus joined forces to challenge the authority and legitimacy of the Soviet state. Although the odds favoring the creation of such a political coalition might have been high under any circumstances, Gorbachev's political tactics probably contributed inadvertently to this outcome. By allowing 1990 republican legislative elections that were substantially more democratic than the federal legislative elections of 1989, and by postponing the first direct election for his own federal presidential post until 1994, Gorbachev unwittingly paved the way for an electoral alignment between democratic and separatist forces. Had he pushed for a more rapid transition to the fully democratic election of federal officials, he might have reduced the chance that newly enfranchised voters would come to think of democracy as a distinctive attribute of the national republics rather than of the central government.[62] Yeltsin understood the significance of this contrast, and his unprecedented popular election as President of Russia in mid-1991 gave him a clear political advantage over Gorbachev so long as the rules of the political game continued to evolve in a liberal direction.

These internal political developments were closely intertwined with developments in the international arena. As an aid to their efforts at internal reform, Gorbachev and Foreign Minister Eduard Shevardnadze had adopted an international strategy of sweeping concessions and political accommodation with other major powers, especially the United States. This strategy was Janus-faced. Domestic liberalization and the acceptance of human-rights issues as a legitimate topic of East-West diplomacy won increased credibility for Soviet international initiatives and undercut the influence of the hardline opponents of the USSR in the United States and other Western democracies. At the same time, the dramatic improvement in East-West relations served to weaken the domestic position of those Soviet bureaucracies, including the party apparatus, the KGB, and the armed forces, which had a vested interest in maintaining a high level of tension with the outside world. It also allowed Gorbachev and Shevardnadze to argue that further internal democratization was necessary in order to buttress the USSR's public standing in the West.[63] In other words, these reformers were pursuing a strategy of promoting political liberalization from the outside in, as well as from the bottom up.

The fundamental change in the tenor of East-West relations, however, deprived Moscow of its strongest traditional argument for the preservation of the domestic empire. Whereas the siege atmosphere of the Cold War had justified the need to maintain a centralized state, the buoyant optimism of the "new political thinking" provided no compelling geopolitical justification for the maintenance of the union. This was particularly true after 1989, when Gorbachev and Shevardnadze elected to allow the East European empire to crumble without significant Soviet resistance, let alone military intervention. More than any other single event, this development persuaded Western hard-liners that a profound political change had transpired in Moscow. By the same token, however, it strengthened the belief that had been growing in the non-Russian segments of the USSR that Moscow would hesitate to use force to maintain the domestic empire as well.

The dissolution of the Soviet state reached a watershed at the end of 1990. In a desperate search for means by which to counter the country's political disintegration and shore up his own diminishing power, Gorbachev aligned himself with party and military conservatives and apparently acquiesced in a limited military crackdown in the Baltics in January 1991. Two months later he attempted to staunch the continuing leakage of central power by initiating a carefully worded referendum that produced substantial majorities for the preservation of the USSR in the nine republics that participated, including Ukraine.[64] By April, however, snowballing popular hostility to the Communist "center" and Gorbachev's reluctance to use massive force compelled the party general secretary to strike a bargain with his reformist critics, headed by Yeltsin. The terms of this bargain called for a radical decentralization of power that would turn the USSR from a unitary pseudo-federation into an authentic confederation of sovereign republics. Whether attempts to implement the bargain would have stabilized the relations between the old central institutions and the newly empowered republics remains uncertain.[65] The abortive coup of August 1991 prevented the new formula from being put to the political test.

The small group of party, police, and military officials who tried to seize power in August aimed to preserve the Soviet state. Had they acted in 1987 or 1988, they might well have succeeded. By 1991, however, the cumulative effects of *glasnost'* had undermined the key institutions that might have halted the process of political disintegration by the large-scale use of violence. Six years of public debate and criticism had so eroded the political cohesion of the institutions of coercion that they could no longer be counted on to obey orders, especially when those orders called for the use of force against constitutional and/or democratically elected leaders.[66] Although courageous resistance from President Yeltsin, St. Petersburg mayor Anatoliy Sobchak, and other democratic activists provided an indispensable rallying point for resistance to the coup, conservative politicians in several non-Russian republics and the majority of the local governments in Russia either endorsed the conspiracy or adopted a neutral stance toward it. The key cause of the coup's failure was not massive popular resistance but deep political rifts within the military and police establishments and the reluctance of some commanders to use force against civilians in the service of an unconstitutional political cabal.[67]

Instead of preserving the Soviet state, the coup attempt accelerated the USSR's disintegration. Within six months a surge of anti-

Communist and separatist sentiment produced declarations of independence in virtually all the Soviet republics. Meanwhile Yeltsin, now the country's dominant leader, and Gorbachev, eclipsed and crippled by the dramatic events of August, vied to shape the postcoup distribution of political power. In early December 1991, after several months of fruitless negotiations involving representatives from most of the republics, Yeltsin met with the leaders of Ukraine and Belarus and declared the dissolution of the USSR and the establishment of the Commonwealth of Independent States (CIS). This declaration provoked dissatisfaction among the Central Asian republics, which gave signs of organizing an international political entity of their own but were then quickly admitted to the Commonwealth with the title of founding members. By the end of December a total of eleven republics had joined the CIS.[68] Although the vagueness of the guidelines for the new organization indicated that many key issues concerning the relations among the former republics remained unresolved, it was clear that the Soviet era had ended. Stripped of its traditional sources of cohesion – Marxist-Leninist ideology and state-sponsored Russian nationalism – the Soviet state, once rightly regarded as a leviathan and a juggernaut, dissolved with scarcely a whimper, and the peoples of the former USSR entered a new and uncertain era.

1

The Legacies of History

Although the destruction of the Soviet empire has created dramatic possibilities for the establishment of peaceful relations among the states of Eurasia, it has also unleashed long-suppressed national feelings and reopened age-old controversies. For this reason, historical scholarship must play an important role in efforts to understand the volcanic changes occurring in Eurasia. If it is true, as one practitioner has remarked, that the study of history can be defined as "the intersection of what was expected with what was not,"[1] history can help analysts explain the geopolitical earthquakes of the past few years and help them envision the form of future eruptions. Any satisfactory analysis of these upheavals must situate the collapse and transformation of the USSR within a broader context that takes account of the complex legacies of the past.

History influences the behavior of states in at least two ways: as process and as memory. As a natural and social process, history creates physical and social realities that demand political action but also constrain leaders' choices among potential responses. For example, history has created a geographical mingling of ethnic groups within the territory of the former USSR that demands decision-makers' attention but diminishes the possibility of peacefully creating new states based on ethnically homogeneous populations. Similarly, historical processes have bequeathed most of the new states with high levels of economic interdependence that can be repudiated only at great cost. Such an inheritance limits the policies that leaders of the new states can adopt with any plausible hope of success. Objective conditions of this kind can sometimes be altered, but only through concerted action over the long term.

As social memory, history influences a country's political agenda by shaping public perceptions of the society's purposes and problems.[2] It also plays a powerful role in the decision-making of leaders, even when those leaders make choices without any conscious reference to historical

23

events or manipulate historical anologies to justify current objectives.[3] As a rule, historical events exert the strongest influence on attitudes of individuals who have personally experienced them in their formative years, but a country's collective memory of past events is also shaped and transmitted through popular celebrations and commemorations, folklore, the arts, historical writings, and the country's educational system. By these means, major historical events are incorporated into a "grand governing narrative," a general historical outlook that gives the members of the society a sense of their shared origins and of the common goals they are striving to achieve.[4]

Although democracies are generally more truthful than authoritarian regimes in chronicling the past, no country possesses a fully objective understanding of its history.[5] Rather, a country's historical memory is the result of continuous reinterpretation by persons whose attention is guided by contemporary concerns and whose preconceptions frequently shape the "lessons" they draw from historical episodes. At the level of mass consciousness, the interpretation of a country's past involves the commemoration of events and symbols that are chosen – sometimes long after they transpired or first appeared – because of their bearing on contemporary needs.[6] Despite the assumptions associated with the idea of cultural progress, this process of historical recollection is not linear nor necessarily cumulative. Depending on contemporary circumstances, new knowledge of specific historical events and actors may be carefully imparted to a new generation, then forgotten, and still later rediscovered.[7]

Both as process and memory, history will shape the politics of the new states of Eurasia, but that effect will be far from easy to assess. History has bequeathed the new states with so many objective points of conflict and entanglement that it is difficult to discern what the net impact of these factors will be. For example, will the animosities kindled by the oppressive nationalities policies enforced during much of the Soviet era fracture the ties among Russia and other former republics once and for all, or will the high level of economic interdependence built up during the same years gradually neutralize these centrifugal forces and lead to some political reintegration? In pondering such questions, it is essential to remember that "the past" consists of many periods whose relative influence on the present is difficult to establish. In Russia, for example, will the memory of Soviet totalitarianism discredit all forms of authoritarianism, or will the collective memory of tsarism legitimize a form of authoritarianism based on resurgent Russian nationalist sentiments? As these questions imply, at any given moment a country's range of political possibilities is limited by the legacies of the past, but an element of contingency remains, and the choice among those possibilities is influenced by the judgments and decisions of political actors living in the present.[8]

In the post-Soviet states the effects of history are especially complex. This is true not only because the national chronicles of these countries are filled with calamitous events but also because the societal memory of those events has been systematically distorted. Due to the Soviet regime's falsification of history, whole societies must struggle to free themselves from decades of historical propaganda and censorship. For many citizens – particularly nonintellectuals – the historical assumptions absorbed through schooling and public propaganda are likely to have a much longer half-life than the formal principles of Marxism-Leninism, which have been widely though not universally discredited.

In the post-Soviet states even freethinking intellectuals who consciously have reformulated their ideas not only about the history of tsarist Russia and the Soviet empire but about their own nations are likely to be deeply affected by the cultural legacy of the Soviet era. In the words of a Western scholar, "nations themselves *are* narrations. The power to narrate, or to block other narratives from forming and emerging, is very important to culture and imperialism, and constitutes one of the main connections between them."[9] For independent-minded intellectuals in the new states, the challenge is not whether to reject Soviet historical myths, but rather to find new historical interpretations that are not themselves distorted by the impulse to repudiate the official Soviet outlook and to embrace diametrically opposite views.[10]

Any effort to appraise the post-Soviet impact of history, then, is fraught with epistemological and other intellectual difficulties. Still, no assessment of contemporary developments in Eurasia can be complete without reflecting on the multiple legacies of the past and how they may affect the present and the future.

Russia

Without a doubt, the most important historical question for the future of Eurasia is how the legacy of the past will affect Russia's overall international orientation. Due partly to the absence of impassable natural barriers in central Eurasia, Russian history has been marked by a long succession of wars that have threatened the country's existence and have killed millions of its inhabitants. The Mongol invasions of the thirteenth century destroyed the independence of the East Slavic principalities that later became the political core of modern Russia. After the fifteenth century, when Muscovy freed itself from the "Mongol yoke" and began to take control of adjacent territories, the tsarist regime clashed repeatedly with adversaries from Europe, the Middle

East, and Inner Asia. Although some of these wars were forced on the tsarist regime, in the course of four centuries the tsarist government carried out a vast expansion in Europe, the Caucasus, Central Asia, and the Far East. Sometimes the government extended its control through adroit diplomacy and the cooptation of peoples threatened by other enemies; often, however, it established its suzerainty by military conquest.[11]

Despite the long historical lineage of the tsarist polity, circumstances prevented the tsars' Russian subjects from developing a clear-cut sense of political identity. Thanks to the vast openness of the Eurasian steppe, tsarist Russia, in contrast to the pattern later exhibited by West European imperialism, colonized territories that were contiguous rather than physically separate from the metropole. As a result, Russians mingled with non-Russians more extensively than they would have if the colonies had been situated on another continent. Moreover, the formation of the modern Russian nation did not precede the process of tsarist colonial expansion, but instead coincided with it. The simultaneity of the two processes blurred the ethnic and cultural definition of Russian nationality and made Russia's political identity heavily dependent on the tsarist state's imperial exploits.[12] During most of the twentieth century Russian identity continued to hinge on the international power of the state – but now on the power of the Soviet state, whose millenarian ideology contained a strong imperial element.

The question today is whether Russia will adopt a more benign policy toward neighboring countries, or whether it will revert to a hegemonic role. Historically, few nations have given up an imperial mission without undergoing a lengthy crisis of political and cultural identity, and Russia appears to be no exception. Today Russian politicians and intellectuals are seeking to salvage a sense of the nation's greatness in the face of the stunning collapse of the Soviet empire. The success of their efforts will depend not only on the legacy of history as natural and social process – in other words, on the numerous objective political and socioeconomic factors examined in later chapters of this book – but also on how contemporary Russians think about the tsarist past, about Soviet history, and about Russia's historical relationship to other nation-states.

Russian policy-makers and intellectuals are searching for a "usable past" that can both shape and legitimize contemporary Russian foreign policy.[13] The "new political thinking" introduced in the late 1980s by Mikhail Gorbachev marked an important step in this direction but was only a beginning. If in the late 1980s many Russian liberals seemed content to criticize Soviet foreign policy for neglecting the needs of the Russian nation (as well as those of other Soviet nations), following the collapse of the Union, liberal thinkers have felt impelled to hammer out an operational conception of Russia's national interests vis-à-vis other states.[14] This enterprise has inevitably entailed an effort to justify such conceptions by deriving liberal lessons from Russia's past. By the same token, conservative and reactionary thinkers have bitterly attacked the Yeltsin government for purportedly harming national interests and values that they claim are rooted in prerevolutionary Russian and Soviet history.

In Russia, the linkage between the country's "grand governing narrative" and the state's political behavior has always been close. In prerevolutionary Russia the writing of national history was intertwined with the educated public's conception of the state's international mission, and varying public notions of the nation's past were linked with the nineteenth-century debate about whether the country should be developed according to a Western or uniquely Russian pattern.[15] In the Soviet era the connections between politics and historiography became both more immediate and more Byzantine. From the 1930s onward Soviet politicians frequently turned to the regime's initial "Leninist" years (as well as to some aspects of tsarist practice) as a key source of guidance and validation for state policies.[16] At the same time, however, they frequently engaged in the falsification of the historical record in order to legitimize their programmatic or personal objectives.[17]

Embedded in the historical attitudes fostered under the tsars are fundamental assumptions about Russia's relations with other states and peoples. A common feature of the popular histories published during the tsarist period is the emphasis on the disasters inflicted on Russia early in its history, particularly by the Mongol invasions of the thirteenth century, and the justification of later Russian expansion and annexations as a legitimate response to these misfortunes. For example, the early nineteenth-century historian N. M. Karamzin described the states of Western Europe as determined to expand at Russia's expense; he also referred to the peoples of the southern and eastern steppes as dangerous barbarians and predators. Many key Russian military conquests were thus interpreted as a vindication of the manifold wrongs that Russia had suffered at the hands of foreign adversaries.[18]

A related feature of prerevolutionary Russian history was the propagation of the notion of a "patrimony" of territories that had belonged to the Russian state before the Mongol invasions and that Moscow reclaimed in the "gathering of the Russian lands" that commenced in the fifteenth century under Ivan III. This idea played little part in Muscovy's original justifications for its territorial expansion, but by the nineteenth century the myth of the patrimony had become a key element in the ideology of Russian imperialism.[19] Karamzin, in particular, argued that by the eleventh century, Russia's forebears had controlled almost all the territory encompassed by the European portion of the nineteenth-century tsarist empire.[20] Construed elastically, the notion of a Russian patrimony served to justify Moscow's expansion into many regions and performed a legitimizing function not unlike the one fulfilled by the notion of "Manifest Destiny" in American social thought. Even the great tsarist historian V. O. Klyuchevskiy sometimes slipped into this form of reasoning. Colonization of new territories, Klyuchevskiy reportedly observed, was the "basic fact" of Russian history, and "the history of Russia is the history of a country in the process of being colonized."[21] This revealing formula implied that the territories being occupied by Russian soldiers and settlers were already an intrinsic part of Russia. Russia was, as it were, colonizing itself rather than other peoples or countries.

The Russian notion of restoring a preexisting political and cultural order focused above all on the territories currently inhabited by the Ukrainian and Belarusian peoples, fellow East Slavs whose linguistic ties with the forebears of ethnic Russians can be dated as early as the sixth century A.D. According to the Russian outlook prevailing in the nineteenth century, tsarist Russia was the natural successor to Kievan Rus, the East Slavic polity that had started to decline by the time of the Mongol invasion in the thirteenth century, and was therefore entitled to reunify the domains of ancient Rus. This version of history suffered from several logical defects. According to this historical view, statehood was the principal criterion of historical continuity, and since neither Ukraine nor Belarus had possessed an enduring state structure since the end of the Mongol domination, tsarist Russia was the direct successor of Kievan Rus. This interpretation excluded the notion that continuity should be judged by cultural and ethnic criteria as well as by statehood, and that Ukraine and Belarus could therefore rightfully claim to be descendants of ancient Rus. The Russian interpretation also glossed over the fact that the first polity to proclaim the "gathering of the lands of Rus" as its mission was not Muscovite Russia but the Belarusian-dominated Grand Duchy of Lithuania, another partial descendant of Kievan Rus, which asserted this claim a century or more before Muscovy did so.[22]

Russia's claim to be the only successor to Kievan Rus performed an important ideological function by enabling tsarist ideologists to deny that Ukrainians and Belarusians were distinct peoples or that they possessed legitimate political interests separate from those of the Russian populace. During the second half of the nineteenth century, it also buttressed the tsarist decision to suppress growing Ukrainian and Belarusian nationalism by prohibiting the use of the Ukrainian and Belarusian languages in education and by demanding that the geographic designations "Belarus" and "Ukraine" be eschewed in favor of such terms as "Western Russia" or "Little Russia." In a fashion that had no parallel in tsarist policy toward the empire's other minorities, the refusal to accept the separate historical and cultural identities of Ukrainians and Belarusians was rooted in Russians' uncertainty about their own political identity, and the tsarist policy of denial won adherents from all points on the Russian political spectrum.[23]

Apart from references to Russia's patrimony, tsarist historians justified Russian hegemony and expansion into non-Russian regions on several other grounds. Although these rationales ranged from aiding foreign co-religionists to assisting other countries under attack by a third party, Russia's "civilizing mission" was frequently invoked to rationalize expansion into Muslim and Asian territories. Karamzin, for example, argued that just as Spain had charted a new world in the western hemisphere, Russia was exploring "a second new world for Europe" in northern Asia.[24] Other historians contended that Russia was fulfilling a historic mission to turn back Asiatic nomads from the steppes and establish the higher form of culture embodied in sedentary Western civilization.[25] Prominent Russian observers of both conservative and radical persuasions argued that any level of Russian force employed in this process was justified by the primitive and savage nature of the peoples being colonized.[26] Other observers, especially those influenced by the ideas of the Slavophiles, argued – against the evidence – that Russia's imperial expansion had been accomplished strictly by peaceful means. The Russian empire, they contended, differed fundamentally from the other states of Europe because it had been created through love rather than violent conquest.[27]

During the mid-nineteenth century Russian intellectuals wrestled with the question of their country's identity, particularly its relationship to Europe, and this issue produced sharp differences among the Westernizers, the Slavophiles, and somewhat later, the pan-Slavists.[28] Russia's distinctive culture and its location between most of Europe and much of Asia led a number of thinkers to question whether the country could be called, or should become, "European." However, despite such differences, both Westernizers and Slavophiles agreed that Russia was culturally superior to most of the peoples it was colonizing – particularly those to the south and to the east. The Asian borderlands "were perceived by the intelligentsia not as a threat to Russia's European identity but rather as an opportunity to prove that identity. In bringing to her Oriental subjects the fruits of Western civilization, Russia would be demonstrating her membership in the exclusive club of European nations; in absorbing these subjects into the Russian nation, still in the process of formation, Russia would be carrying out her civilizing mission," much as the West was perceived as doing in its colonies.[29]

Although participants in the nineteenth-century debate over Russia's political identity sometimes invoked Russia's geographical location to demonstrate its political and cultural distinctiveness, they did not regard Russia as a part of Asia in a cultural sense. Despite their differences over Russia's proper relationship to Europe, Slavophiles, Westernizers, and pan-Slavists all shared the view that Russia was a Christian country having more in common with Europe than with Asia. During the tsarist era, the "entire 'anti-Western tradition' remained thoroughly Western in its attitude toward Asia. The conflict with the West, which its proponents loudly proclaimed, was essentially a fraternal conflict, perhaps all the more bitter for that reason, but nevertheless fraternal. Self-identification in terms of Orthodoxy, the Byzantine heritage, the Russian people, or Slavdom almost inevitably implied a close relationship to other Christians, other heirs of the classical world, and other European peoples or groups of peoples."[30] In the early twentieth century a fundamentally different outlook was set forth by Russian thinkers who regarded Russia as a distinctive combination of European and Asiatic cultures. This "Eurasian" outlook, however, was formulated among emigres displaced by the 1917 Revolution and played no significant role in the thinking of the prerevolutionary tsarist elite.[31]

Tsarist Russia's nineteenth-century expansion into Central Asia and the Far East was thus a reflection of geopolitical calculations rather than of cultural affinities. Although the defeat of Napoleonic France had made Russia a key actor in the European balance of power during the first half of the nineteenth century, Russia's defeat at the hands of a British, French, and Ottoman alliance in the Crimean War of the mid-1850s sharply reduced the tsarist government's influence in Europe. Partly to compensate, the autocracy stepped up its expansion into the territories of Central Asia. Prompted primarily by strategic and military considerations rather than economic ones, the annexation of peoples and territories in Central Asia allowed Russia to compete against its European rivals, particularly England, on terms more favorable than those possible in Europe. "Central Asia therefore played a subsidiary role in Russia[n] policy-making: its importance was derived not from the intrinsic value of the conquered territories but from the role it played in European affairs."[32]

At several crucial junctures in tsarist history, the distinctive features of the Russian outlook had a major impact on imperial Russian foreign policy. During the 1870s, for instance, pan-Slavic pressures helped draw St. Petersburg into war with the Ottoman Turks, and into a dangerous confrontation with other major European powers over the Balkans. Of greater consequence, imperialist condescension toward the peoples of Asia contributed to the autocracy's aggressive push into East Asia and to its humiliating military defeat at the hands of Japan in 1904–5. Pan-Slavic assumptions, if not passions, also played a part in the tsarist regime's reluctant but politically fatal decision to go to war in 1914.[33]

The foreign policy debates in post-Soviet Russia echo the great debates of the prerevolutionary era. As one Russian legislator has remarked, Russian foreign policy is "an eternal struggle" between the advocates of Westernization and nationalist forces "who want a specific way for Russia."[34] Thanks to the enduring disagreement about Russia's geographic and political identity, contemporary advocates of an "Atlanticist" or a "Eurasian" orientation for Russia appear to be waging a modern variant of the historic struggle that divided Westernizers from the Slavophiles and the pan-Slavists.[35] From the Atlanticist perspective, the West is no longer an adversary of Russia, but a model for Russian emulation and a partner in the post-Soviet world order. By contrast, the exponents of a Eurasian outlook believe that Russia should concentrate on expanding its ties with the nations of the Middle East and Asia, where it can command greater influence and can fulfill its historic calling as an international leader and a great power.

Although historical perspective can shed a great deal of light on contemporary Russian behavior, care must be exercised in drawing direct historical analogies. Like the great debates of the past, the current controversies over Russia's destiny and national interest are multilayered disputes whose policy implications need to be carefully investigated rather than derived a priori from a schematic notion of each side's basic ideas.[36] For instance, failure to exercise due caution could lead analysts to depict all contemporary "Westernizers" in a favorable light while branding all "Eurasianists" as the champions of anti-Western policies based on nationalism and coercion. The real patterns of thought and the political coalitions involved in contemporary Russian foreign policy debates are considerably more complicated than this equation suggests.[37]

Apart from its implications for future relations with long-established states, history has a direct bearing on Russia's relations with the other new states spawned by the Soviet collapse. One Western scholar has drawn a distinction between the Russian "empire savers," who equate Russia's greatness with dominion over neighboring peoples, particularly the East Slavs of Ukraine and Belarus, and the "nation builders," who believe that Russia can achieve its proper place only by shedding the burdens of empire and concentrating on domestic needs.[38] A key question is whether post-Soviet Russians can make an enduring departure from the empire-building mentality, or whether the change in the Russian outlook will prove short-lived. During the first two years following the collapse of the USSR, the Yeltsin government generally avoided any direct attempt to dominate the other post-Soviet states, and Yeltsin himself denounced persons who claimed Crimea and other areas for Russia. Nonetheless, on occasion Yeltsin exhibited a rather combative stance toward charges of Russian imperialism, remarking in this connection that Russia should not allow itself to be insulted in a manner that the USSR would not have tolerated.[39] Together with the strident voices of Russian extremists who proclaim that Moscow must reestablish its suzerainty over the other new states, these debates indicate that the question of which Russian outlook will prevail has not yet been decided. They also suggest that historical memory will play a significant role in shaping policy toward the other former Soviet republics.

Many of the participants in these debates, however, are likely to have a distorted understanding of the historical realities involved. In the decade following the Russian Revolution, Marxist historians such as Mikhail Pokrovskiy harshly criticized Russia's prerevolutionary conquest of neighboring peoples. This new perspective, which marked an important though highly schematic attempt to rectify the imperialist biases embodied in prerevolutionary Russian historiography, was linked with the broader Soviet effort during the 1920s to strike a fairer balance in relations between the Russian and non-Russian inhabitants of the former tsarist empire.[40]

The advent of Stalinism, however, obliterated these initial steps toward a more accurate understanding of Russia's complex relations with the tsarist empire's non-Russian peoples. After consolidating his personal power at the end of the 1920s, Stalin turned to Russian nationalism and Russian cadres as key building-blocks for the construction of the emerging totalitarian state. Intent on the indoctrination of Soviet citizens, he and his minions rejected the critical historical approach of the Pokrovskiy school. Instead they endorsed a "lesser evil" theory that rehabilitated the historical reputations of tsarist statesmen and generals and justified Russia's prerevolutionary expansion on the grounds that it had protected non-Russians from exploitation by Western imperialists.[41] Stalin's ideologists later imposed an even more distorted brand of history that flatly denied that incorporation into the tsarist empire had entailed any costs for the non-Russian peoples.[42] This outlook bore more than a passing resemblance to the strain of prerevolutionary Russian thought that had emphasized the peaceable nature of tsarist expansion and the voluntary nature of the incorporation of the non-Russian peoples into the tsarist empire.

In the post-Stalin era central party ideologists worked to perpetuate the image of prerevolutionary accord in order to buttress Moscow's claims of interethnic harmony under Soviet Communism.[43] Although this effort failed to prevent more skeptical treatment of the tsarist era by some historians after Stalin's death, on the whole it maintained the historical image of interethnic harmony in official propaganda and education. Thus the tendentious historiography of the Stalin era continued to affect interpretations of the historical relations between Russia and the non-Russian territories and peoples. Shifts in some historians' treatment of these issues may well have resonated in the minds of non-Russians who were already attuned to such matters, but the changes were registered in specialized periodicals rather than in the mass media and were too subtle to affect the historical outlook of most Russian politicians and ordinary citizens. Although some Russian dissenters underscored the past wrongs inflicted on the non-Russian peoples, they found the roots of these evils in the Soviet system, not in the Russian nation. As late as 1989, Gorbachev proudly echoed Dostoevsky's praise of Russia's efforts to achieve union with other nations and commended the legacy of "friendship" among the peoples that had been "united" with Russia in the tsarist empire.[44]

Because the dominant Soviet interpretation of past relations between Russians and non-Russians coincides in many essentials with the Russian historical outlook that prevailed before the Revolution of 1917, it seems certain to exercise an enduring influence on the historical memory of Russian policy-makers and citizens alike. As Russians reject ideas and institutions labeled "Soviet," many of them have begun to look to Russia's prerevolutionary heritage for guidance. This proclivity seems especially pronounced among individuals with strong anti-Communist feelings, who often tend to see Russian values and Soviet values as antithetical. However, in this intellectual domain the difference is often illusory. Western observers report that in the confused search for books from which to teach national history to the younger generation, some educational establishments are turning to prerevolutionary history texts. One such text, written by Dmitriy Ilovayskiy and widely used before the revolution, has been endorsed by the Russian Ministry of Education. At the beginning of the century Ilovayskiy was regarded by Russian liberals and members of ethnic minorities "as the quintessential expositor of autocratic rule, intolerant Orthodoxy, and chauvinist Russification."[45] Although other, more enlightened prerevolutionary works are being made available for use in Russian schools, many of these works also embody the imperial attitude toward non-Russians that was almost universally accepted by Russians during the nineteenth century. The main intellectual antidote to this attitude consists of the new histories being prepared by liberal academic institutions, together with the translation and publication of Western historical accounts such as *The Russian Revolution*, by Richard Pipes.[46]

The linkages between historical memory and present policy are well illustrated by the behavior of Russian vice-president Aleksandr Rutskoy. Committed to the tenet that "Russia must be a great state," Rutskoy has warned the new governments embroiled in territorial disputes with Russia that "Russia's thousand-year history" must be the basis for interstate relations. "The demarcation of borders, and nothing but the demarcation of borders . . . will define Russia as a power," he has insisted. "This will be done without fail for the glory of Russia, however the political leaders of national-careerism may try to drive [Russia] back within its twelfth-century borders."[47] Claiming to express Russian popular consciousness, Rutskoy has warned that "the historical awareness of Russian citizens will not allow anyone to implement a mechanical combination of Russia and the Russian Federation, [thus] renouncing all that constituted the glorious pages of Russia's history."[48] Rutskoy has rejected Ukrainian sovereignty over Crimea, insisting that "Crimea was Russian, it's covered with Russian blood, and it must be Russian."[49] Although as of mid-1993 the Yeltsin government was still following a relatively restrained policy toward such territorial disputes, statements such as Rutskoy's have naturally fed neighboring states' apprehensions that sooner or later Russia will attempt to renew its historic domination of the borderlands.

An assertive view of territorial issues is held not only by conservative figures such as Rutskoy, but by some leading Russian liberals. Anatoliy Sobchak, a respected democrat, has stridently criticized the Yeltsin government for failing to defend Russia's historic interests. Implying that border changes made in the Soviet period are illegitimate, Sobchak has called for the Russian government "to openly demand the return to Russia of what it lost during the Soviet totalitarian period," including Ukrainian-held Crimea and territories now part of Kazakhstan.[50] Even a former Soviet dissident such as Zhores Medvedev has lamented the breakup of the USSR as Russia's "greatest national and historic defeat" and has castigated acquiescent Russians for this "self-inflicted" injury. According to Medvedev, Yeltsin has lost the "Russian heartland"; the December 1991 Ukrainian popular vote for independence was "a disaster for Russia"; and efforts to reestablish some form of central authority within the domain of the former Soviet Union are "inevitable."[51]

Even if such statements have not yet led to an aggressive government policy, they show that nationalist desires for a return to the traditions of "glorious Russia" will be a salient element of Russia's politics and foreign relations. Sobchak's statements also suggest that a number of Russian liberals may not embrace a conciliatory policy toward the other new countries that have emerged from the collapse of the Soviet empire. This liberal hostility to political independence for non-Russians has roots in the prerevolutionary history of the Russian liberal movement.[52] It remains to be seen whether contemporary Russian liberals, having made common cause with non-Russian nationalities against the Soviet autocracy, will revert to the attitudes of their liberal forebears in dealing with the political and territorial interests of the new non-Russian states.

The Western Newly Independent States

In contrast to Russia, none of the new states of the western region – Ukraine, Belarus, Moldova, and the Baltic states – has enjoyed a lengthy period of political independence in the modern era. Although the peoples of almost all of these territories can look back to at least one brief episode of independent statehood, for most of the past three centuries they have been ruled by Russia, Austro-Hungary, Germany, or Poland, and their perspectives on history and international politics have been shaped by this reality.[53] Among these peoples historical experience has engendered memories of abuse at the hands of many governments, including the tsarist and Soviet regimes. On the other hand, the official historical accounts that were propagated and taught during most of the Soviet era have accented the themes of national friendship and political partnership within the USSR. This contradictory mixture of historical attitudes has confronted the new states of the western region with problems of political identity that are only slightly less complex than those facing post-Soviet Russia.

During the formative years of the Soviet system politics and historiography were intimately intertwined, particularly in such politically vital regions as Ukraine. During 1917, for example, Mykhailo Hrushevsky, the leading historian of Ukraine and a prominent public figure, returned from exile to become the leader of the newly organized central legislative council that proclaimed an independent Ukrainian People's Republic. Within a year the central council fell from power due to the tides of war and its own political errors – one of the most important being the decision not to organize a regular army from the Ukrainian soldiers who had defected from the tsarist army to support the new Ukrainian government.[54] Hrushevsky was compelled to flee to the West. However, the events that allowed him to return to Soviet Ukraine in the mid-1920s vividly demonstrated the close connection between historical memory and the politics of statehood.

As noted in the introductory chapter, the early and middle 1920s constituted a brief but comparatively liberal phase of Soviet nationalities policy. In the case of Ukraine this period of moderation coincided with early expressions of national consciousness that had begun to crystallize in the late tsarist period despite the tsarist government's oppressive policies. In Soviet Ukraine Hrushevsky used his position as leader of the republic's academy of sciences to promote a fundamentally new interpretation of Ukraine's history and identity – and therefore of Russia's.[55] He rejected the standard Russian claim that the tsarist state was the direct descendent of Kievan Rus and that the post-Kievan history of Ukraine had been strictly subordinate to that of Russia. Instead he argued that the culture of Kievan Rus had initially been preserved by proto-Ukrainian principalities and that tsarist Russia did not represent a direct continuation of the medieval Kievan polity. Hrushevsky also pointed out that Ukraine had developed independently of Muscovite Russia and had come under tsarist control only in the seventeenth century. The Russian failure to acknowledge these historical realities, he contended, had impeded the development of Ukrainian political identity and had done even worse injury to the formation of a distinctive sense of identity among the Belarusian people.[56]

Viewed from a political standpoint, the historical outlook formulated by Hrushevsky implied the possibility of genuine Ukrainian political autonomy, if not outright independence.[57] The political implications of his historical perspective are indicated by the fact that during the short life of the Ukrainian People's Republic in 1917–18, Hrushevsky had made the trident, the ancient emblem of the authority of the Kievan princes, the official symbol of the newly declared Ukrainian state.[58] In the mid-1920s Hrushevsky's central role in the wartime struggle for independence gave his ideas a special political resonance in Ukraine, and the evidence indicates that his scholarly writings aroused the concern of the local division of the Soviet political police and were probably discussed by the political authorities in Moscow.[59]

In any event, such heterodox views became politically untenable once Stalin launched his violent onslaught against all potential sources of resistance to his dictatorial power. During the 1930s the Stalinist regime forced the histories of the non-Russian peoples into an arbitrary new mold that continued to affect patterns of historical thought long after the tyrant's death in 1953. Under this new dispensation, research into the histories of individual non-Russian national movements was strongly discouraged, and the prerevolutionary histories of non-Russian peoples and regions were generally presented as components of the history of the USSR. Along with the anachronistic use of terms such as "Soviet peoples" in accounts of developments before 1917, this approach gave Soviet historical accounts a teleological bias suggesting that the events of earlier eras were no more than a prelude to the formation of the Soviet state.[60] In addition to silencing Hrushevsky and other unconventional historical thinkers who challenged tsarism's imperial role, the consolidation of Stalin's dictatorship produced especially egregious omissions and falsifications in accounts of the fate of various nationalities repressed during the period of Communist rule.[61] As in the case of Russia, the creation of semifictional histories of the USSR's non-Russian peoples was intended to obscure the crimes and human costs inflicted on ordinary citizens by such arbitrary acts as the deportation of large numbers of Ukrainians on the charge that they had aided the USSR's foreign enemies.

To be sure, the historical legacy of the Stalin era was complex and entailed painful moral contradictions. Stalin's policies cost Ukraine millions of lives – not only in the crucible of agricultural collectivization but through the disastrous mishandling of the Nazi attack in 1941. Stalin's drive for territorial expansion also unified Soviet Ukraine with the western Ukrainian territories that were seized from Poland and which, almost a half-century later, spearheaded the Ukrainian independence movement.[62] During World War II the Organization of Ukrainian Nationalists and its Ukrainian Partisan Army fought tenaciously to restore Ukraine's independence from the Stalinist régime that had devastated Ukraine. Yet the OUN was also an ultranationalist organization that collaborated with the Nazis in fighting the Soviet regime. It is estimated that compared with the two million Ukrainians who fought on the Soviet side during the Second World War, as many as 220,000 Ukrainians fought along with the Germans, including the 13,000 members of the SS Volunteer Galicia Division who participated in the extermination of Ukrainian Jews.[63] In the Baltic states, the brutal Soviet 1940 takeover designed to crush resistance had the unintended effect of strengthening Baltic nationalism and substituting Russia for Germany as the object of Baltic national hostility, which found an outlet in a tenacious anti-Soviet partisan movement and ultimately in the successful drive for Baltic independence. Some Baltic partisans and ordinary citizens, however, also participated in the extermination of local Jews.[64] In the western borderlands of the USSR, as in Russia proper, the brutal extremes of the Stalin era led to shocking events that were either excised from the historical record or caricatured for the purposes of Soviet propaganda.[65]

Although Stalin's death opened the way for incremental changes in historical depictions of the various Soviet peoples, especially sensitive issues remained off limits. In the case of Ukraine, for instance, negative assessments of the seventeenth-century Russian-Ukrainian Treaty of Pereyaslav, an important step toward the incorporation of Ukraine into the Russian empire, could not be published, nor could dispassionate accounts that described the decision of Ukrainian Cossack Hetman Ivan

Mazepa to join the Swedish war against Peter the Great as an effort to protect Ukrainian interests rather than as an act of treason against Russia.[66] During the early 1970s a group of historians who had sought to rehabilitate the Ukrainian Cossacks by portraying them in a favorable historical light were censured for nationalist leanings and purged.[67] Historical discussions of events of the Soviet era were subject to even tighter party controls. Any published reference to the secret codicil of the 1939 Nazi-Soviet pact that paved the way for the forcible Soviet annexation of the Baltic states was still forbidden, as were published descriptions of the man-made Stalinist famine that killed several million Ukrainian peasants in 1932–3. Although these subjects were increasingly discussed in the samizdat literature of the dissent movement, they received virtually no attention in official discourse about the Soviet past.[68]

In the late 1980s the relaxation of Soviet censorship opened the floodgates for the recollection and reconsideration of the past. Due to the particular bias of Soviet censorship and many individuals' personal ties to events of the post-1917 period, the historical revelations with the greatest emotional charge concerned the Soviet era. Thus, for example, the disclosure of mass graves in the Kuropaty wood near Minsk led to the creation of an organization called Martyrology of Belarus, which in turn founded the Belarusian Popular Front.[69] As the revelations of Stalinist atrocities mounted, however, public interest in the unwritten history of the Soviet era was increasingly augmented – and in some cases, supplanted – by a deepening interest in national events and traditions that antedated the creation of the Soviet empire.

The revival of historical memory was especially dramatic in Ukraine. Despite opposition from Communist Party elites and old-line historians, many cultural leaders and citizens embraced the views of Hrushevsky and other prerevolutionary Ukrainian historians, as well as more nuanced historical interpretations developed in the Ukrainian diaspora in the West.[70] In this formal sense, the Ukrainian revival of historical consciousness has resembled the analogous process in Russia, where intellectuals and educators also turned to the writings of prerevolutionary historians for guidance. As Soviet political hegemony crumbled, Ukrainian historians set about rewriting the history of the Ukrainian Cossacks in a way that emphasized the theme of independence from tsarist control and attempted to bridge the historical divide between eastern and western Ukraine.[71] The negative Soviet historical evaluation of the wartime Ukrainian military resistance to Soviet forces was increasingly called into question, and one of the OUN leaders, Stepan Bandera, came to be regarded by many persons as a national hero.[72] The disastrous human consequences of the Stalinist collectivization of agriculture received extensive attention, and the view spread that this policy constituted a genocidal attack on the Ukrainian people.[73]

Developments during the twilight of the Soviet regime demonstrated the power of key historical events, particularly those that had been excised from official histories, to capture the imagination of rank-and-file citizens. In Latvia, for instance, during the summer and fall of 1987 large-scale "calendar demonstrations" were held to commemorate key occurrences such as Latvia's declaration of independence in 1918, the signing of the Nazi-Soviet pact in 1939, and the mass deportation of Latvians by the Soviet secret police in 1941. By August 1989, the fiftieth anniversary of the Nazi-Soviet Pact, joint efforts of the three Baltic popular fronts were able to mobilize almost two million people in a human chain linking the Baltic capitals.[74] In Ukraine in January 1990, nearly a million people gathered to form a similar chain between Kiev and Lviv in commemoration of the 1918 Ukrainian declaration of independence and the act of union joining western and eastern Ukraine.[75]

The political leaders of the emerging western states have sought to harness the population's evolving historical awareness to specific national objectives as well as to their own political careers. For instance, around 1990 the Belarusian Popular Front, led by Zianon Pazniak, embraced the goal of establishing an East European Commonwealth linking Belarus with Ukraine and the Baltic republics. The half millennium of history shared by these five nations, Pazniak explained, "tells us more than 200 years of imperial bondage" under Russia. Adopting similar rhetoric, Leonid Kravchuk, a candidate for the Ukrainian presidency who had recently served as ideological chief of the Ukrainian Communist Party, wrapped himself in the mantle of Ukraine's pre-Communist history. Kravchuk extolled the "thousand-year-old tradition of Ukrainian statehood" that had begun with Kievan Rus, and he declared his intention to pursue the political vision set forth by Mykhailo Hrushevsky at the beginning of the twentieth century.[76] The effectiveness of such appeals to history has varied – Kravchuk was elected Ukrainian president, whereas the proposal of the Belarusian Popular Front was overtaken by events – but under the right conditions they have had a major impact.

Although observers from many of the new states share a common impulse to reject Soviet historical orthodoxy, they often evaluate concrete events of the Soviet period in disparate ways. If in the post-Soviet era many Russian observers have construed Stalin's depredations as disasters inflicted by a Marxist-Leninist regime upon Russians and non-Russians alike, many Ukrainian and Baltic observers have regarded several of these shattering events as a direct consequence of Russian chauvinism. For example, Russian observers have rightly depicted Stalin's collectivization drive as a disaster for the Russian peasantry, but Ukrainian observers have argued that the Stalinist regime treated the Ukrainian peasantry with a genocidal animus spawned by vindictive Russian nationalism.[77] By the same token, however, in a few specific instances favorable to their cause – such as Nikita Khrushchev's 1954 decision to cede control of Crimea to Ukraine on the 300th anniversary of the Treaty of Pereyaslav – spokesmen for the new non-Russian states have dismissed Russian arguments derived from prerevolutionary history and have treated the acts of the Soviet regime as a source of historical legitimacy.[78]

The contemporary derivation of the "lessons of history" from the tangled skeins of past events is further complicated by the internal variations that history has wrought within several of the new states themselves. For instance, the western provinces of Ukraine were long dominated by Lithuanian-Polish and Austrian rulers, whereas the eastern provinces were part of the tsarist empire. Due to the resulting differences in ethnic composition and cultural attitudes, many present-day inhabitants of western Ukraine seem determined to assert their country's complete independence from Russia, but the less militant citizens of eastern Ukraine are more eager to maintain good relations with their giant neighbor. In Latvia and Estonia, still deeper cultural differences divide the titular Baltic populations from the large Russian communities that settled there in the Soviet era and regard themselves as full-fledged citizens of their country of residence. These differences are reflected in profoundly different understandings of the Baltic countries' historical balance sheet with Soviet Russia – particularly the balance between the Soviet seizure of the Baltic states under the terms of the Nazi-Soviet pact and the Soviet expulsion of Nazi occupiers near the end of World War II. For instance, during the years after the war many Latvians came to equate the brutalities of Stalinism with the Russian people, whereas some Russians accepted the assertion of Communist Party ideologists that any Latvian expression of anti-Soviet feeling constituted a recrudescence of fascism.[79]

Due to Eastern Europe's turbulent past, the citizens of the new states can recall bitter conflicts with many neighboring countries, and the impact of history will therefore hinge in part on which memories exert the greatest influence on current political attitudes. Like most of the other new states in the western region, Ukraine perceives Russia as posing the most serious potential threat to its security and territorial integrity. Although in 1990 the governments of the Russian and Ukrainian Soviet republics concluded an agreement affirming the existing territorial boundaries between them, political developments since the USSR's collapse have given rise to serious tensions over territorial issues such as Crimea. President Yeltsin has held back from pressing any official territorial claims against Ukraine, but some Russian politicians such as Vice-President Rutskoy have staked out a more assertive position, and the surge in Russian nationalism has provoked some equally inflammatory rhetoric from the Ukrainian side.[80]

In staking Russia's claim to Crimea, Rutskoy and other Russian nationalists have recalled tsarist Russia's costly war in Crimea and have emphasized that the local Crimean population includes a majority of ethnic Russians, many of whom do not wish to be part of an independent Ukraine.[81] The most outspoken Ukrainians, by contrast, are loath to see any territory removed from the control of their fragile new state. These Ukrainians counter Russian references to the Crimean War with the historical argument that the peoples most entitled to the peninsula are the Crimean Tatars and, to a lesser extent, the Soviet Germans, both deported from Crimea by Stalin. Moreover, as the Cossack revival has gained momentum in Ukraine, some Cossack groups have raised claims to the Kuban region of southern Russia, although the Ukrainian government has carefully refrained from endorsing such claims.[82]

Ukraine's eastern Donbas region constitutes another potential source of conflict with Russia. As of mid-1993 there was no significant lobby in the Donbas for political separation from Ukraine, and the residents had succeeded in obtaining a measure of administrative autonomy from Kiev. However, the Donbas has a Russian-speaking majority that contains many ethnic Russians, and the economic and cultural strains of the reform process have produced deepening cleavages between the region and the western provinces of Ukraine. Given the Donbas's strong vote for Ukrainian independence in the December 1991 referendum, the region seems more likely to fight for its interests within Ukraine than to embark on a separatist path of unification with Russia. However, if the political fissures between the eastern and western sections of Ukraine widen further, and if the Donbas receives encouragement from Russia, separatist attitudes in the region could increase rapidly.

Although Russia is the principal focus of Ukrainian apprehensions about the outside world, the legacy of history also provides grounds for concern about other nearby countries such as Germany. For tactical reasons Germany has occasionally favored the idea of Ukrainian independence – for instance, in the closing stages of World War I – but it also has shown a converse inclination to seek a special relationship with Russia at the expense of the rest of Eastern Europe. The 1922 Treaty of Rapallo and the 1939 Nazi-Soviet pact both exemplify this tendency. Ukrainian politicians are keenly aware of the importance of German policy for Ukraine's position vis-à-vis Russia, and they may seek to use Germany as a check on Russian expansionist pressure and territorial claims. President Kravchuk, for example, has attempted to draw Germany into the conflict with Moscow over Crimea by suggesting that the ethnic Germans deported by Stalin from Crimea and other territories could be resettled in the peninsula. However, even though Germany is clearly interested in the fate of Soviet Germans and concerned about Ukraine's role in the European balance of power, it is unclear whether Ukrainian efforts to play a "German card" will in fact win long-term German support for Kiev in its relations with Moscow. Ukraine thus faces a choice about whether Germany best serves Ukrainian interests as a counterweight against Russia or as an "honest broker" in Ukrainian-Russian relations.[83]

Relations with Poland constitute a salient part of the Ukrainian historical legacy. Ukrainian attitudes toward Poland are colored by the memory of Polish-Lithuanian expansion into Ukraine and by a long record of Polish hostility toward Ukrainians under both the Polish monarchy and the modern Polish state created at the end of World War I.[84] Thus far, however, Ukrainian distrust for Poland is less pronounced than distrust of Russia, and Ukrainian leaders have attempted to strengthen relations with Poland in order to buttress their position vis-à-vis Russia.[85] A 1990 treaty with Poland, for example, recognized the existing borders between the two countries.[86] Both nations, however, are imbued with strong patriotic traditions, and both have only recently emerged from a period of protracted domination that has strengthened pent-up national feelings. These circumstances may make each country sensitive to apparent slights and could hamper the two governments' efforts to lay past differences to rest.

Ukrainian relations with Romania are clouded by a territorial imbroglio that has deep historical roots. The tsarist government originally won control over historic Moldova from the Ottoman Empire in 1812, but in 1918 Romania seized the territory and refused to return it despite Soviet claims. In 1940, under the terms of the Nazi-Soviet pact, Moscow annexed the territory east of the river Prut, which included historical territories of Bessarabia, Moldova, and Bukovina; it gave a portion of the territory to the Ukrainian Soviet Socialist Republic and put the remainder under the jurisdiction of another unit, the Moldovan Soviet Socialist Republic, set up expressly for this purpose.[87] Never fully reconciled to the annexation, influential Romanian political groups have pressed, with varying degrees of insistence, for the return of all the annexed territory, and the Moldovan advocates of Moldovan reunification with Romania have backed these claims.[88] The situation has been further complicated by the outbreak of a military conflict pitting the Moldovan government against separatist Russian forces in the trans-Dniester region of Moldova that oppose reunification with Romania.

Acutely sensitive to the risk of fanning pro-Russian separatist sentiment in Crimea and other Ukrainian regions, Kiev has responded to Romanian and Moldovan claims on its territory with "quiet diplomacy." This low-key strategy has been designed to elicit a moderation of Romanian territorial claims in exchange for Ukrainian restraint toward the fighting in the trans-Dniester region, where Romania favors the Moldovan government against the Russian insurgents, and for Ukrainian support of Moldovan president Mircea Snegur, who has distanced himself from Moldovan calls for reunification with Romania.[89] Although the Ukrainian strategy has thus far enjoyed some success, whether Ukraine can continue to insulate itself from the Moldovan conflict and prevent such frictions from souring its relations with Romania remains uncertain.

In certain general respects, Belarus's historical experience resembles that of Ukraine. As one scholar put it, Belarus "has been at one of the crossroads of European history and has suffered accordingly."[90] Fatefully located along one of the principal east-west transit routes linking Russia and Europe, Belarus was the territory through which both Napoleon and Hitler invaded Russia, and its 1940s losses were among the largest of all the Soviet republics in proportional terms.[91] As far as political attitudes are concerned, Belarus's chief difference from Kiev lies in the Belarusians' less-developed sense of national identity and their greater susceptibility to cultural assimilation by other ethnic groups, especially Russians.[92] Together these two historical realities help account for the new Belarusian state's approach to foreign relations.

Although Belarusians dominated the Grand Duchy of Lithuania until the late sixteenth century, Belarus has scarcely any modern historical experience of independence and has long suffered from domination by neighboring powers. The first steps of Belarusian diplomacy in the post-Soviet era have, therefore, naturally aimed at winning international acceptance of the country's borders. Secure borders are needed to provide a firm territorial foundation for the growth of Belarusian ethnonational sentiment. One focus of concern has been Poland. Belarus's past relations with Poland have been difficult – the country's brief taste of independence was terminated in 1919 by a Polish invasion – and shortly after the breakup of the USSR Belarusian officials expressed concern over "Polish chauvinist elements" along the Polish-Belarusian border.[93] Within a few months, however, Belarus managed to defuse this issue by concluding treaties with Poland that secured Belarus's western border and provided for the protection of the Belarusian minority in Poland.[94] Early in 1992 additional territorial frictions arose when Belarusian foreign minister Pyotr Krauchanka announced Belarusian claims on a large part of Lithuania that extended as far as Vilnius, the Lithuanian capital.[95] Krauchanka and other Belarusian leaders subsequently disavowed these claims, perhaps because they wished to reduce their own country's vulnerability to territorial demands. In any case, Minsk demonstrated its concern over its borders with Lithuania and Latvia by establishing a joint border patrol arrangement with Russia.[96]

Despite this incident, the Belarusians' relatively mild sense of their distinctiveness from Russians has generally made them less eager to assert themselves than the Ukrainians. The Belarusian government has moved toward the role of a mediator within the Commonwealth of Independent States (CIS) and a bridge linking Western Europe to Russia and Eurasia. The government also has adopted a posture of international neutrality, although the operational meaning of this notion has become an object of vigorous debate inside Belarus.[97] Keenly aware that its exposed geographical location and economic dependence necessitate sensitivity to Russian and Ukrainian interests, Belarus has sought to balance its position by concluding bilateral military cooperation agreements with both countries.[98] However, Minsk can play a mediating role inside the CIS only if tension between Russia and Ukraine remains within reasonable bounds. If faced with an "either-or" situation vis-à-vis its two East Slavic neighbors, Belarus would almost certainly choose Russia. In 1992 Prime Minister Vyacheslau Kebich stated that new bilateral agreements signed with Russia could mark a step in the direction of a Russian-Belarusian confederation within the CIS.[99]

Although the Baltic countries share the regional historical pattern of foreign domination, their historical experiences of independence between the two world wars have served as a major rallying point for the establishment of new political structures and foreign policies. Combined with the recollection of interwar independence, the opportunity for public discussion of the crimes committed by Stalin's occupying forces and the tenacious postwar resistance mounted by bands of Baltic guerrillas has had a powerful impact on the objectives of the three Baltic states. Following five decades of Soviet-imposed isolation, the Balts are eager to renew their ties to the West, both to overcome economic backwardness and as a hedge against future political domination by Russia.

At the same time, history has created several potential constraints on the Baltic governments' freedom of action. During the interwar period, Baltic relations with other countries of Eastern Europe were sometimes badly strained. Lithuania, in particular, was on the verge of war with Poland several times during this period.[100] Although Lithuanian and Polish leaders have shown a desire to lay these past animosities to rest, such tensions could be rekindled, especially by Polish-Lithuanian ethnic frictions inside Lithuania.[101] Nor is it certain that the Baltic countries will be received with open arms by Western Europe or the United States, now that the Baltic region has ceased to be a bridgehead of East-West struggle.

An equally weighty constraint on the Baltic governments has been created by five decades of Soviet domination. The long period of Soviet hegemony created strong eastward economic, political, and cultural ties that have given Moscow both specific interests and considerable leverage in the region. This situation has posed the difficult issue of how far the Latvian and Estonian governments should go in seeking to ensure the political and cultural cohesion of their citizenry, given the large number of ethnic Russians who still reside in these countries.[102] It also has raised the vexing problem of whether the Baltic states should continue to demand the complete and unconditional removal of Russian military forces from their territories, or whether they should seek to strike a bargain with Moscow to allow the selective basing of Russian military installations on their territories. Given the central role that the 1939 Soviet-Baltic basing agreements played in paving the way for Stalin's seizure of the Baltic countries, this is a particularly sensitive issue.

The Southern Newly Independent States

As a group, the countries of the southern tier are set apart from the European portions of the former Soviet Union by historical and cultural differences much larger than those between Russia and the countries of the western region. Although never unified under a single state with borders coterminous with those of Soviet Central Asia, Central Asia once belonged to a common Islamic civilization that encompassed portions of modern-day Turkey, Iran, Afghanistan, Pakistan, India, Sinkiang, the Caucasus, and the Volga region, and this distinctive cultural heritage is likely to exert a substantial influence on the external relations of the new Central Asian governments. The Caucasus bears a somewhat different stamp, including as it does peoples with ancient ties to Christendom as well as Turkic and non-Turkic Muslims.[103] The resulting historical and cultural mosaic gives the Caucasus certain features in common both with the new states of Central Asia and with the new states situated to the west of Russia.

For many centuries the vast territories of Inner Asia served as a launching point for nomadic invaders who wrought havoc in the adjacent regions in both the east and the west.[104] In the words of one historian, Inner Asia was "the reservoir holding a sea of peoples who, organized into great confederations, from time to time conquered the

Middle East and China" as well as Eastern Europe. "From the second
millennium B.C. to the eighteenth century the history of the region
may be told in terms of ever repeated nomadic conquests, the formation
of empires over oasis and settled populations, and the constant tension
between pastoral and agricultural peoples."[105] The thirteenth-century
Mongol invasion of Europe was perhaps the most dramatic eruption of
Inner Asian peoples into adjacent empires and principalities, but it was
far from being the only episode of this kind. The Chinese and other
East Asian peoples also bore the brunt of repeated nomadic invasions.

After the fourteenth century, however, the Inner Asian empires con-
structed by the Mongols and their ethnic successors began to undergo
a process of political fragmentation that gradually undermined their
military power and profoundly affected the history of Central Asia and
the Caucasus. As the tide of first the Mongol and then the Timuride
empire ebbed, tsarist Russia began to expand eastward and to exert
increasing pressure on the Tatars, Kazakhs, Uzbeks, and other Central
Asian peoples that began to develop distinct identities around the fifteenth century.[106] During the sixteenth and seventeenth centuries Russian emissaries and military forces expanded primarily (though not
exclusively) eastward, moving through the forested northern territories
of Eurasia and conquering such relatively accessible centers of Tatar
and Islamic influence as Kazan and Astrakhan. Starting in the eighteenth century, Russian ambitions turned southward to the semiarid
steppes – a vast region just north of the Black, Caspian, and Aral seas
– where tsarist plenipotentiaries initially caused the Kazakh khanates
to accept Russian suzerainty and later forcibly subordinated the inhabitants to direct Russian rule.[107] Pushing farther south into the nonsteppe
territories during the mid-nineteenth century, Russian generals and
administrators took control of the khanates of Khiva and Kokand, the
emirate of Bukhara, and the remainder of Central Asia. By the 1860s,
Russian forces also wrested control of much of the Caucasus from Persia
and Ottoman Turkey, thereby establishing Russia's sway over Caucasian territories inhabited by Armenians, Georgians, Azerbaijanis, and
various mountain tribes such as the Ossetians.

Russia's expansion into Central Asia and the Caucasus provoked
intense military resistance from some of the indigenous peoples. The
Kazakh population resisted for nearly sixty years; the most famous
Kazakh military campaigns against Russian domination were led by
Khan Kenesary Qasimov between 1837 and 1847. The tsarist conquest
of Bukhara and the Central Asian khanates was also accompanied by
military clashes, although the resistance was apparently less determined
than in the Kazakh regions. In many cases the resistance against Russian
incursions was hampered by rivalries and conflicts among various in-

digenous groups. Some groups sought Russian military support against their local enemies, and during the crucial decade of the 1860s the Central Asian khanates were unable to conclude a mutual assistance pact against the Russian enemy that threatened them all.[108] In the North Caucasus, Russian expansion met tenacious resistance from mountain tribesmen led by Shamil, a legendary figure who fought Russian military expeditions for more than twenty years, whereas other Caucasian groups, particularly the Armenians but also the Georgians, viewed Russian expansion as a welcome counterweight against Turkish domination.

By the late nineteenth century Inner Asia's historic role as a marshalling ground for devastating invasions of Europe and East Asia was brought to an end by the actions of China, Great Britain, and especially Russia. Although politically enfeebled, China succeeded in annexing East Turkestan and incorporating it as the province of Sinkiang. Britain, deeply entrenched in India and increasingly anxious about Russia's southward expansion toward its prize colony, finally reached an agreement with St. Petersburg to make Afghanistan a buffer between the British and Russian empires.[109] Meanwhile Russia moved to transform its Central Asian dominions from an object of foreign policy into a matter of domestic policy, transferring them from the purview of the Ministry of Foreign Affairs to the jurisdiction of domestic ministries and provincial administrations.[110] Central Asian resistance to Russian hegemony subsided for almost half a century. However, in 1916 the Kazakhs and Kyrgyz rebelled against St. Petersburg's attempt to draft Central Asians for service in military labor battalions on the European front during World War I, and they suffered enormous human losses in the repressions that followed.[111]

One circumstance that helped spark the Central Asian uprising was the wave of Russian settlers that flowed into parts of Central Asia beginning in the late nineteenth century. In Kazakhstan more than a million people from European portions of Russia came and settled as farmers in the decade after 1905.[112] Apart from the tsarist government's need to settle land-hungry peasants recently freed from the obligations of serfdom, these migrations were driven by a tremendous growth of the Russian population, which made settlement an effective mechanism for the establishment of imperial control in non-Russian regions. According to some estimates, in the early nineteenth century Russia included around sixty million people, whereas the inhabitants of Central Asia numbered only five or six million, and in the course of the century the number of Russians increased dramatically.[113] During the Soviet era the pressure of migration continued, fueled by Stalin's mass deportations and by ambitious economic undertakings such as Khrushchev's Virgin Lands campaign. The shifts of population did not affect all of Central Asia or the Caucasus in equal measure. The influx of outsiders had a considerably stronger impact in Kazakhstan, for example, than in more distant parts of Central Asia such as Uzbekistan. Nonetheless, the migration of large numbers of Russians and other European settlers had an enduring impact on all the southern borderlands. In the judgment of a leading historian, "nowhere in the Muslim world has colonialism had a more profound and lasting effect."[114]

The impact of the Soviet regime on the region was greater still. Stalin's drive to reconstruct the economies of Central Asia had a disastrous effect on some of the native peoples. This was particularly true of the regime's brutal campaign to collectivize the agricultural practices of the nomadic or seminomadic peoples of the steppe. Approximately two-thirds of the prerevolutionary Kazakh population was killed or forced into exile in the period extending from the Russian Civil War through the collectivization drive of the early 1930s.[115] Although Moscow's central planners decreed that extractive industries should be developed in Central Asia, they did not build processing or manufacturing industries in the region; instead they assigned it a principal role in producing agricultural products, particularly cotton. In short, "Moscow's policy was to use Central Asia as a kind of contiguous Third World which mined and grew raw materials, but did not process them."[116] The social turmoil engendered by these policies was further intensified by the forcible deportation to the region of large numbers of peasant "kulaks" and other politically suspect persons from the European parts of the USSR.

Not surprisingly, the unfolding of this tumultuous history led Russian and non-Russian observers to adopt quite different views of the relations between their homelands. Always hampered by a weak knowledge of the regions and peoples it ruled, the tsarist government displayed a typically imperial attitude toward the Central Asian groups it conquered during the nineteenth century.[117] In championing the notion of Russia's "civilizing" mission toward the area, tsarist historians tended to lump the diverse inhabitants of Central Asia into a single, undifferentiated category – either as nomads, Turks, Muslims, or simply as Asiatics.[118] After the Soviet regime's brief postrevolutionary turn toward a more critical historical appraisal of Russia's colonization of the southern borderlands, Stalin's ideologists once more embraced the notion of tsarist Russia's civilizing mission and accentuated the USSR's even more important role as the bearer of the "internationalist" culture of Marxism-Leninism.

As is often the case in colonial situations, it is more difficult to establish how the inhabitants of the colonized territories regarded these historical changes. One thing that seems reasonably certain is that the historical outlook of the very thin stratum of Central Asians who possessed a significant amount of formal education was fundamentally altered. Apart from propagating the myth of the "great friendship" through propaganda and public education, during the 1930s the Stalinist regime also engineered a change in the Central Asian alphabets from the Arabic to Cyrillic script. At one stroke, this change cut off the access of the younger generation to the native artistic and historical literature that embodied Central Asia's past. The change of alphabets likewise rendered inaccessible the writings and publications of virtually all the neighboring peoples of Inner Asia and the Middle East. As for oral history, which was a central source of historical memory among rural Central Asians, the regime also tried to block the recitation of traditional epic poems extolling the feats of past heroes.[119] Although this effort probably had little effect, it reflects the depth of the Stalinist effort to remold historical consciousness even in the remotest corners of the Soviet empire.

The official historical perspective formulated under Stalin has strongly affected the attitudes of contemporary Russian politicians toward the region. Today some Russian politicians share the belief that Central Asia belongs naturally to Russia – or, at a minimum, to Russia's sphere of influence. For example, Aleksey Surkov, a member of the Russian Supreme Soviet's Committee for International Affairs and Foreign Economic Relations, has described the independence of Central Asia and other former Soviet republics as a "truncation" of the Russian land.[120] Perhaps the most extreme attitude toward the region has been voiced by Vladimir Zhirinovskiy, a virulent Russian nationalist and chairman of the misleadingly named Liberal Democratic Party. With the necessary political power, Zhirinovskiy has said, "in two days, I would do away with such countries as Kazakhstan or Kirghizia, because never ever, there is not a single scholar in the USA or elsewhere . . . who would be able to locate such political entities as Kazakhstan or Kirghizia on the map of the world."[121] To one degree or another, all these views reflect the legacy of the Stalinist notion that a historic "great friendship" united Russia with all its non-Russian dependencies.

Despite the efforts of Stalin's propagandists, Central Asian perspectives on Russia's role in the region are today quite different from the prevailing Russian outlook, and have been for some time. Insofar as one can judge from Western scholarship on the subject, the erosion of Moscow's centrally promulgated historical ideology during the post-Stalin era began earlier and went further in the Soviet Central Asian republics than in the western republics. In the 1960s and 1970s a few unorthodox Central Asian historians put forward stark depictions of tsarist policies in Central Asia, and even their more cautious professional colleagues began to abandon the notion of Central Asia's "voluntary" unification with tsarist Russia in favor of unvarnished references to "annexation" and to tsarist acts of oppression.[122] By contrast, central party ideologists apparently kept historians of Ukraine and the Baltic republics on a much shorter leash.[123] This variation in the treatment of the past probably reflected Moscow's judgment that the disruptive potential of heterodox historical views was greater in the European than in the Central Asian republics.

To be sure, Central Asian and Caucasian political groups have eagerly embraced the goal of rewriting the history of Russian colonialism. In Kazakhstan, for example, a Truth in History Education Society was founded in 1988, and the head of the Kazakh Writers' Union, Olzhas Suleymanov, became an impassioned spokesman for the view that Kazakhs should be compensated for the abuses they suffered in the tsarist era. In Kyrgyzstan during 1990 the Democratic Movement "Kyrgyzstan" pledged to promote a reassessment of Kyrgyz history, especially the revolt of 1916.[124] In Uzbekistan, heterodox thinkers joined other Central Asian historians to challenge the lingering myth of Central Asia's voluntary incorporation into the Russian empire and worked to revive the reputations of Central Asian chieftains who had fought against tsarist military incursions.[125] In the same spirit, Azerbaijani intellectuals began to voice positive evaluations of the short-lived independent Azerbaijani government forcibly deposed by the Bolsheviks in 1920.[126]

The same sort of skepticism has been focused on the events of Soviet history. The Central Asian media have published shocking figures on the numbers of Central Asian deaths that resulted from government policies in the Soviet period. For instance, in 1990 the journal of the Kazakhstan Communist Party published several articles divulging for the first time that millions of Kazakhs had died in the campaign for agricultural collectivization, and it laid responsibility for this human disaster on Moscow and the local Russian population.[127] The history of the Basmachi rebellion, an anti-Soviet uprising that flared up in the early 1920s and was renewed in the 1930s partly in response to the collectivization campaign, has likewise received new attention from Central Asian writers.[128]

Central Asians have also criticized more recent events. For instance, the Birlik (Unity) national movement in Uzbekistan, which played a substantial role in rallying demonstrators in Tashkent to condemn Moscow's January 1990 military crackdown in Azerbaijan, depicted Gorbachev's rule as simply a continuation of the Russian and Soviet historical pattern of exploiting Central Asia's population and natural resources.[129] In the wake of the USSR's collapse, Central Asian disenchantment with Moscow has, according to some reports, intensified further.[130]

On the whole, however, historical revelations and discussions have thus far failed to produce the explosive political results in Central Asia that they caused in the western republics. Although there have been demonstrations in connection with historic events, none of these gatherings appears to have assumed the proportions of the demonstrations in the Baltic states or Ukraine. One reason for the difference is that the halfhearted effort to promote *glasnost'* in most of Central Asia has not led to the kind of no-holds-barred debate that has occurred in most other parts of the former Soviet Union, and many post-Soviet political leaders in Central Asia have personal or broader political reasons to mute historical accounts that put the Soviet past and Central Asian relations with Russia in too bleak a light. However, part of the explanation for the different public response probably lies in the lower receptivity of the Central Asians to nationalist appeals based on historical memory.[131]

Several contemporary Central Asian leaders are dealing with these perturbing historical memories in a fashion that indicates they are interested in disregarding – or at least transcending – the past for the sake of a better future. In June 1992, for example, Kyrgyzstan president Askar Akayev expressed a wish to move beyond the polemical aspects of historical revelations about relations with Russia:

> The history of mutual relations between Kyrgyzstan and Russia will amount to exactly 205 years this year. Two hundred and five years ago farsighted representatives of the Kyrgyz nobility sent their ambassadors to St. Petersburg for the first time to come under the protection of the Russian Empire. Our friendship and cooperation date back to that time. Of course I am far from idealizing these relations. Of course there have been bright moments and moments which now give rise to controversy. Nevertheless, something eternal, bright, and kind is characteristic of our mutual relations.[132]

Similar reactions have come from some Central Asian intellectuals, who have tried to improve Russia's image in Central Asia by contrasting it with the USSR's. Comparing the prerevolutionary Russian and Soviet treatments of Islam, the Uzbek historian T. Saidbayev has stated that "the worst calamities for Islam started after the October Revolution. The Bolsheviks closed mosques, Islamic schools and religious courts. . . . The tsarist authorities, unlike their Soviet counterparts, had never done anything of the kind."[133] Statements of this sort suggest that some Central Asian politicians and intellectuals are attempting to reinterpret the region's historical relations with Russia in ways that, however tenuous intellectually, offer a political middle ground.[134]

This impulse is probably attributable to the pragmatism that has become indispensable to Central Asian officials as they wrestle with their countries' multiplying problems. This pragmatic orientation was articulated by Avdy Kuliyev, at the time Turkmenistan's minister of foreign affairs. "Turkmenistan," he noted, "intends to develop its relations with Russia, proceeding exclusively from . . . pragmatic reasons, trying not to overburden them with any romantic expectations or pledges."[135] No doubt many Central Asian politicians, especially those with political careers reaching back into the Soviet period, will try to cope with the region's massive difficulties by keeping relations with Russia on a reasonably even keel. It remains to be seen whether Central Asian leaders will be able to prevent the widening revelations of Moscow's exploitation and abuse during the Soviet years from harming ties with Yeltsin's Russia, or whether the negative aspects of the tsarist as well as the Soviet eras will feed into a political groundswell that ultimately will undermine those ties.

A sharp deterioration of Central Asian relations with Russia could conceivably be paralleled by Central Asian efforts to close ranks politically, perhaps on the basis of the ideology of pan-Turkism. As shown in Chapter 2, some Central Asian leaders have given lip service to pan-Turkic slogans, and Turkey itself is actively involved in building ties with the region. To judge by the historical record, however, these public gestures to pan-Turkism appear unlikely to produce a significantly higher level of political cooperation among the new states of the region, let alone a politically united Central Asia. On the eve of the Bolshevik Revolution, the predominantly Turkic peoples of Central Asia still identified themselves more by their Islamic faith than by their ethnic Turkic characteristics.[136] Only among the geographically dispersed Tatars, who had no separate territory that they might hope to make their own, did the ideology of a united Turkestan enjoy significant support.[137] Moreover, the annals of Central Asia's history before 1917 contain numerous episodes of conflict and war among the Central Asian peoples themselves, and this legacy is probably no less significant today than is the legacy of Central Asia's conflicts with Russia.

During the Soviet era, differences and tensions among the Central Asian peoples were manifested in the creation of the new national republics of Central Asia. Although historical accounts sometimes suggest that the five republics were created simultaneously by a single stroke of Stalin's pen in the mid-1920s, the process was not so simple. For example, the Uzbeks, who favored the creation of an Uzbek national republic, resisted the notion that a separate Tajik republic should be created from the autonomous Tajik region within Uzbekistan, although they were ultimately overridden.[138] In addition, until 1936 the territories that became the national republics of Kazakhstan and Kyrgyzstan remained "autonomous republics" of the Russian Federation, reflecting their closer demographic and political ties with Russia.

In addition, the tensions among various Central Asian ethnic groups were exacerbated by the way in which the boundaries of the new republics were drawn. In Central Asia Moscow aimed to create national republics that could counteract loyalties to long-existing entities like Bukhara or to any supranational pan-Turkic or pan-Islamic tendency, hoping that these loyalties would themselves be weakened by cleavages among the various indigenous ethnic groups included in the "nation" of each republic. Hence republican boundaries were intentionally designed to divide some large ethnic groups between two or more republics, thereby undercutting the political cohesion of each new national structure.[139]

Apart from long-standing disputes over external Soviet borders with adjacent countries, the Soviet division of Central Asia into separate national republics created a number of internal border disputes among the new political units. For almost seventy years the concentration of political power in Moscow suppressed most of these disputes, but many of them have resurfaced in the wake of USSR's collapse.[140] For example, Kyrgyzstan, in addition to a dozen contested stretches of border with neighboring China, is involved in a running dispute with Tajikistan concerning the border zone in the region of Badken and Isfara. In Uzbekistan, some political groups have raised the question of reclaiming the Kyrgyzstan towns of Osh, Uzgen, Jalalabad, and Karavan. The border between Kyrgyzstan's Talas oblast and Kazakhstan's Zhembyl oblast also has provoked disagreements.[141] Partly because of such border problems, the new Central Asian governments have explored a number of conflict-resolution mechanisms, and some leaders have tended to look to Russia to keep peace and stability in the region.[142] Thus Russia has an opportunity to remain influential in Central Asian affairs by capitalizing on the area's complex political geography. The question that remains is whether a preoccupied Russia will disengage from such disputes, whether it will genuinely attempt to solve them, or whether at some point it will choose to fan such conflicts in order to strengthen its leverage in the region. As shown in Chapter 3, one determinant of Russia's policy will be its instinctive fear of Islamic radicalism.

Perhaps even more than the new states of Central Asia, the new states of the Caucasus are heirs to a tumultuous historical legacy. Due to their relatively small size as well as to the tensions among them, this legacy has often prompted the states of the Caucasus to seek outside alliances rather than to band together. The entire region was devastated by Turkic and Mongol invasions, followed in the sixteenth century by a protracted and destructive struggle for control of the territory between the Ottoman and Persian empires. In the early nineteenth century

Russia seized control of eastern Armenia from Persia, while the western portion of the territory remained under control of the Ottoman Turks. Deeply suspicious of their Armenian subjects, the Turks followed genocidal policies that, by one calculation, killed three hundred thousand Armenians in massacres during 1895-6 and led to the death of another million to 1.5 million Armenians between 1915 and 1917.[143] Having failed in 1917 in an attempt to conclude an alliance with Georgia and Azerbaijan, the Armenian government accepted incorporation into the Soviet Union in 1920 as a means of escaping the threat of renewed Turkish hegemony. These bitter historical experiences long inclined Armenia to look to Russia for aid and protection in conflicts within the Caucasian region.

The most important of those conflicts is with Azerbaijan. For centuries the Azerbaijani lands were part of the Persian empire, but in the early 1800s a portion of this territory was transferred to Russia as a result of tsarist military victories over Persia. Distinguished from Christian Armenia by its Muslim and Persian-influenced culture, Azerbaijan has long-standing ethnic and political ties with Turkey. In 1918 Turkey played a key political and military role in the establishment of an independent Azerbaijani republic. Turkey's collapse at the close of World War I left the new republic increasingly vulnerable to outside pressure, and in 1920 it was invaded by Bolshevik forces and incorporated into the Soviet state.

This complex legacy has significant implications for the present. Some Azerbaijani political groups seek closer association with the adjacent regions of Iran inhabited by their ethnic kin.[144] However, in conflicts with other states in the region, Azerbaijanis also look to Turkey as well as to Russia for aid. This is particularly true of the bitter conflict over whether the predominantly Armenian enclave of Nagorno-Karabakh should remain within the jurisdiction of Azerbaijan, where it was placed by the Moscow authorities during the 1920s, or should be transferred to the control of its kinsmen in Armenia.[145] Since the late 1980s this conflict has led to deadly communal violence and escalating military conflict between the two Caucasian states.[146]

Like Armenia, Georgia early accepted Christianity and enjoyed a period of flourishing political and cultural life during the medieval epoch, but the Georgian principality suffered grave damage from the Mongol invasions and subsequently fell under Persian and Turkish sway. In the late eighteenth and early nineteenth centuries, Moscow's wars against the Persian and Ottoman empires led to Georgia's incorporation into the Russian empire and to a revival of Georgian national life. Like the other main peoples of the Caucasus, the Georgians declared an independent state in 1918, and they refused to support the

White forces against the Bolsheviks. With the removal of British forces from the region, however, Georgia quickly succumbed to a military takeover engineered from Moscow. This fact, coupled with the experience of Communist rule, has made post-Soviet Georgia wary of close ties with Russia, yet needing them in order to cope with economic dislocation and the mounting civil strife inside the fledgling state.

Conclusion

One generalization that can safely be ventured about the historical outlooks within the various post-Soviet states is that they are in flux. Although the credibility of official Soviet accounts of past relations among the peoples of the USSR and other nations was gradually eroded during the final decade or two of Soviet power, these "grand governing narratives" continued to dominate public discourse and public education. After the onset of *glasnost'*, competing and often antithetical historical perspectives were articulated and manifested in large public commemorations in several of the former Soviet republics, particularly the Baltics. In several of the successor states, these differing perspectives are likely to become the foundation for a radically altered understanding of the country's past and its future possibilities. Although the prospects for the creation of a peaceful post-Soviet order in Eurasia depend on a host of objective factors, they depend in part on an ability to transcend historical viewpoints conducive to political conflict.

The post-Soviet reevaluation of history is essential, but it entails two closely related risks. The first is that the revival of prerevolutionary historical traditions in Russia will occur without a critical reappraisal of the political values and assumptions embedded in the "grand governing narrative" of the tsarist era. The visceral popular and intellectual rejection of Communism may produce an equally strong acceptance of the Russian values and traditions that were initially rejected by the leaders of the Bolshevik Revolution. As we have seen, some key Russian traditions, especially the belief in the necessity of an autocratic state and an imperial attitude toward the non-Russian peoples, were reinstated under Stalin. In this important respect, then, the Russian reappraisal of history may produce changes of political attitude that are more apparent than real.

A second risk is that the rejection of the Soviet version of history in the non-Russian successor states may lead to too much change of the wrong kind. Put differently, the intellectuals of some or all of the non-Russian states may veer from a russophilic brand of history to a russophobic understanding of history that oversimplifies the past and exalts values that are narrowly nationalistic. The espousal of such an outlook would undoubtedly complicate even further the task of emerging national elites in charting a course for their fragile new countries.

Whether these outcomes can be avoided will hinge on at least three factors. One is the capacity of cultural elites, particularly in Russia, to devise convincing new historical narratives that take account of the historical experience of other peoples and come to grips with the dark side of their own nation's past behavior. A related factor is the receptiveness of national historians and other cultural figures to the insights of historians and political thinkers, including those of the various national diasporas, living outside the territories of the former USSR. Perhaps most important will be the long-term intellectual effects of the Stalin era. Although these effects are difficult to predict with any confidence, the continuing recollection of the monstrous crimes of Stalinism in Russia and the other new states could serve as a powerful antidote to authoritarian and imperial traditions of non-Soviet as well as Soviet vintage. In short, history as memory may help the citizens of Russia and the other new states to achieve a goal that is frequently associated with the study of history but less often achieved: to learn from the past.

2

National Identity and Ethnicity

Perhaps more than any other problem, fathoming the influence of national identity and ethnicity poses a major challenge, not least because of the complex responses that these notions evoke. One need only think of the divergent normative connotations of the words "nationalism" and "self-determination," or of the ambiguous attitudes of most governments toward the practical application of the principle of self-determination, to sense the complex emotions involved.[1] In the new states themselves, the autocratic legacy of hostility toward manifestations of ethnic sentiment among non-Russians has made the contrast between the pejorative and positive connotations of the native-language terms for "nationalism" and "self-determination" even sharper than it is in English.[2] The value judgments embedded in the terminology commonly used to discuss these controversial issues make it doubly difficult to treat them dispassionately.

Remembering a few general propositions can help analysts avoid such intellectual pitfalls. Despite the assertions of nationalist ideologists, nations are not ancient entities but a product of modern historical processes and contingencies.[3] Rather than being inherent in particular groups of people, national consciousness develops through the efforts of state officials or independent intellectuals to persuade other social groups that they belong to an overarching nation whose members are united by key characteristics.[4] Depending on the circumstances, the features singled out may include citizenship in the same state, shared historical experience, or a common language, religion, or culture. Which features come to be accepted as key markers of national identity in a particular case depends not only on objective social conditions but on the political entrepreneurship of the governmental and cultural elites that seek to shape the nation according to their own political agendas. In other words, nations are social constructions rather than natural entities, and they must be understood as products of societal processes

57

rather than as preexisting organisms that, like Sleeping Beauty, awaken at a prescribed moment.[5]

Recognizing that contingent factors shape national identity opens the way to a fuller understanding of nationalism's political implications. Although membership in a national community provides most inhabitants of the contemporary world with a key source of personal identity, each individual has other social identities that sometimes are at odds with the national one and occasionally override it.[6] Indeed, in multinational political conglomerates such as the Habsburg and tsarist empires, it was not uncommon for some persons to regard themselves as members of two ethno-national categories that outside observers viewed as mutually exclusive.[7] Since the mid-nineteenth century, social changes associated with modernization – particularly the need to select one or a few vernacular languages as a vehicle for mass education, and the cultural effects of competition for upward socioeconomic mobility – have helped crystallize distinctive ethnic and national identities. The expansion of other state activities, such as the government's insistence through censuses and administrative procedures that individuals declare themselves members of one or another ethnic category, have likewise made multiple national identities more difficult for individuals to sustain.[8] Nonetheless, other sources of political identity, such as regionalism, clan membership, or religious affiliation, exert a persisting and occasionally decisive influence that must be taken into account.

Analysts of developments in the new states also must be cognizant that the term "nationalism" does not refer to a single, uniform phenomenon. Rather, nationalism is a category that encompasses related but diverse phenomena, much as the concept of "religion" refers to a wide range of human behavior and that of "ideology" refers to a broad assortment of political outlooks.[9] Specific national movements may vary widely in the ways they define the principal attributes of nationhood, in the intensity of national sentiment, and in the distribution of national sentiment among the social groups and regions that formally belong to the nation. Viewed from this angle, the task of the outside observer is to distinguish different forms of nationalism and their varying political consequences.

It is particularly important to distinguish between two ideal types or models of nationalism that define the essence of the nation in divergent ways. National movements that conceive of the nation as "a sovereign people" emphasize voluntary political choice as a key characteristic of national identity and therefore tend to be receptive to the inclusion of individuals of diverse ethnic and cultural backgrounds. Movements that conceive of the nation as "a unique people," on the other hand, have an exclusive notion of national identity based on ethnic criteria and therefore tend to reject personal political choice as a means by which individuals may become members of the nation.[10] These two models of national identity may be described as "civic nationalism" and "ethnic nationalism." Although neither appears in social life in a pure form, the relative weight of the two approaches in concrete instances helps explain the behavior of the nation in question. Due partly to such variations, nationalist political behavior ranges from a mild form of patriotism conducive to political democracy and a temperate foreign policy to a virulent xenophobia conducive to authoritarianism and belligerent international conduct.

The attachment of ethno-national groups to particular territories varies widely from one case to another. Whether a group regards a particular territory as its homeland depends on the community's "rootedness" – that is, on such factors as the length of time the ethnic community has lived in the territory, whether it is highly concentrated or dispersed among members of other ethnic groups, whether it is attached to the land through agricultural activity, and so forth. This sense of rootedness, in turn, affects whether the members of an ethnic group respond to political pressure from other groups by defending their position through political action, emigrating, or creating a secessionist movement.[11] In contentious circumstances of this kind, much of the struggle often revolves around the definition of whose homeland the territory is – or, put differently, which group is indigenous and which is not. For that reason, this book generally refers to the peoples after which particular countries are named as the "titular" rather than the indigenous nationality, and to other ethnic groups as local minorities.

These observations suggest a number of questions about the impact of national sentiment on the post-Soviet states. Is the level of national consciousness equally high in all the new states, or does it vary significantly? How has the post-Communist surge in national sentiments affected attitudes within the new states toward the major powers of the West and Asia? In view of the multiethnic composition of most of the new states, how have the governing elites approached the problem of national identity, and to what extent have they been challenged by other elites advocating an alternative vision of the nation and its well-being? How inclusively or exclusively have the new states sought to define the national identity of their citizens, and how have these choices affected political trends within the new states and the relations among them? Not least, how have the characteristics of particular titular and minority nationalities shaped these processes? In Chapter 4 we shall explore in more detail the impact of national identity and nationalism on the political culture of the new states and on their prospects for democracy.

Russia

As noted in Chapter 1, Russia's political and cultural relationship with other great powers, especially the major powers of the West, has been an enduring preoccupation and a subject of recurring controversy among Russians. This historical legacy raises several questions about post-Communist Russia. Are contemporary forms of Russian nationalism compatible with a sustained policy of cooperation with such countries as the United States, Germany, and Japan? How will ethnonational sentiments affect Russia's relations with the other new states? And how will Russia cope with the centrifugal regional and ethnic forces that threaten its political integrity, much as earlier manifestations of separatism threatened the Soviet state?

As we have seen, the hostility to the outside world that characterized the Soviet system in the pre-Gorbachev era was nourished not only by Marxism-Leninism but by Russian chauvinism. The appearance of a substantial liberal movement among the new Russian elites and ordinary citizens has thus come as something of a surprise. Foreshadowed by Gorbachev's liberal view of international politics and his desire to promote a partial convergence of the Soviet system with Western political and economic institutions, this liberal impulse has found clearer expression in the policies of the Yeltsin government. Yeltsin and his political allies, despite frequent political zigzags, have pursued a foreign policy grounded on the assumption that Russia's national interests coincide in many essentials with the interests of the advanced industrial democracies. Moreover, he and his domestic supporters have sought to reconstruct Russia's political and economic institutions on the basis of the societal values exemplified by these same polities.[12]

Advocates of this liberal approach have argued against the traditional identification of the Russian nation with an all-powerful state. For instance, when the Democratic Russia parliamentary bloc was formed in the Soviet legislature near the end of 1989, it issued a platform that not only criticized past Soviet abuses of Russians' national feelings but condemned the Soviet identification of the Russian nation "with the totalitarian regime."[13] In the post-Soviet period some intellectuals have argued that the country's political and cultural leaders should strive to create "a new image for Russia and a new role that Russia can play in the future development of mankind." They have urged their countrymen to turn away from Russia's imperial past by treating the upheaval of the late 1980s and early 1990s "not as the disintegration of the former big Russia but as the emergence of a new Russian state."[14] "In our situation," they have asserted, "the greatest patriotism is not to boast about our large territory and resources but to learn how to make proper use of them."[15]

Since the early 1990s the exponents of conservative Russian national attitudes have vociferously attacked this liberal conception of the Russian nation. The most extreme critics have depicted the domestic liberalization during the late 1980s and early 1990s as the outgrowth of malign Western influences working in tandem with subversive liberal forces inside Russia itself. The prominent writer Valentin Rasputin, for instance, has asserted that the breakup of the Soviet Union was the product of a long-standing American plan. Aleksandr Sterligov, co-chairman of the Russian National Assembly, a political group, told the first congress of the organization that due to Yeltsin's implementation of goals set by the United States, "Russia is being destroyed by pro-Western forces. . . . Revival of Russia can be achieved only on one condition: to block any attempt to establish [a] Western political and economic system in the country, as well as to bring Western values that are alien to the Russian people."[16] Another critic has contended that Russia's democrats were suppressing the development of Russian national consciousness. The West, she has claimed, is willing to pay any price to destroy its main rival and "will never help us, because [doing so] is against its . . . interests."[17]

Together with the structure of the Soviet domestic empire, the depth of such differences helps explain why attempts in the late 1980s to form a Russian national front resembling the national fronts in the Baltic and Ukrainian republics were unsuccessful. In the words of one Western scholar, these efforts failed because Russians lacked "a simple ethnic target" against which to unite.[18] Instead of seeking to free themselves from an oppressive state controlled by another national group, Russians had to decide whether to accept the dismantling of the state that they, more than any other nationality, had dominated, and which was an important source of national identity for a significant number of them. The rift between the "empire savers" and the "nation builders" prevented Russians from rallying around a common national program.[19]

During the last two years of the Soviet era conservative nationalists, despite their vitriolic attacks on the views of liberal nationalists, won little popular support for their cause. In federal and Russian republican legislative elections in 1989 and 1990, conservative nationalists fared extremely poorly, thus lending credence to other indications that reactionary, anti-Semitic organizations such as Pamyat were part of Russia's political fringe.[20] In the Russian presidential elections held in mid-1991, right-wing nationalists made a somewhat better showing. Vladimir Zhirinovskiy, their principal standard-bearer, won 7.8 percent of the popular vote, and Army General Albert Makashov, a reactionary figure who may have drawn some voters away from Zhirinovskiy, received 4 percent. Still, Yeltsin won a resounding 58 percent of the vote on a platform that emphasized self-determination not only for Russia but for all the Soviet republics.

Since then, however, the optimism of most Russians has waned. Frustrated by the country's reduced weight in international affairs, by worsening economic conditions, and by continued social disruption, a number of political figures and intellectuals, including some previously counted as liberals, have become convinced that the end of the Soviet empire constitutes a profound international loss for Russia. Harshly criticizing Yeltsin and his supporters for a wide range of alleged foreign policy errors, right-wing nationalists have seized with special tenacity on the Russo-Japanese dispute over four islands in the Kuril chain and on the issue of Russia's purported neglect of its Orthodox Serbian brethren in the war-torn former Yugoslavia.[21] On the issue of the Kurils, public opinion does appear to be strongly opposed to Russian concessions, and such public attitudes have helped convince several careful observers that a broad public shift toward xenophobic nationalism has already gotten under way.[22]

Although the potential for a sea change of the Russian public's attitudes undoubtedly increased during 1992, the evidence available in mid-1993 indicates that thus far such a shift has not occurred. In an opinion survey conducted in June 1991, Russian respondents were asked whether they had positive or negative feelings toward the convergence (*sblizheniye*) of the political positions of the USSR with the political positions of the West. That 88 percent of the respondents said they favored this convergence, whereas only 5 percent said they opposed it, suggests that the proportion of Russian citizens who harbored an ingrained distrust of the West was quite small.[23] Almost two years later, these public attitudes appeared to be little affected by the inflammatory anti-Western rhetoric of right-wing nationalists. In a survey of Russian opinion at the start of 1993, approximately 75 percent of the persons interviewed expressed favorable opinions of the United States, France, and Germany. Moreover, despite the contretemps with Japan over the control of the four disputed islands, two-thirds of the respondents expressed a favorable attitude toward Japan.[24] It should be emphasized that this generally favorable attitude toward the developed democracies did not amount to a blanket endorsement of all the policies or behavior of specific foreign governments.[25] Rather, the evidence suggests that most Russian citizens have welcomed a policy of rapprochement with the West but have also felt that Russia has certain national interests that should not be sacrificed in the quest for international approval and support, even from countries that they otherwise admire.

In general, Russian relations with the other new states appear to be a more neuralgic issue than relations with the Western powers and Japan. Since 1991 a host of controversies have arisen between Russia and the "near abroad" (that is, the other former republics). The controversies that have become most closely intertwined with Russia's search for identity – and those that are therefore potentially the most explosive – concern the determination of which peoples and territories rightfully belong to Russia or to the other new states. Due to the historical pattern of Russian imperial expansion and Soviet rule, more than 25 million ethnic Russians currently reside outside the Russian Federation in the "near abroad."[26] Many of these Russians have demonstrated no obvious desire to be part of the Russian state, nor do they all look to Russia as the defender of their well-being vis-à-vis the new states in which they now live. On the other hand, some Russians in the "near abroad" do harbor these sentiments, and in the Russian Federation their fate has become a matter of concern to politicians of many political persuasions. In a number of cases, Russian disputes with other former republics – such as the argument with Ukraine over Crimea or the controversies with Latvia and Estonia over the treatment of ethnic Russians in those countries – have become entangled with the uncertain fate of Russian military forces based in these same territories.

Having committed himself to the principle of self-determination, President Yeltsin has generally followed a comparatively restrained policy toward the other new states. Although other influential Russian politicians have demanded that Ukraine return Crimea to Russia, Yeltsin himself has refrained from asserting a Russian claim to that territory, and despite some political posturing he has sought to resolve Russian-Ukrainian differences over the control of military forces and nuclear systems in a nonconfrontational fashion. In dealing with the Baltic states, Yeltsin has withdrawn a large number of troops from the region and has avoided the use of military threats. On the other hand, Yeltsin has implicitly linked further Baltic troop withdrawals to the treatment of the local Russian minorities, and he has used Russia's economic muscle to exert political pressure on several of the post-Soviet states.

Yeltsin's measured policy has provoked the anger of right-wing Russian nationalists. For instance, Sergey Baburin, a leading figure in the Russian Supreme Soviet, has argued that the Russian Federation is "an unnatural formation" spawned by "Bolshevik experiments" and that the real Russia "is the former Soviet Union."[27] A like-minded commentator has declared that "the history of mankind is the history of empires. As long as there is mankind, there will be empires. . . . Empires change and their forms evolve, but it is only within their framework that the merciless alchemy of history takes place."[28] Yet another exponent of this outlook has argued that the borders among the new states should be revised "immediately" in order to assure that, at a minimum, all ethnic Russians be included within Russia's territory and that, at a maximum, all peoples faithful to "Russian civilization" be brought under the aegis of "Russian might."[29] Some prominent Russian political figures such as Vice-President Rutskoy and Arkadiy Volskiy, chairman of the Russian Union of Industrialists and Entrepreneurs and a leader of the Civic Union political coalition, have expressed sympathy for such views.[30]

The issue of protecting ethnic Russians in the "near abroad" against discrimination poses an especially serious threat to relations between Russia and the other new states. More than other sources of friction, this issue appears to have caused second thoughts among many liberals who previously defended self-determination for the non-Russian republics. Sergey Stankevich, for example, has insisted that "Russia is responsible" for the fate of these expatriate Russians, and he has threatened that Russia will use force to protect "a thousand-year history [and Russia's] legitimate interests."[31] Under such pressures, even Foreign Minister Andrey Kozyrev has been forced to assert that Russia "will be protecting the rights of Russians in other CIS states. This is a top priority. We shall be protecting their rights firmly and will be using power methods if need [be]."[32] Imperial views are being espoused both by right-wing statists who favor Russia's continual territorial expansion and by some liberals who believe it is Russia's fate to be a great power. Like the writer Tatyana Tolstaya, these liberals reject the argument that just because the Soviet system failed, Russia has made no contribution, and has no right, to the lands in which Russians now live. Tolstaya's view that "the existence of a world culture is somehow dependent on what some people would call imperialism" is indicative of the thinking of a significant number of leading Russian liberals.[33]

One concrete reflection of the increasing pressures for a more assertive policy toward the other new states is the growing influence and militancy of the Russian Cossack movement. In June 1992 Yeltsin himself acknowledged the Cossacks' increasing influence by signing a decree that fully rehabilitated the Cossack movement and by allowing the reintroduction of Cossack units into the Russian army and frontier guards.[34] The Cossacks seek a return to their role in tsarist days as defenders of Russian interests and of territorial conquests along contested borders. In the period since the breakup of the Soviet Union, they have become heavily engaged in supporting the local Russians fighting in the trans-

Dniester region of eastern Moldova, the pro-Moscow forces fighting in the North Caucasus region of Ossetia, and the local minorities waging a political struggle to protect their privileged position in the northwestern and northeastern regions of Kazakhstan.[35] In mid-1993 a Cossack leader in the trans-Dniester region of Moldova, Aleksandr Bulgakov, declared that the Russian Cossacks "will continue to maintain the Russian empire's borders from the Pacific to the Baltic Sea" and "do not recognize any republics or independent states on this [Moldovan] territory."[36] The activities of the Cossacks may have especially serious consequences in Central Asia, where traditional Cossack territories span the border between Russia and Kazakhstan.[37]

However, other segments of the Russian population do not appear to harbor the sort of militant sentiments exhibited by the Cossacks. In 1991, although a majority of Russian citizens appeared to favor the preservation of the USSR and endorsed the need for a strong central authority capable of establishing order, polls also suggested that a majority of Russians did not believe that force should be used to hold the Union together – at least where the Baltic states were concerned.[38] In the summer of 1992, a survey examined the opinions of Russian citizens about the means that should be used to handle the conflicts with other new states over Crimea, the trans-Dniester region, and South Ossetia. Forty-six percent of the respondents expressed the view that Russia should use only peaceful means in these disputes, and another 19 percent stated that Russia should avoid any involvement whatsoever. Only 19 percent answered that it should use any necessary means, including war.[39]

For reasons of ethnic and cultural affinity, members of the Russian elite have shown special reluctance to accept the idea of an independent Ukraine and, to a lesser extent, of an independent Belarus. As one observer remarked, for Russia "the main issue is whether Russia as a civilization embraces only the Russian Federation or [whether] it also includes Ukraine and Belarus. . . . Will Russia be able to remain a great power without preserving common identity with them? Most probably no."[40] This attitude has also received considerable support among ordinary Russian citizens, at least in the period before the disintegration of the USSR. In February 1991, shortly after the limited crackdown in Lithuania, one public opinion organization surveyed attitudes within the Russian republic toward the permissibility of allowing non-Russian republics to secede from the USSR. Although the respondents divided more or less evenly over the possibility of independence for the Baltic republics, Armenia, and Georgia, they rejected the idea of Ukrainian independence by a ratio of almost three to one.[41] Some Russians have expressed similar feelings about Kazakhstan, or at least about the northern portion of Kazakhstan inhabited primarily by Russians and other Slavs. In 1991, for example, Aleksandr Solzhenitsyn proposed a new confederation including Russia, Ukraine, Belarus, and the northern zone of Kazakhstan. Although Solzhenitsyn was careful to specify that such a confederation could be created only by peaceful means, many right-wing Russian nationalists have not renounced the idea of using force as a means of incorporating regions such as Crimea, the trans-Dniester region, and northern Kazakhstan into Russia, and at least one group has advocated the "repatriation," that is, the expulsion, of all Russian Jews.[42]

As in the case of policy toward the West, Russian liberal and conservative elites have become locked in a struggle to sway rank-and-file Russians toward their conception of the Russian nation and its interests. Despite the polemics of conservative nationalists against the Yeltsin government's alleged mishandling of relations with the other new states, sketchy evidence suggests that a majority of Russian citizens approve of how the government has dealt with these issues, and there are few signs of widespread antipathy toward most of the other new states.[43] At the start of 1993 a survey of citizens of the Russian Federation found that strong majorities of the respondents expressed a favorable attitude toward Belarus (75 percent), Kazakhstan (72 percent), and Ukraine (69 percent), and only small minorities expressed negative views. Compared with Kazakhstan, smaller but still significant majorities of the respondents held favorable attitudes toward the other Central Asian states. Thanks partly to the substantial share of respondents who expressed no opinion, the Baltic states did not receive a majority of favorable responses, although the number of persons expressing favorable attitudes toward the Baltic countries still exceeded the number voicing unfavorable views. Only in the case of the Caucasus – more specifically, Azerbaijan and Georgia – did the number of respondents with negative attitudes exceed the number holding positive views.[44]

These data suggest that hostility toward most of the other new states does not presently have a wide popular base in Russia and that moderate Russian leaders have so far managed to prevent a surge of national intolerance in Russian society. Of course, further domestic upheavals within Russia and heightened frictions with the other new states could change this situation; but as of mid-1993, the efforts of right-wing Russian nationalists to win mass support by harping on the alleged tribulations of Russians in the other new states have achieved little success. To judge by the survey findings cited above, the Russian public is less reconciled to independence for Ukraine than for the other former Soviet republics, and if a conservative Russian nationalist groundswell were to develop, it could well crystallize around relations with Ukraine.

The proposition that the ordinary citizens of Russia are not imbued with assertive nationalist sentiments raises an important question about the cohesion of Russia itself. Do the inhabitants of the Russian Federation identify closely enough with the state to preserve Russia's political and territorial integrity, or will Russia succumb to the same sort of centrifugal forces that destroyed the Soviet polity? Although ethnic Russians constitute about four-fifths of Russia's population of 147 million persons, the remaining one-fifth, some 27 million people, belong to ethnic minorities. Many of these non-Russians live in approximately thirty ethnically denominated autonomous republics or other autonomous units that exist uneasily alongside administrative units whose identity is defined solely in territorial terms.[45] During the power struggle between Gorbachev and Yeltsin in 1990, Gorbachev encouraged centrifugal tendencies in the ethnic autonomies in order to weaken Yeltsin's Russian political base, just as Yeltsin encouraged centrifugal tendencies in the Baltics and other non-Russian national republics to weaken Gorbachev's Soviet political base. The Russian legislature's mid-1990 declaration of sovereignty vis-à-vis the Soviet government formally espoused an inclusive, civic-territorial conception of Russian citizenship.[46] Nonetheless, a number of signs indicated a persisting tendency in Russia to think of citizenship in ethnic terms, and the declaration of Russian sovereignty was quickly followed by declarations of sovereignty from virtually all the autonomous ethnic units inside Russia's borders.[47]

Since 1991 many of the Russian Federation's constituent units have sought to give political-economic content to their declarations of sovereignty by wresting greater authority from Moscow, and in some of the units there has been talk of declaring complete independence from Russia. Southwest Russia, which encompasses the North Caucasus, has become a hotbed of ethnic antagonisms. In 1991 the small autonomous republic of Chechen-Ingushetia declared its independence from Russia. Voicing a similar demand, the newly formed Confederation of the Mountain Peoples of the North Caucasus has moved paramilitary forces across the Russian border to aid the Abkhazian and South Ossetian separatist movements that are battling for independence from Georgia. Further to the east, along the southern rim of Siberia, comparatively small autonomies such as Tuva and Buryatia have also sought to assert their interests against Moscow. In several cases, the local governments have begun to establish direct economic and political ties with foreign governments.

Separatist impulses have also spread to Siberia proper and to the Far East. As Siberian and Far Eastern political authorities have begun to press for greater freedom from Moscow's dictates, a few radicals have

espoused the goal of full regional independence.[48] In some instances
these pressures have been fueled by rising ethnic feelings among non-
Russians offended by Moscow's failure to provide adequate native-
language schooling and cultural facilities, but in many cases the principal motive is local resentment against the decades of economic exploitation that Moscow has imposed on these territories for the sake of
promoting the rapid industrialization of European Russia. Along with
members of the ethnic minorities, many Russian inhabitants of Siberia
and the Far East have been angered by Moscow's use of their regions
as a vast storehouse of oil and other natural resources without developing
local industry or raising the local quality of life.

The Yeltsin government's efforts to contain these centrifugal tendencies have enjoyed only limited success. Near the end of 1991 Yeltsin's threat to use force to squelch the declaration of independence by
the Chechen-Ingush autonomous republic was quickly repudiated by
the Russian legislature, forcing the president to fall back on negotiations
and political maneuvers to check centrifugal pressures. Although hard
line members of Yeltsin's government, such as Minister of Defense
Grachev, have continued to warn secessionists that abuse of ethnic
Russians within the autonomies would result in the introduction of
Russian troops, others, such as Foreign Minister Kozyrev, have warned
that such measures would provoke heightened ethnic conflict and endanger Russia's survival.[49] In March 1992 representatives of all but two
of the ethnic autonomies and nonethnic regional units signed a new
federal treaty that attempted to spell out the division of authority between the federal and regional governments, and the Russian legislature
subsequently passed a law establishing procedures for negotiating disputes over internal boundaries and setting up a three-year period during
which changes in the internal structure of the Federation were to be
worked out.[50] On the other hand, the treaty failed to resolve conflicting
federal and local jurisdictional claims in some key fields, particularly
taxation and the control of natural resources, and it skirted the vexing
question of political relations among the ethnic autonomies and nonethnic regional units.[51]

Thanks to the public mood and to Yeltsin's increasing tendency to
bid for regional support against his opponents in the Russian legislature,
the diffusion of power from Moscow to regional authorities is almost
certain to continue.[52] However, this does not necessarily signify that
Russia will follow the USSR into the dustbin of history. In the first
place, ethnic Russians account for about 82 percent of the Russian
Federation's population – far more than their 51 percent share of the
population of the former USSR.[53] Because no other ethnic group accounts for more than 4 percent of Russia's population, few of the non-

Russian groups are likely to attain the critical mass and political leverage necessary to secede. Moreover, it remains uncertain whether most citizens of Russia would approve secession by one or another of the autonomies, even if the local decision were made democratically. Surveys conducted in the Russian republic in 1990 indicated that a small majority of the respondents favored allowing autonomies to secede through democratic means, but that a substantially larger majority favored keeping the autonomies within Russia.[54] In a 1993 survey, almost two-thirds of the respondents (63 percent) said they would oppose independence for Siberia even if a majority of Siberians favored it.[55] Many of the autonomies include substantial ethnic Russian populations, and in some instances, Russian majorities. In the autonomous republic of Tatarstan, for instance, Russians constitute nearly as large a share of the population (43.2 percent) as do the Tatars themselves (48.5 percent).[56] The regions in which non-Russian ethnic feelings are running highest may contain only a small proportion of the country's population and territory, but, as in the case of Tatarstan, which lies astride Russia's transportation system, their secession could deal a blow to Russia's standing as a major power. The loss of Siberia and the Far East, which contain a far larger share of Russia's territory and mineral wealth, along with strategic ports, major industries, and nuclear-weapons sites, would be economically catastrophic.[57]

Pressures from regional units within Siberia and the Far East are nearly certain to produce a further diffusion of political and economic power from Moscow. But even though these changes may have a major impact on Russia's foreign relations – for example, by reducing the federal tax revenues available for the maintenance of the Russian military establishment – the odds are that they will not lead to the breakup of the Russian state. In most cases regional leaders appear to be using the rhetoric of independence as a tool in the protracted bargaining with Moscow over new constitutional arrangements and the control of economic resources. Although eager to win more economic benefits from Moscow and to attract investment and trade from China and Japan, political leaders in most of the Siberian and Far Eastern regions will probably stop short of sacrificing the diplomatic leverage and military protection that political linkage with Moscow affords. In the large regions whose leaders have publicly toyed with the idea of complete independence, most citizens seem reluctant to embark on such an extreme course of action.[58] Although the regional disintegration of Russia cannot be completely excluded as a possibility, it is likely to occur only if the central government is immobilized by deep splits that destroy its legitimacy and render it completely incapable of action for an extended period.

The Western Newly Independent States

Next to Russia, Ukraine is the new country whose search for identity has the greatest potential to affect the international politics of Eurasia. Among the former republics, Ukraine ranks second only to Russia in terms of population, economic output, and military capabilities. Moreover, the issues of Ukrainian and Russian political identity are closely intertwined both demographically and culturally. Although approximately three-quarters of Ukraine's population consists of ethnic Ukrainians, many have been strongly influenced by Russian culture. Countrywide, more than 12 percent of ethnic Ukrainians regard the Russian language as their native tongue. In the eastern and southern regions of the country, the share of Ukrainians whose native tongue is Russian exceeds 25 percent, and in the administrative capitals of these regions the share exceeds 40 percent.[59] Over a long period, there also has been extensive intermarriage between ethnic Russians and Ukrainians. In addition to ethnic Russians, who constitute about one-fifth of Ukraine's population, the presence of a large number of russophone Ukrainians is likely to have a major impact on the balance of political forces inside the country.

Despite these cultural differences, at the time of the Soviet breakup, Ukrainian citizens shared a broad consensus on the desirability of national independence. In contrast to Russia, where a slim majority of the population favored independence and about one-third regretted the dissolution of the USSR, in Ukraine about three-quarters of the population welcomed the change, and only about one-sixth regretted it. Even among Ukraine's ethnic Russians, more than 60 percent favored independence, compared with slightly more than a quarter who preferred that Ukraine belong to a union with other former Soviet republics.[60] The widespread impression that Ukrainian independence would raise living standards probably accounts for some of this sentiment, but it doubtless also derived from many local Russians' deep historical roots in the region and their sense that Ukraine was their home.

Ukraine's political and cultural elites do not appear to be seriously divided over the idea of joining Europe and the West. Although there are important regional differences inside Ukraine over the idea of turning away from Russia and joining Europe, this possibility has not provoked the sort of bitter polemics and conservative intellectual backlash that have occurred in Russia. To a greater degree than in Russia, many elite members appear to agree in principle on the desirability of becoming part of the West. This attitude is personified by Ukrainian foreign minister Anatoliy Zlenko, who has asserted that Ukraine is "a purely European country" and has contrasted it with the "Eurasian state" of Russia.[61] Whether the goal of political and economic Westernization is feasible is, of course, a separate question to which we will return in later chapters. Here it suffices to note that most ordinary Ukrainian citizens, particularly those in western Ukraine, appear to share a sense of affinity with the West. In a survey conducted in Ukraine at the start of 1992, more than three-quarters of the respondents expressed a favorable attitude toward the United States. Nearly half of the respondents also agreed that Western countries should become involved in the domestic process of establishing democracy in Ukraine, compared with about a quarter of the respondents who disagreed with this idea.[62]

Ukrainian attitudes toward the external security of the nation appear to be shifting from optimism toward anxiety. As shown in later chapters, members of the political and cultural elite have voiced increasing apprehension about Ukraine's security, especially vis-à-vis Russia. How deeply these expressions of concern have affected the thinking of ordinary citizens is hard to judge. At the start of 1992, almost two-thirds of the respondents to a Ukrainian survey said they felt no concern about the possibility of an attack on Ukraine by another country during the next five years. Asked to evaluate potential threats both inside and outside the country, slightly more than one in five identified the main threat as coming from "a former USSR republic," by which most respondents undoubtedly meant Russia.[63] These relatively upbeat attitudes may have shifted under the influence of Ukraine's disputes with Russia over Crimea and the Black Sea Fleet, but the extent of any such shift is difficult to gauge. At a minimum, the early survey data indicate that at the start of national independence ordinary Ukrainians' concerns centered primarily on domestic affairs.

To date the Ukrainian national movement has not displayed any significant expansionist impulses, although developments in 1993 have somewhat clouded the picture. Various Ukrainian groups disagree about important matters of foreign and defense policy, and there have been instances of inflammatory rhetoric, particularly directed toward Russia.[64] Nonetheless, Ukrainian national feelings have thus far focused primarily on the defense of Ukraine's territorial integrity, and the nationalist movement has played a largely constructive role in rallying the populace around the goal of consolidating the country's independence. In relations with neighboring countries such as Hungary and Romania, the Ukrainian government has sought to defuse potential tensions by adopting an accommodating stance toward the Hungarian and Romanian minorities residing in Ukraine. Moreover, the government has granted an unusually large measure of de facto autonomy to Crimea, in an effort to prevent the treatment of the Russian inhabitants of Crimea from precipitating an escalation of Ukraine's simmering confrontation with Russia over control of the peninsula. On the other hand, some nongovernmental groups in Ukraine have adopted a more expansionist view of territorial questions. Since 1993 there has been a growing movement among Ukrainian Cossacks to claim the Kuban Cossack region of southern Russia for Ukraine.[65] Although this movement has received no encouragement or support from the Ukrainian government, it could cause serious additional frictions in Ukrainian-Russian relations.

Inside Ukraine, the prevailing political impulse has been to establish a conception of national citizenship that is primarily civic-territorial rather than ethnic. Before the breakup of the USSR the Ukrainian national movement sought successfully to attract Ukrainian inhabitants of all ethnic backgrounds, and since then most politicians have continued to favor this approach.[66] At the same time, some ardent nationalists have fought to ensure that Ukraine becomes, first and foremost, the homeland of ethnic Ukrainians. In 1989 the Ukrainian legislature passed a language law decreeing that by the mid-1990s Ukrainian should become the only language used in administration (*dilovodstvo*) in all regions of Ukraine where ethnic Ukrainians constitute a majority of the population – that is, in all regions except Crimea.[67]

The language issue presents a serious potential stumbling block to the establishment of an inclusive notion of Ukrainian citizenship. The law may originally have been passed for reasons that were largely symbolic: In 1989 Ukrainian nationalism was just beginning to gain wide popular support, and a number of legislators may have viewed it as an easy way to establish their nationalist credentials. However, the ardent nationalists who helped push the law through the Ukrainian parliament wish to see it implemented as written. These individuals want the study of Ukrainian to be made compulsory and the language to be "used by the entire population – no matter what the origin or nationality of these people – that is living in Ukraine."[68] Although the parliament's 1991 "Declaration on the Rights of Nationalities of Ukraine" proclaims that non-Ukrainian citizens have the right to use their language freely "in all walks of life," including education, and promises that localities with large concentrations of non-Ukrainians are entitled to use their language on an equal footing with Ukrainian, there is a catch. In many regions of Ukraine, Russian is the language preferred not only by the ethnic Russian minority but also by russophone members of the ethnic Ukrainian majority. However, the law's emphasis on ethnicity rather than on the actual pattern of language use as the determinant of language policy requires that under these conditions the Ukrainian language must be made the region's prevalent form of communication.[69]

The struggle over Ukraine's national identity and the definition of citizenship is closely linked with important differences between various parts of the country. As noted in Chapter 1, Ukraine consists of several regions that are distinct not only linguistically but sociologically. The eastern and southern regions exhibit high levels of linguistic russification among Ukrainians, high concentrations of ethnic Russians, and high measures of urbanization and industrialization. The central and western regions exhibit almost no linguistic russification, have few Russians, and are less urban and industrial.[70] Apart from their impact on the debate over language policy, these regional differences affect the attitudes of citizens toward issues ranging from the structure of the state to economic reform and foreign policy.

Interregional differences are linked especially closely to the Ukrainian debate over federalism, and to perceived threats to the Ukrainian state. Since mid-1991 Ukrainian legislators and politicians have been involved in a dispute over whether the country's unitary state structure should be changed to a federal one. Many legislators have rejected federalism on the grounds that it would alter the character of the state and could lead to Ukraine's dismemberment through a combination of internal centrifugal forces and external pressures. A decentralization of power from Kiev would encourage regional governments to attempt to reverse the 1989 language law, thereby thwarting the desire of the most fervent Ukrainian nationalists.[71] Further, because the eastern and southern regions are located on Ukraine's external borders – adjacent either to Russia or the Black Sea – many Ukrainian nationalists "are convinced that a federal formula would lead to secessionist movements in the peripheral russified regions and to the eventual dismemberment of Ukraine."[72]

Spurred by this fear, the Ukrainian parliament in 1991 quickly followed its declaration of independence with a harsh law that sets criminal penalties for "activities aimed at the violating of the territorial integrity of Ukraine," an elastic category that apparently includes calls for non-violent change.[73] In December 1992 the cochairmen of Rukh, the umbrella movement that led the struggle for independence from Moscow, demanded vigorous enforcement of the law. The leaders urged the Ukrainian procuracy and security organs to take a harder line against what they regarded as separatist organizations in Crimea, Transcarpathia, and the Donbas region.[74] In the meantime, some Ukrainian political parties have embraced the goal of establishing a federal system. The proponents of this step include the "Citizen Congress of Ukraine," a party based primarily in the Donbas and other mining areas of the eastern region.[75]

Despite these tensions over the proper conception of the Ukrainian nation and the structure of the state, ethnic relations inside the country have thus far remained fairly benign. Most Ukrainians have shown no predilection for the ethnic intolerance and exclusivity that characterized much of the Ukrainian national movement in the interwar period. In the rush to rehabilitate key historical figures anathematized by the Soviet regime, a few Ukrainian figures who fought the Soviets and aided the Nazis have been praised as national heroes by some Ukrainian commentators, and a handful of contemporary nationalists have taken up the old integral nationalist theme of "Ukraine to Ukrainians."[76] Nevertheless, the government and most politicians have adhered to a relatively inclusive approach toward the country's non-Ukrainian minorities. The parliament's "Declaration on the Rights of Nationalities of Ukraine" guarantees equal political rights to individuals of all ethnic origins, and the Ukrainian citizenship law is explicitly antidiscriminatory. Rukh has taken a leading role in combating manifestations of anti-Semitism, and the government has accommodated Ukraine's sizable Hungarian and Romanian minorities by granting autonomy to the two southwest districts in which many of these people live.[77] So far there has been no systematic attempt to enforce the requirements of the 1989 language law, although there have apparently been some efforts to implement it in television broadcasting and in university teaching.[78]

However, the comparatively favorable state of ethnic relations inside Ukraine has been seriously threatened by the grave deterioration of the economy. As shown in Chapter 5, the worsening economic crisis has exacerbated relations among the various regions of Ukraine and has generated pressures from the eastern region for the adoption of a more accommodating policy toward Russia. Meanwhile, a coalition led by the Rukh movement has begun to press for a reduction in relations with Russia, withdrawal from the CIS, and a rapid process of marketization that would inflict a very heavy socioeconomic burden on the eastern region.[79] The worsening economic situation could precipitate a fundamental split in the Ukrainian national movement and spur nationalist leaders to try to shore up their personal political standing by adopting a more assertive policy toward Russia. Although President Kravchuk has deftly employed this gambit in the past, under conditions of increasing domestic polarization the possibility of finding face-saving ways out of confrontations with Moscow would diminish. By increasing tensions between ardent nationalists and local Russians in Ukraine, a split in the national movement could also spur hardline politicians in Moscow to step up the pressure for an aggressive Russian policy toward Ukraine. In addition, domestic frustrations might fuel irredentist claims to Bukovina and southern Bessarabia that could set Ukraine on a collision course with Moldova and by extension with Romania.

Developments in Belarus bear some outward similarities to trends in the other new states west of Russia. In the mid-1980s members of the Belarusian intelligentsia began efforts to raise the level of national self-awareness among ethnic Belarusians, and in 1988 a Belarusian National Front was organized.[80] Like the other new states, Belarus declared its sovereignty in 1990, and in the same year the legislature enacted a language law that made Belarusian the official language of state and stipulated that the transition to its use should take place during the next three to ten years.[81]

The underlying dynamics of the Belarusian national movement, however, have been quite different from the dynamics of nationalism in neighboring states. Perhaps more than any other former Soviet republic in the western region, Belarus has a shortage of an ingredient critical to the construction of a durable nation-state: a vigorous sense of its distinctive national identity. Ill-defined in the pre-Communist era, the Belarusian sense of identity was shaped by several decades of russification whose effects were amplified by the catastrophic impact of World War II on the Belarusian population. Although ethnic Belarusians constitute a weighty 78 percent of Belarus's population and ethnic Russians amount to only 13 percent, the share of ethnic Belarusians who know and use their own national language is well below the comparable shares for any of the titular nationalities of the other fourteen new states.[82]

The leaders of the Belarusian government have recognized this national reality. Stanislau Shushkevich, chairman of the presidium of the Belarusian Supreme Soviet, has said that the "new freedom and the current changes will result in the revival of our national self-awareness, culture, and language. However, the complete revival of Belarus is still ahead, and will take a good deal of hard work to achieve."[83] At an international conference on the emergence of the national consciousness of Belarusians held in Minsk in 1992, many participants noted that the absence of a firmly rooted national identity "is preventing [Belarus] from taking its worthy place in Europe."[84] Viewed from this angle, the Belarusian case demonstrates the difficulty of basing a new state on a conception of the nation as a sovereign people when the core population's sense of ethnic distinctiveness is comparatively underdeveloped.

In striving to establish a firm sense of Belarusian national identity, Minsk has charted a foreign policy course that stresses a European orientation. Foreign Minister Pyotr Krauchanka, for example, has insisted repeatedly that Belarus will "build a civilized European state."[85] Rather like the Ukrainians, Belarusians appear to exhibit little of the ambivalence about the West evident in the statements of conservative Russian intellectuals and politicians. An opinion survey conducted in the fall of 1992 found that 80 percent of the respondents had a favorable opinion of the United States, France, and Germany. The survey also revealed that the Belarusian respondents held unusually sanguine views about the international situation and expressed a very low measure of concern about the potential security risk posed by Russia.[86]

Despite this optimistic outlook, or perhaps because of it, the country's leadership has been careful not to carry the emphasis on Belarus's European orientation to lengths that Russia could find threatening. In this respect, the Belarusian approach differs markedly from that pursued in Ukraine. When a Ukrainian citizen asked Chairman Shushkevich why Belarus did not join forces with Ukraine in the struggle "to come out from under the boot of [Russia]," Shushkevich brushed the question aside. Belarus, he insisted, could not discern any "Russian imperial positions that we Belarusians must do battle with," and he observed pointedly that "we must strive to convince the Russian leadership that the sovereignty of Belarus does not contradict Russia's interests."[87] Foreign Minister Krauchanka likewise cautioned that "we have to live together for the next ten to fifteen years, whether we like it or not. Some things are larger than the will of politicians or state ambitions: namely, harsh economic necessity."[88] The political leadership has also worked assiduously to prevent the issue of ethnic minorities from marring its relations with Russia and most other former Soviet republics.[89] This emphasis on the primacy of relations with Russia appears to reflect the attitudes prevailing among Belarusian citizens. Polls conducted in November 1992 found that almost a year after the dissolution of the Soviet state, 80 percent of the respondents agreed with the statement that the demise of the USSR was "a great misfortune," and a strong majority expressed a wish to see the USSR resurrected.[90]

If a key choice for Ukrainian national leaders is between a posture of active opposition to Russia and a posture of neutrality, the choice for Belarusian national leaders is between neutrality and close alignment with Russia. A debate over whether Belarus should join the Russian-led CIS mutual security agreement signed in mid-1992 has divided Belarusian government leaders over the operational meaning of Belarus's commitment to neutrality, but virtually no voices have advocated a confrontational policy toward Russia.[91] Although local Russians have urged that Russian be made a second state language, and some Belarusian intellectuals have demanded wider use of the Belarusian language, there appears to be less popular pressure for a shift to the titular language than in many of the other new states.[92] On the whole, the measured quality of the government's pronouncements indicates that Minsk is likely to accommodate Russia and will remain closely attuned to the potential impact of domestic ethnic affairs on Belarusian foreign relations.

In the Baltic region, on the other hand, questions of ethnicity and national identity are among the most volatile problems facing the new governments. Estonia's population is approximately one-third Russian. In Latvia approximately 30 percent of the population is Russian and another 20 percent consists of other non-Latvian nationalities. Only in Lithuania does a clear majority of 80 percent consist of the titular nationality, with Poles and Belarusians being important minorities. Moreover, in the capital cities of each of the three countries – Tallinn, Riga, and Vilnius – the concentration of Russians is significantly higher than in the country as a whole.[93]

Because of these demographic realities and the history of Moscow's domination of the region, many Latvians and Estonians feel that their national identities are under threat. As they see it, their hard-won independence could easily be subverted by political actions of the non-native residents who previously helped strengthen Moscow's control over the Baltic region. Hence they are determined to ensure that the local Russian populations prove their political commitment and loyalty to the new states. This determination has been intensified by widespread Latvian and Estonian resentment of the Russian military units stationed on their territories and by the inability as of mid-1993 to reach an agreement with Russia on a timetable for complete withdrawal of the troops.

The issue of ethnic relations and national identity has been sharply posed in Estonia. The Estonian government has conferred automatic citizenship only on citizens of the interwar Estonian Republic and their descendants. All other residents desiring citizenship have been required to apply for naturalization. Eligibility requirements for applicants include a two-year period of residence starting in March 1990, a one-year waiting period after application, and demonstration of a basic knowledge of the Estonian language. (At present approximately 15 percent of the local Russian population knows Estonian.)[94] Persons who have worked for the KGB, are presently serving in a foreign military establishment, or have been convicted of violent crimes may not apply. Although the law allows noncitizen residents to participate in local elections, it prevented many local Russians and other non-Estonians (but not all the persons in this category) from voting in the first post-independence national elections in September 1992.[95] The law is also likely to have the effect – which may prove more consequential over the long term – of preventing a large number of local Russians and other non-Estonians from participating in the privatization of state-owned economic enterprises undertaken by the Estonian government.[96]

The Estonian approach to national citizenship has evoked apprehensions that an all-Estonian parliament would impose further legal restrictions on local Russians, particularly in the economic realm. Russian anxieties about economic discrimination have been compounded by the fact that marketization is likely to strike especially hard at the heavy industrial enterprises in which many local Russians are employed. Some reports indicate that many local Russians are more concerned about obtaining adequate protection of their economic welfare than about immediately obtaining full political rights, and some evidence appears to bear this out. By the spring of 1993, only 13,000 permanent residents of Estonia had applied for Estonian citizenship, and only 17,000 had applied for Russian citizenship.[97] Similarly, the Russian residents of the Estonian city of Narva, populated primarily by Russians, initially showed little interest in a campaign to obtain cultural autonomy for their district or secession from Estonia.[98] By mid-1993, however, the campaign for autonomy within Estonia had picked up considerable political momentum.

The Latvian approach to these matters resembles Estonia's. The Latvian draft law on citizenship confers citizenship only on citizens of interwar Latvia and their descendants and requires the naturalization of all other persons who wish to become citizens. By comparison with the Estonian law, the grounds on which naturalization may be refused are wider; they include work as an official of the Communist Party and conviction for spreading chauvinist or Communist ideas.[99] Another significant difference is that applicants for naturalization in Latvia must have resided in the country for at least sixteen years, a large increase from the six-year residency requirement that was first stipulated by the government. Although the more stringent residency requirement was probably instituted in an effort to exclude many local Russians, in actuality it has had only a marginal effect, since 93 percent of all noncitizens have lived in Latvia for longer than sixteen years.[100]

Conflicts of this kind are not an automatic consequence of the rise of Baltic nationalism. Lithuania, which experienced a surge of national feeling during the late Gorbachev period, has adopted an inclusive citizenship law that grants citizenship to most local Russians and other non-Lithuanians. The numerical predominance of ethnic Lithuanians in Lithuania has made this step relatively safe from a political standpoint, and it has led to some Russian efforts, thus far unsuccessful, to use Lithuania to exert diplomatic pressure on Latvia and Estonia. By contrast, in Latvia and Estonia, the close demographic balance between the titular nationality and local Russians has prompted a more restrictive approach to citizenship. It has also contributed to heightened fears among the titular nationalities, and to the informal discussion of more severe measures to restrict the rights of the Russian inhabitants.[101] Although these measures have not been endorsed by the Estonian and Latvian governments, they have served to sharpen the tensions and anxieties between the two countries' Baltic residents and local Russians.

The escalating tension surrounding the citizenship issue has prompted vigorous protests from Moscow, especially from politicians like Vice-President Aleksandr Rutskoy and from centrists such as Yevgeniy Ambartsumov, head of the Russian parliament's Committee on International Affairs and Foreign Economic Policy. Although some local Russians undoubtedly favor the intervention of Moscow officials and may have encouraged it, it is far from clear that most local Russians have welcomed Moscow's involvement. In the spring 1991 plebiscites organized by the Baltic republics, large numbers of local Russians – perhaps even sizable majorities – voted for independence.[102] In 1992 a cross-section of Russians living in the Baltic region told a visiting American delegation that they believed that their situation was being manipulated by politicians in Moscow.[103] On the other hand, if the Estonian and Latvian governments adopt an operational policy that effectively prevents qualified local Russians from obtaining citizenship for many years, they may inadvertently strengthen the tendency toward disloyalty that the citizenship laws are supposedly meant to prevent.

In Moldova the tension between the titular nationality and others, especially local Russians, has led to violent conflict. At the time of independence about two-thirds of the new state's inhabitants were ethnic Moldovans, one-seventh were Russians, and one-seventh were Ukrainians, with the balance consisting of small ethnic groups such as Jews and the Turkic Orthodox Christian Gagauz. As the campaign for Moldovan autonomy from Moscow and the reassertion of the Moldovan language gathered momentum in 1990, the Gagauz and then the Russians and Ukrainians in the trans-Dniester region declared their independence from Moldova. The particular determination of the trans-Dniester Russians to set up their own state was strengthened by their fear, not unfounded, that Moldovan independence would lead to union with Romania. The Moldovan government responded by dissolving the trans-Dniester local government council and declaring presidential rule in the region, much as it did in the territory inhabited by the Gagauz.[104] This confrontation produced an escalation of violence pitting fighters for the Moldovan government against irregular forces from the trans-Dniester region and, increasingly, units of the Russian 14th Army based in the region. The continuing warfare between these forces demonstrated that, under certain conditions, conflicts between titular nationalities and local Russians could lead to violence and civil war.

The Southern Newly Independent States

In Central Asia, the search for national identity has taken place against a distinctive but complex demographic and cultural background. Before the nineteenth century the ties of the various peoples of the region reached far beyond the modern-day boundaries of Central Asia to the Ottoman empire, Persia, and China, and this history has left an imprint on all the new states. Ethnically, most of the peoples of Central Asia are Turkic, and their languages link them with Turkey. At one time or another, many of the region's peoples also have maintained cultural and trading links with Iran. This is especially true of the Tajiks, whose ties with Iran include a variant of the Persian language and many shared traditions. Despite many cultural commonalities, relations between the Persian-related Tajiks and the Turkic peoples of Central Asia have been characterized especially since the Bolshevik revolution by a persistent element of cultural and political rivalry.

During the 1930s Stalin's imposition of a draconian policy of cultural isolation put an end to the extensive cross-border links between Central Asia and its southern neighbors. Even more significant, however, was Moscow's attempt to neutralize the residual cultural affinities, both among the Central Asian peoples and between them and the outside world, that remained embedded in Central Asian literature and customs. By changing the alphabets of the Central Asian languages to the Latin in the 1920s, Moscow made the literatures and publications of many neighboring countries, as well as past writings from Central Asia itself, unintelligible to new generations of Central Asians. The abandonment of the Arabic alphabet eroded Central Asia's waning ties with Persia and diminished its cultural and religious interaction with the Arab world. After 1928 the jettisoning of the new Latin alphabet used by Tajiks and some Turkic groups undercut the region's ties with Turkey, as well as potential links with Europe. By these means, Moscow severed Central Asia's cultural ties with peoples outside the Soviet empire more thoroughly than simply sealing off the borders could have done. The policy of cutural autarky was calculated to buttress Moscow's control over the development of national sentiments among ethnic Central Asians.

As noted in Chapter 1, at the start of the Soviet period none of the Central Asian peoples had a clearly developed sense of nationality, with the arguable exception of the Tatars. Although a handful of intellectuals were committed nationalists, the bulk of the population was more firmly attached either to supranational identities, particularly an association with Islam, or to subnational clan, regional, or tribal loyalties, which exercised the strongest influence on the self-conception of most of the region's inhabitants. Because the Central Asian national republics were created by Moscow's decree, the post-Soviet states of Central Asia still exhibit more marks of artificiality than do countries in which organic development outweighed administrative fiat in the shaping of the state.

Although distinctive Central Asian national identities did gradually coalesce around the national republics during the Soviet era, nationalist impulses in the region remained relatively weak at the time of the USSR's collapse. For instance, national fronts were formed in only some of the Central Asian republics during the late Gorbachev years, and they lacked the capacity for social mobilization that was evident in such western republics as Lithuania and Ukraine.[105] Although this was due in part to the tight political controls maintained by local party chiefs even after Moscow's proclamation of the principle of *glasnost*, it also reflected the tenor of social attitudes within the various Central Asian nationalities. According to Western specialists, national consciousness has developed in the cities of Central Asia, but the identity of rural inhabitants still is defined primarily in terms of religious or regional affiliation and membership in extended families or tribes.[106]

That none of the countries of the region is ethnically homogeneous has fundamental implications for their external relations and domestic development. The ethnic cleavage most familiar to Western observers divides ethnic Russians from ethnic Central Asians. All the new states of the region have sizable Russian minorities, ranging from approximately 8 to 10 percent of the population in Tajikistan, Uzbekistan, and Turkmenistan to approximately 22 percent in Kyrgyzstan and nearly 38 percent in Kazakhstan.[107] The majority of these Russians are not recent immigrants from Russia, but have come to Central Asia in waves of immigration, either in the late tsarist period, in the 1920s and 1930s, or during the Virgin Lands period under Khrushchev. In all the Central Asian countries save Tajikistan, a majority of the Russian residents were born in the country.[108] With fewer family and personal ties in Russia, some local Russians probably regard their country of residence, rather than Russia, as their home, although as a group local Russians express far more regret about the dissolution of the Soviet Union than do ethnic Central Asians.[109] Those local Russians who have a sense of rootedness will probably make different decisions about whether to respond to pressures from ethnic Central Asians by emigrating, by fighting to preserve their position in the country, or by joining a secessionist movement.

The relationship between local Russians and ethnic Central Asians is critical to Central Asia's future not only because of its effect on Russia's political relations with the new states, but because in most cases the economic and technical skills furnished by the local Russians cannot be replaced with indigenous Central Asian manpower. As shown in Chapter 5, Russians make up the bulk of the managerial and technical personnel in mining, energy production, and other key industrial sectors. For this reason, the prospect that Russians will "vote with their feet" by emigrating is probably scarcely less upsetting to many Central Asian government officials than the possibility that Russians will engage in militant political action or attempt to secede.

Several irritants threaten to inflame the relations between ethnic Central Asians and local Russians (as well as other residents of European origin). One is a rise in anti-Russian feeling among ethnic Central Asians. As Moscow's political reach has receded from the region, a new opportunity to express pent-up resentments has appeared. The fact that Communism came to Central Asia primarily as a result of Russian colonialism has ensured that the millions of Russians who were born and still reside there nonetheless are likely to be viewed as colonizers and foreigners, particularly because of their unwillingness to learn the languages and traditions of ethnic Central Asians. Some of the ethnic Central Asians' resentments have focused on Russians' domination of elite managerial and technical jobs at a time when unemployment has assumed grave proportions among non-European residents.[110] Moreover, as historians and journalists reveal more about the destructive impact of the Soviet system on Central Asia's peoples and ecology, the temptation to blame the local Russians will almost certainly increase.

For their part, many local Russians fear that they may become the target of ethnic violence. Although virtually all the episodes of communal violence in Central Asia have thus far pitted Muslim ethnic groups against one another, local Russians have taken little comfort from this fact. Some of the Russians' fears reflect their unease that Central Asians are no longer being properly subservient and grateful to their Russian "benefactors." In addition, authoritarian leaders in some of these countries have done their utmost to frighten the Russians about how they (the Russians) would suffer if the "native" opposition displaced the hardliners. The object is to keep the Russians out of reformist politics. Surveys show a considerably higher level of insecurity among the Russians of Central Asia than among Russians living in the Baltic states, even though many Balts harbor intense hostility toward local Russians.[111] These anxieties have been compounded by pressures on the dominant position of the Russian language in Central Asian affairs.

Since 1989 all the Central Asian governments have adopted new language laws that impinge on the privileged social and political position of local Russians. For instance, the Kyrgyzstan law of 1989 called for most of its provisions to be phased in over time, but one section required that managers and professionals demonstrate a command of the Kyrgyz language immediately. Kazakhstan's new language law, which went into effect in 1990, made fluency in Kazakh a requirement for high-school graduation starting in 1992 and laid out a timetable for a transition to Kazakh as the language of government business by 1994. The other Central Asian states have passed similar legislation intended to upgrade the status of the titular nationality's language.[112]

These declaratory changes in language policy, especially the more sweeping ones, have not been matched by vigorous government attempts to implement the mandated changes, let alone by actual achievement of those changes. In Kazakhstan, for example, vociferous protests from the large Russian population and hard political bargaining diluted the language requirement in education and stretched out the timetable for completing the shift to fully bilingual administration to the year 2000.[113] Nonetheless, the language issue remains highly sensitive. The percentage of local Russians with a working knowledge of the relevant Central Asian language ranges from less than 1 percent in Kazakhstan to a high of 4.6 percent in Uzbekistan.[114] Hence even small moves toward genuine bilingualism by Russians (all other inhabitants already show a high rate of bilingualism) in the Central Asian states tend to evoke deep anxieties and resistance among the local Russian population. The language issue also reveals the essence of Russians' colonial attitude toward Central Asia, in that even those Russians born in Central Asia often cannot speak the language of the titular nationality and are indignant that they be required to learn it. Such resistance, however, may only increase the determination of the most fervent Central Asian nationalists, who are reportedly monitoring this matter carefully, to force the language issue.[115]

The appearance in most of the Central Asian states of political parties and movements organized along pro- or anti-Russian lines is a natural consequence of these circumstances. Examples of pro-Russian movements include Kazakhstan's Edinstvo (Unity), which favors maintaining Russian as a coequal state language and guaranteeing equal access for all citizens to jobs and economic benefits; the combative Cossacks of northwestern and northeastern Kazakhstan; and the Slavic Fund in Kyrgyzstan, which maintains that current laws repress the non-Kyrgyz.[116] Thus far, most of the political parties that represent ethnic Central Asians have remained circumspect about expressing anti-Russian sentiments – in part, perhaps, out of fear that they will be repressed by government leaders determined to keep local Russians in place for economic reasons. However, anti-Russian sentiments have found some organized political outlets. In Kazakhstan, for example, the program of the Alash party demands "priority rights for the Kazakh

[Turkic] nation and Islam."[117] Given Russia's colonial legacy in the area, it would be surprising if such sentiments were not held widely elsewhere in Central Asia.

Since 1989 the number of Russians leaving Central Asia has increased sharply. By one reckoning, between 1989 and 1991 nearly as many Russians emigrated from Central Asia as had left during the preceding decade. Although the number was not overwhelming in absolute terms, the trend seemed a harbinger of trouble. According to these figures the flow of Russians migrating to Russia from Central Asia is now approximately a hundred thousand per year, and may be considerably greater.[118] In Russia the total number of "forced migrants" – that is, persons holding Russian citizenship who have recently returned to Russia as a result of political pressure from all the other former Soviet republics – is officially put at eight hundred thousand and is probably much higher.[119] If these migrants are not already disgruntled when they arrive in Russia, they are likely to become so, because the material resources available to support them in the Russian Federation are inadequate. Should the flow of Russian immigrants continue to increase rapidly, they could become an important factor in Russian politics as a natural constituency for right-wing nationalists advocating punitive action by the Russian government against the Central Asian countries.

The division of the populations of the Central Asian countries between citizens of Central Asian and European origin has had a significant effect on the new states' foreign relations. Together with the countries' desperate economic circumstances, the ethnic cleavage has made the new polities exceptionally fragile and has prompted their government leaders to try to maintain good relations with all the surrounding countries – but especially with Russia. In those countries where the distribution of domestic political forces between ethnic Russians and Central Asians is most delicately balanced, and where the legislatures have succeeded in gaining a modicum of autonomy from the executive branch, the cleavage has also hampered governmental attempts to take clear-cut foreign policy measures. In 1992, for example, the presidents of Kazakhstan and Kyrgyzstan both agreed to participate with Russia and Uzbekistan in a multilateral peace-keeping force intended to help resolve the civil war in Tajikistan. However, apprehensions about the domestic consequences of intervening in Tajikistan prevented both presidents from obtaining their legislature's prompt authorization to implement the military measure, thereby enabling Uzbekistan to establish a dominant position in war-torn Tajikistan.[120]

Important as it is, the cleavage between Russians and Central Asians may be no more significant than the presence of large ethnic Central Asian minorities in several countries of the region. In Tajikistan, for example, Uzbeks constitute nearly a quarter of the total population, making them a far larger minority than the local Russians. In Kyrgyzstan, Uzbeks account for almost 13 percent of the population, and in Turkmenistan for slightly less than 10 percent of the total.[121] Apart from complicating the internal affairs of several of the Central Asian states, the mingling of populations gives some states an ethnic motive for involvement in the affairs of their Central Asian neighbors. For example, more than 20 percent of all Tajiks live in Uzbekistan, as do almost 7 percent of all Kyrgyz; and 7 percent of all Uzbeks live in Tajikistan.[122]

These internal ethnic divisions have major implications for the relations among the new states of Central Asia, including the notion of creating a unified Turkestan. As shown in the introductory chapter, when the USSR collapsed, Nazarbayev and other leaders played on Russian fears of a united Turkestan to lever their way into the Commonwealth of Independent States, and since that time they have periodically paid lip service to the idea,[123] which is also supported by several Central Asian political groups.[124] However, actually creating such a political entity seems nearly impossible in view of the sharp rivalries and suspicions among several of the Central Asian countries. These tensions, which have both ethno-territorial and economic dimensions, center especially on Uzbekistan. With the exception of Kazakhstan, Uzbekistan is the most powerful of the five Central Asian countries, and it is vying with Kazakhstan for regional preeminence and for the role of Central Asia's main spokesman in dealings with Moscow.

The other Central Asian countries distrust Uzbekistan for several reasons. Perhaps the most important is that Uzbekistan has shown clear signs of a desire for self-aggrandizement at the expense of its neighbors. In 1990, for instance, the Uzbek press ran a provocative article suggesting that Uzbekistan should be renamed "Turkestan" or "Turan," thereby implying that all the territory encompassed by the old tsarist region of Turkestan – that is, the territory of all the other Central Asian states save Kazakhstan – belonged within Uzbekistan's domain.[125] Since 1990 the ambitions hinted at in the article have become more palpable. According to one observer, "Uzbek nationalists have . . . been the most active advocates of the recreation of a Greater Turkestan. There appear to be rising concerns among Central Asia's non-Uzbek populations [over] Uzbek attempts to assert that the Uzbek nation should be dominant in the region."[126]

In short, other Central Asian countries regard calls for a pan-Turkic union as Uzbekistan's thinly veiled attempt to gain a dominant and perhaps hegemonic position in the region. In Kyrgyzstan, for example, "uzbekization appears more insidious than russification," and this colors Kyrgyz reactions to all pan-Turkic or pan-Islamic proposals.[127] An additional fault line separates the Turkic Uzbeks from the Persian-speaking Tajiks. Long-standing tensions between Uzbeks and Tajiks in the Fergana Valley and elsewhere have been compounded by the two peoples' tendency not to recognize each other's distinct history; the Tajiks consider the Uzbeks to be "Turkicized Iranians," whereas Uzbek chauvinists claim either that the Tajiks came to Central Asia after the Arab conquest (and therefore are not true Central Asians) or are Turks who were gradually Iranianized.[128]

Uzbekistan's attitude toward ethnic Uzbeks outside the country has given an added edge to the apprehensions of the other Central Asian states. Uzbekistan president Islam Karimov "has articulated a foreign policy similar to that of Russia – the right of Uzbekistan to intervene in the name of protecting Uzbeks, independent of where they might live."[129] Given the presence of significant Uzbek minorities in most of the other Central Asian countries, this policy has contributed to rising tensions between those minorities and their host governments. If ethno-national feelings grow more pronounced in the host countries, "the Uzbek minorities living there will increasingly be faced with the same choices faced by Russians in the [Central Asian] region today: emigrate or separate."[130] Although this scenario need not come to pass – clearly the outcome hinges partly on whether Uzbekistan continues to adhere to its present policy – the scenario does suggest the strength of the centrifugal forces at work in post-Soviet Central Asia. At best, proposals for pan-Turkic cooperation seem destined to prove no more effectual than the postcolonial pan-Arab movement proved to be in the Middle East during the 1960s and 1970s.

The civil war in Tajikistan has added to the uncertainty about Central Asia's future. The war is a matter of deep concern to the other Central Asian governments, primarily because they fear that it might spread to one of their own countries, particularly to adjacent Kyrgyzstan and Uzbekistan. If the war intensifies or spills over into neighboring countries it is likely to put new strains on the fragile ethnic relations both within and among the new states of Central Asia.

By comparison with the Central Asian countries, the states of the Caucasus stand out as a group for their relatively high level of homogeneity. In Georgia, the least homogeneous of the three, 70 percent of the population in 1989 consisted of ethnic Georgians, while the share of the titular nationality in Azerbaijan was 83 percent and in Armenia, 94 percent. In addition, Georgia and Armenia have long maintained a vigorous indigenous cultural life based on written languages that are centuries older than the Russian language. Unlike virtually all other non-Slavic peoples, whose written languages were changed in the 1930s to the Cyrillic script, Georgia and Armenia retained their traditional alphabets, which predated the Russian alphabet by centuries.

Despite these seemingly auspicious circumstances, regional warfare has devastated the Caucasus. In Georgia, the demise of Soviet power has ventilated hostilities between ethnic Georgians and other groups, such as the Abkhazians and Ossetians, that Soviet domination previously kept from spinning out of control. In Tbilisi the vigorous nationalist impulses that sustained the drive for Georgian independence from Moscow produced an intolerant regime intent on the georgianization of non-Georgian ethnic groups. Led by Zviad Gamsakhurdia, a former Georgian dissenter, the government in Tbilisi proceeded on the assumption that Georgians had long been a persecuted minority in their own land and that the time had come to rectify this injustice.[131] The results were government repression and violent communal conflicts that poisoned the politics of the new Georgian state and produced a virtual civil war.

Developments elsewhere in the Caucasus have been no more encouraging. What began in 1988 as a political controversy between Armenia and Azerbaijan over control of Nagorno-Karabakh, a predominantly Armenian enclave located inside Azerbaijan, has been transformed by communal violence and escalating national passions into an exhausting war of attrition that also helped bring down Azerbaijan's first democratically elected president, Abulfaz Elchibey. For its part, Armenia has been especially conscious of the risk that Turkey, its historic enemy, might open a "second front" in the conflict. Perhaps for this reason, Armenia has refrained from demanding direct control of Nagorno-Karabakh and has sought to define the issue as a matter of self-determination for the inhabitants of the enclave – much to the displeasure of the Armenian diaspora outside the former USSR, which has favored a more aggressive posture.[132] Armenia has also sought to obtain Russian military assistance by invoking the 1992 CIS mutual security agreement, but it appears to have received only indirect military support from Russia, not the direct military intervention it desired.[133]

Based on historic cultural and political affinities, Azerbaijan has obtained Turkish political and perhaps military support. This support, however, has been insufficient to prevent a series of military setbacks. In 1992 the setbacks caused Azerbaijan to renounce membership in the CIS in protest against what it saw as Russian favoritism for Armenia. Azerbaijani public anger at a string of military defeats was one of the factors that helped overturn six leaders and governments during 1992 and created political disorder and the overthrow of Elchibey's government in mid-1993. For its part, Georgia has tended to favor the Azerbaijanis out of a concern that secession by Nagorno-Karabakh would set a precedent for the Abkhaz and the Ossetians who are struggling by military and political means to secede from Georgia.

The war between Armenia and Azerbaijan is the clearest illustration in the post-Soviet states of the destructive potential of nationalism. In the Caucasus, nationalist animosities have proved especially complex and inflammatory, entangled as they are with cross-cutting tribal and family loyalties. In most of Central Asia, the governments have thus far avoided hard-and-fast commitments to irredentist causes advocated by subnational groups. In the Caucasus, on the other hand, national governments have been drawn into these disputes and have become locked into ethnic conflicts that cannot be won but that must not be lost.

Conclusion

In all likelihood the search for national identity that has begun in the new states will take decades to reach clear outcomes. In virtually every country, leaders and elites are competing to shape the development of their society's set of self-defining national symbols and myths. Although this process of "nation building" contains serious risks, it is both un-avoidable and potentially very positive; it is a mistake to regard all appeals to national loyalty and national values as parochial and exclu-sionary. Nationalism is indeed a path into modernity, despite the wide-spread Western tendency to think the opposite.[134] Durable states cannot be created without a sustaining sense of common identity to cement political obligations and political institutions. Moreover, in many of the new states, the prevailing impulse has been to adopt an inclusive def-inition of nationality that accepts all willing inhabitants of the territory as citizens of the nation. With good fortune, this approach may ensure that the historic process of ethnic unmixing begun late in the Soviet era – that is, the "return" of ethnic groups to "their" titular national states – does not generate massive population shifts or explosive political consequences.

Even at its best, however, the creation of an inclusive national identity is fraught with difficulty. Too small an admixture of ethnic identity – too weak a sense of the nation as a "unique people" – makes the process of state-building exceptionally difficult, as in Belarus. On the other hand, too powerful an admixture of ethnic consciousness risks per-manently dividing the population along ethnic lines and triggering a spiral of domestic conflict. Such a situation could conceivably come to pass in Latvia and Estonia, despite their formal commitment to the notion of civic nationality and the concept of equal legal treatment of all individuals. It is also a serious danger in the countries of Central Asia, and already an agonizing reality in the new states of the Caucasus.

The conception of the nation as a set of unique people is especially destabilizing in sizable countries with large diasporas, because it invites the inhabitants of the national homeland to intervene abroad in defense of their ethnic kinsmen. Although some problems of this sort exist in almost all the new states, the two cases with the largest potential for politically destabilizing consequences are Russia and, to a lesser extent, Uzbekistan. Although the Russian government has adopted an inclusive attitude toward nationality inside the country, its attitude toward ethnic Russians living abroad reflects a more ethnocentric attitude. Only skillful political leadership, the passage of time, and a substantial measure of luck can ensure that this attitude does not lead Russia into violent conflict with other former republics. The same holds for Uzbekistan's relations with the other countries of Central Asia. Although the imperial mentality may be considerably less developed among contemporary Uzbeks than among Russians, so are the domestic political and institutional restraints that might curb precipitous foreign initiatives on behalf of the nation's kinsmen abroad.

3

The Impact of Religion

Like nationalism, religion can serve as a key component of political identity. Some pioneers in the study of modern nationalism have suggested that nationalism's emergence has coincided with a decline in religiosity, and it probably is true that changes in the psychological role of religion were a precondition for the development of national identities among the adherents of universal religions.[1] However, religion and nationalism do not necessarily occupy the same psychological space in people's minds, and the two phenomena are not mutually exclusive.[2] Although some brands of nationalism have been strictly secular, some of the twentieth century's most passionate nationalists have been religious believers. As a rule, concrete circumstances determine whether religion becomes a salient element of political identity and whether it reinforces or undermines a sense of cohesion within a particular national group.

At least six variables affect the political impact of a given religious confession. One is whether the confession is national or supranational in scope, and therefore how readily it can become a vehicle of national consciousness and political mobilization. A second variable is the institutional structure of the religion, which affects both its capacity to mobilize believers and its susceptibility to state control. A third is the number of adherents of the confession relative to the size of the society as a whole. A fourth is the spiritual content of the particular confession, especially its attitude toward the legitimacy of secular political authority and its tradition of independence or subservience to the state. A fifth variable is whether the confession's religious leaders seek to steer it toward or away from active involvement in worldly affairs. A sixth is whether and how political leaders seek to use religious sentiments and institutions for their own political ends.

Depending on how they are combined, these variables can produce a wide range of political consequences. For instance, if the members of a nation are divided among two or more religious confessions, religion

90

may weaken their sense of national identity. Such religious cleavages may prevent the nation from developing political cohesion vis-à-vis other national or ethnic groups, especially if the members of these other groups are adherents of the same religious confessions. In these circumstances, political and cultural elites aiming to build a sense of distinctive nationhood must play down religion as a marker of national identity in favor of other markers, such as shared language or historical experience, that set the nation apart from surrounding ethnic or national groups.

On the other hand, when national markers such as shared language or historical experience are weak or unavailable, religious beliefs and institutions may become an essential component of national identity and even of national survival. If most members of the nation belong to the same religious confession, the efforts of political and religious leaders may transform religion into a central source of political identity, even if the particular religious confession is supranational in scope. The crucial role of Roman Catholicism in sustaining the Polish nation's sense of identity during more than a century of statelessness and partition among Russia, Prussia, and Austria is a case in point.[3] The sustaining role of Islam among the russophone Muslims of the North Caucasus and Tatarstan is another example. As shown below, similar phenomena occurred among several other ethnic groups inside the tsarist and Soviet empires.

In addition to helping define the social boundaries of the national community, religion can affect the structure of power inside the community. For example, analysts agree that religion can have a major influence on a society's attitudes toward political authority and on the establishment of a democratic or a dictatorial political order. At the same time, they often disagree about the specific effects of religion on the evolution and behavior of particular political systems – for example, the impact of Islam on the polities in which it constitutes the dominant religious tradition.[4] In any case, whatever the country's political system, religion may also serve as the foundation for political parties or groups based on religious outlooks and affiliations. The Christian Democratic parties of Europe exemplify this tendency, as do the diverse Islamic parties of the Middle East. Political groupings of this kind often become the focus of debates about the proper relationship between the "church" – that is, religious confessions of any kind – and the state.

Apart from its impact on national identity and on domestic political arrangements, religion may directly influence the foreign relations of states. On occasion the spokesmen of a religious confession may seek to affect the political behavior of citizens of other countries, especially co-religionists, through direct appeals. More commonly, religious spokesmen may seek to influence the external policies of their own government – for example, by pressing the government to intervene to protect co-religionists abroad. In addition, religious institutions and leaders may influence their government's treatment of other countries based on different religious traditions by interpreting conflicts with those countries in terms that are religious as well as secular. One need only recall the history of relations between Christian and Islamic political forces in the Middle East to grasp the potential impact of religious differences on the relations among the new states of the former Soviet Union. Conversely, religious confessions may press their government to adopt a conciliatory or protective policy toward other countries with which they share a common religious heritage.

The interaction between past and present may make the political impact of religion especially large in the new states of Eurasia. As one observer has noted, "ironically, Communist regimes, despite considerable success against religious practices, have often reinvigorated ethno-religious identity by a combination of religious repression and, in the search for national legitimacy, encouragement of church patriotism."[5] In the post-Soviet era the new states of Eurasia are experiencing a religious revival intensified by the injustices perpetrated under the aegis of Soviet atheism, and many observers have noted that the crumbling of Communist ideology has created a moral vacuum that religion seems suited to fill. In an era marked by fluid political values and weak institutions, religion is likely to have a heightened political effect. However, the extent to which religion will reinforce or undermine the political cohesion of the new states is unclear. Nor is it clear how religion will figure in the relations among the new states as they seek to define themselves and their interests in the outside world.

Russia

In varying degrees, most Western countries are heirs to a tradition of separation between organized religion and the state. Due partly to the conversion of Kievan Rus to the Byzantine variant of Christianity, a very different tradition took root in tsarist Russia. From the sixteenth century the tsars based their rule on an ideology of divine right; and Russian theologians generally adhered to the Byzantine conception that grants the head of state substantial authority in the governance of the church. Also at this time, the Russian Orthodox church declared its independence, or autocephaly, from the Orthodox patriarch of Constantinople. From the seventeenth century onward the church increasingly fell under the bureaucratic domination of the Russian state and played a supporting role in the state's expansion into non-Russian

lands.[6] In exchange for its state-protected monopoly on religious prose-
lytism and censorship of religious works, the church increasingly became a tool of political indoctrination that exercised a strong influence
over the outlook of the tsar's subjects.[7] In particular, religious beliefs
and rituals helped maintain the population's loyalty to "Holy Russia."
This was especially important during the tumultuous early seventeenth
century, when the church rallied the population to save Russia from
the dynastic conflicts and foreign intervention that had shattered the
tsarist state.[8]

Today, as Russia sheds the Soviet legacy of state-enforced atheism
and reaches back into its history for guidance, religion once again seems
destined to play an important political role. Between 1987 and mid-
1992, more than six thousand Russian Orthodox churches were reopened, nearly doubling the number of active parishes.[9] A survey conducted near the end of the Soviet era found that 41 percent of the
Russian respondents in the Russian Federation considered themselves
religious believers, and that the overwhelming majority of these persons
(95 percent) gave their religious confession as Russian Orthodoxy.[10]
Another study conducted about the same time found that almost two-
thirds (64 percent) of the respondents expressed confidence in the
church, compared with much lower levels of confidence expressed in
most other public institutions.[11] Three years later the church, unlike
most other societal institutions, retained its moral standing in the eyes
of the Russian public, and its leader, Patriarch Aleksiy II, ranked ahead
of virtually all the other public figures monitored in opinion surveys.[12]

In keeping with the heightened popular interest in religion, the Russian Orthodox church has attracted widespread public attention as a
panacea for Russia's pressing domestic problems. According to one
observer, "there is no subject, it sometimes seems, on which the media
do not seek an opinion from the clergy, and the Russian government
constantly tries to gain legitimacy or add to its stature by invoking a
blessing from the Russian Orthodox hierarchy on formal occasions."[13]
Patriarch Aleksiy officiated at Yeltsin's inauguration and at the funeral
of civilians killed during the August 1991 coup attempt. In mid-1992
Yeltsin thanked the patriarch for helping revive the Russian state and
signed a decree allocating 200 million rubles to restore the churches on
the Valaam archipelago, for centuries a center of Russian Orthodoxy.[14]
In the fall of 1992 the government gave the patriarchate authority over
all the Kremlin cathedrals and St. Basil's church on Red Square.

Although there are many signs of a new deference to Russian Orthodoxy, the post-Soviet political dispensation has posed some unfamiliar dilemmas for the church. Despite the drastic changes brought
about by the Bolsheviks' revolutionary disestablishment of the Russian

Orthodox church, in both the tsarist and Soviet eras the church hierarchy generally took its political cues from the state.[15] In this respect
the Bolsheviks' adoption of the constitutional principle of separation
of church and state was no more than a political fiction. In the post-
Soviet period, however, the attempt to establish real democracy has
given the principle some genuine substance and has exposed the church
to direct competition from other religious confessions. Moreover, rival
Russian political forces are vying to use the church to advance their
own causes, thereby presenting it with a choice between conflicting
political "lines." This, in turn, has exacerbated the rifts dividing church
reformers and political moderates from the religious obscurantists and
political reactionaries in the church's ranks. The church has received
a novel opportunity to put its stamp on Russia's development, but the
opportunity has been coupled with equally novel challenges.

   Due in part to the church's tribulations in the Soviet era, it will be
hard-pressed to meet these challenges. Although the Russian Orthodox
church at first resisted Bolshevik rule, near the end of the 1920s the
head of the church, Metropolitan Sergiy, pledged the church's unqualified loyalty to the Bolshevik state, thereby causing a deep schism
that prompted several thousand disillusioned believers to go underground and form groups that later came to be known as the True
Orthodox church.[16] Sergiy's effort to reach an accommodation with the
Bolshevik regime also alienated the Russian Orthodox Church Abroad,
a foreign-based branch of Russian Orthodoxy first established as a result
of the exigencies of the Civil War.[17] In the following decades, the Soviet
authorities subjected the church to destructive political pressures that
fluctuated substantially over time but never abated entirely.

   Under Stalin, those pressures came in the form of massive church
closings as well as surveillance by the secret police, who penetrated the
church hierarchy at every level and drastically reduced its nominal
freedom of action.[18] The devastating Nazi military attack in 1941
prompted Stalin to adopt a much more measured policy toward religious
activities in order to mobilize popular resistance against the German
invaders, but at the end of the 1950s Khrushchev mounted another
major offensive against religion that was moderated but not rolled back
by the Brezhnev-Kosygin leadership. In contrast to the attempt to
uproot completely some supranational confessions such as Judaism and
Catholicism, Stalin and his successors ultimately elected to coopt the
Russian Orthodox church and use it as an instrument for managing
political relations with the West and ethnic affairs inside the USSR.[19]
The church paid a high institutional and spiritual price for this "privileged" position, however. As shown in Chapter 4, the road to full
institutional and spiritual health is bound to be long and arduous.

Under the Soviets the Moscow patriarchate was often used as a political tool against foreign religious denominations, but it often fulfilled this role willingly. One recent chapter of the church's historic struggle with Roman Catholicism stretches back to the decision of the Catholic church to support a powerful national-religious challenge to the Moscow patriarchate from the Uniate (or Greek Catholic) church, based historically in western Ukraine. Long banned in the USSR, the Uniate church recognizes the doctrinal and ecclesiastical authority of the pope but follows Orthodox liturgical practices and canon law.[20] Around 1980 Pope John Paul II publicly recognized the banned church's ecclesiastical claims against the patriarchate, thereby angering Russian Orthodox prelates. Patriarch Pimen described the pope's action as an "alien" source of "pain and alarm" that threatened to obliterate ecumenical cooperation. Ten years later Pimen's successor, Patriarch Aleksiy II, accused Rome of "forceful expansionism" for much the same reason.[21] The patriarchate's disinclination to compromise on these matters has probably been further hardened by the criticism emanating from the conservative Russian Orthodox Church Abroad, which bitterly opposes ecumenical ties with non-Orthodox confessions,[22] and by the novel forms of institutional vulnerability that confront it as a result of political liberalization.

Partly because of the patriarchate's perceived complicity with the Soviet regime, the Russian Orthodox claim on Christian believers in Russia has been challenged by foreign-affiliated confessions including not only the Uniates but the Free Russian Orthodox church (a branch of the emigre Russian Orthodox Church Abroad), the Pentecostals, and many other Western-based Protestant confessions. Non-Orthodox congregations have increased in size and number, and a sizable number of Orthodox parishes have switched their allegiance to the Uniates or the Orthodox Church Abroad.[23] The patriarchate has responded to these religious challenges by arguing that the Russian Orthodox Church Abroad collaborated with the Nazis during World War II and therefore lacks any moral basis for condemning the behavior of the patriarchal church under Communism, by reiterating its complaints against the Holy See, and by obtaining legislative limits on the activities of foreign religious denominations, including their access to Russian television.[24] In 1992, after repeated complaints from Orthodox churchmen, the papal nuncio to Ukraine formally renounced any intention to convert Orthodox Christians to Roman Catholicism.[25] Nevertheless, in view of the religious ferment in the former USSR and the Moscow patriarchate's ingrained dislike of religious pluralism, this declaration seems unlikely to heal the rift between the two confessions.[26]

The controversy with the Roman Catholic church and the Uniates is a matter of special importance. During 1988 Russian churchmen became embroiled in a bitter dispute with the Vatican over the celebration of the millennium of the acceptance of Christianity in Kievan Rus and over the role of the Uniate church, long a key source of national identity for many Ukrainians. Viewed from a secular political standpoint, this ecclesiastical controversy was primarily a struggle over the relative standing of the Russian and Ukrainian nations. In 1989–90 the struggle took a further twist when the Uniate church and the Ukrainian Autocephalous Orthodox church, another Ukrainian church long suppressed by the Soviet government, both won recognition as legal organizations, and the Moscow patriarchate countered by creating an allegedly autonomous Ukrainian Orthodox church that in fact remained closely tied to the church hierarchy in Moscow.[27] In the heated struggle that ensued, Russian Orthodox prelates charged that their religious competitors in Ukraine were "separatist extremists" who were leading the churches toward religious "civil war."[28] Moreover, even after the breakup of the USSR, the main journal of the Moscow patriarchate continued to advocate the notion of a "one and indivisible Russia" that still encompassed Ukraine.[29] As shown in the following section, a central motive for the church's conservative nationalist stance was the religious challenge posed to the patriarchate in Ukraine by the Uniate and Ukrainian Autocephalous Orthodox churches.

The larger political stakes in these ecclesiastical controversies were spelled out late in 1991. On the eve of the Ukrainian referendum on independence from the USSR, the Russian Alliance of Orthodox Brotherhoods, a lay organization closely linked to the Moscow patriarchate, urged their Slavic brethren not to vote for independence. "The Slavic peoples of Russia and Ukraine have one history, one fate. . . . Do not let the enemy of our salvation separate us," they pleaded.[30] Speaking for many of his fellows, one Ukrainian believer retorted by extolling the virtues of the Autocephalous church. "The Ukrainian Autocephalous Orthodox church," he asserted, "is the expression of the resolute will of the Ukrainian people to finally liberate itself from the imperial [Russian] Orthodox church which is an instrument of spiritual oppression against the Ukrainian people, aiming at its complete russification and enslavement."[31]

The Ukrainian attempt to merge the Ukrainian Orthodox church with the Ukrainian Autocephalous Orthodox church in June 1992 was designed to weaken Moscow's influence in Ukraine while strengthening church forces loyal to the independence of the Ukrainian state. That was one reason prominent Ukrainian politicians backed the attempted merger.[32] Nevertheless, this measure is unlikely to undo the knot be-

inhabited by peoples of Muslim origin highlights the problematic nature of some nationalists' depiction of Russia as a Christian country. Muslim spokesmen have objected to the close association of the Yeltsin government with the Russian Orthodox church. For instance, near the start of 1992 Sheikh Ravil Gainurtdin, the imam of the Moscow Mosque, complained that "our country still retains the ideology of the tsarist empire, which believed that the Orthodox faith alone should be a privileged religion, that is, the state religion." The imam asserted that the Russian media were slighting the activities of Russia's Muslims, including meetings of Russian Islamic clerics with such international figures as the king of Saudi Arabia and Libya's Muamar Qaddafi, while giving extensive coverage to such events as the meeting of the patriarch with the U.S. president.[44] Although Islamic religious institutions appear to have fared much worse during the Soviet era in Russia than in Central Asia and the Caucasus,[45] the prospects for a revival of Islam have been heightened by its potential linkage with the campaign of several ethnic governmental units inside Russia for greater political autonomy from Moscow and perhaps even for complete independence.

In April 1992 the Islamic Renaissance Party convened a conference in the Russian city of Saratov, located on the Volga. The conference was attended by representatives from several of the new Caucasian and Central Asian states and from several autonomous regions of Russia – including the independence-minded autonomous republics of Tatarstan and Bashkortostan. Its announced purpose was to explore the possibility of unification of Muslims of the former USSR into a single Islamic movement.[46] Although no clear-cut progress was made toward achieving this goal, the gathering's pan-Islamic character and its worrisome political implications for the cohesion of the Russian Federation were not lost on Russian politicians, some of whom had already voiced their fear that Islamic radicalism could spread to Russia.[47] In June 1992 President Yeltsin used the occasion of the Islamic Bairam holiday to call on Russia's Muslims to help to foster "a single Russian community, strengthening civil peace and national accord."[48]

The struggle over political autonomy within Russia has also been fought on the level of religious organization. The Russian Federation is heir to two of the four spiritual boards, or muftiates, established under Stalin to supervise the religious activities of Islamic groups in various parts of the empire. One board is responsible for European Russia and Siberia; the other is responsible for Russia's North Caucasus region. In August 1992 the two most independence-minded of Russia's autonomous republics, Tatarstan and Bashkortostan, withdrew recognition from the spiritual board for European Russia and Siberia and set up their own muftiates. In the North Caucasus, several religious associations had already withdrawn from the muftiate for the North Caucasus and attempted to establish their own muftiates.[49] In November 1992 a large congress of Muslim delegates from Russia condemned the action of Tatarstan and Bashkortostan and called for the preservation of the existing spiritual board for European Russia and Siberia. Asserting that Russian Islam was an important component of Russia "as a multinational and multi-confessional Eurasian state," the delegates adopted an appeal for worldwide peace, pointedly adding the mountain peoples of the North Caucasus to the list of groups to which the appeal was addressed. The episode demonstrated the various ways in which religious groups and institutions might affect Russia's internal cohesion, as well as the potential for external religious influence on the country's political evolution.[50]

Russia's leaders are aware that Muslim citizens of Russia are becoming more involved not only in their country's internal political affairs but in foreign policy issues, particularly the war in the former Yugoslavia. Foreign Minister Kozyrev, for example, has pointedly rejected the notion that Orthodoxy should become a determinant of Russian foreign policy, on the grounds that "it would promote a split in Russia itself" between Orthodox and Muslim believers. On the question of supporting Orthodox co-religionists in Serbia, Kozyrev wondered aloud why Russian Muslims in response should "not be just as reckless in defense of their fellow believers in Bosnia and Herzegovina. Then where would Moscow be? And is not this kind of policy tantamount to shifting the civil war from Yugoslavia to our own motherland?"[51] Not long after Kozyrev sounded this warning note, Muslim organizations in Russia announced their intention to follow up an Iranian diplomatic initiative in support of the Bosnian Muslims by appealing to the Russian government as well as the international community to stop the war. They also stated their intention to picket the Yugoslav embassy in Moscow.[52] These developments suggest that Russian diplomacy may be influenced not only by the views of Russia's various Christian confessions but also, to a lesser extent, by the attitudes of its Muslim citizens, and that some policymakers are mindful of the possible domestic consequences of appearing to take sides with one or another religious confession abroad.

Russian perceptions of the growth of Islam in Central Asia constitute a critical test case for the impact of religious beliefs, or at least of religiously conditioned sensibilities, on Russian foreign policy. In the late Soviet era, many Russian observers anticipated and warned against the prospect of the rise of Islamic radicalism inside the USSR. This expectation was influenced by the Islamic revolution in Iran and by the USSR's protracted war in Afghanistan, where its military adversaries included Islamic radicals. As Islam gained more and more open adherents in the Central Asian republics, many Russians became increasingly convinced – along with some Western scholars – that radical Islam would unify the Muslim population and threaten the survival of the USSR.[53]

Although the events of 1991 graphically disproved this expectation, many Russians have continued to regard the reinvigoration of Islam in the southern tier of new states as a serious political threat to Russia's security.[54] This attitude, which one Russian specialist on Islam labelled "Islamophobia," is partly a result of decades of Soviet atheistic propaganda designed to block any potential centrifugal forces in the non-Russian republics.[55] However, the outlook also is rooted in the history of Christian-Muslim tensions and in cultural stereotypes associated with Russian Christianity. One Uzbek historian has complained of a Russian double standard in religious matters: "The idea of a revival of the Russian people through Orthodoxy is perceived today as something normal, but when the Muslim people return to Islam with the same objective it puts people on guard. This is strange, to say the least."[56] Western scholars have likewise discerned a tendency for Russians to treat the revival of Russian Orthodox traditions as a healthy aspect of civil society but to interpret a growth of Islamic religious observances as evidence of Islamic militancy.[57]

Russian attitudes of this kind have been sharpened by the outbreak of violence in parts of Central Asia, particularly the civil war in Tajikistan, and they could influence the Russian government's behavior in such crises. Following the ouster of Tajik President Rakhman Nabiyev by nationalist and Islamic forces in September 1992, the Russian Foreign Ministry issued a stern warning against "outside interference" in Tajikistan or any other Central Asian state.[58] This declaration appeared to refer to the risk of political intervention by Islamic militants based in Iran or Afghanistan. Although the arrival of large numbers of Tajik refugees in Afghanistan almost inevitably made that country a participant in the war in Tajikistan, other neighboring states apparently have not made serious efforts to use radical religious movements to manipulate Central Asia's internal affairs.[59] The challenge for Moscow is to discern the cases, if any, in which Islamic radicalism represents a real threat to political stability in Central Asia, and whether outside intervention is actually occurring there. As shown in the final section of this chapter, some Central Asian political leaders have played up this risk with the intention of securing firm political backing from Russia. However, Moscow's backing might encourage the Central Asian governments to adopt policies that would intensify the very Islamicist political trends they were meant to thwart.

The growing incidence of interconfessional conflicts has prompted

President Yeltsin to attempt to reduce such tensions inside Russia. In the spring of 1993 Yeltsin convened a large gathering of religious leaders from the Russian Federation. In contrast to some of his past gestures to the Russian Orthodox church, Yeltsin underscored the diversity of the religious confessions represented at the meeting and called upon religion "in all its variety" to contribute to the regeneration of spirituality and morality in Russia. Remarking that some political groupings were trying to mobilize religious organizations for political goals, Yeltsin emphasized that "political confrontation in society should not be compounded by interreligious strife." Although he cautioned impatient religious leaders that the government's return of religious buildings confiscated during the Soviet era would take time, he also promised state help with the "difficult material situation of a number of confessions," especially assistance to reconstruct religious buildings, and set up a special government department to assist with this task.[60] Yeltsin plainly hoped that the state provision of material assistance would soften the conflicts over religious facilities. Viewed from a political standpoint, the gathering represented both a bid for the support of many different confessions and an effort to reduce interconfessional strife.

The Western Newly Independent States

In the new states of the western region, the political dynamics of interconfessional relations have been closely linked with religious developments in Russia but have shown some distinctive variations. Historically, the western region has been a meeting ground where various religious confessions – particularly Eastern Orthodoxy and Roman Catholicism – have intermingled and frequently clashed, but the contest has been waged on terms less lopsided than those in the heartland of Central Russia. Although the numerous Orthodox religious believers in Ukraine and Belarus have historically come under the ecclesiastical authority of the Moscow patriarchate,[61] in recent years the Russian Orthodox congregations in Ukraine have constituted such a large proportion of the total number of congregations in the territory of the former Soviet Union (40–60 percent) that one iconoclast has suggested that the Orthodox church could more properly be called Ukrainian than Russian.[62] In Ukraine and Belarus the two principal religious competitors of the Russian Orthodox church have been the Uniate church, created when, under Polish rule, ecclesiastical union with Rome was decreed at the Council of Brest in 1596, and the Ukrainian Autocephalous Orthodox church, first established during the Russian Civil War. For much of the tsarist period the Uniate church posed a challenge to Russian Orthodoxy in Belarus as well, but during the twentieth century Orthodoxy's main religious competitor in Belarus has been the Roman Catholic church.

During the tsarist era the complex relations among the religious confessions were a key aspect of the politics of the western borderlands. According to one scholar, during the long historical stretches when Ukraine was deprived of its independence, "the church either remained a catalyst of the national consciousness (and its last refuge) or was forced, even manipulated, into being an instrument of assimilation with foreign ruling nations and serving their interests in Ukraine."[63] For example, the Orthodox church in Ukraine was independent of Moscow's control until the late seventeenth century but was then incorporated into the Moscow patriarchate as part of the tsarist state's gradual consolidation of its hold over Ukraine. As a result of this change, most of the church's clergy gradually transferred their loyalty to Moscow and played virtually no role in the rise of Ukrainian nationalism in the nineteenth century. By contrast, the clergy of the Uniate church, which was based primarily in Galicia under the control of the Habsburg empire but was also represented in the territory of modern-day Belarus, played a key part in the rise of the Ukrainian national movement. Although a minority of Uniate clerics looked to Russia for protection against Polish influence and were carefully cultivated by the Russian Orthodox church, most Uniate clergymen favored greater autonomy for Ukraine.[64]

Following the 1830–1 Polish rebellion against tsarism, St. Petersburg promulgated the doctrine of Official Nationality, which included among its three cardinal principles a commitment to Russian Orthodoxy. Adopting an increasingly harsh policy toward the Uniate church, in 1839 the tsarist government coerced the Uniate hierarchy into a purportedly voluntary merger with the Russian Orthodox church.[65] This step reflected the autocracy's increasing determination to deny and suppress the existence of separate Ukrainian or Belarusian nations within the empire. Because the Orthodox ecclesiastical structure in the western borderlands was dominated by the clerical proponents of cultural russification and central political control, the Orthodox church constituted an important instrument for the implementation of St. Petersburg's policy. In Belarus the stratagem of religious repression achieved a political success of sorts; after 1839 most Belarusian adherents of the Uniate church shifted to Roman Catholicism and were gradually Polonized. In Ukraine, however, tsarist religious policy proved less effective against the rise of nationalism. During the early twentieth century the Orthodox church in Ukraine was altered under the influence of the growing Ukrainian nationalist movement and the stirrings of ecclesiastical reform within the Russian Orthodox church. The conciliar reform movement allowed junior clerics and church councils dominated by Ukrainian laymen to exert mounting pressure on the senior prelates in Ukraine who still defended complete religious subordination to the Moscow patriarchate.[66]

The upheaval of the Civil War enabled the Ukrainian adherents of Orthodoxy to establish the Ukrainian Autocephalous Orthodox church – that is, a national Orthodox church independent of the Moscow patriarchate. Widespread dislike of the Russian Orthodox hierarchy's prerevolutionary alliance with anti-Ukrainian Russian nationalists gave the new church strong popular appeal.[67] During the 1920s the Bolsheviks encouraged this trend. The emergence of a Ukrainian national church coincided with the comparatively liberal phase of Soviet nationalities policy, which emphasized tactical accommodations with the non-Russian minorities and the indigenization of local institutions.[68] Moreover, the existence of a separate Ukrainian church helped the Bolsheviks bring the Russian Orthodox church to heel. Thanks to the Bolsheviks' proclamation of the separation of church and state and their disestablishment of Russian Orthodoxy, the Ukrainian Autocephalous Orthodox church was able to appropriate a significant number of churches that previously belonged to the Moscow patriarchate.[69] By denying the patriarchate authority over a sizable share of the parishes formerly within its domain, Bolshevik policy helped undermine the patriarchate's resistance to Communist control.[70]

All this changed under Stalin, who viewed religious and national diversity as a source of vulnerability rather than as a potential strength. Engulfed by the Stalinist assault on Ukrainian "bourgeois nationalism" during the late 1920s, the Ukrainian Autocephalous Orthodox church was purged and forced to declare its self-liquidation in 1930.[71] Briefly restored in 1942 during the Nazi occupation of the western borderlands, the church was again subordinated to the Moscow patriarchate as Soviet armies reconquered Ukrainian territory. The de facto abolition of the Ukrainian church's autocephaly, which Moscow rationalized with accusations of church complicity with the Nazi occupiers, was facilitated by the westward exodus of many Ukrainian Orthodox clergymen and lay leaders near the end of the war. The Belarusian Autocephalous Orthodox church, also set up in 1942 under the Nazi occupation, suffered a similar fate with the reimposition of Soviet control.[72]

For Moscow the outcome of World War II posed the additional question of how to deal with the Uniate church. Although outlawed in tsarist Russia, the Uniate confession had flourished in the Austro-Hungarian empire and survived in the eastern territories of the new Polish state set up at the close of World War I. Many Uniate believers were therefore incorporated into the USSR along with the territory that the Soviet government seized from Poland at the end of World War II. In 1946 Moscow engineered the absorption of the Uniates into the Russian Orthodox church at a stage-managed "Reunion Council" that bore a striking resemblance to the tsarist church assembly that had subordinated the Uniate confession to the Russian Orthodox church in 1839.[73] The Reunion Council, convoked on the 350th anniversary of the Union of Brest, repudiated that linkage as a measure "imposed upon our people in the sixteenth century by aggressive Roman Catholic Poland." Condemning the Roman Catholic church for "siding with bloody Fascism," the Reunion Council presided over the forced dissolution of the official Uniate church, which until the Gorbachev era existed only underground.[74] As the main institutional beneficiary of this forcible merger, the Moscow patriarchate backed the assault on the Uniates and took possession of the numerous church properties seized by the Soviet authorities.[75] The episode revealed the Stalinist regime's growing disposition to use the Russian Orthodox church as a political tool to tighten its hold over the non-Russian components of the empire.[76] Viewed in broader historical terms, "the suppression of the Eastern Catholic [Uniate] church . . . represented but another, this time an eastward, swing of the pendulum of the centuries-long ecclesiastical struggle between Moscow and Rome, seemingly closing a chapter of history that opened with the Union of Brest in 1596."[77]

Toward the end of the 1980s, however, the pendulum of history swung once more in the opposite direction. In 1989–90 Gorbachev's program of political liberalization and Moscow's steady loss of political control led to the legalization and reestablishment of both the Uniate and the Ukrainian Autocephalous Orthodox confessions.[78] Along with the concomitant growth of Roman Catholicism near the end of the Gorbachev era, this turn of events has highlighted the importance of the religious factor in Ukrainian and Belarusian national affairs, and it has given political resonance to matters that appear at first glance to concern only minor points of religious history.

Like the Russian-Ukrainian dispute over the character of Kievan Rus, contemporary Russian-Ukrainian debates over the provenance of Orthodox Christianity underscore the problematic relationship between the Russian and Ukrainian peoples. According to mainline Russian historiography, the arrival of Orthodox missionaries in Kievan Rus in 988 A.D. marked the moment when Russia accepted Christianity. This argument is based on the equation of Kievan Rus with early Russia. According to many Ukrainian church historians, in 988 the Kievan forbears not of the modern Russians but of the modern Ukrainians accepted Christianity, which they subsequently conveyed and taught to Muscovite Russia. To some people this view implies not only that Ukrainian Christianity predates Russian Christianity, but that Ukraine was instrumental in bringing pagan Russia into the Christian fold.[79]

The political implications of these divergent perspectives were thrown into especially sharp relief by the controversy surrounding the celebration of the millennium of the acceptance of Christianity in Kievan Rus. In 1979 Pope John Paul II sent a letter to the exiled head of the Uniate church that called for Catholic celebrations of the event but omitted any mention of the Russian Orthodox church, and in 1980 the Vatican convened a synod that declared the decision of the 1946 Reunion Council to "merge" the Uniate and Orthodox churches invalid.[80] This development heightened Moscow's misgivings over the political impact of the selection of the first Polish pope, who showed an unprecedented interest not only in Moscow's "outer" East European empire, but in the "inner empire" of the western Soviet republics. The development also gave the Moscow patriarchate a compelling argument with which to persuade the Soviet government that the millennium celebrations should be centered not in Kiev but in Moscow under the auspices of the Russian Orthodox church. Organized on a grand scale, the ceremonies were accompanied by a marked relaxation of governmental restrictions on the Russian Orthodox church and were deftly woven into Gorbachev's conciliatory diplomacy toward the Western powers.[81]

Although the millennium celebrations eased the situation of the Russian Orthodox church, they were preceded by a harsh government campaign to suppress the unofficial countercelebrations that groups of Ukrainian Orthodox and Uniate believers organized in Kiev and elsewhere in Ukraine.[82] Backed by Russian Orthodox spokesmen who branded the Uniate confession as "nationalist" and "separatist," Soviet agencies seized a large number of clandestine Uniate churches and transferred them to the jurisdiction of the Moscow patriarchate.[83] The national-political dimension of this religious controversy was reflected in a proclamation issued by the Russian Orthodox patriarch on the fortieth anniversary of the Stalinist regime's forcible merger of the Uniates with the Russian Orthodox church. Addressing the relations among Russians, Ukrainians, and Belarusians, the patriarch said:

> Reaffirmation of our confessional and cultural unity, unity of origin of our three peoples, is especially important in connection with the approaching Millennium of the Baptism of Rus. . . . Our membership in the fraternal family of Soviet peoples encourages the growth of this confessional unity; and the unity of the church also serves to strengthen the friendship of peoples of [the USSR].[84]

The story of the millennium celebrations demonstrates that both the Communist Party leadership and the Russian Orthodox hierarchy grasped the close connection between religious affiliation and political identity. In 1990 the Moscow patriarchate made a belated effort to counter the growth of religiously based national sentiment in the western republics by establishing two allegedly independent national churches, the "Ukrainian Orthodox church" and the "Belarusian Orthodox church," which in fact remained largely under the ecclesiastical control of the patriarchate.[85]

The arrival of national independence in Ukraine and Belarus has changed the dynamics of the interconfessional struggles but has not eliminated them. The decision late in 1989 to legalize the Uniate church and to return previously nationalized church property opened a new chapter of interchurch struggles over religious jurisdictions and material resources. These struggles sparked numerous confrontations over the control of particular churches and cathedrals in both Ukraine and Belarus, as well as charges by both sides that the other had used violence.[86] Leaders of the Uniate and Ukrainian Autocephalous Orthodox churches believed that the newly created Ukrainian Orthodox church was a tool of the Moscow patriarchate, whereas Russian Orthodox prelates appeared to be convinced that the creation of the Ukrainian Autocephalous church was no more than a nationalist gambit abetted by the leaders of the Rukh movement.[87]

In mid-1992, in a surprise move, Metropolitan Filaret, until then the Moscow patriarchate's exarch for Ukraine, announced a merger of the Ukrainian Orthodox church with the Ukrainian Autocephalous Orthodox church. Rising Ukrainian nationalism among Orthodox believers may have helped convince some churchmen that this step was necessary in order to save Ukrainian Orthodoxy from the sort of institutional erosion that was undercutting the Ukrainian Communist Party, another organization with close links to Moscow. However, if this was part of the explanation for the attempted merger, another reason was purely political. Metropolitan Filaret seems to have undergone a spectacular religious metamorphosis not unlike the political conversion experienced by Ukrainian president Kravchuk, a former Communist now purportedly transformed into a democrat. Indeed, the attempted merger of the two churches appears to have been jointly engineered by the two men, partly to preserve Filaret's crumbling political position vis-à-vis the Moscow patriarchate, and partly to solidify Ukrainian political opposition to Moscow. Despite Filaret's long history of attacks on nationalist trends within Ukrainian religious confessions, Kravchuk and the leadership of Rukh quickly hailed the merged church as the only legitimate representative of Orthodoxy in Ukraine.[88] Meanwhile the Moscow patriarch and a majority of local bishops and clergymen continued to recognize the authority of a newly appointed Ukrainian primate.[89] Like most political structures, ecclesiastical structures inherited from the USSR have begun to fragment along national lines.

This tumultuous process, as yet incomplete, appears likely to remain a source of tension in Ukraine's external relations. The Moscow patriarchate will not yield its traditional primacy to the Ukrainian Autocephalous Orthodox church and the Uniates without further religious struggle. For the Russian church the institutional stakes are very high, and Metropolitan Filaret is clearly a political opportunist. Moreover, a substantial number of Orthodox believers in Ukraine do oppose separation from Moscow, at least without following established canonical procedures, and they apparently have remained loyal to the Ukrainian branch of Russian Orthodoxy despite Filaret's defection.[90] Important dioceses loyal to Moscow are located in the Donbas, Crimea, and Odessa. Early in 1993 the chief of the Ukrainian security services observed that certain religious functionaries had "speculated on religion," and remarked that religious conflicts, including those with the Russian Orthodox church, were a powder keg.[91] Even after allowing for possible bias on the part of the speaker, his statement indicates the seriousness of the interconfessional tensions affecting Ukrainian internal politics and relations with Russia.

Religious developments have figured in Ukraine's relations with other countries as well. During the 1980s the pope's vigorous support of the Uniate cause helped repair some of the historic mistrust between Poland and Ukraine. However, the demise of the Soviet state has given rise to new ecclesiastical frictions. The Vatican's decision to subordinate a portion of the Uniate hierarchy to the Warsaw metropoly rather than directly to Rome offended some Uniate church officials, as did the Vatican's appointment of Poles to several bishoprics in Ukraine. According to one account, such tensions led the Lviv City Council to deny landing rights to an airplane carrying Cardinal Glemp, the head of the Polish Catholic church, who had planned to participate in the ceremonial return of the previously exiled cardinal of the Uniate church.[92] Less in need of external religious support than in the past, the Uniates have evidently decided to establish the prerogatives of their confession vis-à-vis their erstwhile ecclesiastical defenders.

The most serious political consequences of interconfessional struggles may be the tensions inside Ukraine between the Uniate and Ukrainian Autocephalous Orthodox churches. Before the demise of the USSR the battle against Soviet religious and national oppression tended to draw the two confessions together.[93] However, the collapse of their common governmental enemy will probably amplify the religious tensions between the two. In 1989 Metropolitan Filaret led the Orthodox attack on the Uniates, and at least one other prelate of the Ukrainian Autocephalous Orthodox church has voiced a view of the Uniates just as harsh as the Moscow patriarch's.[94] Strife between the two confessions has been especially sharp in western Ukraine, where they have vied for control of local parishes and churches.[95] Although the growth of Ukrainian Orthodox parishes in western Ukraine has blurred the old geographical dividing line between Uniates in the west and Orthodox in the east, competition between the two confessions may nevertheless exacerbate the centrifugal economic and political forces inside Ukraine and inhibit the emergence of a countrywide political culture shared by all Ukrainians.

In most other parts of the western region the relationship between religion and national identity has varied considerably. Since the mid-nineteenth century the two main confessions in Belarus have been Roman Catholicism and Orthodoxy. In the post-Soviet period tensions between the two confessions have contributed to frictions in Belarus's relations with both Poland and Russia, as the two countries have sought to use their ties with co-religionists inside Belarus to increase their influence over the new state.[96] In this respect the Belarusian case bears a partial resemblance to the political dynamics of church relations inside Ukraine. However, interconfessional conflicts in Belarus have not assumed the same intensity as in Ukraine, and they are less likely to have a major impact on the country's political evolution and external relations.

In the bitter contest over the future of Moldova, religion has been less a cause than an instrument of political conflict. Orthodoxy is the predominant confession among both the ethnic Moldovans and the local Russians who are the main supporters of the secessionist "Dniester Republic." However, struggles over ecclesiastical governance have become an important aspect of the political battle for Moldova's future. In December 1992 the patriarch of the Romanian Orthodox church publicly asserted his authority over the Orthodox church in Moldova, which he declared to be "under the protection" of Romanian Orthodoxy, and the Moscow patriarchate denounced this step as "internal interference in the affairs of the Russian Orthodox church in Moldova." Due largely to the persisting controversy inside Moldova over the possibility of reunification with Romania, the Romanian patriarch's declaration provoked resistance from President Snegur and other Moldovan politicians seeking to steer a middle path between Russia and Romania.[97]

The case of Lithuania demonstrates how a supranational religious confession initially at odds with the creation of a cohesive national identity can be transformed by historical contingencies into a source of national solidarity. In the nineteenth century Roman Catholic clerics in Lithuania feared that the rise of a Lithuanian national movement directed against Polish cultural dominance would also undermine the position of the Catholic church. In the period following World War I, Lithuanian politics continued to be characterized by major conflicts between the Catholic church and anticlerical Lithuanian nationalists. However, the annexation of the country by the Soviet Union transformed the church into a key element of the national resistance movement during the 1940s.[98] No doubt this transformation was facilitated by the long-standing religious struggle between Catholicism and Russian Orthodoxy and by the Soviet regime's de facto association with the Orthodox religious tradition. In the Gorbachev era Roman Catholic laymen and clerics such as Cardinal Sladkevicius vigorously championed the cause of Lithuanian independence. Although in recent years the Catholic hierarchy has taken steps to avoid too close an association with the nationalist movement, it has responded favorably when Lithuanian political leaders have sought its advice on such sensitive matters as the selection of a new head of the Lithuanian Security Service.[99]

Religion has had a less marked political effect in Latvia and Estonia. In Latvia, the prevailing Lutheran confession had little impact on the dissent movement of the 1970s. In part this was due to Lutheranism's general tendency to defer to state authority, and to its historical association with the ethnic German nobles who dominated Latvia in the pre-Soviet era. Latvian nationalists may also have made a conscious decision not to make religion a centerpiece of the nationalist movement, as this would have divided people associated with the Lutheran tradition from those of Catholic background, who constituted a significant minority of the population. In 1987 Archbishop Mesters dismissed a number of clergymen for founding a "Rebirth and Renewal" movement within the church, but by 1989 a major turnover in the church leadership aligned the church hierarchy firmly behind the drive for national independence.[100] Due partly to the absence of similar changes in the Estonian Lutheran church, the nationalist movement in Estonia remained primarily secular and was little influenced by the church.[101] In addition to these confessions, the local branches of the Russian Orthodox church constitute another source of religious influence on politics in Latvia and Estonia. Because the Orthodox church enjoys a high standing among local Russians, it could conceivably have a significant effect on the political attitudes of the local Russian populations and on Moscow's perception of developments in the region.[102]

The Southern Newly Independent States

Islam is the dominant religion of Central Asia's fifty million inhabitants and one of the two principal religious traditions in the Caucasus. In the pre-Soviet period, Islam constituted an important element in the identity of the Central Asian peoples but did not generate a set of political loyalties that overrode all others. Although in the early twentieth century most Central Asians had a general sense that they belonged to the *umma*, the all-inclusive community of Muslim believers, Islam constituted only one of several markers of identity, with tribal and clan loyalties and attachments to subnational regions often having greater salience.

In Central Asia most Muslims adhere to the Sunni form of Islam; only modern-day Azerbaijan in the Caucasus is predominantly Shiite. While Sunni Islam takes the Koran and Sunna (the sayings and deeds of the prophet) as the main sources of religious authority, Shiite Islam adds the contributions of the prophet Mohamed's son-in-law, Ali, and Mohamed's descendants through Ali. Shiites believe that the rightful rulers of the Islamic world were not caliphs, but a succession of Imams, initially related to Mohamed, through Ali. Because the Shiites suffered enormous losses in their early efforts to wrest control of the Islamic world from Sunni caliphs, martyrdom and opposition to authority became pronounced parts of their beliefs.[103]

Like other religious confessions, Islam was subjected to devastating attacks during the early Soviet era, especially under Stalin. By one reckoning, between 1917 and 1930 more than 80 percent of the twelve thousand mosques in the USSR were closed, and at least 90 percent of the mullahs and muezzins were prevented from performing their religious duties, often because they had been executed or sent to labor camps. By 1941 the country reportedly contained slightly more than thirteen hundred mosques.[104] During World War II Stalin made concessions to Islam that were intended, like his accommodation with Russian Orthodoxy, to use religion to mobilize Soviet citizens against the Nazis. In 1941 Muslim clerics called on the faithful "to pray in the mosques for the victory of the Red Army" and "to defend our country in the name of religion." In return the regime allowed an increase in the number of mosques and established a Central Muslim Spiritual Board, which was soon divided into four regional Muslim spiritual boards – one for Central Asia (including Kazakhstan), one for Azerbaijan, one for the Northern Caucasus, and one for European Russia and Siberia.[105] After the war, however, many of Stalin's concessions were reversed, and in the late 1950s, Khrushchev launched an aggressive new anti-religious offensive that harshly attacked Islamic beliefs and customs.

Nevertheless, a strong attachment to Islam has persisted among the inhabitants of Central Asia and the Caucasus. Part of the explanation is that by comparison with many other religions, Islamic beliefs and observances are woven more deeply into the fabric of everyday life, making them more difficult for antireligious propagandists to root out. Even prior to the collapse of the USSR, Soviet sociological studies had concluded that the level of religiosity remained substantially higher among ethnic Central Asians than among Soviet citizens of European origin.[106]

The demise of Soviet-sponsored atheism has cleared the way for a new Islamic groundswell embodied in the growth of religious observances, the expansion of religious education, and the construction of new mosques.[107] For example, in Uzbekistan, one of the Central Asian territories in which Islam historically sank the deepest roots, 75 percent of the ethnic Central Asian respondents to a 1992 survey identified themselves as believers in Islam.[108] In contrast to the pattern in other countries such as Iran and Egypt, thus far the Central Asians most strongly attracted to the Islamic revival are reported to be the inhabitants of rural rather than urban areas.[109] Perhaps this is due in part to the Soviet regime's success in destroying the more intellectually sophisticated variants of Islam in Central Asia, much as the regime effectively froze the intellectual development of Russian Orthodoxy.[110] In any case, the nature of Soviet rule and the suddenness of the USSR's collapse have created large opportunities for foreign religious authorities and teachers to make a firm imprint on Islamic thought and practice in Central Asia, and the social strata supporting the Islamic movements in the region probably could change dramatically in a fairly short period.[111]

These developments naturally raise the question of how the revival of Islam might affect the internal evolution of the Central Asian states and the international relations of the region as a whole. The history of the Islamic world shows that a country's adherence to Islam does not by itself determine whether the government will follow a radical or a moderate line in the international arena. Although post-1979 Iran has tended to be virulently anti-Western, conservative Islamic regimes, including many of the Gulf states, have not shared this orientation. Moreover, some of the most radical foreign policy behavior in the Middle East has come from secular regimes – witness Iraq, Libya, and Syria. All this said, the character of the Central Asian Islamic revival is still likely to influence the region's external relations, and the Islamic movement has the potential to take on a radical hue, if only because the domestic crises facing the new states of the region are so severe.

For most leaders of the new Central Asian states, the Islamic revival presents something of a political conundrum. As of mid-1993, four of the five heads of state were former Communist officials who were previously closely identified with the Soviet regime. Moreover, their political support was strongest among the officials and social groups that had been most influenced by the secular cultural values propagated by Moscow. On the other hand, the popular repudiation of Marxism-Leninism and the strengthening of Islamic attitudes have posed a cultural challenge to the legitimacy of the current leaders that demands an effective political response.

In varying ways, most leaders of the new states have attempted to garner personal legitimacy from Islamic traditions while confining Islam to a spiritual plane and blocking the creation of religiously based political movements or parties. Implementing this political strategy has been easiest for the leaders of Uzbekistan and Turkmenistan, whose populations, although ethnically diverse, nevertheless consist primarily of persons of Muslim extraction. President Karimov of Uzbekistan and President Niyazov of Turkmenistan have made widely publicized pilgrimages to Mecca and have traveled extensively in the Arab Middle East. They also have obtained membership for their countries in the Islamic Conference Organization, an international body that admits only Muslim countries.[112] One motive for these steps has been to increase the chances of tapping the wealth of conservative oil-rich Islamic regimes such as Saudi Arabia.[113]

The political management of Islam has been more difficult for President Nazarbayev of Kazakhstan and President Akayev of Kyrgyzstan. Although historically the nomadic peoples of these countries were not as conventionally observant of Islam as were the sedentary natives of present-day Uzbekistan and Turkmenistan, public gestures to Islam can nevertheless earn political capital among the Muslim citizens of the two countries. The catch is that a sizable proportion of these countries' populations – indeed, in Kazakhstan, a majority – consists of people of European extraction who might be alienated by dramatic gestures of this kind.[114] Nazarbayev has made virtually no effort to appeal to Muslim citizens on religious grounds, and Akayev has made relatively few such efforts and kept them low-key. Kazakhstan is the only Central Asian state that does not celebrate any Muslim holidays, and its constitution makes no mention of Islam, in contrast to most of the other Central Asian countries. Moreover, in the post-Soviet period Nazarbayev has made frequent public references to his own atheism.[115] In Kyrgyzstan, Akayev successfully fought an attempt in the national legislature to insert a reference to the guiding role of Islam into the new national constitution adopted in May 1993.[116] He has also resisted domestic pressures for Kyrgyzstan to join the Islamic Conference Organization, citing the fact that his country is composed of non-Muslims as well as Muslims.[117]

Although their political tactics have varied, all the Central Asian leaders are committed to building secular polities, in large part because under an Islamic dispensation they would quickly be shunted aside.[118] Their instinctive wariness about the political impact of Islam has been sharpened by the civil war in Tajikistan, where the Islamic Renaissance Party joined forces with other groups to bring down the government of President Nabiyev in September 1992. Despite the substantial variations in the level of political freedom in the four countries – ranging from the comparatively liberal Kyrgyzstan to the highly oppressive Turkmenistan – all the governments have banned political parties based on Islam (or on any other religion).[119] Even in Tajikistan, arguably the country most open to Islamic influence, where the Islamic Renaissance Party operated legally for one year, the government banned the party once it felt it had the political muscle and the repressive capability to withstand the resulting public discontent.[120]

In addition to the Central Asian heads of state, religious leaders have sought to win Islamic believers to their own views of society. The dominant attitude of the traditional and quiescent Muslim clergy of the region is that Islam must be kept out of direct involvement in politics. For example, during his tenure as head of the Central Asian Muslim Spiritual Board, Mohamed Yusuf Sadiq defended a secular state as the natural form of government in Sunni countries and attributed efforts to create Islamic states such as Iran to the Shiite tradition alien to most of Central Asia.[121] Sadiq and like-minded clerics have attempted to use their influence to calm political passions and especially to counsel against the sort of interethnic violence that broke out among various groups of ethnic Central Asians in Uzbekistan's Fergana Valley in 1989.[122]

Whether this attitude toward the relationship between Islam and politics will prevail is uncertain. If the clerics associated with the Central Asian Spiritual Board and the mosques registered during the Soviet years adopt too passive an attitude toward social problems, they may be eclipsed by more assertive religious leaders determined to make Islam a direct part of day-to-day politics. A substantial proportion of Central Asians suspect that Islamic clergymen trained in the Soviet period were agents of the KGB, and dissatisfaction among laypersons has already precipitated considerable turnover at the top of the "official" Islamic establishment.[123] Just as significantly, the number of trained clerics is small – in the late 1980s estimates put the total number of official clergymen at a mere two thousand for all of Central Asia – so younger clerics, many with foreign training, can be expected to take over religious leadership in the future.

In any case, some members of the Central Asian elites are clearly seeking to rouse Islamic believers and draw them deeper into national politics. In June 1990 a congress of representatives of Muslim communities from throughout the Soviet Union convened in Russia and announced the creation of the Islamic Renaissance Party (IRP). One of the party's principal aims was to secure for Muslim believers the same religious rights that had been extended to Russian Orthodox Christians by Gorbachev.[124] The tone of the party program was comparatively moderate. Although isolated Central Asian voices had previously called for the creation of an Islamic theocracy and some IRP members continued to pay lip service to this goal, the party program did not endorse this objective.[125] Stressing the need to defend Islam against atheistic attacks, it espoused the principle of equal legal treatment for all religions and the notion of political cooperation with other parties.[126] According to some early reports, the new party drew its strongest support from Tajikistan, the North Caucasus, and the Tatars of Russia.[127]

The notion of a political party based on Islam was highly unwelcome to the Central Asian governments both before and after they declared their independence from Moscow. No doubt the leaders of the IRP hoped to convene the party's future meetings in Central Asia and not only in Russia. However, in all the Central Asian countries, the heads of state immediately sought to brand the IRP as a vehicle of Islamic radicalism. This stance, which was a logical extension of the Communist Party's official attitude toward Islam, came naturally to those government leaders who were former Communist officials, and it reflected real fear of the potential political impact of Islam. It also was a useful device for curbing any reformist impulses among the local Russian minorities, and for eliciting political support from Russia, whose own anxieties about Islamic radicalism could be mobilized to shore up the existing regimes of Central Asia. But the depiction of the IRP as a vehicle of Islamic radicalism did not mesh with the party's emerging profile, hazy though that profile sometimes was.

During its first three years, the Islamic Renaissance Party has encountered significant political obstacles but also has achieved substantial gains. Faced with widespread hostility from Central Asian governments, the party has also been compelled to wrestle with the question of how to reconcile its inclusive pan-Islamic aspirations with the existence of separate Central Asian nations and governments. By the end of 1991 the component of the party in Tajikistan, the only country in which the party was ever allowed to operate legally, formed a separate national party, and similar steps were subsequently taken by the party branches operating surreptitiously in other Central Asian states. Nonetheless, the party has managed to win widespread popular support. In a public-opinion survey conducted in Uzbekistan at the start of 1992, the IRP substantially outscored two other major legal parties, Erk and Birlik, among ethnic Central Asians.[128] The relationship between the IRP and radical Islamic splinter groups, such as those that carried out attacks on Uzbekistan government installations in mid-1992 in an effort to force the Karimov government to impose Islamic law, remains uncertain.[129]

The desire of the Central Asian governments to prevent political spillover from the revival of religion has prompted them to try to 'nationalize' Islam by bringing established religious institutions under their direct control. Under the old Soviet dispensation, Islamic religious activities in all five Central Asian states were supervised by a single Muslim spiritual board, or muftiate, headquartered in Tashkent, the capital of Uzbekistan. However, under the influence of the centrifugal forces released by perestroika, Kazakhstan in 1990 established a separate muftiate responsible for Islamic activities in Kazakhstan.[130] Tajikistan also withdrew from the Tashkent muftiate, reducing its jurisdiction to only Uzbekistan and Turkmenistan.[131] In April 1993 the head of the Tashkent muftiate, Mohamed Yusuf Sadiq, was replaced by Mukhtarkhan Abdullaev because, according to one account, President Karimov wished to establish more secure control over the Islamic religious establishment in Uzbekistan.[132] If the local risk of an Islamicist political groundswell appears to increase, further governmental efforts to 'nationalize' the administration of Islam are likely to ensue, even though such an effort may inadvertently strengthen the very sort of radical Islamic movement that it is intended to prevent.

Islam has played its most salient political role in Tajikistan. In September 1992 Islamic activists joined with regional and democratic forces, and finally succeeded in ousting the president of the republic, Rakhman Nabiyev. Members of the Islamic Renaissance Party played an active part in the coalition of groups that resisted Nabiyev's repressive regime; further, some have advocated that religion should be the central guide for foreign policy.[133] Yet they have not openly advocated the establishment of an Islamic state. Akbar Turadzhanzade, the highest Islamic authority in Tajikistan, has refused appeals to run for national president and has called for the creation of a secular state with full human-rights guarantees, reportedly out of a belief that any move toward Islamic government in Tajikistan would be possible only after several decades.[134] The growth of Central Asian interest in Islam has not provided the impetus for the development of radical Islamic political movements in the other countries of the region. According to Western observers, most of the numerous new Islamic movements have a moderate rather than a revolutionary orientation.[135]

Several factors could conceivably change this situation. In the Middle East, the rise of Islamic radicalism has been fostered by declining standards of living, hostility to extensive Western cultural and social influence, and the corruption and insensitivity of the existing political leadership.[136] In Central Asia Islamic militancy could also be fueled by these factors and by the vast social problems confronting the new states, such as mass unemployment, pollution-generated menaces to public health, and rising ethnic tensions, particularly those centering on local Russians. In addition, Islamic radicalism might be spread through the vigorous actions both of governments and religious groups in neighboring Muslim countries such as Iran, Pakistan, and Afghanistan.

To date, domestic and international circumstances have not produced an upsurge of Islamic militancy in any country, not least because the secular leaders of the Central Asian states have taken authoritarian steps intended to thwart the growth of radical Islamic groups.[137] Also, while neighboring countries have been eager to encourage a Central Asian Islamic religious revival by broadcasting readings from the Koran and other Islamic programs, as well as by providing money for scholarships, Islamic schools (*madrasas*), and cultural links,[138] none of the neighboring states has seemed eager to destabilize Central Asia by promoting Islamic radicalism. Iran, perhaps the most likely candidate for this role, has been hampered by the fact that few Central Asians belong to the Shiite branch of Islam, and by its desire to maintain good political, economic, and military relations with Russia, whose preponderance in the area still counts for a great deal. If other Middle Eastern governments have felt any inclination to support radical Islamic groups, they also have remained conscious of their need for circumspection vis-à-vis Russia.[139] Thus far, the limited foreign efforts at radical proselytizing appear to have been primarily the work of nongovernmental political and religious movements, such as the Muslim Brotherhood and the Pakistan- and Afghanistan-based Jamaat el-Islami.[140]

Nonetheless, the prospects that moderate variants of Islam will prevail in the longer run are problematic. By virtually all accounts, the socioeconomic situation in Central Asia will get much worse before it gets better; hence the countries of the region are destined to pass through acute and protracted socioeconomic traumas that could overwhelm efforts to steer the development of Islam in a moderate direction. Over the long term, such shocks will create a substantial possibility of the rise of potent Islamic radical movements in at least some of the countries of Central Asia. One key determinant in the political evolution of Islam will be whether members of the urban population, now the most secular element of Central Asian societies, are won over to Islamicist views and take on leadership roles in radical Islamic movements.

Another key determinant will be whether the secular leaders of Central Asia offer meaningful political participation to Islamic moderates or inadvertently push the moderates toward militancy by excluding them from the political process and forcing them to go underground.

Analysts of Central Asian religious trends must also consider non-Islamic religious groups. Although numerically tiny, the Central Asian Jewish population could become an important focus of political conflict and have a significant impact on Central Asia's relations with the West if Islamic radicalism gains ground.[141] Close attention must also be paid to the behavior of Christian groups in the region, particularly in Kazakhstan and Kyrgyzstan, where persons of European extraction constitute sizable shares of the total population. Some reports suggest that Protestant sects such as the Baptists and Adventists are the fastest-growing Christian denominations in Central Asia.[142] However, a public opinion survey conducted in mid-1991 indicates that the Russian Orthodox church enjoys an extremely high level of trust among the Russian residents of Central Asia and that Russian Orthodoxy is an especially strong marker of national consciousness among Russians living in these Muslim territories.[143] On balance, it therefore appears that the religious stance and political comportment of the Orthodox church will probably be the most important European element of Central Asia's evolving religious-political mosaic.

In the countries of the Caucasus, religion has played an important but variable political role. In the territories of modern-day Armenia and Georgia indigenous forms of Christianity took root long before the acceptance of Christianity by Kievan Rus. Because the Caucasus was a major "shatter zone" in the historical encounter between Christianity and Islam, the significance of religious affiliations was so large that the Georgians and Armenians who over the centuries converted to Islam ceased to be called Georgian or Armenian. After the fourteenth century, when the last independent Armenian kingdom fell to invaders, the Armenian Apostolic church functioned as a key source of Armenian cultural continuity, not least because of the church's relatively democratic ecclesiastical structure.[144] Having played a central part in the early development of the distinctive Armenian alphabet, the church became permanently linked with language as a component of Armenian identity. Due partly to conflicts with the Muslim Turks, Armenian Christians were instrumental in promoting Armenia's subordination to the Russian tsar in the early nineteenth century.[145]

After the Bolshevik seizure of power, the church sustained extensive institutional damage at the hands of the government. However, the two sides ultimately struck a compromise based partly on the church's willingness to support Moscow's policy toward foreign countries – particularly Turkey – and its ability to serve as a link between the USSR and the large Armenian diaspora. From the 1960s onward, the church helped revive the national commemorations of the Turkish genocide – commemorations that frequently went beyond Moscow's preferred treatment of this explosive issue. Nevertheless, the church did not play a central part in the national movement for independence from Moscow during the 1980s, perhaps because it was reluctant to jeopardize the close ties and privileged position it had developed with the Soviet government during the preceding years.[146]

Unlike Armenia, Georgia maintained at least a semblance of independent statehood until the beginning of the nineteenth century, making religion less essential as a marker of national identity. Moreover, the hierarchically organized Georgian Orthodox church lacked the close social ties with the laity that characterized the Armenian church, as well as the sort of distinctive theology that differentiated the Armenian church from other variants of Christianity.[147] Together these characteristics made the Georgian church more susceptible to absorption by the Russian Orthodox church, a step that occurred shortly after Russia conquered the Caucasus in the early nineteenth century. In a broader sense, however, Georgian Christianity has served as a link with Russia, at least in the face of threats from non-Christian states. In the early 1800s Georgian Orthodox Christians pushed for a close political alignment with the Russian empire, although not necessarily for the imperial absorption of their country that actually occurred.[148] During World War II the Georgian church formally regained its autocephaly from the Moscow patriarchate, and in the post-Stalin period it experienced a certain revival. Many Georgians were proud to remind the members of other ethnic groups that theirs was the second-oldest Christian church in the territories of the USSR (the first being the Armenian rather than the Russian Orthodox church). However, the Georgian church never became a central actor in the Georgian national movement in the fashion that, for instance, the Catholic church became a core element of the Lithuanian national movement.[149]

In Azerbaijan Islam has historically been the dominant religion, with adherents of the Shiite tradition outnumbering adherents of the Sunni tradition by about two to one.[150] Although citizens of Azerbaijan have recently shown a widespread interest in Islam, apparently only a tiny percentage of the population supports the notion of creating an Islamic state, according to reports of survey research conducted in the country.[151] In theory the possibility for launching an influential radical Islamic movement inside Azerbaijan should be increased by the country's proximity to Iran. However, the comparatively high level of secularization in Azerbaijan and the significant linguistic and cultural links with secular Turkey diminish this possibility.[152] Moreover, as shown in Chapter 2, Iran has special reason to proceed cautiously in dealing with the inhabitants of "Northern Azerbaijan." For Iran the risk is that religious proselytizing among the citizens of Azerbaijan could generate powerful centrifugal forces inside Iran by spurring Azerbaijanis on the Iranian side of the border to seek reunification with their northern brethren.[153] Hence religion is likely to exert a less substantial influence on Azerbaijan's foreign relations than might appear probable at first glance.

Islamic-Christian religious differences have undoubtedly contributed to the tensions in the Caucasus, particularly to the armed conflict between Muslim Azerbaijan and Christian Armenia. However, it would be an oversimplification to equate the sometimes negative impact of religious affiliations with the effect of religious institutions per se. At least some religious leaders have tried to cooperate to move the Armenian-Azerbaijani war toward resolution. For instance, the mufti of the Transcaucasian Spiritual Board and the head of the Armenian Apostolic church agreed at the end of 1992 to discuss means of establishing peace between the two countries.[154] Contacts of this kind might conceivably help end this protracted war.

Conclusion

Historically, religion has had a complex impact on the development and relations of the peoples within the Russian and Soviet orbits. Over long stretches of history, Russian Orthodoxy has played the role of a supplementary instrument of control extending from Moscow into non-Russian territories, and in the post-Soviet period it has not yet abandoned this tendency nor found a satisfactory alternative national role. Conversely, for several peoples of the former USSR, religion has been an especially important source of identity in periods when the national group was controlled by a nonindigenous state – as in Ukraine, Lithuania, and Armenia – or when the national group possessed a state of its own that was on the verge of collapse, as in Armenia after World War I and even during certain turning points in Russia's history. In other cases, religion has not served as a marker of sociopolitical identity. In Latvia, for instance, no religious institution was fully suitable as a rallying point for political activism, and the advocates of Latvian national independence avoided emphasizing religious appeals that might create fissures between Lutheran and Catholic Latvians. For rather different reasons, an equally peripheral political role has been played by the Georgian Orthodox church. Lacking special ecclesiastical or theological features that sharply distinguished it from Russian Orthodoxy, the Georgian church never became a central symbol of Georgian political identity. Nevertheless, such was the extent of religious revival in the USSR during the late 1980s that even in Georgia groups called for an increase in the church's active involvement in politics.[155]

Given the social and spiritual disruption occasioned by the collapse of the Soviet empire, several religious confessions could potentially exert a strong influence on the emergence of new political identities in the post-Soviet states. However, formidable impediments may hamper their ability to do so. In all the new states religious institutions and confessions have entered a tumultuous stage marked by internal struggles between generations, contentious debates about religious culpability for political misdeeds of the Soviet era, and a "war of laws" among and within ecclesiastical structures not unlike the jurisdictional conflict among secular institutions. In countries as different as Ukraine and Uzbekistan, supranational religious confessions have experienced centrifugal pressures that are causing them to fragment along national lines. The contest over the organization of religious institutions is part of the larger struggle to shape the political identities of peoples now emerging from decades of confinement within the exoskeleton of the Soviet autocracy.

In some of the new states where religion has served as an important marker of political identity, unfamiliar freedoms have come as a mixed blessing. Liberated from Moscow's oppressive political and religious policies, those new states in which two or more religions are widely practiced face the risk that religion may become a source of internal division rather than of political solidarity. In Ukraine, the tensions between Russian and Ukrainian Orthodox, and between Orthodox and Uniates, exemplify this danger. In a broader sense having more to do with religious and cultural sensibilities and less with specific religious institutions, Kazakhstan presents another example of the same risk.

Religion has directly affected the foreign policy orientations of the new states in at least four ways. First, it has sometimes inhibited governmental action, as with the initial hesitation of Kazakhstan and Kyrgyzstan to participate in joint peacekeeping operations in Tajikistan. Second, it has predisposed governments in favor of foreign countries to which they are religiously akin – as with Russia's policy toward Armenia – although the religious factor has often been overridden by economic, strategic, or other foreign policy calculations. Conversely, confessional differences have sometimes hardened the enmities between political or military antagonists, as with the clash between Armenia and Azerbaijan and, to a lesser extent, the conflict between Russia and Ukraine. Finally, in the best of cases – exemplified, perhaps, by the limited interconfessional dialogue in the Caucasus and by calls in Russia for the Orthodox church to mediate the dispute between the president and parliament – religious leaders and institutions have sought to counter such enmities and to pave the way for reconciliation between conflicting parties.

4

Political Culture and Civil Society

Perhaps the most striking feature of Mikhail Gorbachev's effort to reform the Soviet system was his decision to invite public discussion of the fundamental political issues that his predecessors had masked for decades behind a facade of public unanimity. By abandoning the ideological myth of a "solidary society" whose members are united around a single political goal,[1] Gorbachev's campaign for *glasnost'* and reform from below electrified a profoundly alienated citizenry and opened a path toward what one scholar has aptly called the "reinvention of politics."[2] As a result, Soviet political culture entered a period of tremendous ferment, and voluntary political participation grew exponentially. These developments, which far exceeded Gorbachev's original intent, ultimately contributed to the public's repudiation of the Communist order and to the creation of fifteen independent states.

However, the depth of the domestic changes and their implications for the behavior of the new states remain uncertain. On first glance, the foreign policy implications of democratic versus dictatorial political outcomes in the new states seem clear. If the new states evolve into full-fledged, stable democracies, war among them will be less likely. Coupled with the higher level of public discourse and information fostered by democratic debate, the citizenry's reluctance to suffer the human and material costs of war will make military aggression a more difficult option for decision-makers to choose. This, however, is not the whole story. Although a substantial body of evidence supports the proposition that democracies do not wage war on each another, they have often waged wars – and not just defensive wars – against non-democratic states, partly because they distrust those states on ideological grounds and regard them as illegitimate.[3] Moreover, democracies are likely to have particular difficulty maintaining peaceful relations with other democracies when demographic and territorial boundaries are at issue.[4] On balance, then, it seems plausible that conflicts may not be avoided but will be easier to resolve under a democratic than under an authoritarian dispensation.

The establishment of an enduring democratic order in some or all of the new states will depend heavily on the creation of constitutional institutions such as a freely elected legislature, an executive branch with powers clearly defined and limited by law, an independent judicial system, and an impartial civil service. Most of the post-Soviet states have taken steps to create at least some of these institutions, and in some instances the progress has been impressive. Nonetheless, the fate of the new political institutions remains uncertain in all the new states. Passionate debates have erupted over the distribution of authority among governmental institutions and over the democratic legitimacy or illegitimacy of key government bodies, particularly the legislatures formed in the twilight of the Soviet era, and these issues have become intertwined with fundamental conflicts over economic reform.

The prospects for democracy in the new states hinge not only on constitutional developments and economic trends, but also on the emergence of supportive public attitudes often described as a "civic culture."[5] Citizens imbued with a civic culture believe in the government's duty to serve the people, in their own capacity to influence government decisions, and in their obligation to participate in national political life. They also believe in the general trustworthiness of their fellow citizens, in the universal right to engage in political activity, and in the impermissibility of violence as a form of political action.

Historical experience suggests that revulsion against past tyranny and a stalemate among contending political factions can prompt a country to set up democratic institutions even in the absence of a civic culture. Many recently established democracies began in this fashion, and it is arguably the way some "classic" European and North American democracies originated as well.[6] However, the presence of a protodemocratic political culture facilitates the building of democratic institutions, and the political consolidation of a democratic order becomes possible only if such values have been internalized by a large segment of the public. A civic culture buffers the political order against clashes over the institutional division of political power and against the fluctuations in "performance legitimacy" that oscillations in economic growth and other social benefits invariably entail.[7]

Whether a protodemocratic culture exists in some or all of the post-Soviet states is both important and uncertain. On the one hand, liberalism was a weak strand of the pre-Soviet political tradition in almost all the new states, and before the late 1980s most of the citizens were relentlessly indoctrinated with the profoundly antidemocratic ideology of Marxism-Leninism.[8] That many former Communist Party functionaries have rapidly transformed themselves into "democratic" national leaders also raises doubts about whether the prevailing political culture has really changed; or it may indicate that Soviet political indoctrination was not as effective as some assumed. Opinion surveys conducted in Eastern Europe during the early 1990s suggest that many other post-Communist publics have gravitated toward political values that bear a striking though incomplete resemblance to the democratic values of West Europeans.[9] These findings lend credibility to the proposition that "Communist efforts at resocialization [of citizens] . . . have been counterproductive in the sense of having created strong liberal propensities in countries such as Poland and Hungary where those orientations were relatively weak in the prerevolutionary era."[10]

The development and preservation of a civic culture depend heavily on the existence of a civil society. In most historical cases, a civic culture has emerged in conjunction with a civil society, but the two concepts have different meanings that deserve to be kept distinct.[11] By "civil society" we mean a dense network of nongovernmental associations and groups established for the autonomous pursuit of diverse socioeconomic interests and prepared to rebuff state efforts to take control of these activities. The components of a civil society include independent media, churches, business and professional associations, labor unions, schools and universities, and the political parties that seek to aggregate these diverse societal interests through the political process. In a stable democracy, these organizations institutionalize the values and ethos of the civic culture outside the formal structures of government. They possess the organizational knowledge and skill needed to perform essential socioeconomic functions and, equally important, to counter government efforts to dominate society.

In all societies, social groups pursue some of their objectives at the expense of other social groups. It is this quality of self-seeking individualism and particularism that has led some Western political theorists to exalt the state over society as the true representative of the general good. The existence of a civil society thus depends not only on the presence of large numbers of associations and organized groups but on the spirit in which they act. They must acknowledge the legitimacy of the interests of other social groups and must exercise a certain political self-restraint. Above all, they must support the rule of law, understand the benefits of obeying laws, eschew communal violence, and avoid using the government's military and security forces for the violent resolution of their disagreements with other social groups.

The remainder of this chapter sketches the evolution of the main political institutions, the content of the political culture, and the condition of civil society in the new states. Our central concern is whether domestic political changes are moving each country toward or away from a democratic order, and how these changes may affect interstate relations. The chapter inquires whether the leaders of these polities are disposed and able to govern on the basis of consent rather than coercion, and whether the governmental means of coercion are under reliable political control. It also considers the domestic political impact of interstate conflicts, particularly whether democratic trends or general political stability have been undermined in the countries involved in such conflicts.

Russia

Since 1990 Russia has made major strides toward the establishment of representative institutions. The parliamentary elections held in the spring of 1990 marked a significant step toward authentic democracy. Unlike the other Soviet republics, Russia adhered to recent Soviet precedent by providing for the indirect rather than direct election of its standing legislature, the Supreme Soviet, which was chosen by a larger, popularly elected Congress of People's Deputies.[12] Despite this structural deviation from international democratic norms, the congress itself had a plausible procedural claim to democratic legitimacy. Although some Communist Party officials took advantage of rural electoral districts to win "safe" seats and obstructed the campaigns of reformist candidates, virtually all the congressional seats were contested, with the number of candidates averaging more than six per seat.[13] The elections led to the creation of an outspoken liberal bloc in the Supreme Soviet alongside a larger conservative bloc. The June 1991 Russian presidential election marked a dramatic further advance. Vigorously contested, the balloting marked the first time in Russia's history that its political leader had been chosen by means of popular democratic election, and it gave President Yeltsin an aura of democratic legitimacy that virtually no other politician in the former Soviet Union could match.

Nevertheless, Russia's political institutions are not yet fully formed nor accepted as completely legitimate by the Russian populace. The elections of 1990–1 set the stage for a bitter struggle between President Yeltsin and his legislative opponents. This struggle has been reflected in a running battle for control of government appointments and policy, particularly economic policy, as well as in a protracted debate over several proposed drafts of a new constitution.[14] As in a number of other new states, the constitutional debate has centered on whether the country should have a parliamentary system dominated by a strong legislature or a presidential system dominated by a powerful chief executive. Intertwined with this issue has been another matter at least as vexing

– the division of authority between the federal government in Moscow
and the governments of Russia's regions and autonomous republics.
Meanwhile economic disorder and the collapse of old moral guidelines
have corroded the state bureaucracy, undermining the government's
ability to implement its policies and providing ample grounds for the
opposition's attacks on governmental corruption.[15]

The result of these overlapping controversies has been a deepening
deadlock over the division of governmental powers and the pace of
economic reform. In the fall of 1991, after rallying the country to defeat
the August coup attempt, President Yeltsin looked virtually unchal-
lengeable. In November the Congress of People's Deputies voted Yeltsin special powers for a year, authorized him to occupy the posts both
of president and prime minister, and endorsed the presidential blueprint
for rapid marketization drawn up by Deputy Prime Minister Yegor
Gaidar. However, as economic reform generated mounting social hardships, parliamentary speaker Ruslan Khasbulatov and other critics
sought to curb Yeltsin's power. Yeltsin attempted to defuse these pressures by offering a trade-off. In exchange for the parliament's agreement
in principle to the adoption of a new constitution that would alter the
political system, in mid-1992 he shifted the balance between radical
reformers and centrists in his government, adding three new cabinet
members from Civic Union, a centrist coalition that spoke for many
state industrial managers and favored slowing the pace of economic
reform.[16]

Despite this adjustment, relations between the president and the
parliament continued to worsen. In December 1992 the Congress of
People's Deputies refused to renew Yeltsin's special presidential powers. Meanwhile members of the newly formed National Salvation Front
called for Yeltsin's removal from power, and centrists in the congress
subjected him to intense criticism. Under these conditions, some of
Yeltsin's radical democratic advisors urged him to declare direct presidential rule and dissolve the Congress of People's Deputies.[17] Although
a new compromise reinstated Yeltsin's special powers and put the constitutional referendum back on the political agenda, Khasbulatov and
other opponents soon reneged on this understanding and again derailed
the proposed referendum.[18]

The crisis came to a head in March 1993, when a frustrated Yeltsin
declared a "special presidential regime" that he apparently hoped would
enable him to override legislative resistance to his reform program.
Apparently Yeltsin contemplated dissolving the parliament and declaring a full state of emergency.[19] For several days his intent remained
uncertain, contributing to an irrevocable split with his vice-president,
Aleksandr Rutskoy, and with some other members of the government.

In the end, however, Yeltsin chose not to take the fateful step of proroguing the parliament. Instead he decided to hold a referendum on his leadership, his socioeconomic program, and the desirability of early presidential and legislative elections; the Congress finally acquiesced in the decision to hold the referendum.

The immediate outcome of this clash between the president and his opponents had both positive and negative aspects. On the one hand, Yeltsin and his opponents, despite their bitter denunciations of one another, sought a compromise and attempted to resolve the issue by political means rather than by force. By giving Yeltsin a resounding vote of confidence in his leadership, the plebiscite momentarily defused the political crisis and gave a new impetus to the drive for political and economic reform. On the other hand, the referendum did not resolve the two-year-old struggle between Yeltsin and his opponents over the allocation of governmental authority. The question of a new constitution was not addressed in the referendum, leaving Yeltsin and his supporters with no obvious avenue by which to try to resolve this issue. What's more, the constitutional draft endorsed by Yeltsin in mid-1993 called for a presidency so powerful that it could have emasculated the legislature.[20] If this was Yeltsin's real objective rather than a negotiating ploy, its enactment would have dealt a blow to the prospects for establishing constitutional government in Russia.

Given the depth of the conflicts between the pro- and anti-Yeltsin camps, the political disposition of the military and security establishments has become potentially important. Despite the political shakeup after the August 1991 coup attempt, two years later Russia's military and police establishments were not yet under firm civilian control. The officer corps has remained divided among groups ranging from outspoken reformers to die-hard reactionaries.[21] In the confrontation between Yeltsin and the parliament, Minister of Defense Pavel Grachev indirectly signaled his support for Yeltsin and showed a clear desire to neutralize any active opposition to the president in the armed forces.[22] But Grachev showed no inclination actually to use the army against Yeltsin's political foes, nor apparently did Yeltsin ask him to do so. Although a reactionary fringe group, the Union of Officers, has publicly called for the ouster of Yeltsin and Grachev and has developed links with parliamentary speaker Khasbulatov,[23] most senior officers have hesitated to thrust themselves into the political arena. The memory of the participation of some senior officers in the failed August coup may constitute a psychological deterrent of sorts, although the military's reputation survived the coup attempt with remarkably little damage.[24] Other formidable obstacles are the military's lack of competence to deal with the country's enormous socioeconomic problems and the prospect that intervention could easily shatter the military establishment, thereby precipitating civil war.

The potential role of the former KGB in domestic political conflicts also remains problematic. Since the USSR's collapse Yeltsin has backed away from his earlier commitment to a radical reform that would prevent the security police from being utilized in domestic politics.[25] Despite some significant structural changes, the Russian Ministry of Security, which has absorbed a large portion of the old KGB apparatus, has not been subjected to effective control through legal statutes and legislative monitoring.[26] There has been little turnover in the ranks of the former KGB, and the turnover that has occurred, particularly before the dismissal of Minister of Security Barannikov in July 1993, has weakened reform-minded security officials more than reactionary ones.[27] One consideration that may have prompted Yeltsin to drop the idea of reforming the security apparatus was that it constituted an important check on instability within the military establishment.[28] Especially for this reason, Yeltsin must have wanted to avoid reform measures that could have driven the security forces into the arms of such political opponents as Khasbulatov at a time when the confrontation with these adversaries was reaching a boiling point.[29] No doubt Yeltsin has also regarded the Ministry of Security as a useful instrument for dealing with centrifugal forces in the regions and autonomies considering secession, as well as an important tool in government efforts to combat official corruption.[30]

Unless they resort to large-scale coercion, Russia's political leaders can generate the power needed to carry out systemic reforms only by mobilizing mass political support. Skillful use of the media and other devices may help rouse the public, but political parties are indispensable for generating real political power. Although political thinkers of diverse persuasions have sometimes suggested that parties exert a divisive and destructive influence on public life, the opposite is closer to the truth.[31] Any modern polity that lacks political parties is highly susceptible to debilitating crises, and the defects traditionally enumerated by the theoretical opponents of parties are actually characteristic of polities having weak rather than strong party systems. In democratic polities, strong political parties are a key agency for meaningful public participation in political life.[32]

Despite Russia's substantial progress in fashioning representative governmental institutions, it lacks an effective multiparty system capable of channeling and structuring mass participation in those institutions. Toward the end of the Gorbachev era, quasi-political parties did emerge in Russia, and since the failed coup, new parties and interest groups have continued to form.[33] Substantively, party alignments have been most strongly affected by the heated debates over economic reform, over the distribution of power within the Russian government, and, to a lesser extent, over Moscow's loss of control over the other former republics. However, most parties consist of fragmented elite groups that depend heavily on individual personalities and are susceptible to frequent internal splits and mergers with other political organizations. In 1992–3 the number of party factions in the Congress of People's Deputies fluctuated between fourteen and eighteen. These factions were loosely grouped into four legislative blocs. By one count, the "left-wing" coalition favoring radical political and market reforms included about 220 deputies; two centrist blocs favoring a more measured rate of marketization totaled approximately 370 deputies; and the right-wing bloc vigorously opposed to the Yeltsin government and its policies included about 375 deputies.[34]

Russia's parties have been slow to establish an effective grass-roots political structure that elicits popular support on the basis of the party's program or patronage. Reports indicate that a few parties, such as the centrist Democratic Party of Russia and right-wing Communist Party of the Russian Federation, are developing substantial regional and local networks of supporters.[35] However, none of these parties has yet developed a strong link with large numbers of Russian voters. When asked which political party or group from a long list was closest to their own views, 41 percent of the Russian respondents to a mid-1992 survey said "none." At the start of 1993 the percentage of respondents giving this answer increased to 47 percent. In mid-1992 the radical reformist Democratic Russia bloc garnered the largest share of positive responses with a mere 7 percent of the total. At the start of 1993 "the former Communist Party of the Soviet Union" (which in fact no longer existed) won the greatest share with 6 percent of the total. Following behind were Democratic Russia, which had slipped to 5 percent, the Democratic Party of Russia, also with 5 percent, and the Civic Union, a centrist political movement led by industrialist Arkadiy Volskiy and others, with 3 percent.[36]

The tendency toward party factionalism and isolation from the electorate has several causes. These features bear some resemblance to the early stages of party evolution in many established democracies, where contending leadership factions gradually built party organizations to mobilize public electoral support against their rivals within the political elite. One major obstacle to the current development of effective Russian parties has been the shortage of elections as a focus for party-building. The primary motive for forming and maintaining mass parties is to win elections, yet most of the Russian parties were established after the 1990 parliamentary elections, in the wake of the formal abolition of the Communist Party's legal monopoly of power.[37] New elections could serve as a stimulus to the creation of stronger party organizations. Depending on the structure and timing of the elections, the resulting party organizations could either span or reinforce the regional political cleavages afflicting Russia.

The weakness of Russian political parties, however, is due to more than the momentary absence of elections. Although parties had already been legal for more than a year at the time of the Russian presidential election, that contest appears to have done little to strengthen most party organizations. After resigning from the CPSU in 1990 Yeltsin proclaimed himself above party matters, and he and most of the other contenders treated the 1991 presidential election as a "supraparty" affair. Although the efforts of the Democratic Russia movement contributed a great deal to Yeltsin's victory, that party gained little institutional strength from the contest. In this respect the process of party-building in Russia resembles the difficulties encountered in most of the post-Communist countries of Eastern Europe.

As his power weakened during the fall of 1992, Yeltsin recognized the need to build support among parliamentary fractions for his embattled reform program, and he endorsed a new bloc, Democratic Choice, that included Democratic Russia and was intended as a counterweight to his opponents in the parliament.[38] However, Yeltsin devoted little time to this bloc; and his political lieutenants apparently did not make much effort to build up its organizational resources. Perhaps because of bitter past experiences with the CPSU, many Russian leaders and ordinary citizens appear to harbor an instinctive feeling that parties are enemies of the common good. The distaste felt by ordinary citizens has been strengthened by the tendency of most parties, perhaps unconsciously mimicking the CPSU, to require that individuals become formal party members rather than to accept a looser form of affiliation based on political outlook and voting behavior. In the aftermath of the April 1993 referendum, there was a flurry of discussion among reform-minded politicians about the organization of new parties or groups to back the cause of reform, but it remained uncertain whether these organizations would display more coherence and institutional strength than existing parties.

In addition, many of the social groups and associations that are the natural building blocks for party organizations are still comparatively weak or underdeveloped. The Russian Orthodox church, for example, might help draw large numbers of politically inactive Russians into national politics. Although the political mobilization of the members of Orthodox parishes would generate support primarily for center-right and right-wing political parties rather than for radical democratic parties advocating stepped-up reforms, it could provide a channel for the participation of conservative citizens in organized politics.[39] However, the church is organizationally weak, and its real hold on the allegiance of the millions of persons who identify themselves as Russian Orthodox believers remains uncertain.[40] As for other sectors of society, during the late 1980s and early 1990s energetic individuals established independent professional, research, and educational organizations at a rapid rate, and there has been an upsurge in voluntary organizations engaged in charitable and philanthropic activities. However, these trends have begun from an extremely modest baseline. A great deal of time will be required to generate a network of social organizations and associations comparable to those in the Western democracies and Japan.

The media, which play a crucial role in any political system, have gained a large measure of freedom but are not yet securely established. By mid-1993 the legislature had adopted a strong press law that offers protection of the rights of the print media, and it had begun considering legislation to regularize the licensing process for television and radio broadcasters. Although these measures represent steps in the right direction, a clear political boundary has not yet been drawn between government and the media. This problem was typified by the battle between the staff of *Izvestiya* and the leadership of the parliament for control of the newspaper – a battle that the staff ultimately won in late 1992 with Yeltsin's backing. The difficulty of establishing independent media has been compounded by the harsh impact of inflation, which has forced a number of newspapers to turn to the government for operating subsidies, and by a precipitous decline in the status of the print media in the eyes of Russian citizens since the heyday of *glasnost'*.[41] Television, which accounts for the lion's share of the news that reaches ordinary citizens, appears vulnerable to government pressure, and both the parliament and the Yeltsin government have pressed broadcasters to give their activities favorable coverage.[42]

Nor has the process of economic reform yet produced the extensive private property and free labor markets that are major bulwarks of a strong civil society in most democratic countries.[43] During 1992 the process of privatizing state enterprises was impeded by political and bureaucratic resistance. As for labor, Russian workers endured the privations of the first year of attempted economic reform with remarkable patience; according to Yegor Gaidar, the rate of strike activity was a mere one-sixth of the level in 1991.[44] However, most workers remain locked into the official trade union structure inherited from the Soviet period, due to the official unions' persisting legal stranglehold over the provision of social security benefits.[45]

The acceleration of the process of privatization in 1993, however, promises to change this state of affairs. As noted in Chapter 5, by mid-

1993 one-quarter of Russia's workers were employed in private enterprises producing one-third of the country's output. Private entrepreneurs have become the source of the Yeltsin government's most committed supporters, and the shift toward private ownership of production facilities has been reflected in the establishment of an association of private enterprises chaired by Gaidar to exert political pressure on the legislature.[46] As for the labor union structure, an effort has been launched to break the old unions' legal hold over social security benefits.[47] If it succeeds, workers' natural distrust of the Soviet-era union structure could lead to a substantial increase in the strength of new, independent labor unions – provided that those unions demonstrate their ability to advance workers' interests.

Although this evidence suggests that Russia has only an embryonic civil society in a structural sense, the trends in Russian political culture are nevertheless encouraging. An opinion survey conducted in mid-1990 asked respondents from various parts of the Soviet Union a series of questions about democratic values. Two-thirds of the respondents stated that people should have the right to demonstrate on behalf of political causes. Roughly six in ten (57 percent) agreed that a multiparty system was necessary, and a slightly higher proportion (62 percent) affirmed that individuals should have the right to publish newspapers of any political orientation. On a composite index of support for democratic rights, 61 percent of Russians gave answers indicating that they were strong or moderate supporters of such rights, compared with 30 percent whose support for democratic rights was weak.[48] The survey found that support for the values of a civic culture was strongest among those with high levels of education, the young, residents of cities, and men.[49] On the whole, members of these social categories have also been the most active participants in Russian politics.

Political and economic turmoil has tempered, but not negated, the Russian public's support for democratic values. At the beginning of 1992 a survey found that support for a multiparty system had declined slightly (to 50 percent) as some previous supporters moved into the "don't know" category, although direct opposition to a multiparty system had not increased from previous levels.[50] At the start of 1993 another survey found that 65 percent of the respondents agreed with the statement that political opposition is essential in a democracy; the level of support for this proposition among persons with higher education was more than 80 percent. The same survey found that 73 percent of the respondents agreed with the proposition that citizens should have the right to publish newspapers of any political orientation.[51]

On the other hand, opinion surveys showed signs of ambivalence or resistance to democracy within some segments of the Russian public.

Despite the broad-based endorsement of freedom of speech, there was a worrisome increase in support for the proposition that some ideas are too dangerous for society and should therefore be banned.[52] Moreover, about one-fifth of the respondents to another poll showed a persisting attachment to the idea that Communism was the best system for Russia.[53] Perhaps most important, surveys demonstrated that a large percentage of respondents regarded economic prosperity as a key component of democracy. When asked which single characteristic they regarded as the most important feature of democracy, more respondents chose "economic prosperity in the country" than any political characteristic of the governmental system.[54] Although a declining share of respondents identified government provision of citizens' basic needs as a key element of democracy, this response suggested that at some point a continuing decline of living standards would undercut public support for democratic institutions – even though how soon such a backlash might occur remained uncertain.[55]

In any case, the high level of turnout in the April 1993 referendum appeared to disprove the notion that the Russian public had become politically apathetic or had concluded that political democracy was not worth the economic price. Two-thirds of the electorate of 107 million participated in the referendum. The final results showed that 65 percent of the voters endorsed Yeltsin's leadership. Whereas slightly less than half voted for an early presidential election, more than two-thirds of the voters approved early legislative elections, though prior procedural rulings by the parliament and the Constitutional Court prevented the vote on legislative elections from being legally binding.[56] Perhaps most strikingly, 53 percent of the participants in the referendum voted for Yeltsin's economic policies. Exit polls indicated that though the level of support for Yeltsin and his policies varied somewhat among socioeconomic groups, he apparently won the vote of confidence among members of all major socioeconomic groups. Even pensioners and the unemployed, two of the groups hardest hit by the economic downturn, cast about half their votes in favor of Yeltsin's economic program.[57] On balance, the referendum revealed a new level of political maturity and patience that diverged sharply from the images of a volatile and ill-informed mass public in many accounts of the Russian past.[58]

Although subject to various interpretations, the referendum had an immediate impact on the political balance of the country. Stung by the result of the plebiscite, one of Yeltsin's foremost critics, Nikolay Travkin of the Civic Union coalition, resigned his seat in the Congress, called on other deputies to do the same, and advocated holding new parliamentary elections in the fall of 1993.[59] Although no surge of parliamentary resignations followed, influential parliamentary leaders began to break with speaker Khasbulatov and to discuss the possibility of compromise with Yeltsin on the writing and ratification of a new constitution.[60] Yeltsin quickly convened a conference of the representatives of Russia's eighty-seven federal units to approve his preferred draft of the constitution. Under the draft proposed by Yeltsin, ethnic republics within Russia, like Tatarstan, would have greater autonomy and control over their resources than would nonethnic federal units. This disparity produced a flurry of regional proclamations in which virtually all the nonethnic federal units declared themselves republics, too.[61] Meanwhile, Yeltsin's opponents in the parliament, realizing the extent of the challenge to their political survival, attempted to block the process of constitution-writing by court action, but failed to do so. The resulting free-for-all became so intense that by the time the draft constitution was approved by the regional representatives in July, only eight of the twenty ethnic republics and two-thirds of the nonethnic federal units had initialed the draft.[62] As of mid-1993 it remained uncertain whether the referendum and the constitutional conference would actually overcome the tangle of factional and regional conflicts and lead to a new constitutional order for Russia. What seemed clear was that the referendum had altered the terrain of Russian politics and that the deepening deadlock between the parliament and the president could not long continue.

The Western Newly Independent States

Since 1990 most of the new states of the western region have exhibited tendencies that bear significant similarities as well as some dissimilarities to the political trends in Russia. In Ukraine, the March 1990 legislative elections for a new Supreme Soviet, although marred by electoral improprieties, were vigorously contested and allowed the Democratic Bloc, an anti-Communist coalition movement, to capture one-quarter of the seats.[63] The election of December 1991 entailed authentic electoral competition and direct popular election for the newly created position of president of Ukraine. Won by Ukrainian Communist Party official and parliamentary chairman Leonid Kravchuk against a field of opponents including two prominent former Ukrainian dissidents, the election was a milestone in the shift toward the creation of a genuinely democratic governmental structure.[64] The unevenness of this shift, however, has provoked controversy over the legitimacy of the legislature and over the division of authority among the legislature and other governmental institutions.

The debate over the division of governmental authority has been reflected in the shifting content of the constitutional drafts proposed for the country. In June 1991 the Ukrainian legislature approved the "concept" or outline of a new draft constitution that provided for a careful balancing of powers between the parliament and the presidency. By early 1992, however, changes in the draft strengthened the powers of the president, partly to provide a political counterpoise to the emergency powers the Russian legislature had recently vested in President Yeltsin.[65] These changes were also promoted for personal reasons by Kravchuk, who was moving his power base to the executive branch of government.

Although the initial deliberations over the proposed constitution avoided the proliferation of competing drafts that occurred in Russia, public discussion since late 1992 has revealed serious disagreements about the provisions of the fundamental law. As in Russia, the parliament, though deeply divided over many substantive issues of policy, has achieved a measure of consensus against the numerous powers reserved for the president. Moreover, the constitutional draft has sharpened the disagreement over a unitary versus a federal state that some politicians had previously tried to finesse.[66] Many regional officials have faulted the draft for neglecting to spell out the powers of local government, and the Crimean legislature has demanded that the draft be amended to stipulate that the Ukraine is a federal state, as well as to provide for dual citizenship. Ivan Plyushch, chairman of the parliament, has encouraged the demands of the localities as a means of checking the power of Kravchuk.[67]

Paralleling this constitutional debate has been a struggle over the legitimacy and political survival of the current parliament. As in Russia, the parliament's election in the twilight of Soviet power and a public perception that it is incapable of coping with the country's multiplying problems have convinced some political activists that it should be dissolved and a new legislature elected.[68] In September 1992 Rukh, the umbrella organization that had led the fight for Ukrainian independence, and New Ukraine, a movement dedicated to accelerating the pace of economic reform, launched a campaign to force new legislative elections by collecting the 3 million signatures required by law.[69] Although this drive failed to obtain the necessary signatures within the legally mandated time period, Rukh pledged to begin a new recall campaign to dissolve the legislature in 1993.[70]

Although Ukrainian politics has been characterized by numerous controversies and partisan political maneuvers, one fundamental issue has stood out: whether to give priority to strengthening the unity and cohesion of the Ukrainian state or to accelerating the pace of democratization and economic reform. President Kravchuk has paid lip service to reform slogans but in practice has emphasized state-building. By exploiting carefully chosen disagreements with Russia but always striking face-saving compromises before the controversy spins out of control, Kravchuk has aimed to demonstrate Ukraine's independence and bolster his own nationalist credentials. Reluctant to seize the painful nettle of economic reform, he has undercut officials, such as Deputy Prime Minister Volodymyr Lanovyi and Prime Minister Leonid Kuchma, who have attempted to come to grips with the country's rapidly deteriorating economy by slashing the state budget deficit and speeding up economic liberalization.[71]

In 1992 differences over such fundamentals precipitated important realignments in Ukrainian politics. Having fought successfully for independence, the Rukh movement was split by a dispute between those who backed Kravchuk as chief spokesman for Ukrainian statehood and those who distrusted the president because of his Communist past and wanted to speed up domestic change. This split in Rukh prompted an exodus of Kravchuk supporters that substantially narrowed the political base of the Rukh movement.[72] In August 1992 defectors from Rukh joined in establishing a new political coalition called the Congress of National Democratic Forces (CNDF). Committed to a strong institutional presidency and to Kravchuk personally, the CNDF has advocated a unitary state, creation of a strong military establishment, and Ukrainian withdrawal from the CIS.[73] At about the same time, the remnant of Rukh assembled a coalition of parties intended to promote the legislative referendum and force the formation of a more inclusive government, and the New Ukraine movement held its first congress.[74] Less concerned with strengthening the country in military or narrowly political terms, the New Ukraine movement has called for accelerated marketization and economic reform, the creation of a federal state, and cooperation with Russia and other CIS members. It also has declared its political opposition to Kravchuk.[75]

Up to the summer of 1993 Ukrainian constitutional and political controversies did not produce a confrontation as intense as the one in Russia, nor did the organs of coercion appear to play a significant role in such disputes. However, the mechanisms of civilian control over the military and security establishments in Ukraine appear no more reliable than those in Russia. After winning over a very large contingent of Russian officers with promises of generous benefits and equal treatment for all citizens regardless of ethnicity, the Ukrainian government has found itself pressed to reduce the size of the military establishment and make room for Ukrainian officers returning from other former republics. The promotion of ethnic Ukrainians in the officer corps, in which ethnic Russians and other non-Ukrainians still fill 70 to 90 percent of the top posts, has become an especially delicate issue, and since mid-1992 President Kravchuk has appointed several ethnic Ukrainians to the high command.[76] Demands for the ethnic ukrainianization of the armed forces have come from the Union of Ukrainian Officers, a nationalist group with links to the Ukrainian Republican Party and the Rukh movement. In addition, members of the Union have reportedly played an important role in the monitoring of the armed forces by the counterintelligence branch of the National Security Service (NSS), successor to the Ukrainian KGB.[77]

Although not opposed in principle to civilian control of the military establishment, the Union of Ukrainian Officers has urged that the NSS and the Ministry of Internal Affairs take more decisive action to ban anti-Ukrainian political organizations in regions such as Crimea, and its affiliates have reportedly been involved in training a paramilitary group that has fought in the self-proclaimed "Dniester Republic."[78] These developments raise the possibility that ethnic Russian officers upset by Kravchuk's acceptance of some of the Union's demands might bring strong counterpressures to bear on the civilian leadership. They also raise the possibility that some of these officers, frustrated with their worsening career prospects, might transfer their loyalties to Russia.

Similar problems may exist with the National Security Service. Despite vague reports that the security apparatus has been cleansed by the removal of some former KGB officers, most NSS personnel were carried over from the KGB, and their chief during the Soviet era became first deputy minister of security in Moscow.[79] Moreover, the Ukrainian legislation governing parliamentary oversight of the security police has apparently been modeled on the Soviet legislation adopted under Gorbachev. Like that legislation, it contains large loopholes and major weaknesses.[80] In a full-blown Ukrainian political crisis, the Ukrainian institutions of coercion might therefore play an uncontrolled and perhaps a critical role.

Ukrainian political parties, the main potential vehicles for public participation in national politics, remain fairly weak. A survey conducted at the beginning of 1992 inquired which of several movements and parties inspired a great deal or a fair amount of trust in the respondents. The Socialist Party of Ukraine, as the former Ukrainian Communist Party was now called, received an expression of trust from 15 percent of the respondents. The comparable ratings for the Ukrainian Republican Party and the Democratic Party of Ukraine – two organizations that later joined the political bloc supporting Kravchuk – were 15 and 16 percent, respectively. The Rukh movement, many of whose members later adopted a critical stance toward Kravchuk, received an expression of support from 18 percent of the respondents.[81] A separate survey that asked a similar question found that the New Ukraine movement, which also took a critical line toward the Ukrainian president, received expressions of full or partial trust from about 10 percent of the respondents.[82] These results suggest that party organizations in Ukraine had links with the public that were probably no stronger than those of Russian political parties.[83]

In Ukraine the media have played a somewhat different role in shaping political attitudes than they have in Russia. During Gorbachev's campaign for *glasnost'*, the Ukrainian press never matched the openness and vigor of the Russian press, and Ukraine has lagged behind Russia in adopting reform legislation to protect press rights.[84] Inflation and commercial pressures also may have influenced the press by stimulating some publications to seek to attract readers through sensationalism.[85] Perhaps most important, control of Ukrainian television and radio broadcasting facilities has remained in the hands of conservatives. The government's tight rein on the electronic media has been justified partly by pointing to the "information siege" that allows Russia to beam TV broadcasts into Ukraine but prevents Ukraine from broadcasting its programs to Russia.[86] This policy toward television and radio exemplifies the argument that Ukraine must create a strong state capable of resisting Russian pressure.

Despite these problems, the broad trends in Ukraine's political culture appear to be favorable. A 1990 survey found that Ukrainian citizens favored democratic values by a ratio of almost two to one, approximately the same level of support as existed at the time in Russia.[87] At the end of 1992, 70 percent of Ukrainian respondents agreed that a multiparty system was an important attribute of democracy, compared with 15 percent who disagreed. The level of support for the freedom to publish any sort of newspaper was high (66 percent), and support for freedom of speech, even speech that increased social tensions, was still higher (78 percent). However, some of these attitudes were clearly ambivalent, in that 50 percent of the respondents also agreed with the statement that some ideas were too dangerous for society and should therefore be prevented by the government from being published.[88] To an even greater degree than the Russians, Ukrainian respondents described economic prosperity as a vital part of democracy.[89]

More dramatically than opinion surveys, events during the summer of 1993 underscored that the economy is the Achilles' heel of the Ukrainian political system. During 1992 and the first half of 1993 neither President Kravchuk nor the parliament was willing to confront the country's fundamental economic problems and introduce decisive reforms. As a result the economy spun increasingly out of control, even by comparison with the economic decline in Russia and several other new states. In June 1993, despite the government's recent conclusion of a pact with the old-style trade union federation, the government's belated attempt to reduce the ballooning budget deficit through major price increases provoked a strike by miners and workers in other heavy industries.[90]

Threatening to paralyze the country with a general strike, the miners demanded a referendum on popular confidence in Kravchuk and new parliamentary elections by the end of 1993.[91] After first seeking to face down the miners by stripping Prime Minister Kuchma of political authority and concentrating executive power in his own hands, Kravchuk was forced to retreat and accept the political concessions offered by the parliament.[92] In a move obviously influenced by Russian political developments just a few months before, the parliament initially agreed to conduct a referendum on public confidence in the presidency and in the parliament itself – but not new parliamentary elections.[93] Although this conflict gave a new impetus to political change within Ukraine's central governmental institutions, it also deepened cleavages among the regions and intensified centrifugal political forces. Its long-term effect on the shape of the polity therefore remained difficult to gauge.

In Belarus political change has occurred at a slower pace than in Russia and Ukraine. Although the Belarusian public has gradually become more active politically, the 1990 legislative elections produced a parliament with a smaller share of reform-minded deputies than in the other Slavic republics, and as of mid-1993 Belarus remained the only CIS member that had not established a presidency.[94] In the legislature the main organizational advocate of reform has been the Belarusian Popular Front (BPF), which won about 35 of that body's 360 seats; another 65 to 70 deputies have sometimes voted in favor of legislation favored by the BPF.[95] Convinced that the parliament is a major roadblock on the path to democracy and a market economy, Belarusian reformers have pressed for new legislative elections; in 1992 the BPF gathered enough signatures to require that a public referendum be held on this question.[96] When the petitions were delivered, however, the parliament refused to schedule the plebiscite. In October 1992 it did set a date for new parliamentary elections in March 1994, one year ahead of schedule; but it rejected the call for immediate elections on the pretext that advocates of the referendum had committed procedural violations of the law in collecting signatures. This arbitrary act produced a public reaction described by outside observers as "muted, to say the least."[97]

Beginning in 1992 a livelier public debate developed over the shape of a proposed new constitution. One key issue was whether the state should create a powerful presidency and a strong premiership, as proposed in the constitutional draft under discussion in mid-1993. Parliamentary head Shushkevich and the BPF have argued that the introduction of a strong presidency should be delayed for several years in order to avoid the risk of a slide back into authoritarianism.[98] In any case, the draft constitution under consideration in mid-1993 contained some positive features, such as a long list of political rights and the requirement that members of parliament serve as full-time deputies rather than combine their posts with work in the government bureaucracy, as about 70 percent of the deputies have done under the existing constitutional dispensation.[99] However, the draft undercut these positive features by declaring that the rights of individuals may be restricted in the interest of public morals, national security, and public order. It also stated that parties and social organizations could be banned if they infringe on the independence of the state, advocate war, or distribute several types of propaganda.[100]

The constitutional debate has been more temperate in Belarus than in Russia, and the military and security establishments apparently have not been drawn into the political fray. However, the weakness of civilian control of the armed forces and security police could lead to this eventuality should a political show-down occur over constitutional issues. Despite reformers' calls for parliamentary oversight of the military, the 1993 draft constitution contains crucial deficiencies. Although it states that the chairman of the government becomes commander in chief in case of a declaration of martial law, it also calls the minister of defense the highest military commander in the land, and it does not spell out the chain of command in case of actual war.[101] Calculations about the likelihood of political interference by the military are difficult to make because the share of ethnic Russians in the Belarusian officer corps is somewhere between 50 and 80 percent. On the one hand, these officers would appear to be less likely to enter the political fray in a country where they are not members of the titular majority. On the other hand, should relations with Russia deteriorate, their loyalty would be called into doubt and could cause friction in the military. Indeed, protests against the number of Russian officers were raised by the Belarusian Association of Servicemen (set up in 1991) and echoed by the BPF.

Confronted with the potential for intramilitary ethnic tensions like those in Ukraine, the Belarusian civilian leadership initially temporized. It delayed administering a loyalty oath to military officers until the end of 1992, and the wording of the oath that it finally administered did not specify that a Belarusian officer must be a citizen of Belarus.[102] However, the minister of defense has since laid out what appears to be a demanding timetable for steps to indigenize the officer corps, and some concrete movement in this direction has apparently taken place.[103] The impact of these measures on civil-military relations remains to be seen.

Civilian control over the new state's security apparatus appears even more problematic. Still known as the Belarusian KGB, it is headed by Eduard Shirkouskiy, who signed the Belarusian Communist Party's appeal in support of the August 1991 coup attempt; and little if any turnover occurred in the agency following independence.[104] Only beginning in late 1992 were Belarusian KGB officers required to take an oath of loyalty to the new state, and the agency was still not subject to any meaningful parliamentary oversight.[105]

Since 1991 party competition in Belarus has increased, but the establishment of an effective multiparty system seems a distant prospect. Although several political parties exist, most are quite small and unknown to the general electorate. In March 1992 the legislature noted that "the process of the emergence of political parties is only beginning. They are small, are gathering experience, and do not yet reflect the full range of the population's interests. So it is too soon to speak of a real multiparty system in our society."[106] Apart from other obstacles, the persistence of government control over the bulk of the media undercuts political parties' ability to generate public support. As of early 1993 the Supreme Soviet had passed no legislation setting out the rights of the media, and almost all newspapers had become heavily dependent on state subsidies that made them both vulnerable to governmental pressures and politically cautious.[107] The electronic media remained under government control, and the only competition to state-run television came from broadcasters based in Moscow, not in Belarus.[108]

Since independence the Belarusian polity has experienced a certain measure of polarization. "All society, from top to bottom," remarked one observer with considerable exaggeration, "is split into 'radicals' and 'conservatives'."[109] Although the Belarusian advocates of reform and of the status quo were clearly moving apart in 1993, the level of political conflict within the country was still mild by comparison with Ukraine, not to mention Russia. The sense of political inertia has been compounded by the caution of the principal governmental leader, parliamentary chairman Stanislau Shushkevich, who has shown little inclination to take on the surviving elements of the party *nomenklatura* and other entrenched political interests for the sake of economic reform.[110] In the spring of 1993 Shushkevich did become involved in a vigorous struggle with Prime Minister Vyacheslau Kebich and other officials over whether Belarus should hew closely to its previous declaration of international neutrality or join a pending CIS security pact in order to obtain more advantageous terms of trade with Russia, and thereby shore up its troubled economy. However, this debate over guns versus trade had far less military significance than comparable debates in Ukraine.[111] Creation of a popularly elected presidency might help overcome the inertia, but the prospects for this step depend on the timetable for the adoption of a new constitution, which remained uncertain in mid-1993.[112]

Viewed primarily in terms of political culture, the prospects for democracy are no worse in Belarus than in Russia or Ukraine. Belarus appears less vulnerable to the risk of political disintegration along regional lines, and opinion surveys reveal that democratic values are held by a proportion of the citizenry that equals or slightly exceeds the comparable levels in Russia and Ukraine.[113] However, the pace of democratization in Belarus has been palpably slower. This halting progress demonstrates how heavily political liberalization depends on dynamic political leadership to mobilize public opinion and propel the process forward. Although apparently quite committed to constitutional values, parliamentary leader Shushkevich has not taken on this role, nor have many other Belarusian leaders. Because the country had almost no dissent movement during the pre-Gorbachev years, it entered the post-Soviet era with relatively few experienced political activists ready to fight vigorously for political liberalization.

The situation in the Baltic states is fundamentally different. That all three Baltic countries look back on a period of independence, and that they maintained a stronger European orientation than most parts of the former Soviet Union, has given them a head start in taking steps to energize civil society. This is especially true of the mass media and the creation of effective political parties. In the period of perestroika, the Baltic republics took the lead in forming autonomous groups in a wide range of social sectors, such as environmental protection, and they created the first political parties inside the USSR. On balance, the Baltic states also have made more progress than the other former republics in encouraging entrepreneurship and privatizing state assets.

As a group, the Baltic states are further along than most other former republics in installing new constitutions that are politically meaningful. In June 1992 Estonia became one of the first former Soviet republics to adopt a post-Communist constitution, and in the fall of 1992 Lithuanian voters approved a constitution for their country.[114] In Latvia, where legislators adopted a constitution only in July 1993, constitution-making was slowed by basic disagreements about the role of the presidency and the proper political mechanism for deciding the criteria for citizenship and naturalization. Still, on balance the Baltic states stand out from the other former Soviet republics, which in mid-1993 were either wrestling with the task of preparing new constitutions or had adopted constitutions that were ideological facades rather than blue-prints for real societal relationships.[115]

The dynamics of constitution-making shed light on the impact of the Baltic states' political experiences before the imposition of Soviet control in 1940. All three countries wrestled with the central issue of whether to establish a powerful presidency. In the period leading up to the Estonian constitutional referendum, several constitutional variants that included this feature were proposed. However, these proposals were quickly rejected, partly on the ground that the Estonian constitution of 1938, which some fervent nationalists wanted to revive, had demonstrated the risks of a turn toward authoritarianism.[116] In Lithuania, the attempt of parliamentary chairman Vytautas Landsbergis and the Sajudis national movement to win public approval for a strong presidency was also criticized – again, partly on the grounds that the internal disintegration of Lithuanian democracy during the 1930s illustrated the risks of a domestically created dictatorship. Instead Estonian voters approved a strong parliamentary system, and the Lithuanian electorate approved a mixed presidential-parliamentary system weighted toward parliamentary rule.[117] In Latvia, following the June 1993 elections, the new parliament (the Saeima) voted to reinstate the constitution of 1922, which contained provisions for a weak presidency. These events appear to support the argument of Western scholars that the establishment of a democratic order is aided by prior national experience with democracy, even if that experience proved unsuccessful.[118]

During the two years following independence the political complexions of the Baltic governments diverged substantially. The September 1992 Estonian legislative elections, the first post-Soviet legislative elections anywhere in the former USSR, were contested by four major party groupings. Despite the spiraling economic hardships, the elections produced a stable majority coalition committed to accelerating the transition to a fully capitalist economy.[119] In a major upset, the Popular Front, which had led the fight for Estonian Independence, won only 15 of 101 parliamentary seats. The reformist successor to the Estonian Communist Party, known as Left Opportunity, fared even worse, suffering a crushing defeat that prompted one wag to suggest it should be known as "Lost Opportunity." It became the first Communist successor party of Eastern Europe to be completely excluded from a post-Communist parliament.[120] The principal winner in the balloting was Pro Patria, a coalition of parties favoring scaled-back government and the free market, which won 29 seats in the new legislature.[121] In Estonia economic hardship appeared to increase the population's determination to be rid of socialist or quasi-socialist economic arrangements.

Events in Lithuania took the opposite course. In the fall 1992 elections Landsbergis and the Sajudis movement, which had sustained the long struggle for national independence, suffered a decisive defeat. They were defeated, however, not by the forces of the "right" but of the "left." The victor in the elections was the Lithuanian Democratic Labor Party, the successor to the pro-independence Lithuanian Communist Party trounced by Sajudis in the legislative elections of 1990. Moreover, soon afterward Lithuanians elected as their new president Algirdas Brazauskas, the erstwhile reformist leader of the Lithuanian Communist Party. This political turnabout did not signify a move back to authoritarianism, but it did suggest that economic hardships had undermined the prevailing free-market outlook of the preceding three years and had created a Lithuanian government more prepared to compose its differences with Moscow. The divergence between the electoral outcomes in Estonia and Lithuania demonstrated not only the distinctive character of the two countries, but the capacity of varying electoral systems to produce substantially different political results.[122]

In Latvia, the elections of June 1993 produced an outcome midway between the results in Lithuania and Estonia. The balloting for the 100-member Saeima produced a plurality of 36 seats for the Latvian Way Party, the successor to the reformist wing of the Latvian Communist Party. The Ravnopravie (Equal Rights) Party, the vehicle of local Russian inhabitants, won seven seats. On the other hand, the National Independence Movement and the Fatherland and Freedom Party, both right-wing nationalist groups, captured a total of twenty-one seats, and various centrist parties won the balance.[123] Former Latvian Communist Party official Anatolijs Gorbunovs was elected chairman of the parliament; his deputies came from the National Independence and Farmers' parties. After a three-way split in which none of the candidates for president won a parliamentary majority, the Saeima elected Guntis Ulmanis, a former Communist Party member but also a descendant of the last president of independent Latvia, as head of state.[124]

On balance, the Baltic states appear to have the best chances for a successful transition to democracy of any of the new states of the western region. Although ethnic divisions in Estonia and especially Latvia could become a major obstacle to the creation of a reasonably unified citizenry sharing basic democratic values, the cultural conditions favoring democracy seem to be much more deeply ingrained in the Baltic countries than in Belarus, Ukraine, and Moldova. In all three Baltic states, a civic sense of political restraint has been reflected also in the absence of political violence against people, especially the local Russians, whom many Balts strongly dislike.

The importance of such restraint is demonstrated by the case of

Moldova. Due to its prominent role in the campaign for political autonomy, the Moldovan Popular Front held key legislative and executive posts in the government at the time the country declared its independence from Moscow. The MPF came to power with a strong disposition to seek Moldovan union with Romania, which led to an escalation of tensions and violence between the government and the break-away pro-Russian regime in the trans-Dniester region. Over time, however, Moldovan public opinion has gradually shifted against unification, splitting the MPF and leading to a reshuffling of the government in central Moldova.[125] The coalition government of Andrey Sangheli, who assumed power during July 1992, differed significantly from its predecessors. Depicting itself as a "government of national consensus" representing all the inhabitants of Moldova, the new government pledged to act on a multinational basis and to observe the civil and political rights of all persons regardless of ethnicity. In line with this policy, it proposed to block MPF proposals for Moldovan unification with Romania by conducting a public referendum on this question.[126]

The new government enjoyed the support of 180 to 190 deputies in the 240-member parliament.[127] Its ministers were chosen on the basis of consultation with parliamentary fractions as well as with political clubs and ethnic groups outside the parliament. The political salience of parliamentary fractions and the weakness of grass-roots political parties is likely to persist for the foreseeable future. The deputies supporting the government belong to the Agrarian Club, which includes chairmen of agricultural cooperatives; the Democratic Club and the Independent Club, which consist mainly of individuals who have broken with the MPF; the Soglasiye (Accord) Club, which consists of the numerous Russians and Ukrainians from the right bank of the Dniester who are loyal to Moldova; and a fraction of Gagauz deputies from the south of the country.

The new government's more conciliatory and inclusive approach may lay the basis for reconciliation with non-Moldovan minorities in central Moldova and undermine the domestic political position of the trans-Dniester regime. In August 1992 a cease-fire in the military conflict took effect, and the struggle between Chisinau and Tiraspol assumed a more political form. At the start of 1993 the commander of the Russian 14th Army based in the trans-Dniester region, Lieutenant General Aleksandr Lebed, condemned several members of the region's civilian government for alleged corruption and rejected the notion that the army should refrain from intervening in domestic politics.[128] Lebed's support for a minority civilian faction within the trans-Dniester regime may have been intended to pave the way for a more flexible public posture designed to counter the Sangheli government's political offensive.[129]

However, the general's record of comments and behavior made it virtually certain that he remained set against any genuine reconciliation with the Moldovan government. Barring unexpected pressures from Moscow for a settlement, the conflict between the government and the breakaway regime thus seemed destined to continue, although in a less violent form.

The Southern Newly Independent States

On the whole, the sociopolitical situation in the countries of Central Asia differs markedly from that in Russia and most of the other new states. Although the expansion of political participation and the depth of the anti-Communist political movement have varied substantially among Russia and the countries of the western region, in nearly all instances these developments have surpassed the analogous political phenomena in Central Asia. If political and economic holdovers from the Communist system are at least under siege in the western states, they have a much surer hold on power in most of Central Asia. Just as Central Asia did not undergo a social revolution similar to Russia's in 1917, during the past five years it has not experienced a democratic revolution similar to the one occurring in Russia and several other post-Soviet states.[130]

Developments in the Caucasus have shown more resemblance to developments in Russia and the western region – chiefly by virtue of the greater strength of the Caucasian nationalist movements and the success of their initial assaults on the old Communist order. However, the Caucasus has exhibited an exceptionally high level of political instability and communal violence that sets it apart from most of the western region except for Moldova, and from most of Central Asia except for Tajikistan. In a sense, the Caucasus and Central Asia typify two different problems of trying to foster a civic culture and build a civil society. In the Caucasus the reaction against the Communist order was so strong that it has erupted into large-scale violence; in most of Central Asia the reaction has been so weak that the countries of the region may not escape the pull of past authoritarian practices and attitudes.

Central Asia is distinguished from most of the rest of the former Soviet Union by its comparatively traditional social structure. As a group, the countries of the region are far less urbanized than the other new states. Overall, less than 40 percent of the Central Asian population was urban in 1989, compared with an average of almost 66 percent for the other former Soviet republics.[131] Due to low migration rates from the countryside to the cities and exceptionally rapid population growth in rural areas, the degree of Central Asian urbanization actually declined during the 1980s.[132] As a result, ethnic Central Asians remain disproportionately concentrated in rural areas, and residents of European origin are disproportionately concentrated in the cities.

Despite the pain and disruption inflicted on the peoples of the region after the 1917 revolution, the Soviet regime did not transform the social structure in Central Asia as it did in European parts of the former USSR. In Central Asia Soviet totalitarianism adapted itself "with a particular 'feudal-authoritarianism' that has lasted to this day. . . . [T]he only 'traditional custom' that was left to grow was a clan-oriented nepotism that flourished to an unprecedented degree."[133] Notwithstanding some variation among the Central Asian countries, in all of them ties to family, tribe, clan, and locality are far stronger elements of the social fabric than in more developed societies. That the flag of post-Soviet Turkmenistan contains five stars, each representing one of the principal tribes of the country, is more than a quaint detail.[134]

Due to this sociopolitical legacy, the post-Soviet democratic forms introduced in the region have frequently lacked democratic substance. In May 1992 Turkmenistan became the first former Soviet republic to adopt a post-Communist constitution, and during the next fifteen months Uzbekistan, Kazakhstan, and Kyrgyzstan followed suit. The debates in Kyrgyzstan between the parliament and President Akayev were open and lively,[135] but Uzbekistan's legislature unanimously adopted the new constitution after only a perfunctory discussion. The Uzbek resemblance to Soviet practice was underlined by the constitutional clause that barred any social group or individual from claiming to speak for the nation and reserved that right to the president and the legislature.[136] In Turkmenistan, shortly before the adoption of the new constitution a number of crucial articles dealing with such matters as freedom of the press and a constitutional court were excised, and one-third of the articles that remained depended on the discretion of government agencies for their implementation.[137] The constitution endorsed the principle of the separation of powers, but two anomalous political bodies have been created under the president's control and endowed with both legislative and executive functions. Since that time, most formal decisions in the legislature have been made by unanimous votes.[138]

Most of the Central Asian elections conducted since 1990 reflect popular inability to effect democratic change. The 1990 legislative elections did not provide a springboard for new democratic forces and critics of the status quo. In Kazakhstan and Uzbekistan the elections were conducted on the basis of the pseudodemocratic Soviet practice of reserving a large bloc of seats for the representatives of various "social organizations." Moreover, in Uzbekistan, almost one-third of the remaining seats were uncontested, and in Turkmenistan, most of them were. Although all five Central Asian states have held popular elections for the new institution of the presidency, in all but one instance the election has merely draped a mantle of democratic legitimacy over a former leader of the country's preindependence Communist Party. In three cases – Turkmenistan, Kazakhstan, and Kyrgyzstan – the winner of the election was the sole candidate for the new office. In Uzbekistan, the strongest non-Communist political competitor was arbitrarily excluded from the race in favor of a weaker, "showcase" candidate. In only one instance, Tajikistan, was there a contest between two leading political figures, and that election was clouded by claims of electoral fraud.[139]

Under these political conditions, it comes as no surprise that the institutions of coercion have not been subjected to meaningful civilian political control. In mid-1992 the Kazakhstan legislature adopted a law on the organs of national security that gave the former republican KGB virtually a free hand. Defining the security agency's mission in sweeping terms, the law declared that citizens' constitutional rights could be circumscribed in extreme circumstances but did not spell out the concrete cases to which this provision applies. It also authorized the security agency to continue recruiting informers and underscored the obligation of individuals in private as well as governmental organizations to assist the security apparatus. Perhaps most striking was the grant of authority for the agency to jam almost any foreign or domestic radio or television broadcasts.[140] A similar political outlook was reflected in the declaration of the head of Uzbekistan's National Security Service that every level of society was urging his agency to squelch any attempts at destabilizing the country.[141]

Despite these resemblances to the Communist era, Central Asia has experienced significant changes, and the states of the region have not developed in political lockstep. The very presence of opposition parties, which exist in some form in all the Central Asian countries, was unthinkable under the old Soviet dispensation. The amount of change has varied, ranging from the autocratic immobilism of Turkmenistan and the increasingly oppressive authoritarianism of Uzbekistan to the more enlightened authoritarianism of Kazakhstan and the relatively benign political regime in Kyrgyzstan. Although all the governments save Tajikistan have never allowed religiously based parties to be legally registered and have been reluctant to countenance opposition parties of other sorts, their approaches to such political groups have differed. Some have allowed several political groups to register as parties and operate legally in that capacity; some have preferred to deny most political groups registration, thereby compelling them to operate in a crippling condition of semilegality; and at least one government has chosen to suppress all independent parties except the ruling party. Significant differences also exist in the governments' treatment of the media.

The harshest standard in these matters has been set by the regime of President Saparmurad Niyazov in Turkmenistan. The only legally sanctioned party of any consequence, the Democratic Party, is essentially the Communist Party of Turkmenistan in different clothing. The constitution authorizes the government to ban any groups that "encroach on the health and morals of the people," and the only other registered party is a "Peasant Justice Party" set up to foster the illusion of multiparty activity.[142] Unregistered parties, such as Agzybirlik (Unity) and the (non-Communist) Democratic Party of Turkmenistan, do engage in subterranean political activities, but they have been forced to hold their major political gatherings in Moscow and to publish a jointly edited magazine from there as well. All of Turkmenistan's media have remained under government control and reportedly are censored as rigorously as in the Soviet era.[143]

In Uzbekistan the government of President Islam Karimov, although outwardly less monolithic, has adopted an increasingly authoritarian approach. After a brief postindependence flirtation with the idea of political liberalization, Karimov turned toward a repressive policy that he claimed was justified by the political upheavals in Afghanistan, Azerbaijan, and especially Tajikistan.[144] The regime has followed a divide-and-conquer policy toward political parties. Although refusing to register the Birlik (Unity) movement as a political party, it has registered the Erk (Freedom) party, which earlier split from Birlik over whether to make parliamentary politics or mass demonstrations the centerpiece of oppositional activity.

By mid-1992, however, the Karimov regime's increasing repressiveness prompted Erk's leader, Mohamed Salih, to resign his legislative seat and to join Birlik and the Islamic Renaissance Party in a campaign of public demonstrations designed to force new parliamentary elections. Birlik also sought to appeal to Uzbekistan's nascent business class.[145] The regime responded to this new coalition by redoubling its efforts to convince the public and the international community that all three parties were intent on establishing an Islamic theocracy. It also subjected leaders of the opposition parties to a program of continuous harassment and severe beatings.[146] Drawing on the repertoire of Communist tactics, the government organized and expeditiously registered new "independent" parties designed to syphon off support from the opposition movement.[147] It also shut down several domestic newspapers and banned or confiscated selected issues of Moscow newspapers containing material regarded as politically offensive.[148] In 1993 this campaign of repression continued.[149]

In Kazakhstan, the government of President Nursultan Nazarbayev has followed a less bare-knuckled approach. By the end of 1992 three parties were legally registered: the dominant Socialist Party, successor to the Kazakh Communist Party and still effectively controlled by Nazarbayev despite his nominal "nonparty" stance; a Social Democratic party consisting primarily of Kazakh and Russian intellectuals; and the People's (or National) Congress of Kazakhstan, an inclusive party that grew out of the country's environmental movement and has sought to appeal to both Russians and ethnic Kazakhs. It is significant that all these parties are committed at least nominally to bridging the dividing line between the country's ethnic Russian and Kazakh communities. Most other political organizations consist primarily of a single ethnic group such as Kazakhs or Russians.[150]

The Nazarbayev regime has been unwilling to sanction the activities of most of these other organizations by registering them as political parties.[151] It has barred the Alash party, which has advocated the expulsion of the local Russian population.[152] For a long time the government likewise resisted registering the Zheltoksan (December) movement, which grew out of the December 1986 mass demonstrations, and which claims to speak for ethnic Kazakhs, but has taken a less hardline stance on the question of Russian emigration. After wavering, the government also refused to register the Edinstvo (Unity) party, which has taken up the cause of local Russians against the perceived threat of being made second-class citizens.[153] At the end of 1992, the Zheltoksan party joined with others to form the Azat (Free) Republican party, dedicated to the "true decolonization" of Kazakhstan.[154] In February 1993, a new political party, Popular Unity of Kazakhstan, was established with President Nazarbayev at its head, designed to give the president a broad base of support and prevent political fissures along ethnic lines. Whether future political alignments in Kazakhstan develop on the basis of transethnic coalitions or form primarily along ethnic lines will have a major impact on the country's future stability and territorial integrity. Although the government has maintained the legal and political instruments necessary to thwart any criticism from the media, society has reportedly enjoyed more media freedom in Kazakhstan than in several other new states of the region.[155]

In a number of respects Kyrgyzstan has moved farthest along the path of democratization. Approximately 80 percent of the seats in the 1990 legislative elections were contested.[156] Although President Askar Akayev won the presidency in an uncontested election, he has nevertheless fostered a relatively tolerant political atmosphere.[157] By comparison with other regimes in the region, Akayev has allowed more political parties to be registered. Thanks to the timing of the 1990 elections, most of these groups, such as the Kyrgyzstan Party of National Regeneration and the "Free Kyrgyzstan" Democratic Party, are virtually unrepresented in the parliament, whereas the russophone party known as the Slavic Fund holds about one-fifth of the legislative seats. New legislative elections could change this situation fundamentally, but as of mid-1993 Akayev had rebuffed pleas for new elections on the grounds that they would be politically destabilizing. A number of independent newspapers have been permitted to publish, and foreign monitors have found few complaints of government violations of human rights.[158] Akayev has worked hard to smooth relations among the country's ethnic groups by blocking legislation biased in favor of ethnic Kyrgyz, and also by refusing to register the Social-Democratic Party, which is made up primarily of ethnic Russians and which the government regards as extremist.[159]

Tajikistan illustrates the process of escalation from struggles waged by political means to confrontations settled by recourse to violence. At the start of 1990 the Communist government in Tajikistan used rising communal tensions and public demonstrations as a pretext for a harsh crackdown and the exclusion of all opposition candidates from the republican legislative elections, thus ensuring a solidly conservative parliament. Nonetheless, three reform-minded parties – the Rastokhez (Rebirth) Party, the Democratic Party of Tajikistan, and also the Islamic Renaissance Party – were registered during the second half of 1991. After the legislature chose a former Tajik Communist Party leader, Rakhman Nabiyev, as the country's new president, these parties staged demonstrations against Nabiyev and his authoritarian policies, including his decision to reinstate the outlawed Communist Party of Tajikistan. Temporarily forced to step down as president, Nabiyev ran for the presidency in popular elections held in November 1991. In balloting whose fairness has been challenged by his critics, Nabiyev won a majority of 58 percent against the opposition candidate's 30 percent.

From this stage onward political methods of struggle steadily gave way to violence. In the spring of 1992, after a series of demonstrations, Nabiyev became involved in a deadlock with the minister of internal affairs, whom he tried unsuccessfully to remove from office. In May, escalating demonstrations by the opposition met with government repression. After the death of about a dozen protesters, the head of the National Guard broke with Nabiyev, sided with members of the opposition, and distributed weapons to them from government stocks. Nabiyev likewise set up and armed an irregular military force recruited largely from the Kulyab region. When Nabiyev hesitantly agreed to the opposition's demand for new legislative elections in December 1992, this force rejected the compromise and refused to part with its weapons.[160] Consequently both sides in the conflict became heavily armed. In September Nabiyev was forced to flee, and was replaced by Akbarsho Iskandarov, who himself was forced to step down in November and was replaced with Imam Ali Rakhmanov, a Nabiyev supporter. In June 1993 the parliament outlawed all opposition parties. Despite continued efforts to reach a compromise, the country remained engulfed in an increasingly destructive civil war.

This pattern of events bears some resemblance to the countries of the Caucasus, which one observer has described as "a Yugoslavia that has already begun to happen."[161] In Georgia the parliamentary elections in the fall of 1990 were conducted peacefully on the basis of liberal political platforms. From the beginning, however, some Georgian political groups refused to recognize the legitimacy of the legislature and of Zviad Gamsakhurdia, the former Georgian dissident who won the presidency in a landslide vote in mid-1991. Led by other former dissidents, these groups formed their own representative organ, known as the National Congress, and organized public demonstrations and hunger strikes against Gamsakhurdia's policies.[162] Gamsakhurdia met these actions with repression, and the conflict in central Georgia soon became intertwined with the government's military campaign to suppress Abkhazian and South Ossetian inhabitants attempting to secede from the country. In the fall of 1991 Gamsakhurdia's ambivalent response to the coup attempt in Moscow undermined his political position and crystallized an anti-Gamsakhurdia coalition strengthened by the defection of National Guard units from the president's camp.[163] Following physical battles for the parliament building in Tbilisi, Gamsakhurdia was pronounced deposed by his opponents and escaped from the capital, finally arriving in his political stronghold in western Georgia.

For the better part of 1992 Georgia was governed by a military council headed by Eduard Shevardnadze, who returned to the country in the spring of that year. In August Shevardnadze attempted to bring the various anti-Gamsakhurdia irregular militias under the control of the Ministry of Defense. In October he succeeded in conducting new legislative elections and was himself popularly elected to the chairmanship of the new parliament. Nonetheless, a sizable contingent of the old legislature has remained committed to Gamsakhurdia; other forces opposed to both Shevardnadze and Gamsakhurdia have coalesced around the deposed minister of defense Tengiz Kitovani; and violent conflict has continued throughout the country. The prospects for taming the militias and achieving civil peace in Georgia depend also on finding a solution to the conflicts in southern Ossetia and Abkhazia. By mid-

1993 these conflicts remained far from resolution, although the introduction of a trilateral peacekeeping contingent (of Georgians, Ossetians,
and Russians) in Ossetia, and a cease-fire backed by the United Nations,
did reduce hostilities somewhat in the two areas for a time.

Military conflicts have also affected the shape of the political order
in Azerbaijan. The conflict with Armenia over the fate of Nagorno-
Karabakh, an area located inside Azerbaijan but inhabited primarily
by ethnic Armenians, was the driving force behind the rise of the
Azerbaijani Popular Front (APF), which accused the republic's Communist leadership of sacrificing the country's interests in the conflict.
Battlefield defeats at the hands of Armenian military forces and a massacre of several hundred Azerbaijanis in February 1992 precipitated the
fall of former Communist Party chief Ayaz Mutalibov. In June, following a violent clash that blocked Mutalibov's attempt to return to
power, a presidential election was held. The winner was APF chairman
Abulfaz Elchibey, running against six other candidates on a platform
that espoused liberal-democratic principles. The management of the
war with Armenia figured prominently in the campaign, and Elchibey
met an unexpectedly stiff challenge from Nizami Suleymanov, an ally
of former Azerbaijan Communist strongman Gaidar Aliyev.[164] Shortly
after the election Azerbaijan mounted a large-scale offensive against
Armenian emplacements.[165]

Although Elchibey ran on a democratic platform, the war with Armenia and domestic conflict have increasingly made the organs of coercion a law unto themselves. About the time of Elchibey's election
Iskandar Hamidov became minister of interior. In that capacity Hamidov instigated acts of violence against journalists whose writings he
disliked. Despite protests from newspaper editors and members of the
government, Elchibey proved incapable of disciplining the security
chief. The attacks were hushed up and Hamidov was promoted to the
rank of two-star general, partly on the strength of his military accomplishments in the struggle over Nagorno-Karabakh. In 1993, setbacks
in the conflict over the enclave prompted Elchibey to attempt to disarm
a group of Azerbaijani irregulars that was allegedly responsible. Charging Elchibey himself with mishandling the war, the irregulars resisted
the presidential order, and the military high command refused to support Elchibey, prompting him to flee Baku. The parliament then turned
to its recently elected head, Aliyev, former chief of the Azerbaijani
Communist Party and the republican KGB, to lead the country.[166] The
episode illustrates the difficulty of attempting political liberalization
under conditions that both strengthen the organs of coercion and make
the government liable to charges of betraying the nation.

Armenia, Azerbaijan's main opponent in the war, has faced a similar challenge. Armenia started the post-Soviet era with reasonably democratic institutions. The legislature elected in 1990 includes a spectrum of political parties and movements, and Levon Ter-Petrossyan, chairman of the Armenian National Movement, was elected president in an election that outside observers believe was basically fair.[167] Like the government leadership of Azerbaijan, Ter-Petrossyan has come under political fire for failing to bring the war over Nagorno-Karabakh to a victorious conclusion. The Armenian Revolutionary Party, which has a long history and strong roots in the large Armenian diaspora, has attacked Ter-Petrossyan for allegedly failing to build up the professional armed forces and undercutting the country's military potential.[168] However, this conflict has remained a political dispute, bitter though it is, and none of the sides has resorted to violence to resolve the disagreement. Due partly to memories of the Turkish genocide, Armenian public support for the war has been stronger than public support in Azerbaijan, and during 1992 the tide of war moved in Armenia's favor. The Armenian public's relatively democratic values have probably also reduced the likelihood of a violent overthrow of the established government.[169]

As elsewhere in the former Soviet Union, developments in the states of the southern tier hinge not only on the stratagems of political leaders and elites but on the society's underlying political culture. In the southern region this variable appears to take on added importance in view of the suggestion by some prominent observers – vigorously disputed by others – that Muslim cultures are incompatible with, or at least inhospitable to, democracy.[170] In the post-Soviet countries, one of the several conceptual difficulties entailed by this sweeping proposition is whether societies emerging from more than seven decades of atheistic propaganda and aggressively secular education may accurately be described as "Muslim."

The results of public opinion surveys do not establish a specific relationship between belief in Islam per se and adherence to democratic or antidemocratic values. What they often do suggest is that the population of Central Asia is traditionally more conservative and respectful of authority. In 1990 a survey of Soviet citizens of various national origins found that on a composite index of democratic values, Estonians (the only Baltic group sampled) far outstripped the Belarusians, Ukrainians, and Russians, who in turn far outdistanced the Kazakhs and other Central Asians. Of the Estonian respondents, 98 percent qualified as strong or moderate supporters of democratic values. Among the various Slavic nationalities, the corresponding figure ranged from 61 to 74 percent. However, for ethnic Kazakhs the percentage dropped to only 30 percent, and among other Central Asians, such as the Uzbeks and

Turkmen, to a mere 17 percent.[171] Part of the explanation is that the Central Asians as a group were less educated and more rural – two intervening variables that are generally associated with a nondemocratic outlook. Even after controlling for these factors, however, researchers found that ethnic identity, which for some Central Asian respondents included adherence to Islam as one component, had a strong impact on political attitudes – almost twice as strong as the effect of educational level, and considerably stronger than that of age.[172]

Compared with respondents from other areas, Central Asian respondents also generally tended to show more deference to authority and a considerably milder inclination to lay the blame for socioeconomic hardships on specific political leaders and institutions. In 1990, for example, 50 percent of Kazakhs and 60 percent of other ethnic Central Asians expressed substantial confidence in various Soviet political institutions, compared with levels of 33 percent and lower for other ethnic groups.[173] At the start of 1992, a striking 86 percent of ethnic Uzbek respondents expressed strong confidence in President Karimov. This result may be partly due to respondents' prudence in answering questions about a government whose leaders are hostile to criticism, but that is not the whole story, because Karimov's approval rating among non-Uzbek residents of Uzbekistan was substantially lower.[174] These results may reflect greater Uzbek deference to authority. On the other hand, they may simply be a product of the non-Uzbek population's greater disenchantment with the new political order in Uzbekistan.

Other evidence challenges the notion that the Islamic component of Central Asian political cultures renders these societies incompatible with adherence to democratic values. The Tatar populations in the Crimea and in the Kazan region, whose adherence to Islamic traditions helped them to survive statelessness and dispersement at both tsarist and Soviet hands, exhibited a remarkably high level of activism and commitment to democratic values. In 1990 the share of Tatar respondents endorsing democratic principles was 77 percent, second only to the Estonians.[175] Since the Tatars were the tsarist empire's main Muslim advocates of reforming and adapting Islamic traditions to modern-day life, this suggests that certain strains of Islam may be more compatible with liberal political values, much as some strains of Christianity are more conducive to individualism and tolerance than are others.[176] Moreover, surveys conducted at the start of 1992 found a much smaller discrepancy between the political values of respondents in Uzbekistan and in European portions of the former USSR than had been indicated by previous polls.[177] Wherever democratic parties or institutions have been allowed by the regimes in Central Asia and Azerbaijan, they have been embraced by sizable numbers of Muslims, many of whom were prepared to risk physical harm protecting advances made. Demonstrations in support of democracy, and human rights abuses against activists supporting democratic transition, whether in Azerbaijan or in Central Asia, show the extent to which the lure of democracy has quickly established itself. Although there are antidemocratic features present in Central Asia as elsewhere among the new states, on balance the information available about the new states of the southern region suggests that analysts should be wary of assuming that widespread adherence to Islam necessarily constitutes an obstacle to these countries' development along a democratic path.

Conclusion

The political cultures of the former Soviet republics are in a state of tremendous flux. Marxism-Leninism has been thoroughly discredited and shown to have been an ideological screen for a multitude of political crimes and abuses perpetrated in the name of the Soviet state. Although the erosion of Marxist-Leninist ideology was well under way in the late Brezhnev years, the public dismantling of the ideology has had a profound impact on most of the inhabitants of the former Soviet Union. Deprived of an all-encompassing system of political and economic principles, they are searching for new political values in the experiences of foreign countries and in their own past. Reinforced by a profound socioeconomic upheaval, this situation has made the political cultures of Russia, Ukraine, and the other new states susceptible to a rate of change that is historically unusual and perhaps historically unique.

In several of the new states, some of the preconditions for the emergence of a full-fledged civil society are present. These include the existence of a governmental structure that allows for the public selection of legislators and the head of state through free, competitive elections. Most of the new states have experienced a dramatic increase in the number of societal groups eager to participate in the formulation of policy, foreign as well as domestic. To varying degrees, the media in the former Soviet republics have taken on a role in political life that is far more constructive than the part played by the media under Communism.

On the other hand; important preconditions for the creation of a durable civil society are missing from nearly all of the new states. Prominent among these is the existence of a system of strong political parties competing against one another on the basis of distinct and reasonably consistent political platforms. Equally important is the absence of a solidly entrenched system of private property and widespread public commitment to observe the laws adopted by the national legislature.

Nor are the media on a firm political and economic footing that ensures their independence.

Within these broad outlines, some of the new states have clearly moved much farther from the legacy of authoritarianism than have others. The degree of competition and fairness in elections has varied widely. So has the ability of Communist elites to maintain or reestablish their power in post-Soviet conditions. By mid-1993 all the new states were headed by former Communist officials except Belarus, Kyrgyzstan, Latvia, Armenia, and Estonia. The phenomenon of the "return of the Communists" does not have identical implications in all countries. Clearly it is a much more serious obstacle to democratization in Central Asia than, say, in Lithuania. Much depends on whether the Communists in question were among the advocates of genuine reform in the era of perestroika and whether the changes in the rules of the political game have made a return to authoritarianism politically risky or impossible. Under the latter conditions, Communist elites, particularly regional and local elites, may plunge into democratic politics in an effort to retain their hold on power and may ultimately be coopted into the democratic political process.[178] Under less propitious circumstances, such as those in much of Central Asia, Communist elites are likely to fight to reverse the process of democratization rather than adapt to it.

In all the countries the legitimacy of particular governmental institutions has been vigorously and sometimes fiercely debated. This is especially true of the legislatures elected in the twilight of Soviet power. Attacking them as vestiges of Communism that are inherently undemocratic, critics have demanded that they be dissolved and that new legislative elections be held. As shown above, the critics' charges are well founded in some cases, but wide of the mark in others. In many new states such accusations have become standard tools in running battles over the future political order. At one time or another these battles have tempted almost all the participants to try to resolve political stalemates through the use of force. Even in Russia, Ukraine, and several other states of the western region where legislatures and their rivals in the executive branch have thus far drawn back form violence and have concentrated on political means of competition, the temptation to use force is great. To the extent that the political collisions among these contending groups produce a "democratic escalation," in the form of public referendums and stepped-up timetables for new elections, the slow institutionalization of such practices may gradually decrease the probability of attempts to decide disputes by force.

In some cases, political confrontations have already led to the large-scale use of violence. Among the factors that have contributed to this are the willingness of leaders to resort to force, the political balance within the country and inside the organs of coercion, the attitudes of the public, and especially preexisting military conflicts with a secessionist movement or with another state. Although indigenous causes can fully explain the authoritarian path of a Turkmenistan or an Uzbekistan, a country's involvement in large-scale military conflict strongly increases the temptation to resort to force in the central domestic political arena as well. It often creates a useful pretext, as in Azerbaijan, and it also creates some of the key actors, as with the rise of free-lance militias in Azerbaijan and Georgia. Although it is too early to be certain, the absence of a large professional military establishment may contribute to such a turn of events at least as often as the presence of powerful professional forces. Militias have no ethos of noninvolvement in civilian politics, in contrast with large segments of the former Soviet military establishment in Russia, Ukraine, and Belarus, strained though that ethos may be. More important, militias have little to lose institutionally from civil war, whereas a violent conflict that shatters the armed forces goes directly against the institutional interests of professional military officers.

The volatile domestic politics of the new states are certain to affect their external relations. In some cases it may make individual countries' foreign policies unpredictable and/or self-contradictory. To the degree that civil societies take firm root in the new states, those states are likely to behave more cooperatively toward each other and toward other countries. This will hold true particularly for Western democracies, with which the new democratic states would have a close political affinity. Conversely, a sharp turn toward authoritarian political values and practices is likely to exacerbate tensions among the new states and in their relations with the democratic members of the international community. Such a turn would probably produce significant changes in Western military policies and reduce if not eliminate Western economic support for the economic revitalization of the former republics of the USSR. By the same token, a shift toward authoritarianism might improve relations with political dictatorships such as China and might contribute to a reorientation of strategy for the economic reconstruction of the new states.

Economic trends will strongly affect the new states' prospects for democratization or a return to authoritarianism. Successful privatization of a substantial proportion of the national economy can contribute to the creation of components of a genuine civil society, especially if it is associated with a palpable improvement of the standard of living. The persisting public adherence to notions of "positive constitutional rights" indicates that in order to survive, democratic governments in the new states must produce a sense of economic improvement. The results of the Russian referendum indicate that the public may be willing to wait some time for such an improvement, but the strong public identification of democracy with economic well-being means that the public will not wait interminably. At a minimum, citizens must be given a plausible reason to believe that the economic situation is starting to improve, even if there is a long way to go. In times of upheaval, the public's perception of trends may be more important than its perception of absolute levels.

5

The Impact of Economics

Just as many social theorists believe that liberal democracies are less likely than authoritarian regimes to initiate wars against other states, many observers believe that a developed market economy and a high degree of international economic integration make countries less prone to resort to military force, domestically and externally.[1] In the countries of the former Soviet Union, this proposition may receive a serious test.

The post-Soviet states inherited relatively high levels of economic interdependence that made them far more reliant on each other for trade than on the outside world.[2] However, the Soviet era has also bequeathed a legacy of animosity that has caused some of the new states to pursue the objective of complete independence, especially from Russia, the country they perceive as most responsible for the political and economic damage done during the Soviet period. For their part, most Russians view their neighbors as economic burdens for which Russia has sacrificed its own economic health for decades.

Operating alongside this mutual animosity, however, is the equal, or greater, desire by the populations of these new countries for economic security, which outranks military security as a source of public concern.[3] The task facing all these countries, therefore, is to develop their economies by transforming economic dependency and national enmities into normal international economic relations with the other new states and the outside world. In this way, economic interaction may potentially serve as a vehicle both for economic recovery within the new states and for ethnic and national peace among all the states of Eurasia. However, given the economic crises in the new states, the hostility of some leaders to economic reform, and the growth of interethnic and international conflict, these objectives may be unrealizable for the foreseeable future.

Because many outside observers regard the creation of democratic polities and market economies as a potential source of international stability in Eurasia, Western governments have placed such changes high among their objectives for the region. However, a cloud of uncertainty still surrounds the questions of how these two goals can be achieved and whether or not they are mutually compatible with one another. Economic hardships, which have been exacerbated by efforts at market reform, may provoke political instability that will undercut efforts to create a democratic order. By the same token, the absence of a stable democratic system may deprive policy-makers of the authority needed to implement economic reforms. Although the existence of free markets and democracy may indeed increase the prospects for international concord, the transitional effects of marketization and democratization are uncertain and potentially dangerous.

What is certain is that economic developments will profoundly affect relations among the post-Soviet states and the other countries of Eurasia. The distribution of economic benefits and hardships – a central issue in any political system – is especially critical in countries experiencing the combined turmoil of falling economic output and attempted economic transformation. As a major determinant of domestic political alignments, economic issues help shape the coalitions that support or oppose particular foreign policies. Moreover, economic crises can result in social unrest and a turnover of political elites that may scuttle an established foreign policy agenda. Alternatively, leaders may try to deflect domestic discontent onto foreign as well as domestic scapegoats. All of these foreign policy effects are likely to be manifested in the volatile international politics of the new states.

The condition of the new states' economies will influence their external relations in other ways as well. Economic performance will constrain the amount of resources that each government can expend in the pursuit of foreign policy goals, and it also will shape those goals in more subtle ways. In times of economic crisis, a government's economic choices entail sharp trade-offs between domestic and foreign policy objectives. However, domestic turmoil and the inexperience of policy-makers may prevent these trade-offs from being properly weighed, or even from being perceived as trade-offs at all. De facto policy trade-offs of this sort can produce international consequences that may be all the more profound for being unintended. One important question, therefore, is whether policy-makers in Russia and the other post-Soviet states can gradually develop a clear understanding of the foreign policy trade-offs confronting them.

The collapse of the Soviet system has also left many thorny international economic issues that the new states must address, no matter what their policy toward economic reform. One problem is the division of the assets previously owned by the Soviet central government, including not only industrial enterprises and physical facilities but also vital natural resources and important financial assets. The tendency has been for each new state to claim the physical facilities and resources on its territory, and for Russia to acquire the lion's share of other assets, but some of these matters remain to be resolved. Meanwhile, the new states, prompted by foreign creditors, have had to confront the question of their individual responsibilities for servicing and paying off the USSR's $70–80 billion in foreign debts. Although earlier efforts to solve this problem encountered many setbacks, by November 1992 it appeared that common ground had been reached. By agreement, Russia assumed full responsibility for the external Soviet debt in exchange for the shares of external assets and foreign debt repayments that had previously been proportionally allotted to each new state following the USSR's collapse.[4]

In addition, the new governments must also resolve disputes over each state's rights to ship goods via transportation routes and pipelines that traverse the territory of other former republics, as well as disputes over the charges that the countries transited are entitled to levy these goods. This issue is central in the energy field, where virtually every state except Russia depends upon energy imports and is transited by oil and gas produced elsewhere. Conflicts arise, therefore, between the wish to charge world prices in hard currency for one's own energy exports and for transit fees, on the one hand, and the desire to pay for energy imports at subsidized ruble rates on the other. The map of energy resources and pipelines illustrates this basic energy and infrastructural interdependence. In tracing the interaction between foreign policy and economic change, it is necessary to keep in mind the impact of such sectoral issues as well as the broader effects of economic reform.

Russia

In January 1992, President Yeltsin, realizing the need for macroeconomic stabilization, gambled on a strategy of complete and rapid transformation to a market economy. Yegor Gaidar, who subsequently became acting prime minister of Russia, was chosen by Yeltsin to implement this strategy. Popularly known as shock therapy, it was designed to boost economic performance in the shortest possible time through stabilization of the money supply, privatization of property and enterprises, and liberalization of the laws governing economic activity. Advocates saw this approach as the quickest way to move to a free-market system, and they favored using subsidies only to provide a minimal safety net for persons in dire need. Price controls were indeed lifted on most producer and consumer goods. Budget restraints were advocated that would have reduced, then eliminated, subsidies on inefficient enterprises and would have led to widescale bankruptcies and

Energy resources and pipelines

mass unemployment. Some Western economists estimated that if the "hard budget constraints" proposed had been applied, 90 percent of enterprises and 60 percent of banks would have gone bankrupt.[5] Alongside the lifting of price controls and the cutting of subsidies, a new tax system and measures to liberalize foreign trade were also announced.

This strategy had the backing of Westernizers and liberals within the Russian elite. It was also supported by some Western economists and officials within the U.S. government, and by economic agencies such as the World Bank and the European Bank for Reconstruction and Development (EBRD).[6] Several other former Soviet republics hesitantly followed Russia's lead in economic reform, but their lack of enthusiasm caused their economic policy to move in fits and starts. Inside Russia itself, the concept of shock therapy, not surprisingly, became the focal point of intense political conflict.

Although Western specialists are divided over the potential effectiveness of shock therapy, most observers agree that Russia's attempts to implement such a strategy in 1991–2 failed to achieve the strategy's main goals with respect to economic performance.[7] Measured by the decline of net material product (NMP) produced, Russian economic output had already diminished by 4 percent in 1990 and 11 percent in 1991.[8] In 1992 the physical size of the economy shrank even further, losing approximately 20 percent of national income and industrial production, as indicated in Table 5.1. This trend continued into 1993. Soaring prices and the collapse of money also accompanied this decline. By one reckoning, the wholesale price index of industrial enterprises in 1992 was 2,049 percent of 1991 prices, with barter accounting for an estimated one-half of all trade in the first half of 1992.[9] During 1992 exports dropped by 16 percent, and imports fell by 15 percent.[10]

More telling, however, was the Gaidar team's inability to achieve its main economic goals of cutting state expenditures and capping inflation. The refusal of the Congress of People's Deputies, with its influential factions of ex-Communist regional bosses and industrial managers, to pass budgets that curtailed subsidization of inefficient state-owned industries under its control, and its related decisions to order the Russian Central Bank, which it also controlled, to print more money to pay for these subsidies, fueled inflation. With inflation at 20 percent a month and central bank interest rates at a mere 20 percent per year, it is not surprising that enterprise directors found that massive borrowing was the surest hedge against bankruptcy.

The Gaidar team's attempt to block these moves set off a bruising political battle between the advocates and opponents of shock therapy that lasted for the remainder of 1992, and resulted ultimately in the Congress' refusal to confirm Gaidar as prime minister in December.

Table 5.1. *Basic socioeconomic statistics of former Soviet republics for
1992 (as a percentage of 1991 totals)*

Country	GDP	Net material product	Gross industrial production	Consumer goods production	Wholesale price index of industrial output
Azerbaijan	75	72	76	76	1,400
Armenia	66	57	47	46	1,047
Belarus	87	89	90	79	2,465
Estonia	—	—	61	—	1,103
Georgia	—	—	—	—	—
Kazakhstan	85	86	85	79	2,469
Kyrgyzstan	89	74	73	64	1,764
Latvia	56	—	65	—	788
Lithuania	39	—	48	—	1,077
Moldova	74	79	78	84	1,311
Russia	81	80	81	85	2,049
Tajikistan	66	69	76	72	1,423
Turkmenistan	90	85	83	86	1,094
Uzbekistan	80	87	94	91	2,500
Ukraine	86	85	91	91	2,500

Sources: Delovoy mir (Moscow), 2 March 1993, in *FBIS-USR*, 21 April
1993, 5; *Kaubaleht* (Tallinn), no. 4, 12–19 February 1993, in *FBIS-
USR*, 14 May 1993, 97; *RFE/RL Daily Reports*; *RFE/RL Research
Reports*; *Plan Econ Report*, 9, nos. 19–21 (10 June 1993); *Argumenty i
fakty*, no. 34 (August 1993), 3.

The ranks of his opponents included many directors of major state
enterprises, who feared – often correctly – that shock therapy's fiscal
objectives would create high risks of bankruptcy and large-scale unemployment at their enterprises. These directors found a voice in Civic
Union, a centrist coalition led by Arkadiy Volskiy and others, which
espoused a slower transition to a privatized, market economy.[11]

The mobilization of the opponents of shock therapy undercut the
government's efforts to pursue a coherent economic strategy. In June
1992 the contingent of radical reformers within the government was
diluted by the appointment of several new deputy prime ministers
opposed to shock therapy.[12] Moreover, despite repeated attempts, Gaidar and his reform allies failed to gain control of the Russian Central

Bank, which remained under the authority of the Russian parliament and its speaker, Ruslan Khasbulatov. Although in the spring of 1992 the Gaidar team managed to limit the issuance of new state credits, this achievement proved transitory.[13] After a three-month political deadlock over control of state credit policy, the bank's chairman resigned and was replaced with Viktor Gerashchenko. In July and August Gerashchenko dealt the Gaidar reform effort a major blow by granting state enterprises 1 trillion rubles in Central Bank credits. State enterprises had previously been granting each other loans in efforts to avoid bankruptcy. This situation had produced an extremely high level of indebtedness and fragility within the interenterprise system, so that if one enterprise went bankrupt, it could bring down dozens of others that might otherwise have been able to survive. The granting of credits from the Central Bank was, therefore, designed to strengthen the interenterprise system, but also contributed to high inflation. These and virtually all other efforts by Gaidar to slash the state's deficit spending were derailed by political resistance.[14] By September 1992 the monthly inflation rate had risen to about 20 percent, where it remained with some month-to-month fluctuation through mid-1993.[15]

These events opened a new chapter in the struggle between the advocates of shock therapy and their political opponents. In September 1992 Yeltsin appeared to take an uncompromising stance in this dispute, when he criticized the "cheap credits and unrealistic social programs" favored by Gaidar's critics. At the same time, Yeltsin doubled the price of Russian oil, thereby moving partway toward a controversial, long-standing demand of the IMF.[16] However, as political resistance continued to mount, Yeltsin took a new tack. In November 1992, as the convocation of the Congress of People's Deputies drew near, Yeltsin showed signs of searching for an accommodation with Volskiy and the other centrists of the Civic Union. News reports indicated that Yeltsin was exploring a deal that would keep the Gaidar team in office but fundamentally alter the government's economic strategy. In the end, this political maneuver failed, and Gaidar was replaced as prime minister by the more conservative Viktor Chernomyrdin, who attempted to reimpose price controls on certain items.

The radical reformers' failure to win full control of economic policy in December 1992 allowed the conservatives to state that they had protected the country from some of the traumas of shock therapy. At the same time, however, it became clear in 1993 that the conservatives had no policies that would diminish inflation rates, resolve economic uncertainty within both Russia and the CIS, or increase confidence in Russia within international agencies such as the IMF.[17] During the first half of 1993 efforts to gain control of the money supply largely failed.

The Russian Central Bank, still under the Congress's control, continued to accommodate demands for credit, and the budget deficit climbed to 25 percent of the Gross Domestic Product (GDP). One of the commitments that the Russian government had undertaken in order to qualify for the disbursement of $1.5 billion from the IMF was to reduce the country's budget deficit to only 10 percent of GDP. The inability of the government to reduce subsidies and increase revenues put the relationship with the IMF at risk.

In early 1993 the promotion of two radical reformers, Boris Fyodorov and Anatoliy Chubais, to the positions of deputy prime ministers in charge of finance and privatization restored the emphasis on market-oriented reform. Trends toward privatization increased, with as many as six thousand of the country's largest enterprises preparing privatization plans that would give 51 percent controlling shares to the managers and workers. The April referendum, which unexpectedly gave President Yeltsin a 52 percent vote in favor of his "socioeconomic policies," was claimed to reflect the population's general acceptance of the policy of privatization and the movement to a market economy. By mid-1993, there were 950,000 private businesses, associations, and joint stock companies, of which approximately 60,000 were totally private shops, restaurants, and enterprises. A quarter of the nation's labor force was employed in these new forms of enterprises, and they were responsible for producing one-third of the country's total output in mid-1993.[18] This shift of economic activity began to have political consequences, as individuals and groups having a stake in privatization organized to counter those within the Congress who were trying to impede shock therapy. In June 1993, proponents of privatization established, under the leadership of Yegor Gaidar, the All-Russia Association of Privatizing and Private Enterprises, with the avowed purpose of forming a "capitalists' lobby" to pressure the Congress and speed up privatization.[19]

Another major trend in 1993 was the continuing disintegration and the emerging regionalization of the Russian economy. There are eighty-seven oblasts, okrugs, krais, and republics within Russia, each on average about the same size and population as Estonia.[20] Although their economic progress was clearly dependent upon the overall stabilization of the Russian economy, many of these regions began to pursue policies independent of the center, seeking local improvements in economic well-being that had the potential to contribute to, or undermine, overall economic success.[21] Often overriding federal laws and edicts they dislike, the leaders of regions and autonomous republics have emerged as major actors in the country's domestic and external affairs. Areas such as Tatarstan, Bashkortostan, Sakha (Yakutia), Chechnya, and Karelia moved forward with their own plans to issue local currencies and levy taxes. They have challenged Moscow's right to control economic activity in their regions. Some have set up trade and tariff controls; others have established links with foreign investors that are often completely independent of the center. Virtually all the twenty-one republics and many of the provinces within Russia have claimed sovereignty and some degree of control over their natural resources, and all are eager to establish economic links abroad to shore up their own economies and minimize the extent of central direction in their economic lives.[22]

This trend, which has produced some notable economic successes in Nizhniy Novgorod and other areas, also has exacerbated the general decline in the authority of the center and deprived Moscow of both power and revenues. Politically, this has been reflected in the establishment of the Council of the Federation, which comprises local representatives and which was chosen by Yeltsin as the forum for debating his new draft constitution, thereby reflecting Yeltsin's decision to embrace decentralization and genuine federalism as a means of breaking the power of the Congress of People's Deputies. In 1992 and 1993, the bypassing of central economic authority produced a situation in which trillions of rubles escaped central taxation and, as acknowledged by the head of Russia's state taxation service, companies engaged in foreign trade failed to pay some $10 billion due in taxes in 1992.[23] The increased unwillingness of the regions to contribute to central government revenues led Deputy Prime Minister Boris Fyodorov to state that Russia's relations with Tatarstan concerned him more than Russia's relations with Ukraine. He has warned that efforts to withhold revenues were totally unacceptable and would produce "major upheavals ahead."[24] The declining ability of central authorities to gather taxes (which in mid-1993 led to the hiring of 1,500 crack airborne troops to provide "physical security" for tax collectors[25]) meant that they lacked sufficient funds for capital investment, social security and other programs, including, of course, defense.

The difficulty of gaining revenues to maintain the military and security services led to the emergence of private or local militias and produced many speeches by interior-ministry and military officials about the need to safeguard the power of the state.[26] It also threatened to throw the military and security services behind the conservative forces striving to recentralize the economy. Continuing economic pressures made the military more aware of the need to finance its own activities through authorized and unauthorized arms sales, loan-service personnel arrangements, and agreements with local separatist leaders in regions outside Russia, such as trans-Dniester and Abkhazia, for the provisioning of Russian troops on their soil.[27]

Other military and foreign policy issues have been deeply affected by the downward economic spiral. The worsening condition of the economy has sharpened Russian interest in negotiated – or at any rate, parallel – arms reductions with the United States and other Western powers. By the same token, however, it has given persons employed in military research and development (R&D) and defense production, who number about 7 million people out of a total Russian labor force of 72.3 million, an added stimulus to find ways to protect their jobs.[28] They can do this either through converting their industries to civilian use – a process that has thus far produced more failures than successes – or they can continue to produce military output, but primarily for export.[29] Table 5.2 indicates the extent to which the Russian economy emerged out of the USSR as particularly dependent on military-industrial production. In 1991 Russia accounted for 61 percent of the total Soviet economic activity in terms of GNP;[30] yet every statistic in Table 5.2 shows that more than 61 percent of military-industrial enterprises, capital stock, R&D expenditures and number of employees came from Russia.

One in ten workers throughout the country, therefore, has been involved in military production, providing an enormous pressure group for the continuation and increase of arms sales. The struggle to rescue the economy has caused radical economic reformers – whose political liberalism might ordinarily predispose them against Russian arms exports – to champion weapons exports as a means of earning desperately needed hard currency, including money to fund conversion of military plants to civilian use. The liberal temptation to support large-scale arms exports may be all the stronger if such exports help reformers surmount the intense resistance of military industrialists to radical economic reform at home. The center's need for hard currency is matched by the regions' efforts to prevent the bankruptcy of what was previously their most lucrative source of revenue. Although it may seem paradoxical, the dynamics of the economic crisis may have broadened the support for the military-industrial complex on this specific issue, and although arms sales abroad declined in 1992, support for them can be expected to continue.[31] That the basic foreign policy concept paper presented by the foreign ministry in March 1993 for parliamentary approval accepted "the possibility of friction [with the West] on specific questions in areas where Russian enterprises prove competitive (space, arms export and others)" indicates the broad support for Russia's role as a major arms trader.[32]

Table 5.2. *The defense complex of the former USSR and of Russia*

Category	Soviet total	Russian total	Percent of Soviet total
Number of military-industrial enterprises and institutions			
1. Production associations and enterprises	1,327	888	67.0
2. R&D institutions and scientific-production associations	969	714	73.6
3. Others	71	33	46.5
4. Total	2,367	1,635	69.0
Value of capital stock invested in defense sector (millions of rubles)			
5. In industry only	153,173	107,911	70.4
6. In R&D	33,058	29,128	88.1
7. Total	186,231	137,039	73.6
Annual expenditures on research and development (millions of rubles)			
8. National output	32,474	28,560	88.0
9. For defense programs only	17,958	16,215	90.2
No. of employees (in thousands)			
10. In defense industry	8,014	5,673	70.8
11. In military R&D	1,756	1,500	85.3
12. Combined 10 & 11	9,770	7,173	73.4

Source: Calculated from *Moscow News*, no. 9, 1992, 10; and Michael Checinski, *Military-Economic Implications of Conversion of the Post-Soviet Arms Industry*, Research Paper No. 75, The Marjorie Mayrock Center for Soviet and East European Research, The Hebrew University of Jerusalem, Winter 1992, 3.

Russia's economic policies have a major impact on the economies of the countries of the "near abroad." Two policies in particular deserve analysis: Russia's attitude toward the ruble zone, and energy policy. The move to introduce shock therapy in January 1992 was taken with little regard for the preferences of the other new states. At the same time, however, Russian elites appeared unenthusiastic about proposals to abolish the ruble zone, even though the ruble credits issued by the other new states' central banks created an enormous additional obstacle to efforts to implement an effective economic strategy inside Russia. Moreover, as much as 10 percent of the ruble credits issued by the Russian Central Bank went to the non-Russian states in 1992.[33]

During the first half of 1992 Russia devoted considerable political energy to ultimately unsuccessful attempts to coordinate and regulate the monetary policies of CIS member states.[34] The movement away from the ruble zone, therefore, was seen by many Russian and Western economists as necessary to curb the fiscal crisis in Russia. Some Russian politicians hesitated to dismantle the ruble zone, in part perhaps because they regarded it as an important symbol of Russia's great-power standing and one of the last remnants of Russia's imperial greatness.[35] In the eyes of some Russians, the ruble zone contains the seeds of the ultimate political reconstitution of the Soviet empire. However, others, including President Yeltsin, came to understand that the monetary vestiges of the Soviet empire carry a very high price tag for Russia itself.[36] In mid-1992, Pyotr Aven, then minister of foreign economic relations, advocated either establishing the monetary authority of the Russian government throughout the ruble zone or forcing other CIS members to introduce their own currencies.[37] The gradual introduction of national currencies, a process indicated in Table 5.3, continued despite the pleas of Gerashchenko for the other CIS states to remain in the ruble zone.[38]

The greatest shock to the stability of monetary relations among the new states occurred in July 1993, when the Russian Central Bank announced that Soviet and Russian banknotes issued before 1992 would be taken out of circulation or deposited in savings banks and could only be transferred to new rubles after six inflation-ridden months. Although the decree was subsequently softened, that no prior warning of the move had been given to other countries within the ruble zone hastened the determination of many leaders to leave it. Those leaders who announced their willingness to stay within the zone despite the catastrophic economic situation created by the de facto attempt of the Russian Central Bank to confiscate or cancel their bank holdings left themselves open to charges of personal collusion and corruption.[39]

Having long benefited from access to cheap supplies of Russian energy, most of the other new states are dependent on Russian energy, as indicated by Table 5.4. They are also highly sensitive to the price Russia charges for its oil and gas, as a rapid shift to world prices would impose a very heavy burden on their economies.[40] As President Yeltsin has stated, Russia is moving toward the use of world prices in its trade with other republics, but some major products have continued to be sold at prices below world levels.[41] According to the chairman of the

Table 5.3. *Introduction of national currency units in the former Soviet republics*

Country	Currency unit	Date of introduction
Armenia	Russian ruble	Plans to introduce the dram as the national currency were announced on 25 March 1992
Azerbaijan	Manat	15 June 1993. On 15 August 1992, Azerbaijan placed the manat in parallel circulation with the Russian ruble
Belarus	Russian ruble and Belarusian zaichik are in parallel circulation	25 May 1992
Estonia	Kroon	20 June 1992
Georgia	Georgian coupon	2 August 1993. The Georgian coupon is a temporary currency. Plans to introduce the lari as the national currency were reaffirmed
Kazakhstan	Russian ruble	Plans to introduce the tenge as the national currency were announced in July 1993
Kyrgyzstan	Som	10 May 1993
Latvia	Lats	5 March 1993. On 7 May 1992, Latvia placed the rublis in parallel circulation with the Russian ruble, and made it the sole currency on 20 July 1992
Lithuania	Litas	On 28 April 1992, Lithuania placed the talonas in parallel circulation with the Russian ruble, and replaced the provisional talonas with the litas in July 1993

Table 5.3. (*continued*)

Country	Currency unit	Date of introduction
Moldova	Moldovan coupon and Russian ruble are in parallel circulation	10 June 1992. Plans to introduce the leu were announced in July 1993
Russia	Ruble	In July 1993 Russia announced it would gradually withdraw all pre-1993 rubles
Tajikistan	Russian ruble	
Turkmenistan	Russian ruble	Plans to introduce the manat as the national currency by October 1993 were announced in July 1993
Ukraine	Karbovanets	The karbovanets was introduced on 12 November 1992 as a temporary currency, and is expected to be replaced eventually by the hryvnya
Uzbekistan	Russian ruble	Plans to introduce a national currency were announced on 3 June 1992

Sources: New Times (Moscow), no. 48 (November 1992), 20; *FBIS* reports; *RFE/RL Research Reports.*

Russian Oil Industry Committee, states in the ruble zone in mid-1993 were paying roughly one-half of the world price for Russian crude oil and one-third of the world price for Russian gas. This meant that in 1992 Russia was subsidizing other members of the CIS to the tune of some $15 billion.[42]

Russia's pricing policy reflected its interest both in promoting stability in the former republics and in continuing to use energy as a lever of political influence. As Table 5.5 indicates, oil and gas production in the new states, although not expanding, has not been as badly affected as other sectors of these economies. Together with national variations in energy reserves, these figures indicate that, given stability and in-

Table 5.4. *Energy imported from Russia as a percentage of consumption*

Country	Natural gas	Crude oil
Armenia	0	*
Azerbaijan	0	14
Belarus	100	91
Estonia	100	*
Georgia	27	82
Kazakhstan	0	0
Kyrgyzstan	0	*
Latvia	100	*
Lithuania	100	94
Moldova	100	*
Tajikistan	0	*
Turkmenistan	0	16
Ukraine	56	89
Uzbekistan	0	55

*These countries have no oil refineries and import refined oil products, primarily from Russia.

Note: All the new states of the former USSR – with the exceptions of Turkmenistan, Russia, Kazakhstan, and Azerbaijan – in 1990 had a ratio of indigenous energy production to consumption less than 100.

Sources: Mikhail Korchemkin, University of Pennsylvania; *PlanEcon*; *U.S. News and World Report*, 19 July 1993, 45; Jeffrey W. Schneider, "Republic Energy Sectors and Inter-State Dependencies of the Commonwealth of Independent States and Georgia," Joint Economic Committee, Congress of the United States, *The Former Soviet Union in Transition*, Washington, D.C.: U.S.G.P.O., 1993, 480–4.

vestment, energy production could serve as a catalyst for the growth of several of the new states. The beneficiaries of such a policy could include Russia, Azerbaijan, Kazakhstan, and Turkmenistan, and even Kyrgyzstan, which is already a net exporter of hydroelectric power. On the other hand, a number of countries such as Armenia, Ukraine, Moldova, Georgia, Belarus, and the Baltic states, have much less potential in the energy sector. In these countries, dependence on imported – mainly Russian – energy supplies is likely to remain high, and to exert a strong influence on bilateral relations with Moscow. Even in these cases, the production asymmetries favoring Russia do not eliminate the political and economic incentives for Russia to engage in regional energy cooperation. Inasmuch as Russia's oil and gas deliveries

Table 5.5. *1992 production of fuel and energy resources by CIS principal extracting states (as percentage of 1991 totals)*

Country	Petroleum, incl. gas condensate	Gas	Coal
Azerbaijan	95	91	—
Kazakhstan	97	103	97
Russia	86	99.6	95
Turkmenistan	96	71	—
Uzbekistan	116	102	79
Ukraine	91	86	97

Source: Delovoy mir (Moscow), 2 March 1993, in *FBIS-USR*, 21 April 1993, 12. Overall, CIS petroleum extraction dropped 14% from 1991 totals, which themselves were 10% lower than 1990 levels. Gas extraction remained at virtually the same level from 1990 to 1991, but fell 3% in 1992. Coal extraction fell by 10% in 1991, and by an additional 5% in 1992.

to Europe and to the outside world have to traverse the territories of some of these countries, Russia also has an interest in maintaining a stable relation in the energy sector with these states. In the final analysis, however, the absolute dependence of these economies on Russian energy cannot be overemphasized, thereby giving Moscow a powerful lever for influencing their actions.

The prospects for energy cooperation among the new states will be influenced by broader international trends such as the move toward developing a European Energy Charter that gained momentum in the summer of 1993. If created, the charter will provide both a legal and regulatory framework for the entire area from the Atlantic to the Pacific, as well as short-term subsidies from the G-7 states for non-Russian CIS members to cushion the increase to world price levels. Moves such as this offer the best hope for creating regional stability of supply and integration of the former Soviet energy sector into the world market.[43]

The Western Newly Independent States

Second in economic and political importance only to Russia, Ukraine illustrates the non-Russian states' difficulty in reconciling a drive for complete sovereignty with the high level of economic interdependence inherited from the Soviet regime. In 1988 Ukraine relied on the other republics to purchase approximately 39 percent of its NMP produced and to supply approximately 37 percent of NMP used, including energy imports obtained from Russia at a fraction of the world price.[44] Nonetheless, Ukraine entered the era of political independence with high hopes of reducing its economic reliance on Russia and integrating itself into the world economy. The various recipes for reorienting the national economy involved a major expansion of exports to Western markets, particularly markets for agricultural goods, large infusions of Western aid, and over the longer term, membership in the European Community.[45] The country's initial period of independence, however, has cast doubt on the feasibility of all these economic ideas.

Since 1991, Ukrainian economic strategy has consisted of two major schools of thought. Initially, the first school, supported by the most ardent nationalists and some of their allies among the former Communists, dominated Ukrainian policy-making. This school has maintained that political independence and economic reform can be safeguarded only if Ukraine uncouples itself economically from Russia. Proponents of this view have argued that Russia could use close economic relations as an instrument to reinstate its political hegemony, that Ukraine could be exposed unwillingly to negative economic side effects from other former republics (as happened after Russia's January 1992 decision to decontrol most prices), and that Ukraine should not tie its economic fate to Russia's because of the ethnic turmoil that might ensue if that strategy should fail. A competing school of thought, supported by such leaders as former first deputy prime minister Volodymyr Lanovyi, former Ukrainian presidential candidate V. Grinyov, and sections of the New Ukraine movement, has maintained that rapid market reform is essential for Ukraine's long-term international survival and that a rational economic strategy must include continued commerce with Russia.[46]

The story of Ukrainian economic strategy since 1991 is largely a chronicle of the struggle of the exponents of the first school of thought against recalcitrant economic realities. Although the Ukrainian economy is fairly well developed in terms of its sectoral structure, by world standards most sectors have fundamental economic and technological deficiencies that invalidate many of the economic nostrums proposed at the dawn of political independence.[47] During Ukraine's first nine or ten months of independence the political elite pursued a conservative approach to domestic issues and resisted most of Russia's efforts to coordinate monetary policy through the CIS framework.[48] Gradually, however, the Ukrainian political leadership was forced to recognize that competing in world markets is entirely different from operating inside the protected Soviet market and that economic relations with the West cannot be substituted for fundamental economic reforms or for the maintenance of economic ties with Russia.

In the meantime, the economy has been battered by an accelerating decline. After contractions of 3.6 percent in 1990 and 11.2 percent in 1991, net material product dropped by 15 percent in 1992. This figure would have been larger had it not been for the continued production of industrial goods for which there were no customers. In 1992 the process of contraction, which in previous years affected primarily investment goods, strongly affected consumers. The rate of inflation rose to between 30 and 40 percent per month, significantly higher than the rate in Russia. As a result, prices for consumer goods in February 1993 were 1,305 percent of the prices for the same goods in February 1992. This was the highest rate of inflation recorded in any of the new states.[49] While Ukrainian heavy industry produced unmarketable goods, output of food products declined 13.5 percent in 1991, 15.6 percent in 1992, and at an annual rate of 15.2 percent in the first quarter of 1993.[50]

President Kravchuk and his political allies were initially reluctant to acknowledge the seriousness of the domestic economic crisis. In March 1992, Kravchuk paid lip service to the idea of fundamental economic reforms and even appointed a first deputy prime minister, Volodymyr Lanovyi, who was committed to rapid marketization and privatization. In retrospect, however, the appointment of Lanovyi appears to have been part of a political maneuver intended to buttress Kravchuk's domestic political position. Within a few months, Kravchuk fired Lanovyi and installed a far more conservative politician, Valentin Symonenko, in his place. After his appointment, Symonenko endorsed the notion of an incremental strategy combining the reduction of budget deficits with the reintroduction of wage and price controls throughout the economy.[51] Symonenko's efforts to justify this approach included the assertion that ordinary Ukrainians were not culturally prepared for radical reform.[52]

As in Russia, the issue of public support for reform was not as simple as it might first have appeared. Popular dissatisfaction with the mounting economic difficulties was not focused solely on reform as the source of hardship. Many citizens of Ukraine believed that the downward economic spiral was due at least partly to the government's halfhearted measures and the absence of genuine economic reform. The segments of Ukrainian society that have favored market reforms from the beginning have included the relatively small group of genuine entrepreneurs and a sizable component of the younger generation who understand that their long-term interests are best served by economic liberalization. The proreform coalition has also encompassed some high-level politicians and intellectuals, particularly those associated with the New Ukraine movement led by Volodymyr Filenko.

In October 1992, mounting political and economic pressures forced a change of government and imparted at least some momentum to the previously stalled proposals for serious economic reform. Early in the month an upsurge of dissatisfaction in the Supreme Soviet forced Prime Minister Vitold Fokin and the entire cabinet to resign. Chosen to succeed him was Leonid Kuchma, the head of a major rocket-manufacturing enterprise whose local political base was primarily in eastern Ukraine and who assembled a coalition of reform-minded parliamentarians from the Rukh movement's liberal wing and from the New Ukraine movement.

Although Kuchma's abilities as an economic manager seemed strong, his contradictory statements showed little understanding of the basics of economic policy. On the one hand, he praised the Chinese economic model, thereby implying a belief in a distinctly authoritarian approach to economic reform, and stated that the economic emergency militated against the dismantling of Ukraine's collective farms. However, Kuchma also endorsed liberal economic principles, and his operational approach to monetary and foreign economic policy has been comparatively enlightened. He called for tight budget and wage controls, for an end to enterprise subsidies, and for a swifter pace of economic privatization. In addition, he tried to suspend the ruble within Ukraine by making the possession of rubles by individuals illegal and by declaring that the ruble would be replaced with a temporary currency, known informally as the karbovanets, until conditions become favorable for the introduction of the hryvnya as Ukraine's permanent currency. This step met resistance from traders, who had even less confidence in the value of the karbovanets than in the ruble, and consequently the ruble effectively stayed in circulation. Meanwhile the government did nothing to shore up the value of their new currency; the number of karbovanets in circulation jumped from 383 billion in October 1992 to 1.048 trillion in February 1993, fed mainly by the massive credits granted to uneconomical state enterprises. As a result, the government's deficit, according to Western estimates, jumped to almost 30 percent of GDP.[53]

Kuchma did move to mend fences with Russia by reaching an agreement on the division of foreign debt and restoring the sort of Ukrainian-Russian barter trade, such as the Donbas region's provision of machinery in exchange for coal from mines in the Kuzbas region, that Fokin had blocked.[54] Perhaps most important, Kuchma extracted wide-ranging emergency powers from the legislature for a period of six months. The emergency powers gave him control of Ukraine's Central

Bank, and with it the potential to introduce and enforce strict monetary discipline.

His failure to use these emergency powers to good effect, however, produced a crisis in mid-1993 in which Kravchuk demanded his resignation. Inflation was rampant, the Ukrainian currency had less value than the ruble, industrial production was plummeting, and relations with Russia on key debt and energy issues were very tense.

The disagreement with Russia centered on the inability of Ukraine to pay its formidable and growing debt to Russia. As Table 5.6 indicates, in mid-1992 Ukraine was the largest single debtor to Russia. While Russia was dependent on Ukraine for some items, this was overshadowed by Ukraine's overwhelming dependency on Russian energy. Energy was a sore spot because it is a hard-currency good already provided to Kiev at prices substantially below world levels. Ukraine's incurring of massive debts for energy provided even at reduced rates, therefore, caused enormous tension in the two countries' relations. By mid-1993, Russian officials unilaterally stated that henceforth they would provide oil and gas to Ukraine at world market prices, for hard currency only, and that this price policy would take effect retroactively to cover all energy supplied to Ukraine since 1 April 1993. This meant that Ukraine's debt to Moscow, which Moscow already calculated as amounting to 2.5 billion dollars (Table 5.6 indicates that 159.3 billion rubles of debt had been accumulated by mid-1992), was going to increase massively. Although Ukraine could counter dependence on Russia by increasing its importation of gas from Turkmenistan, the Turkmens were also moving the price of their gas toward the world market prices that Ukraine was unable to afford. In addition, Russia continued to cut energy supplies to Ukraine, with officials reporting that Russian supplies were down by one half during the first six months of 1993 compared to the same period in 1992.[55] Ukraine likewise suffered from rapidly falling natural gas production and electric energy capacity, which in turn threatened the ability of the country's energy-intensive heavy industries to maintain output levels.

Many Ukrainians have begun to realize that the country would not be able to weather the disruption of energy supplies without a drastic decline in living standards and an excruciating restructuring of the economy. This realization has produced pressure in the more russophone eastern part of the country to improve relations with Russia. In January 1993, during the discussions among CIS members of the possibility of strengthening the commonwealth, representatives of several Ukrainian political parties convened in the eastern city of Donetsk to protest against the government's threats to leave the CIS. Attacking the government for following an isolationist policy that had "already

Table 5.6. *Indebtedness of former Soviet
republics to Russia through mid-1992 (in billions
of rubles)*

Country	Amount
Ukraine	159.3
Kazakhstan	46.7
Belarus	22.0
Turkmenistan	18.1
Azerbaijan	15.9
Uzbekistan	13.9
Georgia	11.3
Lithuania	9.0
Moldova	4.6
Kyrgyzstan	4.5
Tajikistan	3.7
Estonia	3.7
Armenia	2.3
Latvia	1.4

Source: Nina Plekina, "Their Cotton, Our Oil,"
New Times (Moscow), no. 48 (November 1992),
20.

driven the country into a blind alley," the gathering asserted that the cost of living was now two or three times as high as in Russia or Kazakhstan and warned that withdrawal from the CIS would lead to "mass poverty and destruction" in Ukraine.[56] An extensive miners' strike in the Donbas region in summer 1993 voiced similar concerns, and ended only when the government promised massive subsidization of living standards in the region.

To the north of Ukraine, the political leadership of Belarus has rhetorically proclaimed an independent-minded approach to economic reform. In actuality, Belarus has as many intractable economic difficulties as Ukraine. In mid-1992, Supreme Soviet chairman Shushkevich proclaimed that "we have decided in principle that we are moving toward a market economy, but we are not doing it in the way our western and eastern, or northern and southern, neighbors do. We have decided that we will have a Belarusian way,... using our Belarusian intellectual power."[57] Shushkevich held out "South Korea's economic miracle" as the model Belarus should follow in its economic reforms. In the same breath, however, he called for "a sensible, comprehensive and detailed five-year plan of development providing for annual targets and policy corrections."[58] Although these contradictory pronouncements suggest considerable intellectual confusion, in Belarus there is a greater elite consensus over broad economic strategy than there is in Russia, Ukraine, and some of the other new states. If sustained over time, this consensus will make Belarus a concrete test of the feasibility of carrying out a slow but deliberate move from a centrally planned to a mixed market economy.

The outlook for the economy is nevertheless bleak. During 1992 net material product fell by 11 percent, industrial production declined by 10 percent, and the volume of commodities traded shrank by 26 percent, while the wholesale price index for industrial goods jumped to 2,465 percent of 1991 levels.[59] Moreover, even though the grain harvest in 1992 was 15 percent higher than in 1991, Minsk was forced to declare a "state of emergency" in agriculture and buy essential supplies from Kazakhstan, Russia, and elsewhere.[60] The emergency was caused by the government's misguided attempt to keep food prices far below those in Russia and Ukraine. In August 1992 the government tripled the prices, but by that time a large share of Belarusian agricultural output had been exported to Ukraine and Russia by middlemen. An additional financial burden has been imposed by the necessity of grappling with the legacy of Chernobyl. According to a Belarusian official, Belarus's political independence means that it will have to foot the bill for the continued Chernobyl cleanup, estimated to be 16 billion rubles for 1992 alone.[61]

Coupled with these economic pressures, Minsk's high level of economic dependence and the low level of support for ethnic separateness have led the Belarusian government to adopt an international economic approach that is more cooperative and less confrontational than, say, the approach initially adopted by Ukraine. Before the collapse of the USSR, Belarus's level of economic dependence on other Soviet republics exceeded the levels of nearly all other republics. In 1988 Minsk shipped 69.5 percent of NMP produced to other republics, and it counted on the others to supply 64.2 percent of the NMP used.[62] This pattern of trade explains why Vladimir Zalomay, Belarusian state secretary for CIS affairs, stated that Belarus intends to make "maximum use of CIS structures" in order to stabilize and reform the economy. It also explains why Belarus promoted the idea of establishing a Slavic economic union of Belarus, Ukraine, and Russia when the Central Asian states appeared in the summer of 1993 to be moving toward the Middle Eastern and South Asian-oriented Economic Cooperation Organization.[63]

Almost all the potential answers to Belarus's economic vulnerability involve cooperation with neighboring states, thus dictating a significant part of Minsk's foreign policy. In March 1992 Supreme Soviet chairman Shushkevich and Prime Minister Vyacheslau Kebich wrote a plea to Yeltsin complaining about critical shortfalls in supplies of raw materials and energy supplies from Russia.[64] Economic pressures of this kind prompted the government to explore several alternative policies. It simultaneously sought to negotiate better terms with Russia, to import oil through pipelines in Latvia, to find suppliers in the Middle East (such as Saudi Arabia and Kuwait), to establish an oil port at the Polish port of Gdansk, and to link up with a prospective Baltic natural-gas market that would supply gas from Norway.[65] Together with Russia's subsequent price increases for oil, energy shortfalls have even led Belarusian officials to consider turning to nuclear power, although painful public memories of Chernobyl have thus far blocked this option.[66]

Given its dire economic situation, Belarus has been among the most enthusiastic supporters of closer economic integration with other states of the former USSR – both through bilateral arrangements and through closer CIS ties. In March 1993, Prime Minister Kebich proposed an economic "confederation" with Russia and heartily endorsed closer economic integration among CIS member-states. Belarus, he noted, "cannot exist alone without close cooperation with [Russia, Ukraine, and Kazakhstan]."[67] Moreover, Minsk's primary emphasis has been placed on relations with Russia. As Kebich has acknowledged, "it is not Russia that needs Belarus . . . it is we who need Russia."[68] At the same time, like Russia, Belarus seeks to meet IMF conditions to qualify for the nearly $100 million in promised IMF credits, conditions that include Belarusian imposition of strict monetary restraints and the curtailment of government credits to enterprises that are not economical.

The economic situation in Moldova is critical. As stated by Moldova's deputy prime minister in November 1992: "Drought and civil strife have sucked away up to 80 percent of Moldova's national income; the country's reserves are completely exhausted."[69] The GDP declined 25 percent in 1992 over 1991 levels, and by some reports the civil war and the drought cost the country 80 billion rubles in 1992 out of a total GDP of 100 billion rubles. The country's net material product declined 20 percent in the first half of 1993 compared with the same period of 1992; agricultural output fell by 36 percent. Unemployment rates in cities reached 50 percent by the end of the year, making most of the labor force available for recruitment into local militias and gangs run by organized crime. The former KGB chief in Moldova claimed publicly that the entire economy was controlled by Mafia-like organizations. Although his statement was not meant to apply to the trans-Dniester, the high numbers of KGB and OMON officers who have flocked to the self-proclaimed "Dniester republic" to establish smuggling routes, including many who were literally on the run from criminal prosecution in the Baltic states, have given this area's economy a particularly lawless character. For example, the minister of security of the "Dniester republic," when asked about his plan to stabilize the country, replied that "to stabilize the situation in the country it is necessary to knock a certain number of people out of circulation."[70] Nevertheless, the IMF acted in July 1993 to move forward with a credit scheme to help ease Moldova's transition to a market economy.

Of all the non-Russian countries of the former Soviet Union, Western analysts believe that Estonia, Latvia, and Lithuania probably enjoy the best long-term economic prospects. Like Belarus, the three Baltic states all have economies that are highly dependent on trade with components of the former USSR, and all suffered painful economic downturns and increased inflation after reestablishing their independence.[71] In the near future, these hardships are likely to continue and perhaps worsen, partly as a result of changes in the Baltic countries' terms of trade with other CIS members, particularly Russia.[72] Over the long run, however, the Baltic countries have favorable prospects for diversifying their economic ties and making a successful transition to capitalism. Geographically and institutionally, they are better positioned than the other new states to carry out economic reforms and build profitable economies. To a large extent the Baltic states see themselves as stepping-stones between Russia and Europe, and favorable transportation routes should enable them to function as economic go-betweens linking Europe with Eurasia. In particular, Finland, Sweden, Denmark, and Germany have demonstrated an active interest in developing strong commercial relations with the three Baltic countries. Estonia has been the most successful in establishing trading relations, and remarkably, has succeeded in reorienting its trade away from Russia in just one year. Thus 21 percent of Estonian exports were to Finland in 1992, compared with 20 percent to Russia.[73] Trade relations have been bolstered by the greater fiscal stability in the Baltic states, due partly to the fact that the gold reserves that the Baltic states deposited in the Swiss-based Bank of International Settlements prior to 1940 have remained intact and can now be used to support their currencies. It is also a reflection of the Baltics' role as a smuggling route for goods out of Russia – and as a stable avenue into Russia for Western companies that have chosen to headquarter their business operations in the more comfortable, safe, and stable Baltic capitals rather than in Moscow or other regional cities.[74]

The Baltic states have also taken the lead in economic reform. All three countries have unusually high levels of commercial entrepreneurship and a long-standing legal tradition that has assisted steps to construct an effective market economy. In the late 1980s, when cooperative businesses became legal in the USSR, the Baltics and the Caucasian republics accounted for a disproportionately large number of the new enterprises that were formed. Privatization programs have been significant throughout the Baltic region. In addition, because the three countries are small, the modest amounts of outside aid provided can have a larger economic effect, and for political and cultural reasons the three are likely to receive a disproportionate share of the Western aid that becomes available.

Estonia was the first former Soviet republic to leave the ruble zone and establish its own currency, tied to the Deutschmark and under-written by a $40 million loan from the IMF and a $30 million credit line from the World Bank. Latvia followed in late 1992, and succeeded in bringing its monthly inflation rate down from 67 percent in January 1992 to only 4.2 percent in January 1993.[75] Lithuania, which was far more dependent on Russia (64 percent of Lithuanian imports were from Russia, compared with 28 percent of Estonian imports, for example[76]) hesitated and remained essentially within the ruble zone, suffering a double shock of imported inflation and declining energy supplies.[77] Consequently it finished 1992 in the worst shape of the three Baltic republics, suffering an annual inflation rate of 1,100 percent and a GNP only 39 percent of 1991 levels. This trend continued into 1993, with production levels continuing to drop; by June, Lithuania's industries worked at only 52 percent of capacity.[78]

Apart from short-term economic hardships, the main threat to the Baltics' long-term economic transformation lies in Russia. Although to a certain degree the Baltics benefit from being Russia's "Hong Kong," because the three are small and highly dependent on foreign trade, they are also more sensitive to economic disruption in Russia and to economic pressure as Russia seeks to shape the bargaining over the withdrawal of Russian troops stationed in the region and the treatment of the Russian inhabitants residing there. The Baltic states' policies toward the reform and/or privatization of local factories that belonged to the Soviet military-industrial complex are a case in point. These large fac-tories were built by the Soviets and were manned overwhelmingly by Russians. Withdrawal of subsidization has been favored by the gov-ernments of these countries as a way of moving toward marketization in general, but such a move has been resisted both by these firms' Russian employees and by the Russian government.

Although especially acute in the Baltics, this kind of conflict is present in many of the other new states where Russian factory workers pre-dominate. Marketization could lead to the bankruptcy of a number of these firms and to unusually high rates of unemployment among ethnic Russian employees, who are heavily represented in the work forces of these plants. According to the Bank of Estonia, 75 percent of Estonia's large enterprises are insolvent, and enterprise debts have been increasing due to ruble inflation and to Russia's general cessation of payments for goods shipped to it.[79] The fate of such defense enterprises will probably entail special negotiations with Russia and may require special treatment in the economic reform plans of the Baltic governments.

The Southern Newly Independent States

Most of the countries of Central Asia face an even more difficult economic future than do the new states of the western region. In the Soviet era, Moscow's policy toward the Central Asian republics called for them to specialize in a few primary sectors, notably cotton growing, and to import industrial equipment and other inputs from the European and Siberian portions of the empire. This policy has inflicted a high price on the region in both economic and health terms. Chemical fertilizers have been applied in massive doses that have polluted water and lands and caused severe health problems among the inhabitants of the region. Water supplies have been used profligately, destroying the Aral Sea and causing injurious salination of a vast tract of contiguous farmland.[80] In per capita terms, the Central Asian states are the poorest countries of the former Soviet Union. The countries of the region are yoked together by a single water system and a common electrical grid, which means that in periods of economic shortage the political conflicts over scarce resources are likely to be magnified.[81]

On the other hand, some elements of the current economic situation do favor the Central Asian countries. The agricultural situation in 1992 was not as bleak in Central Asia as it was in the rest of the former Soviet Union. All the Central Asian countries except Tajikistan reported an improvement in all main sectors of agriculture except meat production in 1992 over 1991. And while the GDP and national figures presented in Table 5.1 show a decline in all Central Asian countries equal to the decline elsewhere, these countries nevertheless have mineral and energy reserves that allow for a more optimistic long-term economic forecast. As shown in Table 5.4, none of the Central Asian states is dependent on Russian gas or (with the exception of Uzbekistan) crude oil. In particular, Turkmenistan and Kazakhstan have large deposits of oil and gas; if properly exploited, these resources could become the driving force behind broad-based economic development.[82]

Thus far, however, the Central Asian states as a group have made only modest progress in marketizing and privatizing their economies. Uzbekistan, for example, has professed a commitment to marketization and has been pushed in this direction by Russia's price liberalization;

nonetheless the Uzbek government has resisted such important components of the reform process as privatization and the elimination of state orders.[83] In their search for foreign models that they might emulate, several Central Asian states have focused on the authoritarian market systems of Asia – notably South Korea and China – but without privatization and other measures aimed at economic liberalization. Only Kyrgyzstan and Kazakhstan have moved toward privatization and only the former has introduced its own currency, a move that slowed the monthly inflation rate to less than 20 percent by mid-1993, compared with an average 30 percent rate in neighboring – and richer – Kazakhstan. None of the Central Asian regimes, however, has taken bold steps to introduce either Asian model of market reform, which in any case would be very difficult to emulate.[84]

Much of the Central Asian governments' attention has centered on foreign economic relations. Because the region's economies are basically more similar than not, the governments have looked farther afield for partners to help diversify their trade and provide foreign investment. Kazakhstan, for instance, has succeeded in reaching agreement with three major international petrochemical companies – Chevron, British Petroleum, and Agip – to develop the country's energy resources.[85] The country is also negotiating with American, South Korean, and several other national companies over joint ventures to mine industrial and precious metals.[86] The quest for diversified foreign economic ties has encompassed even the poorest and most Islamic-oriented among them, Tajikistan. Despite a sharp drop in the production of energy, food, and construction,[87] a Tajik presidential economic adviser, Rustam Mirzoyev, emphasized before the ouster of President Rakhman Nabiyev that Tajikistan wanted to open itself to the outside world. Having employed an American economic adviser, President Nabiyev traveled to Pakistan and Iran to finalize agreements for a half-billion-dollar-credit deal with Islamabad and a $50 million loan agreement with Tehran to complete the Rogun hydroelectric power station (which is slated to supply Iran with power).[88] Although this policy has not been renounced by Nabiyev's successors, the Tajik civil war has frightened off potential investors and demonstrated the close link between domestic political stability and expanded foreign commerce.

However, even if ultimately carried through to fruition, large-scale energy, mining, and infrastructure projects pose a serious limitation for the leaders of Central Asian governments. Major projects of this sort will require a long time to be completed, and in the meantime they will have no significant positive effect on the standard of living in Central Asia. The leaders of the region need benefits that will help compensate for the loss of legitimacy they have suffered as a result of the USSR's collapse, a loss that cannot be fully offset through gambits designed to appeal to local nationalist sentiment.[89]

This problem conceivably could exacerbate another consequence of reorienting foreign economic policy to attract foreign investors, namely, an imbalance between the domestic- and trade-oriented sectors of the economy. Some Central Asian states have already adopted laws that clearly favor the external sector. This policy has sparked complaints from opposition groups that Central Asia should not repeat the experience of some Third World countries, in which multinational corporations increased the scope of their projects without commensurate benefits to the rank-and-file citizens of the host country. Despite this concern, the governments have moved ahead with trade liberalization measures. For example, in the summer of 1992 Uzbekistan issued a decree lifting import taxes for one and a half years, exempting enterprises with foreign investments from income tax for the first five years of operation, and stipulating that foreign investors will have the right to buy factory facilities and housing, as well as the opportunity to take out long-term leases on plots of land.[90]

Like a number of other former Soviet republics, the new states of Central Asia have been overly optimistic in appraising the possibilities for rapid internationalization of their economies and for the rapid diversification of international partners. It is true that many countries have shown an interest in the region and that the Central Asian countries and Azerbaijan have joined the Economic Cooperation Organization designed to expand international commerce in the region.[91] However, as the first glow of independence dimmed, Central Asian leaders began to recognize that economic relations with Russia remain extremely important, especially for the immediate future. Expressing concern about the deterioration of Kazakhstan's economic relations with Russia and the rush to establish relations with other countries, President Nazarbayev asked:

> Why have we stopped trusting one another and now show more confidence in the West? After all we had a common history, we had good mutual relations. I very much want the reforms in Russia to succeed and would like every one in Russia to look at these difficulties with understanding because our economies are strongly interwoven and they depend on the position and the victory of the reform in Russia.[92]

Central Asia's close economic links with Russia are reflected in the fact that most Central Asian leaders have opted to remain within the ruble zone even after Russia imposed restraints on the ruble supply in mid-1993; Kazakhstan in particular has continued to press for economic integration with Russia and other CIS states.[93] The risk of relying too heavily on trade ties with Russia is that if these ties are maintained for other than mutually beneficial economic reasons, they are likely to perpetuate the overspecialization and sectoral disproportions that have kept Central Asia in a semicolonial economic status for more than a century.

For this reason, over the longer term the new states of the region may seek to move away from their close economic relationship with Russia. Not only will they expand their economic relationships with the wealthy countries of the Middle East and some of the dynamic capitalist economies of Asia; they also are likely to experience a large increase in financial and trade relations with China. In contrast to the bleak economic situation in Russia, the Chinese economy is growing at any extraordinarily rapid rate and is likely to continue to do so. China enjoys one of the highest domestic savings rates in the world, and its entrepreneurs may wish to diversify their economic risks by investing abroad. Unless disrupted by a major internal political upheaval, the Chinese economy could become a source of vital trade and investment for the new Central Asian states.

This scenario is rendered even more plausible by China's demonstrated interest in supporting Communist parties in Mongolia and other parts of Asia. No doubt one motive for this sort of assistance is the Chinese oligarchy's fear of geopolitical isolation stemming from the demise of Communism in other parts of the globe. China may therefore be eager to help stabilize and expand those Central Asian regimes that, although nominally democratic, retain many political features of Communist systems. By 1993 it had already become the major non-CIS trading partner of several Central Asian states. A major economic realignment of Central Asia, however, could strain relations between Russia and China. Under conditions of tension between the two great powers, it could also become a source of serious internal friction within the Central Asian states, especially in countries such as Kazakhstan and Kyrgyzstan, where ethnic Russians constitute a substantial proportion of the population.

Like the rest of the Soviet successor-states, the Caucasian states of Georgia, Armenia, and Azerbaijan were battered by the chaos unleashed by the Soviet breakup. The disruption of traditional trading links with Russia and the other former Soviet republics, coupled with the severe catapult in prices following liberalization, proved economically crippling. What has set the countries of the Caucasus apart, however, and what has transformed their economic hardship into collapse, has been the war of attrition in each of the states. Augmented by the strains and stresses of price liberalization and disrupted trade, the socioeconomic burden of war has devastated the economies of the three countries. Faced with plummeting living standards, spiraling inflation, and mounting political instability – all in the midst of unrelenting war – the leaders of the three countries have found their foreign policy capabilities and options far more limited than they would otherwise be prepared to accept.

The bitter war with Azerbaijan over Nagorno-Karabakh has proven disastrous to Armenia. In 1992, its GNP fell nearly 40 percent, national income declined 42 percent to equal the level attained in 1975, and industrial and agricultural production fell to levels attained in 1971 and 1976, respectively.[94] The human and economic costs of the conflict have been heightened by Armenia's landlocked location, wedged as it is among states ranging from unsympathetic to hostile. Given its dire economic straits, the crippling economic blockade imposed by Azerbaijan, and the fact that it is dependent on imports for 96 percent of its energy needs, the government of President Levon Ter-Petrossyan concluded that Armenia must promote privatization and reach out to its neighbors as the only realistic means of overcoming its perilous situation. Erevan's most controversial initiative has been its attempted rapprochement with Turkey. The Azerbaijani closing of a pipeline supplying 80 percent of Armenia's gas has forced Erevan into precarious dependence on a single pipeline – which has been routinely sabotaged – running through an Azerbaijani-populated region of Georgia.[95] Armenian discussions with Turkey have yielded limited results; a Turkish decision to supply Armenia with electricity was reversed following an intense domestic and Azerbaijani backlash. Turkey briefly allowed humanitarian shipments of food and fuel to transit its territory to Armenia, but terminated the relief operation following Armenian offensives in western Azerbaijan in April 1993.[96]

Armenian relations with Russia, Georgia, and Iran have also been affected by the economic crisis. Relations with Georgia have fallen sharply due largely to Armenian suspicions that Tbilisi has tilted toward Baku in the Karabakh struggle and conspired with Azerbaijan's gas blockade of Armenia. Despite a growing perception in Erevan that Moscow has limited its aid in order to balance its southern diplomacy, Russia remains the preeminent force in the Armenian economy.[97] Erevan's acute dependence on Russia for ruble credits and assistance has provided Moscow with a significant lever for its Caucasian diplomacy.

The Georgian economy has been shattered by secessionist conflicts in Abkhazia and South Ossetia. Industrial production in 1992 plummeted 67 percent from the 1990 level, inflation ran at some 50 percent a month, and unemployment was an estimated 20 percent. The secessionist conflicts, augmented by the political instability that plagued Georgia throughout much of 1992 and 1993, have blocked the influx of foreign aid and investments that Georgian officials doubtless expected after the accession of former Soviet foreign minister Eduard Shevard-nadze to power in March 1992. Rather, the country was by 1993 running a 70 percent budget deficit, with the war in Abkhazia alone estimated to be costing the country 50 million rubles per day.[98] Instead of capitalizing on Shevardnadze's international prestige and on privatization measures to shift its foreign economic relations westward, Georgia has been forced to remain tethered to Russia, on which it depends for energy supplies and trade in industrial goods. Although Georgia adamantly refused to join the CIS and withdrew from the ruble zone in July 1993, the acute economic crisis has forced it to remain dependent on a state, Russia, which it accuses of aiding the Abkhazian secessionist forces. Shevardnadze, for one, has cautioned that whatever difficulties emerge in Russo-Georgian relations, Tbilisi's national interests mandate good relations with Moscow. "If we break our links with Russia," he has warned, "our economy will come to a halt."[99]

Although Azerbaijan appears not to face as troubling an economic future as either Armenia or Georgia, economic factors will likely continue to influence its foreign policy choices. The bloodless seizure of power by the pro-Turkish, anti-Russian Azerbaijani Popular Front (APF) in May 1992 and the election of its head, Abdulfaz Elchibey, as president in June sparked rumors of a complete Azerbaijani break with the CIS countries and a concurrent realignment with its Middle Eastern neighbors. By the fall of 1992, however, Azerbaijan's economic situation had compelled it to conclude a series of economic and trade agreements with Russia. As deputy parliamentary chairman Tamerlane Karayev explained, "economics have made us partners for centuries."[100] Although GNP fell by some 20 percent in 1992, Azerbaijani prime minister Rahim Huseynov noted signs of stabilization emerging at the end of 1992, and predicted that Baku would achieve overall economic growth for 1993. That 60 percent of CIS oil and gas field equipment, including the newest CIS technology, is manufactured in Baku gives Azerbaijan the potential for strong economic relations with Russia and the rest of the CIS.[101] However, this potential did not prevent the government from collapsing in June 1993, and the debilitating war with Armenia continued to impose a heavy toll on the Azerbaijani economy and limit its foreign policy options.

Economic relations with Central Asia, Turkey, and Iran have come more naturally, due to shared ethno-linguistic and religious ties, for Azerbaijan than for Armenia and Georgia. President Elchibey attempted to reorient Baku's economic relations toward these countries; instead of purchasing grain from Canada, for example, he suggested importing it from Kazakhstan. He also endorsed the idea of forming a community of Central Asian states that would encompass Azerbaijan.[102] Partly for

economic reasons, the APF shelved its oft-cited irredentist claims to
northern Iran and signed a number of bilateral economic and trade
accords with the Iranian government.[103]
Convinced that both the West and Moscow have tilted toward Armenia, Azerbaijan has sought to increase its economic links with the
Turkic world for political and military, as well as economic, reasons.
In November 1992, Baku joined in the creation of a loose "Turkic
Common Market" formed in Ankara and consisting of Turkey, Kazakhstan, Uzbekistan, Turkmenistan, and Kyrgyzstan.[104] On the same
visit, Elchibey received a $250 million credit line from Turkey, with
assurances that another $250 million in credits would soon be issued.[105]
Political considerations, however, cut both ways in the relationship with
Turkey. For example, in November 1992 Foreign Minister Tofik Ga-
symov called Ankara's decision to supply Armenia with electricity "a
stab in the back of Azerbaijan." Turkish officials hastily called off the
deal and reassured the Azerbaijanis that "Azerbaijan has a priority
position in Turkish foreign policy."[106]

Conclusion

It has correctly been observed that "taking the Russian trunk out of
the tree of the former Soviet economy would leave the branches and
roots in a perilous state."[107] For most of the period since 1991, Russia,
because of its size, relative wealth, and tradition, has set the pace of
economic interaction and reform among the post-Soviet states. In the
other states the strength of the domestic forces favoring rapid marketization and privatization has varied widely. The level of political support has ranged from strongly committed countries such as Estonia and
Armenia, through less committed countries like Kyrgyzstan and Belarus, to uncommitted countries such as Ukraine and Turkmenistan.
Nevertheless, by virtue of Russia's sheer economic weight, the economic
course that Russia follows will have a profound impact, as a necessary
but not sufficient condition, on the success of radical economic reform
in most other post-Soviet states. That Russia, with all its resources,
was unable to avoid taking harsh Western advice for monetary stabilization, liberalization, and privatization also had a significant effect on
the other new states.
    This does not signify that a small country such as Estonia could not,
with extensive Western support, break loose and reorient itself completely toward the world economy. Western governments, however,
command neither the economic resources nor the domestic political
consensus necessary to finance the reform process in the larger former
Soviet republics. Although the West can assist the new states' reform

Conclusion 193

efforts, the economic outcomes will ultimately depend on developments in Russia and on the skill and political stamina exhibited by the governments of the countries themselves.

For advocates of fundamental economic reform, the central political challenge appears to be whether governments in democratizing countries can sustain the traumatic and protracted process of economic change. Given that the most authoritarian post-Soviet governments have shown the least inclination to undertake marketizing reforms, the experience of the new states raises serious doubts about the feasibility of achieving economic reform through political authoritarianism. Although this strategy has succeeded in countries like South Korea or Chile, many of the postsocialist countries lack the pool of skilled entrepreneurs, the banking and legal institutions, and the prior experience with markets that have allowed other capitalist – but authoritarian – countries to implement such an approach. Whether a democratic approach to economic reform will prove significantly more effective remains uncertain.

Although the initial efforts in Russia and some other countries to implement shock therapy failed to attain their main objectives, a good deal has been revealed about the requirements of a successful transformation process. First, although much political resistance has been generated, major political movements in most of the former republics appear to agree on the principal goal: creation of a modern, mixed, private-enterprise economy. The major disagreement is over the pace and sequence of reform. Second, many observers now realize that macroeconomic stabilization is impossible without the full support of the state's central bank. This lesson has been impressed on a number of policy-makers as a result of the harsh experience of Russia and Ukraine, although whether the post-Soviet governments can muster the strength to exercise the necessary control over budgetary and credit policy is uncertain. Third, a number of policy-makers now realize that Russia must either obtain close collaboration in economic policy from the members of the CIS or go it alone. That is, the central banks and the government budgets of all the interdependent states must be coordinated for economic stabilization to succeed, or, alternatively, Russia itself will be obliged to dismantle the ruble zone. Fourth, few if any major figures in the new states expect the Western powers, the IMF, the World Bank, the EBRD, or any other international agency to pave the way with dollars. At the same time, a general acceptance of the need and desirability of foreign involvement and partnership has marked the transition process. The internationalization of the former Soviet space has deeply undermined, though not eliminated, the impulse toward autarky. Fifth, the new states are beginning to realize that they must cooperate to achieve the solution to basic problems, particularly in meeting energy needs. Sixth, many leaders in the post-Chernobyl former Soviet Union recognize that economic development cannot be achieved at the cost of environmental destruction. Although the temptation to cut corners is still great, the populations and media of these countries have mobilized in an effort to safeguard public health and the environment.

At least as much as the military policies of the new states, the results of these economic struggles will have a profound effect on the shape of the international politics of Eurasia. Given the high level of interdependence among the post-Soviet economies, economic exchange and economic resources offer a powerful source of political leverage. Not only Russia, but such states as Georgia and Azerbaijan have attempted, with widely varying degrees of subtlety, to manipulate their economic ties with other new states for political advantage. The tendency of several countries to rely on economic tools in relations with other new states has been strengthened not only by a reluctance to initiate interstate war but by the perilous condition of the new national military establishments, which have been demoralized by economic cutbacks as well as by the confusion of loyalties generated by the breakdown of the old Soviet order.

In short, the economic upheaval in the new states of Eurasia will have pervasive effects on their external relations, even though the precise nature of those effects is difficult to predict. It remains to be seen whether, having declared their sovereignty, the new non-Russian states will make a successful transition from limited to full-fledged independence, or whether continuing economic reliance on Russia will produce a variety of political dependency resembling the phenomenon of European neocolonialism in the postcolonial Third World. In any case, the post-Soviet economic upheaval will play a pivotal role in shaping the relations of all the new states with established regional and global powers. No more striking case could be found to illustrate the common adage that domestic and foreign policies are inextricably linked, or to underscore the maxim that politics and economics cannot be separated. In an era when volcanic economic forces have been set in motion in the territories of the former Soviet Union, a new generation of national policymakers must work with these truths in mind.

6

Foreign Policy Priorities and Institutions

Decision-making never occurs in a vacuum. In stable democracies, foreign policy is the end result of a process by which historical memories, contemporary pressures, and domestic political life are sorted out and turned into policy. The interests upon which a state's leaders forge foreign policy are subject to differing interpretations and misinterpretations in even the calmest of environments: The turbulence gripping the new states of the former Soviet Union has further complicated this critical task.

Struggling to define their nations' interests, to build new institutions out of a contested past, in an environment where effective regional security structures do not exist, the leaders of the new states face almost insurmountable difficulties. They have often been forced to make foreign-policy decisions before a clear consensus on national priorities has been reached. These decisions, in turn, have had an impact on the political elites in neighboring states, who also have been taking only the first tentative steps on the international stage. For any state making the transition to independence, there are enormous pressures on its new leaders, groups, and institutions. When not just one but fifteen states are simultaneously making choices that will affect the region's total decision-making environment, the potential for a downward spiral of misperception, misinformation, and mistrust is considerable.

This potential is increased because of the fragility of the new institutions at the apex of the state structures. The leaders in all the new states have moved to assert their control over foreign policy and have often done little to overcome the widespread inexperience and lack of resources of the ministries of foreign affairs. Even in a country such as Russia, where the new Ministry of Foreign Affairs (MFA) has established a strong institutional basis and has the confidence of its president, it has come under intense attack from other powerful institutions. New parliaments, opposition political parties and movements, and military-industrial establishments are just some of the institutional actors that have been promoting quite different foreign policies.

As the new parliaments and governments, including the foreign ministries, seek to mediate between diverse and sometimes conflicting policy objectives, societal groups on all sides, in a pattern typical of their role in a democracy, clamor to have their views taken into account in the formulation of policy. In a stable democracy, institutions not only withstand such pressure but are renewed by it. When the institutions are fragile, however, there is a risk that if pressures become too great, the institutions will collapse into the societies they seek to represent, ceasing to serve the function of aggregating diverse interests and instead becoming simply additional political actors representing their own narrow interests. In a strong democratic system, external actors interact with a country through the mediating role of the state. In particular, the leaders of a democracy enjoy the popular legitimacy that enables them to represent the national interest of the state in dealing with foreign countries. But when, as is the case in most of the new states of the former Soviet Union, there is no consensus on what "the national interest" is, and when, in addition, the leaders of the new states often lack the enthusiastic support of their populations, policies toward foreign countries can become pawns in domestic politics.

This is true, of course, not only of the newly independent states. In the United States, for example, trade with Japan became a salient domestic issue as the popularity of the Bush administration declined and the country's budget deficit grew. In Russia, some people's image of the United States as imperious and overbearing is at least as much a reflection of the decline in power of Russia's own leadership and the country's general crisis as it is of U.S. policies. In Ukraine, the leadership has had to balance the fact of the country's economic dependence on Russia against the negative image of Russia held by some core elites and sections of the population. The power of this negative image effectively deters Ukrainian leaders from making decisions that might be in Ukraine's short-term economic interest but would also significantly diminish the legitimacy of the leaders themselves. In Central Asia, leaders who scaled the career ladder as anti-Islamic Communists now must balance the popular pressure to improve relations with Islamic states and movements against the knowledge that, if an increase in relations with the Islamic world bolsters the positive image of Islam among the population, this might undermine their own authority. In this fashion, images of the external environment are filtered back into a society and form part of the domestic political debate. And this debate can have an especially significant impact on foreign policy when the institutions normally responsible for mediating between the domestic and external environments are weak.

With the breakup of the USSR, the new states' need to establish independent yet stable relationships among themselves has become the lens through which all other ties with the outside world are viewed. If in the Soviet era, the establishment of "good-neighborly relations" with countries on the Soviet periphery allowed Soviet foreign policy to range farther afield, the very absence of these relations makes it imperative for the leaders of the new states to put the management of regional politics at the top of the list of foreign policy priorities.

The management of regional politics has been made more difficult because so many of the countries that lie just beyond the boundaries of the former USSR are themselves under significant external and internal pressure. The countries of east-central and east-southern Europe seek the transformation of their economies and are braced against the spread of civil war from territory of the former Yugoslavia. Eager to join Europe, they can be seen as competitors with the post-Soviet states for Western aid, investment, and coveted membership in the European Community. Their leaders are torn between the recognition that economic collapse in the east could engulf their own economies and the impulse for tactical reasons to lobby against aid to the former Soviet states as a "lost cause" or "bottomless pit" in an effort to maximize their own short-term economic advantage.

To the south of the new states, Turkey, Iran, Afghanistan, Pakistan, and other countries in the Middle East and South Asia are intrigued by the prospect that Inner, South, and Southwest Asia may now have the opportunity for greater cooperation. However, none of these countries has shown an inclination to share in the massive financial effort necessary to reorient the economies of the former Soviet republics. Furthermore, as a group of countries, the nations along the new states' southern periphery are deeply divided and unlikely to form a unified bloc that could put together a political and financial package having the same result. The same is true of the countries to the east of the former Soviet Union – Japan, South Korea, Taiwan, and China – all of which have great economic potential, but none of which has shown an interest, for a variety of reasons, in making a large-scale investment in economic reform.

Given the narrow range of options, the number-one challenge facing all the countries of the former Soviet Union is not, therefore, whether or not to break with the other new states, but how to manage forced and reluctant interdependence among them. The success of each of their economies is held hostage to the success of all the others. Equally, the well-being of ethnic kinsmen living outside their own countries is dependent upon other governments' policies toward national minorities. The ability of each country to establish democracy and an effective economic system is thus affected by the success or failure of reform in the rest.

At the center of this web of interdependence is Russia, which arguably is in the best geopolitical position to offer leadership to the other new states. Russia has the most experienced diplomatic corps, the highest concentration of intellectual expertise about the outside world, and the most developed industrial and communications infrastructure. However, it is also the subject of special misgivings by the other new states and is itself beset by divisive internal debates about its own international role. More than any other factor, this dialectic between the need for a Russian renaissance and the fear of it shapes the debate between Russia and the new states.

Russia

In most of the countries of the former Soviet Union, the process of foreign policy-making lacks a firm institutional structure. New governments, ministries, legislatures, and leaders are only slowly establishing clear-cut institutional arrangements for foreign policy-making. This should have been less true in Russia than elsewhere, because as the inheritor of so many Soviet institutions and personnel, less time should have been needed for institutions to establish interests and priorities. Nevertheless, even in Russia the policy-making process has thus far been amorphous.

The difficulty for Russia is not so much that the country lacks institutions per se, but that with the collapse of Communism and the demise of the Soviet empire, the *raison d'être* of these institutions has also disappeared. Therefore, although Russia enjoys enormous advantages over all the other successor states in the numbers and level of training of its diplomats and officers, the effectiveness of these officials has been stymied because of the lack of direction and consensus over Russia's foreign policy priorities among the top leaders. One distinctive feature of the totalitarian model was the absence of independent mediating groups between the individual and the state. A key feature of post-totalitarian politics in Russia is the inability of most state institutions to formulate unified policies that reflect the stable long-term corporate interests of the state as distinct from more inchoate and transient, if strongly pluralist, popular inclinations – inclinations that have flourished with the help of the unprecedentedly free mass media. Because of the state's weakness and its inability to set a carefully calculated external policy, many of Russia's ancient dilemmas and motivations, ranging from pan-Slavic messianism to Slavophile isolationism, have an unusually large potential to shape Russian foreign relations.

These circumstances make it necessary to examine the broad outlines of the larger debate that has taken place since Gorbachev abandoned crucial elements of Marxism-Leninism and opened the Soviet Union to the West after 1986.[1] This leadership debate has mirrored and been influenced by the wider debate within Russian society as a whole, which has been discussed in Chapters 2–4. Once Russia was removed from the "road toward socialism," spokesmen for contending and frequently mutually exclusive outlooks were left to pursue an answer to a traditional Russian dilemma: What is Russia, and where is it going?

A major difficulty in analyzing the elite debate on Russia's foreign policy priorities is that differing views cannot accurately be equated with single institutions. Thus, for example, while the foreign ministry is frequently associated with the Atlanticist, pro-Western orientation of its foreign minister, Andrey Kozyrev, this equation does not capture the full range of opinions about priorities in the foreign ministry.[2] The same holds true for the views of Defense Minister Pavel Grachev and the Russian military establishment. Nor has the prestige of President Yeltsin remained high enough to allow him to impose his own foreign policy priorities "from above," as has remained the case in many of the other successor states. On sensitive issues such as relations with Japan, Yeltsin's long-standing affinity for a foreign and economic policy that would promote close interaction with Japan as one of the developed industrialized countries came under severe domestic pressure beginning in late summer 1992, when he was obliged to postpone his September trip to Tokyo. Yeltsin continued to be criticized whenever he tried to reschedule the trip throughout the following year (although he did attend the meeting of the leaders of the seven major industrial states [the G-7] in Tokyo in July 1993).

Later in this section the limits on Yeltsin's power and the effect of institutional policy differences on foreign policy will be considered. Before doing so, however, it is important to examine the various orientations toward foreign affairs that have emerged. One can identify broad and competing schools of thought about Russia and its future foreign policy direction that cut across institutions and that reflect broader alignments within society. One major intellectual current comes from individuals who want Russia to have an activist foreign policy, but not an expansionist one, and to interact with the other former Soviet states on the basis of equality, mutual recognition and respect, according to the maxim enunciated by Foreign Minister Andrey Kozyrev: "the better off my neighbor is, the better off I am."[3] This view is sometimes identified as Westernizing, but its adherents conceive its scope to be much broader. They seek greater pragmatism in foreign policy, a clearer definition of national interests as they affect specific policy choices, and a rejection of a messianic conception of Russian destiny. This approach, initially associated with Foreign Minister Kozyrev, former state secretary Gennadiy Burbulis, and sometimes with President Yeltsin himself, emphasizes pragmatism and compromise to secure, in Yeltsin's words, Russia's "entry into the civilized community."[4] Supporters of this trend tend to see relations with Europe and the West as benefiting domestic political reform, and they have voiced concern that a reliance on cooperation with the conservative regimes of Central Asia will encourage the revival of conservative political forces in Russia and lead, in the words of one Russian policy forecast, to "the postponement, if not collapse, of the market reforms in Russia."[5] This group has, moreover, tended to be more averse to the use of force than others, leaving them open to the criticism that they have sacrificed Russia's national interests for the sake of pleasing the West. For example, critics severely castigated this approach for "lacking even minimal virility"[6] when Kozyrev and like minds declined immediately to commit Russian troops to neighboring "hot spots" in order to protect Russian citizens. Such accusations, when added to many others, led to the hardening of Russian policy in the fall of 1992. Yeltsin himself has been obliged to warn the West that Russia "is not a country which can be kept in the waiting room" and that the Western view that Russia is a state "that only says 'Yes!,' silently swallowing affronts and even insults" is "impermissible."[7] In response to criticism, Kozyrev too began to soften his "Atlanticist" orientation, claiming in a report to parliament that in 1993 the major foreign policy goals of his ministry would be integration within the CIS and the protection of ethnic Russians abroad.[8] Following the forced resignation of liberal acting prime minister Yegor Gaidar in December 1992 and the strongly anti-Western speeches of the seventh and eighth sessions of the Russian Congress of People's Deputies, it became more difficult to pursue an Atlanticist policy without challenge.

A second school of thought also sees Russia as developing along liberal democratic lines, but with a more active and assertive foreign policy, as befits a great power. Russia is conceived as a multiethnic state: secular, pluralist and cosmopolitan by social orientation, but with interests and responsibilities focused, above all, in the new states of the "near abroad." Most members of this school believe that all the new states belong to Russia's sphere of influence. Leaders most closely associated with this view have been State Counselor Sergey Stankevich, St. Petersburg mayor Anatoliy Sobchak, head of the Parliamentary Committee on International Affairs and Foreign Economic Policy Yevgeniy Ambartsumov, ambassador to the United States Vladimir Lukin, leader of the Democratic Party of Russia Nikolay Travkin, secretary of the Constitutional Commission Oleg Rumyantsev, and even Kozyrev's own adviser and media liaison, Galina Sidorova.[9] Yeltsin's claims of a special role for Russia as the peacekeeper in the borderlands indicate the ascendancy of this point of view.

A third school of thought also sees Russia as a great power, but one resting on an ethnically defined domestic base, with authority residing in a strong state. This view, associated with Speaker of Parliament Ruslan Khasbulatov, Vice-President Aleksandr Rutskoy, and the Civic Union movement, lays special emphasis on the need to take all steps necessary to protect from violence and discrimination the 25 million-strong Russian population living in neighboring states. This school does not necessarily accept the current borders of Russia as natural or permanent. As Rutskoy reminded an audience in Omsk: "Those people dreaming of 'forcing' the country back into the borders that existed before Ivan the Terrible's day should remember that we were also ruled by Peter the Great."[10] Nor does this school of thought acknowledge the right of neighboring states to live alongside Russia in equal security. Its strong emphasis, as contained in the Civic Union's foreign policy program, on Russian ethnicity, the presumption of "natural Russian rights" and the promotion of foreign policy activism highlight the potential for conflict between Russia and its post-Soviet neighbors.[11]

This school's reliance on messianic and pan-Slavic historical roots has created a particular psychological barrier to the acceptance of an independent Ukraine and Belarus. As one commentator remarked, for Russians everywhere, irrespective of their political orientation, the "most painful act in the collapse of the USSR was the separation of Ukraine."[12] "I am absolutely sure," Christian Democratic Movement leader Viktor Aksyuchits has insisted, "that Belarusians, Ukrainians, and Russians even today continue to belong to one great Russian nation, formed during our joint history on the basis of the Orthodox faith."[13] As pan-Slavic ideologist Anatoliy Glivakovskiy has argued, "the whole of Ukraine . . . , Belarus, and European Russia is a single homogeneous space – homogeneous in every respect, even in the anthropological one."[14] Coming to terms with these losses is even more difficult because the relationship between Moscow and Kiev is fraught with territorial, economic, and military disputes.

A fourth school of thought sees Russia as being in the midst of a spiritual rebirth, its economic and spiritual capital having been squandered by the previous periods of expansion and terror. This group is isolationist, Slavophile, and focused on domestic reconstruction and revival. Its foremost representatives, as discussed in Chapter 2, include intellectuals such as the mathematician Igor Shafarevich, and writers like Vasiliy Belov, Valentin Rasputin, and Aleksandr Solzhenitsyn, but the view resonates within parts of the Orthodox church hierarchy and outside Moscow among some segments of an exhausted and increasingly demoralized population. Anti-Westernism and xenophobia remain a strong current within this school.[15]

Elements within both the third and fourth schools have, to a certain extent, been coopted by a fifth school on the extreme right, many of whose leaders and members are former Communists, but who now identify with right-wing and protofascist groups that tend to blame all of Russia's current problems on foreigners, Jews, and, in the words of one tract, "esoteric entities related to the Vatican, the Maltese Knights Order and Masonry."[16] These groups joined together in the summer of 1992 to form a National Salvation Assembly under the leadership of an ex-KGB general, Aleksandr Sterligov, who went on record with the view that Russia "needs imperial thinking," that "Slavic Ukraine, Belarus, and Russia, plus Kazakhstan" should be reunited, albeit voluntarily, that "Jews are desecrating our basic values," and that Yeltsin's government should be forcibly overthrown.[17] Many Russian officials believe that such extreme right-wing views have considerable support in the military and the security services. Indeed, the Yeltsin government demonstrated its apprehension over the potency of right-wing extremism by immediately banning the National Salvation Front, an umbrella organization linking extreme right- and left-wing groups, just two days after its founding congress in late October 1992.[18] The views of its members, however, continued to circulate freely in the media and to find support among right-wing intellectuals, and in February 1993 the Constitutional Court overturned Yeltsin's ban.[19]

Although contemporary Russian foreign policy-making is highly personalized and focused on the interactions and rivalries between key leaders who express views that cut across institutions, foreign policy is made within an institutional context. The primary institution for foreign policy decision-making in Russia is the Ministry of Foreign Affairs, headed by Foreign Minister Andrey Kozyrev. After numbering fewer than a hundred staff members in November 1991, the ministry swelled to more than three thousand a year after the collapse of the USSR. As with all the other institutions in the metropole, non-Russian employees were given the choice of staying on and working in conditions they were accustomed to, or returning home to native capitals in which many had not resided since childhood. Most opted to stay in Moscow. As a consequence, the Russian foreign ministry enjoys a distinct organizational advantage over neighboring foreign ministries. It even provided policy evaluation papers to other foreign ministries and seconded diplomats to serve in the foreign service of some new states as they were establishing their own ministries in 1992.[20]

Whatever its advantages vis-à-vis its counterparts in neighboring states, the MFA's authority to make foreign policy has been challenged by other Russian leaders alarmed at the MFA's apparent failure to prevent the growth of conflict along Russia's borders. Some, including Khasbulatov and Stankevich, even went so far as to demand the establishment of a separate ministry for CIS affairs. "The CIS must be dealt with on a daily basis, and not in between trips to London and Paris," Stankevich argued.[21] The MFA's handling of ethnic conflicts in the trans-Dniester region and the Baltics has been "dilatory, weak, and often, in my view, wrong," Stankevich has further noted.[22] Although detractors did not succeed in obtaining the establishment of another ministry, they did succeed in forcing the MFA to focus more urgently on the "near abroad" and in curbing its authority in this domain.

Three other institutions have asserted their right to shape policy toward the "near abroad": the Russian Security Council, the Russian Supreme Soviet (backed by the Congress of People's Deputies), and the military. The Security Council was created by presidential edict upon the recommendation of the Second Congress of People's Deputies and was designed to resemble the inner cabinet within the old CPSU Politburo – a comparison made by, among others, Yuriy Skokov, the first secretary of the council. The council, composed of voting (permanent) and nonvoting members, is formally empowered to coordinate and control the execution of major foreign policy decisions.[23] Reportedly the Security Council was behind the effort to wrest control of diplomacy toward the "near abroad" from the Ministry of Foreign Affairs. Additional reports noted that the Security Council had passed votes of no confidence in both Kozyrev and his then-first deputy, Fyodor Shelov-Kovedayev, and was pressing Yeltsin to demand their resignations. Not surprisingly, Kozyrev scoffed at the Security Council's attempt to control foreign policy, replying that the MFA was acting with the consent of the Russian government as a whole.[24] Nonetheless, Shelov-Kovedayev did resign under circumstances suggesting that he had been forced out by opponents of his relatively conciliatory line toward the other former republics. The firing in November 1992 of Galina Starovoytova, Yeltsin's adviser on ethnic affairs and one of the few leaders publicly to advocate accepting the loss of Crimea, and her replacement by the more conservative Sergey Shakhray, was also hailed as a victory for hardline opinion in the run-up to the December 1992 meeting of the Congress of People's Deputies.[25] Moreover, as critical decisions began to be made in late 1992 to send or retain troops in warring areas in Moldova, North Ossetia, and Abkhazia, the Security Council, with its interagency coordinating capability, was at the center of the deployment decisions.[26]

The authority of the Security Council was bolstered in December 1992 by the creation of the Interdepartmental Security Council Foreign Policy Commission. Subordinate to Yeltsin, then-chairman Skokov and the Security Council itself, the commission was empowered by Yeltsin to coordinate the drafting of foreign policy decisions, process information, elaborate proposals to safeguard Russia's national interests, and prepare forecasts concerning potential crises on Russia's periphery. The further creation by the council of an Interregional Commission for the North Caucasus, chaired by Sergey Shakhray, who also headed the State Committee for Ethnic Policies, indicated Yeltsin's concerns about the deteriorating situation in that region and showed the growing role of the council.[27] In general, the creation and strengthening of the Security Council and its subsidiary bodies were a reflection of Yeltsin's desire to maintain control over key foreign policy issues, and of his discomfort with the inability of the Ministry of Foreign Affairs to coordinate policy within a political environment that was shifting to the right.[28] Although the foreign ministry subsequently gained in power vis-à-vis the Security Council, even ministry personnel at the time admitted that their agency ultimately "lacked the necessary powers to overcome interdepartmental conflicts."[29]

The emergence of a nascent institutional separation of powers between the Russian executive and legislative branches has obstructed attempts to build a consensus over Russian foreign policy. Prominent critics of Russian foreign policy include Parliamentary Speaker Ruslan Khasbulatov, State Counselor Sergey Stankevich, Constitutional Commission chairman Oleg Rumyantsev, former Deputy Supreme Soviet Chairman and later Yeltsin chief of staff Sergey Filatov (who formerly sat on the Security Council), Yevgeniy Ambartsumov, the chairman of the Supreme Soviet Committee on International Affairs and Foreign Economic Relations, and hardline nationalist People's Deputy Sergey Baburin. Seeking to protect parliamentary prerogatives and to increase his own power vis-à-vis Yeltsin, Speaker Khasbulatov has noted the "particular responsibility" of parliamentarians "to raise their voices" on foreign policy and crucial state matters.[30]

Beginning in January 1992, the Supreme Soviet held several hearings on Russian foreign policy, and Kozyrev and his deputy foreign ministers were regularly called to testify. On the contentious issue of the Kuril Islands, for example, the Supreme Soviet in late July called a closed-door hearing on the matter, ostensibly "to assist the government and the president to draw up a true package of ideas and decisions," in

Oleg Rumyantsev's words. In reality, the hearings turned into a nationalist warning from the parliament to Yeltsin not to return the islands to Japan. Filatov asserted that the constitution gave the parliament the right to dispute "operational decisions" of foreign policy, and Rumyantsev asserted that "it must be guaranteed that there will be no surprises during the visit," a transparent warning against making concessions to Japanese territorial claims.[31] Parliamentary opposition played a significant role in Yeltsin's abrupt decisions to postpone both this and a subsequent visit to Japan.

Parliamentary critics have also spoken out on other issues ranging from the protection of Russians outside Russia to the historic January 1993 strategic arms accord with the United States and the bitter conflict in the former Yugoslavia. In early August 1992, a parliamentary delegation led by Yevgeniy Ambartsumov and Oleg Rumyantsev visited the Balkans and castigated the Russian government's position as being too Western-oriented. "One would think naturally that Russia, which has its own state interests, would not find it necessary at all to duplicate the U.S. position," Ambartsumov complained. Instead, he and other self-identified democrats began to argue that Russia should adopt a much more active policy favoring Serbia, given their common Slavic heritage.[32] This coalescence between Communists and democrats within the parliament on Yugoslavia constrained governmental action and produced a tangible shift in Russian policy toward Serbia, resulting in a December 1992 parliamentary resolution demanding that existing international sanctions against Serbia be extended to all the warring sides in former Yugoslavia, that Russia use its United Nations Security Council veto if the question of armed intervention should arise, and that humanitarian deliveries to Yugoslavia begin within two weeks.[33] The decree elicited a protest from the Ministry of Foreign Affairs that parliament was making foreign policy "by word of mouth," without the input of any experts.[34] Although Yeltsin did not implement the parliamentary resolution in toto, Russian pronouncements and actions became more supportive of the Serbian position after this date. As for the arms treaty with the United States, hardline nationalist Nikolay Pavlov, head of the rightist Russian People's Assembly, was among those who warned that Yeltsin could be overthrown "if the parliament does not prevent Russia from coming under America's nuclear umbrella" by rejecting the treaty.[35]

Although the parliament proved capable of making overt political threats and asserting its rights – as in the case of Yegor Gaidar – to refuse to confirm a presidential appointee whose policies it did not agree with, the fact remained that in the realm of foreign policy, particularly toward the "near abroad," the parliament was capable of inflaming passions and reflecting popular frustrations, but less able to provide an alternative and coherent vision of Russia's national interest. The overwhelmingly negative vote against the parliament in the April 1993 national referendum indicated popular dissatisfaction with the parliament's apparent inability to play a constructive role.

The military has also actively attempted to influence foreign policymaking on a wide variety of issues. Many of these issues are covered in Chapter 7. It should be noted here, however, that the relationship between Kozyrev and Grachev had so deteriorated by fall 1992 that Yeltsin publicly upbraided Kozyrev for the foreign ministry's continued inability to work with the defense ministry, even though, according to Yeltsin, it had been a "non-Yazovist" (i. e. nonmilitarist) organization for some time.[36] High military involvement in decision-making for the "near abroad," combined with frustration over the slowness or absence of resolution of core issues relating to military reorganization and doctrine, have further galvanized the military. For example, the officer corps' frustration was starkly evident in the results of an opinion poll in summer 1992 of leading public figures, in which 96 percent of respondents from the military command regarded normalization of relations with the CIS as Russia's first priority, yet only 3 percent of all respondents felt that Russia had achieved any success in this aim.[37]

Nonetheless, military efforts to influence policy have frequently been marked by a level of internal discord that matches or exceeds the comparable phenomenon inside the Ministry of Foreign Affairs. The military's anger at the virtual collapse of its previous status and role has made it fertile ground for internal politicization, exemplified by the formation of a liberal Independent Union of Servicemen and a highly conservative Union of Officers.[38] But this process has made it harder for the military to speak with a single voice. Although senior officers certainly have a powerful impact on decisions concerning matters in which they possess the greatest expertise, such as nuclear weapons and troop withdrawals, they too are fundamentally split. On a wide spectrum of issues, ranging from arms control and foreign policy to domestic economic reform, military officers have entered the political arena, but not as a single political force. Individual commanders speak out for or against particular policies, but with the possible exception of the welfare of servicemen, the military establishment does not exist as a unified political institution.

Evidence about the roles of the Foreign Intelligence Service (FIS) and the security ministry in shaping foreign policy has been contradictory. As a major purveyor of information from the outside world into the highest echelons of the decision-making process, these agencies are influential in any country. The involvement of the KGB and its former director, General Kryuchkov, in the attempted coup against Mikhail Gorbachev in August 1991 underlined the threat the agency still posed to democratic transformation. It was broken into two separate ministries dealing with security affairs (headed by Viktor Barannikov) and foreign intelligence (headed by Yevgeniy Primakov), and efforts were made to bring both under at least a modicum of legislative control. It seems clear nevertheless that both remain bastions of conservative views, and that in foreign policy their voices have most often been raised in favor of Russian nationalist positions. Some have suggested that the effectiveness of the intelligence services is enhanced by the fact that there are fewer policy debates and splits within its ranks than, say, in the military. Moreover, whereas the military is in disarray with withdrawal and reorganization issues, the foreign intelligence service has, since 1991, been recruiting agents in the new states, apparently often drawn from old KGB networks.

The Western Newly Independent States

The Baltics, Ukraine, Moldova, and Belarus share many common perspectives and policies, but warrant separate discussion. In Ukraine following the declaration of sovereignty by the Supreme Soviet on 16 July 1990, Kiev's priority goal was to establish Ukraine's independence and to guarantee its territorial integrity. These broad objectives have been supported by the majority of the state's new political parties, despite differences regarding the speed and tactics to be applied. In contrast to Russians, there has existed a greater overall consensus among Ukrainians that their identity is basically European. The view has been generally expressed that Ukraine, as pointed out by one Ukrainian political scientist, belongs more to the West than to the Eurasian empire, which is seen as extending eastward from Moscow.[39] Ukraine's leaders have worked to achieve broad international recognition of the new republic, to improve Ukraine's image in the United Nations and other international organizations, and to integrate Ukraine into regional European structures. They also see the need to normalize bilateral relations with countries on its immediate periphery, to promote external economic policies that would aid domestic economic growth, and to strengthen Ukrainian security. Most of all, however, they have sought to establish sovereignty over Ukrainian territory and everything in it, and they have felt the need to mobilize the international community to accept Ukraine as having the need for unique security guarantees against future Russian expansion. In pursuing these goals, Ukraine has faced enormous internal constraints and external pressures, above all from Russia.

Although there may have been a broad Ukrainian consensus on ma-croissues in the period after independence, more disagreement has emerged on specific policies, including the central issue of Ukraine's policy toward Russia. The faction of Rukh headed by Vyacheslau Chornovil has been unbending in its antagonism toward Russia, its identification with a pro-Western foreign policy, and its anti-Communist domestic policy. Chornovil garnered 23 percent of the popular vote in the December 1991 Ukrainian presidential elections (the victor, Leonid Kravchuk, received 61 percent). Despite internal splits, Chornovil went on to transform his faction of Rukh from a movement into a party, and strengthened his grass-roots support among younger Ukrainians and residents of western Ukraine.[40] Among these segments of the population, the demand has been for more rapid economic reform, new parliamentary elections (which they believe would sweep away former Communists), and a more assertive policy toward Russia.

A more centrist opposition bloc was formed after the presidential elections to pressure Kravchuk to open up the decision-making process and to press for more extensive economic reform. This group went under the umbrella name of "New Ukraine," and included the reformist wing of the former Communist Party of Ukraine (called the Party of Democratic Rebirth of Ukraine), the Green Party, and other social democratic and liberal parties, as well as industrial and business lobbies. New Ukraine drew its support primarily from Kiev and from eastern Ukrainians who were less resentful of russification and who sought to prevent a confrontation with Russia that they believed Ukraine could only lose.

A conciliatory posture toward Russia has also been endorsed by the economically more conservative Civic Congress, whose social base lies in Donetsk and other areas with large ethnic Russian and Russian-speaking communities. The Civic Congress advocated, for example, that Ukraine remain within both the CIS and the ruble zone, insisting that close ties with Russia had been the bulwark of Ukrainian policy "for hundreds of years."[41] At their congress in December 1992, members called for Russian to be accorded equal status with Ukrainian as a language for government business and in the education system. They also supported closer ties with Russia and the other CIS countries.[42]

With the deterioration in Ukrainian-Russian relations, however, it has become politically more difficult to be pro-Russian in orientation. By January 1993, at a meeting in Kiev prior to the CIS summit, the representatives of twenty-four out of twenty-six political parties and movements supported the decision not to agree to a Russian-sponsored effort to create a stronger suprastate structure within the CIS framework to coordinate relations.[43] The Green Party and Rukh were identified in public opinion polls as the most popular parties,[44] and with their increasing tendency to form an alliance with the centrist parties to support President Kravchuk and to isolate the substantial group within parliament favoring close relations with Russia, the lines of domestic cleavage have shifted against those who favor continued close cooperation with Russia.

Despite some controversies over foreign affairs, the process of Ukrainian foreign policy decision-making has remained remarkably stable and largely the prerogative of the president and a few top officials. The legacy of strong authoritarian rule and the incomplete emergence of institutional checks and balances have afforded President Kravchuk increased latitude in foreign affairs even as the domestic economic situation deteriorated.[45] Nevertheless, while Kravchuk has appeared to have the final word on most major decisions, his decisions, especially on security matters, have been the product of an institutional structure consisting of the parliamentary commission on defense matters, the Ministry of Defense, the National Security Service, the State Committee for the Defense of State Borders, and the security adviser to the president. Even when the majority of government ministries were reshuffled in October 1992, both Foreign Minister Anatoliy Zlenko and Defense Minister Konstantin Morozov maintained their positions, suggesting that along with Kravchuk, they formed a strong triumvirate in foreign and defense affairs. The appearance of coordination in the foreign policy field has contrasted with the realm of economic reform, which has been in much greater disarray and marked by disagreements among executive and legislative agencies and diverse societal interest groups.[46]

In the period after independence, Ukrainian foreign policy was focused on a variety of tasks that included gaining diplomatic recognition, establishing a Ukrainian presence in the major regional and international organizations, and signing treaties with neighbors guaranteeing the inviolability of borders (including the maintenance of Ukraine's hold on Crimea). The government also started negotiating Ukraine's military and nuclear status.[47] As the months passed and as the political barometer in Moscow shifted in favor of nationalist and even imperialist sentiment, the relationship with Russia deteriorated and increasingly became the lens through which all other issues were viewed.

Severe strains on key issues have continued to afflict Ukrainian-Russian relations, despite the repeated statements by President Kravchuk and others that the two countries, whether they like it or not, are "fated to live together" as "equal partners"[48] and that "divergence from Russia is impossible both from the economic and the political standpoint."[49] Ukrainian policy during this period has been aimed at preventing a complete break in relations with Russia and supporting

Russian political forces that have been willing to accept Ukrainian independence, while simultaneously enhancing Ukraine's military potential and pursuing an activist policy designed to gain regional and Western support for Ukraine's position on such key issues as the future status of the CIS, economic cooperation, Crimea, Moldova, the Black Sea Fleet and the transfer of nuclear weapons.

The Commonwealth of Independent States, having been created to coordinate relations among the newly independent states, soon became a point of contention for them. Kiev has been willing to have a structure to coordinate relations, but has consistently vetoed the formation of any suprastate institutions that might infringe upon Ukrainian independence. Kravchuk specifically opposed the signature of an open-ended draft charter on the grounds that it had a "military connotation" and would only undermine the sovereignty of member states.[50] The Ukrainian position has been that a network of strong bilateral relations must be established in political-military affairs, with the CIS operating primarily to coordinate the management of the enormous economic and energy problems posed by the disruption of ties among the former Soviet republics.

Ukrainian resistance to the notion of supranational CIS institutions has been intensified by controversies with Russia over such matters as Crimea. Crimea, which has an ethnic Russian majority, has received close attention from the Russian parliament and government, neither of which has been prepared unconditionally to accept Ukrainian sovereignty over the ancient region.[51] The May 1992 Russian Supreme Soviet resolution annulling the 1954 decision to transfer the region to Ukraine produced a renewal of Ukrainian claims, and increased efforts by the pro-Russian Crimean parliament to declare its own independence from Ukraine.[52] The ownership of the Black Sea Fleet (see Chapter 7) was the subject of heated exchanges in the spring of 1992. The conflict over Crimea was temporarily defused in summer 1992 by agreements reached between Yeltsin and Kravchuk, at their summits in Dagomys and Yalta, to concentrate on political and economic cooperation and to postpone the final disposition of naval units and facilities until 1995. Russia's use of facilities in Sevastopol – a naval port claimed by Ukraine – has continued, however, to provide almost daily irritants to the relationship. The decision by the Russian Congress of People's Deputies in December 1992 to investigate the legality of Ukraine's claim to Sevastopol, and the congress's subsequent action in July 1993 (by a vote of 166 to 1) declaring it a Russian city, produced further heated exchanges between Kiev and Moscow. It also gave succor to the pro-Russian forces in Crimea that have been seeking independence from Ukrainian rule.[53]

Ukraine's foreign policy priorities to its west have focused on establishing sound relations with the countries on its border, both to improve state-to-state relations and to reduce the temptation any of these states might have to foment ethnic and separatist unrest among the Slovak, Hungarian, Polish, Ruthenian, or Moldovan minorities in Ukraine's western and transcarpathian regions. Of particular concern has been the potential for ethnic conflict and state fragmentation spreading from Moldova into the western regions of Ukraine. That the most pro-Western and independence-minded among the Ukrainian population also reside in the west of the country has made it imperative for the Kiev leadership to seek firm guarantees from Poland, Slovakia, Hungary, and Romania that they recognize existing state borders and will refrain from supporting separatism. Romanian and Ukrainian policy objectives in Moldova are, however, not identical, and while neither wants the Russian Fourteenth Army in the trans-Dniester region, Kiev is sympathetic to the desire of the Slavic population there to avoid cultural assimilation with the Moldovans. The fragmentation along ethnic lines in Moldova threatens to spill over and adversely affect more salient aspects of Ukraine's relations with its Western neighbors.

Kiev has also sought to improve relations with Germany, which it considers both a source of economic support and a potential counterweight to Russian pressure. Ukrainian policy-makers have expressed concern about the need to prevent another Rapallo (or another Molotov-Ribbentrop pact) in which Germany and Russia make strategic decisions to cooperate at the expense of "the lands between."[54] Their strategy has been aimed at soliciting German economic and political investment in Ukraine, while simultaneously maintaining Kiev's commitment to a powerful independent conventional, and perhaps nuclear, force. The combination of the two, Ukrainian leaders calculate, might prove sufficient to convince German leaders that henceforth their relations with Ukraine should go through Kiev and not Moscow.[55]

Ukraine has also sought to use its relations with the so-called Visegrad group of Poland, the Czech Republic, Slovakia, and Hungary as a bridge to Europe. These four countries had agreed to cooperate with each other in seeking entry into the European Community. The harsh realities of life in the European market, however, have increasingly forced them to fall back on links with their eastern neighbors. Nevertheless, the Visegrad countries have shown little enthusiasm for improving trade with any of the new states, believing that reliance on partners with which they were formerly forced to trade would represent a considerable setback in their strategic goal of reorientation toward the West. There was also a feeling in Eastern Europe that the European Community (EC) would be less likely to support entry for the Visegrad countries if they appeared to be trying to get Ukraine or Belarus "under the tent," too. In reality, however, none of the Visegrad states, with the possible exception of the Czech Republic, is likely to be accepted by the EC, making all of them potential trading partners for Ukraine and the other new states.

Beyond economic cooperation, Ukraine's rift with Russia has produced an increased awareness of the need for military allies to the west. Ukraine has sought security guarantees from NATO countries and has worked hard to establish military relations with Russia's historic enemy to the west, Poland. As Russian domestic politics shifted toward the right and Ukrainian-Russian relations deteriorated, it became more common to hear leading Ukrainian and Polish leaders define each other as "strategic partners" and to talk of the need for military cooperation between the two countries.[56] Despite such proclamations, however, Warsaw has also sought to maximize its role in eastern and central Europe through bilateral ties with Russia – a policy that precludes a hard and fast commitment to Ukraine. Polish president Lech Walesa, for example, called for "a Warsaw-Moscow axis" in the region and emphasized that "I would like Poland and Russia to be the pillars in eastern Europe."[57]

Kiev has also explored the establishment of a regional cooperation pact stretching from the Baltic to the Black Sea. Such a pact might include Ukraine, Belarus, the Baltic states, and Turkey. Although an accord of this kind could generate great economic benefits for Kiev, it has provoked sharp hostility from Moscow. The chairman of the Russian parliament's Defense and Security Committee, Sergey Stepashin, for example, has depicted the Ukrainian proposal as a blatant attempt to impose a *cordon sanitaire* around Russia.[58] Indeed, given the increased contentiousness of Ukrainian-Russian relations in the Black Sea region, Moscow remains likely to regard a pro-Ukrainian tilt by NATO member Turkey – which controls egress from the Black Sea to the Mediterranean – with particular alarm.

In the period since independence, Ukraine and other successor states have faced an additional dilemma. On the one hand, they have had to contend with the West's tendency to regard Russia as the political (as well as legal) successor of the former Soviet Union and to make Russia the centerpiece of Western policy toward Eurasia. On the other hand, they have had to reassure Russia that their own relations with the West have not been designed to undermine Russian security or to isolate Russia economically or politically. Russian sensitivity on this score has been illustrated in a memorandum from Russia's envoy in Washington, Vladimir Lukin, to Ruslan Khasbulatov, speaker of the Russian parliament, expressing apprehension that Ukraine might follow the example of Eastern Europe and move "without us" to the West.[59] Sensitivity to Russian concerns has been equally necessary in considering the viability of any Baltic-to-Black Sea regional cooperation agreement. The likelihood that such a zone would be anti-Russian has increased as troop withdrawals and other thorny Baltic-Russian issues have remained unresolved. Moreover, neither Ukraine nor any of the other new western states could afford to alienate Russia without risking even further severe economic dislocation. For some time Russia will remain the major source for energy and raw materials and the major market for exports from this area. It was this fact, plus the real pressure from eastern Ukrainians who sought to prevent a rift with Russia, which explained why in his first statement after forming a new government in October 1992, Ukrainian prime minister Leonid Kuchma pledged an end to the "cold war" in economic relations with Moscow.[60] This continuing economic reliance on Russia underlies Ukraine's hesitation in promoting a more open break.

Belarus, more than Ukraine, has seemed determined to maintain stable relations with Russia, especially in the short-to-medium term, while simultaneously laying the basis for establishing a long-term economic corridor to the European community.[61] Foreign Minister Pyotr Krauchanka has stated that Belarus is "coming back to the family of European peoples,"[62] and has claimed that "Belarus has begun serious preparation to join the European Community," including reforming the domestic economy, sending diplomats for training in a number of Western countries, "and adopting other European standards."[63] Chairman of the Supreme Soviet Stanislau Shushkevich has underlined that in terms of priority relations, Russia ranks first, followed by a second tier consisting of Ukraine, Germany, and France, and then by Poland, Lithuania, and other neighboring states.[64] Although Russia may for a long time rank first in its foreign policy priorities, Shushkevich also said that Belarus was "interested, first and foremost, in addressing the issues which may enable us to rapidly integrate ourselves into Europe."[65]

European aspirations and current economic and political realities, however, have been two different matters, and the Belarusians, more than other new states in the western region, are keenly aware of the distinction. Belarusian politicians constantly have referred to "geopolitical realities" and the resultant restrictions imposed on foreign policy. "We are solving issues here [in Belarus]," Shushkevich noted, "taking into consideration where we are located. It cannot be otherwise."[66] As Shushkevich stated elsewhere, "We cannot survive without close links with Russia. . . . We now supply to Russia more than 80 percent of our manufactured output. . . . Neither we nor Russia has any hard currency, and an abrupt switch to world prices and payment in dollars could prove disastrous to both countries."[67]

The most contentious issue in Belarusian foreign policy since independence has been the collision between the country's constitutionally enshrined goal of neutrality and the belief among a growing number of Belarusian officials that a close "confederation" with Russia is Minsk's only salvation. Supreme Soviet head Shushkevich, who is in the first camp, has argued that "the principle of neutrality . . . should define Belarusian foreign policy for centuries to come," and has insisted that the "political sovereignty, military sovereignty, and the independence of Belarus do not contradict our aim of having close relations with Russia."[68] Shushkevich has sharply castigated the proposed "confederation" with Russia as endangering Minsk's sovereignty; such an arrangement, he admonished, would mean future Belarusian policies would be "determined in Moscow."[69] Moreover, Shushkevich has warned, such a confederation would gravely harm Minsk's relations with its immediate European neighbors, including Poland, Romania, Moldova, Hungary, Latvia, Lithuania, and Ukraine, most of which harbor a deep historical suspicion of Russia.[70]

Among the advocates of a closer alignment with Russia are Prime Minister Vyacheslau Kebich and Foreign Minister Krauchanka, the country's security apparatus, members of the powerful Belarusian military-industrial complex, and former Communist and pan-Slavic officials and organizations. These officials argue that an economic and defense confederation with Russia and possibly Kazakhstan should be the primary objective of Belarusian foreign policy, rather than an inflexible pursuit of the principle of neutrality, which they see as an abstract and distant goal.[71] Kebich has argued that "only collective security can guarantee our independence."[72] KGB chief Eduard Shirkouskiy, who has heartily endorsed entente with Moscow, has painted a more stark choice for Belarus: "either Russia or NATO."[73]

The conflict in the Belarusian leadership between neutrality and confederation with Russia has been reflected in Belarusian society, which generally exhibits stronger pro-Russian sentiments than one might find among citizens of the titular nationality in Ukraine or Kazakhstan. A survey conducted in late October 1992, for example, by the Belarusian Social, Economic and Political Research Institute asked whether the public considered the resurrection of the USSR "necessary." Remarkably, it found that nearly half of the 1,130 people surveyed "did consider the resurrection of the USSR a necessity," 22 percent did not, and another 29.5 percent "could not decide."[74] Other polls, however, have shown hesitation toward the idea of a "confederation" with Russia. One nationwide poll taken shortly after the Belarusian parliament voted on 9 April 1993 to sign the CIS collective security pact found that 55 percent of those surveyed agreed with Shushkevich's contention that to sign the accord violated Belarus's neutrality.[75]

Nonetheless, the attraction of a Belarusian-Russian entente has found considerable resonance in many strata of Belarusian society, particularly within political parties and institutions that favor a Russian and Slavic orientation, and that have linked up with like-minded groups in Russia.[76] For example, General D. A. Ivanov, head of the pan-Slavic and anti-independence Union of Officers of Belarus, appeared before a February 1993 meeting of the conservative Russian Union of Officers in Moscow to denounce proindependence and proneutrality Belarusian officials for wanting to "tear Belarus away from Russia." Belarus, Ivanov declared, has no future without "a renewed political, economic, and military union with all countries of the CIS, above all, with Russia."[77] Similarly, the chairman of the Committee on Volga Salvation, Sergey Shatokhin, came to Minsk to urge Belarusian rejection not only of the proposed Baltic-to-Black Sea Federation (which he said was part of the West's "geostrategic plans"), but also of improved ties with Poland, which had allegedly come "under the wing of the German eagle." Shatokhin's statements acknowledged Belarus's centrality by stating that "the key to the fulfillment or failure of the West's geostrategic plans and the key to Slavic unity is today in the hands of Belarus."[78]

The issue of the practicality of neutrality for Belarus has also sparked a fierce battle over control of Belarusian foreign policy. In late September 1992, parliamentary head Shushkevich barred the Ministry of Foreign Affairs "from developing conceptions of Belarus's foreign political and foreign economic activities," and declared that the "parliament is the only government organ able to govern foreign policy."[79] After Foreign Minister Krauchanka sided with Prime Minister Kebich in endorsing the confederation with Russia, Shushkevich bitterly castigated Krauchanka and the Foreign Ministry for posing a threat to Belarusian national interests, and accused the ministry of shoddy diplomacy, insufficient attention to the CIS, and failing to provide a foreign policy concept for the country.[80] In response, Krauchanka accused Shushkevich of seeking "to establish daily control over [the Foreign Ministry's] work."[81]

Despite the internal struggles over control of Belarusian foreign policy, the desire to maintain close relations with Russia has continued to resonate in Minsk.[82] Combined with the government's commitment to become a nonnuclear and neutral state, this predisposition has meant that Belarus has not come under severe pressure from any external source. It has, therefore, some latitude for dealing with the severe economic situation and the catastrophic long-term ecological and health damage caused by the nuclear-reactor fire at Chernobyl.

At first glance, the foreign policies of the Baltic states appear to face great constraints. The small size of the three republics has greatly complicated the achievement of their foreign policy objectives. In all three countries, resources have been stretched tight. Nevertheless, the goal of reestablishing their independence and their long-accepted international position as north European countries has given a natural direction to their foreign policies. Well before the Soviet collapse, they had extensive contacts throughout the Nordic region. They also benefited from the existence of active emigre communities, particularly in North America, which functioned as sources of political and economic support. Since independence, they have upgraded ties with the Western nations to full diplomatic relations and have joined several international organizations, including the Conference on Security and Cooperation in Europe (CSCE), the United Nations, the European Bank for Reconstruction and Development, the International Monetary Fund, the World Bank, the Baltic Sea States Council, and the Council of Europe.[83]

The Baltic states clearly hope to establish international ties that would mitigate Russian influence. This effort began prior to the breakup of the Soviet Union as they fostered contacts with the United States, their Nordic neighbors, and the European community, especially through CSCE. Although they enjoyed initial success in dealing with Russian president Boris Yeltsin both prior to and following the dissolution of the USSR, relations between Russia, on the one hand, and Estonia and Latvia, on the other, deteriorated over the contentious issues of the withdrawal of the Russian army and the treatment of ethnic Russian communities in these Baltic states. Continued failure to satisfactorily resolve these issues has placed considerable strains on relations with Moscow.[84] At the end of October 1992, President Yeltsin issued a decree suspending the withdrawal of Russian troops from the area and expressed "profound concern over numerous infringements of rights of the Russian-speaking populations."[85] The Russian Foreign Ministry stated that Russia would not link withdrawals to ethnic issues, and indeed despite the hardening of rhetoric,[86] troop withdrawals did continue.[87] However, the continued focus of the Russian and Baltic media and parliaments on the issue of troop withdrawal and citizenship laws indicated that most did not believe that the two issues had, in fact, been delinked. In Estonia, residents of the enclave around the northern cities of Narva and Sillamae, populated almost exclusively by ethnic Russians, have organized a number of demonstrations and referenda calling for greater autonomy within Estonia. These events indicate a growing fear of marginalization and discrimination among some Russian inhabitants of the Baltic region. In Russia, right-wing forces have seized on these developments to justify calls for an economic blockade of the Baltic states and for the use of Russian military units to safeguard the local Russian populations.[88]

The Baltic states' long-term prospect of normalizing relations with their immediate neighbors has also depended upon the solution of territorial claims beginning to surface, including Polish and Belarusian claims on southern Lithuania. These claims include pointed reminders that Lithuania's very capital, Vilnius, previously belonged to another country. Moreover, Kaliningrad's status as a heavily armed Russian enclave surrounded by Poland and Lithuania is certain to remain an issue, particularly if Moscow's relations with these states deteriorate further. Russian foreign minister Kozyrev took the occasion of his visit to Kaliningrad to declare the enclave an "indivisible and undisputed part of Russia." Kozyrev's further statement that Russia needs to maintain an "imposing presence" in Kaliningrad in order to avoid being "squeezed out" of the region alarmed Baltic leaders, who feared that Moscow would use its presence in Kaliningrad to justify continued troop stationing throughout the area. A subsequent explanation from Kozyrev that Russian troops would be needed to protect Kaliningrad against German and other countries' territorial claims did little to assuage Baltic concern.[89]

The conflict in Moldova that spilled over into civil war in the summer of 1992 served as a forewarning of the possible result of failures by the new national elites to resolve disputes over borders and the treatment of Russian-speaking minorities. Conflict between the government of Moldovan president Mircea Snegur and Russian separatists in the trans-Dniester region created thousands of refugees, precipitated external Cossack involvement, and decreased the likelihood that the Russian authorities would withdraw the Fourteenth Army from the republic. The rapidity with which the presidents of Russia, Moldova, Romania, and Ukraine met to defuse the crisis in June 1992 showed the potential for decisive conflict management when political leaders believe the situation warrants it.[90]

Equally, however, the growing political support from Russia, including that from erstwhile liberals, for the Dniester separatists, has made it less likely that negotiations to resolve the conflict will succeed.[91] Indeed, in a February 1993 summit meeting with Moldovan president Mircea Snegur, President Yeltsin linked any timetable for the withdrawal of the Russian Fourteenth Army directly to the future status of the trans-Dniester region and implied that the army would remain as long as Russian-speaking citizens were perceived to be threatened with a forced unification with Romania.[92]

The Southern Newly Independent States

In Central Asia and the Caucasus, postindependence foreign policy decision-making has been deeply affected by restricted international capabilities and by a domestic political environment that has prevented many political parties and interest groups from organizing freely to influence the setting of national priorities. Moreover, civil strife and separatist wars have raged in both regions, hampering the ability of elites in these and neighboring states to make long-term policy. Throughout Central Asia and the Caucasus, traumatized by the growing conflict and still affected by their authoritarian past, political leaders have attempted to monopolize decision-making in both the foreign and domestic-policy realms. Social movements and political parties created after the collapse of the Soviet Union have sought to prevent any single leader from exercising absolute control over the decision-making process, often taking to the streets in escalating cycles of violence. As the level of conflict in the two regions has risen, so have the strains on centralized authority grown. Leaders have tried to achieve and maintain dominion even as the economic situation has deteriorated and the threat of civil and intraregional wars has increased. This is the backdrop against which foreign policy has been made in the post-Soviet period.

From the beginning, political elites in Central Asia have concentrated on pursuing foreign policies that would stabilize their own rule and attract foreign assistance to their beleaguered economies. Such an outlook has ensured that the foreign policies of these states would be based on interest rather than ideology. For example, in discussing his republic's international strategy, President Nursultan Nazarbayev of Kazakhstan indicated that the foreign policy of his country would "be developed in the following, virtually equivalent directions: 1) the CIS, 2) Asian-Pacific region, 3) Asian, 4) European, and 5) American."[93] Pragmatism has also been ably displayed by President Askar Akayev of Kyrgyzstan, who has deftly pursued the goal of building relations with both the East and the West. Although Akayev has not hidden his desire that his country's foreign policy should be oriented toward the secular and capitalist West, he has sought to build ties with Muslim and Eastern countries in order to maximize Bishkek's international links and meet some of the demands of domestic oppositional forces. According to Akayev, these forces have been "trying to deflect us toward the Islamic countries, often criticizing us for our attraction to the West."[94] Akayev, like some of his counterparts in other Central Asian states, has been interested in improving relations with Islamic countries, in large measure because of the money that might flow in from confessional ties. In an interview Akayev bluntly admitted his own seemingly instrumental attitude toward Islam, a view clearly shared by several other Central Asian governmental leaders:

> Interviewer: Do you have plans for the coming period? What will you be doing in three days' time, say, at three p.m.?
>
> Akayev: I will be meeting with the king of Saudi Arabia and asking him for money.
>
> Interviewer: Of course, you have decided not to fall behind your neighbors – Niyazov and Karimov – and go on a hajj?
>
> Akayev: No, I haven't thought about that. Although if the success of my mission depends on it or I am given a credit of a hundred million dollars for it, I will go on a hajj without a minute's thought.[95]

Despite the limited success of some political groups and national parliaments in expanding their political influence, the Central Asian presidents have continued to play the key role in the policy-making process. As shown in Chapter 4, the desire of the Central Asian leaders to create a strong presidency has informed the debates on new constitutions throughout the region, with many states also passing laws "protecting the dignity and honor of the president" that severely limit the ability of the opposition or the mass media to criticize presidential authority or policy.[96] Kazakhstan president Nazarbayev has spoken about legitimizing the "de facto presidential rule" under which "the president of the republic, as the head of the state, should have all the necessary levers for the exercise of effective leadership."[97] Under such arrangements, Nazarbayev envisaged that the three main legal parties (the Socialist Party, which replaced the Communist Party; the Social-Democratic Party, which grew out of environmental groups; and the Party for the National Unity of Kazakhstan) would act not as competitors for political power but as suppliers to the government of information about societal demands.[98] This political picture has been repeated with some variations in the other Central Asian states. In Kyrgyzstan, where groups have enjoyed more legal rights, President Akayev was nevertheless the only candidate in presidential elections in October 1991. His advisers and inner circle, many of whom were Communist officials in the Soviet era, openly sought a constitution that would codify and enhance presidential powers.[99]

In Uzbekistan, President Islam Karimov has established dominion over the making of both foreign and domestic policy. In 1992, the Uzbek national movement, Birlik (Unity), accused Karimov of "betraying the interests of kindred Azerbaijan" by signing the CIS treaty of collective security, which calls for the establishment of a multilateral armed forces ostensibly under CIS jurisdiction but essentially under Russian control. Karimov responded by organizing a terrorist campaign against opposition leaders and political activists that included an attempt to assassinate Abdurrahim Pulatov, the cochairman of Birlik.[100] Along with many democratic principles, the constitution of Uzbekistan passed in October 1992 contains an article (number 10) stating that "only the popularly elected Supreme Council [or Soviet] and the president of the republic may speak on behalf of the people of Uzbekistan. No part of society, nor any political party, public association, movement or individual may speak on behalf of the people of Uzbekistan."[101] This provision has ensured that the ability of any group outside the government to influence foreign policy would be severely circumscribed.

Among Central Asian leaders, Turkmenistan's Saparmurad Niyazov has emerged as the most authoritarian and the leader with the greatest control over the setting of his country's foreign policy priorities. In June 1992 presidential elections Niyazov ran unopposed, and official state returns gave him 99.5 percent of the vote.[102] Since independence, Niyazov has refused to allow any autonomous political parties to officially register, despite the fact that most of them have remained far less assertive than their counterparts in neighboring states.[103] However, unlike Kazakhstan or Uzbekistan, where authoritarianism has been combined with a pro-CIS inclination, in Turkmenistan Niyazov has consistently shunned closer integration within the CIS. The combination of greater economic potential and greater geographic distance from the other capitals has given Turkmenistan's foreign policy more freedom to maneuver than that enjoyed by the other Central Asian states. Turkmenistan has recognized, however, the utility of maintaining bilateral links with Russia. In July 1992 it concluded a treaty of friendship and cooperation with Moscow calling for increased economic, diplomatic, and security cooperation. "I believe that we should have special relations with Russia," Turkmen foreign minister Khalykberdy Atayev explained. "They [the Russians] can be counted on in troubled days. . . . If it weren't for Russia, we would have confronted great problems in our defense policy. It's become a geographic reality that we are defending Russia's southern border."[104]

Rakhman Nabiyev, the former president of Tajikistan, proved more vulnerable to societal pressures than any other Central Asian leader. Sensing his precarious status, in May 1992 Nabiyev sought to defuse popular discontent by bringing into the government 33 representatives of groups that had previously been excluded, including representatives from the country's southern and eastern regions, members of the Islamic Renaissance Party, and intellectuals from Dushanbe. The deputy chairman of the Islamic Renaissance Party, Davlat Usmon, was named vice-premier. In that capacity he attempted to gain adherents to his view that religious affiliation should be the basic determinant of Tajikistan's foreign policy, and that, as a result, "Tajikistan should turn toward

Iran, Afghanistan, and Pakistan."[105] A graphic example of the Islamists' influence during this period was their demand that Nabiyev, who had not paid a single visit to any foreign state, should first visit the Islamic Republic of Iran. Indeed, in early July 1992 Nabiyev did visit Iran and Pakistan for his inaugural visit abroad, which resulted in the signing of loan and technical agreements with both countries.[106]

Nabiyev's move to coopt Tajik Islamic forces ultimately, however, proved insufficient to keep him in power. In September he became the fourth head of state of a former Soviet republic to be forcibly ousted from power in 1992 – following Zviad Gamsakhurdia in Georgia (January), Ayaz Mutalibov in Azerbaijan (March), and Mutalibov's replacement, Yakub Mamedov (May). (Lithuanian Supreme Council chairman and later acting president Vytautas Landsbergis also lost power during the year – but at the ballot box.) Nabiyev's subsequent appearance before the Tajik parliament, where he formally submitted his resignation, allowed Imam Ali Rakhmanov to take power constitutionally, but it did not alter the fact that the changeover of leaders had been paid for by the loss of thousands of lives.[107] All of this naturally meant that foreign policy in Tajikistan became an adjunct of the civil war.

In Tajikistan, it was neither primarily religious nor ethnic tensions that spilled over into open conflict, but instead regional and clan rivalries exacerbated by the near-total absence of effective controls at the Tajik-Afghan border, which allowed weapons and Tajiks from Afghanistan, hardened by ten years of civil war, to flood into the southern provinces and the capital of Dushanbe. The Tajik fighters' hatred of Russians made the remaining Russian garrisons a particular target. The participation of Russian troops in joint peacekeeping operations that were perceived as supporting the Nabiyev government increased the vulnerability not only of the troops but of the Russian civilians they were increasingly called upon to protect.

The rapidity with which Russian troops and civilians were targeted in Tajikistan demonstrated the weakness of Russia's ability to act as a neutral security guarantor in the region. Moscow has increasingly sought to keep troops in these areas to promote its own interests or to protect the sizable Russian minorities. The presence of Russian troops has been welcomed by those pro-Russian leaders who have deep roots in the Soviet period, and who have believed, as Nabiyev did, that under some circumstances Russian troops would be a more reliable guarantor of their power than native forces. The Tajik events, however, appeared to demonstrate that Russian troops had no standing orders to take any military actions except those required for self-defense, and that by the time orders were received from a confused and divided leadership in Moscow, Russian troops could be endangered and local leaders overthrown. This proved fatal for the governments that might have counted on Russian garrisons for support, but it was also dangerous and frustrating for the local garrison leaders themselves. In Tajikistan and elsewhere these commanders have increasingly taken matters into their own hands, operating without central authority in order to protect their own families, to promote a military solution more favorable to the expatriate community, and also, sometimes, to obtain money or goods. This situation produced the direct entry of Russian troops into the fighting in Tajikistan in the summer of 1993.

The Tajik events and the Russian response have demonstrated to Central Asian leaders the need to coordinate their own regional security policies. Under the chairmanship of Nursultan Nazarbayev, the Central Asian states, often with Russian participation, have met to discuss the dispatch of peacekeeping forces to Tajikistan, as well as the creation of a regional, Asian-based security system modeled on the CSCE (which in Nazarbayev's conception would "include first Kazakhstan, Uzbekistan, Kyrgyzstan, Turkmenistan, Turkey, Iran, Pakistan, and later possibly Russia, China, India, and Mongolia").[108] Moreover, ministers of internal affairs from Russia, Ukraine, Latvia, Estonia, Armenia, Georgia, and the Central Asian states held a summit meeting in Erevan in May 1993 to discuss joint measures to increase the security of CIS borders with the outside world as a means to stem the rising flow of arms, illicit drugs, and other contraband.[109] Noting the larger consequences of failing to halt these breaches, Tajik head of state Imam Ali Rakhmanov has admonished that "the Tajik-Afghan border is also the CIS's southern border. That is well understood in Almaty (Alma-Ata), in Moscow, in Tashkent, and in other CIS capitals."[110]

Although the establishment of a CSCE-style process doubtless would take many years to come to fruition, the fighting in Tajikistan throughout the fall of 1992 underlined the urgency of constructing peacekeeping and conflict-resolution mechanisms among the Central Asian states. Consequently, discussions both inside the region and with the United Nations about the training and organizing of peacekeeping forces have assumed a greater urgency. These discussions have been based on the realization that multiethnic states might be more fragile than previously thought, and that popular demands to redraw borders, particularly those in the Fergana Valley region, could be a source of future conflict among them.[111] As Uzbek president Islam Karimov frankly admitted, the situation arising from the conflict in Tajikistan is a "time bomb which could cause another conflict like Karabakh here, but a hundred times worse. . . . At all events, it is impossible to redraw the borders of our states without starting a bloodbath. Uzbekistan is inhabited by 800,000 Kazakhs, another 800,000 Tajiks, plus smaller numbers of

Kyrgyz and Turkmen. Several million Uzbeks live in the other four republics."[112] Given the demands of Tajiks and Uzbeks in the northern province of Leninabad to join Uzbekistan, the demands of Tajiks in and around Samarkand to leave Uzbekistan, and the pressure of hundreds of thousands of refugees in Afghanistan, Kyrgyzstan, and in Russia, the civil war in Tajikistan and its sociopolitical consequences are likely to dominate the foreign policy priorities of these countries for the foreseeable future and increase the likelihood that stability will be sought at the price of democracy.

In the Caucasus, leaders have struggled to fashion a foreign policy against the backdrop of ethnic and religious revivals, separatism, civil war, and socioeconomic collapse. Under such circumstances, foreign policy has been formulated both to ensure the survival of individual regimes and to promote the interests of whole nations that perceive themselves as facing the threat of annihilation. In Azerbaijan, foreign policy has been centered on three central objectives, beyond its ongoing war with Armenia: the maintenance of stable, if not improved, relations with Russia; the acquisition of foreign allies and sources of material support; and the concurrent weakening of Armenia's external backing. From January 1990 until his ouster in March 1992, president and former Communist Party boss Ayaz Mutalibov pursued a policy that was hard-line domestically and pro-Moscow externally. The combination of the two, plus popular criticism of his handling of the war with Armenia, spurred the growth of the Azerbaijan Popular Front, led by Abulfaz Elchibey. The APF adopted an avowedly anti-Russian and pro-Turkish foreign policy orientation, so much so that one Azerbaijani legislator expressed fear that an APF government would adopt "an openly anti-Russian foreign policy."[113] A short-lived government that ruled after Mutalibov's forced resignation in March 1992 vowed to prevent anyone from attempting "to sow discord between Azerbaijan and Russia."[114]

Presidential elections in June 1992 brought Elchibey to power. Although the new president initially resisted the improvement of relations with Russia, which he blamed for supporting Armenia in Nagorno-Karabakh, the APF-dominated government soon realized that Azerbaijan's interests lay in better ties with Moscow. The abrupt turnabout was succinctly explained by Tamerlane Karayev, a leading APF official, who soberly noted that "history, politics, and economics have made us [Russia and Azerbaijan] partners for centuries."[115] Bilateral agreements were signed on trade and economic policy, as well as in the area of mutual security, with Baku using its economic advantage as an energy exporter to gain leverage both in Moscow and in energy-starved Ukraine.[116] The Azerbaijani government also presented itself as the protector of Russians living in the south Caucasus. Its foreign ministry expressed concern over the safety of Russian villages along the Azerbaijani-Armenian border and asserted that although the Russians were thousands of kilometers from the Nagorno-Karabakh conflict, they nonetheless had come under heavy shelling by Armenian forces since August 1992.[117]

Nonetheless, Azerbaijan remained fearful and distrustful of Russia, an attitude exacerbated by separatist stirrings among Muslim communities in neighboring Daghestan, which lies inside Russia. A proposal by Yeltsin in June 1992 to confirm the border between Russia and Azerbaijan sparked massive protests among the ethnic Lezgin community that populates southern Daghestan and northeastern Azerbaijan.[118] Moscow ultimately retracted its border proposal in response to Daghestani and Azerbaijani government appeals that such a move would seriously destabilize the situation in both areas.[119] Nonetheless, the incident clearly shook the Azerbaijani leadership; though Russia has encountered its own troubles with separatist Muslim communities in the North Caucasus, Baku recognized that Moscow had discovered an ethnic card that it could choose to play against Azerbaijan. Already embroiled in a desperate war to preserve Azerbaijani territorial integrity from separatism in Nagorno-Karabakh, Baku understood it could not open a second front to its north. Consequently, the incident prompted Azerbaijani opposition figures and members of the government to start talking about the need for alliances with neighboring Georgia and Chechnya, both of which feared Russian military encroachments.

In its relations with states outside the Caucasus other than Russia, Baku has focused more on its own "near abroad" than on distant countries, including those in the West, which it has regarded as being blatantly pro-Armenian. "The eastern aspect [of Azerbaijani foreign policy] must be given special attention," President Elchibey noted in January 1993. He criticized Baku's previous trade policy as too Western-oriented, saying, for example, that Azerbaijan should import grain from Kazakhstan, not from Canada, and welcoming the idea of forming a community of Central Asian states, an idea that was unlikely to gain adherents in either Armenia or Georgia.[120]

Azerbaijan's relations with Turkey have remained strong because of the two countries' shared Turkic origins, their geographic proximity, the centuries-old trading links between Baku and Istanbul, and their mutual antipathy toward Armenia.[121] Relations with Iran, on the other hand, have been affected by the APF's long-standing demand for unification with the Azerbaijani population of northern Iran. Before taking power, Elchibey was jailed for organizing anniversary celebrations of the founding of an independent republic in Southern Azerbaijan (northern Iran); and as president, he has called on Teheran to grant the region cultural autonomy.[122]

Another aspect of Azerbaijan's foreign policy has been the growing independence of the leadership of Nakhichevan in formulating policy sometimes at odds with Baku. The Nakhichevan region, which is under the control of Azerbaijan but separated from it by Armenian territory, borders on Iran and Turkey. With the escalation of Azerbaijan's blockade of Armenia, Nakhichevan in turn was put under blockade by Armenia. Isolation forced the enclave to find its own means of support, and increased the rift between Elchibey and the enclave's leader, Gaidar Aliyev (previously the KGB chief of Azerbaijan and a member of Mikhail Gorbachev's Politburo, and therefore a person not without means or connections). Aliyev sought and received humanitarian assistance from Iran, Turkey, and the United States. He also entered into negotiations with Armenia to withdraw forces from strategic heights along their mutual border and allowed cargo shipments from Iran across Nakhichevan to Armenia, apparently without Baku's approval.[123] Aliyev's popularity and independence prompted Elchibey to try to impose his own control. Riots broke out in Nakhichevan in October 1992 when APF forces and Aliyev's supporters clashed over Baku's efforts to place Interior Ministry officials in the enclave. The Azerbaijani minister of interior threatened that "I will introduce proper order in Nakhichevan, and, if necessary, I will blow out G. Aliyev's brains."[124] Aliyev's response was to establish an opposition political party called "New Azerbaijan,"[125] and to extend his influence beyond Nakhichevan into all of Azerbaijan. In June 1993, President Elchibey was forced to flee Baku after a rebel military leader, Surat Huseynov, joined with Aliyev to oust him.[126] All this has made any coherence in foreign policy extremely difficult.

In the postindependence period, Georgian foreign relations have been seriously impeded by war, stemming from the two separatist conflicts in Ossetia and Abkhazia. In both cases Georgia has found itself facing a potential conflict with Russia, a factor that has sharply limited Tbilisi's foreign policy horizons. Because leading Western powers are not likely to intervene in any significant way in opposition to Russia, Georgian leaders have been forced to look elsewhere for allies. Indeed, given Moscow's looming presence in both the Ossetian and Abkhazian conflicts – as well as Georgia's own economic dependence on Russia – Georgia has been compelled to conduct what head of state Eduard Shevardnadze termed a "reserved policy" toward Russia.[127] Certainly, Russia's role in helping obtain and maintain a ceasefire in Ossetia paid dividends for Georgia. Nonetheless, the potential for escalated conflict with Russia has prompted Georgian leaders to seek to broaden external ties. While defending the need to maintain constructive relations with Russia, Shevardnadze has simultaneously emphasized the need to seek out additional ties – particularly with neighboring Iran, Turkey, and Azerbaijan – "in order to provide a necessary balance."[128]

In early 1993, Georgia's involvement in the war between Armenia and Azerbaijan shifted from a "neutral" posture favoring Armenia to one favoring Azerbaijan. While denying any "problems" in the relationship with Armenia, head of state Shevardnadze pointedly noted that Georgia had more pressing concerns at the moment and thus "we simply do not have time to formulate our contacts and common interests in agreements." The Georgians did find time, however, to prepare an economic cooperation agreement with Azerbaijan, with Shevardnadze noting that "our interests complement each other," and citing Georgia's need for Azerbaijani rail connections to Russia, as well as Baku's need for access across Georgia to the Black Sea for the shipment of exports to Turkey and the West.[129]

In early February 1993, Shevardnadze visited Azerbaijan, where he signed some two dozen bilateral agreements, including a treaty on friendship and cooperation and one calling for the safeguarding of the national minorities in each state.[130] It was the first state visit from a Georgian leader to Baku in three years.[131] Tbilisi's motivation in securing firmer relations with Baku was hinted at by Azerbaijani president Elchibey, who pointedly reminded Georgia that the large Azerbaijani population in Georgia's eastern Marneuli region is anxious to merge with Azerbaijan. "Our Georgian friends who are in power should not forget that, if it were not for the [APF], today Georgia would be faced with the need to open a third front."[132]

The gas pipeline on which Armenia heavily depends runs from Russia through this Azerbaijani-populated region. It is probably no coincidence that the pipeline was blown up in this region by saboteurs on at least three separate occasions in early 1993. Georgia's protests that it was unable to ensure the safety of the pipeline were rejected by Armenia,[133] which saw the matter as tacit confirmation of a Georgian-Azerbaijani alliance.

The shifting alliance structure within the Caucasus has done little to lessen the conflicts, and Shevardnadze has been forced to concede the obvious: "If we fail to resolve problems plaguing the Caucasus on our own, they might grow into large-scale conflicts in which great powers will get involved."[134] Improving relations with Russia remained the immediate task, but in recognition of the fact that this was becoming increasingly difficult, the Georgian leader also emphasized the need (echoing then-President Elchibey of Azerbaijan) to "intensively develop bilateral relations with the republics of Central Asia," as well as with Turkey, Iran, and Azerbaijan.[135]

Armenian foreign policy has been guided since 1988 (the year that Nagorno-Karabakh's Armenian-dominated Supreme Soviet voted to join Armenia) almost exclusively by its undeclared war with Azerbaijan over Nagorno-Karabakh. The war has decisively shaped Erevan's foreign policy options, yet it has simultaneously polarized the country's foreign policy establishment, with three different foreign ministers being named in the winter of 1992–3 alone.[136] The most contentious issue was whether formally to recognize Nagorno-Karabakh's December 1991 declaration of independence, a move that would undoubtedly put Armenia and Azerbaijan in a formal state of war. The government of President Levon Ter-Petrossyan has resisted such a move, but in so doing has come under mounting pressure to do so from the increasingly vociferous and powerful Armenian Revolutionary Federation (the Dashnaks). Dashnak pressure on this issue grew so intense that by summer 1992, Ter-Petrossyan's political position was seriously threatened.[137]

Nonetheless, Armenian leaders have continued to seek foreign alliances to alleviate pressure on their country. They have looked first to Russia, the country's traditional protector in the Caucasus.[138] Moscow's promise to provide more fuel was deeply appreciated, but with fuel deliveries being interrupted in Georgia both by terrorist actions and by Georgian officials demanding ever-higher portions of the transported fuel, the assistance from Russia arriving in Armenia has been small. Armenian officials have also hoped for improved relations with Turkey, but they have faced a difficult task in surmounting Armenians' historical enmity for Turks and distrust of Ankara's motives. Moreover, Erevan's diplomatic initiatives have caused powerful ultranationalist forces within Turkey to bring sustained pressure to bear on the Turkish government to withhold even humanitarian assistance from Armenia.[139] Notwithstanding their own antipathy toward Armenians – and despite their ethnic affinity with Azerbaijanis – Turkish leaders have recognized the constraints they face in the Armenian-Azerbaijani conflict. As then-prime minister Suleyman Demirel observed, "[while] we are not indifferent to the suffering of the Azerbaijanis, . . . one step too many by Turkey would put the whole world behind Armenia."[140] When Azerbaijani leaders called for Turkish military assistance to halt Armenian offensives in April 1993, Demirel expressed sympathy, but curtly explained that such aid "would solve nothing," as it would only prompt other states to likewise aid Armenia.[141]

Entering its fifth year in 1993 with little prospect of abatement, the undeclared war in the south Caucasus illustrates the fashion in which military violence has come to consume the lion's share of all the region's political and economic energies, leaving neither time nor resources for the pursuit of broader, long-term national interests.

Conclusion

Throughout Central Asia and the Caucasus, leaders have struggled to establish foreign policy priorities in a sea of instability. Not only have their own regimes been plagued by political turmoil, but their neighbors have lacked the kind of rudderlike stability of Scandinavia and Western Europe, which serve as a clear and tangible model for the Baltics and the western NIS. Although Turkey, Iran, Afghanistan, Pakistan and China have presented a range of alternative models from "market" Communist to Islamicist regimes, they themselves have been subject to domestic instability and economic constraints. Consequently, there has been no clear-cut trend among the new states in the southern tier to adopt one model at the expense of the other, or to ally themselves with one country on the CIS perimeter at the expense of the others.

The same has been true to a lesser degree of the western NIS. No single neighboring country has emerged as the guarantor or ally of choice. This has been due partly to the efforts of the Group of Seven (G-7) industrialized states to provide a single multilateral package of aid and assistance to the new states. This has also been the case because the new western states' aspiration to make the transition from "East" to "West" has not been matched by reality. Despite these states' clearly enunciated foreign policy objective to move westward, all remain tethered to Russia. The poor performance of these states' own domestic economies has increased their acute dependence upon Russia and simultaneously diminished their attractiveness to the West. Post-Soviet Western policy toward the NIS has remained essentially russocentric, and attempts by the western NIS to establish political or security alliances without Russian participation have been spurned as unacceptably anti-Russian. In any event, these states have been unable to compete with Russia in the international political arena, where diplomats of the Russian Foreign Ministry (many of them non-Russians) often outshine and always outspend them.

Politically, opposition groups and political parties throughout the new states believe, probably correctly, that their ability to move toward democracy depends upon the continuation of Russia's democratic transformation. Existentially all the new elites understand that the very independence and survival of their states are to a large degree in the hands of Russian leaders. "When there's frost in Russia on Thursday,"

Ukrainian president Kravchuk has noted of Russia's long shadow, "by Friday there's frost in Kiev."[142]

The objective understanding that Russia wields dominant influence in the Eurasian region has been universally accepted by heads of state of both the western and southern states. This is one reason they have tried to maintain uniformly good relations with the other countries on their peripheries. Understanding that in any future conflict with Russia, they would need not one but many sources of external support, leaders have struggled to build and strengthen their political bases while looking to the West, the Islamic world, Japan, and China for both economic assistance and political guarantees in case Russia once again takes up its imperialist mantle. The shift in Russian foreign policy toward a more assertive and nationalist line that began in late summer 1992 has exacerbated fears within the non-Russian states of a renewed Russian revanchism. Of particular concern have been calls from Russian political figures of both liberal and political persuasion for Russia to adopt a "Monroe Doctrine" as the basis of its policy in the "near abroad." The initial proponent of this concept, Yevgeniy Ambartsumov, the chairman of the parliamentary Committee on International Affairs and Foreign Economic Relations, has insisted that Russia

> must base its foreign policy on a doctrine which declares the entire geopolitical space of the former Soviet Union to be a sphere of its vital interests (along the lines of the U.S. 'Monroe Doctrine' in Latin America) and must strive to secure the world community's understanding and acknowledgement of its special interests in this space. Russia must also strive to secure from the international community the role of political and military guarantor of stability throughout the territory of the former USSR. It should strive to secure the G-7 countries' support for these functions of Russia, including hard currency subsidies for its rapid reaction forces (the Russian 'blue berets').[143]

Moreover, the weakening of President Yeltsin's political position in 1993 obliged him, beginning in a speech to the Civic Union, to insist that the international community "grant Russia special powers as guarantor of peace and stability in the regions of the former USSR."[144]

Most of the leaders and political elites of the new southern and western states have clearly recognized that in the context of the power struggle within Russia, their choice is between Yeltsin and someone worse. "Always remember," Ukrainian president Kravchuk has admonished, "that after Yeltsin's Russia can come Zhirinovskiy's Russia."[145] Boris Shikhmuradov, the deputy prime minister of Turkmenistan, has likewise acknowledged that "we're praying day and night for Yeltsin to stay in power. Any of those who might come after him, all of them have an ax in their hand."[146]

The risk that conflicts will escalate and eclipse all these states' other foreign policy priorities remains manifest. A particularly troublesome event in this regard emerged in late January 1993 when separatist factions from Abkhazia, trans-Dniester, and the Gagauz region concluded a treaty of friendship and cooperation.[147] The pact, the first of its kind between multinational insurgent movements in the CIS, threatens to bring Russia, Georgia, Moldova, possibly Ukraine, and perhaps additional governments, into direct armed conflict should its clause calling for military assistance in the event of an attack be exercised.[148]

The problem is particularly serious for Russia, which is involved both directly and indirectly in the politics of each of these new states. Should these new states perceive Russian interference in their internal affairs as being too blatant, for example, they may elect to take retaliatory measures similar to the Dniester–Gagauz–Abkhazian pact by concluding similar accords with separatist regions within the Russian Federation.[149] One potential catalyst for instability is the visible presence of Russian troops, who are in the republics under the agreement of the existing governments. These forces have become the object of attack and resentment by the native populations, particularly when they are ordered by their own commanders to take actions not authorized by indigenous authorities (such as the protection of Russian civilians, the arming of pro-Russian insurgents, the removal of military equipment now claimed by national armies, or the slowing of troop withdrawals to exert pressure for improved conditions for local Russian residents). As a consequence, the Russian presence, rather than acting primarily as a stabilizer, has also become a source of potential conflict and instability. It likewise underscores the fundamental issue posed at the beginning of this chapter: As long as Russia is unable to resolve its internal debate on its national identity, its borders, and its rights and responsibilities toward its neighbors, the other new states will be forced to conduct their own foreign policies with the knowledge that a new era of ethnic conflict and Russian imperial behavior could quickly destroy their independent status. This dilemma is shared both by the successor states whose independence could be compromised by the presence of Russian troops and by Russia itself, as it struggles to synthesize the demands of competing and increasingly polarized interest groups into a coherent set of foreign policy priorities.

7

Military Issues

During the Soviet era outside observers commonly remarked that one of the Soviet system's most distinctive features was its unprecedented drive to accumulate military power. Today the military legacy of that drive poses a series of domestic and international problems that together constitute what is arguably the gravest challenge to the countries of Eurasia.

The Soviet military legacy may be most obvious in the struggle of several of the new states to claim former Soviet military units based on their territories and in the continued stationing outside Russia of about 250,000 Russian Federation troops. The failure of any multinational command to emerge has shifted the latter forces from Soviet to Russian military control. These Russian troops may nominally be CIS units, but the fact that most are slated to be withdrawn to Russia and are under Russian command underscores whom they truly represent.

The authority of the political leaders in the new states is undermined by the stationing on their soil of large numbers of foreign troops who are reluctant to return home. The officers in these units, mainly but not only Russian, have frequently spent their whole lives outside of Russia, on the highly-armed periphery of the Soviet Union, and have frequently married and settled in these areas. Russian officers are naturally resistant to the idea of redeploying their troops and families back to Russia where, due to the lack of housing, they must often live in tent camps.

Some, therefore, have become active in supporting a renewed Russian or Soviet imperial drive that might enable them, if the independence of these states can be undermined or ended altogether, to remain in place. Others have allied themselves, sometimes as mercenaries, with local Russian or Cossack populations to promote the rights of these minorities within the non-Russian new states, sometimes against the wishes both of the leaders of the new states and of central Russian military authorities. Still others have reacted to the fear of great eco-

231

nomic hardships by selling off their equipment to black marketeers, thereby fueling local conflicts. Finally, others have abandoned the Russian military altogether, taking oaths of allegiance to new national authorities.

Local elites have responded to the presence of former Soviet forces in different ways, but one of the most troubling and widespread developments has been the rapid emergence of local military establishments with a large appetite for extremely scarce resources. Interactions with the outside world, instead of being focused solely on the search for economic partners, have also been dominated by the search for security guarantors. In these tangible ways, the legacy of the vast Soviet military complex is undermining both the authority and viability of the new states, as well as the ability of Russia to move from an imperial past to a postimperial future.

Even without this legacy, the new states face enormous challenges in constructing a role for new military establishments. In all the states, governments of uncertain political viability face harrowing socioeconomic problems. They are also burdened with high levels of insecurity and conflict among ethnic, regional, and clan-based groups that are part of the centrifugal force that pulled the USSR apart. Consequently, military power assumes new importance not only as an arbiter of conflicts between subnational groups that could be available to protect minority rights, but also as an instrument of state-building capable of halting the process of disintegration and separatism. In contributing to the process of state-building, however, it is by no means clear that military involvement in politics would be any more likely to support democratic transitions in the post-Soviet states than it has elsewhere. Clearly, then, the military has the capacity to exert a major and perhaps decisive impact on the internal evolution of many of the post-Soviet states.

Such an impact is being felt at the same time that these states are seeking to delineate the formal role of the armed services in the lives of these countries. It is difficult enough to write a new military doctrine when a country is stable and at peace (debates about the role of NATO in the post-Cold War era come to mind), but when regimes are fragile, and there is often little military expertise at the political apex, this task becomes fraught with special difficulties.

Among the challenges facing all the new states are the elaboration of a new military doctrine, the division of responsibility for internal and external defense between the various services, issues of territorial defense that cannot be settled until it is decided which borders are most vulnerable, and the role of civilian oversight and control. The military establishments are themselves hampered by their inability to ensure national security without clear guidance from the political authorities, who are often divided over what their countries' national interests are or should be.

Military forces are likely to play a key role in the relations among the new states, both as objects of interstate competition and as instruments for the domination of some states by others. Not least important, post-Soviet military forces will influence the new states' relations with an arc of neighboring countries extending from Germany to Japan, as well as with the United States.

Russia

Both as an international actor whose "comparative diplomatic advantage" lies in the generation of military power, and as a nation deeply scarred by traumatic invasions, Russia has traditionally emphasized the military as the most important instrument of its foreign policy, and has assigned a supporting role to diplomatic, economic, and cultural instruments. The military has always held a special place in Russian political culture as a primary guardian of the nation.[2] In an interview upbraiding military commanders for "impermissibly" delaying the implementation of military reform and instead trying to play "the army card" in domestic and foreign policy, President Yeltsin nevertheless repeated the standard litany that "there is scarcely any other country in the world that has been subjected so often over the centuries to piratical raids or large-scale armed aggression. . . . [The military's] heroic feats of arms have gone down forever in the annals of the country's history and have made a deep imprint on our entire cultural and spiritual life."[3]

Even in the Soviet period, however, elite consensus on the centrality of military power was sometimes strained by disagreements over the relative emphasis to be given to military versus political and economic instruments of policy.[4] Not surprisingly perhaps, such disagreements have been carried over into the internal deliberations of the now-sovereign Russia, although in many cases the specific issues at stake differ fundamentally from those of the Soviet era. Among the issues at stake are the role of force in Russian foreign policy, especially toward neighboring countries, and the content of military doctrine, a draft of which has been in circulation and under discussion since spring 1992. Also under discussion are military withdrawals from the "near abroad" and the role of the military in regional conflicts, including the role of paramilitary groups like the Cossacks. All of these debates take place against the backdrop, discussed in this chapter, of a decline in military cohesion and morale, and of a socioeconomic environment incapable of supporting the large outlays necessary to maintain Russia's traditional military-industrial base.

The debates on the use of force in general, and the circumstances under which its use would be justified in the "near abroad" in particular, have been central to Russia's larger discussion of its identity as a great power in the region and the world. Stating that the "cessation of armed clashes and the settling of conflicts around Russia" has become "the most important foreign policy problem" facing the country, the Russian Foreign Ministry, in its "Foreign Policy Concept" paper submitted to the Supreme Soviet in March 1993, strongly eschewed the use of force. It urged the "regulation" of Russia's military presence in neighboring countries, the "exclusion of military force" from the arsenal of policy instruments, and the use of "political means of security for Russia in all dimensions." At the same time, however, the Foreign Ministry document stated that although the use of force continues to play "a definite role in the provocation and escalation of conflicts," force is also instrumental in the "blocking of conflicts" and in their regulation.[5] It goes without saying that such a proposal has been viewed with trepidation by the leaders of most of the other new states.

Before such a role could be formalized, the armed forces would first have to agree on their own doctrinal statement. The Russian Ministry of Defense was created only in May 1992, after it became clear that CIS military structures would not succeed in serving all of Russia's interests. Consequently, it is not surprising that fully a year later the military still had not been able to agree on a formal military doctrine that could stand alongside, and support, the foreign policy concept prepared by the Foreign Ministry and approved by the Security Council. This lacuna led President Yeltsin to lament that as long as Russia does not have a military doctrine, "we will be forced to adopt a defensive position, but the Russian Armed Forces have never conducted themselves this way."[6]

Debates over the content of Russia's military doctrine have been extensive, exhaustive, and inconclusive, producing splits within the military itself and inviting the intervention of parliamentary, governmental, and political groupings.[7] At the core of any military doctrine must be a clear definition of the threats facing the state and nation. Only then can posture and force structure be elaborated. As the debate on doctrine unfolded it was clear that consensus could not be reached on four crucial issues: the extent and nature of threats from the West, the best response to threats to Russia's territorial integrity, military rights and obligations to protect Russian minorities abroad, and the nature of threats to Russia's national security from the "near abroad."

During much of the era of detente in the 1970s, Soviet political thinking preached accommodation with the West while military doctrine continued to identify the West as the single greatest threat to Soviet national security. The striving for strategic parity and conventional superiority were a reflection of this threat assessment. Since even before the collapse of the Soviet Union, however, Moscow's political-military establishment has been split over the question of whether the West is a threat at all.[8] Debates about this, as discussed in Chapter 6 and elsewhere, go to the core of Russia's own search for identity; and the military has been a party to that debate, taking a wide array of positions.

Those officers within the military who see the West as a threat do so on a number of grounds. Some are concerned because the West has continued the modernization of strategic systems that remain targeted on Russia. Others object to what they see as America's unilateral assumption of the role of the world's policeman, seeking militarily to impose its interests on areas of the world where Russia's own ties and interests could be diminished.[9] In particular there is the fear that the West may at some point seek to escalate tensions around Russia's borders in an effort to increase Russia's isolation and dependency, perhaps with an eye to using conflicts in neighboring countries as springboards for future intervention in Russia itself. Finally, some officers believe that the West seeks democratization and marketization of Russia not to aid the revival of Russia's great-power status but precisely in order to prevent its reemergence. From these views flows the argument that the Russian military should continue to maintain strategic parity with the West, air defense on the outer perimeter of the former Soviet Union, and a conventional military capability both to prevent the West from using neighboring countries as staging points for an attack on Russia and to support the authority of the state, along with internal security services, if called upon, against Western subversion.

Between the start of 1992 and mid-1993, the members of the military and political elite who espoused such views did not succeed in making them dominant. However, the opposite view, that the West poses no military threat, also did not take hold. Rather, the tendency toward lessening the calculation of the likelihood of direct military confrontation with the United States on specific issues grew stronger at the same time that general misgivings about Western intentions increased. This paradox was due primarily to the tendency to see the greatest risk of general war in the possibility that regional wars on the Russian perimeter would escalate to involve foreign, including possibly Western, intervention. It may also have been due to the tendency of civilian decision-makers to shy away from the crushing budgetary implications of the more somber threat assessment at a time of plummeting economic output.

The emphasis on regional conflict was reflected in important military documents. For instance, the draft statement of Russian military doctrine published in May 1992 defined Russia's national interests in regional rather than global terms, thereby implicitly downgrading the possibility of conflict with the United States. Moreover, in several respects the draft statement corresponded more closely to the concept of "defense sufficiency" than did the revised military doctrine hammered out under Gorbachev.[10] Given Russia's desperate need for Western political and economic assistance, the comparatively restrained tone of the Russian military's comments on policy toward the West may have betokened a measure of genuine, if incomplete, consensus.

All this said, differences over some aspects of military relations with the West have persisted among both uniformed officers and civilian policy-makers. Yeltsin did not engender any trust among conservatives when just one week after assuring senior army officers that he would uphold "the idea of strategic [nuclear] parity" with the United States, he explicitly abandoned the concept at the June 1992 Washington summit when he signed an arms-reduction agreement that, among other things, obligated Russia to dismantle its revered SS-18 ICBMs.[11] Nor was the justification for the dichotomy between Yeltsin's words and deeds likely to win military support: "The audience changed," his spokesman explained.[12] Moreover, the inability of the military to agree on a redrafted military doctrine indicated the extent of disquiet about the nature of Russia's real interest in declaring the West no longer to be a threat.

The recasting of military doctrine has been hampered not only by the absence of consensus about a Western threat, but also by the lack of agreement over the military's mission at and beyond Russia's borders. The heart of the problem has been the difficulty of formulating doctrine for the protection of borders that have been defined only since 1991, and that are not fully recognized either by constitutional arrangements or by international treaties upheld by the current Russian government. There are many political and military leaders who would like to extend these borders, and to extend Russia's mission beyond them. Militarily, it is impossible to develop plans for the defense of borders without becoming party to the political debate about demarcation. Politically, it has become increasingly difficult to build a consensus on the question of the point at which Russia must stop shrinking or start growing again. Public opinion is split between those who are willing to see additional territorial concessions and those who believe that although losing the

Soviet Union was bad enough, losing any part of the Russian Federation would be intolerable.[13]

It is not surprising that the military, on the whole, has supported those who reject territorial concessions. In particular, the Kuril Islands in the east and Crimea in the west are two pieces of territory that have riveted its attention. It is incontestible that Russia's prospects for economic recovery would be aided by an infusion of aid and investments from Japan; yet in both 1992 and 1993, Yeltsin was obliged to put off trips to Japan largely under the pressure of military and conservative civilian opinion in Russia, which feared that he would barter away the four most southern islands in the Kuril chain and probably regarded this possibility as a dangerous precedent for other territorial disputes, such as the one over Crimea.

In late July 1992, as Yeltsin was finalizing plans for his forthcoming state visit to Japan, the Russian General Staff circulated a document sharply rejecting any concessions to Japan over the ownership of the islands and insisting that the islands "are a most important element in ... ensuring the stability of [Russia's] strategic defense in the Far East."[14] Ultimately, Yeltsin had to postpone his trip, even though the document sparked a response from experts denying the strategic value of the islands.[15] His 1993 trip was postponed for the same reason. A similar pattern of dispute emerged in military concerns over Crimea, where the military establishment was even more adamant about the centrality of Sevastopol for Russia's ability to control shipping in the Black Sea and prevent attacks from the southwest.

Doctrinal disagreements have also occurred over the circumstances under which Russia would be justified in projecting force beyond its borders. Clearly Russia no longer has the will or capacity for a global projection of conventional forces. Two other issues have been at the center of doctrinal discussions: namely, the circumstances under which force should be used to protect the 25 million Russians who now find themselves living in the other new states, and the extent to which Russia has other "vital interests" in the "near abroad" that, if violated, would demand the use of military force.

Members of the Russian military elite have, on the whole, supported an activist foreign policy to protect Russians abroad. There are many reasons military feelings run deep on this issue. The military has traditionally seen itself as responsible for protecting Mother Russia above all other nations during both the prerevolutionary and Soviet periods, so while military indoctrination may have encouraged internationalism during the Soviet period, military tradition ensured that Russia remained the central concern. The military is also now focused on the "near abroad" because of the large and vocal communities of retired military officers and their families who have settled in areas that are now outside Russia (particularly in Crimea and in Latvia and Estonia) and who stand to be politically, economically and culturally disenfranchised in these new states.[16]

Military support extends often beyond ethnic Russians to all Russian speakers abroad, giving the military a wide mandate. As Russian defense minister Grachev remarked: "The Russian Armed Forces are carrying the main burden of interethnic conflicts . . . on territories of those states which used to be part of the USSR." "This is happening," he went on to say, "first, because the Russian Army, in fact, is the only manageable unit of the former USSR that can fulfill practical tasks, including those of stopping bloodbaths. . . . Second, as I said before, and as I am about to confirm again: In all states where interethnic conflicts take place, there is a large community of Russian speakers – not a very fashionable word – whom we have the right and the duty to defend."[17]

In addition to this conception of Russia's interests, some officers have argued that Russia has other vital interests at stake in the "near abroad." In the keynote speech at a May 1992 conference on Russia's military security, Colonel General I. N. Rodionov, head of the General Staff Academy, stated that from the military and security point of view, it would be a violation of Russia's "vital interests" if Russia's new neighbors blocked free exit from seaports, allowed third-country military forces on their territory, joined military blocs aimed against Russia, violated the civil rights of the Russian population in these states, or created a *cordon sanitaire* blocking Russian interaction with countries of the West, South, or East. Rodionov also stated that local conflicts arising within or near Russian borders deriving from religious, national, and ethnic unrest constituted a clear threat to Russia's vital interests and were one of the most likely scenarios for a future large-scale conventional war. Rodionov's warning that Russian national security policy must be made only with Russia's security in mind and not in a public-relations attempt to "seek to increase trust in us by the world community" indicated differences among political-military elites in assessing the risk that the West might capitalize on the upheavals in Russia's borderlands to create dangerous new military bridgeheads immediately adjacent to the Russian frontier.[18]

The difficulty of reaching agreement on threat assessments and doctrine has undermined Russia's ability to pursue a coherent strategy toward the related questions of Russian troop withdrawals from areas outside Russia and Russia's role in conflicts in the "near abroad," particularly in those areas where Russian troops are still stationed. In May 1992 Russia signed a collective security agreement with five other CIS members that was intended to regularize the role of Russian military

forces in the signatory countries.[19] The treaty was designed to allow
for Russia to maintain a military presence in the signatory countries,
and thus ease pressures from isolationist-minded groups within Russia
for withdrawal of all Russian troops stationed abroad. However, the
agreement was limited in its effectiveness because some countries of
greatest strategic interest to Russia – Ukraine, Moldova, and the Baltics
– were unwilling to sign. And those countries willing and even eager
to sign, like Turkmenistan and Kazakhstan, did so primarily in order
to use Russian troops as a substitute for the formation of their own
national armies, or as in the case of Armenia, to impel Russian involvement on Armenia's side in its conflict with Azerbaijan.

By May 1993, the collective security treaty had lost its supporters
even within the Russian military. At a meeting of defense ministers of
CIS states, Marshal Shaposhnikov was not able to gain the support of
the Russian high command for a proposal to create a standing CIS
force. Despite the support of the other five signatories to the treaty,
Colonel General Boris Gromov, the Russian representative, rejected it,
noting that Russia alone would bear the brunt of fielding such a force
because the other signatories had not built up their own national
armies.[20] The change in Russia's attitude, combined with the hesitation
of the parliaments of several signatory states to ratify the treaty, prevented the creation of a multilateral legal basis for the continued presence of the Russian troops stationed abroad.[21]

The position and role of Russian forces abroad, therefore, have failed
to be regulated by any overarching treaty. As a result their status and
functions are different in virtually each of the states in which they are
stationed. In the Central Asian states that border on Iran and Afghanistan, Russian soldiers have continued to act as border troops under
agreement with local authorities, and have on the whole received local
support in their efforts to stem the flow of illicit arms, drugs, and other
contraband across these borders.[22] In the Caucasus, Russian troops are
stationed in both Armenia and Georgia. The Armenians have tried, but
so far failed, to draw Russian troops into their battles with Azerbaijan.
Upon Baku's request, Russian troops were withdrawn from Azerbaijan.
One regiment has been stationed in Abkhazia, the autonomous republic
lying along Georgia's northern Black Sea coast. In August 1992, the
renegade Georgian minister of defense, Tengiz Kitovani, launched an
assault on Abkhaz separatists in their capital, Sukhumi. Local Russian
military commanders, apparently eager to "punish" Kitovani and other
ultranationalist and anti-Russian segments of the Georgian hierarchy,
have tacitly supported the side of Abkhazia, reportedly even bombing
Georgian troops that fired on their positions in Sukhumi beginning in
the spring of 1993.[23] In an effort to quell the fighting while maintaining

Georgian control over Abkhazia, Georgian head of state Shevardnadze
was obliged to travel to Moscow to urge President Yeltsin to try to
bring his local commanders under control, while reaffirming that under
the existing bilateral agreement, Russian troops would not be withdrawn
completely until at least 1995.[24]

The situation has been equally complicated in some western new
states, including Ukraine, Moldova, and the Baltics, where Russia and
indigenous elites have been unable to conclude bilateral treaties governing all aspects of the status of Russian troops. Here concern has
been particularly high that Russian troops might refuse to withdraw
under the pretext of the need to protect the local Russian population.
Many of the non-Russian citizens of these states fear that Russian troops
deployed on their territory may be used to shape their internal politics
and, in the worst case, to expand Russia's current borders through
military reconquest. That such views have been freely voiced by sections
of the Russian political-military elite further reinforces anxiety in these
countries.[25]

This highly fluid and conflict-ridden political setting also has worked
to increase the vulnerability of Russian forces stationed abroad to attacks, and commensurately has increased the tendency of local Russian
leaders to take matters into their own hands, both to protect their own
troops and to promote objectives they feel Moscow has neglected. Following exchanges of gunfire between Russian soldiers and national
guardsmen in Lithuania and Estonia, for example, "shoot-to-kill" orders were issued to Russian troops in the event they should again come
under fire, and the incidents stopped.[26] The former CIS commander
of the Black Sea Fleet, Admiral Igor Kasatonov, consistently criticized
Ukrainian efforts to claim some or all of the fleet and insisted that it
was indivisible long after top Russian and Ukrainian political leaders
had agreed, at some point in the future, to divide it. Kasatonov was
eventually recalled.

In bitter fighting between Russian speakers and Moldovans along the
Dniester River in eastern Moldova, the local Russian military has played
a direct role.[27] Units of Russia's 14th Army stationed there have openly
joined the Russian-speaking minority in attempting to establish a separate Russian enclave, and the army's hard-line commander, Lieutenant
General Aleksandr Lebed, has explicitly challenged the Russian Federation's official policy toward the conflict. Asserting that "the Dniester republic [is] itself a small part of Russia," Lebed has rejected
Yeltsin's policy of "going with an outstretched hand to the world's
cabinets, instead of building up a great power capable of imposing its
will."[28] Yeltsin has hinted at his own incomplete control of the residual
14th Army units by remarking that "for my part, I will do everything

to ensure appropriate behavior by the Russian Army there [in the trans-Dniester region]."[29] "Appropriate behavior," however, apparently has not included forcing the army to withdraw, as indicated by Lebed's own admission in May 1993 that the 14th Army was engaged in building housing for its officers in Moldova – this despite the oft-repeated fiction that one reason the Russians had not withdrawn earlier was that they lacked money to build housing for officers in Russia.[30] On the contrary, the inaction (or connivance) of the center allowed Lebed to claim in March 1993 that he would not leave trans-Dniester until its status and borders were assured.[31]

The presence of Russian troops in the Baltics has been a vexatious issue, not least because at their height Soviet troops in these three small states numbered more than 130,000 (compared with the smaller force of 55,000 troops, for example, that had previously been stationed in Poland).[32] These figures did not include family members and a huge contingent of retired Russian military personnel and Russian workers in defense industries. In September 1992 protracted parallel negotiations between Russia and the three Baltic states appeared to reach a watershed when Russia agreed on a timetable for withdrawing its troops from Lithuania. From the start it seemed unlikely that this withdrawal agreement would soon usher in similar agreements with Estonia and Latvia. As shown in Chapter 2, Lithuania had granted citizenship to all its residents regardless of ethnicity, whereas Latvia and Estonia had denied automatic citizenship to most Russians living there, and Russia drew a direct connection between the withdrawal and citizenship issues.[33]

In any case, in October 1992 Russia broke off its talks with Estonia and Latvia and formally suspended implementation of the accord it had already signed with Lithuania. The Russian Supreme Soviet had refused to ratify the agreement, forcing Yeltsin to publicly break off talks, while in fact troop withdrawals continued. Yeltsin dealt with the imbroglio by pledging that a full withdrawal would occur but also by pleading for patience and understanding on the part of the citizens of the Baltic states and their supporters in the West. To achieve a withdrawal, he remarked, "we need to resolve all the social problems" connected with the relocation of troops – such as the provision of housing and retraining. "We simply cannot withdraw 100,000 soldiers to an open field. In this case they will simply be our enemies."[34] Negotiations were resumed, and produced many points of agreement, although with the exception of Lithuania, where the two sides agreed that all Russian troops would be withdrawn by 31 August 1993, no final dates for the completion of withdrawal were agreed. The issue of withdrawal is manifestly more complicated than references to logistical problems and to the quite genuine shortage of housing suggest. It is entangled with the question of Russia's future military posture in northern Europe, with possible Russian political designs on Baltic territory, and with the future of Kaliningrad.

Many natives of the Baltic states fear that Russia has ulterior motives for keeping substantial numbers of troops in their countries – specifically, a desire to retain permanent control of certain military assets and an intent ultimately to reconquer the region by force. It is plausible that the Russian military as a whole supports the first goal, and quite clear that at least some members of the military, as well as some right-wing Russian politicians, cherish the second.[35] At the same time, it is also evident that the numerous retired Russian officers living in Latvia and Estonia fear that they will face discriminatory policies designed to force them to return to Russia.[36] Despite the persisting political controversy, Russian troop withdrawals continued, although the date for the final withdrawal of all troops remained contested.[37] In October 1992, the U.S. State Department announced that about 40 percent of the estimated 130,000 troops recently situated in the Baltic states had already withdrawn, leaving some 52,000, of whom 25,000 were scheduled to return to Russia before the end of 1993.[38] By July 1993, only 28,000 remained, and of these the 7,000 in Lithuania were due to be withdrawn by 31 August, leaving 6,000 in Estonia and 15,000 in Latvia. Of this 28,000 total, only 11,000 were combat troops, the rest being mainly logistical and support staff and officers whose troops had been withdrawn.

Clearly some of these troops would move south and not east to Russia – in other words, Russia would pull out of the Baltic states at least partially by shoring up and strengthening its military presence in Kaliningrad, the enclave of the Russian Federation located between Lithuania and Poland. In particular, the loss of Lithuania's Klaipeda 3d Coastal Defense division, the Liepaja and Riga naval bases in Latvia, and the Tallinn base in Estonia would be compensated for by an increased presence in the Baltiysk base in Kaliningrad. The groundwork for such a redeployment was laid by obtaining Lithuanian agreement to build housing units for 10,000 troops in Kaliningrad in exchange for military hardware to form the basis of a Lithuanian navy.[39] Reflecting the extent of political-military agreement on maintaining its presence in Kaliningrad, Foreign Minister Kozyrev, speaking in Baltiysk, spoke of the necessity for Russia to maintain an "imposing military presence" in Kaliningrad, which he characterized as "an indivisible and undisputed part of Russia."[40]

The growth of militant nationalism within the Russian political-military elite has also been reflected in the Cossack revival in Russia. Historically fierce defenders of Russian territory, the Cossacks have joined Russian military units in armed clashes in the trans-Dniester region and are heavily engaged in fighting in the Ossetian region of the North Caucasus. They are also active in northwestern and northeastern Kazakhstan. Two separate Cossack movements exist in Russia, although some reports have suggested that they will probably merge in the near future.[41] Decrees by Yeltsin in June 1992 and March 1993 paved the way for the active incorporation of these Cossack units into the Russian military and into the frontier border guards. Additional reports indicate that former KGB officers are joining the Cossacks, making the revival a potential vehicle for an antidemocratic, ultranationalist movement.[42] This is one major reason military authorities have resisted Cossack autonomy, insisting that Cossack units, whose reemergence they have welcomed, nevertheless be strictly subordinated not to traditional hetmans, but to military authorities.[43]

All of these debates over doctrine, and all of the activities relating to Russia's potential role in conflicts abroad, have taken place against the backdrop of a decline in civilian patriotism, in military cohesion and morale, and in the military-industrial base that traditionally has supported Russia's global reach. The military is not only "downsizing," it is in danger of collapse. Thus fully 75–80 percent of Russian youth evaded compulsory military service in 1992.[44] The collapse of units has been combined with efforts to achieve orderly restructuring, but the combination of the two has resulted in the announcement by the defense minister that 270,000 officers would have to be discharged from the military.[45] This has produced a decline in morale and an increase in organizations lobbying within the military for a wide range of social, political, and economic objectives, thereby producing a politicization of the officer corps unprecedented in Russian history. Indeed, such is the level of dissatisfaction that a poll of officers conducted by the army journal *Armiya Rossii* found that 73 percent of the respondents "consider it a mistake that they did not storm the White House in August 1991."[46] So-called strike committees have been formed with the avowed purpose to "psychologically prepare personnel for the possibility of the authorities being overthrown."[47] It should be noted that activities of this type were not unknown in the period before the August 1991 attempted coup, which in fact received little support from junior and middle-grade officers.

Even assuming that some fears of the army entering politics are exaggerated, nevertheless such fears have worked to increase the ability of the army to pressure the political authorities not to diminish its economic base. This addresses the military desire to maintain a strong military-industrial complex and an active arms-sales program. Although a public campaign for the conversion of the military-industrial complex has been under way since 1988, the results of the effort to date have been rather meager. Critics complain that the campaign has frequently entailed a mindless shift of high-technology industrial facilities to the manufacture of technically unrelated products, thereby causing economic hardship and the dispersal of exceptionally talented research and production teams. Proponents of more radical conversion measures have countered that most of the conversion effort to date has been a sham exercise carried out under the protection of continued central planning of the defense-industrial sector.[48]

Of equal concern to the military have been sales of arms and high technology to outside states. With the yield from such sales estimated at some $8 billion for 1992, even the most liberal members of the government, such as former acting prime minister Yegor Gaidar, have come to understand that Russia must depend upon this industry as one of the few sectors capable of generating hard-currency revenues in the collapsing Russian economy.[49] As discussed in Chapter 5, Yeltsin's decree that part of the proceeds from arms sales will go toward constructing housing for returning Russian troops, and for education and retraining programs, has further boosted the incentive to expand arms exports. Presumably any qualms the high command feels about selling sophisticated military equipment to potential adversaries such as China are more than counterbalanced by the desire to maintain faltering military industries and cushion the officer corps against economic hardship.

A policy of encouraging sales of arms and military-applicable technology to generate hard currency, however, has created friction with other nations, particularly the United States. One such conflict broke out in May 1992, when the United States pressured Russia to cancel a $250 million deal to supply India with cryogenic rocket boosters. Washington charged that the sale violated the Missile Technology Control Regime, and threatened Moscow with economic sanctions if the sale went through. Another conflict between the United States and Russia developed over Moscow's sale of Kilo-class diesel submarines, SU-24 bombers, and nuclear power reactors to Iran. Although one U.S. defense analyst concluded that "the Russians will sell anything to anybody to earn hard currency and to keep production lines going,"[50] in fact they abided by U.N. sanctions against Iraq and the former Yugoslavia.

Russia and the United States eventually worked out a modification of the sale to India, but the incident left Moscow with some doubt about its new relationship with its erstwhile enemy. "A real trade war is on," the head of Glavkosmos, the Russian state agency responsible for the deal, said of the U.S. action. The Americans "would like to force us out of India and then from other countries."[51] Politicians as diverse in political leanings as Vice-President Aleksandr Rutskoy and

St. Petersburg mayor Anatoliy Sobchak have maintained that a reduction of arms exports runs counter to Russian national interests and, in the words of Sobchak, has "played into the hands" of Russia's competitors in the United States and Germany.[52] Efforts by arms manufacturers in the West, supported by their governments, to maintain and expand their own shares of the global arms market bode ill for Western efforts to persuade Russian political leaders to sign international agreements limiting the sales of advanced weapons.

The Western Newly Independent States

Given Ukraine's history of coerced mergers and forced annexation by Russia, Poland, and other neighboring states, it is hardly surprising that on the day Ukraine's leaders declared absolute sovereignty and full independence from Moscow, they simultaneously moved to create an armed force capable of defending the new state.[53] Following the 1 December 1991 referendum that overwhelmingly favored independence, Ukrainian leaders moved quickly to establish an autonomous military and national defense structure. On 6 December, the parliament passed a number of laws on the formation of the armed forces, and six days later President Kravchuk declared himself commander-in-chief of all nonstrategic (meaning nonnuclear) forces on Ukrainian soil. At that time, 20 of the 124 divisions of the Soviet army stationed within the USSR were based in Ukraine, including some of the country's most battle-ready and best-equipped troops. It was from these divisions that Ukraine sought to fashion its new army. By early January, Kiev was well on its way to creating its own army.[54] That these acts to create a military force occurred against the backdrop of the creation of the Commonwealth of Independent States (CIS)[55] served as a clear notice of how seriously Ukraine viewed its sovereignty and how vigorously it was prepared to defend it.

Ukrainian thinking on the establishment of a national defense force actually emerged in the late Gorbachev years, and thus was in no way an impulsive reaction to the collapse of the USSR. Indeed, given Ukraine's long-suppressed aspirations for independence and statehood, as well as the bitter memory of its ignominious defeat at the hands of the Bolshevik Red Army in 1917–19, one may posit that Ukrainians had been thinking for a long time about the necessity of having a strong military force for national and territorial defense.[56]

In asserting its sovereignty over the estimated 670,000 Soviet military personnel stationed on its territory,[57] Ukraine overnight claimed control of the second-largest armed force on the European continent. Put into comparative perspective, such a military force was "larger than British and French forces combined and two and a half times the size of the entire complement of U.S. forces in Europe."[58] The sheer task of reducing and shaping these divisions into a military force that would serve the country has proved formidable. As of spring 1993, the Ukrainian army consisted of 525,000 men. Even if Ukraine were to receive pledges of loyalty and retain only half of these forces, such military potential would prompt concern among Ukraine's neighbors, given the historical record of antagonisms and disputed borders. A force of 450,000, the target figure on which Ukrainian officials agreed after some initial fluctuation, would not be part of any CIS force, and would be fully independent of Russia.

Ukrainian efforts to formulate a military doctrine have been hampered by fundamental disagreements over the disposition of the Black Sea Fleet with Russia and the terms under which Ukraine should accept the status of a nonnuclear neutral state. Inside Ukraine, political disputes have broken out over whether the country can afford to maintain half a million men under arms, especially if, as the military doctrine states, Ukraine has no enemies. A Ukrainian government minister announced that it "will take a sum total of more than 2 trillion rubles to fulfill the concept of the doctrine. This is in excess of the entire Ukrainian budget."[59]

Cognizant that the greatest potential threat to its territorial integrity lies in the east, Ukraine has reoriented its forces and sought to reach military agreements with neighbors to its west. Ukraine concluded a friendship treaty with Poland that "confirms the inviolability of borders and the rejection of all territorial claims," and calls for mutual consultation on matters of defense and national security.[60] Moreover, Ukrainian defense minister Konstantin Morozov flew to Warsaw to convey assurances that Kiev would be a nonnuclear power, would reject military force as a foreign policy option, and would abide by international arms reduction treaties such as the Conventional Forces in Europe (CFE) treaty. In response, then-Polish defense minister Jan Parys, all too aware of the distinction between statement and practice, remarked ironically that "once [these declarations] are implemented, Poland will certainly not be in danger from the Ukrainian armed forces."[61]

Romania and Moldova are other border states concerned over the size and intentions of the new Ukrainian army. Romania is the only state to have made official claims on present Ukrainian territory, specifically on northern Bukovina and parts of southern Bessarabia. Such claims, which are also endorsed by Moldova, have unquestionably affected Kiev's military thinking. A summit in October 1992 between Ukrainian president Leonid Kravchuk and Moldovan president Mircea Snegur specifically allowed for the future discussion of the status of the disputed former Moldovan and Romanian territories of Bukovina and Bessarabia.[62] However, it is improbable that Moldovan leaders would reveal their real attitude toward such territorial disputes while Moldova is embroiled in the trans-Dniester conflict with Russia – a conflict in which Moldova has actively courted Ukrainian support as a deterrent against Russian intervention or secession by the trans-Dniester regime.[63]

Ukraine is faced with a dilemma in Moldova. On the one hand, it has not supported the emergence of military cooperation between Moldova and Romania and would probably oppose Moldovan unification with Romania, particularly if Romanian politics continue to be influenced by ultranationalist, irredentist, and protofascist parties.[64] Even leaving the issue of Romanian domestic politics to one side, Ukraine has shown sympathy for the plight of the Slavs (Russians and Ukrainians) in Moldova who do not want to be ruled by Romanian-speaking and Romanian-oriented Moldovans. However, the stationing of the remnants of the Russian 14th Army in trans-Dniester and its apparent refusal to withdraw effectively give Russia the ability in the event of conflict with Ukraine to force Ukraine to fight on two fronts.

As for international disarmament obligations, in July 1992 Ukraine formally ratified the CFE arms-reduction treaty, which places ceilings on five categories of conventional weapons. That Kiev acceded to a treaty that had been signed and ratified by twenty-nine NATO, Warsaw Pact, and former Soviet states may have eased the suspicion of some of Ukraine's neighbors about its military intentions, but the ceilings for Ukraine give it holdings of major armaments higher than Germany or France. Ukrainian deputy foreign minister Boris Tarasyuk, moreover, insisted that Kiev would preserve an army of more than 400,000 troops even after making reductions, thereby maintaining the second-largest army in Europe after Russia.[65] Tarasyuk's remark suggests that Ukraine plans to peg the size of its military to that of its most likely opponent – Russia.

The creation of a Ukrainian military force has had a profound impact on the military structures and defense orientations of the other post-Soviet states. President Kravchuk's adamant refusal to submit Kiev to a joint CIS military force effectively crippled that organization; likewise, Ukraine's determined insistence on creating an army not only galvanized Russia into doing the same, but also produced a tangible increase in sentiment against Ukraine on the part of Russian elites. St. Petersburg mayor Anatoliy Sobchak, for example, called Kiev's decision to create its own military force "a huge threat to mankind as a whole."[66] As might be expected, Kiev's commitment to establish a sovereign military force by essentially confiscating former Soviet military equipment and forces has exacerbated tensions with Russia. The schism with Russia has had two core components: Moscow objected to the process by which Ukraine started building its armed forces, as well as to the very existence of an independent Ukrainian military force.

The focal point of Kiev's move to establish a loyal military was its controversial promulgation of an "oath of allegiance" to Ukraine. Officers and soldiers who refused to take the oath were hastily relieved of their posts and told to leave the country, thereby creating even more pressures in the receiving states. That the frontline Soviet forces armed with the most advanced weapons, equipment, and technology were based primarily in Ukraine prior to the USSR's collapse also made Kiev's annexation of these units more troubling for Moscow.[67]

The oath created other problems. One was that by April 1993, as part of the general move by Ukraine to take control of the nuclear weapons on its territory, the Ukrainian high command was insisting that forces operating these strategic weapons also take an oath of loyalty to Ukraine, increasing both Russian and Western concern about whether Ukraine would eventually accept an obligation to divest itself of all remaining nuclear weapons.[68] The other issue that caused concern, this time within the Ukrainian command itself, was the reliability of the military men who had taken the oath. Defense Minister Morozov himself expressed the view that a considerable portion of the officer corps had sworn loyalty to Ukraine to avoid repatriation to Russia, where they would be homeless, and in the belief that the two armies would in any case be united within the CIS.[69] Such concerns produced an increase in efforts to improve the morale and the cohesion of the new force, partially by building on Ukraine's Cossack legacy.[70] The increased sentiment in the Ukrainian parliament against Russia fueled this trend, with the parliament rejecting the military's draft defense doctrine in April 1993, at least partially because of the desire by some members to see Russia identified by name as a threat to Ukrainian security, and partially because of the concern of some deputies that Ukraine should not state in its doctrine that the country was committed to a nonnuclear course.[71]

The struggle over ownership of the post-Soviet Black Sea Fleet has been the most serious point of contention between Russia and Ukraine since the collapse of the Soviet Union. Although the fight over the division of vessels remains real enough, the most burning issue has been base facilities, above all the Fleet's main base at Sevastopol. This issue was seriously exacerbated by the simultaneous demand of Russian politicians for the return of the Crimean peninsula or at least Sevastopol, where the fleet is based, to Russian jurisdiction.[72] In January 1992, Russian and Ukrainian officials met to discuss the distribution of fleet forces, which resulted in an agreement that Kiev had the right to an unspecified number of vessels. In mid-March, a battle of decrees was waged, with each side asserting complete sovereignty over the entire fleet.

In late June 1992, Russian president Boris Yeltsin and Ukrainian president Leonid Kravchuk held a summit meeting at Dagomys and agreed in principle to share the Black Sea Fleet. At the summit Yeltsin implicitly acknowledged Crimea to be an internal Ukrainian matter by not even raising the topic with Kravchuk. Exactly one month later, however, two Black Sea Fleet ships were hijacked and defected to Ukraine, prompting other ships to give chase and to open fire on the fleeing vessels. As the hijacked vessels neared Odessa, Ukrainian aircraft and warships raced out to challenge the pursuing ships and to escort the defecting vessels to port, bringing Russian and Ukrainian forces to the brink of armed conflict.[73] The pro-Russian commander of the fleet called the "super-serious" situation "increasingly explosive," while Ukrainian defense minister Konstantin Morozov acknowledged that "a situation of clear confrontation has taken shape, and it is highly probable that there will be conflicts involving weapons."[74]

Yeltsin and Kravchuk were therefore obliged to meet yet again, this time in Yalta in August, to discuss the status of the fleet. At Yalta they decided to remove the fleet from CIS jurisdiction and transfer it to a joint Russian-Ukrainian command for a period of three years, until tensions had eased enough so that a division of forces could be more readily achieved.[75] Critical problems, however, remained, with practically daily incidents flaring up between the two sides in Crimea.[76] On 11 November Kravchuk acknowledged that despite the agreements at Dagomys and Yalta, negotiations on the Black Sea Fleet "remain difficult."[77] Meanwhile, after a protracted silence, Russian vice-president Rutskoy again reiterated Russian claims to Crimea, averring that sooner or later the region would revert to Russian control.[78]

Ukraine's reaction has been equally tough, with Defense Minister Morozov stating that unless Russia stops removing large amounts of materiel from the Black Sea Fleet without Ukrainian agreements and negotiates an equitable division of assets, "Ukraine would demand that Russia withdraw all its naval forces from Ukraine. . . . I don't see on what terms Sevastopol, Kharkov, or Sumy could be leased to any country."[79] The problem that Ukraine faces, however, is that the overwhelming majority (90 percent) of officers in the Black Sea Fleet do not support the "Ukrainianization" of the fleet. On the contrary, although 87 percent reportedly are in favor of dual citizenship and a dual fleet, 45 percent are for Sevastopol's belonging to Russia, 43 percent for the restoration of a single state, and only 7 percent believe Sevastopol must belong to Ukraine.[80] Such a clear-cut feeling among officers is a major constraint on Ukraine's actual ability, beyond mere declarations, to take control of the fleet.

Developments affecting the defense industry could also contribute to the destabilization of the domestic and international situation. As discussed in Chapter 5, Ukraine is economically ill-equipped to sustain the tremendous former Soviet military force it inherited, yet Kiev has shown strong resistance to parting with any of it. One motive lies in the importance of sovereignty and an intrinsic aversion to compromise on such a key element of nationhood. On an economic level, however, Kiev may well plan to sell off some of the more advanced pieces of the former Soviet arsenal for desperately needed hard currency. Admiral Kasatonov, formerly commander of the Black Sea Fleet, charged that "in Ukraine they look at the fleet as a commercial commodity, which can be profitably sold or exchanged for oil." The Ukrainians countered that submarines and land-assault ships from the contested Black Sea Fleet have been sold off by Russian authorities.[81] Rumored deals involving the sale of the incomplete advanced aircraft carrier *Varyag* (in a Ukrainian shipyard) to China or France have been denied by Ukraine, but such assurances do not inspire much confidence.[82] Moreover, the October 1992 appointment of Leonid Kuchma as prime minister engendered a stronger tilt toward the sale of former Soviet armaments as a source of hard currency earnings. As the former director of the world's largest missile production plant,[83] Kuchma viewed such sales as a positive contribution to the crumbling Ukrainian economy. And given the widespread view among the Ukrainian population that economic problems within Ukraine are a far greater threat to the country's national security than that posed by any foreign country, a move to lower defense expenditure would be welcome.[84]

Belarus also made known its intention to establish its own armed forces and to subordinate former Soviet troops in Belarus to Belarusian authority (except for strategic forces). Minsk has been careful not to repeat Ukraine's example of creating an armed force that might antagonize Russia. Above all, in contrast to Ukraine's plan to establish a force of half a million men, the Belarusian military is not planned to exceed 100,000.[85] In addition, Minsk, with a few exceptions, has not laid claim to expensively equipped military units; there is no navy to fight about; and Minsk has proven amenable to the removal of nuclear weapons.

Belarus is also trying to avoid the sort of problems that Russia faces in attempting to absorb thousands of troops stationed on its soil as well as thousands more wishing to return home. As of July 1992, Minsk reported that some fifteen thousand servicemen in the republic were homeless, and in response it passed laws forbidding the further transfer to Belarus of servicemen for whom accommodations are not available, and appealed to Belarusian servicemen in other CIS states to "not immediately return to the republic."[86]

Minsk has concluded an agreement with Russia that provides for Russian troops to be withdrawn from Belarus over a seven-year period, thereby averting a tense standoff with Russia over the presence and disposition of Russian forces. Although violence has broken out in other states aimed at expelling the Russian "occupiers," Belarus has instead sought to use the Russian troops as the basis for its own armed forces. "An independent state cannot exist without its own armed forces," Chairman Shushkevich has argued. "Clearly, this is 90 percent a question of relations between Belarus and Russia," he said of the need for professional soldiers to help train and establish a Belarusian army.[87] For example, in the Belarusian Defense Ministry, in mid-1992 only one of nine deputy defense ministers was an ethnic Belarusian; the rest were almost all Russians.[88] This ethnic imbalance was found in other areas of the Belarusian military. For example, only 30 percent of the Belarusian office corps was ethnic Belarusian; half of the rank-and-file was ethnic Russian; and just 20 percent of the defense ministry staff was ethnic Belarusian.[89] Although Minsk began conscription in July 1992 and decreed that all Belarusian military forces would take an oath of allegiance in December 1992, it has also striven to avoid contention with Russia over the seizure and inheritance of former Soviet army divisions and equipment. Minsk has said that all service personnel who want to serve a state other than Belarus are free to do so prior to the oath-taking, and it has sought to defuse the rising tensions between ethnic Belarusian and ethnic Russian officers.[90]

Minister of Defense Pavel Kozlouskiy has said that Belarus will reduce the number of troops by 40 percent over the next few years. He has declared that previously "the offensive potential of Belarus was considered to be the greatest in Europe" and thus post-Soviet Minsk needed to adopt a defensive military doctrine.[91] This is consistent with the views of Deputy Defense Minister Pyotr Chaus, who has said that Belarus did not sign the CIS agreement on collective security because of his nation's adherence to the principle of neutrality, and because Belarus sees national armed forces as an attribute of statehood and a part of the overall European security system.[92]

In the Baltic states, the presence in mid-1993 of 28,000 soldiers of the former Soviet army still cast a shadow over the new governments' sovereignty, but a diminishing one (this figure is down from the 130,000 originally stationed in the region). The size of the Baltic countries and their extremely limited economic capabilities militate against the creation of sizable national forces. All three countries are concentrating, in the first stage, on creating border guards whose main function is to prevent smuggling. Moreover, the Russian commander of the northwest group of forces, Valeriy Mironov, asserted that all equipment was the property of his group, and that it would be repatriated to Russia or sold to meet the resettlement costs of his men. Efforts by local authorities physically to prevent equipment from leaving in some cases have created further rifts in relations between Moscow and Latvia and Estonia.[93]

The Baltic states, like Ukraine, have been striving to reduce their military dependence and vulnerability to Russia. They have signed joint defense agreements among themselves, have entered into long-term negotiations over NATO membership, and individually have sought to reduce their reliance on Russian arms by building ties with Western suppliers. Their defensive strategy and military posture would certainly not eliminate their fundamental geopolitical and economic vulnerability to Russian pressure, but shifting to dependence on the West is seen as providing a hedge against such pressure.[94]

The Southern Newly Independent States

The decision by most of the Central Asian and Caucasian states to join the CIS rather than seek unfettered independence was affected as much by military considerations as by economic factors. For most of the southern states, these considerations included the lack of an established military doctrine, the absence of both an adequate arsenal and an independent military-industrial base, and a nonexistent or an insufficiently trained officer corps. Many of these factors were most serious in Central Asia. In the Caucasus, where more than two years of fighting in Nagorno-Karabakh had stimulated the emergence of local militias and national armies, the desire on the part of Armenia in particular to join the CIS stemmed more from the calculation that such a move would evoke Russian support for Armenia's goals vis-à-vis Azerbaijan. For the same reason, Azerbaijan moved to cut military ties with Russia.

In 1992 and early 1993, debates were still focused on such core issues as: Which states are potential enemies and which states are potential allies? Should Russia be regarded as an enemy or as a military guarantor? What military doctrine should any given state develop? What size of military force would be sufficient to meet security requirements, and how would the need to spend on security square with the fiscal requirements of economic reform?

Although the answers to these questions hinged in part on an assessment of real external threats, they also depended on the domestic political calculations of the leaders of the new states. Analysts have often observed that political elites may manufacture contrived security threats in order to divert public attention from intractable domestic problems.[95] This tactic is all the easier when the external environment actually is uncertain or hostile, as in Central Asia and the Caucasus.

The three potential external sources of threat to the new states of the southern tier are from Russia, other Central Asian or Caucasian countries, and other neighboring nations such as Iran, Afghanistan, Turkey, and China. Many Central Asian and Caucasian leaders realize that too close an association with their former Russian "master" may weaken their own states' movement toward independence and will be viewed by domestic opposition leaders as a sign of continued subservience. However, so long as these governments cannot afford military forces of their own, they must pursue a dual strategy. On the one hand, leaders of some of these states have gone out of their way to emphasize their desire for close cooperation with Russia. For example, Turkmenistan's defense minister, Danatar Kopekov, declared that "Turkmenistan firmly adheres to the position of concluding a military treaty with Russia." Moreover, the minister stated that Russia could send soldiers and officers to serve in Turkmenistan if they expressed a wish to do so.[96] Most important, in negotiations between President Saparmurad Niyazov and Russian defense minister Pavel Grachev, the Turkmen side not only supported the creation of a joint command over the troops on its territory (the Soviet army had in Turkmenistan four motorized rifle divisions and one airborne brigade), but agreed to allow Russian control over air-defense formations and airborne units.[97]

Often, however, agreements are easier to sign than to implement. In the case of Turkmenistan, no sooner was the agreement signed than the Turkmen side demanded the subordination of this command to Turkmen authority.[98] Before leaving Ashgabat, Grachev signed a protocol creating a joint command but did not approve its subordination to Turkmenistan. To satisfy Turkmenistan's national pride, the two sides discussed the idea of creating a small Turkmen army, to be staffed primarily by Russian officers.[99] Furthermore, Turkmenistan has disagreed with Russia over border forces, which Russia has sought to maintain under its own jurisdiction. For President Niyazov, "such an approach is unacceptable because it can infringe upon our national dignity: in the near future border troops will consist 90 percent of Turkmenistan citizens."[100]

Other Central Asian states have shown a similar ambivalence in their policies toward Moscow. For example, after concluding a treaty of friendship and cooperation between Russia and Kyrgyzstan, President Akayev reported that both states would cooperate in guaranteeing the reliable defense of the two countries and would preserve and maintain CIS strategic military forces under joint command (in Kyrgyzstan, one motorized rifle division was stationed). Moreover, the treaty indicated that "Russia and Kyrgyzstan will cooperate in providing a joint defense policy on the basis of the fact that the territory of both states lies in a joint military strategic space."[101] In Kazakhstan, President Nazarbayev also initially stated that Kazakhstan recognizes "the community of military-political and economic interests with Russia and other countries of the CIS."[102] Central Asian countries, however, began moving to take more control over CIS forces stationed on their territory (four motorized rifle divisions are stationed in Kazakhstan. In Uzbekistan, there is one such division.) In addition there were some fears on the Kazakh side regarding the growing military activity of both the Union of Cossacks and the Union of the Cossack Armies of Russia (UCAR) in western Kazakhstan.[103] The role of Russian (and other) mercenaries in the fighting on both sides in the Georgian-Abkhazian dispute, along with Russian units whose activities were often disavowed by Moscow, carried the lesson for Central Asian leaders that reliance on a military establishment that is itself disintegrating could spread disorder rather than eliminate it.[104]

Unlike the Caucasus, where Azerbaijan, Armenia, and Georgia are all involved in one or more local conflicts, the Central Asian states not only are attempting to rule out military activity against each other, but also are trying not to depict each other as potential enemies. That all the Central Asian states except Turkmenistan signed the CIS collective security treaty brings them closer in the area of military security. Central Asian leaders seem concerned to construct a web of military and security arrangements that will bolster and not undermine territorial integrity and national sovereignty.[105] For instance, the Kazakhstan National Security Committee has signed a bilateral agreement on mutual assistance with a similar body in Kyrgyzstan. The chairman of the National Security Committee reported that analogous agreements would be signed with other sovereign republics of the commonwealth, a development that would include the other three Central Asian republics.[106]

With the exception of Afghanistan, neighboring countries like Iran, Pakistan, and China have tried to influence Central Asian states more through cultural and economic means than through military methods. Tajik authorities have accused Afghanistan of numerous violations of the borders between the two countries. In the period up to July 1992, approximately four thousand border infractions had been reported.[107] The aim of such violations has been to channel weapons (AK-47s, RPGs, and plastic mines) from the mujahidin in Afghanistan to opposition groups inside Tajikistan.[108] President Nabiyev accused Muslim militants in both countries of threatening his country's stability and reached an agreement with the Russian military to maintain the 201st motorized rifle division and Russian border guard units in Tajikistan.[109]

Whereas Kazakhstan and the Caucasian states have established military forces composed of several military branches,[110] the other southern states have established limited military contingents rather than complete forces. One important reason for this is their participation in the larger security framework of the CIS. For example, in May 1992, before endorsing a plan to build a national army in July 1992, President Akayev of Kyrgyzstan stated that "we are, perhaps, the only CIS country which has made a decision not to create an army of its own."[111] Even after agreeing on the idea of having a national army, Akayev declared that the Kyrgyz army would be made up of professionals and conscripts and would number just 8,000 men.[112] Another justification for founding only small-scale armies came from Valeriy Otchertsov, member of the Turkmenistan Presidential Council and deputy head of government:

> For small Turkmenia, surrounded on all sides by larger neighbors, the creation of its own armed forces guaranteeing the reliable defense of its sovereignty from outside aggression would be highly dubious. The optimum scenario would be for Turkmenistan to have a small formation capable of stopping unauthorized incursions by bandit formations that do not come under any government's jurisdiction.[113]

A further reason for the limited size of Central Asian military establishments is the almost complete absence of a trained indigenous officer corps.[114] This contrasts with the situation in Belarus, for example, where at the meeting of the Coordinating Council of the Union of Belarusian Soldiers, 39,000 officers of Belarusian origin scattered throughout the CIS command are reported to have expressed their willingness to return home in the event of Russian aggression against Belarus.[115] It also contrasts sharply with the situation in the Caucasus, where the military has begun to exert such an influence on politics that civilian governments are destabilized. In Georgia, head of state Shevardnadze was faced with the need either to oust Minister of Defense Kitovani or himself be overthrown.[116] In Azerbaijan, Surat Huseynov, who had been relieved of his post as commander of the Azerbaijani forces in Nagorno-Karabakh, took over the country's second-largest city, Gyandzha, and then the rest of the country, forcing the resignation of Prime Minister Panakh Huseynov and toppling President Elchibey.[117]

Conclusion

Faced with an uncertain international environment, each of the fifteen new states has taken steps to set up its own military forces. This process has entailed the creation of new institutional structures and loyalties in conditions of political turbulence and rapidly declining economic output. In most of the post-Soviet states it also has encountered the fundamental intellectual difficulty of planning and structuring a military establishment in the absence of any trustworthy guidelines about the external military challenges that the armed forces must be prepared to meet.

In all the new states the armed services are nominally subordinate to the civilian political authorities. However, in Russia, as in most of the other new states, civilian control of the military remains informal and is based on weak institutional mechanisms. In view of this fact, it should not be forgotten that the 1991 coup attempt involved not only the conservative wing of the Soviet Communist Party but also the Soviet minister of defense, the chief of the general staff, nine deputy ministers of defense, and ten military district and fleet commanders. In all, more than three hundred high-ranking military officers were relieved of their posts as a result of the episode.[118] Although the failed coup may have created a new deterrent to future coup attempts by highlighting the grave risk of intramilitary violence, many of the grievances that led a substantial segment of the officer corps to support the August coup attempt remain.

At a minimum, this situation is likely to generate continuing turbulence in relations between civilian politicians and military officers, not only in Russia but in other new states as well. Strong centrifugal forces are at work within many of the new military establishments, and the desire of military commanders to protect their personal and institutional positions against severe socioeconomic pressures has led to heightened military activism in the politics of nearly all the new states. If they continue to increase, these trends threaten to undermine the democratic transformation of the new states and intensify the insecurity among neighboring countries.

Economic collapse has affected the military as much as any sector of society; and with hundreds of thousands of officers and soldiers returning to their national homelands without housing or social services, their economic situation in some cases is worse than that of the local population. Units that have guns and no butter, and cannot "return to the barracks" because the barracks have not been built, will be highly susceptible to the influence of subnational groups that can provide such basics as adequate food and shelter. The prospect of so-called rogue commanders taking charge of "units, formations, and even districts" has become a real concern, particularly in Russia, where central military authorities have long believed that the breakup of the Russian military may have "absolutely unpredictable consequences when the threat of antagonism 'between one and all' becomes reality."[119] As the new states attempt to define the role of their military and security forces, the dwindling level of institutional cohesion, morale and professionalism will face major new tests.

The severe deterioration of economic performance and the skewed distribution of military-industrial resources among the former Soviet republics have created major obstacles for the makers of military policy. In all the new states, decision-makers face severe resource constraints on their capacity to plan for various military contingencies, not least because of the trade-off between expenditures on the welfare of servicemen and on weapons and maintenance. In Russia, intense pressures on the defense budget have been one motive for recasting military doctrine to devote more attention to potential regional conflicts; in other post-Soviet states the economic constraints have been even stronger. Although Ukraine possesses a share of the former Soviet military-industrial complex second only to Russia's, it is by no means clear that the country can shoulder the burden of paying servicemen's salaries, let alone maintaining and modernizing a large military establishment. For the most part, the countries of Central Asia have inherited only a small fraction of Soviet military-industrial facilities. This problem is compounded by an acute shortage of ethnic Central Asians with the training needed to run such facilities or command modern military forces. Kazakhstan's declaration that it lacks the resources necessary to independently operate the Baikonur missile test site illustrates this point. If regional instability were to propel any of the new governments into arms races with other former republics or nearby countries, the problem of generating sufficient resources for military budgets would be sharply exacerbated.

However, this does not signify that new regional military conflicts involving the post-Soviet states are unlikely to occur. A large number of the hard-line proponents of Russian military action in the "near abroad" are Afghan war commanders (Defense Minister Grachev; his deputy, General Gromov; commander of the 14th Army in Moldova, Lieutenant General Lebed; and Vice-President Aleksandr Rutskoy). It remains to be seen whether the much-vaunted "Afghanistan syndrome" will prevent another cycle of intervention in conflicts beyond Russian borders, particularly if it is Russian residents of the "near abroad" and not foreign Communists who are imperiled. It is at this point that the new states on Russia's borders will test both their ability to defend their own territorial integrity and the success of their efforts to seek external sources of support to deter possible Russian aggression. The potential for involvement by the West, China, Afghanistan, and by the Middle Eastern states is significant, and, as discussed in the Conclusion, is fraught with risks for an escalation of tensions and competition among outside powers.

8

The Nuclear Factor

When the Soviet Union fell apart, citizens in the newly independent states began to focus on democracy, economic reform and state-building. However, for strategic planners all over the world, the central issue posed by the disintegration of the USSR was the future control of the nuclear warheads in the Soviet arsenal.[1] If the decade of the 1970s was the era of strategic arms limitations and the 1980s the era of arms reductions, transparency and verification regimes, the 1990s has returned to a major concern of the 1960s: nonproliferation. The difference between the two decades, however, is enormous. In the 1960s, existing nuclear powers established a regime to prevent all other countries from becoming nuclear-armed powers. The success of that regime rested on the agreement among existing nuclear powers that they would not pass nuclear technology on to nonnuclear states. In the 1990s, however, the international community is trying to convince two countries – Ukraine and Kazakhstan – that already have nuclear weapons in their territories to give them up and accept a third, Russia, as the only post-Soviet nuclear state. Belarus, the fourth Soviet successor state with nuclear weapons on its territory, agreed early on that those weapons were Russian, that they should be moved to Russia according to a mutually agreed schedule, and that Belarus would remain nonnuclear. Belarus also agreed that the international community would monitor the removal of all nuclear weapons located on its territory.

The major challenge, therefore, is in getting the leaders of Ukraine and Kazakhstan to agree to one of two options. First, it could be agreed that the weapons are not owned by Ukraine and Kazakhstan, and that therefore, they can be removed from the territory of these countries for deployment and/or destruction by their "real" owner, Russia. The second, and more difficult, option would come into effect if the leaders of either of the two states decide, for whatever reason, that they wish to claim ownership of these weapons. This option would apply even if the state lacks the technical expertise to control them. In this case,

258

Russia, the United States, and the rest of the international community would either have to accept the fact of proliferation (and probably watch the entire nonproliferation regime unravel elsewhere in the world as a consequence), or pursue what might be termed a dispossession strategy. Although the United States and Russia have committed themselves to reduce nuclear stockpiles massively in recent years, the international community has had great difficulty in getting any state that already has nuclear weapons to give all of them up; so such a strategy would be fraught with difficulties.

The likelihood of such a strategy succeeding has been further complicated by the fact that the leaders of the three nuclear inheritors are divided over the desirability of looking to the fourth, Russia, for any kind of Eurasian nuclear umbrella. On the contrary, some circles, particularly in Ukraine, see Russia itself as a threat against which nuclear weapons might provide the only deterrent. The centrifugal forces in Russia and the disintegration of the Russian military further diminish confidence in Russia's ability to exercise stable control over all nuclear weapons and facilities in the former Soviet Union. Such doubts have naturally led some leaders, especially in Ukraine, to question the basis of the West's support of what would be a Russian nuclear monopoly. All of these factors have worked to undermine the credibility of nonproliferation strategies.

The nonproliferation environment is also vastly different in the 1990s from what it was in the 1960s. By the 1990s there were thousands more warheads, dozens more countries with either the political will or the technological capability to "go nuclear," and hundreds of potential new sources for nuclear materials and components – including many within the fragmented Soviet Union.

The disposition of the enormous Soviet nuclear arsenal poses a great challenge to the stability of the Eurasian continent. Literally overnight, Ukraine, Belarus, and Kazakhstan emerged from the ruins of the former Soviet Union not only as newly independent states, but as potential nuclear powers with sizable nuclear arsenals stationed in their territories. The leaders of these countries have struggled with the dilemma that although transferring these weapons to Russia might aid global stability, it would also entail the sacrifice of a powerful symbol of global status and a major deterrent against future external threats.[2]

With the high level of uncertainty surrounding the collapse of the USSR and the increased potential for conflict in and among the new states, the international community sought assurances beginning in early 1992 that Belarus, Kazakhstan, and Ukraine would transfer all nuclear weapons to Russia, the only CIS country that under the plan would remain nuclear. Russia and the United States agreed from the outset, with the general support of the international community, that Russia would, or should, be the only nuclear successor state to the USSR. They reasoned that because among the former Soviet republics Russia alone possessed the ability to control nuclear materials and systems at all the stages leading from production to deployment and from storage to destruction, the weapons stationed in other former republics should logically be transferred to Russia.

Initial negotiations for transfer to Russia went smoothly, and in December 1991, a mere three weeks after the creation of the CIS, a CIS nuclear agreement was signed. The agreement called for joint command of strategic forces by the CIS and control over those forces by the commander in chief of the CIS (at that time yet to be named)[3] and the Russian president, in agreement with other CIS presidents. It also stipulated that tactical nuclear weapons should be moved to Russia by July 1992 and strategic nuclear weapons in the Ukraine should be dismantled by the end of 1994. By 7 May 1992, all the tactical nuclear weapons scattered across the former USSR were reported to have been transferred to Russian control, marking a major advance toward the agreed objective of asserting unified control over the former Soviet Union's nuclear arsenal.

The arms-control debate then turned to the issue of putting the considerable number of strategic nuclear weapons stationed outside Russia under CIS control and arranging for their eventual repatriation and destruction in Russia (see Table 8.1 for the number of warheads in each country).[4] It soon became apparent, however, that the CIS as an institution did not command sufficient authority and legitimacy, largely because of Ukraine's refusal to join. Ukraine's leaders were concerned that the CIS would not act in an evenhanded way to serve the interests of all member states. Throughout 1992 and into 1993, multilateral negotiations were held within the framework of the CIS, but the appointment of two Russian officers, Marshal Yevgeniy Shaposhnikov and Colonel General Yuriy Maksimov, to be, respectively, commander in chief of the CIS joint armed forces, and commander of the strategic forces of the CIS joint armed forces, only hastened the demise of the CIS as a possible source of unified cooperation and control.[5]

Russia's effort to establish the CIS as a vehicle for nuclear weapons control coincided with parallel Western attempts to ensure that Ukraine, Belarus, and Kazakhstan would sign the START-I treaty and accede to the Nuclear Non-Proliferation Treaty (NPT) as nonnuclear states. All the Western governments were extremely concerned about the effect of the breakup of the USSR on command and control of nuclear weapons. They were also concerned that the reductions envisaged under the

Table 8.1. *Strategic nuclear weapons in republics of the former Soviet Union*

Country	Weapon type	Weapon no.	Warhead no.
Russia	ICBMs	1,003	5,800
	SLBMs	456	2,400
	Bombers	100	1,300
Ukraine	ICBMs	176	1,240
	SLBMs	0	0
	Bombers	41	667
Belarus	ICBMs	81	81
	SLBMs	0	0
	Bombers	0	0
Kazakhstan	ICBMs	104	1,040
	SLBMs	0	0
	Bombers	40	*

ICBMs: Intercontinental ballistic missiles
SLBMs: Submarine-launched ballistic missiles
*U.S. officials believe that the 320 warheads aboard the long-range bombers stationed in Kazakhstan were removed and returned to Russia, without negotiating their formal removal, at the same time that tactical nuclear weapons were withdrawn. Bruce Blair, *The Logic of Accidental Nuclear War*, Washington, D.C.: The Brookings Institution, 1993, 63; and Steven Miller, "Western Diplomacy and the Soviet Nuclear Legacy," *Survival*, 34, no. 3 (Autumn 1992), 6.
Sources: International Institute for Strategic Studies, London, from *The Economist*, 3 April 1993, 52; Robert Norris and William Arkin, "Nuclear Notebook," *Bulletin of Atomic Scientists*, July-August 1993, 57; *Nezavisimaya gazeta*, 3 June 1993; William C. Potter, *Nuclear Profiles of the Soviet Successor States*, Monograph No. 1, Monterey, Calif.: Program for Nonproliferation Studies, Monterey Institute of International Studies, May 1993.

first strategic arms reduction treaty (START-I), which the United States and Soviet Union concluded in July 1991, might not take place. To address these security concerns, the West, led by the United States, directly engaged each of the former Soviet republics having strategic nuclear weapons on its territory in an effort to transfer those missiles to Russia for destruction. All four new nuclear-weapons states were incorporated into START-I. On 23 May 1992, the Lisbon Protocol to the START-I treaty was signed by Ukraine, Belarus, Kazakhstan, Russia, and the United States, thereby binding all the Soviet successor states with nuclear weapons on their territory to observe the terms of START-I. In signing the protocol, Ukraine, Belarus, and Kazakhstan agreed to cede all strategic nuclear weapons based on their territory to Russia for destruction. They also agreed to join the Nuclear Non-Proliferation Treaty as nonnuclear weapons states "in the shortest time possible." It was further agreed, however, that the protocol and the treaty had to be ratified by all the signatories before its obligations came into effect. From the moment that the last party ratified the treaty and protocol, all sides would then have seven years to meet the provisions of the treaty, provisions that would involve the total elimination of strategic nuclear offensive weapons from the territory of Ukraine, Belarus, and Kazakhstan.

The ratification debates began immediately after the signing of the Lisbon Protocol. By May 1993, all the parties, with the notable exception of Ukraine, had ratified both START-I and the protocol. The continued worsening of Russian-Ukrainian political relations throughout 1992 and into 1993 made it less likely that Ukrainian leaders would surrender the weapons. Although not rejecting the protocol and the treaty outright, Ukrainian leaders came to regard them, in the words of one opposition figure, as "nuclear muscles"[6] and as bargaining chips to be exchanged, if at all, only for firm security guarantees from the West, as well as for greater financial compensation from both the West and Russia.

Partly in an effort to assuage the fears of the non-Russian nuclear states, Russia and the United States negotiated to further reduce their own stockpiles of strategic nuclear weapons below the levels agreed to in START-I. A treaty, START-II, was signed by Russia and the United States in January 1993, and in it, both sides pledged to reduce their strategic arsenals to between 3,000 and 3,500 warheads each, equaling a 50 percent reduction below the level called for in START-I. However, START-II cannot come into effect unless and until START-I goes into force, making both treaties dependent on the Ukrainian ratification and implementation of the Lisbon Protocol and associated measures. In the meantime, Russian nationalist opinion began to mobilize against the reduction of nuclear forces. Even before START-II was signed, Deputy Foreign Minister Grigoriy Berdennikov, the chief Russian negotiator in arms reduction talks with the United States, was forced to admit that the arms control environment in Russia had changed: "A large portion of public opinion believes that we've done too much disarming already, especially with the troop withdrawals from Eastern Europe. So the situation is really different."[7] Others were more concerned about specific requirements of the treaties. In particular, they were upset by the requirement that Russia eliminate all its MIRVed SS-18 missiles (missiles equipped with multiple independently targetable reentry vehicles, with each missile capable of carrying at least ten warheads), while the United States would only "download" its own MIRVed counterforce Trident SLBMs (submarine-launched ballistic missiles) by reducing the number of warheads on each missile. The SS-18s were the main Russian counterforce weapons – that is, weapons having a potential to destroy a large number of hardened U.S. strategic weapons sites. The deputy chairman of the Russian Supreme Soviet Committee for International Affairs and Foreign Economic Relations, Iona Andronov, went so far as to call this provision a "trick" designed to allow the West to maintain its superiority at Russia's expense.[8]

Additional concerns regarding the economic costs of destroying a large part of the strategic-weapons inventory have been raised by political figures from a cross-section of the political spectrum in all four countries. It was these concerns that led Russian officials to back away from some of START-II's initial provisions calling for the destruction of missile silos. Officials began to recognize that the timetable for destruction of the estimated 30,000 warheads, which would yield roughly a hundred tons of plutonium, was unrealistically short;[9] but as long as START-I is not ratified by Ukraine, the dismantling and destroying of weapons will not begin in Russia, and the economic costs, therefore, will not be incurred.

If strategic-weapons agreements cannot be brought into effect, it will be even more difficult to construct regional or international regimes for monitoring and controlling the proliferation of nuclear weapons, materials, and know-how. START-II implementation is slated to begin concurrently with START-I reductions, but START-I cannot go into effect until several preconditions are met. First, Ukraine, Belarus, and Kazakhstan all have to accede to the Nuclear Non-Proliferation Treaty (NPT) as nonnuclear states. Second, all three have to ratify START-I and agree on a dismantling schedule before Russian ratification, which occurred in November 1992, can go into effect. Third, a schedule for implementation that would include agreements on verification measures and allocation of costs has to be agreed on before the transfer of strategic weapons can begin. So long as Ukraine and possibly Kazakhstan claim ownership of the nuclear weapons on their territories, they may not be able to join NPT as nonnuclear states until the weapons are disposed of. In this way, START-I and NPT are tied to, and dependent on, one another; and although Kazakhstan and Belarus have largely agreed to meet their obligation and have ratified START-I, Ukraine's refusal to do likewise until significant security guarantees and compensation packages are negotiated prevents all other agreements from going into effect, and essentially blocks further movement toward strategic stability and nuclear nonproliferation.[10]

Moreover, although it is generally agreed that only Russia has the capability to launch the strategic weapons currently stationed outside its borders, what is less clear is whether these states could use the nuclear materials and components of the weapons systems on their territories to build primitive nuclear weapons at some point in the future, should they obtain full control over them. If any of them decided to do so, one obstacle they would face would be the acquisition of weapons-grade plutonium or uranium.[11] One source would be the warheads of the strategic missiles to be dismantled by Russia. This may help convince Ukrainian and possibly Kazakh leaders that if they wish to keep their options open about going nuclear in the future, asserting control over the weapons on their territory will provide them with the core material necessary to exercise this option.

Once these weapons are given up, any future decision to build new national nuclear forces would be more difficult to achieve. It would not, however, be impossible. As Table 8.2 shows, there are significant parts of the nuclear-production chain spread throughout the territory of the former Soviet Union. There are numerous nuclear-power reactors in Ukraine, Lithuania, Kazakhstan, and Armenia (although the Armenian facilities are not operational). Additionally, there are research reactors outside Russia, in Ukraine, Belarus, Latvia, Kazakhstan, Uzbekistan, and in Georgia (where the facilities have been closed down). Experts believe that some of these nuclear-power and research-reactor facilities are capable of producing quantities of weapons-grade plutonium.[12] Uranium mining and milling centers are located in seven of the fifteen new states, and most of these nuclear facilities are known to be under the control not of Russia, but of the local national authorities. Although nuclear expertise is obviously greatest in Russia, it is by no means certain that scientists and other experts who formerly worked for the USSR and now live outside Russia will necessarily decide to return there. Some may seek to emigrate altogether and others may be willing for patriotic or personal economic reasons to participate in developing incipient nuclear programs in the countries of the "near abroad." While figures are lacking, the problem was deemed serious enough to warrant the release of a major report on proliferation by the Russian Foreign Intelligence Service calling for various measures to ensure that nuclear-arms expertise remains a Russian monopoly.[13] This means that, although Kazakhstan and Ukraine may not be able to construct a massive arsenal of nuclear weapons, they do possess some

Table 8.2. *Nuclear assets of the Soviet successor states*

Country	Nuclear weapons	Nuclear power reactor	Nuclear research reactor	Nuclear weapons design	Uranium mining, milling	Uranium enrichment capability	Fuel fabrication facility	Plutonium production, handling	Heavy water production	Other NSG* controlled material	Nuclear research center	Nuclear test site	Acceded to NPT	NSG member
Armenia		a							e		x			
Azerbaijan													x	
Belarus	x		x								x		x	
Estonia					x								x	
Georgia			b								x			
Kazakhstan	x	x	x		x		x	d		f	x	x		
Kyrgyzstan					x									
Latvia			x								x		x	
Lithuania		x											x	
Moldova														
Russia	x	x	x	x	x	x	x	x	x	x	x	x	x	x
Tajikistan					x				x					

Table 8.2 (continued)

Country	Nuclear weapons	Nuclear power reactor	Nuclear research reactor	Nuclear weapons design	Uranium mining, milling	Uranium enrich- ment capability	Fuel fabrica- tion facility	Plutonium production, handling	Heavy water produc- tion	Other NSG* controlled material	Nuclear research center	Nuclear test site	Acceded to NPT	NSG member
Turkmenistan														
Ukraine		x	x		x				x	g	x			
Uzbekistan			x		x	c					x		x	

[a]The two Armenian reactors were shut down in 1989 for safety reasons, but the Armenian government has announced its intent to restart them.
[b]The IRT-M Tbilisi was shut down in 1990.
[c]A uranium enrichment facility, of at least an experimental nature, probably operated at Navoi during the 1970s and 1980s.
[d]A hot cell is reportedly located at the Semipalatinsk test site.
[e]Although one report of an Armenian heavy water site has appeared in print, there has been no additional confirmation.
[f]The Ulbinsky Metallurgy Plant in Ust-Kamenogorsk produces beryllium and possibly zirconium.
[g]Zirconium, hafnium, and ion exchange resins are produced in Ukraine at the Pridneprovsky Chemical Factory.
*Nuclear Suppliers Group

Source: Updated from William C. Potter, Nuclear Profiles of the Soviet Successor States, Monograph No. 1, Monterey, Calif.: Program for Nonproliferation Studies, Monterey Institute of International Studies, May 1993.

of the key materials and capabilities required if the political will exists to create a limited number of cruder nuclear bombs.

In addition to disarmament problems, there also exists the potential for proliferation, if not of entire missiles or warheads, then of component fissile material such as plutonium and enriched uranium. As discussed in Chapter 5, the leaders of all four states with nuclear weapons on their territories have expressed their countries' need to engage in weapons sales as a means of acquiring the hard currency required to back marketization and economic stabilization. Certainly Belarus, and even Kazakhstan, can neither acquire nor disassemble these warheads to get the fissile material to sell. Although further discussion of this matter may be speculative, one cannot rule out entirely the possibility that Ukraine, or Russia, could sell nuclear-warhead materials if the price were right. And given the current chaos surrounding the political and military command structures of these states, such transactions, as discussed in the next section, could also take place without being officially sanctioned.

Russia

The issue of Russian nuclear weapons has as much a psychological as a political impact upon the Russian polity. "Historically," as one Russian commentator noted, "the notion of a state's 'greatness' has always been connected with its military might."[14] As Russian foreign minister Andrey Kozyrev acknowledged, the USSR's superpower status had existed "largely by virtue of a single criterion – the nuclear criterion."[15] The implosion of the Soviet Union still left Russia with the world's largest arsenal of nuclear warheads, which to many Russians constituted a continuing sign of greatness.

However, the Yeltsin-Kozyrev strategy for fulfilling Russia's perceived mandate for greatness has emphasized domestic reform and international influence more than military might and nuclear standing. One positive step in this direction occurred on 4 November 1992, when the Russian parliament, following U.S. ratification a month earlier, voted overwhelmingly to ratify the strategic arms reduction treaty (START-I) negotiated by the United States and the then-USSR in July 1991.

Ratification, however, did not come about without a heated debate. START-I was bitterly criticized by hardline opponents suspicious of Western intentions, who depicted the "arms surrender" as a sellout to the West that left Russia defenseless and deprived of foreign influence. *Pravda*, for example, called the agreement "a hasty, unjustified concession to Washington – and the final loss of Russia's status and its significance as a superpower."[16] Nevertheless, the treaty was ratified by a vote of 157 to 1, with 26 abstentions, showing the sharp distinction between rhetoric and deed.

The decision by President Yeltsin to further reduce the number of warheads from the 7,000–9,000 allowed both the United States and Russia under START-I to the 3,500 envisaged under START-II, therefore, has to be seen as an act requiring considerable political courage on his part. It provoked vigorous nationalist opposition; *Pravda*, for example, called the signing of the accord tantamount to a "total and unconditional surrender."[17] In signing START-II, Russia agreed to eliminate completely the most formidable weapons in the former Soviet nuclear arsenal – the 154 land-based multiwarhead SS-18s that would remain after the first 154 were destroyed under the terms of START-I – in addition to all other land-based multiwarhead ICBMs.[18] In essence, the Yeltsin government was gambling that Russia's perceived historically mandated great-power status could be maintained, if not enhanced, through a more stable strategic environment, through reliance on a restructuring of ground forces to meet the greater challenges facing military planners on the Russian periphery, and through non-military means – specifically economic growth and democratization. "The real challenge to our security today," Foreign Minister Kozyrev has argued, "lies in regional conflicts. . . . all this nuclear arsenal has absolutely no importance whatsoever – either in Tajikistan, Ossetia, Abkhazia, or in Dniester."[19]

START-II was a gamble that many Russian politicians would have been unwilling to see their country take had it not been for Russia's reliance on plants now outside its borders for maintaining the SS-18 and SS-24 forces. Contributing to their decision may also have been the leaders' increased anxiety that other new states might acquire ownership, and ultimately operational control, over the sizable number of former Soviet nuclear weapons and production facilities now based outside Russia. "Russia," Foreign Intelligence chief Yevgeniy Primakov has noted, "is not interested at all in the emergence of new states possessing WMD [Weapons of Mass Destruction] along the perimeter of its borders."[20] Arms-reduction agreements with the United States, therefore, served the Russian nationalists' purpose of gaining control, even if for the purpose of destruction, of potentially contested nuclear weapons, thereby maintaining Russia's nuclear monopoly within the lands of the former USSR. In addition, it was calculated that the agreements would also have the effect of speeding the closure of sensitive nuclear facilities that might give countries other than Russia some increased potential for nuclear capability in the future. All of the SS-18s, for example, were made in Ukraine, at the Yuzhmash factory headed by Leonid Kuchma, who subsequently became Kiev's prime minister in October 1992. The Russian signing of START-II, with its plans for the total elimination of SS-18s, thus targeted for permanent cessation of missile production a plant in a country other than Russia. In this way, if START-I, START-II, the Lisbon Protocol, and the Nuclear Non-Proliferation Treaty are ratified and go into effect, they will have the consequence not only of transferring those weapons now located in neighboring countries to Russia, but also of severely limiting the capability of neighboring states to maintain the parts of the nuclear-arms production cycle now in their territory. Moreover, any installation with nuclear potential would be subject to strict international safeguards and monitoring.

Russia's interests in this regard have become much more focused, moving from a generalized desire to work with the United States to assert unified control over all nuclear facilities and weapons, to three particular concerns: the proliferation of nuclear capability, the smuggling of nuclear materials, and the security and safety of nuclear facilities under Russian control in areas of conflict both inside and outside of Russia.

Of all the concerns, the single greatest is the potential of Ukraine to develop an independent nuclear capability. Although President Yeltsin confirmed in late 1992 that "for the foreseeable future, . . . nuclear weapons will remain an essential component of international security,"[21] it is unlikely that he intended to extend this logic to Ukraine, or for that matter to Kazakhstan or Belarus. Ukrainian "administrative control over the [nuclear] weapons on its territory . . . worries us," confided Russian deputy foreign minister Grigoriy Berdennikov, because "the officers who sit there with the key will be Ukrainians."[22] State Counselor Sergey Stankevich further noted that Kiev's hardening position on the issue of strategic nuclear missiles makes "the nuclear equation . . . more complicated than before. If Rukh comes to power in Ukraine, I do not know what to expect. If some slippery nationalist forces come to power in Kazakhstan, I do not know what to expect. We [Russia] should simply be more careful."[23] Despite the enormous technical difficulties involved in acquiring and developing nuclear weapons, Russian concerns are often mirrored in the West, where, as in one report, it is sometimes concluded that "even if all nuclear weapons are removed to Russia and/or dismantled, some of the non-Russian republics may retain substantial nuclear assets that could permit the rapid development of nuclear weapons."[24] Given this mutual reinforcement, it is likely that this will remain an abiding Russian concern for some time to come.

Russia has also taken additional steps in the worrisome matter of potential smuggling of warheads and fissile material.[25] In late 1992,

U.S. senator Sam Nunn, chairman of the Senate Armed Services Committee, stated that he had learned during a trip to Belarus that officials there had thwarted an attempt to smuggle uranium to Poland. Subsequently, the CIA confirmed that there had indeed been one attempt to smuggle out a small quantity of enriched uranium.[26] To construct a nuclear device with a yield equal to that of Hiroshima, only 15 kilograms (33 pounds) of highly enriched uranium or 5 kilograms (11 pounds) of plutonium are needed.[27] To address the proliferation of nuclear material and know-how, Russia has established a special branch of its intelligence service responsible for arms control and nonproliferation.[28] The head of this new department, Gennadiy Yevstafiyev, has asserted that only a few dozen people have knowledge of nuclear secrets. He also has said that his division would closely monitor the development of nuclear weapons capabilities in neighboring countries and would prevent attempts to export controlled materials.[29] However, it remains to be seen whether a set of institutions that once relied heavily on isolating all of society to prevent the leakage of nuclear secrets and materials to the outside world can quickly be converted to provide protection in a country whose international business and human contacts are growing at a tremendous pace. Moreover, because Russian border guards are not at all CIS borders, their ability to monitor smuggling operations from neighboring countries to the rest of the world will be severely limited.

The Western Newly Independent States

It is Ukraine's position on, and provisions for, nuclear disarmament that have prompted the highest level of anxiety in both Russia and the international community. Despite repeated professions of intent to denuclearize, a growing number of ambiguous remarks and hardening demands by senior Ukrainian officials and parliamentarians have increased doubt about Kiev's real plans. The increased sentiment among some Ukrainian decision-makers to retain nuclear weapons, however, has to be seen against the backdrop of a continued strong belief among the Ukrainian population that post-Chernobyl Ukraine should be a nuclear-free state. Public-opinion polling has found continued widespread agreement that "Ukrainian territory should be free of all nuclear weapons" (72 percent agree, 20 percent disagree) with fairly consistent results over the twelve-month period after independence.[30] In trying to understand the shift away from the decision to relinquish nuclear weapons, therefore, one has to look at the deterioration of economic conditions domestically and the heightening political tension with Russia.

Ukraine's reconsideration of its nonnuclear pledges has been fueled in particular by apprehension about Russian intentions, as well as by

Russia's political turmoil, rising nationalism, and territorial claims on Crimea. Irresponsible statements in the early postindependence days by a handful of Russian nationalists (such as the warning from the parliamentarian and hardliner Sergey Baburin that "either Ukraine reunites with Russia or there will be war"[31]) quickly escalated into a torrent of statements from Russian hardliners who wished to impede, if not eliminate, Ukrainian independence altogether. Such statements, no matter how great the effort to dismiss them as unrepresentative or designed for domestic consumption, nonetheless could not help but cast considerable doubt on the wisdom of surrendering to Russia a formidable nuclear arsenal.

The short history of Ukrainian denuclearization diplomacy has been marked by moments of tension and high drama. The key variables affecting Kiev's ambiguous position are fears of Russian designs regarding Ukraine, the instability of the Russian political system, and a growing sentiment that the economic incentives and security provisions offered by the West constitute inadequate compensation for the sacrifice of strategic nuclear weapons. "This has been a unique historical event for a country to unilaterally renounce nuclear weapons," insisted Deputy Foreign Minister Boris Tarasyuk, Kiev's chief nuclear-arms negotiator. "The international reaction should be as brave."[32]

The debate on Ukrainian nuclear disarmament has been deeply affected by the level of amity or animosity in the mutual relationship between Russia and Ukraine at any given time. Kiev has been acutely aware that many political elites in Moscow acknowledge Ukrainian independence only with difficulty; the rising tide of hard-line nationalist and irredentist sentiment in the Russian polity has not engendered any additional faith in Kiev on this matter. The wisdom of relinquishing its nuclear deterrent to Russia – though called for in the START-I treaty and the Lisbon Protocol – has therefore come under increasing doubt in Ukraine, even though Ukrainian officials apparently accepted that they lack the capability to target Russia with the remaining missiles, and that they are not able to control the launching of these weapons from Ukrainian territory.[33] The argument over the missiles has therefore become an argument not only about acquiring a tangible or immediate nuclear capability, but even more about the symbolic and psychological expression of sovereignty and power that the ownership of nuclear weapons is believed to confer.[34]

Ukrainian expressions of concern over surrendering nuclear weapons to Russia are not new. As early as March 1992, President Kravchuk announced that Kiev was suspending the transfer of tactical nuclear weapons to Russia because Ukraine "cannot be certain that the missiles being sent away by us [to Russia] are being destroyed and not falling into unfriendly hands." He further insisted that weapons transfers from Ukraine "will never make anybody stronger or more powerful than at present."[35] Specifically citing Russian "claims to our territory," Kravchuk complained that while Ukraine received the world's applause for agreeing to surrender the missiles, "we have also weakened ourselves."[36]

Though Kiev did in fact ultimately relent and hand over all tactical warheads to Russia by the early spring, Ukrainian leaders have since called the move a mistake and have vowed not to repeat it with strategic nuclear missiles. "What did Ukraine get in exchange [for this]?" Prime Minister Leonid Kuchma complained. "This is what is troubling the population and members of the parliament. I am for ratification [of START-I], but if we go to parliament with nothing it will be a fiasco."[37] "In order for Ukraine to complete its disarmament," President Kravchuk has added, "we must have some material benefit and fixed guarantees for its security." Kiev cannot afford to transfer its strategic nuclear weapons to Russia "without recompense" as it had done with its tactical nuclear weapons.[38] Nor, Kravchuk has vowed, will Ukraine any longer seek to "appease" Western calls for denuclearization at the expense of Ukrainian national security. "We will not take a single step backward no matter whom it pleases or displeases. We are defending Ukrainian interests."[39]

Regarding strategic nuclear bombers and missiles, originally President Kravchuk promised to remove all such weapons from Ukraine by 1994, although this pledge did not last long. The 1994 deadline was soon scrapped in favor of the longer seven-year deadline called for in START-I, to which Kiev acceded by signing the Lisbon Protocol in May 1992. Defense Minister Konstantin Morozov sought to blame the West for Kiev's shift, saying that while Kiev had wanted to eliminate its nuclear stockpile by the end of 1994, it had received no financial assistance for such an undertaking. Consequently, Kiev was forced to abandon its ambitious earlier pledge and instead join START-I.[40]

Perhaps in response to the increasingly nationalist tenor of Russian foreign policy, in fall 1992 Kiev vigorously reiterated its financial and security concerns over denuclearization. Ukrainian officials declared with increasing adamancy that Kiev would not part with its nuclear stockpile without substantial economic assistance and some form of defense guarantee. "We in Ukraine are now counting every kopek, every dollar," First Deputy Prime Minister Igor Yukhnovskiy insisted. "Ukraine doesn't seek nuclear [military] power, but given the status quo, . . . [we cannot] just get rid of that which we have."[41]

Alarmingly, Yukhnovskiy suggested that Ukraine auction off its nuclear warheads to the highest bidder among existing nuclear states. Although his statement was immediately disavowed by the Ukrainian government, his words were hardly reassuring.[42] Even if Kiev opts not to sell entire warheads, it has suggested selling the enriched uranium and plutonium extracted from the missiles abroad for hard currency. "You cannot push a state that is trying to rise to its feet to the wall," Yukhnovskiy has warned. "We know that what we have is a treasure, and on this we will insist." He has specifically called into question the Ukrainian commitment to denuclearization, warning that nonnuclear pledges may not apply if the existing nuclear states decline to buy on the auction block.[43]

Ukraine's security concerns increased in October 1992, when the Russians insisted on unilateral command and control over all nuclear forces. At the Bishkek summit of CIS leaders in early October 1992, CIS commander in chief Yevgeniy Shaposhnikov proposed that the command and control of nuclear weapons in Belarus, Kazakhstan, and Ukraine be transferred from the CIS to Russia, thereby foreclosing the possibility of multinational control under the CIS umbrella. Belarus agreed, and Kazakhstan consented to take the matter under consideration, but the proposal was rejected outright by Ukrainian officials.[44] "If Russia takes over the strategic structures [in Ukraine], it will leave us with two options," remarked one top Ukrainian disarmament official. "We can again become a colony of Russia or we will be forced to become a nuclear state."[45] As part of this effort, Defense Minister Morozov called for all the personnel stationed at the 43d Missile Army command center that controls the nuclear missiles in Ukraine either to swear their loyalty to Ukraine "or resign."[46]

It remains uncertain whether Ukraine would, or could, succeed in actually gaining control of these weapons, although by mid-1993 both U.S. government and Russian sources suggested that an effort to do so was under way. At least some of Ukraine's rhetorical challenges, apart from being part of the escalation of tensions between Moscow and Kiev, have been aimed at obtaining security and economic assistance from both Russia and the West. As the Ukrainian ambassador to the United States said: "We want a guarantee that the powers will never use nuclear weapons against Ukraine, never resort to conventional force or the threat of force, will abstain from economic pressure in a controversy and respect our territorial integrity and the inviolability of borders. So far, the guarantees Moscow offers have not met our minimal demands." If Ukraine is going to make the elimination of nuclear weapons dependent upon, for example, Russian unconditional affirmation of Kiev's sovereignty over Crimea, or cushioning the price of oil, then it is easy to suppose that the weapons will remain an issue of contention for some time. In June 1993 Prime Minister Kuchma reportedly told a closed meeting of the parliament that Ukraine should become "a temporary nuclear power" by ratifying the START-I agreement and the Lisbon Protocol but deferring accession to the Non-Proliferation Treaty as a nonnuclear state.[47]

As for the United States and other Western countries, Ukraine has demanded that the United States provide further security guarantees in exchange for eliminating the forty-six SS-24 missiles on its soil, missiles that in the Ukrainian view do not necessarily have to be eliminated under the terms of START-I, although they are included in the Lisbon Protocol. Kiev has also expressed concern that Russia's ability to sell highly enriched uranium to the United States for the U.S. nuclear program represents a substantial profit from disarmament that Kiev and others should be able to share. As Prime Minister Kuchma noted: "We removed the tactical nuclear weapons and what happened? The Russians got a contract to supply the U.S. with nuclear fuel. Where is at least a minimal program of aid similar to Russia's? . . . Our people are not fools."[48] The American response was to promise $175 million in aid to defray the costs of dismantling and transferring the weapons. Disbursement was agreed in July 1993 once Ukraine committed to dismantling all 130 of its SS-19s, allowing the country, in the words of the Ukrainian ambassador, to avoid having to choose between two alternatives: "invest in a healthy economy or put billions in our currency, provided by taxpayers, in a mammoth disarmament project, with few security gains."[49] It was clear which choice he and much of the Ukrainian population increasingly wished to make.

Unlike its Ukrainian neighbor, Belarus has not felt the need to reconsider or modify its pledges of nuclear disarmament. Within a strict framework of denuclearization, however, some Belarusian spokesmen have sought to extract the maximum benefit for the fledgling state. The existence of such weapons on Belarusian territory has, in their opinion, called world attention to a state that is struggling to develop its own concept of national identity. Deputy Defense Minister Pyotr Chaus, for example, expressed the opinion that Minsk should not "be hasty in the withdrawal of strategic nuclear missiles. The presence of such a powerful weapon in our country will at first help Belarus to establish itself. The whole world treats us as a nuclear power."[50] This view was nevertheless overridden within the Belarusian government.

Like Ukraine, Belarus has promised to become a nonnuclear state and to renounce the possession of nuclear weapons. Unlike Kiev, however, Minsk has more than lived up to its word. All tactical weapons, for example, were removed to Russia by May, well ahead of schedule.[51] Moreover, Belarus announced in October 1992 that it would relinquish all strategic nuclear warheads to Russia in two and a half years, even though the START-I treaty and the Lisbon Protocol allowed for a seven-year timetable.[52] In short, by the end of 1994 Belarus will have no strategic nuclear arms stationed on its territory. Until then, Minsk has further ceded all administrative and operative control – including unilateral launch authority – to Russia.[53] Indeed, the chairman of the Belarusian parliament, Stanislau Shushkevich, was strongly critical of Ukrainian recalcitrance in refusing to ratify START-I and repatriate strategic weapons, stating that these weapons were Russian and it was inappropriate for Belarus, or Ukraine, to demand compensation for them.[54]

Nonetheless, some Belarusian officials questioned the wisdom of so readily surrendering the nuclear weapons, particularly in light of the growing level of conflict among the former Soviet republics. "Considering the touchy political situation in the world," Deputy Defense Minister Pyotr Chaus cautioned against withdrawing strategic nuclear weapons "in the near future." "There aren't any nations in the world who wouldn't like to have nuclear weapons," he added. "Quite the contrary, they are all trying to get them."[55] Henadz Danilou, head of the department of Civilian Rights, Civil Security, and Defense Work in the Cabinet of Ministers, has expressed resentment of Western disarmament pressures, complaining that "the impression being created is that one side is doing all the eliminating, while the other side just sends inspectors to control the fulfillment of these obligations."[56] Although some Belarusian military officials echoed Ukrainian concerns about the status of the tactical nuclear weapons being transferred to Russia,[57] Minsk nonetheless completed the transfer ahead of schedule (as did Ukraine). In February 1993, at a time when the Ukrainian parliament was deadlocked and the Russian parliament was trying to mount a procedural coup against Boris Yeltsin, the Belarusian parliament ratified START-I and the Lisbon Protocol, and approved Belarus's adherence to the Nuclear Non-Proliferation Treaty. Despite considerable parliamentary debate on the issue (with 218 votes in favor and only 1 against, but as many as 60 abstentions),[58] Chairman Shushkevich was able to shepherd it through, a credit to the high degree of consensus on this issue in Belarus. In light of these actions it therefore appears improbable that Belarus will attempt to gain control of the nuclear weapons on its soil, particularly because of the strong antinuclear sentiment that developed within the population after Chernobyl.

The Southern Newly Independent States

Of all the countries of Central Asia and the Caucasus, only Kazakhstan has on its territory both strategic nuclear weapons (including 104 SS-18 ICBMs, each armed with ten warheads, and 40 Tu-95 Bear bombers) and many testing and production facilities. These include nuclear-power and research reactors as well as facilities for uranium mining and milling, fuel fabrication, and plutonium production and handling; Kazakhstan does not have facilities for reprocessing or for nuclear-weapons production. Many of these assets are located at or near the Semipalatinsk test site, which until it was closed in August 1991 was the USSR's primary location for underground nuclear tests.[59] All tactical nuclear weapons have been removed from Kazakhstan and the other states in Central Asia that had them stationed on their territory.

Among the other countries of the southern tier of new states, as shown in Table 8.2, a number have uranium mining and milling facilities, heavy-water production and uranium-enrichment capability, and nuclear research reactors.[60] Although many of these countries have in their territories some nuclear facility, strategic material necessary for nuclear production, or a reactor containing a weapons-grade uranium core, the probability that any of them could develop an independent nuclear capability that could in the near future serve as a real deterrent or a viable instrument of foreign policy is extremely low. There are, of course, huge transnational environmental issues associated with nuclear pollution.[61] Also, individual acts of sabotage to, or smuggling from, nuclear facilities might take place. Additionally, the conflicts in the Caucasus, for example, might provide an impetus for obtaining a nuclear deterrent. These issues and risks are relatively small, however, when compared with the overwhelming and more immediate task of negotiating the denuclearization of Kazakhstan, whose territory – even after the withdrawal of all tactical and some strategic nuclear weapons – still holds a huge arsenal of weapons and materials.

Issues of proliferation and nuclear-weapons control and transfer have dominated the analysis of Kazakhstan's nuclear capability. Several factors interact to shape the debate: issues of national security and identity, economic interest, and environmental concern. Revelations about significant environmental damage and nuclear contamination led to the closure by President Nazarbayev of the Semipalatinsk nuclear test site in August 1991. "Scores of our people have suffered as a result of nuclear tests conducted in Kazakhstan for decades," Nazarbayev explained in shutting down Semipalatinsk. This is "a serious reason for the striving of the people of Kazakhstan to eliminate weapons of mass destruction . . . on their soil."[62] A strong antinuclear popular reaction has been balanced by the awareness that Kazakhstan's ability to serve as a leader of Central Asia might be increased if it were able to counter the nuclear capability of Russia, China, Pakistan and India with a capability of its own. Although Nazarbayev never said he would refuse to give up his strategic weapons, he also emphasized the need for regional security guarantees that would ensure that Kazakhstan would not be disadvantaged by giving up its missiles. He also, initially at least, insisted that "I am absolutely against having any single republic control all nuclear weapons by itself."[63]

Nazarbayev subsequently became more amenable to the idea of transferring his tactical and strategic nuclear missiles to Russia after receiving guarantees of territorial integrity from Russia and China, as well as statements of support from the United States.[64] In a meeting with CIS leaders in March 1992, he reportedly declared that "his vast nation straddling Europe and Asia will seek to become a non-nuclear state."[65] It was during this early period that the 320 nuclear weapons designed for the forty bombers based in Kazakhstan were quietly returned to central storage in Russia (the same types of weapons were reportedly dismantled in place in Ukraine).[66] On a later occasion, Kazakh state adviser Tulegen Zhukeyev and defense minister Colonel General Sagadat Nurmagambetov emphasized to a visiting U.S. Defense Department delegation that strategic nuclear missiles still deployed in Kazakhstan would be eliminated.[67] During the same visit, the American delegation received confirmation from Kazakh prime minister Sergey Tereshchenko that his country's military doctrine would be firmly based on the principle of nuclear nonproliferation.[68]

Nonetheless, Kazakh officials remain acutely aware of the dilemma that without nuclear weapons, many fewer Western leaders would have courted Kazakhstan. "If we did not have nuclear weapons, [U.S. secretary of state James] Baker would not have come here twice. Neither would [British prime minister Margaret] Thatcher. Or [French foreign minister Roland] Dumas," said one Kazakh official.[69] "Let's face it," added a concurring presidential adviser, "the fact that Kazakhstan has nuclear weapons is one reason why the rest of the world is paying attention to us. This is the best card in Nazarbayev's hand."[70]

Leaders in Almaty have also come under growing public criticism for giving up nuclear weapons without significant economic compensation. The leader of the opposition Zheltoksan party, Hasan Kazhahmetov, for example, has called for Kazakhstan to retain the weapons and has blasted Nazarbayev for "making a gift" of nuclear weapons to Russia, thereby endangering Kazakh independence.[71] Additionally, the Kazakh public is divided over retaining nuclear weapons, with a plurality (43 percent in one poll) of ethnic Kazakhs expressing the view that "Kazakhstan should have its own nuclear weapons in the future," and 50 percent of ethnic Russians living in Kazakhstan opposed to retaining nuclear weapons.[72]

Finally, given the occasional demands to absorb northern Kazakhstan that come not only from the nationalist right wing in Russia but also from officials considered moderate liberals,[73] Nazarbayev and other Kazakh officials have alluded to Almaty's inherited nuclear weapons as a deterrent. Following a statement from Russian president Yeltsin's spokesman in late August 1991 that Russia would seek to redraw borders with states declaring independence, Nazarbayev publicly warned Yeltsin not to press territorial claims on Kazakhstan, pointedly noting that "particular danger lies in the fact that Kazakhstan is a nuclear republic."[74] As a consequence, Nazarbayev has suggested that his country wants a strategic nuclear force kept by Russia in Kazakhstan for another fifteen years or so, until Almaty can be assured of their destruction.[75] "Our neighbor China has nuclear weapons, our neighbor Russia has nuclear weapons," Nazarbayev has explained. "Some Russian politicians have territorial claims to Kazakhstan. There are Chinese textbooks that claim parts of Siberia and Kazakhstan belong to China. Under these conditions, how do you expect Kazakhstan to react?"[76] Underscoring that Almaty was surrounded by nuclear powers, presidential adviser Burkutbay Ayagonov remarked that Kazakhstan would "always feel safer with nuclear-tipped strategic missiles on its territory than without them."[77] Given the extent of China's military buildup in 1992 and 1993, and the burgeoning arms trade between China and Russia, it is not difficult to understand Kazakh concern.

Nevertheless, all tactical nuclear weapons in Kazakhstan were withdrawn to Russia (assuming that the reports that three warheads were transferred to Iran are indeed "spurious," as experts have claimed).[78] President Nazarbayev also signed the Lisbon protocol to START-I in May 1992, obligating Almaty to remove all strategic nuclear weapons from its territory by 1999. Kazakhstan, moreover, became the first of the Lisbon signatories to ratify START-I and the Lisbon Protocol – doing so in early July 1992 – though by August 1993 it had not signed and ratified the NPT.[79] In the meantime, Marshal Shaposhnikov implied that in the CIS summit discussed above, Kazakhstan had in effect agreed to cede command and control of nuclear weapons to the Russian Strategic Rocket Forces,[80] although this had not been confirmed by any authoritative Kazakh source.

The leadership in Kazakhstan clearly has become emboldened by Ukrainian defiance, worried by the Russian slide to the right, and impressed with the extent to which the mere threat to keep the weapons that are already on Kazakh territory increases Kazakhstan's status in international affairs.[81] Nuclear "rhetoric" has become commonplace even where there is almost no capability to back the claim. For example, Azerbaijani former interior minister Iskandar Hamidov has claimed that Azerbaijan has six nuclear weapons that will be used against Erevan if the Armenians "don't come to their senses."[82] Both Azerbaijan and

Armenia are listed by nuclear experts as perhaps having the will but generally lacking the capability of building nuclear weapons.[83] However, indigenous development and manufacture are not the only way to obtain nuclear armaments. Indeed, with highly enriched uranium selling at approximately $250,000 per kilo – and with so much of it available from mining and warhead extraction – the threat of the proliferation of enriched uranium on the part of states as well as individual actors is tangible.[84] Doubtless it was the allure of such profit that prompted Kyrgyz president Askar Akayev to offer to sell enriched uranium from Kyrgyz mines to states such as India.[85]

Fortunately, other Central Asian countries have declared their willingness to become nonnuclear states. For example, Uzbekistan's new defense law, which took effect in August 1992, states that Uzbekistan will accept and behave according to three nonnuclear principles: not to deploy, not to produce, and not to acquire nuclear weapons.[86] Another manifest example was Turkmenistan's new regulations on importing and exporting certain products in its territory. The list of products approved by President Niyazov banned the import of many items, including nuclear materials.[87]

Kazakhstan, therefore, is likely for the foreseeable future to remain the only state on Russia's southern frontier to have nuclear weapons on its territory; these weapons will nevertheless most probably stay under Russian control even if their ownership remains vague. The situation is dictated as much by economic stringency as by political will. Moreover, the continued discovery of the ecological disasters inflicted on Kazakhstan – with an official survey of environmental conditions listing 529 sites where dumping of millions of tons of radioactive waste has taken place[88] – is likely to serve as a salutary lesson to its neighbors of the enormous human cost involved.

Conclusion

Considering the record of historical mistrust, ethnic strife, and political unpredictability, it is possible that Ukraine – and perhaps Kazakhstan – may find some way of obtaining control over a nuclear arsenal, both to attract continued attention from the West and to deter possible Russian territorial aggression, especially given the high level of political uncertainty in Russia. With the emergence of a separate Ukrainian military establishment, moreover, a new lobbying group for the retention and/or acquisition of nuclear weapons has also been created. Ukraine's defense minister, Konstantin Morozov, reflected this view when he told a meeting of NATO defense ministers in March 1993 that "the West will take heed of what Ukraine says only as long as there are nuclear weapons on its soil."[89] If Ukrainian military strategists are asked to plan seriously for the country's defense against Russian invasion, nuclear weapons would almost undoubtedly form a major component of that plan, not necessarily for first use, but as a deterrent to Russian use. Nuclear weapons would carry an additional appeal to Ukrainian planners insofar as the worsening economic situation in the country has made the notion of maintaining a large conventional force against Russia seem less feasible. A nuclear deterrent based on gaining control of former Soviet nuclear weapons sited in Ukraine would be far cheaper. What remains unclear is whether strategists will conclude that the attempt to create such a nuclear force would do more to invite Russian attack than deter it.[90]

Even if Ukraine ratifies START-I, the time lag to the realization of the required denuclearization stipulated in it and in the Lisbon Protocol is quite long (seven years). Given the unpredictable nature and rapidity of developments in this part of the world, it is likely that the nuclear environment will be uncertain in all of the new states throughout and beyond this period. The longer it takes to ratify and implement strategic-arms-reduction and nonproliferation agreements, the more difficult it will be both to denuclearize Ukraine and Kazakhstan, and to prevent the spread of nuclear weapons to neighboring countries. Public opinion, reacting to high levels of insecurity brought on by economic collapse and interethnic as well as international conflict, may come to view nuclear weapons as a shield against attack. National elites who favor the incorporation of nuclear weapons into their countries' military planning may pursue a strategy of dragging out promised nuclear disarmament until the idea of additional nuclear powers becomes palatable to the West. At such time, these elites may be gambling that in the future the West will no longer have the political will to actively force them to adhere to their previous disarmament agreements. And if Russia does turn to the right, elites may also be calculating that the West would actually be grateful if, for example, Ukraine and Kazakhstan could rely on their own nuclear deterrents and not on the West for security guarantees.[91] Such hedging on signed treaties, however, could fuel Great Russian chauvinism, and heighten tensions in the region.

Conclusion

The political and social upheaval in the lands of the former USSR constitutes one of the greatest historical changes of the twentieth century, combining a chaotic imperial collapse with simultaneous attempts to build new nation-states. Given the complexity of this process, no observer can pretend to foretell its outcome or its larger consequences. However, analysts can identify some of the key features of the process and the underlying factors that may push developments in the new states toward chaos or stability. In this chapter several major aspects of the Soviet Union's disintegration and post-Soviet state-building are discussed. Next this process is briefly compared with previous twentieth-century instances of imperial collapse and political realignment. On the basis of these comparisons, the chapter closes with an evaluation of the implications for the future of Russia and the other new states.

The Eurasian Upheaval as Process

One important characteristic of the upheaval taking place in Eurasia is that it is virtually certain to continue for many years. Whether judged in terms of the formation of political and legal institutions, the recasting of national economies, or the emergence of new norms of intrasocietal and government–society relations, all the new states are experiencing the kind of revolutionary transformation that has historically required decades to complete.[1] Those countries that make a successful transition to an open, democratic, and market-oriented society integrated into the international community cannot expect to reap the full benefits for two or three decades. Almost certainly some of the countries will not complete the transformation, and a handful may not even seriously attempt it.

Much depends on the disposition of Russia. If the process of democratization in Russia falters and the country reverts to authoritarianism, this will give succor to like-minded leaders and groups elsewhere. Moreover, should authoritarian rule be reestablished in Russia, the desire for a new "gathering of the Russian lands" is likely to be part of the ideological basis of the regime, which would threaten the independence of several new states to which ultranationalist Russians currently lay claim – especially Ukraine, Belarus, and Kazakhstan. Given the current severe limitations on Russia's military capabilities, Moscow could not quickly or easily reestablish direct control over its principal former Soviet dependencies. Nevertheless, the rise of an ultranationalist authoritarian regime in Russia would undoubtedly trigger a cycle of increased expenditure on military buildups in all the new states; it could legitimize the imposition of emergency powers for leaders of the other new states; and it would derail efforts to shift these countries from reliance on state-controlled heavy and defense industries to consumer-oriented market economies. In the worst-case scenario, it could lead to interstate or civil war throughout the territories of the former USSR.

Russia has, however, made enormous strides away from its centuries-old legacy of authoritarian rule. For reasons to be discussed, it may be able to avoid a slide back into autocracy. Even if Russia continues its movement toward democracy, though, other states may not. The new states' steps toward democratic political norms and market-oriented economic practices have already shown a tremendous variation. Just as most of the East European states that won independence after the First World War – and a sizable number of the Asian and African states that gained it after World War II – soon abandoned their new democratic institutions and reverted to authoritarianism, some of the post-Soviet states may prove unable to overcome the authoritarian legacy of the past.[2] In the absence of a reassertion of Russian military rule over many of the former Soviet republics, the political tides in Eurasia will consist of a tumultuous ebb and flow that will make the underlying direction of change difficult to discern.

Just as the post-Soviet upheaval will last for a long time, it will reverberate in many corners of the globe. Because of the vastness and military might of the USSR, its collapse has already jarred and altered diplomatic alignments in many important arenas of world politics. The emergence of six new (and poorer) states east of Prague has expanded the East European region and widened the economic disparities within it, thereby diminishing the likelihood that all the states of the region might be admitted to the European Community. Unsettled by the macroeconomic implications of integrating the low-wage countries of Eastern Europe, by the possibility of excessive immigration from the east, and by the economic aftershocks of German reunification, public opinion in Western Europe no longer supports the granting of membership in the European Community to most of the new post-Communist states. Clearly, the prospect of constructing a single, united Europe on terms contemplated until recently by governments from Moscow to London appears increasingly unlikely.[3]

In the Middle East, the Soviet collapse and Russia's pro-Western policy have undercut the position of several regional powers that previously depended on Cold War hostility to sustain a plentiful flow of weapons and military advisors from Moscow. The collapse of the superpower that often supported a "rejectionist" stance against Israel has made those regimes, such as Syria, more susceptible to American pressure and more mindful of the need to explore political solutions to regional conflicts. The emergence of independent states in the Caucasus as well as in Central Asia has expanded the number of players in the region, sparked new clashes that could draw the established countries into large-scale wars, and moved the region's political center of gravity northward toward Turkey and Iran.

Farther to the east, the effects of the Soviet imperial collapse have been scarcely less important. In Inner Asia the advent of new states with predominantly Muslim populations has created opportunities for new alliances among these states and Afghanistan and Pakistan; simultaneously it has raised concerns in predominantly Hindu India that a "great game" may once again have to be played, this time by forging a strategic alliance with Russia to prevent Islamic regimes from dominating politics on both sides of the Khyber Pass.[4] Developments in Central Asia have created new diplomatic opportunities for China but also have raised the risk of increased political instability and separatist tendencies inside the People's Republic, particularly among the Uyghur population in the strategically important province of Sinkiang.[5] In the Far East, Russia's new foreign policy philosophy and need for trade and investment have led to a near-total reversal of Moscow's traditional posture toward the two Koreas.[6] Although as of mid-1993 the post-Soviet upheaval had not ushered in any basic change in Russia's relations with Japan, by sharply reducing the perceived military threat from Russia in East Asia it had given free play to the economic conflicts undermining the Japanese–American security alliance.

Much of the diplomacy in the regions along the periphery of the former USSR will be shaped by the historical legacies of the new states and their neighbors, a subject discussed in Chapter 1. But as shown in Chapter 2, the course of events will also be strongly affected by the character of the nationalist movements in the new states and the form of identity that nationalist leaders succeed in instilling in their followers. The volatile process of nation-building is still in its early stages, and its long-term consequences remain uncertain. Nevertheless, the ethnic variations that are already apparent in the former Soviet republics suggest that future forms of nationalism in the new states are likely to display wide differences. To begin with, the sheer intensity of national sentiment – not to be confused with its political coloration – varies widely, ranging from the high levels seen in countries such as Estonia and Ukraine to much lower levels in others such as Belarus and Turkmenistan.

In several countries, including Russia, Ukraine, and the Baltic states, nationalism has thus far taken a relatively benign form. In Russia, right-wing nationalists have attempted to rally the population around a xenophobic and aggressive national program by incorporating the alleged mistreatment of Russians in the other new states into their political indictment of the Yeltsin government. As of mid-1993, although right-wing rhetoric had become increasingly shrill and some influential members of the liberal elite had been swayed by it, most citizens of Russia did not appear to accept this conception of Russia's national identity and international role. The situation was quite different in such countries as Moldova, where the interplay of intolerant forms of nationalism, including chauvinism on the part of influential members of the local Russian population and local units of the Russian army, contributed to the eruption of civil war. In Georgia the dynamic of relations between ethnic Georgians and local non-Slavic minorities was somewhat similar, although in this case members of the titular nationality seemed more clearly at fault for the outbreak of political violence.

Whether virulent nationalism will develop in Russia and other new states hinges on a number of factors. One is the predilections of national political and cultural elites, and their skill in imparting their ideas to ordinary citizens through political action, public symbolism, rewriting the nation's history, and other cultural activities. Another determinant is the actual treatment of nontitular ethnic groups (and not only Russian minorities) by their "host" governments. This treatment has become a core issue in the relations among the new states because governments are demanding the easing of any pressures on their ethnic kinfolk abroad, and also because of the political and social pressures on those states experiencing in-migration. The political coloration of nationalism in the new states is especially dependent on the public's receptivity to various types of nationalist appeals, which will be affected by economic trends. The interaction of these variables may produce many new twists and even reversals of public attitudes. To date, however, the most important news is that militant forms of nationalism – those that emphasize ethnic exclusivity rather than a civic conception of national identity – have become predominant in only a few of the small post-

Soviet states rather than in such large countries as Russia, Ukraine, and Kazakhstan.

Like nationalism, the growth of religiousness and public interest in religion has had a major impact on the domestic politics and external relations of several of the new states. That impact is multifaceted, as shown in Chapter 3. One of the most important effects of a revival of religiousness has been to help restore a sense of personal morality and individual obligation in societies with a heritage of rampant corruption and widespread evasion of personal responsibility. At the same time, interconfessional differences have generated friction in Russia's relations with countries such as Ukraine and Moldova, and have affected relations between Muslims and non-Muslims in Central Asia. Religiously based sensibilities have played an important part in Russia's perception of conflicts on its southern borders, clashes often portrayed by Russian parliamentarians and commentators as being between Orthodoxy and Islam. In the Caucasus, despite tentative peace-making attempts by clerics of different faiths, conflicting religious loyalties have reinforced the popular animosities that have fueled the war between Armenia and Azerbaijan, as well as that between Christian Georgians and separatists in Abkhazia and South Ossetia, many of whom are Muslims.

The revival of religion has the potential to influence the internal political evolution of all the new states. How it does so depends on the forms it assumes, which in turn hinges partly on the existence or absence of unobstructed popular participation in politics. The dominant trend in Western orientalism tends to accept Christianity as promoting and buttressing democracy, while viewing Islam as likely to undermine the prospects of establishing democratic political systems.[7] However, it is unwise to analyze international affairs primarily in terms of the relations among whole civilizations, or to suggest that entire religious traditions either promote or obstruct democratic political development.[8] Because analyses framed in these terms almost invariably oversimplify the diverse strands of tradition that exist within a single culture, they obscure the seeds of cultural and political change.[9] Christianity, for example, has supported authoritarian regimes (not least in tsarist Russia) but also movements for democracy, and some currents of political reformism within contemporary Islam resemble reformist trends inside the Roman Catholic church.[10] The impact of religion on national political dynamics must be evaluated in context, alongside such factors as the level of economic development, the performance of existing political institutions, the influence of international actors, and the "snowballing" effect of trends in other countries.[11]

In large measure, the future geopolitics of Eurasia will hinge on the political systems that become established inside the post-Soviet states. As shown in Chapter 4, many of the new states exhibit a number of conditions favorable to the development of democracy and civil society. These include hard-fought constitutional struggles that by mid-1993 had resulted in the ratification of new fundamental laws in some countries; a real, though conflict-ridden, division of authority between executive and legislative institutions; news media that are freer than in the past and serve as an outlet for vigorous public debate; the growth of interest groups and associations beyond government control; and substantial public support for democratic principles among rank-and-file citizens, especially the younger and better educated.

At the same time, some elements necessary for the consolidation of democracy are weak or absent. With the arguable exception of the Baltic countries, none of the new states possesses a coherent system of developed political parties that can channel and sustain mass participation in national politics, and very few have well-developed institutional mechanisms of civilian control to bar military officers and the security police from intervention in domestic politics. Equally important, most countries still lack a system of private property and banking that can guarantee civic groups and associations the independent economic resources needed to resist arbitrary acts of government, although stepped-up privatization may remedy this deficiency in Russia and a few other countries.[12] In addition, the fate of democracy will hinge on the emergence of skilled new political elites and able political leaders – not least in the new elections that are slated to occur in most of the post-Soviet states by 1996 and that may be held substantially earlier in Russia and elsewhere.

Despite the new states' proud claims of political independence, the economies of most of these countries are likely to remain highly interdependent for the foreseeable future, as shown in Chapter 5. Although several countries have attempted to expand their economic relations with the outside world and curtail their relations with other post-Soviet states, especially with Russia, this objective has proved exceedingly difficult to attain. In Ukraine, for instance, economic pressures have undercut the strong nationalist impulse to sever ties with Russia and have reportedly caused a significant portion of the population to regret the collapse of the USSR.[13] Even in Estonia, which has enjoyed an unusual measure of success in reorienting its economy away from the CIS countries, the economic relationship with Russia remains critical. Although Russia under President Yeltsin has refrained from military action against other new states, it has used economic leverage for political objectives, as it did by restricting energy supplies in an effort to force Estonia to modify its legislation on citizenship and naturalization. In the absence of massive external assistance, most of the new states will be compelled to endure such pressures in order to prevent the total collapse of their economies and societies.

On the other hand, close economic interaction among the new states has positive potential as well. Although Azerbaijan has exploited economic leverage to the hilt by blockading Armenia, in other bilateral relationships that have not reached the point of outright military warfare, the very level of interdependence has often given the new states an incentive to avoid a spiral of self-defeating economic blows against each other. Moreover, all the new states, despite their distinctive histories and cultures, face a common challenge: the task of constructing a modern economy using the fractured building blocks of a failed Communist regime. Although the advanced capitalist countries can teach them about the functioning of an advanced market economy, the West has considerably less knowledge about the creation of market economies, especially from the detritus of a bankrupt socialist order. In this respect, the post-Soviet states may learn as many useful lessons in political economy from observing one another and the countries of Eastern Europe as from listening to advice from the West.

The pace of political and economic change has posed special challenges to the makers of foreign policy in the new states. Decision-makers in all the states lack time-tested guidelines to help them judge what constitutes their countries' national interests; even Russia's leaders have been hard-pressed to reach consensus on this basic issue. In all the post-Soviet countries, diplomacy has been shaped by the need to obtain foreign economic aid and support while avoiding external political and military commitments that could break the back of the national economy. In many of the non-Russian states, policy has also been affected by a desire to cultivate external powers as a counterpoise against any future Russian attempts to reestablish control. Most governments have therefore worked to develop and maintain friendly relations with all the established states beyond the borders of the former USSR. This diplomatic strategy has proved more difficult to follow in relations with the other new states, where the legacy of political, ethnic, economic, and military entanglements has provoked serious frictions and, in the Caucasus, interstate war.

Developments in the national military forces reflect the contradictory political and economic processes at work in the new states. The paucity of operational definitions of the national interest and the reluctance of governments in most of the new states to specify any major foreign power as a prospective enemy have stymied military planners and accentuated the marked shift toward a focus on potential regional rather than global conflicts. Efforts to establish national military forces are being carried out under conditions of acute economic stringency and uncertainty about Russia's future political relations with Ukraine and a host of other new states. Although the Russian military is gradually withdrawing from former republics such as the Baltic countries, it has also played an active role in military conflicts along Russia's border in the North Caucasus and in other new states, and has served as a mechanism for the maintenance or reimposition of Russian influence. Meanwhile, however, the institutional cohesion of all the post-Soviet military establishments has been undermined by declining morale and mounting economic hardships, raising the risk that the chain of command may dissolve as an increasing number of units ally themselves with local civilian authorities who can ensure their welfare.

The question of nuclear armaments has become a touchstone for the national aspirations and anxieties triggered by the breakup of the Soviet Union. In the first flush of optimism following the breakup, the Soviet stocks of tactical nuclear weapons were removed from all the non-Russian states and transferred to Russia. A comparable measure of change, though, has not occurred in the realm of strategic weaponry. Noteworthy progress has been made in planning for the reduction of Russia's strategic nuclear arsenal through arms control agreements with the United States and for the elimination of strategic armaments from other post-Soviet states. But the fate of the strategic weapons based in Ukraine – and to a lesser extent those in Kazakhstan – remains hostage to larger political forces. Of the three non-Russian states in which such weapons are currently situated, only Belarus has clearly undertaken to divest itself of them.

One reason for Ukrainian and Kazakh reluctance to part with these weapons is that they are a politically valuable means of holding the West's attention and eliciting larger quantities of Western economic assistance. However, the reluctance to give them up also reflects real military dilemmas and uncertainties. Unless much higher levels of trust are achieved with Russia, the prospects of nuclear divestiture, particularly by Ukraine, are problematic. Whatever the justification in terms of Ukraine's immediate security interests, its acquisition of operational nuclear capabilities would most likely derail scheduled Russian–American arms reductions, precipitate a fundamental reevaluation of the military situation in countries such as Germany and Poland, and lead to the breakdown of the antiproliferation regime embodied in the Nuclear Non-Proliferation Treaty.

The Upheaval in Comparative Perspective

Comparing the Eurasian upheaval with the disintegration and aftermath of other twentieth-century continental empires can help put the dynamics of the contemporary process in perspective. By the end of the First World War, four empires lay in ruins – the German Second Reich, Austro-Hungary, Ottoman Turkey, and tsarist Russia. The cases of Austro-Hungary and Ottoman Turkey are particularly germane because these polities consisted of contiguous territories and had multinational populations.[14] The contemporary parallels with Imperial Germany are less obvious, primarily because the Second Reich had relatively few subjects who were not ethnic Germans. None of these historical cases, of course, corresponds in all the essentials with the contemporary Eurasian upheaval, but they can help pinpoint some of the principal social and political forces at work in the current situation.

The disintegration of the USSR and its immediate aftereffects appear to have a number of similarities as well as dissimilarities to these three other episodes of imperial collapse and political realignment. (The collapse of the tsarist empire was analyzed in the Introduction, and hence has been omitted from the discussion here.) Several aspects of each case warrant attention: first, the domestic ramifications of the empire's competition with other states, particularly where this leads to involvement in a protracted general war; second, changes in the relationship between the imperial state and its subject peoples, including especially the main national group; third, the international outlook of the principal nation-state that emerges from the breakup of the empire; fourth, the impact of the existence of ethnic kinfolk of the dominant group living beyond the empire's core territories; and finally, the role of scavenger states that seek to take advantage of the collapse by appropriating elements of the fragmented empire.

The pressure of competition against other states exerted a powerful effect on all the empires in question.[15] By the late 1960s the USSR was laboring under mounting pressures from its rivalry with states that possessed more plentiful resources and higher levels of technology, and these stresses helped precipitate the process of liberalization that led ultimately to the empire's collapse.[16] In this sense the Soviet case resembles the Ottoman and Habsburg experiences. During the nineteenth century the international power of the Ottomans and Habsburgs steadily declined; in each instance efforts of varying seriousness were undertaken to modernize inherited political and economic institutions, but the reforms proved inadequate to shield the empire from the shocks of international politics.[17] However, in the Soviet case the period of international decline was much briefer, even allowing for the fact that

Soviet censorship obscured the onset of the USSR's internal crisis, and the crumbling of the Soviet system occurred quite differently from the breakup of the other polities under discussion.

The collapse of the other empires was precipitated by involvement in an exhausting general war; the Soviet collapse was not.[18] The enormous political, economic, and psychological strains generated by participation in World War I, a "total war" that mobilized all members of society and all national resources, were a crucial contributing factor to the demise of the Ottoman, Habsburg, and Imperial German political systems.[19] By contrast, the Soviet collapse occurred in the absence of the extraordinary societal strains generated by such warfare. Indeed, the USSR's prodigious military effort in the titanic clash with Nazi Germany during World War II constitutes one of the few genuinely heroic episodes of its history. By this standard, the war in Afghanistan was relatively inconsequential, and defeat in that conflict had only marginal importance for the fate of the Soviet empire.[20] The principal causes must be found elsewhere.

One of the most important causes of imperial collapse is the withdrawal of support for the imperial state by its subject peoples. Such a withdrawal played a critical role in the demise of both the Ottoman and Habsburg dynasties. In each case the stresses of geopolitical competition and protracted war were multiplied by the imperial elite's inability to create a durable shared political identity for all the subjects of the empire. Under heavy external pressure during the nineteenth century, the Ottoman empire was compelled to loosen its control over the Arab Middle East; it completely lost control of a series of territories inhabited primarily by such non-Turkic groups as Greeks in the 1820s, Romanians in the 1850s, and Bulgarians and Serbs in the 1860s. During the same period the Habsburg empire also came under powerful centrifugal pressures from its subject peoples, especially the Hungarians, Czechs, and Poles. In neither empire was the imperial government able to establish a supranational political identity capable of subsuming the burgeoning nationalist sentiments among its nontitular ethnic peoples. The Ottomans carried out forced population exchanges with Greece that were meant to eliminate these problems, and the Habsburg dynasty, through the compromise of 1867, elevated the Hungarians to a position more or less equal to that of the ethnic German inhabitants of Austria. Nevertheless, such measures failed to resolve the tensions stemming from the dissatisfaction of other peoples inside each empire. Soviet efforts to bring about the assimilation of the various ethnic groups into a supranational identity were far more systematic, though in the long run not much more successful.

The reason for the Soviet empire's collapse even in the absence of overwhelming external pressures lies primarily in the long-term impact of the Stalinist regime's systematic repression of its subject populations. For all their hegemonic impulses, none of the other empires under discussion treated their subjects with anything like the brutality displayed at the height of the Stalinist terror. The Habsburg dynasty's abuses were mild by comparison with the massive executions and untold deaths from freezing and starvation in the concentration camps of the Stalinist regime.[21] Ottoman Turkey comes somewhat closer to the Soviet experience by virtue of the genocidal policies it applied to its Armenian subjects in the early twentieth century. However, this policy centered on one national subgroup within the empire, not on the whole range of non-Turkic nations under Ottoman control.

Neither the Habsburg nor the Ottoman regime, moreover, used mass terror against the imperial nationality itself. This distinguishes the Ottoman case from the Soviet experience and helps explain why the full revelation of Stalin's crimes contributed to the rapid dissolution of ethnic Russian support for a powerful Soviet state. The monumental human costs of the Soviet empire for the Russians themselves made its achievements far dimmer than the accomplishments of the Habsburg and Ottoman empires seemed to members of their core national groups at the start of the twentieth century.[22] Consequently, large segments of the imperial nationality at both the elite and the mass level lost – at least temporarily – the desire to rule the minority nationalities previously subjugated or coopted by the empire.

Yet another subject that bears examination is the international outlook of the principal nation-state that emerged from the breakup of the empire. A feature that links the Soviet collapse with past cases of imperial disintegration is the development of paranoid explanations of the empire's demise. As we have seen, some right-wing Russian nationalists have blamed the breakup of the Soviet empire on the machinations of Western capitalists and intelligence services, thus echoing the rhetoric of the Stalin era. Interwar Germany offers the clearest example of the way that such xenophobic interpretations of military defeat can contribute to the rise of authoritarian regimes with aggressive international agendas. Postwar political attitudes were mixed in Austro-Hungary, where the demise of the empire led to the creation of independent Austrian and Hungarian states. Due to the loss of large amounts of territory in the postwar peace settlement, Hungary developed a strong revanchist movement, but the new state was too weak to take action on its own. In Austria, by contrast, no paranoid theory developed, mainly because many ethnic German inhabitants of Austria wanted to become part of Germany rather than restore the Habsburg empire. In Turkey the revanchist impulse fal-

tered for somewhat different reasons. The new Kemalist regime became the only country defeated in World War I that was allowed to
participate in peace negotiations, and it succeeded at the Lausanne
conference in overturning the punitive terms imposed on its Ottoman
predecessors under the Treaty of Sevres.[23]

In the post-Soviet political situation, there is also an important difference from the conditions that gave rise to revanchist movements in
Germany and Hungary. The Soviet breakup occurred in the absence
of military conflict with the outside world. More precisely, it transpired
during a period of international amity without precedent in the USSR's
prior history. That the USSR was not destroyed by foreign invaders
means the persecutionist interpretation lacks any tangible link to the
personal experience of ordinary Russians. As of mid-1993, one feature
of mass attitudes in Russia and several other new states was the public
sense that the international environment was relatively benign and that
the real dangers to the country's survival came from within. If these
attitudes endure, revanchist elements will find it difficult to persuade
the public of the need to adopt an aggressive posture toward the other
new states. On the other hand, the rise to power of a chauvinist leadership might be facilitated by full-fledged efforts of important parts of
Russia to secede and become independent states. Under these conditions, it is easy to imagine that nationalist leaders determined to preserve
Russia's integrity by violent means might rise to power, and that conflicts within Russia could spill over into the other new states, and into
neighboring countries as well.

Another of the general factors that influences the political denoue-
ment of imperial collapse is the existence of ethnic kinsmen living
beyond the empire's core territories. The existence of such groups can
have a major effect on the strength of the core nation's impulse to
recreate the empire or even expand beyond the empire's previous
boundaries. One of the advantages of Ataturk and the other reformers
who wished to renounce Ottomanism was that there were no major
concentrations of ethnic Turks in the parts of the empire outside Anatolia. That pan-Turanism (a movement to unify all speakers of Turkic
languages) had ceased to be a major political trend by the 1920s helped
the advocates of Turkish nation-building in Anatolia avoid political
claims from the scattered Turkish communities that did exist in and
beyond the empire's peripheral territories.[24] The advocates of building
a predominantly Turkish nation-state also benefited from the Turkish
population's weariness with the burdens of empire, popular resentment
of the governmental advocates of Ottoman imperialism who had led
Turkey into the disastrous defeat of World War I, and ethnic Turkish

dislike of Arabs and other non-Turkic groups commonly thought to have benefited unjustifiably from inclusion in the empire.[25]

In this respect the aftermaths of the Austro-Hungarian empire and the German Second Reich may offer more apt parallels with the contemporary upheaval in Eurasia. After 1867, changes in the structure of the Habsburg empire essentially gave the Hungarians status as a co-imperial nation along with Austria's ethnic Germans.[26] As noted above, the post–World War I dismemberment of the Habsburg empire left Hungary truncated and susceptible to the rise of a xenophobic nationalism. The probability of this turn of events was enhanced because the imperial breakup left large concentrations of ethnic Hungarians outside the country's remaining territorial core, thereby creating a focus of Hungarian revanchist sentiments. Hungarians living within the boundaries of the diminished Hungarian state considered themselves responsible for the well-being of Hungarians living elsewhere and for the cultivation of conditions that would eliminate or moderate threats to the welfare of the Hungarian inhabitants of the Carpathian basin, which historically constituted the Crownlands of St. Stephen, the first Christian king of Hungary.[27] In the same vein, it is commonly accepted that the military defeat of Imperial Germany and the historical existence of a far-flung population of ethnic Germans in East Central Europe contributed to the rise of an even more revanchist and aggressive German regime in the 1930s.

Nevertheless, the presence of ethnic kinsmen abroad is not necessarily an all-powerful magnet that drives the homeland state, regardless of its political complexion, to seek their incorporation or reincorporation into the state. The nature of the central polity that emerges from the ruins of empire is at least as important. Kemalist Turkey chose not to base its legitimacy on the ingathering of Turkic peoples, for example; indeed, it maintained its relations with Soviet Russia even as Turkic peoples there were denied cultural and political rights. Political leaders and elites predisposed to imperial expansion are likely to seize on the pretext of rescuing kinsmen abroad; leaders who oppose expansion and wish to focus on domestic needs will seek ways to resist and deflect pressures for such intervention. Although the existence of democratic institutions in the principal successor state is no guarantee against the adoption of a policy of "rescuing" ethnic kinsmen – and with them, the old empire – a democratic polity is less likely to adopt such a stratagem than is an authoritarian, xenophobic regime.

The final factor that differentiates the Soviet collapse from several previous episodes of failed imperialism is the relative caution displayed by potential scavenger states that might pull components of the disintegrating empire into their own political and military orbits. Part of the explanation for this caution is that several of these states are themselves politically fragile and could be destabilized by overzealous efforts to gain direct control over elements of the Soviet empire. The rather temperate behavior of Iran toward the new states is a case in point. China likewise has put good relations with Russia ahead of the manipulation of the new states of Central Asia as possible tools to be used against Russia. Much of the explanation is that Russia remains militarily powerful, not so much by virtue of its crisis-ridden conventional military establishment as because of its vast nuclear arsenal. The result has been to make most neighboring countries careful about cultivating ties with the other former republics at the expense of Russia. For the non-Russian new states, there has been little danger that they will become the object of a scramble for control by other powers; the risk of being neglected by the outside world has been considerably greater.

Although this pattern of international behavior has no parallel in the Ottoman and Habsburg cases, it does bear a certain resemblance to the conduct of the Western powers toward post-Imperial Germany, which emerged during the 1920s as the only country in central Europe of major interest to these governments. In a somewhat similar fashion, Russia has become the central focus of Western concerns today. Following the Locarno Conference and the Kellogg–Briand Pact, Germany was pushed onto center stage, and all its neighbors to the east became dependent on the power of their sponsor, France. Today Russia has also emerged as the East's major independent interlocutor for the West. All the other successor states and countries of Eastern Europe have been marginalized to a greater or lesser degree, and the West is dealing with them primarily through the prism of its policy toward Russia. Some 200 million inhabitants of these regions are dependent on what happens in Russia and how the West perceives it, just as 50 million were sidetracked by the Western focus on post-Imperial Germany in the interwar period. Indeed, the West's geopolitical preoccupation with Germany became so acute that it turned a blind eye to the rise of fascism. Although the West today is more concerned about the fate of democracy, geopolitical calculations might keep Western diplomacy focused on Russia even if authoritarianism were to return there.

Russia, the West, and the Future of Eurasia

These observations raise the question of the future of democratization in Eurasia. Because of the centrality of Russia to the other new states and its position as the core national successor to the failed USSR, it deserves special discussion. In an effort to divine the character of Russia's future political system, some observers have drawn an analogy between Russia and the fate of the fragile democratic republic of Weimar Germany, established after the military defeat and collapse of the imperial Second Reich. Significant parallels exist. Many Russian intellectuals and public figures are suffering from what a distinguished student of German history termed "the politics of cultural despair."[28] Like Weimar Germany, post-Soviet Russia has suffered rampant inflation and plummeting economic production that threaten to undermine its fledgling democratic institutions. Like Weimar, Russia has experienced a steep decline in its international power, though the drop was arguably far more precipitous in postimperial Germany than it has been in post-Soviet Russia. Because in the span of a few years the political crisis of the early 1930s transformed Weimar Germany into the totalitarian juggernaut of Nazism, these parallels are both striking and unsettling.

However, in juxtaposing Weimar Germany with post-Soviet Russia some important distinctions must be borne in mind. The difference in historical sequence is especially important. Germany's disillusionment and repudiation of the Weimar republic came against the backdrop of memories of a relatively prosperous prewar Germany presided over by an emperor of the nineteenth-century European type. In other words, in Germany the overthrow of liberal democracy – which was not inevitable even under the adverse circumstances of the 1930s[29] – preceded the catastrophic experience of Nazism. In Russia, by contrast, the attempt to democratize the political order comes in the aftermath of Stalinism and its terrors. Comparing the process of democratization in several countries, some scholars have argued that in the eyes of many citizens the most compelling reason for democratization is not democracy's socioeconomic benefits, but the protection it offers against dictatorial abuses of power.[30]

If true, this proposition means that democracy may possess a hidden reservoir of support among Russian citizens. Some of these citizens lived through the fires of the Stalinist crucible, and all of them have been inundated since 1987 with shocking accounts of the horrors perpetrated by the Stalinist regime. The depth and suddenness of these revelations, so lethal to the legitimacy of the Soviet state, may give democratic trends in Russia more durability than they otherwise might possess.

Memories and recollections of the terrors of Stalinism are no guarantee against a resurgence of authoritarianism. If they were, such trends would not be visible in some other former Soviet republics, such as Georgia. However, thus far most citizens of Russia and a number of other new states have not surrendered to the sort of messianic nationalism that sprang up in Georgia after the USSR's collapse, and it may be that Russia will be among the countries that the laws of historical probability exempt from this path of development.

A great deal will depend on the way in which Russian leaders, intellectuals, and ordinary citizens reconstruct the "grand governing narrative" of their national history. If Stalinism comes to be widely viewed as a simple aberration from the positive historical developments of the tsarist era, then right-wing Russian nationalism could simultaneously assume an anti-Communist hue and serve to legitimize the creation of an ultranationalist authoritarian regime. The outcome might be quite different, however, if the leaders and citizens of Russia recognize that Stalinism was rooted partly in Russia's own authoritarian traditions, rather than exclusively in an alien Marxist ideology imported from abroad. Acceptance of this reality would facilitate the reappropriation of the strain of Russian political liberalism that constitutes a subsidiary element of Russia's historical legacy and contributed to the country's halting efforts to establish constitutional democracy before World War I. By resurrecting Russian liberalism, Russian thinkers and activists might create a new foundation for the interpretation of Russia's past and help the country move beyond its long chronicle of harsh misfortunes.[31] In short, as with previous cases of postimperial state-building, Russia's path of development will be strongly influenced by intellectual and cultural developments, not only by fluctuations in economic output or the day-to-day tactics of political leaders.

In this process the leaders and citizens of Russia will be compelled to struggle with a recurring issue of their history: the relationship of Russia to the West. It is tempting to conclude that, as in the past, Russia will follow a path fundamentally different from the advanced industrial democracies. However, it is important to remember that even those Western governments with the least-sullied historical pedigrees passed some important signposts on the path to full-fledged democracy only rather recently.[32] Even more important, two pillars of the present-day international community of industrial democracies – Germany and Japan – were, within living memory, governed by aggressive fascist dictatorships. The failure to recall such realities can obscure the possibilities for democratic change. Authoritarian systems can become democracies, particularly when those regimes have discredited themselves by inflicting deep suffering on their citizens.

This does not signify that Russia will indeed become "like the West." However, it is important to recognize that the impulse to rebuild Russia along democratic lines is incomparably stronger today than ever in the past. Moreover, this effort is occurring in an international political setting dominated by the presumption that democracy and market economies are the supreme form of political organization, quite in contrast to the Depression-ridden 1930s, when the *Zeitgeist* glorified the authoritarianism of the Italian fascist and Nazi regimes – as well as that of the Stalinist system – and helped destabilize European democracies by undercutting their legitimacy.[33] Much will depend upon how the issue is framed by Russian thinkers and citizens – whether democracy and a mixed economy are regarded as the essential institutional ingredients of any modern nation-state, or as societal features that violate the essential qualities of the Russian nation and must therefore be rejected. Although the outside world cannot exert a decisive influence over how Russians think about such questions, it is in the interests of the advanced industrial democracies to ensure that large numbers of Russians are personally exposed to as many working national versions of democracy and the market economy as possible. Multifaceted exposure of this kind will bring home to Russians the wide number of countries in which such social arrangements exist; it will help Russians choose those specific arrangements that mesh best with their distinctive cultural and political traditions; and it will reduce the chances that liberalization will come to be regarded as a blueprint for the imposition of an alien cultural pattern – American, German, or some other – on the Russian nation. It is worth noting that contemporary Germans and Japanese do not consider themselves any less German or Japanese for living in a democracy, even though in an earlier era many citizens of these countries would have regarded the institutions of democracy as alien influences that the nation should avoid.

Thus, to a degree unparalleled since at least 1917, the future of Russia, and with it the future of Eurasia as a whole, hangs in the political balance. The other post-Soviet states must wrestle with political and economic challenges similar to those in Russia, and their struggles will affect the course of events inside Russia itself. The upheaval in Eurasia is one of the greatest dramas of modern history, and its results will have an enduring impact not only on the peoples of Eurasia but on the peoples of the entire world.

Chronology of Events, January 1992 to October 1993

Griffin C. Hathaway

Dates for international visits in general reflect dates on which delegation heads met with their counterparts. Leadership changes and elections are listed in Appendix B.

January 1992

2 Russia and Ukraine free prices on most retail goods and services.

3 Ukraine claims control over all nonstrategic military forces on its territory.

3 Russia assumes control over all former Soviet embassies abroad.

4 Ukraine claims control of Black Sea Fleet.

6 Prices on most retail goods and services freed in Kazakhstan and Azerbaijan.

8 Ukraine agrees to remove tactical nuclear weapons by July 1992 and strategic weapons by 1994.

8 Lithuania frees prices for retail goods and services.

9 Russian president Yeltsin claims Black Sea Fleet for Russia.

10 Turkmenistan frees prices for retail goods and services.

11 Russia and Ukraine agree that part of Black Sea Fleet belongs to Ukraine.

15 Ukrainian prime minister Fokin visits Greece.

17 Lithuanian head of state Landsbergis visits Russia.

19 Belarusian prime minister Kebich visits China.

19 British foreign minister visits Ukraine and Kazakhstan on nuclear matters.

20 Student riots occur in Uzbekistan.

21 Lithuanian head of state Landsbergis visits Great Britain.

23 Russian parliament votes to reconsider transfer of Crimea to Ukraine.

23 Azerbaijani president Mutalibov visits Turkey.

25 Moldovan president Snegur and Romanian president meet in Moldova.

30 Russian president Yeltsin visits Great Britain.

31 Russia begins troop withdrawal talks with Baltics.

Griffin C. Hathaway is a doctoral candidate at the University of Maryland at College Park.

February 1992

4 Ukrainian president Kravchuk visits Germany.
6 Russian president Yeltsin visits France.
6 Russian parliament begins review of 1954 transfer of Crimea to Ukraine.
8 CIS summit in Moscow.
12 Opposition stages demonstrations in Tajik capital of Dushanbe.
14 CIS summit in Minsk, Belarus.
17 U.S. secretary of state visits Russia and Central Asia.
18 Moldovan president Snegur visits U.S.
25 Armenian irregular forces massacre Azerbaijani civilians in Khodzhaly.
26 Kazakh prime minister Tereshchenko visits China.
28 Lithuanian head of state Landsbergis visits Germany.

March 1992

3 Russia begins troop withdrawal from Lithuania.
4 Russia claims jurisdiction over Soviet forces in Germany, Poland, Mongolia, and Cuba.
5 Moldovan and separatist trans-Dniester forces clash.
6 Council of Baltic Sea States formed.
12 Uzbek president Karimov visits China.
12 Ukraine suspends transfer of tactical nuclear weapons to Russia.
13 CIS summit meeting in Moscow.
17 Lithuanian prime minister Vagnorius visits Sweden.
18 Belarus creates national army.
20 CIS summit in Kiev, Ukraine.
21 Russian republic of Tatarstan votes for independence.
28 Antigovernment demonstrations occur in Dushanbe, Tajikistan.
31 Eighteen Russian republics sign federal treaty; only Tatarstan and Chechnya refuse.

April 1992

1 Russia places 14th Army in Moldova under its control.
5 Russian vice-president Rutskoy visits trans-Dniester and Crimea.
6 Sixth Russian Congress of People's Deputies opens.
6 Ukraine lays claim to Black Sea Fleet.
6 Kyrgyz president Akayev visits Germany.
7 Russia counters Ukraine, asserts its own control over entire Black Sea Fleet.
9 Russia and Ukraine suspend decrees claiming Black Sea Fleet; agree to negotiate.
11 Uzbek president Karimov visits Saudi Arabia.
13 Finnish president visits Latvia.
16 Ukraine resumes transfer of tactical nuclear missiles to Russia.
22 Lithuanian head of state Landsbergis visits France.

23 Central Asian leaders hold summit in Bishkek, Kyrgyzstan.
23 Belarusian-Polish friendship treaty signed.
26 Ukrainian president Kravchuk visits Iran.
27 Demonstrations and counterdemonstrations continue in Dushanbe, Tajikistan.
28 Turkish prime minister visits Kyrgyzstan and Uzbekistan.
30 Russian president Yeltsin calls for national referendum to dissolve Congress of People's Deputies.

May 1992

1 Georgia announces parliamentary elections for 11 October.
2 Turkish prime minister visits Central Asia and Azerbaijan.
3 Ukrainian president Kravchuk visits Turkey.
5 Major clashes occur in Dushanbe between opposition and Nabiyev forces.
5 Russian Security Council established.
5 Crimea declares independence and schedules referendum for 2 August.
5 Armenian-Azerbaijani summit held in Teheran.
6 Ukrainian president Kravchuk meets with President Bush in Washington.
11 Latvian head of state Gorbunovs visits United States.
13 Kyrgyz president Akayev visits China.
13 Ukrainian parliament annuls Crimean independence decision and referendum plans.
13 Estonian prime minister Vahi visits China.
15 CIS summit in Tashkent; collective security pact signed by Russia, Armenia, Kazakhstan, Kyrgyzstan, Tajikistan, and Uzbekistan.
18 Ukrainian president Kravchuk visits Poland.
19 Romanian president Iliescu visits Moldova.
19 Kazakh president Nazarbayev meets with President Bush in Washington.
19 Crimea rescinds declaration of independence; alters referendum question.
19 Ukrainian prime minister Fokin meets with Yeltsin in Moscow.
19 Lithuanian head of state Landsbergis visits Sweden.
21 Russian parliament annuls 1954 transfer of Crimea to Ukraine.
22 Polish president Walesa visits Russia.
23 United States, Russia, Ukraine, Belarus, and Kazakhstan sign Lisbon Protocol to START-I.
23 Cease-fire broken in trans-Dniester; heavy fighting resumes.
25 Russia and Kazakhstan sign treaty of friendship.
25 Belarus introduces Belarusian ruble to cocirculate with Russian ruble.
25 Czechoslovakian prime minister visits Ukraine.
26 Ukraine and Estonia sign friendship agreement.

June 1992

4 Russian republic of Ingushetia declares independence.
5 Russian president Yeltsin and Lithuanian head of state Landsbergis meet.

8 Russia and Turkmenistan sign military cooperation pact.
12 Azerbaijan launches offensive in Nagorno-Karabakh.
16 Ukrainian president Kravchuk visits France.
16 Uzbek president Karimov begins trips to South Korea, Indonesia, and Malaysia.
17 United States-Russia summit in Washington produces Joint Understanding that leads to START-II treaty.
19 Moldovan prime minister Muravschi visits United States.
20 Estonia introduces national currency, the kroon.
21 Russian 14th Army aids in separatist seizure of Bendery.
23 Russian president Yeltsin and Ukrainian president Kravchuk meet in Dagomys.
23 Belarusian head of state Shushkevich visits Poland.
24 Russian president Yeltsin meets Georgian leader Shevardnadze, North and South Ossetian leaders.
25 Black Sea Economic Cooperation Community formed.
26 CIS summit in Minsk.
28 Lebed named new commander of Russian 14th Army in Moldova.
30 Tajik president Nabiyev visits Iran.
30 Lithuanian prime minister Vagnorius visits United States.

July 1992

1 Poland and Latvia sign treaty of friendship and cooperation.
2 Russian ruble allowed to float at single exchange rate.
3 Moldovan president Snegur visits Moscow.
6 CIS summit in Moscow.
7 Russian president Yeltsin grants broad powers to Russian Security Council.
7 Russian president Yeltsin attends G-7 summit in Munich.
7 Georgia rejects CIS membership.
8 Armenian parliament votes not to recognize independence of Nagorno-Karabakh.
9 Russian president Yeltsin says all Russian troops to be out of Baltics by summer 1993.
9 Crimean parliament suspends 2 August referendum on independence.
14 Russian vice-president Rutskoy visits Chisinau and Tiraspol in Moldova.
14 Shooting occurs between Russian and Estonian troops in Estonia.
20 Belarusian prime minister Kebich meets with Gaidar in Moscow.
20 Armenian offensives launched in Nagorno-Karabakh.
20 Latvia introduces its own currency, the Latvian rublis.
21 Russian president Yeltsin and Moldovan president Snegur sign peace agreement over trans-Dniester conflict.
23 Georgian republic of Abkhazia declares independence; rejected by Georgia.
27 Russian and Estonian forces exchange gunfire in Estonia.
30 Turkish prime minister visits Georgia.

August 1992

3 Russian president Yeltsin and Ukrainian president Kravchuk meet in Yalta to discuss Black Sea Fleet.
13 Uzbek president Karimov visits Pakistan.
14 Georgia seizes control of Abkhazian capital of Sukhumi.
19 Moldovan prime minister Sangheli visits Romania.
19 Russia and Kazakhstan sign military cooperation pact.
20 Belarusian head of state Shushkevich visits South Korea.
21 Armenian president Ter-Petrossyan meets Russian president Yeltsin in Moscow.
22 Latvia and Lithuania establish joint coordination in national defense matters.
24 Turkmen president Niyazov concludes visit to Iran.
25 Russian president Yeltsin meets in Moscow with Kyrgyz president Akayev.
25 Ukraine and Uzbekistan sign treaty of friendship and cooperation.
26 Moldovan prime minister Sangheli meets Dniester separatists in Tiraspol.
27 Armenian and Azerbaijani foreign ministers reach cease-fire in Almaty.
28 Moldovan president Snegur meets Romanian president in Romania.

September 1992

1 Yeltsin and Moldovan president Snegur meet in Moscow to discuss trans-Dniester conflict.
3 Russian president Yeltsin, Georgian leader Shevardnadze meet in Moscow with Abkhazian and regional North Caucasus leaders.
8 Russia concludes agreement with Lithuania to have all troops out by 31 August 1993.
9 Acting under extreme parliamentary pressure, Russian president Yeltsin abruptly cancels trip to Japan.
18 Moldovan president Snegur holds talks with Gagauz separatists.
19 Azerbaijan launches major offensive in Nagorno-Karabakh.
22 Kazakh president Nazarbayev visits Germany.
25 Crimean parliament opts to stay part of Ukraine.
28 Lithuanian prime minister Abisala visits Poland.
29 CIS commander in chief Shaposhnikov calls for sole Russian control of nuclear weapons.
30 Russian acting prime minister Gaidar visits Azerbaijan and Armenia.

October 1992

1 Russia begins distribution of vouchers for its privatization program.
1 U.S. Senate ratifies START-I.
3 Gaidar meets with Ukrainian president Kravchuk in Kiev.
6 Abkhazian forces continue offensive against Georgian troops.
7 Azerbaijani National Assembly overwhelmingly rejects CIS membership.
9 CIS summit in Bishkek, Kyrgyzstan.

12 Russian president Yeltsin and Azerbaijani president Elchibey meet in Moscow.
13 Belarus announces all nuclear arms will be transferred to Russia by end of 1994.
15 Russian president Yeltsin and leaders of Russian Federation republics meet in Moscow.
16 Ukraine restarts reactor at Chernobyl nuclear power plant.
19 Russia extends moratorium on nuclear testing until 1 July 1993.
22 Russian acting prime minister Gaidar and Kazakh prime minister Tereshchenko meet in Moscow.
23 Ukraine and Moldova sign pact respecting each state's territorial integrity.
24 Armenian president Ter-Petrossyan meets with Russian president Yeltsin in Moscow.
24 Ukrainian prime minister Kuchma meets Russian president Yeltsin and Russian acting prime minister Gaidar in Moscow.
24 Azerbaijani Interior Ministry forces launch failed operation to control Nakhichevan.
27 Russian president Yeltsin bans right-wing National Salvation Front.
29 Russian president Yeltsin suspends Baltic troop withdrawal; cites inadequate housing in Russia.
31 Turkey, Azerbaijan, Turkmenistan, Kazakhstan, Kyrgyzstan, and Uzbekistan discuss formation of Turkic Common Market.

November 1992

2 Russia declares state of emergency in North Ossetia and Ingush republic.
2 Tajik acting president Iskandarov meets with Russian acting prime minister Gaidar in Moscow.
4 Russian parliament ratifies START-I treaty.
4 Gerashchenko confirmed as head of the Russian Central Bank.
4 Moldova and Kazakhstan sign trade treaty in Almaty.
9 Russian president Yeltsin visits Great Britain.
10 Lithuanian prime minister Abisala visits United States.
10 President Kravchuk says Ukraine needs compensation and security guarantees to ratify START-I.
11 Moldovan president Snegur visits Kyrgyzstan.
12 Ukraine leaves ruble zone and introduces its own currency, the karbovanets.
18 Russian president Yeltsin visits South Korea.
18 Polish prime minister visits Belarus.
23 Russia and Ukraine reach agreement on former Soviet foreign debt.

December 1992

1 Seventh Russian Congress of People's Deputies opens in Moscow.
1 Fighting erupts anew in Dushanbe, Tajikistan.
3 Georgia's declaration of martial law throughout Abkhazia rejected by separatists.

16 German chancellor Kohl visits Moscow.
18 Russian president Yeltsin visits China.
21 Belarus and Moldova conclude a treaty of friendship and cooperation.
23 Ukraine says it needs at least $1.5 billion for denuclearization.
24 Moldovan president Snegur calls for referendum on reunification with Romania.
29 Kazakhstan and Ukraine sign several trade agreements.
31 Ukraine abrogates agreement with Russia on former Soviet debt.

January 1993

1 Russia charges world prices for its oil and natural gas; states with separate pacts with Russia remain unaffected.
3 United States and Russia initial START-II treaty in Moscow.
3 Central Asian states hold summit meeting in Tashkent, Uzbekistan.
4 Azerbaijan announces plans to expand trade relations with Iran.
7 Armenia announces parliamentary and presidential elections for fall 1993.
8 Belarusian head of state Shushkevich visits China.
8 Lithuanian prime minister Lubys meets with Polish prime minister in Poland.
9 Russian prime minister Chernomyrdin and Kazakh prime minister Tereshchenko meet in Russia.
10 Armenian president Ter-Petrossyan meets with Russian president Yeltsin in Moscow.
12 Ukrainian prime minister Kuchma meets Polish prime minister in Kiev.
13 Tajik head of state Rakhmanov meets with Kazakh president Nazarbayev in Almaty.
14 Ukrainian prime minister Kuchma meets Russian prime minister Chernomyrdin in Moscow.
15 Russian president Yeltsin and Ukrainian president Kravchuk hold summit meeting in Moscow.
15 Russian vice-admiral Eduard Baltin named commander of Black Sea Fleet.
18 Ukraine and Moldova sign military cooperation pact.
20 Tajik head of state Rakhmanov announces plans to create national army.
20 Georgian head of state Shevardnadze completes visit to Iran.
21 Meeting of CIS Nuclear Policy Committee; Ukraine refuses to cede nuclear arms control to Russia.
22 CIS summit meeting in Minsk. Russia, Belarus, Kazakhstan, Kyrgyzstan, Uzbekistan, Tajikistan, and Armenia sign CIS Charter; Ukraine, Moldova, and Turkmenistan do not.
22 Abkhazia, the "Dniester Republic," and Gagauz officials sign cooperation agreement.
23 Explosion destroys critical gas pipeline from Georgia to Armenia.
25 Latvia and Lithuania create free trade zone between the two states.
26 Estonian president Meri visits France.
27 Tajik head of state Rakhmanov visits Turkmenistan.

28 Russian president Yeltsin visits India; refuses to drop controversial rocket
   deal.
29 Tajikistan declares state of emergency along country's Afghan border.
30 Moldovan president Snegur visits France.

February 1993

 3 Turkey allows shipments of Western relief aid to cross Turkish territory
   into Armenia.
 3 Ukraine and Poland conclude a defense cooperation agreement.
 4 Belarus ratifies the START-I treaty and concurrent Lisbon Protocol.
 9 Russian president Yeltsin links 14th Army withdrawal to political status of
   "Dniester Republic."
10 Ukrainian president Leonid Kravchuk visits Great Britain.
15 Russia and Ukraine fail to resolve division of former Soviet debt.
16 Uzbekistan announces readiness to introduce national currency if ruble zone
   collapses.
18 Romania presses territorial claims on Ukraine.
19 Ukraine and Moldova conclude an extensive military cooperation pact.
19 United States agrees to purchase uranium extracted from dismantled Russian nuclear warheads.
20 Sweden extends an offer to assist in training Estonian defense, border, and
   police forces.
22 Ukraine reaches agreement with Kazakhstan and Uzbekistan for energy
   imports.
24 Estonia, Latvia, and Lithuania agree to conduct joint training exercises in
   May 1993.
25 Ukrainian prime minister Kuchma visits Turkmenistan.
26 Ukrainian president Kravchuk visits Hungary.
26 Kyrgyz prime minister Chyngyshev completes tour of Europe.
27 Kazakh president Nazarbayev visits Russia.
27 Georgian prime minister Sigua visits Turkmenistan.

March 1993

 1 Latvian head of state Gorbunovs visits France.
 2 Tentative cease-fire reached in Nagorno-Karabakh.
 3 German chancellor Kohl visits Moscow.
 4 Georgian prime minister Sigua visits Ukraine.
 5 Latvia introduces its national currency, the lat.
 7 Tajik head of state Rakhmanov visits China.
10 Gagauz and Dniester separatists reject Moldovan offer of limited autonomy.
12 CIS summit in Moscow.
12 Armenian president Ter-Petrossyan visits France.
15 Abkhazian forces launch offensive to take Abkhaz capital Sukhumi, held
   by Georgia.

15 Estonian prime minister Laar meets with Latvian prime minister Godmanis in Latvia.
16 French president Mitterrand visits Moscow.
16 Council of Baltic Sea States meets in Helsinki.
17 Moldovan president Snegur visits India.
17 Lithuanian president Brazauskas visits Denmark and Iceland.
19 Ukrainian prime minister Kuchma visits Moldova.
19 Russian prime minister Chernomyrdin visits Uzbekistan.
19 Armenian president Ter-Petrossyan visits Kyrgyzstan.
20 Kazakh prime minister Tereshchenko meets Ukrainian counterpart Kuchma in Crimea.
21 Turkmen president Niyazov begins visit to United States and Great Britain.
24 Slovak prime minister Meciar visits Moscow.
26 Georgia introduces state coupons in parallel circulation with Russian ruble.
30 CIS summit in Minsk.
31 Estonian president Meri visits Great Britain.

April 1993

2 Lithuanian president Brazauskas visits Russia.
3 Armenian forces seize Azerbaijani town of Kelbadzhar.
5 Russian president Yeltsin concludes Vancouver summit with U.S. president Clinton.
7 Turkish president Ozal begins tour of Central Asian states.
9 Belarusian parliament approves membership in CIS collective security pact.
13 Georgian head of state Shevardnadze concludes trip to Ukraine.
14 Turkish president Ozal visits Azerbaijan.
14 Ukrainian prime minister Kuchma tours Persian Gulf states seeking oil supplies.
14 Lithuanian president Brazauskas visits Great Britain.
14 Uzbek president Karimov visits Turkmenistan.
16 CIS summit in Minsk is held to show support for Russian president Yeltsin in 25 April referendum.
17 Baltic prime ministers confer in Vilnius, Lithuania.
21 Azerbaijani president Elchibey and Armenian president Ter-Petrossyan meet in Turkey.
21 Moldovan prime minister Sangheli visits United States.
22 Tajik prime minister Abdullodzhanov visits Moscow.
23 Kyrgyz president Akayev visits Japan.
26 Latvian prime minister Godmanis visits Poland.
27 Lithuanian prime minister Slezevicius visits Norway.
28 CIS summit in Minsk.
28 Uzbek president Karimov visits Germany.
30 Ukrainian president Kravchuk meets Hungarian prime minister Antall in Ukraine.

May 1993

3 Defense representatives from Ukraine, Latvia, Lithuania, Estonia, Moldova, Belarus, Poland, Romania, the Czech Republic, and Slovakia confer in Latvian capital of Riga.

6 Belarusian head of state Shushkevich visits Romania.

6 Estonian president Meri visits Poland.

6 Moldovan prime minister Sangheli visits Israel.

7 Summit of Baltic Sea States concludes in Tallinn.

10 Kyrgyzstan introduces its national currency, the som.

10 Belarusian prime minister Kebich begins trip to United Arab Emirates.

10 Moldovan president Snegur and prime minister Sangheli meet with leaders from "Dniester Republic."

14 CIS summit in Moscow; economic union planned.

14 Georgian head of state Shevardnadze meets with Russian president Yeltsin in Moscow.

14 Belarusian prime minister Kebich visits India.

15 Moldovan president Snegur meets with Russian president Yeltsin in Moscow.

18 Kyrgyz president Akayev visits the United States.

19 Kazakh president Nazarbayev visits Turkmenistan.

19 Georgian head of state Shevardnadze visits Armenia.

21 Several Black Sea Fleet ships raise Russian naval flag, sparking a new dispute about the fleet.

23 Azerbaijani prime minister Huseynov visits Great Britain.

24 Indian prime minister Rao visits Uzbekistan.

24 Tajik head of state Rakhmanov visits Moscow.

24 Polish president Walesa visits Ukraine.

25 Armenian president Ter-Petrossyan visits Moscow.

25 Indian prime minister Rao visits Kyrgyzstan.

26 Armenia, Azerbaijan accept U.S.-Russian-Turkish peace plan; rejected by Nagorno-Karabakh representatives.

26 Kazakh president Nazarbayev visits Uzbekistan.

27 Uzbek president Karimov and Kyrgyz president Akayev meet to resolve crisis over som.

28 Turkmen president Niyazov concludes visit to France.

30 Estonian prime minister Laar and Kyrgyz president Akayev meet in St. Petersburg.

31 Russian ruble falls to more than 1,000 per U.S. dollar.

31 Baltic states conclude first ever joint military exercises.

June 1993

2 Georgian head of state Shevardnadze visits Kazakhstan, then travels on to China.

2 Baltic heads of state meet to seek membership in European Community.

3 Ukrainian parliament opens debate on START-I ratification.
6 Lithuanian prime minister Slezevicius visits Finland.
8 Kyrgyz president Akayev visits Kazakhstan.
10 German chancellor Kohl visits Ukraine.
12 Intense fighting breaks out along Nagorno-Karabakh's borders.
14 Nagorno-Karabakh reconsiders, then accepts peace plan agreed to by Armenia and Azerbaijan.
14 Lithuanian prime minister Slezevicius visits Belarus.
14 Estonian prime minister Laar visits Finland.
15 Azerbaijan leaves the ruble zone.
15 CIS Joint Military Command dissolved; Russia assumes control of all CIS forces.
15 Lithuanian president Brazauskas visits France.
15 Tajik prime minister Abdullodzhanov visits Moscow.
16 Prime ministers of Kyrgyzstan and Uzbekistan meet in Tashkent.
17 Kravchuk and Yeltsin in Moscow agree to equally split Black Sea Fleet beginning in September 1993.
18 Lithuanian president Brazauskas visits Switzerland.
21 Estonia adopts law on foreigners; Russia threatens sanctions.
21 Kyrgyz president Akayev visits Iran.
21 Hungarian president Goncz visits Russia.
21 Lithuanian prime minister Slezevicius visits the United States.
22 Georgian head of state Shevardnadze visits Belgium.
24 Russian prime minister Chernomyrdin cancels U.S. visit over disputed Indian rocket deal; instead, Chernomyrdin meets with Ukrainian prime minister Kuchma and Ukrainian president Kravchuk in Ukraine.
24 Georgian head of state Shevardnadze visits Germany.
25 Lithuania introduces its national currency, the litas.
26 Georgian head of state Shevardnadze meets with Ukrainian president Kravchuk in Ukraine.
28 Polish president Walesa visits Belarus.
28 Estonian prime minister Laar visits Germany.
29 Russian president Yeltsin visits Greece.
29 Slovak president Kovac visits Ukraine.
30 IMF approves $1.5 billion loan to Russia.

July 1993

1 Abkhaz forces launch major offensive against Georgian forces in Sukhumi.
1 Belarusian prime minister Kebich visits Moscow.
2 Ukrainian parliament declares ownership of nuclear weapons on Ukrainian territory.
5 Muslim Economic Cooperation Organization summit held in Turkey.
6 Georgian head of state Shevardnadze declares martial law throughout Abkhazia.
6 Ukrainian prime minister Kuchma begins tour of Baltic states.
8 Russian president Yeltsin arrives in Tokyo for G-7 summit.

9 G-7 nations offer $3 billion in aid to Russia.
9 United Nations Security Council approves sending military observers to Abkhazia.
9 Russian parliament declares Crimean port of Sevastopol to be a Russian city.
10 Prime ministers of Russia, Ukraine, and Belarus agree to form joint economic space; insist that Central Asian states must choose between joining them or remaining in ECO.
10 German chancellor Kohl meets with Russian president Yeltsin at Lake Baikal, Russia.
12 Kyrgyz president Akayev completes visit to Mongolia.
13 Tajik rebels and Afghan mujahidin destroy Russian border post along Tajik-Afghan border.
13 Estonian prime minister Laar visits Israel.
13 Indian president Sharma visits Ukraine.
14 Russian prime minister Chernomyrdin visits Germany.
15 United States and Russia agree to restrictions on Russian sale of rocket engines to India.
16 Georgia launches full offensive against Abkhaz forces surrounding Sukhumi.
17 Predominantly Russian towns of Sillamae and Narva in Estonia conclude referendum; more than 90 percent vote to declare themselves autonomous regions within Estonia.
17 Moldovan president Snegur and prime minister Sangheli visit Romania.
21 Belarusian head of state Shushkevich visits United States.
21 Kazakh prime minister Tereshchenko visits Lithuania.
22 Belarus formally joins NPT.
23 Kazakh prime minister Tereshchenko visits Australia.
23 Armenian forces seize strategic Azerbaijani town of Agdam.
24 Russian Central Bank announces withdrawal from circulation of all banknotes issued between 1961 and 1992.
24 Kazakh president Nazarbayev visits Thailand.
26 Lithuanian prime minister Slezevicius visits Poland.
27 Cease-fire reached between Georgian and Abkhazian forces.
27 Ukraine announces it is dismantling ten SS-19 ICBMs and will store the warheads in Ukraine.
28 Kazakh president Nazarbayev and Uzbek president Karimov call for emergency CIS summit to discuss Russian ruble exchange and Slavic economic union.
29 Bulgarian president Zhelev visits Kazakhstan.
30 Ukrainian president Kravchuk declares that forty-six SS-24 ICBMs are not covered by START-I.
31 Bulgarian president Zhelev visits Kyrgyzstan.

August 1993

2 Georgia leaves ruble zone; will introduce its currency, the lari, when country is stable.

Appendix A

4 Moldovan parliament narrowly fails to approve economic membership in CIS.
6 Russia, Uzbekistan, and Kazakhstan agree to form ruble monetary union.
7 Russian president Yeltsin and Central Asian leaders meet in Moscow to discuss growing conflict along Tajik-Afghan border.
7 Estonian president Meri meets Latvian president Ulmanis in Estonia.
10 Belarus announces it will introduce national currency, the zaichik.
11 Estonia invalidates referendum held 16–17 July in Narva.
11 Ukrainian prime minister Kuchma meets with Russian president Yeltsin in Moscow.
13 Latvian president Ulmanis visits Lithuania.
14 Kyrgyz president Akayev and Uzbek president Karimov meet in Osh, Kyrgyzstan.
16 Lithuanian prime minister Slezevicius meets Latvian prime minister Birkavs in Riga.
17 Georgian head of state Shevardnadze begins visits to Turkmenistan and Azerbaijan.
19 Belarusian head of state Shushkevich meets with Russian president Yeltsin in Moscow.
22 Russia suspends agreement to withdraw all troops from Lithuania by 31 August.
23 Slovak prime minister Meciar visits Moscow.
23 Georgian head of state Shevardnadze meets with Russian president Yeltsin in Moscow.
24 Russian president Yeltsin visits Poland.
31 Authorities in Azerbaijan and Nagorno-Karabakh agree to cease-fire.
31 Russia completes its troop withdrawal from Lithuania.

September 1993

2 Russian prime minister Chernomyrdin visits the United States.
3 Russian president Yeltsin and Ukrainian president Kravshuk meet in Crimea.
4 Pope John Paul II begins tour of all three Baltic States.
7 Russia, Armenia, Belarus, Karakhstan, Tajikistan, and Uzbekistan agree to form new ruble zone.
16 Abkhazian forces break cease-fire; launch attack on Sukhumi.
17 Russia completes its troop withdrawal from Poland.
20 Azerbaijan joins the CIS.
21 Russian president Yeltsin dissolves the Congress of People's Deputies.
24 CIS summit held in Moscow; members agree to form economic union.
27 Abkhaz take Sukhumi; Gamsakhurdia forces renew attacks in west Georgia.

October 1993

4 Russian president Yeltsin orders stroming of parliament building following armed opposition attacks; opposition leaders arrested.

Compendium of Leadership and Institutional Changes in the Eurasian States, January 1992 to October 1993

Griffin C. Hathaway

Political figures are those holding the positions identified as of 7 October 1993.

Armenia

PRESIDENT: Levon Ter-Petrossyan
VICE-PRESIDENT: Gagik Arutyunyan
PRIME MINISTER: Hrant Bagratyan
SPEAKER OF PARLIAMENT: Babken Ararktssyan
FOREIGN MINISTER: Vahan Papazyan
DEFENSE MINISTER: Sergey Sarkissyan
INTERNAL AFFAIRS MINISTER: Vanik Siradegyan
SECURITY MINISTER: Eduard Simonyants
CHAIRMAN, FOREIGN AFFAIRS COMMITTEE: David Vartanyan
CHAIRMAN, DEFENSE AFFAIRS COMMITTEE: Gevork Bagdasaryan

Elections to the 240-seat, unicameral Armenian Supreme Council were held in May 1990; in July 1991 the parliament created the posts of president, vice-president, and prime minister. On 16 October 1991, Armenian National Movement candidate Levon Ter-Petrossyan, then parliamentary chairman, was elected president with more than 80 percent of the vote. Relations between the government and parliament grew tense in 1992, erupting in late April after the parliament rejected for the third time the government's economic program. Prime Minister Gagik Arutyunyan submitted his resignation in protest, but Ter-Petrossyan refused to accept it. The parliamentary opposition, led by the Armenian Revolutionary Federation (the Dashnaks), united to form the National Alliance bloc, and organized massive rallies calling for Ter-Petrossyan's resignation over his refusal formally to recognize the independence of Nagorno-Karabakh. On 30 July, Khosrov Arutyunyan was named prime minister, succeeding Vice-President Gagik Arutyunyan, who had also been serving as acting prime minister since November 1991. Fighting in Nagorno-Karabakh in August set off demonstrations demanding a national referendum of confidence in Ter-Petrossyan's leadership. The parliamentary opposition declined to vote for the referendum when Ter-Petrossyan announced that if he won, he would dissolve parliament and hold new elections. On 16 October, Foreign Minister Raffi

Hovannisian resigned over what he felt was Erevan's too-conciliatory approach to the Nagorno-Karabakh conflict, and was replaced by Arman Kirakossyan on 10 November. On 21 October, former prime minister Vazgen Manukyan, who had resigned in September 1991 over policy disputes with Ter-Petrossyan, was named to replace Vazgen Sarkissyan as defense minister. On 2 February, Ter-Petrossyan dismissed Prime Minister Khosrov Arutyunyan for his opposition to the government's economic proposals, and replaced him with First Deputy Prime Minister Hrant Bagratyan. On 16 February, Eduard Simonyants was appointed head of the National Security Agency. On 26 February, Vahan Papazyan replaced Arman Kirakossyan as foreign minister. In March, parliamentary debate began on adopting a new constitution. In early July, Norat Ter-Grigoryants replaced Defense Minister Manukyan in an acting capacity. On 21 August Ter-Petrossyan named Sergey Sarkissyan as defense minister. In September the parliament rejected new parliamentary elections in early 1994.

Azerbaijan

PRESIDENT: Gaidar Aliyev (acting)
PRIME MINISTER: Surat Huseynov
SPEAKER OF PARLIAMENT: Gaidar Aliyev
FOREIGN MINISTER: Hasan Hasanov
DEFENSE MINISTER: Mamedrafi Mamedov
INTERNAL AFFAIRS MINISTER: Vagif Novruzov
SECURITY MINISTER: Nariman Imranov
CHAIRMAN, FOREIGN AFFAIRS COMMITTEE: Namik Akhundov
CHAIRMAN, DEFENSE AFFAIRS COMMITTEE: Mamed Kuliyev

Elections to Azerbaijan's unicameral, 360-seat Supreme Council were held in September 1990; Ayaz Mutalibov, the former first secretary of the Azerbaijani Communist Party, had already been named as president by the Supreme Council in May. On 8 September 1991, Mutalibov was popularly elected without opposition to the presidency. In late November, opposition rallies led by the nationalist Azerbaijani Popular Front (APF) forced the creation of a 50-member National Assembly to serve as a standing legislative component of the Supreme Council. Following the February 1992 killing of some 400 Azerbaijani civilians by Armenian fighters in the town of Khodzhaly, Mutalibov was forced to resign on 6 March. Elmira Kofarova also resigned as parliamentary chairwoman. Yakub Mamedov was named acting president. Mamedov appointed Hasan Hasanov as prime minister, but then dismissed him on 4 April, replacing him with Feyruz Mustafayev. Following further losses to Armenian forces in Karabakh, on 14 May Mutalibov and his supporters in the Supreme Council attempted a coup. The parliament declared Mutalibov's resignation invalid, returned him to the presidency, and named Mamedov to his prior parliamentary chairman's post. Mutalibov then declared a state of emergency and cancelled postponed presidential elections scheduled for 6 June. The opposition was able to turn back Mutalibov's coup, with the APF seizing power the next day. The APF dissolved the

Supreme Council, transferred power to the National Assembly, reinstated Mamedov as acting president, lifted the ban on the 6 June presidential election, and promised new parliamentary elections in the fall. On 18 May, the Azerbaijani Supreme Council met for the last time, accepted Mamedov's resignation, named Isa Gambarov as acting president and parliamentary chairman, and then ceded its legislative power to the National Assembly. Presidential elections for 6 June went ahead as scheduled, with APF chairman Abulfaz Elchibey winning with 60 percent of the vote. On 30 December, Elchibey proposed to eliminate the prime ministership and the cabinet of ministers. In response, Prime Minister Rahim Huseynov resigned on 26 January 1993, and was replaced in an acting capacity by his first deputy, Ali Masimov. On 19 February Defense Minister Rahim Gaziyev resigned and was replaced by Dadash Rzaev. On 15 April, Interior Minister Iskandar Hamidov was forced to resign following a personally led attack on several journalists in late March. Hamidov was replaced by Abdullah Allahverdiyev. On 28 April Panakh Huseynov replaced as prime minister Ali Masimov. On 4 June, former commander of the Nagorno-Karabakh theater Surat Huseynov launched an insurrection in the city of Gyandzha, and after taking control of the city, marched on Baku. Under pressure, Prime Minister Huseynov resigned on 7 June; parliamentary speaker Isa Gambarov resigned on 13 June. Former Soviet Politburo member and Nakhichevan leader Gaidar Aliyev was elected parliamentary chairman by the National Assembly on 15 June. In response to opposition demands, Elchibey dismissed Security Minister Fakhreddin Takhmazov and Internal Affairs Minister Allahverdiyev, but Huseynov continued his drive on Baku. On 18 June, Elchibey fled Baku, though he refused to resign as president. On 24 June, the National Assembly stripped Elchibey of presidential authority and transferred it to Aliyev. Foreign Minister Tofik Kasymov and Defense Minister Rzaev were dismissed; Aliyev replaced them in acting capacities with Albert Salamov and Safar Abiyev, respectively. On 30 June, the assembly named Surat Huseynov prime minister. On 3 July, Aliyev appointed Vagif Novruzov as minister of internal affairs and Nariman Imranov as minister of security, and arrested virtually all high-ranking members of the former government. On 29 August Elchibey was rejected in a national vote of confidence. Two days later Aliyev named Hasan Hasanov as foreign misnister and Mamedrafi Mamedov as defense minister. On 20 September Azarbaijan joined the CIS. On 3 October Aliyev was elected president with 99 percent of the vote.

Belarus

HEAD OF STATE AND PARLIAMENTARY CHAIRMAN: Stanislau Shushkevich
PRIME MINISTER: Vyacheslau Kebich
FOREIGN MINISTER: Pyotr Krauchanka
DEFENSE MINISTER: Pavel Kozlouskiy
INTERNAL AFFAIRS MINISTER: Vladzimir Yahorau
SECURITY MINISTER: Eduard Shirkouskiy
CHAIRMAN, FOREIGN AFFAIRS COMMITTEE: Pyotr Sadouskiy
CHAIRMAN, DEFENSE AFFAIRS COMMITTEE: Mycheslau Hryb

Belarus is one of three former Soviet states – Georgia and Tajikistan are the others – that does not have a presidency; the head of state is the chairman of the Supreme Council (a 360-seat, unicameral body elected in March 1990). Debate in Belarus has favored the creation of a presidency since the Supreme Council announced in June 1991 that Belarus intended to become a presidential republic, although there quickly emerged strong disagreement as to the powers of the post as well as the timetable for its introduction. Parliamentary chairman Stanislau Shushkevich has argued for a weak presidency, and has sought to delay its introduction. Prime Minister Vyacheslau Kebich, on the other hand, has advocated a strong presidency to be introduced rapidly. There has been remarkably little political change in Belarus since independence; most top officials remained unaffected by the failed August 1991 Moscow putsch. One notable exception was Mikalai Dzemyantsei, who was forced to resign as parliamentary chairman on 25 August 1991, owing to his support for the Moscow coup leaders. He was replaced on 18 September by deputy parliamentary chairman Shushkevich. The fall of 1991 saw numerous calls for the resignation of the government and the parliament because of both institutions' overwhelming conservative orientation. On 7 January 1992, the opposition Belarusian Popular Front (BPF), led by Zianon Pazniak, launched a referendum campaign to oust the Communist-dominated Supreme Council and hold early elections. On 11 January Belarus created a ministry of defense, and on 28 January named Pyotr Chaus to head it in an acting capacity. On 22 April, Pavel Kozlouskiy was named as defense minister, and Chaus was appointed deputy defense minister. In early May, the BPF's referendum petition was considered by the Supreme Council, which was required by law to designate the date of the vote within one month. Instead, the Supreme Council simply tabled the referendum until late October, when the planned date for the new parliamentary elections called for in the referendum had passed. On 29 October the parliament announced that the referendum petition was illegal (though its legitimacy had been recognized by the parliament in May), and thus rejected holding the vote. Instead, the parliament voted to hold elections to the body in March 1994, one year earlier than scheduled. At the same time, the parliament announced that a new constitution would be adopted by the end of 1993. As 1993 began, Belarusian politics split into two polarized camps: conservative Communist deputies aligned with Prime Minister Kebich against parliamentary chairman Shushkevich; and the BPF and other opposition movements, which sided with Shushkevich. On 22 March 1993, the draft version of the new constitution was finally completed; over Shushkevich's objections, it establishes a strong presidency with broad powers. On 9 April, again over Shushkevich's strong opposition, the Supreme Council approved membership in the 15 May 1992 CIS collective security pact. Arguing that signing the pact contradicted Belarus's neutrality, Shushkevich called for a national referendum on the issue. If the public supported the pact, Shushkevich said, he would resign. On 12 May, eight opposition parties endorsed Shushkevich's call for a referendum, but sought to broaden it to include questions on the dissolution of parliament and new elections. On 1 July, the Supreme Council overwhelmingly passed a vote of no-confidence in Shushkevich. The vote was not legally binding, however, as a quorum was not present, and so Shushkevich was not forced to resign. On 7 July, Shushkevich agreed to postpone until fall 1993 his planned referendum on Belarusian neutrality, because a referendum on the new constitution would also be held then.

Estonia

PRESIDENT: Lennart Meri
PRIME MINISTER: Mart Laar
SPEAKER OF PARLIAMENT: Ulo Nugis
FOREIGN MINISTER: Trivimi Velliste
DEFENSE MINISTER: Juri Luik
INTERNAL AFFAIRS MINISTER: Lagle Parek
SECURITY MINISTER: Juri Pihl
CHAIRMAN, FOREIGN AFFAIRS COMMITTEE: Vello Saatpalu
CHAIRMAN, DEFENSE AFFAIRS COMMITTEE: Peeter Lorents

Estonian politics following Soviet recognition of the country's independence on 6 September 1991 were polarized between the Estonian Popular Front (a coalition founded in 1988 to attain independence), and the Congress of Estonia (another coalition formed in opposition to the 105-member, unicameral Supreme Council elected in March 1990 Communist-dominated elections). On 16 January 1992, after intense debate, the Estonian parliament voted to grant Prime Minister Edgar Savisaar emergency powers for up to three months. After the parliament, however, refused to authorize these new powers, Savisaar and his government resigned. On 27 January, Tiit Vahi was confirmed as the new prime minister, and he retained most of Savisaar's cabinet. On 23 March, Lennart Meri resigned as foreign minister following strident parliamentary criticism. He was replaced on 6 April by Jaan Manitskiy. Following the parliament's inability to decide on a defense minister, Uno Veering was named acting defense minister on 27 April. Subsequently, the parliament confirmed Ulo Uluots as defense minister. On 28 June, the new Estonian constitution was confirmed by referendum. Drawn up by a constituent assembly equally divided between the Supreme Council and the Congress of Estonia, the constitution defined the country as a parliamentary republic with a largely ceremonial presidency. The first president would be elected by popular vote, but thereafter would be selected by the parliament. The constitution also replaced the Supreme Council with a 101-seat State Assembly called the Riigikogu. Presidential and parliamentary elections were held on 20 September, in which, due to citizenship laws, more than 40 percent of voting-age residents – mostly ethnic Russians – were ineligible to participate. Nonetheless, no presidential candidate emerged with the requisite majority of the vote. Parliamentary chairman Arnold Ruutel received 43 percent, followed by center-right Lennart Meri, the former foreign minister, with 29 percent. The Riigikogu, now dominated by Meri's Isamaa

(Fatherland) party, then elected him as president at its first session on 6 October. On 8 October, Mart Laar was selected as the country's new prime minister; on 21 October he announced his new cabinet, including Trivimi Velliste as foreign minister, Hain Rebas as defense minister, and Lagle Parek as minister of internal affairs. On 16 June 1993, Internal Affairs Minister Parek survived a parliamentary vote of no-confidence. In early August, Defense Minister Rebas was replaced by Juri Luik. Also in early August, the Riigikogu defense affairs committee voted no-confidence in its chairman, Rein Helme. Unable, however, to agree upon Helme's replacement, the committee named Peeter Lorents as head for three months, after which Helme was due to resume the position.

Georgia

HEAD OF STATE AND PARLIAMENTARY CHAIRMAN: Eduard Shevardnadze
PRIME MINISTER: Otar Patsatsia
SPEAKER OF PARLIAMENT: Vakhtang Goguadze
FOREIGN MINISTER: Aleksandr Chikvaidze
DEFENSE MINISTER: Giorgi Karkarashvili
INTERNAL AFFAIRS MINISTER: Eduard Shevardnadze (acting)
SECURITY MINISTER: Irakli Batiashvili*
CHAIRMAN, FOREIGN AFFAIRS COMMITTEE: Thomas Gamkrelidze
CHAIRMAN, DEFENSE AFFAIRS COMMITTEE: Nodar Natadze

The state's first Supreme Council, a unicameral, 250-seat body, was elected in October 1990; it in turn voted its chairman, former dissident Zviad Gamsakhurdia, as president in April 1991. Gamsakhurdia won 87 percent of the vote in a popular election for the post one month later; but in late 1991 opposition forces moved to oust him. After three weeks of heavy fighting in the heart of Tbilisi, Gamsakhurdia on 6 January 1992 fled the country, making Georgia the first former Soviet republic to overthrow a popularly elected leader. Rebel commanders then formed a ruling Military Council that suspended the constitution and created a parallel Coordinating Council, consisting of moderate political leaders, to serve as a provisional parliament. In late February, council officials announced that Georgia would abolish the presidency and adopt a parliamentary form of government. Both councils, however, lacked popular legitimacy; and as a result, the Democratic Union (the successor party to the Georgian Communist Party) in early March 1992 invited former Soviet foreign minister Eduard Shevardnadze to return to Georgia to form a new government. Both the Military and Coordinating councils then dissolved themselves and created a single State Council holding both legislative and executive power. The State Council then dissolved the Supreme Council elected in October 1990.

*Georgia does not maintain a ministry of security, but instead has a Bureau of Information and Intelligence.

On 8 May, Tengiz Kitovani replaced Levon Sharashenidze as minister of defense. On 11 October, unopposed candidate Shevardnadze was elected chairman of parliament with 90 percent of the vote; after the vote, the State Council formally dissolved itself. The strongest political faction in the 235-seat parliament was the Peace bloc, led by the Democratic Union. On 6 November, the new parliament confirmed Shevardnadze as chairman of the parliament with powers of head of state, Vakhtang Goguadze as speaker of the parliament, and reelected Tengiz Sigua as prime minister. The parliament also amended its election process, voting subsequently to elect the chairman by itself, and not through a general election, as was done on 11 October. On 6 May 1993, Shevardnadze dismissed his rival Tengiz Kitovani as defense minister, replacing him with Giorgi Karkarashvili. In mid-June, however, the Georgian National Independence Party and other opposition groups began demanding the resignation of Shevardnadze over his handling of the economy and separatist strife in Abkhazia. In response to the economic crisis, on 2 July, parliament granted Shevardnadze broad powers to issue decrees and choose all ministers except the prime minister. In late July, parliament refused to pass the government's budget, prompting the resignation of Prime Minister Sigua and his entire cabinet on 6 August. On 20 August Otar Patsatsia was approved as prime minister. Shevardnadze in September formed a new cabinet and assumed the post of acting Internal Affairs Minister. The parliament on 14 September endorsed a two-month state of emergency and agreed to suspend itself for 3 months after Shevardnadze threatened to resign.

Kazakhstan

PRESIDENT: Nursultan Nazarbayev
VICE-PRESIDENT: Erik Asanbayev
PRIME MINISTER: Sergey Tereshchenko
SPEAKER OF PARLIAMENT: Serikbolsyn Abdildin
FOREIGN MINISTER: Tuleutai Suleymanov
DEFENSE MINISTER: Sagadat Nurmagambetov
INTERNAL AFFAIRS MINISTER: Vladimir Shumov
SECURITY MINISTER: Bulat Bayekenov
CHAIRMAN, FOREIGN AFFAIRS COMMITTEE: Serikhan Zhakupov
CHAIRMAN, DEFENSE AFFAIRS COMMITTEE: Bulat Dzhanasayev

The unicameral, 358-seat parliament, called the Supreme Council, was elected in March 1990 elections. Dominated by Communists, parliament named Kazakh Communist Party head Nursultan Nazarbayev as president in April 1990. On 1 December 1991, Nazarbayev won an uncontested election for the presidency, receiving 99 percent of the vote. On 7 May 1992, Nazarbayev transformed the State Defense Committee into the Ministry of Defense, and named Sagadat Nurmagambetov as its minister. In early June, the Supreme Council, headed by Speaker Serikbolsyn Abdildin, approved for debate a draft constitution that would establish a strong presidency with limited legislative checks on the executive branch. On 10 June, the opposition organizations Azat (Freedom), Zheltoksan (December), and the Republican Party staged large demonstrations in Almaty demanding a coalition government. By 17 June, some five thousand protestors had gathered in front of the parliamentary building demanding the resignation of the government of Prime Minister Sergey Tereshchenko and of the Supreme Council. The demonstrations were forcibly broken up by Kazakh security forces the next day. On 28 January 1993, the Kazakh parliament adopted a new constitution granting the president broad powers. Opposition forces had insisted that parliamentary elections be held before the constitution's adoption, since the parliament had been elected in March 1990 Communist-dominated elections. On 6 February, a new political organization, Popular Unity of Kazakhstan, was created, with Nazarbayev as its nominal head. Nazarbayev has kept a tight leash on opposition political movements; in addition to the ones involved in the June 1992 protests, other organizations under strict watch include the Kazakh nationalist party Alash and the Russian nationalist movement Edinstvo (Unity). In October a new political party, the National-Democratic Party, was created. Headed by a former leader of Azat, the party pledged to focus on environmental concerns and interethnic relations.

Kyrgyzstan

PRESIDENT: Askar Akayev
VICE-PRESIDENT: Feliks Kulov
PRIME MINISTER: Tursunbek Chyngyshev
SPEAKER OF PARLIAMENT: Medetkan Sherimkulov
FOREIGN MINISTER: Ednan Karabayev
DEFENSE MINISTER: Myrzakan Subanov*
INTERNAL AFFAIRS MINISTER: Abdybek Sultalinov
SECURITY MINISTER: Anarbek Bakayev
CHAIRMAN, FOREIGN AFFAIRS COMMITTEE: Alikbek Dzhekshemkulov
CHAIRMAN, DEFENSE AFFAIRS COMMITTEE: Beksultan Ishimov

The 350-seat, unicameral Supreme Council was elected in March 1990; riots later that summer in Osh between Kyrgyz and Uzbeks led to widespread demonstrations for the government's resignation. When the parliament convened in October to select a president, it narrowly defeated a bid for the post by hard-line Communist Absamat Masaliyev. Instead, the parliament named Askar Akayev, the former head of the Kyrgyz Academy of Sciences. Akayev, Central Asia's only postindependence head of state who was not a former top Communist Party official, subsequently won the presidency in an unopposed election on 12 October 1991 with 95 percent of the vote. On 11 February 1992, Akayev abolished half the ministries and departments, named himself head of government, and demoted the newly appointed prime minister, Tursunbek Chyngyshev, to the post of deputy head of government. Dzhanybek Umetaliyev

*Kyrgyzstan was the only former Soviet republic not to establish a ministry of defense; it maintains only the State Committee for Defense Questions.

was named chairman of the State Committee for Defense Questions on 26 February. On 27 February, Akayev named Feliks Kulov to replace German Kuznetsov as vice-president. On 29 June, protestors demanded Akayev's resignation and new elections. In December 1992, Marat Saralinov was replaced as foreign minister by Ednan Karabayev. On 25 January 1993, eleven major opposition parties and movements united into a single front to promote democratization in the country; the coalition split in late February over support for the government. One faction led by Erkin (Free) Kyrgyzstan and the Asaba (Banner) National Renaissance Party called for the government's resignation; the other faction, led by the Kyrgyzstan Democratic Movement, thought this demand too destabilizing. On 15 April, the Supreme Council began the second reading of the draft constitution, in the process stripping Akayev of most of the presidential powers enshrined in the first draft. In response, Akayev demanded that either a constituent assembly complete the constitution, or that new parliamentary elections be held. On 5 May, however, the two sides reached agreement; Akayev ceded his position as head of government to Prime Minister Chyngyshev, while the Supreme Council dropped its challenges to the president's powers and removed a phrase proclaiming the country's adherence to Islamic values. The two sides also agreed that their terms in office will expire in 1995. On 22 July, Akayev dismissed State Defense Committee chair Umetaliyev and replaced him with his first deputy, Myrzakan Subanov. Calls for the government's resignation were repeated by Erkin Kyrgyzstan in mid-July.

Latvia

PRESIDENT: Guntis Ulmanis
PRIME MINISTER: Valdis Birkavs
SPEAKER OF PARLIAMENT: Anatolijs Gorbunovs
FOREIGN MINISTER: Georgs Andrejevs
DEFENSE MINISTER: Valdis Pavlovskis
INTERNAL AFFAIRS MINISTER: Girts Kristovskis
SECURITY MINISTER: Juris Vectirans
CHAIRMAN, FOREIGN AFFAIRS COMMITTEE: Aleksandrs Kirsteins
CHAIRMAN, DEFENSE AFFAIRS COMMITTEE: Ivars Silas

Prior to the Soviet recognition of Baltic independence on 6 September 1991, the first Supreme Council was elected in March 1990, with the proindependence Popular Front winning the majority. Originally, the parliament held 201 members; 20 were subsequently dismissed for their pro-Soviet actions. On 21 October 1992, the government of Prime Minister Ivars Godmanis survived a no-confidence vote from the Supreme Council. Also singled out but surviving were Foreign Minister Janis Jurkans and Internal Affairs Minister Ziedonis Cevers. On 27 October, however, despite surviving the no-confidence vote against him, Foreign Minister Jurkans resigned, citing discord between himself and parliament over foreign policy, especially toward Russia. He was replaced on 10 November by Georgs Andrejevs. On 18 May 1993, twenty deputies from various parliamentary blocs demanded a vote of no-confidence in Prime Minister Godmanis. On 25 May, the parliament declined to take such a vote, which, if successful, would have dismissed Godmanis and transferred the prime ministership to Supreme Council chairman Anatolijs Gorbunovs until a new government was formed. Many deputies felt it unnecessary to create such a governmental crisis so close to elections. On 5–6 June 1993, Latvia held elections to the new, 100-member Saeima, which replaced the Supreme Council. Parties winning the most seats were the center-right Latvian Way (36 seats), led by parliamentary chairman Gorbunovs and Foreign Minister Andrejevs; the center-right National Independence Movement (15); the center-left Concord for Latvia (13), led by former foreign minister Janis Jurkans; and the center-right Farmer's Union (12), led by Guntis Ulmanis. On 6 July, the new Saeima convened with a coalition between Latvian Way and the Farmer's Union, and elected Gorbunovs as chairman. The Saeima also reinstated the Constitution of 1922, which contained a weak presidency. After three ballots, Guntis Ulmanis was chosen president on 7 July. The next day, the Saeima approved Ulmanis's selection of Valdis Birkavs as prime minister. On 20 July, Birkavs's cabinet was confirmed; Andrejevs was retained as foreign minister, while Valdis Pavlovskis was named defense minister and Girts Kristovskis was named minister of internal affairs.

Lithuania

PRESIDENT: Algirdas Brazauskas
PRIME MINISTER: Adolfas Slezevicius
SPEAKER OF PARLIAMENT: Ceslovas Jursenas
FOREIGN MINISTER: Povilas Gilys
DEFENSE MINISTER: Andrius Butkevicius
INTERNAL AFFAIRS MINISTER: Romasis Vaitekunas
SECURITY MINISTER: Jurgis Jurgelis
CHAIRMAN, FOREIGN AFFAIRS COMMITTEE: Kazys Bobelis
CHAIRMAN, DEFENSE AFFAIRS COMMITTEE: Saulius Peceliunas

Elected in February and March 1990, the 141-member, unicameral parliament, called the Supreme Council, witnessed the gradual unraveling of the once-dominant Sajudis coalition. In dispute were efforts by parliamentary chairman and Sajudis leader Vytautas Landsbergis to establish a strong presidency. A referendum on the matter showed popular support for Landsbergis, but failed to garner the necessary majority. By summer 1992, increasing political paralysis and declining economic fortunes found Landsbergis and his Sajudis faction in the minority, and on 14 July parliamentary opposition forced the resignation of Prime Minister Gediminas Vagnorius. On 21 July the parliament elected

Aleksandras Abisala as prime minister, and subsequently approved a largely unchanged cabinet of ministers. In two rounds of voting on 25 October and 16 November, the Lithuanian Democratic Labor Party (LDLP), the successor party to the Lithuanian Communist Party, scored a stunning upset against Sajudis. The 25 October voting also approved a new constitution that created a presidency. In its first session on 25 November, the new, 141-seat parliament – called the Seimas – elected as its chairman LDLP head Algirdas Brazauskas. Brazauskas then became acting president pending presidential elections on 14 February 1993. Until then, the deputy chairman of parliament, Ceslovas Jursenas, served as acting chairman of parliament. On 2 December, Bronislovas Lubys replaced Aleksandras Abisala as the new prime minister. On 10 December, Lubys announced his new government: Defense Minister Andrius Butkevicius was retained, while Povilas Gilys was named foreign minister and Romasis Vaitekunas as minister of internal affairs. On 3 January 1993, Landsbergis unexpectedly declined to run for president. Instead, he endorsed Stasys Lozoraitis, then ambassador to the United States. On 14 February, Brazauskas easily defeated Lozoraitis for president; he was inaugurated on 25 February. The same day, Jursenas was confirmed as parliamentary chairman. On 26 February, Prime Minister Lubys resigned and was replaced by Adolfas Slezevicius, who was confirmed by the Seimas on 10 March. On 31 March, the Seimas confirmed Slezevicius's cabinet, which contained virtually no changes. Defense Minister Andrius Butkevicius resigned on 21 September, though he agreed to stay in his post while President Brazauskas considered his resignation.

Moldova

PRESIDENT: Mircea Snegur
PRIME MINISTER: Andrey Sangheli
SPEAKER OF PARLIAMENT: Petru Lucinschi
FOREIGN MINISTER: Nicolae Tiu
DEFENSE MINISTER: Pavel Creanga
INTERNAL AFFAIRS MINISTER: Constantin Antoci
SECURITY MINISTER: Vasile Calmoi
CHAIRMAN, FOREIGN AFFAIRS COMMITTEE: Alexandru Buruiana
CHAIRMAN, DEFENSE AFFAIRS COMMITTEE: Anatol Simac

Moldovan politics since the Soviet collapse have been marked by tension and violence over the ultimate fate of the new state: independence, membership in the CIS, or unification with Romania. Unification has been advocated by the Moldovan Popular Front (MPF) and the Congress of Moldovan Intellectuals. They have held disproportionate influence in the parliament and have been able to paralyze parliamentary activity due to a boycott by Russian separatist deputies from the self-proclaimed "Dniester Republic" on the left bank, to the east, of the Dniester River. The 366-seat, unicameral Supreme Council was elected in February 1990, and it subsequently named Mircea Snegur as president. Throughout 1991, political debate centered on the new constitution; a presidential republic was favored by Snegur and his supporters, while a parliamentary republic was advanced by Prime Minister Mircea Druc and the opposition MPF. In May 1991, parliamentary supporters of Snegur ousted Druc as prime minister, and replaced him with Valeriu Muravschi, effectively ending the debate. The parliament voted to turn the government previously answerable to the Supreme Council into a cabinet of ministers subordinate to the president. On 8 December 1991, Snegur ran unopposed for president and won with 98 percent of the vote. On 28 January 1992, the parliament granted Snegur the power to appoint and dismiss cabinet ministers without legislative approval. Rising discontent over declining living standards forced the government of Prime Minister Muravschi on 8 June to resign, though the ministers of defense, internal affairs, and national security remained. The parliament approved Snegur's new prime minister, Andrey Sangheli, on 1 July, and Sangheli began to compose a government of "national consensus" between July and November, incorporating more ethnic and political diversity from parties and blocs such as the Agrarian Democratic Party and the Social Democratic Party, as well as the sizable Russian, Ukrainian, and Bulgarian communities on the right bank of the Dniester river. On 16 July, Snegur dismissed Defense Minister Ion Kostash and Security Minister Anatoliy Plugaru in an unsuccessful attempt to convince separatist Russian parliamentary deputies from the left bank to end their parliamentary boycott and join Sangheli's national consensus government. Five days later, the parliament confirmed Pavel Creanga as the new defense minister and Vasiliy Calmoi as minister of security. Despite popular consensus against either unification with Romania or full membership within the CIS, suspicion over the government's ultimate intentions has remained. On 18 November, parliament refused to grant emergency powers to Snegur and Sangheli. On 24 December Snegur proposed holding a national referendum in 1993 that would ask voters to decide whether Moldova would be independent, unite with Romania, or join the CIS. On 29 January 1993, parliamentary chairman Alexandru Mosanu resigned after a parliamentary majority threatened to walk out if Mosanu did not support the holding of the referendum. Mosanu, along with the opposition MPF, favored unification with Romania – a position that had scant support in Moldova. He was replaced by Petru Lucinschi on 4 February. In March, parliament completed debate on the first draft of a new constitution declaring Moldova to be an independent state. On 19 March, Snegur described Moldova's status in the CIS as an associate member and a nonsignatory to the charter. In July, Snegur asked parliament to ratify Moldovan economic membership in the CIS. After bitter debate, on 4 August the parliament failed by four votes to obtain the simple majority required to ratify the CIS pact. A small minority of deputies favoring unification with Romania took advantage of the continued boycott of pro-Russian deputies from the trans-Dniester region to stymie the vote. In response, on 10 August the majority of deputies attempted to dissolve the parliament and force new elections; failing again, the majority of deputies walked out and vowed not to return. The walkout left the parliament technically alive, but far short of the quorum needed to pass legislation.

Russia

PRESIDENT: Boris Yeltsin
VICE-PRESIDENT: Aleksandr Rutskoy*
PRIME MINISTER: Viktor Chernomyrdin
SPEAKER OF PARLIAMENT: Ruslan Khasbulatov*
FOREIGN MINISTER: Andrey Kozyrev
DEFENSE MINISTER: Pavel Grachev
INTERNAL AFFAIRS MINISTER: Viktor Yerin
SECURITY MINISTER: Nikolay Golushko
CHAIRMAN, FOREIGN AFFAIRS COMMITTEE: Yevgeniy Ambartsumov*
CHAIRMAN, DEFENSE AFFAIRS COMMITTEE: Sergey Stepashin*

In March 1990, Russia held elections to the 1,068-seat Congress of People's Deputies (CPD); from its ranks the CPD then elected 252 members to a Supreme Soviet that serves as a full-time legislature between CPD sessions. In May, the Supreme Soviet named Boris Yeltsin its chairman. In March 1991, after a nationwide referendum established the post of president, Yeltsin became acting president and was succeeded as parliamentary chairman by Ruslan Khasbulatov. On 12 June, Yeltsin won a popular election for the presidency with 57 percent of the vote. Following the failed August putsch, Yeltsin emerged as the central political figure in Russia, and was granted emergency powers to govern by the Supreme Soviet in November 1991. Yeltsin at this time assumed the post of prime minister. On 16 March 1992, Yeltsin created a Russian ministry of defense and named himself as acting defense minister. In April the Sixth Congress of People's Deputies sought to reduce Yeltsin's power base. By the end of the tumultuous session, the congress had rescinded the emergency powers granted Yeltsin in 1991 and then reversed itself; it also initially demanded the resignation of the cabinet of ministers and then likewise changed its position. In a compromise, the congress extended Yeltsin's emergency powers until December 1992 on the condition that he step down as prime minister. Yeltsin subsequently named Deputy Prime Minister Yegor Gaidar, the architect of the government's reform policy, acting prime minister on 15 June. On 5 May, Yeltsin created the Russian Security Council and granted it broad powers over foreign and security policy. Yuriy Skokov was named as secretary of the Security Council. On 18 May, Yeltsin named Pavel Grachev as defense minister. In June, Yeltsin responded to challenges from the center-right industrial lobby Civic Union by appointing three conservatives as deputy prime ministers. Also shifting in and out of the opposition camp was Yeltsin's own vice-president, Aleksandr Rutskoy, whose People's Party of Free Russia was a founding member of the Civic Union coalition. In December, the Seventh Congress of People's Deputies refused to confirm Gaidar as prime minister, prompting Yeltsin to announce a national referendum in January 1993 to endorse either him or the congress. A compromise mediated by Constitutional Court chairman Valeriy

*These officials held these positions until President Yeltsin's 21 September decree dissolving parliament and his 3 October dismissal of Rutskoy.

Zorkin selected 11 April 1993 as the date for a broader referendum on a new Russian constitution. Yeltsin also named Deputy Prime Minister Viktor Chernomyrdin to replace Gaidar, and the CPD readily confirmed the choice. On 23 December, Yeltsin and Chernomyrdin announced the new cabinet of ministers, which contained virtually no changes. On 10 March 1993, the Eighth Congress of People's Deputies canceled the 11 April referendum and further curtailed Yeltsin's powers as president. On 20 March, Yeltsin declared on Russian television a period of special presidential rule. Yeltsin did not dissolve parliament, but declared invalid any legislative actions opposing his decrees. Yeltsin also announced a plebiscite for 25 April, which would ask for a vote of confidence in the president, a draft constitution, and new parliamentary elections. The next day, the Supreme Soviet in emergency session called for the CPD to initiate impeachment proceedings against Yeltsin. Most government ministers supported Yeltsin; notable exceptions were Vice-President Rutskoy and Security Council secretary Skokov. Although no written decree had yet been published, the Russian Constitutional Court on 23 March ruled Yeltsin's television statement unconstitutional. The text of the decree was finally published the next day, and noticeably contained no reference to the introduction of "special rule." The text did, however, mention the 25 April plebiscite. On 26 March, the Ninth Congress of People's Deputies failed by only 62 votes to remove Yeltsin from office. On 29 March, the CPD approved four questions for the rescheduled 25 April referendum. On 21 April, the Constitutional Court ruled that early elections (asked for in questions three and four) could only be mandated by the referendum if a majority of all eligible voters (not just those voting) supported such a move. The results of the 25 April voting were as follows, with percentages of those voting yes listed first, followed by the percentage of all eligible voters listed parenthetically: support of Yeltsin, 59 percent (37.3); support for the government's socioeconomic program, 53 percent (34); early presidential elections, 49 percent (32); and early parliamentary elections, 67 percent (43). Yeltsin announced that the results gave him a renewed mandate to adopt his version of a new constitution, which he published on 29 April. The next day, the parliamentary Constitutional Commission issued its own competing version. Yeltsin also set out to punish those officials who had opposed him; on 11 May, he dismissed Skokov as Security Council secretary. Two days later, he relieved Vice-President Rutskoy of his duties, although Rutskoy officially retained his post. On 5 June, Yeltsin convened the Constitutional Assembly, composed of representatives of Russia's eighty-seven federal units, to discuss his draft constitution. The three main stumbling blocks that quickly emerged concerned the extent of presidential powers; federal relations between the center and the periphery; and the desire of the nonethnic regions for equal status with the twenty ethnically designated republics of the Russian Federation. On 12 July, the Assembly reluctantly approved a draft version that grants the president broad powers and eliminates the vice-presidency. The draft was then sent to the local parliaments within the Russian Federation for approval. The summer also saw disputes over governmental appointments. On 11 June, Yeltsin named CIS Commander in Chief Yevgeniy Shaposhnikov to replace Skokov as secretary of the Security Council; the parliament, which had favored Skokov and distrusted

Shaposhnikov's ardent support for Yeltsin, refused to confirm him. On 27 July Yeltsin dismissed Security Minister Viktor Barannikov because of the latter's suspected support for conservatives within the parliament; he named Nikolay Golushko to replace him. The Supreme Soviet, however, refused to accept Barannikov's dismissal, asserting it possessed the right to appoint and dismiss the ministers of security, foreign affairs, defense, and internal affairs. On 12 August, Yeltsin called for parliamentary elections to be held in the fall of 1993, declaring that he would take this step if the parliament refused. On 13 August, Yeltsin won the support of republican leaders to create a Federation Council of representatives from the 87 federal units within Russia. In September Yeltsin suspended Rutskoy, named First Deputy Prime Minister Oleg Lobov as secretary of the Security Council, and replaced him with Yegor Gaidar. On 21 September Yeltsin dissolved the CPD and set dates for elections to a new 450-seat Duma and for early presidential elections. After naming Rutskoy president, parliamentary forces launched armed attacks on 3 October. The next day Yeltsin ordered the parliament building stormed and arrested Rutskoy, Khasbulatov, and other opposition leaders.

Tajikistan

HEAD OF STATE AND PARLIAMENTARY CHAIRMAN: Imam Ali Rakhmanov
PRIME MINISTER: Abdumalik Abdullodzhanov
FOREIGN MINISTER: Rashid Alimov
DEFENSE MINISTER: Aleksandr Shishlyannikov
INTERNAL AFFAIRS MINISTER: Yakubdzhon Salimov
SECURITY MINISTER: Seidamir Zukhurov
CHAIRMAN, FOREIGN AFFAIRS COMMITTEE: Unknown
CHAIRMAN, DEFENSE AFFAIRS COMMITTEE: Unknown

The Tajik Supreme Council was elected in March 1990, and subsequently named Kakhar Makhmedov president. Makhmedov, however, was forced to resign on 9 September 1991 due to his open support for the Moscow coup plotters. He was replaced by parliamentary chairman Kadridden Aslonov, who himself was ousted by parliament days later following his banning of the Communist Party. The parliament then named former Communist Party leader Rakhman Nabiyev parliamentary chairman and acting president pending elections in November. Nabiyev quickly repealed the ban on the Communist Party, sparking fierce demonstrations. Opposition groups forced Nabiyev to step down as president on 6 October since he was a candidate for the post. On 24 November, Nabiyev defeated opposition coalition candidate Davlat Khudonazarov, 58 percent to 30 percent. Violent opposition to Nabiyev erupted again in February 1992, however, with demonstrations calling for the resignation of the government and the parliament. After Interior Minister Mamadayez Navzhuvanov was dismissed by Nabiyev and parliament in late March, the demonstrations increased. Protestors, led by the Democratic Party of Tajikistan, the Islamic Renaissance Party, and the nationalist movement Rastokhez (Rebirth), now called for the resignation of parliamentary speaker Safarali Kendjaev, as well as the entire Supreme Council. In April the government agreed to hold a special parliamentary session to consider the opposition's demands. On 21 April, following a parliamentary decision to renege on its promise to take up the matter of seeking Kendjaev's resignation, opposition forces stormed the parliamentary building and took several officials hostage. The next day, Kendjaev resigned and the opposition freed its hostages. The crisis began anew, however, after Nabiyev restored Kendjaev to his post on 3 May, and a fierce battle for control erupted in Dushanbe. By 7 May, opposition forces had seized most of the Tajik capital, and on 11 May Nabiyev was forced to concede. The opposition was given one-third of the ministries, including defense and internal affairs. A 70-seat interim legislature – the Popular Assembly – was also created to replace the Supreme Council until parliamentary elections could be held in December 1992. Seats between government and opposition supporters were evenly split. Though Nabiyev remained as president, his supporters in the Khodjant (formerly Leninabad) and Kulyab regions of the country refused to accept the coalition government, and launched armed insurrections against it. On 25 July, Nabiyev named Khudoyberdy Khaliknazarov as the new foreign minister. On 11 August, the coalition Tajik parliament finally convened its session after months of trying, and officially accepted Kendjaev's resignation of 22 April. In his place it named Akbarsho Iskandarov as the new parliamentary speaker. The parliament also stripped Nabiyev of the emergency powers granted to him at the last, precoalition parliamentary session. On 30 August Prime Minister Akbar Mirzoyev, who was a close associate of Nabiyev's, resigned. On 2 September, amid heavy fighting from pro-Nabiyev forces throughout the country, the presidium of the Tajik parliament removed Nabiyev from office and announced plans to convene a full parliamentary session to formalize the decision. On 7 September, Nabiyev was captured and forced to resign as president. Parliamentary chairman Akbarsho Iskandarov was named acting president. Iskandarov then named Abdumalik Abdullodzhanov as acting prime minister. On 24 October, forces loyal to Kendjaev launched a coup attempt in Dushanbe; after two days of fierce fighting, the coup was defeated. On 10 November, the cabinet of ministers and Supreme Council presidium resigned, and agreed to hold a special parliamentary session in Khodjant on 16 November to resolve the continuing political strife in the country. On 19 November, the parliament removed Iskandarov from his posts as parliamentary chairman and acting president. In his place it named Imam Ali Rakhmanov, a Nabiyev supporter. It also confirmed Abdullodzhanov as prime minister. On 20 November, the parliament voted to annul Nabiyev's September resignation as president; deputies then forced Nabiyev to resubmit it, which they then accepted. On 27 November, the parliament abolished the post of president, and made Tajikistan a parliamentary republic, with the chairman to serve as head of state. On 21 January 1993, Rakhmanov named Aleksandr Shishlyannikov as defense minister, replacing Farouk Rakhmanov. On 16 June, Tajikistan held parliamentary by-elections to the Supreme Council to replace deputies who were killed or who fled during the civil war. Opposition groups were not allowed to participate; indeed, on 21 June Tajikistan officially banned the country's four main opposition parties – the Islamic Renaissance Party, the Democratic

Party, Rastokhez, and Lali Badakhshan. On 23 June, the Supreme Council convened in Dushanbe for the first time since March 1992, and subsequently voted to annul all decrees issued under former acting president Iskandarov. In September Rakhmanov called for a new constitution and for parliamentary elections to be held in 1994.

Turkmenistan

PRESIDENT and PRIME MINISTER: Saparmurad Niyazov
VICE-PRESIDENT: Boris Shikhmuradov
SPEAKER OF PARLIAMENT: Sakhat Muradov
FOREIGN MINISTER: Khalykberdy Atayev
DEFENSE MINISTER: Danatar Kopekov
INTERNAL AFFAIRS MINISTER: Kurban Mohamed Qasimov
SECURITY MINISTER: Saparmurad Seidov
CHAIRMAN, FOREIGN AFFAIRS COMMITTEE: No such committee
CHAIRMAN, DEFENSE AFFAIRS COMMITTEE: No such committee

In October 1990, Supreme Council chairman Saparmurad Niyazov won an uncontested election for the presidency, thus becoming the first leader of a Soviet republic to be popularly elected. On 27 January 1992, Turkmenistan created a ministry of defense and named Danatar Kopekov to head it. In May, the Turkmen Supreme Council adopted the first constitution of the post-Soviet republics, which granted the president broad powers of government. The constitution established a People's Council, headed by the president, with powers to supersede the legislature. Elections to the People's Council were held on 6 December 1992. The constitution also reinstated the traditional Council of Elders, whose members are to be chosen by Niyazov. The Council of Elders was granted the power to propose presidential candidates to the Supreme Council, which in turn has the exclusive right formally to nominate presidential candidates. Presidential elections were held in Turkmenistan on 21 June 1992. Niyazov was the sole candidate once again, and official government returns gave him 99.5 percent of the vote. On 4 August, Foreign Minister Avdy Kuliyev resigned over policy disputes with Niyazov. He was replaced by Khalykberdy Atayev. Opposition political parties such as Agzybirlik (Unity) and the Democratic Party of Turkmenistan (not to be confused with the renamed Communist Party of the same name) were refused official registration. On 2 April 1993, Niyazov dismissed Serdan Chariyarov as internal affairs minister on charges of corruption, and replaced him with Kurban Mohamed Qasimov. Chariyarov was then, however, named deputy defense minister. On 12 April, the Turkmen parliament voted to transfer its authority to issue decrees on matters under its jurisdiction to Niyazov.

Ukraine

PRESIDENT: Leonid Kravchuk
PRIME MINISTER: Efim Zvyahilskiy (acting)
SPEAKER OF PARLIAMENT: Ivan Plyushch
FOREIGN MINISTER: Anatoliy Zlenko
DEFENSE MINISTER: Vitaliy Zaretskiy
INTERNAL AFFAIRS MINISTER: Andrii Vasylyshyn
SECURITY MINISTER: Yevhen Marchuk
CHAIRMAN, FOREIGN AFFAIRS COMMITTEE: Dmytro Pavlychko
CHAIRMAN, DEFENSE AFFAIRS COMMITTEE: Valentyn Lemish

The 450-seat, unicameral parliament (Rada) was elected in March 1990, and subsequently chose Leonid Kravchuk as its chairman. On 1 December 1991, Kravchuk was popularly elected president, defeating his nearest challenger, nationalist Rukh candidate Vyacheslau Chornovil, 61 percent to 23 percent. Rising dissatisfaction with economic performance, however, plagued the government of Prime Minister Vitold Fokin throughout 1992; as early as 7 February the Rada censured Fokin. In June, demonstrators in Kiev demanded that Fokin step down, and a motion of no-confidence in the government was signed by a third of the Rada. In response, Kravchuk dismissed Deputy Prime Minister and Minister of Economics Volodymyr Lanovyi. Parliamentary pressure on Fokin's government continued, however, and on 30 September, Fokin resigned. The next day, over Kravchuk's strong objections, the Rada forced the cabinet of ministers to do likewise. On 13 October, Leonid Kuchma was confirmed as the new prime minister. In early November, Kravchuk dismissed First Deputy Prime Ministers Valentyn Symonenko and Konstantin Masik; replacing both with Igor Yukhnovskiy. On 18 November, the Rada voted to grant Kuchma emergency powers over the economy for a six-month period. On 28 January 1993, the Rukh faction headed by Chornovil voted to support Kravchuk and Kuchma, and announced plans to force a referendum on new parliamentary elections. On 16 February, Kravchuk called for a new constitution as well as for new presidential and parliamentary elections to be held in 1993. On 17 March, Kravchuk dismissed First Deputy Prime Minister Yukhnovskiy, and named Deputy Prime Minister Vasyl Yevtukhov to replace him in an acting capacity. In spring 1993 Ukrainian politics became increasingly affected by the decline in the economy. On 20 May, Kuchma tendered his resignation after the Rada refused to extend the special powers it had granted him in November 1992. The same day, Kravchuk proposed the abolition of the prime ministership, with himself taking over the position as head of government, and the creation of a vice-presidency. The Rada rejected both Kuchma's resignation and Kravchuk's proposal, though it did grant the president some additional powers over the economy. On 1 June, when the Rada reconvened, Kuchma again attempted to resign, but the parliament again rejected his request. While the political stalemate continued in Kiev, strikes that had begun in the Donbas spread across Ukraine. The strikers demanded a national vote of confidence in Kravchuk, Kuchma, and the Rada. In response, Kravchuk named Efim Zvyahilskiy as first deputy prime minister. The strikers, however, were not appeased, and on 14 June, the Rada agreed to their demand to hold a referendum. The next day, Kravchuk rejected the referendum as too expensive, and instead proposed new parliamentary and presidential elections. On 16 June, Kravchuk abruptly issued a decree placing himself as head of government and shifting Kuchma to head a special economic commission. In response, Kuchma on 18 June yet again offered his resignation. On 21 June, after fierce ministerial and parliamentary opposition, Kravchuk withdrew his 16 June decree. On 13 July, Kravchuk asked the Rada to cancel the referendum on the presidency, though not the one on the parliament. On 9 August, the Central Electoral Commission made the point moot by ruling that there was insufficient time available to prepare for the 26 September referendum. Kuchma once again resigned on 9 September after the Rada tabled his plea for special powers. On 21 September the Rada accepted Kuchma's resignation and asked Kravchuk to take the post of prime minister and form a new government. On 24 September the Rada voted to hold early elections to a new 450-seat unicameral parliament on 27 March 1994 and presidential elections on 26 June 1994. Kravchuk named Zvyahilskiy as acting prime minister, although he named himself as head of government. Kravchuk retained the ministers of foreign affairs, internal affairs, and security. On 4 October Defense Minister Konstantin Morozov resigned and was replaced by Vitaliy Zaretskiy.

Uzbekistan

PRESIDENT: Islam Karimov
PRIME MINISTER: Abdulkhashim Mutalov
SPEAKER OF PARLIAMENT: Shavakt Yuldashev
FOREIGN MINISTER: Said Mukhtar Said Qasimov
DEFENSE MINISTER: Rustam Akhmedov
INTERNAL AFFAIRS MINISTER: Zakirzhon Almatov
SECURITY MINISTER: Gulam Aliyev
CHAIRMAN, FOREIGN AFFAIRS COMMITTEE: Pulat Khabibullayev
CHAIRMAN, DEFENSE AFFAIRS COMMITTEE: Vilor Niyazmatov

Uzbekistan's unicameral, 360-seat Supreme Council was elected in February 1990; the next month, Communist Party head Islam Karimov was named president. Popular elections to the post were held on 29 December 1991; Karimov was elected with 86 percent of the vote. His only competitor, Mohamed Salih, chairman of the opposition Erk (Will) party, received 12 percent. On 8 January 1992, Karimov restructured the Uzbek government, replacing Foreign Minister Shakhlo Makhmudova with Ubaydulla Abdurazzakov. Karimov also abolished the post of vice-president following policy disputes with the then-incumbent Shukrullo Mirsaidov. Mirsaidov was moved to another post. Karimov also created the post of prime minister, and on 13 January named Abdulkhashim Mutalov to that position. In mid-January, Tashkent was beset by violent student demonstrations. Fearful that the civil war in neighboring Tajikistan might spill over into Uzbekistan, Karimov unleashed a wave of repression against political opponents, including most notably Birlik (Unity) cochairman Abdurrahim Pulatov, who suffered a vicious attack in June. On 8 December, the Uzbek Supreme Council adopted a new constitution that granted the president broad powers of government. In May 1993, the parliament amended the law on the cabinet of ministers, naming the president as the head of government instead of the prime minister. In early May, Birlik's other cochairman, Shokhrat Ismatullaev, was hospitalized following an attack similar to the one against Pulatov. In another case of intimidation, former vice-president Mirsaidov was put on trial on 27 May for alleged corruption; he was convicted on 18 June, but immediately pardoned. On 23 July, Karimov named Said Mukhtar Said Qasimov as foreign minister. Elections to a new parliament, the 150-seat Oliy Majlis, which will replace the current Supreme Soviet, are scheduled for 1994.

Soviet Census Data, Union Republic
and ASSR, 1989

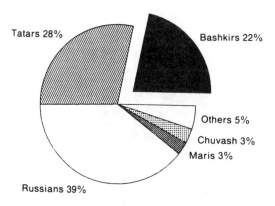

Tatars 28%

Bashkirs 22%

Others 5%

Chuvash 3%

Maris 3%

Russians 39%

1. Bashkir ASSR 1989 population 3,043,133

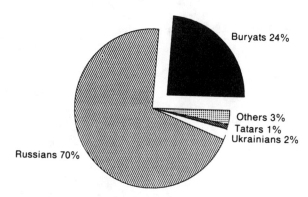

Buryats 24%

Others 3%

Tatars 1%

Ukrainians 2%

Russians 70%

2. Buryat ASSR 1989 population 1,038,252

Source: Daria Fane, "Soviet census data, union republic and ASSR, 1989," in Ian Bremmer and Ray Taras, eds., *Nations & Politics in the Soviet Successor States*, New York: Cambridge University Press, 1993, 550–60.

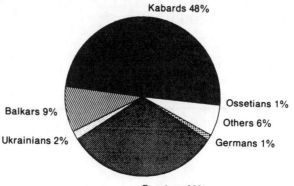

Kabards 48%

Ossetians 1%

Others 6%

Balkars 9%

Ukrainians 2%

Germans 1%

Russians 32%

3. Kabardino-Balkaria ASSR 1989 population 753,531

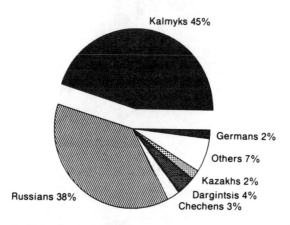

Kalmyks 45%

Germans 2%

Others 7%

Kazakhs 2%

Russians 38%

Dargintsis 4%

Chechens 3%

4. Kalmyk ASSR 1989 population 322,579

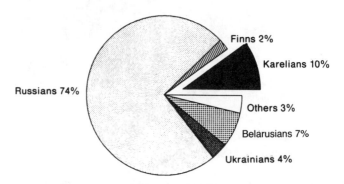

Finns 2%

Karelians 10%

Russians 74%

Others 3%

Belarusians 7%

Ukrainians 4%

5. Karelia ASSR 1989 population 790,150

332

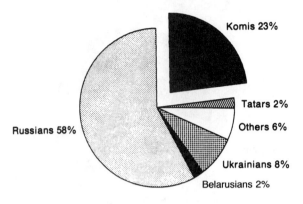

6. Komi ASSR 1989 population 1,250,847

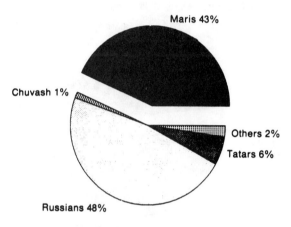

7. Mari ASSR 1989 population 749,332

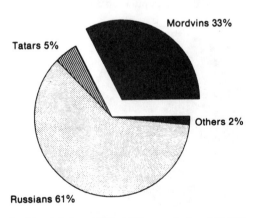

8. Mordvinian ASSR 1989 population 963,504

333

9. North Ossetia ASSR 1989 population 632,428

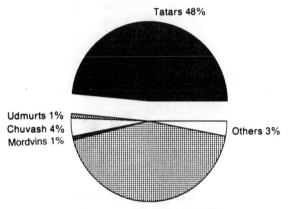

10. Tatar ASSR 1989 population 3,641,742

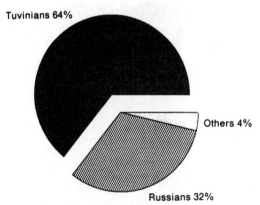

11. Tuva ASSR 1989 population 308,557

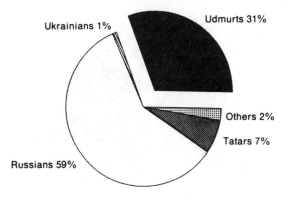

12. Udmurt ASSR 1989 population 1,605,663

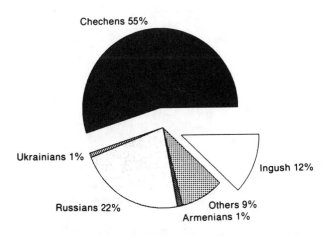

13. Chechen Ingush ASSR 1989 population 1,338,023

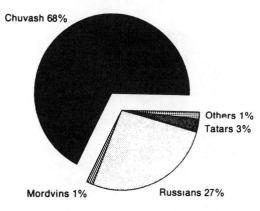

14. Chuvash ASSR 1989 population 1,338,023

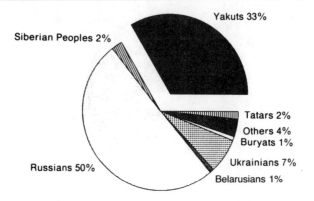

15. Yakut ASSR 1989 population 1,094,065

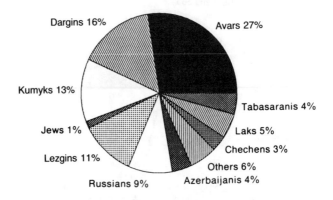

16. Daghestan ASSR 1989 population 1,802,188

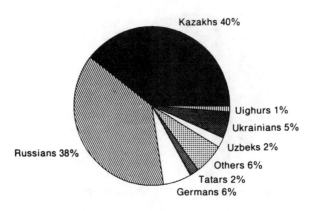

17. Kazakhstan 1989 population 16,463,115

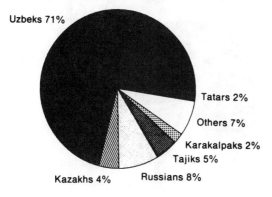

Uzbeks 71%

Tatars 2%

Others 7%

Karakalpaks 2%

Tajiks 5%

Kazakhs 4%   Russians 8%

18. Uzbekistan 1989 population 19,808,077

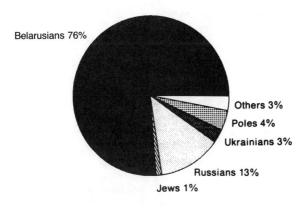

Belarusians 76%

Others 3%

Poles 4%

Ukrainians 3%

Russians 13%

Jews 1%

19. Belarus 1989 population 10,149,248

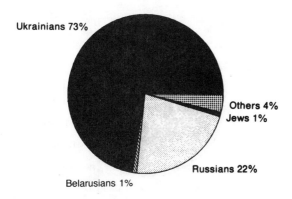

Ukrainians 73%

Others 4%

Jews 1%

Russians 22%

Belarusians 1%

20. Ukraine 1989 population 51,449,479

337

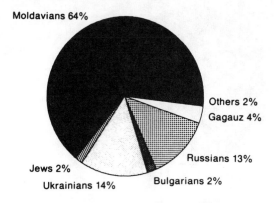

Moldavians 64%

Others 2%
Gagauz 4%

Russians 13%

Jews 2%

Ukrainians 14%   Bulgarians 2%

21. Moldavia 1989 population 4,322,363

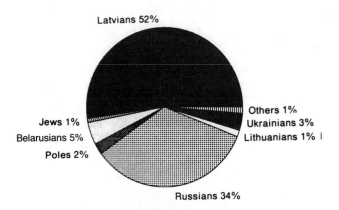

Latvians 52%

Jews 1%
Belarusians 5%
Poles 2%

Others 1%
Ukrainians 3%
Lithuanians 1% |

Russians 34%

22. Latvia 1989 population 2,666,567

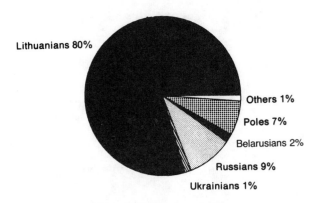

Lithuanians 80%

Others 1%

Poles 7%

Belarusians 2%

Russians 9%

Ukrainians 1%

23. Lithuania 1989 population 3,673,362

338

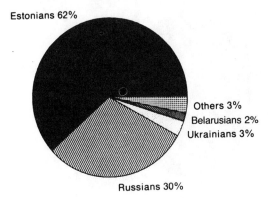

24. Estonia 1989 population 1,565,662

25. Turkmenistan 1989 population 3,512,190

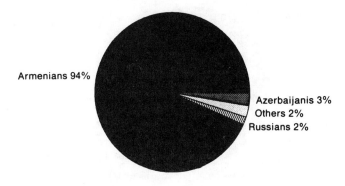

26. Armenia 1989 population 3,304,353

339

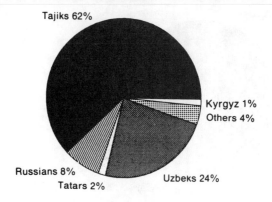

27. Tajikistan 1989 population 5,089,593

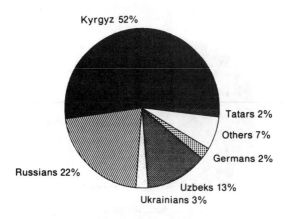

28. Kyrgyzstan 1989 population 4,257,755

29. Georgia 1989 population 5,395,841

340

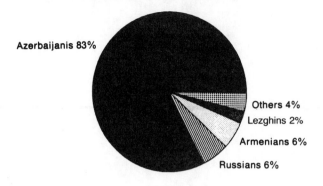

Azerbaijanis 83%

Others 4%
Lezghins 2%
Armenians 6%
Russians 6%

30. Azerbaijan 1989 population 7,019,739

Notes

Introduction

1. Charles Tilly, ed., *The Formation of National States in Western Europe*, Princeton, N.J.: Princeton University Press, 1975.
2. For a classic exposition of the various perspectives from which international relations may be studied, see Kenneth Waltz, *Man, the State, and War: A Theoretical Analysis*, New York: Columbia University Press, 1959. See also Joseph Nye, Jr., "Neorealism and Neoliberalism," *World Politics*, 40, no. 2 (January 1988), 235–51.
3. As shown later in this chapter, the official position of the Baltic states is that their forcible incorporation into the USSR in 1940 was illegal and that they therefore never ceased to exist as states. However, given that for almost fifty years the Baltic countries were effectively deprived of operational sovereignty, we believe it is sensible to describe them as new states in a political sense.
4. For a comprehensive interpretation that traces the growth of civic consciousness within the educated elite but understates the importance of the peasantry as an ingredient in the emergence of a civil society, see Marc Raeff, *Understanding Imperial Russia*, New York: Columbia University Press, 1984. For a discussion of the notion of civil society, see Chapter 4.
5. Edith Clowes, Samuel Kassow, and James West, eds., *Between Tsar and People: Educated Society and the Quest for Public Identity in Late Imperial Russia*, Princeton, N.J.: Princeton University Press, 1991.
6. For an interpretation that emphasizes Russian expansionism, see Richard Pipes, *Russia under the Old Regime*, New York: Scribner, 1974, 80–4.
7. Nicholas Riasanovsky, *Nicholas I and Official Nationality in Russia, 1825–1855*, Berkeley and Los Angeles: University of California Press, 1959.
8. S. Frederick Starr, "Tsarist Government: The Imperial Dimension," in Jeremy Azrael, ed., *Soviet Nationality Policies and Practices*, New York: Praeger, 1978, 3–38.
9. For example, calculations by the eminent historian V. O. Klyuchevskiy show that of 930 noble families in the late sixteenth century, only 33 percent were of Great Russian origin; 24 percent were of Ukrainian, Belarusian,

Polish, or Lithuanian origin; 25 percent were Germans and other West Europeans; and 17 percent consisted of Tatars and other persons drawn from the Volga region. (V. O. Klyuchevskiy, *Kurs russkoy istorii*, vol. 2, Moscow: Mysl, 1988, 193.) This pattern of elite recruitment persisted into the nineteenth century. See John Armstrong, "Mobilized Diaspora in Tsarist Russia: The Case of the Baltic Germans," in *Soviet Nationality Policies and Practices*, 74–7.

10. This point is made by Starr, "Tsarist Government: The Imperial Dimension," 3–4. For instance, Michael Doyle's large comparative study of nineteenth-century imperialism (*Empires*, Ithaca, N.Y.: Cornell University Press, 1986), does not incorporate the case of imperial Russia into its analysis.

11. For the background, see Hans Rogger, *National Consciousness in Eighteenth-Century Russia*, Cambridge, Mass.: Harvard University Press, 1959. For a discussion of the concept of nationalism and its analytical uses, see Chapter 2.

12. Sergei Maksudov and William Taubman, "Russian–Soviet Nationality Policy and Foreign Policy: A Historical Overview of the Linkage Between Them," in Michael Mandelbaum, ed., *The Rise of Nations in the Soviet Union*, New York: Council on Foreign Relations, 1991, 22.

13. Hugh Seton-Watson, *The Russian Empire, 1801–1917*, London: Oxford University Press, 1967, 705–15, 723–5; Bernard Pares, *The Fall of the Russian Monarchy*, New York: Knopf, 1939.

14. Richard Pipes, *The Russian Revolution*, New York: Vintage, 1990, 431–8.

15. Bohdan Nahaylo and Victor Swoboda, *Soviet Disunion*, New York: Free Press, 1990, 44–7.

16. William O. McCagg, Jr., "The Soviet Union and the Habsburg Empire: Problems of Comparison," in Richard Rudolph and David Good, eds., *Nationalism and Empire: The Habsburg Monarchy and the Soviet Union*, New York: St. Martin's, 1992, 57.

17. Nahaylo and Swoboda, *Soviet Disunion*, 44–65.

18. Bolshevik cultural policy was probably least accommodating in the realm of religion, but even there significant concessions were made by comparison with the policies followed during the Civil War. For details, see Chapter 3.

19. John-Paul Himka, "Nationality Problems in the Habsburg Monarchy and the Soviet Union: The Perspective of History," in *Nationalism and Empire*, 86–7.

20. On foreign policy, see Hélène Carrère d'Encausse and Stuart Schram, *Marxism and Asia*, London: Penguin, 1969; and E. H. Carr, *The Bolshevik Revolution*, vol. 3, New York: Macmillan, 1953.

21. Himka, "Nationality Problems in the Habsburg Monarchy and the Soviet Union," 86–7; Orest Subtelny, *Ukraine: A History*, Toronto: University of Toronto Press, 1988, 428–36.

22. Tadeusz Swietochowski, "Azerbaijan: A Borderland at the Crossroads of History," Russian Littoral Project Working Paper No. 8, draft, University

of Maryland, College Park, and the Johns Hopkins School of Advanced International Studies (hereafter UMCP/SAIS), May 1993, 9.

23. This was true of one of the major Bolshevik theoretical works on the national question, written by Stalin in 1913.

24. Given Stalin's future hostility to the non–Russian nationalities, it should be noted that he differed sharply with Lenin over the wisdom of this policy. Nahaylo and Swoboda, *Soviet Disunion*, 46, 48–51.

25. Victor Zaslavsky, "Success and Collapse: Traditional Soviet Nationality Policy," in Ian Bremmer and Ray Taras, eds., *Nations and Politics in the Soviet Successor States*, Cambridge University Press, 1993, 33–4.

26. For example, "as a result of the ethnic–territorial basis of the Soviet federal structure, local cultural minorities such as the Armenians in Azerbaijan found themselves treated as factually non-indigenous, and excluded from republic–based cultural development." (Nora Dudwick, "Armenia: The Nation Awakens," in *Nations and Politics in the Soviet Successor States*, 274.)

27. Zaslavsky, "Success and Collapse," 36; Nahaylo and Swoboda, *Soviet Disunion*, 78–9.

28. Zaslavsky, "Success and Collapse," 34, 36.

29. Ibid.; Kendall Bailes, *Technology and Society under Lenin and Stalin*, Princeton, N.J.: Princeton University Press, 1978, 205–10; Nahaylo and Swoboda, *Soviet Disunion*, 66, 72–5; Robert Conquest, *The Great Terror*, New York: Macmillan, 1968, 251–9.

30. Robert Conquest, *Harvest of Sorrow*, New York: Oxford University Press, 1986, 87–282; Martha Brill Olcott, *The Kazakhs*, Stanford, Calif.: Hoover Institution Press, 1987, 184–7.

31. In a 1930 discussion of Soviet language policy, for example, Stalin called attention to the irredentist challenge posed by the presence of a sizable Ukrainian and Belarusian population in Poland: "There is a Ukraine in the USSR. But there is another Ukraine in other states [sic]. There is a White Russia [i.e., Belarus] in the USSR. But there is a White Russia in other states [sic]. Do you imagine that the question of the Ukrainian and White–Russian languages can be settled without taking these peculiar conditions into account?" (J. Stalin, "Extract from a Report Delivered at the Sixteenth Congress of the CPSU, June 27, 1930," as quoted in Gregory Gleason, "Evolution of the Soviet Federal System," in Rachel Denber, ed., *The Soviet Nationality Reader*, Boulder, Colo.: Westview, 1992, 115.)

32. June Teufel Dreyer, "Ethnic Minorities in the Sino–Soviet Dispute," in Brian Silver and William O. McCagg, eds., *Soviet Asian Ethnic Frontiers*, New York: Pergamon, 1979, 201–3. See also Chapter 1.

33. Adam Ulam, "Nationalism, Panslavism, Communism," in Ivo Lederer, ed., *Russian Foreign Policy*, New Haven, Conn: Yale University Press, 1962, 41.

34. Thus, for example, Soviet citizens of Chinese and Korean origin were deported to special penal colonies on the suspicion – highly implausible, in view of East Asian history during the previous four decades – that they

were agents of an expansionist Japan. Nahaylo and Swoboda, *Soviet Disunion*, 79.

35. See Abraham Brumberg, "Not So Free at Last," *New York Review of Books*, 22 October 1992; and Chapter 1. It should also be noted that a substantial number of captured Russian soldiers joined the Nazi–sponsored anti–Soviet Russian Liberation Army led by General Andrey Vlasov. See Catherine Andreyev, *Vlasov and the Russian Liberation Movement*, Cambridge University Press, 1987; and Herbert Ellison, *History of Russia*, New York: Holt, Rinehart, and Winston, 1964, 448–9.

36. Nahaylo and Swoboda, *Soviet Disunion*, 81–94, 96–100.

37. On Moscow's policies in Eastern Europe see Zbigniew Brzezinski, *The Soviet Bloc: Unity and Conflict*, New York: Praeger, 1961; and Karen Dawisha, *Eastern Europe, Gorbachev, and Reform: The Great Challenge*, Cambridge University Press, 1990, 81–127.

38. Nahaylo and Swoboda, *Soviet Disunion*, 101.

39. Robert Conquest, *Power and Policy in the USSR: The Study of Soviet Dynastics*, London: Macmillan, 1962, 140, 164; Yehoshua Gilboa, *The Black Years of Soviet Jewry, 1939–1953*, Boston: Little, Brown, 1971, 311–35.

40. Nahaylo and Swoboda, *Soviet Disunion*, 109–128.

41. In the late 1970s there were no non-Russian secretaries of the party Central Committee, although non-Russian Slavs (Ukrainians and Belarusians) were represented at lower levels of the Central Committee apparatus. Seweryn Bialer, *Stalin's Successors*, Cambridge University Press, 1980, 219; John H. Miller, "Cadres Policy in Nationality Areas: Recruitment of CPSU First and Second Secretaries in Non-Russian Republics of the USSR," in *The Soviet Nationalities Reader*, 183–209.

42. Peter Reddaway, "The Development of Dissent in the USSR," in William Griffith, ed., *The Soviet Empire: Expansion and Detente*, Lexington, Mass.: Lexington Books, 1976, 57–84.

43. In 1976, for instance, more than three-quarters of the members of all the republican party bureaus and presidiums of the republican councils of ministers consisted of persons belonging to the titular nationality. (Bialer, *Stalin's Successors*, 214).

44. Zaslavsky, "Success and Collapse," 37.

45. Yaroslav Bilinsky, "The Soviet Education Laws of 1958–1959 and Soviet Nationality Policy," *Soviet Studies*, 14, no. 2 (October 1962), 138–57.

46. Grey Hodnett, "The Debate over Soviet Federalism," in *The Soviet Nationalities Reader*, 121; Nahaylo and Swoboda, *Soviet Disunion*, 185.

47. One study of the second secretaries of republican party organizations found that in 1964, 93 percent of these officials had prior work experience in the Moscow apparatus, whereas 42 percent had prior experience in high executive provincial posts. By 1976, the percentage of second secretaries with prior experience in the Moscow apparatus had dropped to 14 percent, whereas the share with provincial executive experience had increased to 86 percent. (Bialer, *Stalin's Successors*, 217). Starting in the 1960s, many

republican party first secretaries occupied the same post for periods as long as twenty or twenty–five years. (Ronald Grigor Suny, "State, Civil Society and Ethnic Cultural Consolidation in the USSR: Roots of the National Question," in Alexander Dallin and Gail Lapidus, eds., *The Soviet System in Crisis*, Boulder, Colo.: Westview, 1991, 421, 429n).

48. A. S. Bruk and V. M. Kabuzan, *Migratsionnyye protsessy v Rossii i SSSR*, vol. 1, Moscow: INION, 1991, 108–12, as cited in Zaslavsky, "Success and Collapse," 39. This process was not uniform in all the non-Russian republics, however. See Chapter 2 for details.

49. Between 1966 and 1981, republics in which KGB officials belonged to the republican party politburo increased from about one-quarter of the republics to virtually all of them. Bruce Parrott, "Civil–Military Relations and Political Change," in Timothy Colton and Thane Gustafson, eds., *Soldiers and the Soviet State*, Princeton, N.J.: Princeton University Press, 1990, 77.

50. See Alec Nove and J. A. Newth, *The Soviet Middle East: A Model for Development?*, London: Allen & Unwin, 1967.

51. Nahaylo and Swoboda, *Soviet Disunion*, 126–7; Grey Hodnett and Peter J. Potichnyj, *The Ukraine and the Czechoslovak Crisis*, Canberra, Australia: Australian National University, 1970.

52. Karen Dawisha, *The Kremlin and the Prague Spring*, Berkeley and Los Angeles: University of California Press, 1984.

53. William Griffith, *The Ostpolitik of the Federal Republic of Germany*, Cambridge, Mass.: MIT Press, 1978. For the most comprehensive history of the whole process, see Raymond Garthoff, *Detente and Confrontation: American–Soviet Relations from Nixon to Reagan*, Washington, D.C.: The Brookings Institution, 1985.

54. Dreyer, "Ethnic Minorities in the Sino–Soviet Dispute," 211–15.

55. In the negotiations leading up to the CSCE agreement, the Soviet side sought Western concessions concerning the two "baskets" that dealt with East–West security arrangements and trade and technology transfers. The Soviet delegation tried to turn aside Western pressure over "basket three," which dealt with human rights, but in the end the Soviets were forced to undertake new human–rights obligations in order to achieve their foreign policy objectives.

56. Peter Duncan, "The Rebirth of Politics in Russia," in Geoffrey Hosking, Jonathan Aves, and Peter Duncan, eds., *The Road to Post–Communism: Independent Political Movements in the Soviet Union, 1985–1991*, New York: Pinter, 1992.

57. Jerry Hough, "The Soviet System: Petrification or Pluralism?" *Problems of Communism*, 21, no. 2 (March–April 1972), 24–45; John Bushnell, "The 'New Soviet Man' Turns Pessimist," in Stephen Cohen, Alexander Rabinowitch, and Robert Sharlet, eds., *The Soviet Union Since Stalin*, Bloomington: Indiana University Press, 1980, 179–99.

58. Konstantin Simis, *USSR: The Corrupt Society: The Secret World of Soviet Capitalism*, New York: Simon & Schuster, 1982.

59. Between 1960 and 1986, the number of specialists with higher education

increased fourfold, reaching a total of some 15 million persons. During the same period, the total labor force increased by approximately two and a half times. (Moshe Lewin, *The Gorbachev Phenomenon: A Historical Interpretation*, Berkeley and Los Angeles: University of California Press, 1988, 48–9.)

60. We use the term "semidemocratic" because the nonparty legislative candidates still ran up against many bureaucratic obstacles in local electoral districts, and because only two–thirds of the members of the Congress of People's Deputies were selected through competitive popular elections. Elected every five years, the congress was to convene periodically to approve or disapprove the decisions and rulings made by the Supreme Soviet. The members of the Supreme Soviet, the standing legislature, were selected by the congress from its membership through a process that generally did not involve competitive candidacies and was manipulated by Gorbachev and his lieutenants.

61. Alexander Motyl, "Totalitarian Collapse, Imperial Disintegration, and the Rise of the Soviet West: Implications for the West," in *The Rise of Nations in the Soviet Union*, 45.

62. Juan Linz and Alfred Stepan, "Political Identities and Electoral Sequences," *Daedalus*, 121, no. 2 (Spring 1992), 123–39.

63. Bruce Parrott, "Soviet National Security under Gorbachev," *Problems of Communism*, 37, no. 6 (November–December 1988), 1–36.

64. The referendum was boycotted in the Baltic republics, Armenia, Georgia, and Moldova. Given the volatility of public opinion in this period, the meaning of the vote was open to debate. For example, in a separate question on the ballot, Ukrainians voted heavily to remain in the USSR, but on the terms laid out in the Ukrainian parliament's declaration of state sovereignty.

65. Mark Beissinger, "The Deconstruction of the USSR and the Search for a Post–Soviet Community," *Problems of Communism*, 40, no. 6 (November–December 1991), 29.

66. In particular, the vigorous public debates since 1987 had led to a tremendous divergence of views between the older officials at the top of these hierarchies and the junior officials at the bottom. This divergence held not only for the armed services but also for the party apparatus and the KGB as well. See especially *Argumenty i fakty*, no. 20 (1990) for a study of voting trends by Russian republican legislators. Also see Stephen Meyer, "How the Threat (and the Coup) Collapsed: The Politicization of the Soviet Military," *International Security*, 16, no. 3 (Winter 1991/1992), 5–34; and Olga Kryshtanovskaya, "A Closer Look at the KGB," *Moscow News*, no. 44 (1991), 4, for a description of an internal survey of opinion among KGB officers conducted several months before the attempted coup.

67. Although Yeltsin called during the coup for a general strike, most Russians did not heed his call. A study commissioned by Yeltsin after the coup concluded that 60 percent to 70 percent of the regional government councils in Russia had either supported the coup or remained neutral. See *Report on the USSR*, 3, no. 44 (1 November 1991), 31–2.

68. Those that never joined were the Baltic states and Georgia. Azerbaijan signed but subsequently refused to ratify the pact. Moldova also signed but as of mid–1993, had not ratified the agreement.

1. The Legacies of History

1. John Lewis Gaddis, *Tectonics, History, and the End of the Cold War*, Occasional Paper, Ohio State University: The Mershon Center, 1992, 3.
2. See Harvey Kaye, *The Powers of the Past: Reflections on the Crisis and the Promise of History*, Minneapolis: University of Minnesota Press, 1991.
3. Robert Jervis, *Perception and Misperception in International Politics*, Princeton, N.J.: Princeton University Press, 1976, chapter 6; George W. Breslauer and Philip E. Tetlock, eds., *Learning in U.S. and Soviet Foreign Policy*, Boulder, Colo: Westview, 1991; Richard E. Neustadt and Ernest R. May, *Thinking in Time: The Uses of History for Decision–Makers*, New York: Free Press, 1986.
4. The term "grand governing narrative" was coined by Kaye, *The Powers of the Past.*
5. J. H. Plumb, *The Death of the Past*, Boston: Houghton Mifflin, 1970.
6. Eric Hobsbawm, "Mass-Producing Traditions: Europe, 1870–1914," in Eric Hobsbawm, ed., *The Invention of Tradition*, Cambridge University Press, 1983, 271–3.
7. Jacques Le Goff, *History and Memory*, New York: Columbia University Press, 1992, 101–15. This point is illustrated by Frances FitzGerald's penetrating analysis of the various historical interpretations embedded in the shifting curricula of American secondary schools since the 1800s. In the mid–1800s, the most commonly used history texts "described the [American] frontier as a fairly crowded and war-torn place – a country disputed by the French, the Spanish, the English, various Indian nations, and later the Canadians and the Americans. Then, in the late nineteenth century, the text writers, telescoping the Colonial period into one or two chapters and making it a mere introduction to the history of the United States, stopped writing the history of these conflicts, and so left the impression that 'the Americans' went forth into a land without people or previous history." The result was a picture of "the English colonies as standing quite alone at the edge of a vast – indeed, continental – wilderness." Since the 1960s, the peoples and events omitted from this brand of historical narrative have been rediscovered and partially reincorporated into the high school American history curriculum. Frances FitzGerald, *America Revised: History Schoolbooks in the Twentieth Century*, New York: Vintage, 1980, 76–7, 90–1, 132–3.
8. Barrington Moore, *Political Power and Social Theory*, New York: Harper, 1958.
9. Edward Said, *Culture and Imperialism*, New York: Knopf, 1993, xiii. Emphasis in the original.
10. See R. W. Davies, *Soviet History in the Gorbachev Revolution*, Bloomington: Indiana University Press, 1989, 187–92; Mark von Hagen, "The Stalin

Debate and the Reformulation of the Soviet Past," *The Harriman Institute Forum*, 5, no. 7 (March 1992), 4.

11. S. Frederick Starr, "Tsarist Government: The Imperial Dimension," in Jeremy Azrael, ed., *Soviet Nationality Policies and Practices*, New York: Praeger, 1978, 3–38.

12. Richard Pipes, "Introduction," in Zev Katz, Rosemarie Rogers, and Frederick Harned, eds., *Handbook of Major Soviet Nationalities*, New York: Free Press, 1975, 1–2.

13. The term "usable past" was coined by S. Frederick Starr in a discussion of the linkage between pre-1917 Russian liberalism and political reform under Gorbachev. See Starr, "A Usable Past," *The New Republic*, 15 May 1989, 24–7.

14. Stephen Sestanovich, "Inventing the Soviet National Interest," *The National Interest* (Summer 1990), 3–16; Suzanne Crow, "Russia Debates Its National Interests," *Radio Free Europe/Radio Liberty* (hereafter cited as *RFE/RL) Research Report*, 1, no. 28 (10 July 1992), 43–6.

15. Seymour Becker, "The Muslim East in Nineteenth-Century Russian Popular Historiography," *Central Asian Survey*, 5, no. 3/4 (1986), 25–47; Seymour Becker, "Russia Between East and West: the Intelligentsia, Russian National Identity and the Asian Borderlands," ibid., 10, no. 4 (1991), 47–64; Andrzej Walicki, *The Slavophile Controversy*, New York: Oxford University Press, 1975, chapter 1.

16. Franklyn Griffiths, *Genoa Plus 51: Changing Soviet Objectives in Europe*, Toronto: Canadian Institute of International Affairs, 1973; Robert Tucker, *Stalin in Power: The Revolution From Above, 1929–1941*, New York: Norton, 1990; Lowell Tillett, *The Great Friendship: Soviet Historians on the Non-Russian Nationalities*, Chapel Hill: University of North Carolina, 1969.

17. Cyril Black, ed., *Rewriting Russian History*, New York: Praeger, 1956.

18. Becker, "The Muslim East," 30–1.

19. For a penetrating critique of the proposition that Muscovy originally claimed the right to "gather the Russian lands" because it was the descendant of ancient Kievan Rus, see Edward Keenan, "On Certain Mythical Beliefs and Russian Behaviors," Russian Littoral Project Working Paper No. 1, draft, University of Maryland, College Park, and the Johns Hopkins School of Advanced International Studies (hereafter UMCP/SAIS), May 1993. In the nineteenth century, Russian historians did not seriously inquire whether Muscovy was the legitimate claimant to all that territory, or whether the loose confederation of pre-Mongol principalities had to be gathered into a highly centralized empire.

20. Becker, "The Muslim East," 31.

21. V. O. Klyuchevskiy, *Sochineniya*, vol. 1, part 1, Moscow: Politicheskaya Literatura, 1956, 30–2. Compiled by his students, this volume of Klyuchevskiy's history of Russia was originally published posthumously in 1904.

22. Orest Subtelny, *Ukraine: A History*, Toronto: University of Toronto Press, 1988, 72, 75.

23. Roman Szporluk, "The Ukraine and Russia," in Robert Conquest, ed., *The Last Empire: Nationality and the Soviet Future*, Stanford, Calif.: Hoover Institution Press, 1986, 153–5; Hugh Seton–Watson, *The Decline of Imperial Russia, 1855–1914*, New York: Praeger, 1965, 81–2. For a discussion of the thirteenth-century origins of a distinctive Belarusian culture and language, see Ivan S. Lubachko, *Belorussia under Soviet Rule, 1917–1957*, Lexington: University Press of Kentucky, 1972, 1–12.

24. N. M. Karamzin, *Istoriya gosudarstva Rossiyskovo*, 5th ed., St. Petersburg, 1842–1843, vol. 9, 217–19, 226–8, as quoted in Becker, "Russia Between East and West," 49.

25. Becker, "Russia Between East and West," 50.

26. The exponents of this view included the writer Pyotr Chaadayev, the political radical Nikolay Chernyshevskiy, and the nationalist historian and publicist Mikhail Pogodin, during his early years. See Becker, "Russia Between East and West," 52, 59, and "The Muslim East," 34; Nicholas Riasanovsky, "Asia Through Russian Eyes," in Wayne Vucinich, ed., *Russia and Asia*, Stanford, Calif.: Hoover Institution Press, 1972, 14.

27. The thinkers who advanced this argument included S. M. Solovyov, the preeminent figure in Russian historiography during the second half of the nineteenth century; Mikhail Pogodin, a leading nationalist historian of the same period; and the great Russian novelist Fyodor Dostoevsky. See Becker, "Russia Between East and West," 50, 61; Edward C. Thaden, *Conservative Nationalism in Nineteenth Century Russia*, Seattle: University of Washington Press, 1964, 25–37, 73–86.

28. See Walicki, *The Slavophile Controversy*, 11–14 on the origins and limits of the terms "Slavophile" and especially "Westernizer."

29. Becker, "Russia Between East and West," 61–2.

30. Riasanovsky, "Asia Through Russian Eyes," 17.

31. Ibid., 19.

32. Dietrich Geyer, *Russian Imperialism: The Interaction of Domestic and Foreign Policy, 1860–1914*, trans. by Bruce Little, New Haven, Conn.: Yale University Press, 1987, 94–5; also Firuz Kazemzadeh, "Russia and the Middle East," in Ivo Lederer, ed., *Russian Foreign Policy*, New Haven, Conn.: Yale University Press, 1962, 492–519; Firuz Kazemzadeh, "Central Asia's Foreign Relations: A Historical Survey," Russian Littoral Project Working Paper No. 5, draft, UMCP/SAIS, May 1993, 23.

33. Geyer, *Russian Imperialism*, 65–85, 315–18.

34. *Washington Post*, 9 April 1992.

35. See Alexander Rahr, " 'Atlanticists' versus 'Eurasians' in Russian Foreign Policy," *RFE/RL Research Report*, 1, no. 22 (29 May 1992), 17–22. For an illustrative debate about Russia's European or Asiatic character, see the roundtable discussion among the leaders of several Russian political parties in *Mezhdunarodnaya zhizn*, no. 7, 1990, 3–23.

36. Walicki, *The Slavophile Controversy*, 6.

37. See Vera Tolz, "Russia: Westernizers Continue to Challenge National Patriots," *RFE/RL Research Report*, 1, no. 49 (11 December 1992), 1–9; and Chapter 6.

38. Roman Szporluk, "Dilemmas of Russian Nationalism," *Problems of Communism*, 38, no. 4 (July–August 1989), 15–35.
39. These paraphrases of Yeltsin's remarks are from *RFE/RL Daily Report*, no. 208 (28 October 1992).
40. As shown in the Introduction, this policy gave greater latitude to non-Russians in culture, education, and the staffing of local institutions – but not self–determination.
41. Konstantin F. Shteppa, "The 'Lesser Evil' Formula," in *Rewriting Russian History*, 107–22; Tillett, *The Great Friendship*, 35–40; John Dunlop, *The Faces of Contemporary Russian Nationalism*, Princeton, N.J.: Princeton University Press, 1983, 3–28.
42. S. Enders Wimbush, *Contemporary Russian Nationalist Responses to Non-Russians in the USSR*, Rand Paper P–941, Santa Monica, Calif.: Rand Corporation, 1978, 2.
43. Tillett, *The Great Friendship*, 418–22; Lowell Tillett, "Russian Imperialism and Colonialism," in Samuel Baron and Nancy Heer, eds., *Windows on the Russian Past*, Columbus, Ohio: American Association for the Advancement of Slavic Studies (hereafter AAASS), 1977, 104–21.
44. *Izvestiya*, 24 December 1989, as quoted by Stephen Velychenko, *Shaping Identity in Eastern Europe and Russia: Soviet-Russian and Polish Accounts of Ukrainian History, 1914–1991*, New York: St. Martin's, 1993, 216.
45. Elizabeth Valkenier, "Teaching History in Post-Communist Russia," *The Harriman Institute Forum*, 6, no. 8 (April 1993), 5.
46. Ibid., 5–6. According to the headquarters of Alfred A. Knopf, the U.S. publisher of the Pipes book, the Russian publisher has contracted to print at least fifty thousand copies. (Personal communication, July 1993.)
47. *Pravda*, 30 January 1992. The border areas in dispute between Russia and other CIS countries include Crimea and areas of the Caucasus and northern Kazakhstan.
48. Ibid.
49. Quoted in "Weekly Review 5–11 August 1992," *RFE/RL Research Report*, 1, no. 33 (21 August 1992), 74. See also *RFE/RL Daily Report*, no. 223 (19 November 1992).
50. Interfax, 9 April 1992, in Foreign Broadcast Information Service, *Daily Report: Soviet Union* (hereafter *FBIS–SOV*), 10 April 1992, 31.
51. *Washington Post*, 12 January 1992. For a less dire view of Russia's new political geography, see Sergey Rakovskiy, "New Neighbors, New Problems," *New Times* (Moscow), no. 34 (August 1992), 19–21.
52. Terence Emmons, *The Formation of Political Parties and the First National Elections in Russia*, Cambridge, Mass.: Harvard University Press, 1983, 42, 105–6, 206–9; Richard Pipes, *The Formation of the Soviet Union*, rev. ed., New York: Atheneum, 1968, 29–30.
53. During the Russian Civil War independent Ukrainian and Belarusian republics were declared but were overturned by hostile Bolshevik and German forces. (Pipes, *The Formation of the Soviet Union*, 114–54). The Baltic states were politically independent between World Wars I and II.
54. Subtelny, *Ukraine: A History*, 345–53.

55. Hrushevsky had developed many of his basic ideas in the pre–Soviet period. He presented the most concise statement of his views on Ukrainian and Russian history in 1904.
56. Mykhailo Hrushevsky, "The Traditional Scheme of 'Russian' History and the Problem of a Rational Organization of the History of Eastern Slavs," in *From Kievan Rus' to Modern Ukraine: Formation of the Ukrainian Nation* (reprinted essays), Cambridge, Mass.: Harvard University Ukrainian Studies Fund, 1984, 355–64; Subtelny, *Ukraine: A History*, 52–4.
57. It was during this same period that other leading intellectuals such as Mykola Khvylovyi argued that Ukrainian culture must turn away from Russia and toward the West. Subtelny, *Ukraine: A History*, 391–2.
58. Serhii Plokhy, "Historical Debates and Territorial Claims: Cossack Mythology in the Russian–Ukrainian Border Dispute," Russian Littoral Project Working Paper No. 10, draft, UMCP/SAIS, May 1993, 7.
59. James Mace, *Communism and the Dilemmas of National Liberation: National Communism in Soviet Ukraine, 1918–1933*, Cambridge, Mass.: Harvard University Press, 1983, 235.
60. Tillett, *The Great Friendship*, 41–3; Sergei A. Romanenko, "National Autonomy in Russia and Austro–Hungary: A Comparative Analysis of Finland and Croatia–Slovenia," in Richard Rudolph and David Good, eds., *Nationalism and Empire: The Habsburg Empire and the Soviet Union*, New York: St. Martin's, 1992, 110.
61. Tillett, *The Great Friendship*. For an analysis of similar distortions in the history of the Soviet Communist Party, see Nancy Whittier Heer, *Politics and History in the Soviet Union*, Cambridge, Mass.: MIT Press, 1971.
62. Yaroslav Bilinsky, "The Soviet Years and Their Impact on the Foreign Policy of Ukraine," Russian Littoral Project Working Paper No. 12, draft, UMCP/SAIS, May 1993, 1–2.
63. Abraham Brumberg, "Not So Free at Last," *New York Review of Books*, 22 October 1992, 59; Subtelny, *Ukraine: A History*, 471–3.
64. On the shift of Baltic hostility from Germany to Russia, see Romuald Misiunas, "National Identity and Foreign Policy in the Baltic States," Russian Littoral Project Working Paper No. 11, draft, UMCP/SAIS, May 1993, 2, 5. On the wartime atrocities, see Nils Muiznieks, "Latvia: Origins, Evolution, and Triumph," in Ian Bremmer and Ray Taras, eds., *Nations and Politics in the Soviet Successor States*, Cambridge University Press, 1993, 184; and John Hiden and Patrick Salmon, *The Baltic Nations and Europe: Estonia, Latvia and Lithuania in the Twentieth Century*, New York: Longman, 1991, 117–20.
65. Soviet publications' treatment of the wartime and postwar Ukrainian and Baltic movements of resistance to the reimposition of Soviet power fall in this latter category. The equation of Ukrainian and Baltic nationalism with fascism became a staple of Soviet postwar propaganda.
66. A few of these topics were, however, addressed in samizdat writings. Bohdan Nahaylo and Victor Swoboda, *Soviet Disunion*, New York: Free Press, 1990, 169; Stephen Velychenko, "Perestroika and the Interpretation

of Russian–Ukrainian Relations," paper presented at the annual AAASS convention, Washington, D.C., 1990, 6.

67. Plokhy, "Historical Debates and Territorial Claims," 18; Frank Sysyn, *The Ukrainian Orthodox Question in the USSR*, Cambridge, Mass.: Harvard Ukrainian Studies Fund, 1987, 17.

68. For example, in the samizdat work, *Internationalism or Russification?*, Ivan Dzyuba presented a critical historical account of the Soviet government's treatment of Ukraine. See M. Davies, ed., *Internationalism or Russification? A Study in the Soviet Nationalities Problem*, by Ivan Dzyuba (translated from the Ukrainian), London: Weidenfeld and Nicolson, 1968.

69. Michael Urban and Jan Zaprudnik, "Belarus: A Long Road to Nationhood," in *Nations and Politics in the Soviet Successor States*, 110–11.

70. Zenon Kohut, "History as a Battleground: Russian–Ukrainian Relations and Historical Consciousness in Contemporary Ukraine," Russian Littoral Project Working Paper No. 9, draft, UMCP/SAIS, May 1993, 12–13. One Western work that has been used widely in education is Orest Subtelny's comprehensive history of Ukraine.

71. The Rukh movement was especially active in the effort to use Cossack traditions to link the russophone inhabitants of eastern Ukraine to the Ukrainian national movement. Kohut, "History as a Battleground," 13–14.

72. David Marples, "New Interpretations of Ukrainian History," *RFE/RL Research Report*, 2, no. 11 (12 March 1993), 59.

73. Kohut, "History as a Battleground," 15; Marples, "New Interpretations of Ukrainian History," 57.

74. Muiznieks, "Latvia: Origins, Evolution, and Triumph," 191, 198.

75. Bohdan Krawchenko, "Ukraine: The Politics of Independence," in *Nations and Politics in the Soviet Successor States*, 77.

76. *Belarus*, no. 375 (November 1990), New York: Belarusian–American Association, as quoted in Michael Urban and Jan Zaprudnik, "Belarus: A Long Road to Nationhood," 116; Krawchenko, "Ukraine: The Politics of Independence," 95.

77. Such writers note, for example, that at the height of the 1933 famine in Ukraine Soviet troops closed off the Ukrainian border with Russia in order to prevent starving peasants from seeking food in the Russian agricultural regions to the northeast, which purportedly suffered rather lightly in comparison with the Ukrainian districts. (Nahaylo and Swoboda, *Soviet Disunion*, 69–70.)

78. For Kravchuk's tactics on the historical aspect of the Crimean issue, see Plokhy, "Historical Debates and Territorial Claims," 5–6.

79. Muiznieks, "Latvia: Origins, Evolution and Triumph," 184.

80. In the fall of 1991, for example, Ivan Drach, a leading spokesman for the Ukrainian independence movement, gave an interview to a Polish newspaper in which he warned that "only Polish–Ukrainian reconciliation and understanding" could deter "the [Russian] imperial monster, which will again surface, regardless of whether it is a communist or democratic one." *Tygodnik powszechny* (Warsaw), 13 October 1991.

81. In Ukraine as a whole, the December 1991 referendum produced a resounding majority for national independence, but in Crimea only 54 percent of the voters cast their ballots in favor of secession from the USSR. For further discussion of the Crimean issue see Chapter 2.

82. Plokhy, "Historical Debates and Territorial Claims," 26–8.

83. For more on this topic, see Chapter 6.

84. Subtelny, *Ukraine: A History*, 188–92; Norman Davies, *Heart of Europe: A Short History of Poland*, New York: Oxford University Press, 1984, 120, 125, 127, 132.

85. Abraham Brumberg, "Not So Free At Last," 57.

86. Krawchenko, "Ukraine: The Politics of Independence," 91.

87. In 1924 the Soviet government established a Moldovan autonomous region within the boundaries of the Ukrainian national republic. In 1940 the autonomous region was upgraded to the status of a separate national republic within the Soviet federal structure.

88. Daria Fane, "Moldova: Breaking Loose from Moscow," in *Nations and Politics in the Soviet Successor States*, 128–31, 138; and Nicholas Dima, *From Moldavia to Moldova: The Soviet–Romanian Territorial Dispute*, Boulder, Colo.: East European Monographs, 1991, 133–55.

89. A summit in October 1992 between Ukrainian president Kravchuk and Moldovan president Snegur specifically allowed for the future discussion of the status of the disputed territories. (*RFE/RL Daily Report*, no. 208, 28 October 1992.) For its part, Romania must exercise caution in pressing such claims because of the possible ramifications for Hungary's claims on the ethnically Hungarian Transylvanian region of Romania.

90. Ralph S. Clem, "Belorussians," in Graham Smith, ed., *The Nationalities Question in the Soviet Union*, London, England: Longman, 1990, 109.

91. During the war, one-quarter of the Belarusian population was either killed or deported. Michael Urban and Jan Zaprudnik, "Belarus: A Long Road to Nationhood," 107.

92. Ibid., 111, 115.

93. Quoted in Kathleen Mihalisko, "Belarus Moves to Assert Its Own Military Policy," *RFE/RL Research Report*, 1, no. 11 (13 March 1992), 49.

94. "Weekly Review of Events, 22–28 April 1992," *RFE/RL Research Report*, 1, no. 19 (8 May 1992), 60; "Weekly Review of Events, 17–23 June 1992," *RFE/RL Research Report*, 1, no. 27 (3 July 1992), 73.

95. Kathleen Mihalisko, "The Outlook for Independent Belarus," *RFE/RL Research Report*, 1, no. 24 (12 June 1992), 10.

96. *Nezavisimaya gazeta*, 24 March 1992.

97. See Chapters 2 and 6 for details.

98. "Military and Security Notes," *RFE/RL Research Report*, 1, no. 31 (31 July 1992), 60.

99. "Weekly Review of Events," *RFE/RL Research Report*, 1, no. 31 (31 July 1992), 74. Kebich made this statement in response to a similar statement by Russian acting prime minister Yegor Gaidar.

100. Richard Krickus, "Lithuania: Nationalism in the Modern Era," in *Nations and Politics in the Soviet Successor States*, 165.

101. Ibid., 176–7.
102. For a discussion of this issue, see Chapter 2.
103. Here and elsewhere we use the term "Caucasus" (rather than "Trans-caucasus") to designate the region immediately south of the Caucasus mountains that includes Georgia, Armenia, and Azerbaijan. We use "Northern Caucasus" (rather than "Ciscaucasus") to designate the territory immediately north of the Caucasus mountains that is part of the Russian Federation and includes numerous non-Russian ethnic groups.
104. In this book the term "Central Asia" denotes the territories encompassed by contemporary Kazakhstan, Turkmenistan, Uzbekistan, Kyrgyzstan, and Tajikistan. We use "Inner Asia," a more general and less precise term, to denote not only Central Asia but Afghanistan, Mongolia, and China's Sinkiang province.
105. Ira Lapidus, *A History of Islamic Societies*, New York, Cambridge University Press, 1988, 415.
106. Ibid., 414–19; Elizabeth E. Bacon, *Central Asians under Russian Rule*, Ithaca, N.Y.: Cornell University Press, 1966, 1–116.
107. Kazemzadeh, "Russia and the Middle East," 489–529.
108. Edward Allworth, "Encounter," in Edward Allworth, ed., *Central Asia: A Century of Russian Rule*, New York: Columbia University Press, 1967, 47.
109. Previous British attempts to subjugate Afghanistan had failed.
110. Allworth, "Encounter," 51–2.
111. Up until that time, Central Asians had been exempt from military service. The Russian loss of life in the uprising was about three thousand persons. By contrast, an estimated 100,000–120,000 Kyrgyz lives were lost. (Hugh Seton-Watson, *The Russian Empire, 1801–1917*, Oxford University Press, 1967, 722; Gene Huskey, "Kyrgyzstan: The Politics of Demographic and Economic Frustration," in *Nations and Politics in the Soviet Successor States*, 400.)
112. Martha Brill Olcott, "Kazakhstan: A Republic of Minorities," in *Nations and Politics in the Soviet Successor States*, 316.
113. Allworth, "Encounter," 15.
114. Lapidus, *A History of Islamic Societies*, 784.
115. Martha Brill Olcott, "Nation-Building and Ethnicity in the Foreign Policy of the New Central Asian States," Russian Littoral Project Working Paper No. 20, draft, UMCP/SAIS, June 1993, 4.
116. Ibid., 5.
117. The central government's ignorance of regional affairs and its non-Russian subjects is pointed out by Marc Raeff, *Understanding Imperial Russia*, New York: Columbia University Press, 1984.
118. Becker, "The Muslim East in Nineteenth-Century Russian Popular Historiography," 43.
119. The use of Chagatai, a Turkic language with deep literary roots in Central Asia, was also proscribed. See Shirin Akiner, "Uzbeks," and Annette Bohr, "Turkmen," in *The Nationalities Question*, 216–17, 231.
120. *Rossiyskaya gazeta*, 12 June 1992, in *FBIS-SOV*, 16 June 1992, 9.

121. "Conversation: Challenge From the Right: Interview with Vladimir Zhir-inovskiy," *The MacNeil/Lehrer Report*, 13 January 1992.
122. Tillett, "Russian Imperialism and Colonialism," 116–17.
123. Compare ibid. with Velychenko, "Perestroika and the Interpretation of Russian–Ukrainian Relations."
124. Olcott, "Kazakhstan," and Huskey, "Kyrgyzstan," in *Nations and Politics in the Soviet Successor States*, 321, 406.
125. One Uzbek writer approvingly quoted nineteenth-century praise for Timur (Tamerlane), the leader of a devastating invasion of European Russia in the fourteenth century. James Critchlow, *Nationalism in Uzbekistan: A Soviet Republic's Road to Sovereignty*, Boulder, Colo.: Westview, 1991, 132; Martha Brill Olcott, "Perestroika in Kazakhstan," *Problems of Communism*, 39, no. 4 (July–August 1990), 69.
126. Audrey Altstadt, "Rewriting Central Asian History in the Gorbachev Era," paper presented at the AAASS convention, Washington, D.C., 1990, 6–7.
127. Olcott, "Kazakhstan: A Republic of Minorities," 321. These figures put the human cost of collectivization in Kazakhstan on a par with the enormous costs of the policy in Ukraine. However, as in other former republics, the precise scale of the Stalinist regime's destruction of the native population remains to be established. Cf. Lapidus, *A History of Islamic Societies*, 805.
128. Azade-Ayse Rorlich, "Islam and Atheism: Dynamic Tension in Soviet Central Asia," in William Fierman, ed., *Soviet Central Asia: The Failed Transformation*, Boulder, Colo.: Westview, 1991, 203.
129. Yaacov Ro'i, "The Islamic Influence on Nationalism in Soviet Central Asia," *Problems of Communism*, 39, no. 4 (July–August 1990), 57.
130. Marie Bennigsen Broxup, "Comrade Muslims!" *Wilson Quarterly*, 16, no. 3 (Summer 1992), 39.
131. For details, see Chapter 2.
132. Russian Television, 1 June 1992, in *FBIS–SOV*, 3 June 1992, 55.
133. *Pravda*, 3 December 1991, translated in *The Current Digest of the Soviet Press*, 1 January 1992, 12.
134. Saidbayev's statement holds for some periods of tsarist history, but as a description of the whole tsarist period it is incorrect. See Lapidus, *A History of Islamic Societies*, 422–3; and Chapter 3.
135. Interfax, 2 June 1992, in *FBIS–SOV*, 5 June 1992, 82.
136. "In 1917, . . . when the democratic Provisional Government exhibited no signs of administrative intervention, the continued use of religious rather than national terminology [by the indigenous inhabitants of Central Asia] only reflected the insufficient appeal of a purely national plan for the still deeply traditionalist Muslim population of Russia. The decision of the First All-Russian Muslim Congress in May 1917 to call its executive organ a Muslim and not a Turko-Tatar Council was the most eloquent demonstration of the weakness of Turkic nationalist feelings among Russia's Turks." Serge Zenkovsky, *Pan-Turkism and Islam in Russia*, Cambridge, Mass: Harvard University Press, 1960, 271, 274–5.

137. Lapidus, *A History of Islamic Societies*, 793.
138. Muriel Atkin, "Religious, National, and Other Identities in Central Asia," in Jo-Ann Gross, ed., *Muslims in Central Asia: Expressions of Identity and Change*, Durham, N.C.: Duke University Press, 1992, 50.
139. Olcott, "Nation-Building and Ethnicity," 3; *Afghanistan and Post–Soviet Central Asia: Prospects for Political Evolution and the Role of Islam*, Special Report of the Study Group on the Prospects for Conflict and Opportunities for Peacemaking in the Southern Tier of Former Soviet Republics, Washington, D.C.: U.S. Institute of Peace, 1992, 13–14.
140. Some of these disputes were aired during the Soviet period, however. See, for instance, Ann Sheehy, "Tadjiks Question Republican Frontiers," *Radio Liberty Research Bulletin*, 11 August 1988.
141. Radio Rossii, 30 May 1992, in *FBIS–SOV*, 1 June 1992, 53.
142. For example, Uzbekistan's president, Islam Karimov, has remarked that "for us, Russia is the guarantor of stability and peace in our region and the inviolability of our borders." *Pravda*, 2 June 1992.
143. Nora Dudwick, "Armenia: The Nation Awakens," in *Nations and Politics in the Soviet Successor States*, 264–6.
144. Tamara Dragadze, "Azerbaijanis," in *The Nationalities Question in the Soviet Union*, 172.
145. In 1921 Armenia received control over the disputed region; in 1923 this decision was rescinded and Azerbaijan received control of the area.
146. For further details, see Chapter 2.

2. National Identity and Ethnicity

1. On the tendency of Western liberal intellectuals to view nationalism in a negative light, see Benedict Anderson, *Imagined Communities: Reflections on the Origin and Spread of Nationalism*, London: Verso, 1983, 128. See also E. J. Hobsbawm, *Nations and Nationalism since 1780: Programme, Myth, Reality*, Cambridge University Press, 1990, 29–32.
2. We are indebted to Professor Roman Szporluk for calling this point to our attention.
3. Hobsbawm, *Nations and Nationalism*, identifies eighteenth-century France and the United States as the earliest nations in the modern sense of the word. Liah Greenfeld, *Nationalism: Five Roads to Modernity*, Cambridge, Mass.: Harvard University Press, 1992, argues that England made the transition to modern nationhood roughly two centuries before these other countries did so.
4. Hobsbawm, *Nations and Nationalism*; Miroslav Hroch, "Language and National Identity," in Richard Rudolph and David Good, eds., *Nationalism and Empire: The Habsburg Monarchy and the Soviet Union*, New York: St. Martin's, 1992, 65–71.
5. We have borrowed this analogy from Ronald Grigor Suny, "State, Civil Society and Ethnic Cultural Consolidation in the USSR: Roots of the National Question," in Alexander Dallin and Gail Lapidus, eds., *The Soviet System in Crisis*, Boulder, Colo.: Westview, 1991, 416.

6. Hobsbawm, *Nations and Nationalism*, 8.
7. Paul Robert Magocsi, "A Subordinate or Submerged People: The Ukrainians of Galicia under Habsburg and Soviet Rule," in *Nationalism and Empire*, 97–8.
8. Anderson, *Imagined Communities*, 164–170.
9. Ibid., 14–39.
10. Greenfeld, *Nationalism: Five Roads to Modernity*, 8–12. See also Rogers Brubaker, *Citizenship and Nationhood in France and Germany*, Cambridge, Mass.: Harvard University Press, 1992.
11. For a useful discussion of these matters, see Rogers Brubaker, "Aftermaths of Empire and the Unmixing of Peoples: Historical and Comparative Perspectives," in Jeremy Azrael, ed., *Migration Within and From the Former USSR*, Santa Monica, Calif.: The Rand Corp., forthcoming.
12. See Chapters 4 and 5.
13. Quoted in Jonathan Aves, "The Evolution of Independent Political Movements after 1988," in Geoffrey A. Hosking, Jonathan Aves, and Peter J. S. Duncan, *The Road to Post-Communism: Independent Political Movements in the Soviet Union, 1985–1991*, New York: Pinter, 1992, 96.
14. Grigoriy Pomerants in *Polis*, no. 3, 1992, as quoted in Vera Tolz, "Russia: Westernizers Continue to Challenge National Patriots," *RFE/RL Research Report*, 1, no. 49 (11 December 1992), 8.
15. Marina Pavlova-Silvanskaya in Yuriy Afanaseyev et al., eds., *God posle avgusta, gorech i vybor*, Moscow: Literatura i politika, 1992, as quoted in Tolz, "Russia: Westernizers Continue to Challenge National Patriots," 3.
16. *Literaturnaya Rossiya*, no. 3, 1992, 2–3, and *Russkiy vestnik*, no. 25, 1992, 4–5, as quoted in Tatyana A. Shakleina, "American–Russian Relations: Confrontation or Cooperation," unpublished paper, Institute of the USA and Canada, Moscow, 1992, 2, 4–5.
17. K. Myalo in *Literaturnaya Rossiya*, no. 11, 1992, 4, as quoted in Shakleina, "American–Russian Relations: Confrontation or Cooperation," 5–6.
18. Geoffrey Hosking, "The Beginnings of Independent Political Activity," in *The Road to Post-Communism*, 18, 22–3. Cf. Duncan, "The Rebirth of Politics in Russia," ibid., 108.
19. John Dunlop, "Russia: Confronting the Loss of Empire," in Ian Bremmer and Ray Taras, eds., *Nations and Politics in the Soviet Successor States*, Cambridge University Press, 1993, 57, 62.
20. Duncan, "The Rebirth of Politics in Russia," 88. Despite extensive coverage given to Pamyat in the Western media, one public opinion survey during 1990 showed that Pamyat and similar protofascist organizations were supported by only 1 or 2 percent of the RSFSR population. (Dunlop, "Russia: Confronting a Loss of Empire," 62, 69).
21. Japan refers to these islands as the Northern Territories; Russia refers to them as the Southern Kuril Islands. Russia's control of the other islands in the Kuril group is not contested. In the remainder of this book we follow common English usage and refer to the four islands as part of the Kuril chain. See Chapter 6 for a discussion of the Russian government's handling of the island controversy.

22. One poll conducted in the fall of 1991 showed that Russian citizens opposed returning the islands to Japan by a ratio of more than five to one. See *Mir mnenii i mneniya o mire* (newsletter of the Moscow public opinion research service "Vox Populi"), no. 10 (1991), 1. The debate about the extent of growth in the imperial-authoritarian current of Russian nationalism is dealt with in Igor Torbakov, "The 'Statists' and the Ideology of Russian Imperial Nationalism," *RFE/RL Research Report*, 1, no. 49 (11 December 1992), 10–16; Paul Goble, "Russian Culture and the Redefinition of Moscow's Foreign Policy," Russian Littoral Project Working Paper No. 13, draft, May 1993; and Alec Guroff and Greg Guroff, "The Paradox of Russian National Identity," Russian Littoral Project Working Paper No. 16, draft, May 1993.

23. Approximately 80 percent of the persons interviewed expressed support for enlarging the role of the United Nations in resolving international problems. (Note that the survey was based on interviews with inhabitants of Russia from all backgrounds, not just interviews with ethnic Russians. In 1989 non–Russians constituted approximately 19 percent of the residents of Russia.) *Mir mnenii i mneniya o mire*, no. 7 (1991), 3.

24. *Opinion Research Memorandum*, Office of Research, U.S. Information Agency, 2 April 1993, 1.

25. Thus, for instance, 50 percent of the respondents to one questionnaire disapproved of the increased international influence of the United States, and only 24 percent expressed approval; other respondents answered "it's hard to say." *Mir mnenii i mneniya o mire*, no. 7 (1991), 3. See also ibid., no. 11 (1992), 2.

26. This figure is based on the 1989 Soviet census.

27. *Nezavisimaya gazeta*, 9 January 1992.

28. Shamil Sultanov, "The Spirit of a Eurasian," *Nash sovremennik*, July 1992, 147, as quoted in Torbakov, "The 'Statists' and the Ideology of Russian Imperial Nationalism," 12.

29. *Sovetskaya Rossiya*, 12 July 1992, as quoted in Torbakov, "The 'Statists' and the Ideology of Russian Imperial Nationalism," 12.

30. Ibid., 12.

31. *Washington Post*, 19 July 1992, and "Weekly Review of Events 17–23 June 1992," *RFE/RL Research Report*, 1, no. 27 (3 July 1992), 72.

32. ITAR–TASS, 1 April 1992, in *FBIS–SOV*, 1 April 1992, 18.

33. Tatyana Tolstaya, "Common Historical Roots," *Partisan Review*, 59, no. 4 (1992), 572–3.

34. *New York Times*, 25 July 1992.

35. See "Last Call," *Eastern Europe Newsletter*, 6, no. 15 (20 July 1992), 1; "Kazakhstan: In Chile's Footsteps?" ibid., 6, no. 17 (24 August 1992), 4.

36. *RFE/RL Daily Report*, no. 115, 21 June 1993.

37. "The Cossacks," *Eastern Europe Newsletter*, 6, no. 15 (20 July 1992), 1, 5; Gene Fishel, "The Russian Cossack Revival," *Geographic Notes*, 2, no. 3 (1992), 19–21; *Washington Post*, 23 March 1992; *New York Times*, 25 July 1992.

38. See *Mir mnenii i mneniya o mire*, no. 6 (1991), 4; no. 7 (1991), 4. Just days

after the January 1991 crackdown by Soviet troops in Lithuania, a survey of public opinion in several RSFSR cities revealed that less than a third of the respondents (29 percent) approved of the crackdown and more than half (55 percent) condemned it. (*Komsomolskaya pravda*, 18 January 1991.) For the RSFSR citizenry as a whole, opinion was probably more evenly divided, since Russia's rural areas are consistently more conservative politically than are the cities.

39. *Mir mnenii i mneniya o mire*, no. 11 (1992), 4.

40. Konstantin Pleshakov, "The Russian Dilemma," *New Times* (Moscow), no. 7 (February 1992), 15.

41. *Mir mnenii i mneniya o mire*, no. 17 (1991), 5.

42. This position has been endorsed by the "Russian Party of the RSFSR," founded in May 1991. (Dunlop, "Russia: Confronting the Loss of Empire," 61.)

43. In a survey conducted in February and March 1992, Russian citizens were asked how they assessed the Russian government's efforts to stabilize relations with the other former republics via the CIS. Of the respondents, 56.5 percent answered "excellent," "good," or "fair;" 22.5 percent answered "bad" or "very bad." (*Mir mnenii i mneniya o mire*, no. 5 [1992], 5.) These findings seem clear-cut, but the poll was conducted before some of the disputes between Russia and the other new states heated up.

44. The percentage shares of positive and negative responses for each former republic were as follows: Belarus, 75, 6; Kazakhstan, 72, 8; Ukraine, 69, 13; Uzbekistan, 58, 16; Kyrgyzstan, 57, 15; Turkmenistan, 56, 16; Tajikistan, 48, 26; Latvia, 48, 30; Moldova, 47, 30; Estonia, 46, 30; Lithuania, 45, 32; Armenia, 41, 37; Azerbaijan, 38, 39; Georgia, 36, 41. *Opinion Research Memorandum*, Office of Research, U.S. Information Agency, 2 April 1993, 2–3.

45. These ethnic-territorial units encompass approximately one-third of Russia's land mass. The remainder falls within the jurisdiction of the non-ethnic administrative units. Jim Nichol, "The Russian Federation: Will it Hold Together?," *CRS Report for Congress*, Washington, D.C.: Congressional Research Service, 5 October 1992, 1.

46. Rather than refer to the Russian nation, the declaration proclaimed that Russia's sovereignty flowed from its "multinational people." (Duncan, "The Rebirth of Politics in Russia," 92–3.)

47. Edward W. Walker, "The New Russian Constitution and the Future of the Russian Federation," *The Harriman Institute Forum*, 5, no. 10 (1992), 5, 8; Dunlop, "Russia: Confronting a Loss of Empire," 50–1.

48. Walker, "The New Russian Constitution and the Future of the Russian Federation," 9; Michael Bradshaw, "Siberia Poses a Challenge to Russian Federalism," *RFE/RL Research Report*, 1, no. 41 (16 October 1992), 7.

49. Nichol, "The Russian Federation: Will It Hold Together?" 13.

50. Walker, "The New Russian Constitution and the Future of the Russian Federation," 10–11. The only two units that refused to sign were the autonomous republics of Tatarstan and Chechnya.

51. Ibid., 19–20, 22.

52. For more on Yeltsin's approach to political reform, see Chapter 4.

53. Lee Schwartz, "USSR Nationality Redistribution by Republic, 1979–1989: From Published Results of the 1989 All–Union Census," *Soviet Geography*, 32, no. 4 (1991), 210–12.

54. Approximately 56 percent of the respondents said that the autonomies should be allowed to leave the federation; about 28 percent said this should not be permitted, and another 24 percent responded that "it's hard to say." Asked for their own preferences, 20 percent said the autonomies should have only their current powers, 57 percent said those powers should be broadened without denying the Russian republic the final say, and 20 percent said the autonomies should receive independence. (Dunlop, "Russia: Confronting the Loss of Empire," 62–3.)

55. *Opinion Research Memorandum*, Office of Research, U.S. Information Agency, 4 June 1993, 1. Only 20 percent said they would favor granting independence under these conditions.

56. Walker, "The New Russian Constitution and the Future of the Russian Federation," 6–7; Ron Wixman, "The Middle Volga: Ethnic Archipelago in a Russian Sea," in *Nations and Politics in the Soviet Successor States*, 438–43.

57. Nichol, "The Russian Federation: Will It Hold Together?" 24.

58. Vera Tolz, "Regionalism in Russia: The Case of Siberia," *RFE/RL Research Report*, 2, no. 9 (26 February 1993), 1–9.

59. Dominique Arel, "Federalism and the Language Factor in Ukraine," paper presented at the annual convention of the American Association for the Advancement of Slavic Studies, Phoenix, Arizona, November 1992, 12. Countrywide, slightly less than 60 percent of the Ukrainians whose mother tongue was Russian also knew Ukrainian. (Calculated from Krawchenko, "Ukraine: The Politics of Independence," in *Nations and Politics in the Soviet Successor States*, 86. All figures are based on 1989 census data.)

60. These conclusions are based on surveys conducted between December 1991 and February 1992. See *Research Memorandum*, Office of Research, U.S. Information Agency, 20 April 1992, 2, 7. Also see Algimantas Prazauskas, "The Influence of Ethnicity on the Foreign Policies of the Western Littoral States," Russian Littoral Project Working Paper No. 23, draft, University of Maryland, College Park, and the Johns Hopkins School of Advanced International Studies (hereafter UMCP/SAIS), June 1993.

61. Interfax, 13 November 1992, in *FBIS–SOV*, 16 November 1992, 66.

62. *Research Memorandum*, Office of Research, U.S. Information Agency, 11 June 1992, 1–2. Of the respondents 45 percent said Western countries should be involved; 27 percent had no opinion on the matter.

63. Ibid., 1–2. The remainder of the responses identified the main threat as follows: threat from a foreign country outside the former USSR, 5 percent; no threat at all, 15 percent; don't know or no opinion, 18 percent.

64. In 1991, for example, Rukh leader Ivan Drach warned that no matter what sort of government came to power in the Russian Federation, Russia would remain "a totalitarian monster." (*Tygodnik powszechny* [Warsaw], 13 October 1991.)

65. Serhii M. Plokhy, "Historical Debates and Territorial Claims: Cossack Mythology in the Russian–Ukrainian Border Dispute," Russian Littoral Working Paper No. 10, draft, UMCP/SAIS, May 1993, 25–7.
66. Krawchenko, "Ukraine: The Politics of Independence," 92–3.
67. Arel, "Federalism and the Language Factor in Ukraine," 6.
68. Quoted in David Marples, "The Shevchenko Ukrainian Language Society: An Interview with Dmytro Pavlychko," *Report on the USSR*, 1, no. 30 (1989), 36.
69. *Izvestiya*, evening edition, 2 November 1991; Arel, "Federalism and the Language Factor in Ukraine."
70. The eastern and southern regions are the home of 80 percent of Ukraine's ethnic Russian population. Russians constitute only 5 percent of the population in the western region and 8.5 percent in the central region (excluding Kiev), compared with 22 percent of the population countrywide. (Arel, "Federalism and the Language Factor in Ukraine," 8–9, 11; Krawchenko, "Ukraine: The Politics of Independence," 80, 84–5.)
71. Arel, "Federalism and the Language Factor in Ukraine," 11–12.
72. Ibid., 13.
73. Ibid., 13, 14n.
74. *Narodna hazeta*, no. 45 (74), November 1992, 1, in *FBIS–SOV*, 15 December 1992, 33. The statement was signed by Ivan Drach and Vyacheslau Chornovil.
75. Arel, "Federalism and the Language Factor in Ukraine," 6.
76. One contemporary politician who has sounded this theme is Valentyn Moroz, head of the Lviv chapter of Rukh. (Ilya Prizel, "The Influence of Ethnicity on Foreign Policy: The Case of Ukraine," Russian Littoral Project Working Paper No. 22, draft, UMCP/SAIS, June 1993, 15.) An example of the rehabilitation of a historical figure is Stepan Bandera, an ultranationalist leader of the OUN, the Ukrainian military force that fought alongside the Nazis against the Soviets in a vain attempt to achieve an independent Ukraine. It should be noted that some present-day Ukrainians have protested against the tendency to lionize the OUN (Abraham Brumberg, "Not So Free at Last," *The New York Review of Books*, 22 October 1992, 58–9; Zenon Kohut, "History as a Battleground: Russian–Ukrainian Relations and Historical Consciousness in Contemporary Ukraine," Russian Littoral Project Working Paper No. 9, draft, UMCP/SAIS, May 1993, 16–17.)
77. Bohdan Krawchenko, "Ukraine: The Politics of Independence," 86.
78. For instance, since 1989 there has been virtually no change in the percentage of pupils taught in Ukrainian and Russian. Roman Solchanyk, "The Politics of Language in Ukraine," *RFE/RL Research Report*, 2, no. 10 (6 March 1993), 2; Brumberg, "Not So Free at Last," 60.
79. Prizel, "The Influence of Ethnicity on Foreign Policy," 15.
80. Ralph Clem, "Belorussians," in Graham Smith, ed., *The Nationalities Question in the Soviet Union*, New York: Longman, 1990, 115–17.
81. Michael Urban and Jan Zaprudnik, "Belarus: A Long Road to Nationhood," in *Nations and Politics in the Soviet Successor States*, 115.

82. Clem, "Belorussians," in Smith, ed., *The Nationalities Question*, 115, and 366, Table 4; Urban and Zaprudnik, "Belarus: A Long Road to Nationhood," 109.

83. Interfax, 10 September 1992, in *FBIS–SOV*, 11 September 1992, 39. See also ITAR–TASS, 24 July 1992, in *FBIS–SOV*, 27 July 1992, 50.

84. *Izvestiya*, evening edition, 24 August 1992.

85. *Komsomolskaya pravda*, 28 August 1992.

86. *Opinion Research Memorandum*, Office of Research, U.S. Information Agency, 7 December 1992, 1–2, and 10 December 1992, 1–2. These results were more optimistic than the answers of Ukrainian respondents polled in a similar survey about a year earlier.

87. Quoted in Kathleen Mihalisko, "The Outlook for Independent Belarus," *RFE/RL Research Report*, 1, no. 24 (12 June 1992), 8.

88. Quoted in ibid.

89. See the statement by Shushkevich in *Komsomolskaya pravda*, 9 January 1992.

90. *Opinion Research Memorandum*, Office of Research, U.S. Information Agency, 18 March 1993, 1–2.

91. Jan Zaprudnik, "Development of Belarusan National Identity and Its Influence on Belarus's Foreign-Policy Orientation," Russian Littoral Project Working Paper No. 21, draft, UMCP/SAIS, June 1993, 7–9; and Jan Zaprudnik, *Belarus: At a Crossroads in History*, Boulder, Colo.: Westview, 1993, 134–41.

92. See the statement of Shushkevich reported by Interfax, 16 November 1992, in *FBIS–SOV*, 18 November 1992, 32–33. According to a public opinion survey conducted in Belarus in June 1992, 70 percent of the respondents expressed the view that both Russian and Belarusian, rather than just the latter, should be official state languages ("Weekly Review of Events 10–16 June 1992," *RFE/RL Research Report*, 1, no. 26 [26 June 1992], 77.)

93. Schwartz, "USSR Nationality Redistribution by Republic, 1979–1989," 230–1. Also see Walter C. Clemens, Jr., "Baltic Identities and Foreign Policy," Russian Littoral Project Working Paper No. 24, draft, UMCP/SAIS, June 1993.

94. Nikolai Rudensky, "Russian Minorities in the Newly Independent States: An International Problem in the Domestic Context of Russia Today," Russian Littoral Project Working Paper No. 15, draft, UMCP/SAIS, May 1993, 6.

95. According to one estimate, one-sixth of the 600,000 ethnic non-Estonians living in Estonia qualify to vote in national elections under the citizenship law. (Romuald Misiunas, "National Identity and Foreign Policy in the Baltic States," Russian Littoral Project Working Paper No. 11, draft, UMCP/SAIS, May 1993, 27.)

96. *News from Helsinki Watch*, 4, no. 7 (15 April 1992), 3.

97. Misiunas, "National Identity and Foreign Policy in the Baltic States," 24.

98. ITAR–TASS, 17 January 1993, in *FBIS–SOV*, 22 January 1993, 88. For

a thorough discussion of the issue, see Philip Hanson, "Estonia's Narva Problem, Narva's Estonian Problem," *RFE/RL Research Report*, 2, no. 18 (30 April 1993), 17–23.

99. *News from Helsinki Watch*, 4, no. 7 (15 April 1992), 3.
100. *Report on Latvia's June 5–6, 1993, Parliamentary Elections*, Washington, D.C.: Commission on Security and Cooperation in Europe, June 1993.
101. For example, some hard-line nationalists in Latvia have considered the possibility of imposing a quota on the number of non-Latvians who may qualify as citizens in any given year. The purpose of this policy would be, at a minimum, to stave off the acquisition of political influence by local Russians, and, at a maximum, to spur many of them to emigrate to Russia. According to one account, in the early 1990s many ethnic Latvians appeared "to have unrealistic expectations about . . . the possible 'repatriation' of Slavic settlers to Russia proper," (Rudensky, "Russian Minorities in the Newly Independent States," 18; Nils Muiznieks, "Latvia: Origins, Evolution, and Triumph," in *Nations and Politics in the Soviet Successor States*, 200.)
102. *Russians in Estonia: Problems and Prospects*, Washington, D.C.: Commission on Security and Cooperation in Europe, September 1992; Dzintra Bungs, "Poll Shows Majority in Latvia Endorses Independence," and Riina Kionka, "Estonia Says 'Yes' to Independence," *Report on the USSR*, 3, no. 11 (15 March 1991), 22–6; Saulius Girnius, "Lithuania Votes for Independence," ibid., 3, no. 8 (22 February 1991), 24–5. The exact size of the Russian vote could not be calculated because the results were not tabulated according to ethnic group.
103. *Russians in Estonia*, 1.
104. Daria Fane, "Moldova: Breaking Loose from Moscow," in *Nations and Politics in the Soviet Successor States*, 138–45.
105. Two arguable exceptions are Birlik, the Uzbekistan national front, and Rastokhez in Tajikistan. In 1992 Birlik's organizers claimed that it had 500,000 adherents. In Tajikistan, Rastokhez played a conspicuous role in the opposition coalition that forced a change in the government in 1992 before being overthrown. See Cassandra Cavanaugh, "Crackdown on the Opposition in Uzbekistan," *RFE/RL Research Report*, 1, no. 31 (31 July 1992), 21; and personal communication from Muriel Atkin.
106. James Critchlow, "The Ethnic Factor in Central Asian Foreign Policy," Russian Littoral Project Working Paper No. 17, draft, UMCP/SAIS, June 1993, 2.
107. Schwartz, "USSR Nationality Redistribution by Republic, 1979–1989," 241–6. These figures are based on the 1989 Soviet census; events since that time may have changed the percentages significantly.
108. In 1989 the percentage of local Russians born in their Soviet republic of residence ranged from 48.5 percent in Tajikistan to 66.6 percent in Kazakhstan, with the percentages for the other republics falling between 50 and 60 percent. The percentages of local Russians born in the given republic or in another Central Asian republic ranged from 56.7 percent in Tajikistan to 68.4 percent in Kazakhstan. (Robert Kaiser, "Ethnic

Demography and Interstate Relations in Central Asia," Russian Littoral
Project Working Paper No. 18, draft, UMCP/SAIS, June 1993, 23, 36.)
109. *Opinion Research Memorandum*, Office of Research, U.S. Information
Agency, 30 September 1992, 10, and 13 January 1993, 4.
110. Tensions were building around this issue even before the USSR's collapse.
See James Critchlow, "Uzbeks Demand Halt to Russian In–Migration,"
Report on the USSR, 2, no. 9 (1990), 18–19. This situation obtains in
most of the Central Asian states. However, Turkmenistan, which is endowed with a wealth of energy resources, may be an exception.
111. A. Vishnevskiy and Zh. Zayonchkovskaya, *Migratsiya iz SSSR: Chet-
vertaya Volna*, vol. 3, Moscow: Tsentr Demografiy i Ekologiy Cheloveka,
1991, 12, as cited in Kaiser, "Ethnic Demography," 22.
112. Martha Brill Olcott, "Kazakhstan: A Republic of Minorities"; Gregory
Gleason, "Uzbekistan: From Statehood to Nationhood"; Muriel Atkin,
"Tajikistan: Ancient Heritage, New Politics"; David Nissman, "Turkmenistan: Search for a National Identity"; and Gene Huskey, "Kyrgyzstan: The Politics of Demographic and Economic Frustration," all in
Nations and Politics in the Soviet Successor States, 320, 341, 365, 391, 407.
113. Olcott, "Kazakhstan: A Republic of Minorities," 320.
114. The statistics for the other republics are 1.2 percent in Kyrgyzstan, 2.5
percent in Turkmenistan, and 3.5 percent in Tajikistan. (Rudensky,
"Russian Minorities in the Newly Independent States," 6.)
115. In Kazakhstan, the language issue is especially thorny because a substantial percentage of ethnic Kazakhs know only Russian and not Kazakh.
Some estimates put the figure as high as 40 percent. See Martha Brill
Olcott, "Nation-Building and Ethnicity in the Foreign Policy of the New
Central Asian States," Russian Littoral Project Working Paper No. 20,
draft, UMCP/SAIS, June 1993, 23–4, 35–6.
116. *Trip Report on Turkmenistan, Kazakhstan and Kyrgyzstan, 23–29 May 1992*,
Washington, D.C.: Commission on Security and Cooperation in Europe,
July 1992, 4 and 7. Also see Nurbek Omuraliev, "The Influence of Ethno–
political Processes on the Foreign Policy of Kyrgyzstan [in Russian],"
Russian Littoral Project Working Paper, draft, UMCP/SAIS, June 1993;
and Kadir Alimov, "The Rediscovery of Uzbek History and its Foreign
Policy Implications," Russian Littoral Project Working Paper No. 6,
draft, UMCP/SAIS, May 1993.
117. *Khak*, no. 2, 1992, as quoted in James Critchlow, "Democratization in Kazakhstan," *RFE/RL Research Report*, 1, no. 30 (24 July 1992), 13–14.
118. The total number of Russians estimated to have emigrated from Central
Asia in 1979–88 was 319,000; the total for 1989–91 was 288,000. (Kaiser,
"Ethnic Demography," 36). The figure of 100,000 or more migrants to
Russia rests on the assumptions that the rate of emigration increased
between 1989 and 1992 and that virtually all the Russians who emigrated
from Central Asia moved to Russia. It should be emphasized that contradictory statistics on outmigration from Central Asia have been publicized by various sources, no doubt partly out of political calculations, and
that the real trends are difficult to determine.

119. Ibid., 23.
120. Olcott, "Nation–Building and Ethnicity," 24–5.
121. Schwartz, "USSR Nationality Distribution by Republic, 1979–1989," 242–4.
122. Calculated from ibid., 241–6. Tajik spokesmen claim that the size of the Tajik population of Uzbekistan has been deliberately understated by the Uzbek government and numbers three to four million rather than less than one million, as is claimed by the government.
123. Although the government of Kazakhstan has advocated this idea of a pan–Turkic commonwealth, it also has maintained that creation of such a commonwealth would not lead Kazakhstan away from the CIS or harm its relations with Russia. To emphasize this intention, Kazakhstan concluded a Treaty of Friendship and Cooperation with Russia, which aims, among many other things, to reassure the anxious Russian inhabitants of Kazakhstan.
124. Among the pan-Turkic groups in the region are Alash, a Kazakhstan-based party that advocates a democratic, multi–party system and unification of all Turkic peoples into a united Turkestan, and the Islamic Party of Turkestan in Uzbekistan, which consists primarily of a coordinating committee with branches in Namangan, Andijan and Kokand in the Fergana valley and in two districts of Tashkent (*Trip Report on Turkmenistan, Kazakhstan and Kyrgyzstan, 23–29 May 1992*, 5; *Eastern Europe Newsletter*, 6, no. 23 [16 November 1992], 8.)
125. James Critchlow, "Will Soviet Central Asia Become a Greater Uzbekistan?" *Report on the USSR*, 2, no. 37 (14 September 1990), 17–19.
126. Kaiser, "Ethnic Demography," 25.
127. Huskey, "Kyrgyzstan: The Politics of Frustration," 409.
128. Muriel Atkin, "Religious, National, and Other Identities in Central Asia," in Jo-Ann Gross, ed., *Muslims in Central Asia*, Durham, N.C.: Duke University Press, 1992, 47–51.
129. Olcott, "Nation-Building and Ethnicity," 33.
130. Kaiser, "Ethnic Demography," 25.
131. Stephen F. Jones, "Georgia: A Failed Democratic Transition," in *Nations and Politics in the Soviet Successor States*, 288–310.
132. Richard G. Hovannisian, "Historical Memory and Foreign Relations: The Armenian Perspective," Russian Littoral Project Working Paper No. 7, draft, UMCP/SAIS, May 1993, 21.
133. Ibid., 38.
134. Greenfeld, *Nationalism: Five Roads to Modernity*, 487–91.

3. The Impact of Religion

1. For a penetrating analysis of the transition from religious to national identities in early modern Europe, see Benedict Anderson's brilliant *Imagined Communities*, London: Verso, 1990.
2. The assumption that they are incompatible is characteristic of the work of such pioneering scholars as Hans Kohn and many recent Western

students of third world nationalism. Literature on this subject, especially in the 1970s, made the assumption that religious influence necessarily wanes with the growth of modernity. (Mark Juergensmayer, *The New Cold War? Religious Nationalism Confronts the Secular State*, Berkeley and Los Angeles: University of California Press, 1993, chapter 1.)

3. Peter F. Sugar, "The Historical Role of Religious Institutions in Eastern Europe and Their Place in the Communist Party-State," in Pedro Ramet, ed., *Religion and Nationalism in Soviet and East European Politics*, rev. ed., Durham, N.C.: Duke University Press, 1989, 51.

4. See Leon T. Hadar, "Is Islam a Threat? No," and Judith Miller, "Is Islam a Threat? Yes," *Foreign Affairs*, 72, no. 2 (Spring 1993), 27–56; Adeed Dawisha, ed., *Islam in Foreign Policy*, Cambridge University Press, 1983; and Chapter 4.

5. S. F. Jones, "Religion and Nationalism in Soviet Georgia and Armenia," in *Religion and Nationalism in Soviet and East European Politics*, 171.

6. Nicholas Riasanovsky, *Nicholas I and Official Nationality in Russia, 1825–1855*, Berkeley and Los Angeles: University of California Press, 1959; S. Frederick Starr, "Tsarist Government: The Imperial Dimension," in Jeremy Azrael, ed., *Soviet Nationality Policies and Practices*, New York: Praeger, 1978, 16–18.

7. Mark Szeftel, "Church and State in Imperial Russia," in Robert L. Nichols and Theofanis G. Stavrou, eds., *Russian Orthodoxy under the Old Regime*, Minneapolis: University of Minnesota Press, 1978, 128–37.

8. Michael Cherniavsky, *Tsar and People: Studies in Russian Myths*, New Haven, Conn.: Yale University Press, 1961, 107, 114; Nicholas Riasanovsky, *A History of Russia*, 4th ed., Berkeley and Los Angeles: University of California Press, 1968.

9. Keith Armes, "Russian Patriarchate and Communist Caesar," *Religious Life in Russia*, ISCIP Publication Series no. 9 (July 1992), Boston University: Institute for the Study of Conflict, Ideology & Policy, 4; Jane Ellis, "Hierarchs and Dissidents: Conflict over the Future of the Russian Orthodox Church," *Religion in Communist Lands*, 18, no. 4 (1990), 311.

10. Mark Rhodes, "Religious Believers in Russia," *RFE/RL Research Report*, 1, no. 14 (3 April 1992), 61.

11. The Communist Party, by contrast, received the trust of only 5 percent of the respondents. (D. Pospielovsky, "Russkaya Pravoslavnaya Tserkov sevodnya i novyy patriarkh," *Vestnik russkovo khristianskovo dvizheniya*, no. 159 [1990], 213.) Another survey conducted in September 1990 showed a somewhat lower rating for "religious organizations" (43 percent) and a somewhat higher rating for the Communist Party (11 percent), but the gap was still striking. (Nikolai P. Popov, "Political Views of the Russian People," *International Journal of Public Opinion Research*, 4, no. 4 [1992], 329.)

12. *Opinion Research Memorandum*, Office of Research, U.S. Information Agency, 18 March 1993, 13. In one survey, the patriarch received a popularity rating second only to that of President Yeltsin, as well as the lowest negative rating among any of the public figures included in the question-

naire. (E. Chekalova, "Tele khochet videt," *Moskovskiye novosti*, 8 March 1992, 15.)

13. Rev. Canon Michael Bourdeaux, "Religion and the Collapse of the Soviet System," in *Religious Life in Russia*, ISCIP Publication Series, no. 9 (July 1992), 21.

14. ITAR–TASS, 14 June 1992, in *FBIS–SOV*, 15 June 1992, 15; Moscow Mayak Radio Network, 12 July 1992, in *FBIS–SOV*, 13 July 1992, 33.

15. In February 1918 a Bolshevik decree nationalized all church property and called for the complete secularization of education, the legal system, and public life.

16. Jane Ellis, *The Russian Orthodox Church: A Contemporary History*, Bloomington: Indiana University Press, 1986, 4.

17. Vladimir Moss, "The Free Russian Orthodox Church," *Report on the USSR*, 3, no. 44 (1 November 1991), 9.

18. Walter Laqueur, *Black Hundred: The Rise of the Extreme Right in Russia*, New York: HarperCollins, 1993, 231–9; Oxana Antic, "Orthodox Church Reacts to Criticism of KGB Links," *RFE/RL Research Report*, 1, no. 23 (5 June 1992), 61; Armes, "Russian Patriarchate and Communist Caesar," 4–8; and Dimitry Pospielovsky, "The Russian Orthodox Church in the Post-Communist CIS," paper prepared for the annual convention of the American Association for the Advancement of Slavic Studies (hereafter AAASS), Phoenix, Arizona, November 1992.

19. Bohdan Bociurkiw, "Nationalities and Soviet Religious Policies," in Lubomyr Hajda and Mark Beissinger, eds., *The Nationalities Factor in Soviet Politics and Society*, Boulder, Colo.: Westview, 1990, 148–74. Apparently Stalin originally intended to destroy all religious confessions and changed his mind only under the pressures of the war. In 1926 not one Roman Catholic bishop remained in the USSR, and by May 1941 only two of the 1,195 Roman Catholic churches operating in 1917 were still functioning. Between 1914 and 1941 the number of Russian Orthodox parishes declined from more than 54,000 to as few as 500, not counting the territories annexed by the USSR in 1939–41, which brought the number to slightly more than 4,000. (Pedro Ramet, "The Interplay of Religious Policy and Nationalities Policy in the Soviet Union and Eastern Europe," in *Religion and Nationalism in Soviet and East European Politics*, 18, 25.)

20. Several names have been used for the church, including Eastern Catholic, Eastern Rite Catholic, and others. None of the names is completely satisfactory from the standpoint of descriptive accuracy and ethical neutrality. (Mark Elliott, "Uniates," *The Modern Encyclopedia of Russian and Soviet History*, Gulf Breeze, Fla.: Academic International Press, 1985, vol. 40, 210.)

21. Quoted in Ivan Hvat, *The Catacomb Ukrainian Catholic Church and Pope John Paul II*, Cambridge, Mass.: Harvard University Ukrainian Studies Fund, 1984, 270; and Oxana Antic, "The Bishops' Synod in Rome and the Crisis in Catholic–Orthodox Relations," *Report on the USSR*, 3, no. 49 (1991), 20. For more on this controversy, see the following section.

22. Moss, "The Free Russian Orthodox Church," 9.

23. Ellis, "Hierarchs and Dissidents," 307–309; Vladimir Moss, "The True Orthodox Church of Russia," *Religion in Communist Lands*, 19, nos. 3–4 (1991), 239–49; Moss, "The Free Russian Orthodox Church," 8–9. The switch to the Uniates has occurred in west Ukraine, not in the rest of the former USSR.

24. In July 1993 the Russian parliament adopted a law to this effect, and liberal deputies announced their intention to appeal the issue to the Constitutional Court (*RFE/RL Daily Report*, no. 133, 15 July 1993). For other charges leveled against the Church, see ibid., no. 75, 21 April 1993; and Pospielovsky, "The Russian Orthodox Church in the Post-Communist CIS." The charges of complicity with the Nazis are valid for one large component of the Russian Orthodox Church Abroad; see Laqueur, *Black Hundred*, 225.

25. Ilya Prizel, "The Influence of Ethnicity on Foreign Policy: The Case of Ukraine," Russian Littoral Project Working Paper No. 22, draft, University of Maryland, College Park, and the Johns Hopkins School of Advanced International Studies (hereafter UMCP/SAIS), June 1993, 7.

26. On the Russian Orthodox hierarchy's attitude toward religious pluralism, see Kent R. Hill, "The Orthodox Church and a Pluralistic Society," in Uri Ra'anan, Keith Armes, and Kate Martin, eds., *Russian Pluralism – Now Irreversible?* New York: St. Martin's, 1992, 165–88.

27. The early history of the UAOC is briefly described in Orest Subtelny, *Ukraine: A History*, Toronto: University of Toronto Press, 1988, 401–2, 417, 464–5. On the status of the Ukrainian Orthodox church, see John B. Dunlop, "The Russian Orthodox Church and Nationalism after 1988," *Religion in Communist Lands*, 18, no. 4 (1990), 297–8.

28. Quoted in David Little, *Ukraine: The Legacy of Intolerance*, Washington, D.C.: United States Institute of Peace, 1991, 40–1.

29. Zenon Kohut, "History as a Battleground: Russian–Ukrainian Relations and Historical Consciousness in Contemporary Ukraine," Russian Littoral Project Working Paper No. 9, draft, UMCP/SAIS, May 1993, 22.

30. Oxana Antic, "Revival of Orthodox Brotherhoods in Russia," *RFE/RL Research Report*, 1, no. 11 (13 March 1992), 62.

31. Anatoly Krasikov, "The Exarch vs. the Patriarch," *New Times* (Moscow), no. 27 (July 1992), 13.

32. Marta Kolomayets, "Orthodox Churches Announce Union," *The Ukrainian Weekly*, no. 26 (28 June 1992), 1, 10. For the convoluted church–state politics that led up to the merger, see Armes, "Russian Patriarchate and Communist Caesar," 9–11, and the next section.

33. Laqueur, *Black Hundred*, 236–7.

34. Western assessments of the role of the church during the coup differ sharply. Compare Oxana Antic, "Church Reaction to the Coup," *Report on the USSR*, 3, no. 38 (20 September 1991), 15–16, with Rhodes, "Religious Believers in Russia," 60, and especially with Armes, "Russian Patriarchate and Communist Caesar," 8.

35. Peter J. S. Duncan, "The Rebirth of Politics in Russia," in Geoffrey A. Hosking, Jonathan Aves, and Peter J. S. Duncan, *The Road to Post-*

Communism: Independent Political Movements in the Soviet Union, 1985–1991, New York: Pinter, 1992, 83.

36. Suzanne Crow, "Russia's Response to the Yugoslav Crisis," *RFE/RL Research Report*, 1, no. 30 (24 July 1992), 31–5.
37. *Rossiyskaya gazeta*, 23 February 1993.
38. "The Way to the Truth, – Or, What the Christian Democrats are Fighting For," *Pravda*, 7 January 1992, translated in *Current Digest of the Soviet Press* (hereafter *CDSP*), vol. 44, no. 1, 30.
39. The two extremist groups that have taken over the leadership of the Union are the St. Sergius Brotherhood of Sergiyev Posad and the Moscow Union of Christian Regeneration. (Pospielovsky, "The Russian Orthodox Church in the Post-Communist CIS," 45.)
40. As stated by Aleksandr Sterligov, cochairman of the ultra–right–wing Russian National Assembly, and quoted in Aleksandr Yanov, "Late by a Century," *New Times* (Moscow), no. 24 (June 1993), 13.
41. Laqueur, *Black Hundred*, 45–52.
42. This position was adopted by Metropolitan Ioann of St. Petersburg and has also received support from clerics associated with the Free Orthodox Church. *Sovetskaya Rossiya*, 20 February 1993; Laqueur, *Black Hundred*, 232–3.
43. Laqueur, *Black Hundred*, 229–30; Pospielovsky, "The Russian Orthodox Church in the Post-Communist CIS," 26; Zoya Krakhmalnikova, "Russophobia, Antisemitism and Christianity: Some Remarks on an Anti-Christian Idea," and Sergei Lezov, "The National Idea and Christianity," *Religion, State and Society*, 20, no. 1 (1992), 7–50.
44. *Pravda*, 3 December 1991.
45. According to Sheikh Gainurtdin, more than fourteen thousand mosques in Siberia and the European parts of the USSR were destroyed or closed during the Soviet era, leaving just eighty still in operation, and thirty thousand Muslim clerics had been "lost" (ibid.).
46. *RFE/RL Daily Report*, no. 70, 14 April 1992.
47. See the editorial note accompanying the interview with T. Saidbayev in *Izvestiya*, evening edition, 28 November 1991.
48. ITAR–TASS, 11 June 1992, in *FBIS–SOV*, 11 June 1992, 33.
49. These included the religious associations for Chechen–Ingushetia, North Ossetia, and others. (Marie Broxup, "Islam in Dagestan under Gorbachev," *Religion in Communist Lands*, 18, no. 3 [1990], 215.)
50. The conference was attended by guests from Saudi Arabia, Afghanistan, Turkey, and Pakistan. (Interlegal Research Center and Postfactum newsletter, *Religious Life in Russia* [Moscow], November 1992.)
51. *Nezavisimaya gazeta*, 20 August 1992.
52. Ibid.
53. For a critical evaluation of Western scholars' views on this question, see Muriel Atkin, "The Islamic Revolution that Overthrew the Soviet State," *Contention*, 2, no. 2 (Winter 1993), 89–106.
54. Not only did the secular leaders of the Central Asian republics seek to preserve the Soviet system, but the head of the Islamic muftiate for Central

Asia also came out in favor of maintaining the union. For evidence of Russian fears of Islam in connection with episodes of violence in Uzbekistan and Tajikistan, see the article by V. Skosyrev, in *Izvestiya*, 8 October 1991.

55. On the existence of widespread Russian "Islamophobia," see *Komsomolets Uzbekistana*, 17 January 1990, as quoted in Paul Goble, "Islamic 'Explosion' Possible in Central Asia," *Report on the USSR*, 2, no. 7 (16 February 1990), 22–3.

56. Talib Sarimsakovych Saidbayev in *Pravda*, 3 December 1991.

57. Muriel Atkin, "Attitudes Toward Soviet Islam in the Gorbachev Era," paper prepared for the 1991 convention of the AAASS, Miami, Florida, November 1991.

58. *Washington Post*, 9 September 1992.

59. *Afghanistan and Post-Soviet Central Asia: Prospects for Political Evolution and the Role of Islam*, Special Report of the Study Group on the Prospects for Conflict and Opportunities for Peacemaking in the Southern Tier of Former Soviet Republics, Washington, D.C.: U.S. Institute of Peace, 1992, 28–34. See also the final section of this chapter.

60. ITAR–TASS, 20 April 1993, in *FBIS–SOV*, 21 April 1993, 21–2.

61. More precisely, the patriarchate headed the church until the early eighteenth century, when it was replaced by Peter the Great with a holy synod staffed with secular officials. The patriarchate was reestablished at the time of tsarism's collapse in 1917.

62. According to one source, during the late 1970s, Ukraine contained about 3,000 of the USSR's total of 7,062 Russian Orthodox parishes, or about 42 percent of the total. (Calculated from Vasyl Markus, "Religion and Nationalism in Ukraine," in *Religion and Nationalism in Soviet and East European Politics*, 146.) According to figures released by the Moscow patriarchate, in mid-1988 there were 6,893 functioning Russian Orthodox parishes in the USSR, of which more than 4,000 were located in Ukraine. Hence the Ukrainian share amounted to at least 58 percent of the total. (Calculated from Dunlop, "The Russian Orthodox Church and Nationalism After 1988," 295.)

63. Vasyl Markus, "Religion and Nationalism in Ukraine," 139.

64. Ibid., 140–1; Michael Urban and Jan Zaprudnik, "Belarus: A Long Road to Nationhood," in Ian Bremmer and Ray Taras, eds., *Nations and Politics in the Soviet Successor States*, Cambridge University Press, 1993, 101–2; Elliott, "Uniates," 212.

65. For details, see Elliott, "Uniates," 212.

66. Frank E. Sysyn, *The Ukrainian Orthodox Question in the USSR*, Cambridge, Mass.: Harvard University Ukrainian Studies Fund, 1987, 11.

67. Ibid.

68. At the same time, however, Bolshevik ideologists sought to widen and exploit the divisions within the Ukrainian church. (Bohdan Bociurkiw, *Ukrainian Churches Under Soviet Rule: Two Case Studies*, Cambridge, Mass.: Harvard University Ukrainian Studies Fund, 1984, 333–5.)

69. Ibid., 324, 331.
70. Sysyn, *The Ukrainian Orthodox Question in the USSR*, 12–13. By 1924 the Ukrainian church included nearly eleven hundred parishes. (Bociurkiw, *Ukrainian Churches under Soviet Rule*, 315.)
71. See Bociurkiw, *Ukrainian Churches Under Soviet Rule*, 317, 335–8 on the religious purge and its aftermath.
72. Markus, "Religion and Nationalism in Ukraine," 144; Jan Zaprudnik, *Belarus: At a Crossroads in History*, Boulder, Colo.: Westview, 1993, 98.
73. Compare Elliott, "Uniates," 212, with Bociurkiw, *Ukrainian Churches Under Soviet Rule*, 97–108.
74. Quoted in Bociurkiw, *Ukrainian Churches Under Soviet Rule*, 105–6. Members were required to join the Russian Orthodox church. Clergy who refused to do so were imprisoned.
75. In the early 1940s the newly annexed territories may have included as many as 2,300 parishes. (Ibid., 90n.)
76. The Russian Orthodox church's numerical strength in Ukraine may be partly explained by the Stalinist regime's eagerness to combat the Uniate faith, and by its corresponding willingness to permit the Russian Orthodox church to operate in the region with fewer hindrances than in other portions of the empire. In later years Moscow's policy of employing Russian Orthodoxy as a weapon against indigenous Ukrainian religious traditions was reflected in government propagandists' disproportionate efforts to discredit the indigenous movements and in the propagandists' relative neglect of Russian Orthodoxy. (Bociurkiw, "Nationalities and Soviet Religious Policies," 159–60.)
77. Bociurkiw, *Ukrainian Churches Under Soviet Rule*, 89.
78. Dunlop, "The Russian Orthodox Church and Nationalism after 1988," 296–7; Serge Kelleher, "Out of the Catacombs: The Greek–Catholic Church in Ukraine," *Religion in Communist Lands*, 19, nos. 3–4 (1991), 253–4. The ecclesiastical governance of the reestablished Ukrainian Autocephalous Orthodox church was more centralized and hierarchical than it had been in the 1920s; the new UAOC, for example, set up its own patriarchate. (Little, *Ukraine: The Legacy of Intolerance*, 35.)
79. Kohut, "History as a Battleground," 9–10.
80. For an insightful analysis of these events, see Bohdan Bociurkiw, "The Ukrainian Catholic Church in the USSR under Gorbachev," *Problems of Communism*, 39, no. 6 (November–December 1990), 6–8; Bociurkiw, "Nationalities and Soviet Religious Policies," 162–5; and Ilya Prizel, "The Influence of Ethnicity on Foreign Policy," 5.
81. Bociurkiw, "Nationalities and Soviet Religious Policies," 162–5. The official millennium celebrations occurred shortly before President Reagan came to Moscow for the June 1988 summit with Gorbachev.
82. The 1888 celebrations of the 900th anniversary had taken place in Kiev, not Moscow or St. Petersburg.
83. Russian Orthodox hierarchs participated in this campaign. See Bociurkiw, "Nationalities and Soviet Religious Policies," 164–5.
84. "Zverennia do Prezydii Verkhovnoi Rady SRSR i Rady Ministriv SRSR,"

Pravoslavnyi visnyk, nos. 7–8 (1986), 26, as quoted in Bociurkiw, "Nationalities and Soviet Religious Policies," 165. The patriarch who issued this statement was Pimen, the predecessor of Aleksiy II.

85. Dunlop, "The Russian Orthodox Church and Nationalism," 297–8; Little, *Ukraine: The Legacy of Intolerance*, 18.

86. For details of the conflicts that took place in Ukraine, see *New York Times*, 23 August 1990; *Christian Science Monitor*, 5 September 1990; and *Reuters Library Report*, 4 October 1991. Chairman Shushkevich, in a speech to the Belarusian Supreme Soviet, admitted that in relations between the 788 Orthodox and 306 Catholic churches, "occasional frictions and claims for church premises do occur, as was the case in Smorgon, Lida, Polotsk, and other locations." Radio Minsk, 31 March 1993, in *FBIS–SOV*, 9 April 1993, 67.

87. Pospielovsky, "The Russian Orthodox Church in the Post-Communist CIS," 19–20.

88. Filaret had long been a key figure in the Moscow patriarchate in his capacity as Metropolitan of Kiev and Exarch of the Russian Orthodox church. In the two years preceding the attempted merger, he castigated the leaders of the Rukh movement as "bandits" and "provocateurs." He also prohibited his clergymen from delivering their sermons in the Ukrainian language, and he conducted a bitter campaign against the Ukrainian Autocephalous church. (Armes, "Russian Patriarchate and Communist Caesar," 10–12; Pospielovsky, "The Russian Orthodox Church in the Post-Communist CIS," 21.)

89. Ibid.; and personal communication from Professor Bohdan Bociurkiw.

90. The number of people in this group is very difficult to determine. According to one source, "thousands of parishioners and whole parishes" protested the move to autocephaly by writing the patriarch. (Ibid., 20.) See also "Ukraine: God's War," *The Economist*, 7 November 1992, 58–9.

91. Security Minister Yevhen Marchuk, speech reported by Interfax, 12 April 1993, in *FBIS–SOV*, 13 April 1993, 59.

92. Kelleher, "Out of the Catacombs: The Greek–Catholic Church in Ukraine," 260.

93. Sysyn, *The Ukrainian Orthodox Question in the USSR*, 9, 16.

94. Ioann, the Lviv metropolitan who launched the initiative to recreate the UAOC in 1989, has stated that the Uniate church was "coercively formed" in the sixteenth century by Polish occupiers of Ukraine (Little, *Ukraine: The Legacy of Intolerance*, 36–7, 40). See also Hvat, *The Catacomb Ukrainian Catholic Church and Pope John Paul II*, 270–1, 278.

95. Little, *Ukraine: The Legacy of Intolerance*, 47.

96. Nicholas P. Vakar, *Belorussia: The Making of a Nation*, Cambridge, Mass.: Harvard University Press, 1956, 58, 130–1; Zaprudnik, *Belarus: At a Crossroads of History*, 137–41.

97. *The Washington Times*, 21 December 1992; ITAR–TASS, 23 December 1992, in BBC, *Summary of World Broadcasts*, 9 January 1993. Survey data show that in Moldova, in contrast to many other former republics, the

local opulation holds the Russian Orthodox church in relatively low esteem – especially by comparison with the Russian army. See Natalia Evdokimova, "National and Religious Self-Identification as a Russian (Findings of the Recent Survey in the Former Republics of the Soviet Union)," paper presented at the Conference on Russian Minorities in the Former Soviet Union, Kennan Institute, Washington, D.C., May 1992, 2.

98. Kestutis K. Girnius, "Catholicism and Nationalism in Lithuania," in *Religion and Nationalism in Soviet and East European Politics*, 114–37.

99. *RFE/RL Daily Report*, no. 4, 8 January 1993; Marite Sapiets, "The Baltic Churches and the National Revival," *Religion in Communist Lands*, 18, no. 2 (1990), 160–2.

100. Ibid., 156–63; Nils Muiznieks, "Latvia: Origins, Evolution, and Triumph," in *Nations and Politics in the Soviet Successor States*, 188.

101. Sapiets, "The Baltic Churches," 156–63.

102. See Evdokimova, "National and Religious Self–Identification as a Russian."

103. For more on the political role and aspirations of Islam, see Edward Mortimer, *Faith and Power: The Politics of Islam*, New York: Random House, 1982.

104. James Critchlow, "Islam in Soviet Central Asia: Renaissance or Revolution?" *Religion in Communist Lands*, 18, no. 3 (1990), 196, 207; Bernhard Wilhelm, "The Moslems, 1948–1954," in Richard Marshall, Jr., Thomas Bird, and Andrew Blane, eds., *Aspects of Religion in the Soviet Union, 1917–1967*, Chicago: University of Chicago Press, 1971, 264. See also Shoshana Keller, "Islam in Soviet Central Asia, 1917–1930: Soviet Policy and the Struggle for Control," *Central Asian Survey*, 11, no. 1 (1992), 25–50, and Alexander Park, *Bolshevism in Turkestan, 1917–1927*, New York: Columbia University Press, 1957.

105. By 1947 one Soviet source put the total number of mosques at three thousand. (Wilhelm, "The Moslems, 1948–1954," 267; Bociurkiw, "Nationalities and Soviet Religious Policies," 157.) By 1985 a mere 240 of the 25,000 mosques that existed in 1917 were still in operation (*Human Rights and Democratization in the Newly Independent States of the Former Soviet Union*, Washington, D.C.: Commission on Security and Cooperation in Europe, 1993, 165).

106. Azade–Ayse Rorlich, "Islam and Atheism: Dynamic Tension in Soviet Central Asia," in William Fierman, ed., *Soviet Central Asia: The Failed Transformation*, Boulder, Colo.: Westview, 1991, 193.

107. *Afghanistan and Post-Soviet Central Asia*, 18; *Human Rights and Democratization*, 165.

108. *Opinion Research Memorandum*, Office of Research, U.S. Information Agency, 30 September 1992, 1. A survey in Turkmenistan carried out during the Soviet era showed 45 percent of the respondents to be believers. (Rorlich, "Islam and Atheism," 190–1.)

109. James Critchlow, "The Ethnic Factor in Central Asian Foreign Policy," Russian Littoral Project Working Paper No. 17, draft, UMCP/SAIS, June

1993, 3; Vitaly Naumkin, "Islam in the States of the Former USSR," *Annals of the American Academy of Political and Social Science*, 524 (November 1992), 135.

110. Naumkin, "Islam in the States of the Former USSR," 131–2; Sergey Poliakov, *Everyday Islam: Religion and Tradition in Rural Central Asia*, Armonk, N.Y.: M. E. Sharpe, 1992, 95–112.

111. In June 1992 more than fifteen thousand pilgrims from the CIS states went to Mecca for the Islamic holiday of Bairam, compared with approximately four thousand persons who made the pilgrimage in 1991. (*RFE/RL Daily Report*, no. 111, 12 June 1992.)

112. Martha Brill Olcott, "Nation-Building and Ethnicity in the Foreign Policy of the New Central Asian States," Russian Littoral Project Working Paper No. 20, draft, UMCP/SAIS, June 1992, 15.

113. Ibid.

114. Russians alone constitute only about 40 percent of the country's population, but other European groups such as Ukrainians and Germans raise the total to about 52 percent.

115. Olcott, "Nation-Building and Ethnicity," 14–15.

116. The proposed clause of the constitution read: "the people of Kyrgyzstan adhere to the moral values of Islam, other religions and national traditions," The final version refers only to "moral values and national traditions." (*The Reuter Library Report*, 4 May 1993.)

117. Martha Brill Olcott, "Central Asia's Catapult to Independence," *Foreign Affairs*, 71, no. 3 (Summer 1992), 124.

118. Thus, for example, Akayev has stated that "there is no basis in Kyrgyzstan for fundamentalism, our people are not contaminated by it." (*Izvestiya*, evening edition, 19 March 1992.) Uzbekistan President Karimov has declared flatly that "Islamic fundamentalism cannot take root in our country." (TASS, 18 March 1992 in *FBIS–SOV*, 25 March 1992, 72.)

119. *Human Rights and Democratization in the Newly Independent States*, 165, 172.

120. *RFE/RL Daily Report*, no. 116, 22 June 1993.

121. *Izvestiya*, evening edition, 8 January 1992.

122. Rorlich, "Islam and Atheism," 211.

123. Naumkin, "Islam in the Former States of the USSR," 135, 140; *RFE/RL Daily Report*, no. 83, 3 May 1993.

124. "USSR: Special Feature on the Disintegration of the Soviet Union," *Middle East Magazine*, 1 September 1990.

125. Naumkin, "Islam in the States of the Former USSR," 135; Rorlich, "Islam and Atheism," 208; *Financial Times*, 14 August 1991.

126. *Komsomolets Tajikistana*, 24 November 1990.

127. *Izvestiya*, evening edition, 8 January 1991.

128. The parties received an expression of confidence from the following percentages of Uzbek and other ethnic Central Asian respondents: Birlik, 34 percent; Erk, 47 percent; IRP, 57 percent. Both the IRP and Erk received substantially more support from Muslim believers than from nonbelievers; Birlik scored almost exactly the same with the two groups. (*Opinion Re-*

search Memorandum, Office of Research, U.S. Information Agency, 30 September 1992, 12–13.)

129. *Eastern Europe Newsletter*, 6, no. 23 (16 November 1992), 8.
130. Critchlow, "Islam in Soviet Central Asia: Renaissance or Revolution?" 208.
131. *RFE/RL Daily Report*, no. 83, 3 May 1993.
132. Olcott, "Nation-Building and Ethnicity," 23; *RFE/RL Daily Report*, 3 May 1993.
133. In mid-1992 Davlat Usmon, the deputy chairman of the IRP, became vice-premier of Tajikistan. Arguing for the centrality of religion in foreign policy making, Usmon asserted that "Tajikistan should turn toward Iran, Afghanistan, and Pakistan." (Interfax, 18 June 1992, in *FBIS–SOV*, 19 June 1992, 69.)
134. Ibid.; and personal communication from Professor Muriel Atkin.
135. *Afghanistan and Post–Soviet Central Asia*, 1.
136. Mary-Jane Deeb, "Militant Islam and the Politics of Redemption," *Annals of the American Academy of Political and Social Science*, 524 (November 1992), 52–65; and Fatima Mernissi, *Islam and Democracy: Fear of the Modern World*, New York: Addison-Wesley, 1992.
137. For a discussion of governmental restrictions on the political activities of religious groups, see Chapter 4.
138. Such broadcasting started late in the Soviet period and was quite effective. For instance, a 1988 sociological survey conducted in Turkmenistan discovered that one-third of all young people listened to Turkmen-language radio broadcasts beamed from Afghanistan and Iran. The broadcasts, designed to encourage religious and national sentiment, were evidently of greater interest to the respondents than local broadcasts. (Annette Bohr, "Turkmen," in Graham Smith, ed., *The Nationalities Question in the Soviet Union*, New York: Longman, 1990, 240.)
139. During the twelfth conference of the heads of Persian Gulf Arab states, a figure close to the Saudi delegation went out of his way to offer assurances that any investment channeled into the new Muslim states would not indicate any "anti-Russian" bias but "could be an important stabilizing factor and help to end the growth of fundamentalism" in the former republics. (*Izvestiya*, 27 December 1991, in *FBIS–SOV*, 7 January 1992, 3.)
140. *Afghanistan and Post-Soviet Central Asia*, 19. For more on these parties see John L. Esposito, ed., *Islam in Asia: Religion, Politics, and Society*, New York: Oxford University Press, 1987.
141. See Robert Freedman, "Israel and the Successor States of the Soviet Union: A Preliminary Analysis," paper presented at the annual conference of the Middle East Studies Association, Portland, Oregon, October 1992.
142. Graham E. Fuller, *Central Asia: The New Geopolitics*, R–4219–USDP, Santa Monica, Calif.: The Rand Corporation, 1992, 33.
143. Evdokimova, "National and Religious Self-Identification as a Russian," 2.

144. S. F. Jones, "Religion and Nationalism in Soviet Georgia and Armenia," in *Religion and Nationalism in Soviet and East European Politics*, 173–4, 184–6.

145. Alfred Rieber, "Struggle over the Borderlands," Russian Littoral Project Working Paper No. 3, draft, UMCP/SAIS, May 1993, 20.

146. Nora Dudwick, "Armenia: The Nation Awakens," in *Nations and Politics in the Soviet Successor States*, 267; Jones, "Religion and Nationalism in Soviet Georgia and Armenia," 185–6.

147. Jones, "Religion and Nationalism in Soviet Georgia and Armenia."

148. Rieber, "Struggle over the Borderlands." 20.

149. Jones, "Religion and Nationalism in Soviet Georgia and Armenia," 191–5.

150. Tadeusz Swietochowski, "Azerbaijan: A Borderland at the Crossroad of History," Russian Littoral Project Working Paper No. 8, draft, UMCP/SAIS, May 1993.

151. An unpublished opinion survey showed that in the capital city of Baku in 1990, a 77 percent majority of respondents wanted to learn more about Islamic culture, but only 3.8 percent endorsed the idea of an Islamic republic and only about 19 percent "favored full integration into the Islamic world." (Eldar Namazov, "Taking the Path of Renewal," unpublished paper, Baku, 1990, as cited in Shireen Hunter, "Azerbaijan: Search for Identity," in *Nations and Politics in the Soviet Successor States*, 238.)

152. For a discussion of the interplay of Islamic and secular forces in this region, see Tamara Dragadze, "Azerbaijanis," in *The Nationalities Question in the Former Soviet Union*, 163–79.

153. Swietochowski, "Azerbaijan," 24–5.

154. Interlegal Research Center and Postfactum newsletter, *Religious Life in Russia* (Moscow), December 1992.

155. Robert Parsons, "Georgians," in *The Nationalities Question in the Soviet Union*, 195.

4. Political Culture and Civil Society

1. Moshe Lewin, *The Gorbachev Phenomenon: A Historical Interpretation*, Berkeley and Los Angeles: University of California Press, 1988. The term "solidary society" was coined by Gregory Grossman.

2. Vladimir Tismaneanu, *Reinventing Politics: Eastern Europe From Stalin to Havel*, New York: Free Press, 1992.

3. Michael W. Doyle, "Liberalism and World Politics," *American Political Science Review*, 80, no. 4 (1986), 1151–69.

4. The right of self-determination cannot solve such disagreements because it assumes a prior consensus about which individuals and lands constitute the "self" entitled to exercise this right. See Robert Dahl, *Democracy and Its Critics*, New Haven, Conn.: Yale University Press, 1989, 147–8.

5. Gabriel Almond and Sidney Verba, *The Civic Culture*, Boston: Little,

Brown, 1965; Ronald Inglehart, *Culture Shift in Advanced Societies*, Princeton, N.J.: Princeton University Press, 1990; and Gabriel Almond, *A Discipline Divided: Schools and Sects in Political Science*, Newbury Park, Calif.: Sage, 1990, chapter 5.

6. Giuseppe Di Palma, *To Craft Democracies*, Berkeley and Los Angeles: University of California Press, 1990.

7. Samuel Huntington, *The Third Wave: Democratization in the Late Twentieth Century*, Norman: University of Oklahoma Press, 1991, 46–50.

8. See Kenneth Jowitt, *New World Disorder: The Leninist Extinction*, Berkeley and Los Angeles: University of California Press, 1992.

9. Mary E. McIntosh and Martha Abele MacIver, *Transition to What? Publics Confront Change in Eastern Europe*, Occasional Paper No. 38, Washington, D.C.: Woodrow Wilson International Center for Scholars, July 1993.

10. Gabriel Almond, "Communism and Political Culture Theory," *Comparative Politics*, 13, no. 1 (1983), 136.

11. Contemporary observers use the term "civil society" in many different ways. For the concept's origins and contemporary meanings, see John Keane, "Introduction," in John Keane, ed., *Civil Society and the State: New European Perspectives*, New York: Verso, 1988, 1–31, and Robert F. Miller, "Civil Society in Communist Systems: An Introduction," in Robert F. Miller, ed., *The Development of Civil Society in Communist Systems*, New York: Allen & Unwin, 1992, 3–6; S. Frederick Starr, *Prospects for Stable Democracy in Russia*, Occasional Paper, Ohio State University: The Mershon Center, 1992, 5; and Tismaneanu, *Reinventing Politics*, 170–4.

12. *Elections in the Baltic States and Soviet Republics: A Compendium of Reports on Parliamentary Elections Held in 1990*, Washington, D.C.: Commission on Security and Cooperation in Europe, 1990, 95; and Blair A. Ruble, "Stepping off the Treadmill of Failed Reforms?," in Harley D. Balzer, ed., *Five Years That Shook the World*, Boulder, Colo.: Westview, 1991, 13–29.

13. Of the 1,068 Congress seats, only 33 were uncontested. *Elections in the Baltic States and Soviet Republics*, 93–112.

14. Edward W. Walker, "The New Russian Constitution and the Future of the Russian Federation," *The Harriman Institute Forum*, 5, no. 10 (June 1992); and Elizabeth Teague, "The Constitutional Debate over the Role of Russia's Regions," Russian Littoral Project Working Paper No. 14, draft, University of Maryland, College Park, and the Johns Hopkins School of Advanced International Studies (hereafter UMCP/SAIS), May 1993.

15. Anders Aslund, "Prospects for a Successful Change of Economic System in Russia," unpublished paper, Stockholm Institute of East European Economics, 30 October 1992, 6–7; Victor Yasmann, "Corruption in Russia: A Threat to Democracy?" *RFE/RL Research Report*, 2, no. 10 (5 March 1993), 15–18; Victor Yasmann, "The Russian Civil Service: Corruption and Reform," ibid., 2, no. 16 (16 April 1993), 18–21.

16. The three were First Deputy Prime Minister Vladimir Shumeyko and Deputy Prime Ministers Georgiy Khizha (responsible for administration

and personnel, defense conversion, industry and space) and Viktor Chernomyrdin (responsible for the fuel and energy complex). Elizabeth Teague and Vera Tolz, "The Civic Union: The Birth of a New Opposition in Russia?" *RFE/RL Research Report*, 1, no. 30 (24 July 1992), 2.

17. Alexander Rahr, "The Roots of the Power Struggle," *RFE/RL Research Report*, 2, no. 20 (14 May 1993), 9–11.

18. Ibid., 11.

19. According to one undocumented report, as early as the end of 1992 Yeltsin considered introducing direct presidential rule but received no encouragement when he broached this possibility with then–minister of security Viktor Barannikov. See Alexander Rahr, "The Revival of a Strong KGB," *RFE/RL Research Report*, 2, no. 20 (14 May 1993), 76.

20. For details see Vera Tolz and Julia Wishnevsky, "Russia after the Referendum," *RFE/RL Research Report*, 2, no. 19 (7 May 1993), 3.

21. Stephen Foye, "Russia's Fragmented Army Drawn into the Political Fray," *RFE/RL Research Report*, 2, no. 15 (9 April 1993), 4–5. Also see Andrei Kortunov, "The Soviet Legacy and Current Foreign Policy Discussions in Russia," Russian Littoral Project Working Paper No. 4, draft, UMCP/SAIS, May 1993.

22. Foye, "Russia's Fragmented Army," 3–4.

23. Ibid., 5.

24. Surveys showed that most of the public held the Communist Party rather than the military responsible for the attempted putsch, and the military's standing in the eyes of the public remained high relative to most other political institutions. *Komsomolskaya pravda*, 25 September 1991.

25. For evidence of Gorbachev's use of the KGB to spy on his political opponents, see J. Michael Waller, "When Will Democrats Control the Former KGB?," *Demokratizatsiya: The Journal of Post–Soviet Democratization*, 1, no. 1 (Summer 1992), 31–2.

26. Structurally, the former KGB branch dealing with foreign intelligence operations has been formally separated from the branch dealing with domestic Russian security. In early 1992 the Russian Constitutional Court blocked Yeltsin's attempt to merge the Russian components of the KGB and the Russian Ministry of Internal Affairs in a single police agency. Nevertheless, legislative oversight remains weak or nonexistent. See ibid., 30–3.

27. Rahr, "The Revival of a Strong KGB," 75–7; Amy Knight, "Russian Security Services under Yeltsin," *Post-Soviet Affairs*, 9, no. 1 (January–March 1993), 45–55; and *Human Rights and Democratization in the Newly Independent States of the Former Soviet Union*, Washington, D.C.: Commission on Security and Cooperation in Europe, 1993, 28–32. The dismissal of Barannikov and his deputy, Andrey Dunayev, was said to have been made due both to the lack of preparation of the Russian border guards along the Tajikistani–Afghanistani border, and because of the continual leaks of classified materials to parliament that were damaging to Yeltsin and his liberal supporters. Oleg Kalugin, a former KGB general, also stated

in summer 1993 that the Security Ministry had not in any way been reformed and that it was trying to regain its former power. See *RFE/RL Daily Reports*, no. 142, 28 July 1993, and no. 145, 2 August 1993.

28. After the putsch military counterintelligence was transferred from the KGB to the armed forces' General Staff, but in January 1992 Yeltsin signed a decree returning this function to the Ministry of Security. See Rahr, "The Revival of a Strong KGB," 75.

29. In February 1992 both the parliament and Yeltsin reportedly issued decrees asserting authority over the Ministry of Security. See ibid., 76.

30. Yasmann, "Corruption in Russia," 16, 18.

31. The critics of conventional political parties as sources of factionalism include not only Marxist-Leninists but also such early American democratic thinkers as Thomas Jefferson and George Washington. See Richard Hofstadter, *The Idea of a Party System*, Berkeley and Los Angeles: University of California Press, 1969; and Samuel P. Huntington, *Political Order in Changing Societies*, New Haven, Conn.: Yale University Press, 1968, 403–4.

32. Huntington, *Political Order in Changing Societies*, 398.

33. Institut massovykh politicheskikh dvizhenii, Rossiysko–amerikanskiy universitet, *Rossiya: partii, assotsiatsii, soyuzy, kluby. Spravochnik*, 1, parts 1 and 2, Moscow: Izdatel'stvo RAU–Press, 1991; Vladimir Pribylovskii, *Dictionary of Political Parties and Organizations in Russia*, ed. Dauphine Sloan and Sarah Helmstadter, Washington, D.C.: Center for Strategic and International Studies and PostFactum/Interlegal, 1992; Vera Tolz, Wendy Slater, and Alexander Rahr, "Profiles of the Main Political Blocs," *RFE/ RL Research Report*, 2, no. 20 (14 May 1993), 16–25. In late November 1992 the Constitutional Court struck down Yeltsin's attempt to ban the CPSU, allowing only a ban on the reestablishment of the old central party organs, and in February 1993 also revoked Yeltsin's October 1992 ban on the ultraconservative National Salvation Front.

34. Nina Belyaeva and Vladimir Lepekhin, "Factions, Groups, and Blocs in the Russian Parliament," *RFE/RL Research Report*, 2, no. 20 (14 May 1993), 18–19.

35. Tolz et al., "Profiles of the Main Political Blocs," 20, 25.

36. *Opinion Research Memorandum*, Office of Research, U.S. Information Agency, 25 March 1993, 12. The "none" response was distinct from "don't knows," which constituted 31 percent of the respondents in mid-1992 and 29 percent at the start of 1993. Apparently the interviewers did not give respondents a choice among the various parties that claim to be descendants of the CPSU.

37. Michael McFaul, "Russia's Emerging Political Parties," *Journal of Democracy*, 3, no. 1 (January 1991), 31–2.

38. Tolz et al., "Profiles of the Main Political Blocs," 17.

39. In a 1991 survey, respondents who identified themselves as Russian Orthodox believers scored lower on values of tolerance and were more inclined to favor authoritarian solutions to social problems. Only 40 percent of the believers expressed support for a multiparty system in Russia, compared

with 58 percent of non-believers. (Mark Rhodes, "Religious Believers in Russia," *RFE/RL Research Report*, 1, no. 14 [3 April 1992], 60–4). These results do not demonstrate that Russian Orthodoxy is the cause of illiberal political values; the highly disproportionate representation of the old and poorly educated among professed believers may be the real cause. Nevertheless, it is clear that the church's heightened involvement in secular affairs would draw increased numbers of political conservatives into national politics.

40. Decades of relentless Soviet pressure on seminaries and local parishes have sapped the quantity and quality of the religious leaders on whom the church's future depends. (Walter Laqueur, *Black Hundred: The Rise of the Extreme Right in Russia*, New York: HarperCollins, 1993, 224; Keith Armes, "Russian Patriarchate and Communist Caesar," *Religious Life in Russia*, ISCIP Publication Series No. 9, Boston University: Institute for the Study of Conflict, Ideology, and Policy, July 1992, 12). Many of the roughly 37 million Russians who identify themselves as Russian Orthodox believers do not participate actively in church life. John B. Dunlop, "The Russian Orthodox Church and Nationalism after 1988," *Religion in Communist Lands*, 18, no. 4 (1990), 295; Rhodes, "Religious Believers in Russia," 61; and Interlegal Research Center and Postfactum newsletter, *Religious Life in Russia* (Moscow), February 1993.

41. Vera Tolz, "The Media After Glasnost: Russia," *RFE/RL Research Report*, 1, no. 39 (2 October 1992), 4–9; Camille Mendler, "The Electronic Broadcast Media in Russia," unpublished paper, Georgetown University, 1992. In 1992 the liberal newspapers *Literaturnaya gazeta* and *Moskovskiye novosti* retained only 26 percent of their subscribers from the previous year. Russian government press subsidies during 1992 amounted to 12 billion rubles, distributed to both liberal and conservative newspapers. *Human Rights and Democratization in the Newly Independent States*, 36–7.

42. *New York Times*, 26 November 1992.

43. Richard Rose, "Toward a Civil Economy," *Journal of Democracy*, 3, no. 2 (April 1992), 13–26.

44. Cited in Elizabeth Teague, "Organized Labor in Russia in 1992," *RFE/RL Research Report*, 2, no. 5 (29 January 1993), 40. This statistic referred to the first ten months of 1992.

45. Ibid., 38–9; Adrian Karatnycky, "The Battle of the Trade Unions," *Journal of Democracy*, 3, no. 2 (April 1992), 48–54.

46. Amy Corning, "The Russian Referendum: An Analysis of Exit Poll Results," *RFE/RL Research Report*, 2, no. 19 (7 May 1993), 8–9. On the association of enterprises, see Chapter 5.

47. Teague, "Organized Labor in Russia in 1992," 39.

48. Richard B. Dobson and Steven A. Grant, "Public Opinion and the Transformation of the Soviet Union," *International Journal of Public Opinion Research*, 4, no. 4 (1992), 304–5.

49. Ibid., 305.

50. *Opinion Research Memorandum*, Office of Research, U.S. Information Agency, 16 March 1992, 2. Twenty-eight percent of the respondents expressed no

opinion on this matter. The level of support in Russia for a multiparty system in February 1991 was 60 percent, compared with 26 percent who opposed such a system and 14 percent who expressed no opinion. *Research Memorandum*, Office of Research, U.S. Information Agency, 3 May 1991.

51. *Opinion Research Memorandum*, Office of Research, U.S. Information Agency, 25 March 1993, 18, 23.

52. Ibid.

53. When asked whether a Communist system was best for Russia, 8.2 percent of the respondents answered "yes" and 13.1 percent said "more yes than no;" 35.6 percent answered "no" and 21.5 percent said "more no than yes." The remaining respondents were undecided. The poll was conducted by the Vox Populi organization in February and March 1993; see *New Times* (Moscow), no. 22 (May 1993), 8.

54. Of the respondents, 32 percent gave this answer, versus 25 percent who picked "a judicial system that treats everyone equally." *Opinion Research Memorandum*, Office of Research, U.S. Information Agency, 25 March 1993, 17.

55. Ibid., 14–17.

56. The legislature stipulated that in order to be binding, all the questions must be approved by a majority of all eligible voters, not just those participating in the referendum. The Constitutional Court ruled that this stipulation would apply only to the questions on holding early elections. In the event, the number voting in favor of new legislative elections amounted to 43.1 percent of the eligible voters. See "Special Reports: Crisis in Russia," *East European Constitutional Review*, 2, no. 2 (Spring 1993), 16.

57. Our generalization about support from various classes is based on the breakdown of exit poll results by educational levels. See Corning, "The Russian Referendum: An Analysis of Exit Poll Results," 6–9.

58. See the comment of Andrei Kortunov in "Special Reports: Crisis in Russia," *East European Constitutional Review*, 2, no. 2 (1993), 19–20.

59. *RFE/RL Daily Report*, no. 81, 29 April 1993.

60. Ibid., no. 105, 4 June 1993.

61. High taxes prevented local governments from receiving full earnings from their hard-currency exports. (Edward W. Walker, "The Neglected Dimension: Russian Federalism and Its Implications for Constitution-Making," *East European Constitutional Review*, 2, no. 2 (1993), 26.)

62. During July 1993, a number of oblasts and regions declared themselves republics (within Russia), including Yekaterinburg, Vladivostok, Krasnoyarsk, Irkutsk, Amur, Vologda, Kaliningrad, Primorkiy krai, and St. Petersburg. *New York Times*, 13 July 1993; *RFE/RL Daily Report*, no. 138, 22 July 1993.

63. In the election, 3,000 candidates competed for 450 legislative seats. *Elections in the Baltic States and Soviet Republics*, 115; David Marples, "The Ukrainian Election Campaign: The Opposition," *Report on the USSR*, 2, no. 10 (9 March 1990), 17–18.

64. *Presidential Elections and Independence Referendums in the Baltic States, the*

Soviet Union and Successor States, Washington, D.C.: Commission on Security and Cooperation in Europe, 1992, 103–6.

65. "Constitution Watch," *East European Constitutional Review*, 1, no. 1 (1992), 6; "Constitution Watch," ibid., 1, no. 2 (1992), 8.
66. Bohdan A. Futey, "Ukraine's Draft Constitution Meets Political Reality," *East European Constitutional Review*, 2, no. 1 (1993), 15.
67. "Constitution Watch," ibid., 11; "Constitution Watch," *East European Constitutional Review*, 2, no. 2 (1993), 14.
68. See the interview of Rukh leader Vyacheslau Chornovil in *Nezavisimost*, 16 September 1992, in *FBIS–SOV*, 30 September 1992, 33.
69. "Constitution Watch," *East European Constitutional Review*, 1, no. 3 (1992), 11.
70. Ibid., 2, no. 1 (1993), 11.
71. Roman Solchanyk, "Ukraine: The Politics of Economic Reform," *RFE/RL Research Report*, 1, no. 46 (20 November 1992), 1–5.
72. Rukh cochairman Ivan Drach sided firmly with Kravchuk. Rukh's other cochairman, Vyacheslau Chornovil, who has since become the unchallenged leader of the surviving Rukh organization, has been far more critical of the president. See Roman Solchanyk and Taras Kuzio, "Democratic Political Blocs in Ukraine," *RFE/RL Research Report*, 2, no. 16 (16 April 1993), 14–15; and Abraham Brumberg, "Not So Free at Last," *New York Review of Books*, 22 October 1992, 61.
73. Solchanyk and Kuzio, "Democratic Political Blocs in Ukraine," 16. See Marta Kolomayets, "Democratic Organizations, Parties Unite in New Ukrainian Coalition," *Ukrainian Weekly*, 9 August 1992, 1, 15.
74. Roman Solchanyk, "Ukraine: The Politics of Economic Reform," 2.
75. Kolomayets, "Democratic Organizations," 16; Brumberg, "Not So Free at Last," 63.
76. For the officer corps as a whole, the share of ethnic non-Ukrainians was reportedly 60 percent or more. Stephen Foye, "The Ukrainian Armed Forces: Prospects and Problems," *RFE/RL Research Report*, 1, no. 26 (26 June 1992), 55–60; Stephen Foye, "Civilian–Military Tension in Ukraine," ibid., 2, no. 25 (18 June 1993), 62–3.
77. Taras Kuzio, "Ukraine's Young Turks – The Union of Ukrainian Officers," *Jane's Intelligence Review*, 5, no. 1 (1 January 1993), 23.
78. Ibid.
79. *Human Rights and Democratization in the Newly Independent States*, 70; Knight, "Russian Security Services under Yeltsin," 59.
80. Knight, "Russian Security Services under Yeltsin." 59.
81. *Research Memorandum*, Office of Research, U.S. Information Agency, 20 April 1992, 12.
82. Kathleen Mihalisko, "Public Confidence in the Ukrainian Leadership," *RFE/RL Research Report*, 1, no. 43 (30 October 1992), 9. At the time of this survey, New Ukraine had existed for only about six months, and both its favorable and unfavorable ratings were lower than the ratings for movements that had existed longer, such as Rukh.

83. The Ukrainian party ratings for "a great deal of trust" ranged between 5 and 9 percent, just slightly above the ratings of the leading political parties in Russia.
84. Bohdan Nahaylo, "The Media after Glasnost: Ukraine," *RFE/RL Research Report*, 1, no. 39 (2 October 1992), 13.
85. Ibid., 15.
86. Ibid., 14.
87. Dobson and Grant, "Public Opinion and the Transformation of the Soviet Union," 304–5.
88. *Opinion Research Memorandum*, Office of Research, U.S. Information Agency, 23 March 1993, 8–11.
89. Of the respondents, 78 percent described economic prosperity as an essential feature of democracy; another 13 percent described it as important but not essential. Ibid.
90. Significantly, the head of the independent union of coal miners refused to sign the April labor pact with the government. *RFE/RL Daily Report*, no. 90, 12 May 1993.
91. *Los Angeles Times*, 12 June 1993.
92. Ibid., 20 June 1993.
93. *The Guardian*, 2 July 1993.
94. Alexander Lukashuk, "The New Draft Constitution of Belarus," *East European Constitutional Review*, 2, no. 1 (1993), 19; "Belarus," *Eastern Europe Newsletter*, 6, no. 5 (2 March 1992), 8; Radio Odin, 24 April 1992, in *FBIS–SOV*, 29 April 1992, 54.
95. *Human Rights and Democratization in the Newly Independent States*, 77.
96. Kathleen Mihalisko, "Political Crisis in Postcommunist Belarus," *RFE/RL Research Report*, 1, no. 22 (29 May 1992), 28.
97. *Human Rights and Democratization in the Newly Independent States*, 84.
98. Ibid., 19; Interfax, 15 January 1992, in *FBIS–SOV*, 16 January 1992, 62.
99. "Constitution Watch," *East European Constitutional Review*, 2, no. 1 (1993), 3; Alexander Lukashuk, "Belarusian Draft Constitution: A Controversial Step Forward," *RFE/RL Research Report*, 1, no. 43 (30 October 1992), 45–6.
100. Lukashuk, "The New Draft Constitution of Belarus," 19.
101. Lukashuk, "Belarusian Draft Constitution: A Controversial Step Forward," 47.
102. Ustina Markus, "Belarus Debates Security Pacts as a Cure for Military Woes," *RFE/RL Research Report*, 2, no. 25 (18 June 1993), 68.
103. Jan Zaprudnik, "Development of Belarusan National Identity and Its Influence on Belarus's Foreign-Policy Orientations," Russian Littoral Project Working Paper No. 21, draft, UMCP/SAIS, June 1993, 4–5; Markus, "Belarus Debates Security Pacts," 72.
104. Knight, "Russian Security Services under Yeltsin," 60.
105. In the fall of 1992 the parliament considered, but did not pass, legislation renaming the KGB, as it was still called, and giving the legislature concrete powers of oversight. See Alexander Lukashuk, "Belarus's KGB: In Search

of an Identity," *RFE/RL Research Report*, 1, no. 47 (27 November 1992), 18–19, 20–1; and *FBIS-SOV*, 6 January 1993, 41.

106. *Nezavisimaya gazeta*, 10 March 1992.
107. *Human Rights and Democratization in the Newly Independent States*, 78.
108. Alexander Lukashuk, "The Media After Glasnost: Belarus," *RFE/RL Research Report*, 1, no. 39 (2 October 1992), 18–21.
109. *Izvestiya*, evening edition, 31 July 1992.
110. See Mihalisko, "Political Crisis in Postcommunist Belarus," 28–9; and "Belarus," *Eastern Europe Newsletter*, 7, no. 14 (6 July 1993), 8.
111. Belarus had already agreed to give up its nuclear weapons and accede to the nuclear nonproliferation treaty. Moreover, in 1993 the CIS mutual security pact already appeared to be a dead letter, and the watered-down form of participation being debated in Belarusian political circles would have terminated Belarus's membership in the pact as soon as it gave up its nuclear weapons. See Markus, "Belarus Debates Security Pacts," 70–1, and Chapter 7.
112. See Radio Rossii, 24 August 1992, in *FBIS-SOV*, 25 August 1992, 39.
113. Dobson and Grant, "Public Opinion and the Transformation of the Soviet Union," 304–5; *Research Memorandum*, Office of Research, U.S. Information Agency, 7 January 1993, 1–11; and Algimantas Prazauskas, "The Influence of Ethnicity on the Foreign Policies of the Western Littoral States," Russian Littoral Project Working Paper No. 23, draft, UMCP/SAIS, June 1993. Also, a poll conducted for the European Community Commission of 18,500 respondents in Russia, the Caucasus, and the western new states of the former Soviet Union found that respondents in Belarus were the least concerned that a dictatorship might take power in the coming year. Only 18 percent expressed concern in Belarus, compared with 40 percent in Moldova, 39 percent in Armenia, 34 percent in Latvia, 33 percent in European Russia, 27 percent in Georgia, 23 percent in Ukraine, 19 percent in Lithuania, and 18 percent in Estonia. *New Times* (Moscow), no. 14 (April 1993), 8.
114. "Constitution Watch," *East European Constitutional Review*, 1, no. 2 (1992), 3; ibid., 1, no. 3 (1992), 18.
115. See Walter C. Clemens, Jr., "Baltic Identities and Foreign Policy," Russian Littoral Project Working Paper No. 24, draft, UMCP/SAIS, June 1993.
116. "Constitution Watch," *East European Constitutional Review*, 1, no. 2 (1992), 3–4.
117. Ibid., 1, no. 3 (1992), 7.
118. Huntington, *The Third Wave*, 42–4.
119. "Constitution Watch," *East European Constitutional Review*, 1, no. 3 (1992), 5.
120. Riina Kionka, "Free-Market Coalition Assumes Power in Estonia," *RFE/RL Research Report*, 1, no. 46 (20 November 1992), 11.
121. Ibid., 7, 9.
122. The intricate Estonian electoral system magnified the scope of Pro Patria's victory and of the Popular Front's defeat.

123. These included thirteen seats for Concord for Latvia, twelve for the Farmers' Union, six for the Christian Democrats, and five for the Democratic Center Party. *RFE/RL Daily Report*, no. 114, 18 June 1993.
124. Ibid., no. 127, 7 July 1993, and no. 128, 8 July 1993.
125. Vladimir Socor, "Moldova: Another Major Setback for Pro-Romanian Forces," *RFE/RL Research Report*, 2, no. 9 (26 February 1993), 15–16.
126. Ibid., 15. According to a September 1992 public opinion poll taken by the Moldovan National Research Institute, 52 percent of the respondents were against unification and considered this "extremely undesirable for Moldova," whereas 20 percent thought it was "a possibility over a lengthy transitional period." Only 8 percent thought that reunification was "inevitable." Interfax, 30 September 1992, in *Human Rights and Democratization*, 85.
127. About eighty deputies, mostly from the breakaway Dniester republic and the Gagauz region, do not attend parliament. Even so the Sangheli government enjoys the support of more than 50 percent of the deputies. See Vladimir Socor, "Moldova's New 'Government of National Consensus'," *RFE/RL Research Report*, 1, no. 47 (27 November 1992), 8.
128. *RFE/RL Daily Report*, no. 5, 11 January 1993.
129. Ibid., no. 6, 12 January 1993.
130. Alexander Park, *Bolshevism in Turkestan, 1917–1927*, New York: Columbia University Press, 1957; *Afghanistan and Post–Soviet Central Asia: Prospects for Political Evolution and the Role of Islam*, Washington, D.C.: U.S. Institute of Peace, 1992, 8–9.
131. Richard Rowland, "Demographic Trends in Soviet Central Asia and Southern Kazakhstan," in Robert A. Lewis, ed., *Geographic Perspectives on Central Asia*, New York: Routledge, 1992, 235–8. In 1989 the national levels of urbanization ranged from 32.6 percent for Tajikistan to 45.5 percent for Turkmenistan and an unusually high 52.5 percent for southern Kazakhstan, where most ethnic Kazakhs live. For a study of this phenomenon and its impact primarily in Uzbekistan, see Nancy Lubin, *Labor and Nationality in Soviet Central Asia: An Uneasy Compromise*, Princeton, N.J.: Princeton University Press, 1984.
132. Rowland, "Demogrophic Trends," 235–8; Shirin Akiner, "Uzbeks," in Graham Smith, ed., *The Nationalities Question in the Soviet Union*, New York: Longman, 1990, 219.
133. *Human Rights and Democratization in the Newly Independent States*, 168.
134. Ibid., 188. See also Gregory Gleason, "Uzbekistan: From Statehood to Nationhood?" in Ian Bremmer and Ray Taras, eds., *Nations and Politics in the Soviet Successor States*, Cambridge University Press, 1993, 331–2; and Kadir Alimov, "The Rediscovery of Uzbek History and Its Foreign Policy Implications," Russian Littoral Project Working Paper No. 6, draft, UMCP/SAIS, May 1993.
135. After lengthy debate, the Kyrgyzstan parliament adopted a new constitution in May 1993. Akayev succeeded in removing a phrase requiring adherence to the moral values of Islam, but in return had to agree that the terms of office of himself, the vice-president and the head of the

Supreme Soviet would end in 1995. *RFE/RL Daily Report*, no. 87, 7 May 1993.

136. *Human Rights and Democratization in the Newly Independent States*, 208.
137. Christopher J. Panico, "Turkmenistan Unaffected by Winds of Democratic Change," *RFE/RL Research Report*, 2, no. 4 (22 January 1993), 7.
138. *Human Rights and Democratization in the Newly Independent States*, 180–1, 187.
139. Ibid., 162, 194, 207, 223. In Tajikistan, Davlat Khudonazarov, a leader of the Democratic Party of Tajikistan, received a reported 30 percent of the vote against President Nabiyev's 58 percent in the November 1991 presidential elections. Despite massive popular demonstrations charging electoral fraud, the election commission let the results stand.
140. Ibid., 198.
141. Ibid., 219.
142. Ibid., 181; Panico, "Turkmenistan Unaffected by Winds of Democratic Change," 6.
143. *Human Rights and Democratization in the Newly Independent States*, 179, 184, 186.
144. Ibid., 210.
145. Cassandra Cavanaugh, "Crackdown on the Opposition in Uzbekistan," *RFE/RL Research Report*, 1, no. 31 (31 July 1992), 21.
146. *Human Rights and Democratization in the Newly Independent States*, 213–14, 217–18.
147. Ibid., 220.
148. Ibid., 216.
149. *RFE/RL Daily Report*, no. 238, 11 December 1992, and no. 7, 13 January 1993.
150. Bess Brown, "Kazakhstan and Kyrgyzstan on the Road to Democracy," *RFE/RL Research Report*, 1, no. 48 (4 December 1992), 20.
151. Martha Brill Olcott, "Kazakhstan: A Republic of Minorities," in *Nations and Politics in the Soviet Successor States*, 320–1.
152. Ibid.
153. *Human Rights and Democratization in the Newly Independent States*, 190–1.
154. Ibid., 190–1.
155. Ibid., 202.
156. Ibid., 170.
157. Brown, "Kazakhstan and Kyrgyzstan on the Road to Democracy."
158. *Human Rights and Democratization in the Newly Independent States*, 174–5.
159. Ibid., 174. Akayev persuaded the parliament to drop a provision from a law that would have denied the right of land ownership to individuals who are not ethnically Kyrgyz.
160. Bess Brown, "Tajikistan: The Conservatives Triumph," *RFE/RL Research Report*, 2, no. 7 (12 February 1993), 10.
161. Walker, "The Neglected Dimension," 25.
162. Stephen F. Jones, "Georgia: A Failed Democratic Transition," in *Nations and Politics in the Soviet Successor States*, 299.

163. Ibid., 302–3.
164. After serving as chairman of the Azerbaijan KGB, Aliyev headed the Azerbaijan Communist Party between 1969 and 1983. When he moved to a political post in Moscow, Mutalibov succeeded him as leader of the party. He was dismissed from the CPSU Politburo by Gorbachev, and after a time returned to become head of the Azerbaijani enclave in Nakhichevan.
165. *Presidential Elections and Independence Referendums*, 169.
166. *New York Times*, 19 June 1993, and 25 June 1993; *Washington Post*, 19 June 1993.
167. *Presidential Elections and Independence Referendums*, 77.
168. *Human Rights and Democratization in the Newly Independent States*, 101; Richard Pipes, *The Formation of the Soviet Union*, rev. ed., New York: Atheneum, 1968, chapter 5.
169. See *Opinion Research Memorandum*, Office of Research, U.S. Information Agency, 22 October 1992, 1, 8–10; ibid., 30 June 1993, 1; and the discussion later in this section.
170. Huntington, *The Third Wave*, 73, 315; Samuel Huntington, "A Clash of Civilizations?" *Foreign Affairs*, 72, no. 3 (Summer 1993), 29–31, 40; Timothy D. Sisk, *Islam and Democracy: Religion, Politics, and Power in the Middle East*, Washington, D.C.: U.S. Institute of Peace, 1992; Adeed Dawisha, "Arab Democracy: A Contradiction in Terms?" paper presented at the Wilson Center for International Scholars, Washington, D.C., 18 March 1993.
171. Dobson and Grant, "Public Opinion and the Transformation of the Soviet Union," 304–5.
172. Ibid., 306.
173. Ibid., 307; *Research Memorandum*, Office of Research, U.S. Information Agency, 4 February 1991, 1, 13, 18.
174. Among non-Uzbeks, Karimov's approval rating was 56 percent, and 23 percent expressed little or no confidence in him (the corresponding percentage was 10 percent among ethnic Uzbeks.) *Research Memorandum*, Office of Research, U.S. Information Agency, 7 August 1992, 11.
175. Grant and Dobson, "Public Opinion and the Transformation of the Soviet Union," 305.
176. On the historical background of the Tatars, see Azade-Ayse Rorlich, "Islam under Communist Rule: Volga–Ural Muslims," *Central Asian Survey*, 1, no. 1 (1982), 5–41.
177. *Research Memorandum*, Office of Research, U.S. Information Agency, 15 June 1992, 1, 5–6; and ibid., 30 June 1993, 1–2. Ibid., 12 January 1993, contains data that suggest that the same may be true of the citizens of Kazakhstan, although most of the survey results are not broken down according to the ethnicity of the respondents.
178. Gavin Helf and Jeffrey Hahn, "Old Dogs and New Tricks: Party Elites in the Russian Regional Elections of 1990," *Slavic Review*, 51, no. 3 (Fall 1992), 511–30.

5. The Impact of Economics

1. This is one of the central theses in Samuel Huntington's book, and is a development of his general view that "the future of democracy depends on the future of economic development." See Huntington, *The Third Wave: Democratization in the Late Twentieth Century*, Norman: University of Oklahoma Press, 1991, 311.

2. In 1988 virtually all of the non-Russian republics shipped at least 50 percent of their net material product (NMP) produced to other republics and received from other republics at least 40 percent of their NMP used. The only significant exception was Russia, which shipped 18 percent of NMP produced to other republics and imported from them 17.8 percent of NMP used. In the same year, none of the republics, including Russia, exported more than 9 percent of NMP produced to foreign markets, and all imported less than 20 percent of NMP used from foreign markets. Matthew Sagers, "Regional Aspects of the Soviet Economy," *PlanEcon Report*, 7, nos. 1–2 (15 January 1991), 8.

3. See *Opinion Research Memorandum*, Office of Research, U.S. Information Agency, 22 February 1993 (Ukraine), 11 August 1992 (Uzbekistan), and December 1992 (Kazakhstan). The data are discussed in Chapter 2.

4. By the end of November 1992, Russia had signed agreements to this effect with Belarus, Kyrgyzstan, Turkmenistan, and Ukraine. Similar agreements had been drafted with Armenia, Azerbaijan, Georgia, Moldova, Kazakhstan, Tajikistan, and Uzbekistan. Ukraine subsequently abrogated the agreement on 31 December 1992, and the dispute remained unresolved. In July 1993, Russian and Western negotiators agreed on a timetable for Russia's partial repayment of arrears on the substantial interest charges. See Stijn Claessens and Sergey Shatalov, "Debt Legacy of the Soviet Empire: A Bumpy Road to Rescheduling," *Transition: The Newsletter about Reforming Economies* (The World Bank), 3, no. 6 (September 1992), 1–3; *RFE/RL Daily Report*, no. 226, 24 November 1992; *ibid.*, no. 1, 4 January 1993; and *ibid.*, no. 145, 2 August 1993.

5. James A. Duran, Jr. "Russian Fiscal and Monetary Stabilization: A Tough Road Ahead," Joint Economic Committee, Congress of the United States, *The Former Soviet Union in Transition*, vol. 1, Washington, D.C.: U.S.G.P.O., 1993, 196–218.

6. The policy of shock therapy is advocated and elaborated for socialist economies in general and Russia in particular by David Lipton and Jeffrey Sachs, "Creating a Market Economy in Eastern Europe: The Case of Poland," *Brookings Papers on Economic Activity*, Washington, D.C.: The Brookings Institution, January, 1990; Jude Wanniski, "The Future of Russian Capitalism," *Foreign Affairs*, 71, no. 2 (Spring 1992), 17–25; and Anders Aslund, *Post-Communist Economic Revolutions: How Big a Bang?*, Washington, D.C.: Center for Strategic and International Studies, 1992.

7. Western specialists agree that the Russian economy is in a profound crisis but differ over the cause. Some attribute Russia's economic turmoil to the introduction and failure of shock therapy. Others contend that shock ther-

apy was never fully introduced by the Russian government and cannot therefore be said to have failed. For an analysis by an exponent of the latter view, see Aslund, *ibid.* For a contrary view, see James R. Millar, "The Economies of the CIS: Reformation, Revolution or Restoration?" in *The Former Soviet Union in Transition*, vol. 1, 34–57; Peter Murrell, "Evolutionary and Radical Approaches to Economic Reform," *Economics of Planning*, 25 (1992), 79–95; and Ronald McKinnon, *The Order of Economic Liberalization*, Baltimore, Md.: Johns Hopkins University Press, 1992. For a volume that contains conflicting views of shock therapy, see Shafiqul Islam and Michael Mandelbaum, eds., *Making Markets: Economic Transformation in Eastern Europe and the Post-Soviet States*, New York: Council on Foreign Relations, 1993. For a cogent economic analysis of the inherent failings of the socialist economic model, see Bartek Kaminski, *The Collapse of State Socialism: The Case of Poland*, Princeton, N.J.: Princeton University Press, 1991.

8. *PlanEcon Report*, 8, nos. 33–4 (3 September 1992), 8.
9. Richard E. Ericson, Paper on Russian Economy, presented at Seminar on Trends in Russia, Meridian House, Washington, D.C., 13 May 1993.
10. According to "Russian Economic Monitor," *PlanEcon*, 9, nos. 5–6 (10 March 1993), 35. *PlanEcon* calculates that the decline is significantly smaller than that indicated by official Russian figures because these figures understate the value of Russian trade with the other new republics of the former Soviet Union.
11. Whether all members of the Civic Union actually favor this declaratory policy is a different question; whether such a policy could actually lead to a market economy also remains a question.
12. The four were Vladimir Shumeyko, Viktor Chernomyrdin, Georgiy Khizha, and Valeriy Makharadze. Anders Aslund, "Prospects for a Successful Change of Economic System in Russia," unpublished paper, Stockholm Institute of East European Economics, 30 October 1992, 6.
13. Maureen Towers, "The Evolution of Banking in Russia," unpublished paper, The Johns Hopkins School of Advanced International Studies, November 1992, 23–5; Aslund, "Prospects for Successful Change of Economic System in Russia," 17.
14. Keith Bush, "The Russian Budget Deficit," *RFE/RL Research Report*, 1, no. 40 (9 October 1992), 30–2.
15. Aslund, "Prospects for a Successful Change of Economic System in Russia," 26; Herbert Levine, paper presented at the George Hoffman Memorial Seminar, George Washington University, 28 April 1993.
16. *New York Times*, 12 September 1992; *Washington Post*, 11 September 1992. The Russian price increase, however, put the price of Russian oil at only about $3.00 per barrel, which was one-seventh that of world market rates. For energy see, Joseph P. Riva, Jr., "The Petroleum Resources of Russia and the Commonwealth of Independent States," and Jeffrey W. Schneider, "Republic Energy Sectors and Inter-State Dependencies of the Commonwealth of Independent States and Georgia," in *The Former Soviet Union in Transition*, vol. 2, 461–91.

17. As part of its reform package, the Gaidar team promised the IMF and Western governments that it would bring inflation firmly under control. In September 1992, although the IMF reportedly promised to "give the government the benefit of the doubt," statements by Gaidar and Gerashchenko that Russia could no longer meet preset conditions for further IMF aid clearly portended new frictions between Russia and the IMF. *New York Times*, 15 September 1992.

18. According to first-quarter economic statistics published by Goskomstat and reported in *RFE/RL News Briefs*, 2, no. 20 (3–7 May 1993), 3; Richard E. Ericson, Paper on Russian Economy; and *Washington Post*, 3 June 1993.

19. *Washington Post*, 3 June 1993.

20. See Alexander Rahr, "The First Year of Russian Independence," *RFE/RL Research Report*, 2, no. 1 (1 January 1993), 52.

21. According to Philip Hanson, paper presented at the George Hoffman Memorial Seminar, George Washington University, 28 April 1993.

22. See *Washington Post*, 25 May 1993, for an excellent analysis of this trend. See also Ann Sheehy, "Russia's Republics: A Threat to Its Territorial Integrity?" *RFE/RL Research Report*, 2, no. 20 (14 May 1993), 34–40.

23. *RFE/RL Daily Report*, no. 144, 30 July 1993.

24. Ibid., no. 105, 4 June 1993.

25. ITAR–TASS, 19 May 1993, in *RFE/RL Daily Report*, no. 97, 24 May 1993.

26. For example, Defense Minister Grachev himself addressed a meeting of "servicemen–internationalists" – troops who have served in Afghanistan and other areas outside the former Soviet Union – and characterized the collapse of personnel recruitment within the army as "almost catastrophic." He stated that the army "must remain a force acting as the guarantor of the preservation of Russian statehood and stability in society." *Krasnaya zvezda*, 6 May 1993.

27. See, for example, Victor Yasmann, "Corruption in Russia: A Threat to Democracy?" *RFE/RL Research Report*, 2, no. 10 (5 March 1993), 15–18; Konstantin Isakov, "Brothel in an Officer's Apartment," *New Times* (Moscow), nos. 12–13 (March 1993), 16–18; and Stephen Foye, "The Defense Ministry and the New Military 'Opposition'," *RFE/RL Research Report*, 2, no. 20 (14 May 1993), 68–73.

28. *Delovoy mir*, 11 March 1993.

29. In June 1993, the Russian Government approved a draft program for submission to parliament that outlined its plans for the conversion of defense industries to civilian use. The plan, which covers 1993–5, is slated to cost 2 trillion rubles (in constant 1993 rubles) and $3 billion. There was no indication of why there was such a mix of rubles and hard currency, or of where the hard currency would come from. *RFE/RL Daily Report*, no. 105, 4 June 1993.

30. *PlanEcon Report*, 8, nos. 11–13, 27 March 1992, 1.

31. On the efforts of the regions to maximize their revenues from arms sales, see Vladimir V. Kachalin, "Defense Industry Conversion in the Russian Federation: A Case Study of Kaluga Region," *Harriman Institute Forum*,

6, no. 10 (June 1993). On the need to keep the arms trade going in order to raise money for conversion, see *Rossiyskaya gazeta*, 6 July 1993. For a general discussion of conversion see *The Former Soviet Union in Transition*, vol. 2, 681–754. Russian arms trade declined sharply in 1992, with China emerging as Russia's number–one customer. The volume declined less for lack of will on the part of Russia than due to partners' concerns about the reliability of Russian weapons and resupply capabilities, the general decline in the economy, Russian adherence to international embargoes, and keen competition from the United States, which in 1992 increased its share of the world arms market from 30 percent to 58 percent (*Izvestiya*, 16 February 1993; *International Herald Tribune*, 21 July 1993; and Stephen Foye, "Russian Arms Exports After the Cold War," *RFE/RL Research Report*, 2, no. 13 [26 March 1993], 58–66).

32. "Foreign Policy Concept of the Russian Federation," dated 25 January 1993, submitted by the Russian Foreign Ministry to the Russian Supreme Soviet in March 1993, in *FBIS–USR*, 25 March 1993, 8.

33. During the first three quarters of 1992, the Central Bank issued credits of about 650 billion rubles to other former republics. In the third quarter alone, the bank extended about 300 billion rubles in credits to the other new states, particularly Ukraine. Aslund, "Prospects for a Successful Change of Economic System in Russia," 10, 24–5. The 10 percent figure is from Philip Hanson, paper presented at the George Hoffman Memorial Seminar, George Washington University, 28 April 1993; and *The Economist*, 27 March 1993, 23.

34. In early May 1992, for example, Russia participated in the creation of an Interbank Coordinating Council of Central Banks of the ruble-zone states. "Economic and Business Notes," *RFE/RL Research Report*, 1, no. 22 (29 May 1992), 50–2.

35. The IMF's initial ambivalence about the idea of dismantling the ruble zone also played an important role in the protracted discussion of this issue.

36. In response to Ukrainian issuance of large quantities of rubles, Yeltsin reportedly issued an ultimatum to other former republics to accept the authority of the Russian Central Bank or introduce their own currencies in coordination with Russia. In October 1992, the CIS summit at Bishkek appeared to establish that five other countries would join Russia in the ruble zone: Belarus, Kazakhstan, Kyrgyzstan, Uzbekistan, and Armenia. Following a change of government in Tajikistan, the new pro-Russian government decided to stay within the ruble zone. Kyrgyzstan subsequently introduced its own currency in May 1993. The status of the other countries, however, has remained uncertain, and despite Yeltsin's earlier ultimatum Russia itself has continued to follow an ambiguous policy. Aslund, "Prospects for a Successful Change of Economic System in Russia," 15, 24–6, 29.

37. Timothy Ash, "Problems of Ruble Convertibility," *RFE/RL Research Report*, 1, no. 29 (17 July 1992), 31.

38. Gerashchenko made appeals throughout 1992 and into 1993. See "Eco-

nomic and Business Notes," *RFE/RL Research Report*, 1, no. 33 (21 August 1992), 40; and *Izvestiya*, 14 April 1993.

39. *Kommersant*, no. 30 (1993) asserted that the central banks of Kazakhstan, Tajikistan, Uzbekistan, and Armenia have agreed to join what amounts to a monetary union under Russian Central Bank leadership. Such leadership might be used to assert greater monetary restraint. But Anders Aslund, a Swedish adviser to the Russian government, charged that the Russian Central Bank had authorized 588 billion rubles of cash credits to former Soviet republics in April and June 1993, presumably in return for kickbacks to bank officials. Aslund suggested that the currency reform was little more than an attempt to cover up the missing money (*RFE/RL Daily Report*, no. 144, 30 July 1993). Stories of corruption in monetary dealings among Russia and the other new states were widespread throughout 1992 and 1993, and this decreased the likelihood that monetary restraints would be heeded.

40. In spring 1992, the governments of Ukraine, Belarus, Moldova, Kazakhstan, Kyrgyzstan, and Uzbekistan, seeking to counter the advice of the IMF, asked the Russian government to delay the decontrolling of oil prices. *Keesing's Record of World Events* 1992, 38876. In September 1992, Russia raised the domestic price of oil to $3.41 per barrel, still far less than the world price of $21 per barrel. *Washington Post*, 11 September 1992. After oil prices were freed from government control in July 1993 their price increased 2.7 times over January levels. Gas prices similarly rose 4.1 times (domestic gas prices still stood at about a tenth of world price levels). New prices were also negotiated with Russia's neighbors. Ukraine, for example, agreed to pay $80 per ton for oil, rising to $100 by December 1993. *RFE/RL Daily Reports*, no. 133, 15 July 1993; no. 136, 20 July 1993; no. 143, 29 July 1993.

41. Yeltsin, at his 14 April 1993 news conference, as reported in *RFE/RL News Briefs*, 2, no. 18 (19–23 April 1993), 2. Also see Aslund, "Prospects for Successful Change of Economic System in Russia," 26.

42. ITAR–TASS, 30 March 1993, in *RFE/RL News Briefs*, 2, no. 18 (19–23 April 1993), 3.

43. John P. Hardt and Richard F. Kaufman, "Introduction: Transition and Integration in Newly Independent States," in *The Former Soviet Union in Transition*, vol. 2, 22.

44. Sagers, "Regional Aspects of the Soviet Economy," 8.

45. Ukraine also tried to lower its dependence on imports of Russian energy by seeking separate energy arrangements with Iran, Azerbaijan, and even the Russian region of Tyumen. However, the effectiveness of such measures was, at best, limited. On Ukraine's energy situation, see "Ukrainian Economic Performance During the First Half of 1992: Not Even Pretending to Reform," *PlanEcon Report*, 8, nos. 35–6 (1992), 14–17.

46. Abraham Brumberg, "Not So Free at Last," *New York Review of Books*, 22 October 1992, 62.

47. On the technical deficiencies of the economy, see Aleksey W. Sekarev, "Die ukrainische Aussenwirtschaft zwischen GUS und Weltwirtschaft,"

Bundesinstitut fuer ostwissenschaftliche und internationale Studien, *Bericht*, no. 20, 1992.

48. "Economic and Business Notes," *RFE/RL Research Report*, 1, no. 11 (13 March 1992), 43; *Financial Times*, 27 June 1992.
49. *Delovoy mir*, 14 April 1993.
50. "Ukrainian Economic Monitor," *PlanEcon*, 9, nos. 19–21 (10 June 1993), 6.
51. "Ukrainian Economic Performance During the First Half of 1992," 6.
52. *New York Times*, 17 August 1992; and *Financial Times*, 11 September 1992.
53. Walter Popiel, "Ukraine in Numbers," *The Ukrainian Legal and Economic Bulletin* (Kiev), 1, no. 4 (April 1993), 41; and *PlanEcon*, 9, nos. 19–21 (10 June 1993), 18.
54. *Financial Times*, 24 November 1992. Kiev abrogated the debt accord with Russia, however, in late December 1992. See *RFE/RL Daily Report*, no. 1, 4 January 1993.
55. *RFE/RL Daily Report*, no. 105, 4 June 1993; and Jeffrey W. Schneider, "Republic Energy Sectors and Inter-State Dependencies of the Commonwealth of Independent States and Georgia," in *The Former Soviet Union in Transition*, vol. 2, 477–91.
56. ITAR–TASS, 10 January 1993, in *FBIS–SOV*, 11 January 1993, 31. The parties represented at the meeting included Ukraine's Civil Congress, the Ukrainian Council of Work Collectives, the Inter-regional Association of Entrepreneurs, and the Party of Slavic Unity.
57. ITAR–TASS, 24 July 1992, in *FBIS–SOV*, 27 July 1992, 50.
58. Interfax, 17 August 1992, in *FBIS–SOV*, 19 August 1992, 54.
59. *Delovoy mir*, 2 March 1993.
60. ITAR–TASS, 3 September 1992, in *FBIS–SOV*, 4 September 1992, 38.
61. "Weekly Review 17–23 January 1992," *RFE/RL Research Report*, 1, no. 5 (31 January 1992), 68.
62. Sagers, "Regional Aspects of the Soviet Economy." 8.
63. *Pravda*, 11 April 1992; *RFE/RL Daily Report*, no. 132, 14 July 1993.
64. *Nezavisimaya gazeta*, 4 March 1992.
65. "Belarus," *Eastern Europe Newsletter*, 6, no. 13 (22 June 1992), 8.
66. See the comments by Deputy Prime Minister Mikhail Hyasnikovich in *Postfactum* (Moscow), 4 March 1992, in *FBIS–SOV*, 6 March 1992, 51; "Belarus," *Eastern Europe Newsletter*, 8. Belarus received 70 percent of the radioactive fallout from the April 1986 Chernobyl disaster.
67. *Respublika* (Minsk), 11 March 1993, in *FBIS–SOV*, 23 March 1993, 37.
68. Radio Minsk Network, 31 March 1993, in *FBIS–SOV*, 1 April 1993, 57.
69. Economist Intelligence Unit, *Commonwealth of Independent States*, no. 4, 1992, 62.
70. *Literaturnaya gazeta*, no. 15, 1993. The state security minister of the "Dniester republic" goes by the name of Vadim Shevtsov, but his real name is Col. Vladimir Antyufeyev, and he is wanted for crimes committed while a senior officer of the OMON unit in Riga. For more on Moldova's

economy see the Economist Intelligence Unit, *Commonwealth of Independent States*, no. 4, 1992; *RFE/RL Daily Report*, no. 138, 22 July 1993.

71. Sagers, "Regional Aspects of the Soviet Economy," 8.

72. One scholar has calculated that the change in the terms of trade will reduce the national income of the Baltic states by 14 percent. David Tarr, *The Terms-of-Trade Effect on Countries of the Former Soviet Union of Moving to World Prices*, Washington, D.C.: The World Bank, September 1992.

73. *Kaubaleht* (Tallinn), 26 March 1993, in *FBIS–USR*, 3 May 1993, 73–4.

74. The smuggling of Russian nonferrous metals through Estonian ports was particularly significant. In the first half of 1993, for example, because reported exports of nonferrous metals (12 percent of Estonia's total exports) were three times greater than imports, it was clear that smuggling was continuing unabated (*RFE/RL Daily Report*, no. 143, 29 July 1993).

75. Dzintra Bungs, "The Lats Returns to Latvia," *RFE/RL Research Report*, 2, no. 16 (16 April 1993), 37.

76. *Lithuanian Weekly* (Vilnius), 26 March–1 April 1993, in *FBIS–USR*, 28 April 1993, 107, and *Kaubaleht* (Tallinn), 26 March 1993, in *FBIS–USR*, 3 May 1993, 73–4.

77. See John M. Kramer, " 'Energy Shock' from Russia Jolts Baltic States," *RFE/RL Research Report*, 2, no. 17 (23 April 1993), 41–49.

78. See Saulius Girnius, "The Lithuanian Economy in 1992," *RFE/RL Research Report*, 2, no. 16 (16 April 1993), 28–32; *RFE/RL Daily Report*, no. 136, 20 July 1993.

79. The Economist Intelligence Unit, *Commonwealth of Independent States*, no. 4, 1992, 100.

80. As detailed in Murray Feshbach and Alfred Friendly, Jr., *Ecocide in the USSR: Health and Nature Under Siege*, New York: Basic, 1992. Also see Graham Fuller, *Central Asia: The New Geopolitics*, R–4219–USDP, Santa Monica, Calif.: The Rand Corporation, 1992, 70–1.

81. Fuller, *Central Asia*, 72.

82. See Bess Brown, "The Central Asian States," and Jeffrey Schneider, "Republic Energy Sectors," *The Former Soviet Union in Transition*, vol. 2, 477–91 and 971–9.

83. Cassandra Cavanaugh, "Uzbekistan's Long Road to the Market," *RFE/RL Research Report*, 1, no. 29 (17 July 1992), 33–8.

84. *Kyrgyzstan: Social Protection in a Reforming Economy*, Report No. 11535–KG, Washington, D.C.: The World Bank, May 1993; Anders Aslund, "The Nature of the Transformation Crisis in the Former Soviet Countries," paper presented at the Kiel Institute of World Economies, Germany, April 1993; *RFE/RL Daily Reports*, no. 133 (15 July 1993), no. 137 (21 July 1993); and Cassandra Cavanaugh, "Uzbekistan Looks South and East for Role Models," *RFE/RL Research Report*, 1, no. 40 (9 October 1992), 11–14.

85. "Kazakhstan: In Chile's Footsteps," *Eastern Europe Newsletter*, 6, no. 17 (24 August 1992), 5.
86. Ibid.
87. "Tajik National Statistics Committee, June 1992 Figures," *Eastern Europe Newsletter*, 6, no. 17 (24 August 1992), 7.
88. Interfax, 9 July 1992, in *FBIS–SOV*, 10 July 1992, 83.
89. Martha Brill Olcott, "The Future of Central Asia," *The Harriman Institute Forum*, 6, no. 2 (1992), 8.
90. Radio Rossii, 2 August 1992, in *FBIS–SOV*, 3 August 1992, 39.
91. The other members of the organization are Turkey, Iran, Afghanistan, and Pakistan.
92. Moscow Central Television First Program and Orbita Network, 24 June 1992, in *FBIS–SOV*, 7 July 1992, 54.
93. Interfax, 3 July 1992, in *FBIS–SOV*, 6 July 1992, 74; Interfax, 24 June 1992, in *FBIS–SOV*, 2 July 1992, 73. Also Sheila Marnie and Erik Whitlock, "Central Asia and Economic Integration," *RFE/RL Research Report*, 2, no. 14 (2 April 1993), 34–44; *RFE/RL Daily Report*, no. 138, 22 July 1993, and no. 150, 9 August 1993.
94. *Vek* (Moscow), 2–8 April 1993, in *FBIS–USR*, 21 April 1993, 80.
95. Elizabeth Fuller, "The Thorny Path to an Armenian–Turkish Rapprochement," *RFE/RL Research Report*, 2, no. 12 (19 March 1993), 50.
96. Ibid. See also *RFE/RL Daily Report*, no. 65, 5 April 1993; and Richard G. Hovannisian, "Historical Memory and Foreign Relations: The Armenian Perspective," Russian Littoral Project Working Paper No. 7, draft, University of Maryland, College Park, and the Johns Hopkins School of Advanced International Studies (hereafter UMCP/SAIS), May 1993, 28.
97. *Nezavisimaya gazeta*, 3 February 1993; Radio Erevan, 26 February 1993, in *FBIS–SOV*, 1 March 1993, 69.
98. Elizabeth Fuller, "Transcaucasia," *RFE/RL Research Report*, 2, no. 1 (1 January 1993), 23; *International Herald Tribune*, 23 September 1992; *RFE/RL Daily Report*, no. 139, 23 July 1993.
99. Interfax, 23 January 1993, in *FBIS–SOV*, 25 January 1993, 67.
100. Fuller, "Transcaucasia," 21; and Elizabeth Fuller, "Azerbaijan's Relations with Russia and the CIS," *RFE/RL Research Report*, 1, no. 43 (30 October 1992), 53. On the other hand, the Azerbaijani National Assembly unanimously voted to reject membership in the CIS.
101. *RFE/RL Daily Report*, no. 14, 22 January 1993; Joseph P. Riva, Jr., "Petroleum Technology in the Former Soviet Union," *CRS Report for Congress*, 19 April 1993, 1.
102. Interfax, 12 January 1993, in *FBIS–SOV*, 13 January 1993, 58; and Turan, Baku, 24 February 1993, in *FBIS–SOV*, 25 February 1993, 77.
103. Assa–Irada, Baku, 4 January 1993, in *FBIS–SOV*, 5 January 1993, 57.
104. *Izvestiya*, evening edition, 4 November 1992.
105. Interfax, 9 November 1992, in *FBIS–SOV*, 10 November 1992, 70.
106. Fuller, "Thorny Path to an Armenian–Turkish Rapprochement," 49.

107. John P. Hardt and Richard F. Kaufman, "Introduction: Transition and Integration in Newly Independent States," 22.

6. Foreign Policy Priorities and Institutions

1. See Karen Dawisha, "Perestroika, Glasnost' and Soviet Foreign Policy," *Harriman Institute Forum*, Columbia University, 3, no. 1 (1990).
2. See Vera Tolz, "Russia: Westernizers Continue to Challenge National Patriots," *RFE/RL Research Report*, 1, no. 49 (11 December 1992), 1-9.
3. *Izvestiya*, 2 October 1991.
4. Yeltsin speech on Russian Television, 13 February 1992, in Suzanne Crow, "Russia's Relations with Members of the Commonwealth," *RFE/RL Research Report*, 1, no. 19 (8 May 1992), 8.
5. Center of International Studies, Moscow State Institute of International Relations, "The Commonwealth of Independent States: Developments and Prospects," unpublished paper, Moscow, September 1992, 18.
6. ITAR-TASS, 8 April 1992, in Crow, "Russia's Relations," 11.
7. Yeltsin's address to the Foreign Ministry Collegium, *Izvestiya*, 28 October 1992.
8. ITAR-TASS, 26 January 1993, in Alexander Rahr, "Russia: The Struggle for Power Continues," *RFE/RL Research Report*, 2, no. 6 (5 February 1993), 4.
9. M. Shakina, "Sergey Stankevich: A First-Wave Democrat Looking for a Second Chance," *New Times* (Moscow), no. 43 (October 1992), 10-14; Crow, "Russia's Relations," 9; and John Lough, "Defining Russia's Relations with Neighboring States," *RFE/RL Research Report*, 2, no. 20 (14 May 1993), 53-60.
10. *Pravda*, 21 November 1992.
11. *Nezavisimaya gazeta*, 19 January 1993.
12. *Nezavisimaya gazeta*, 23 April 1992.
13. Radio Rossii, 7 January 1993, in Vera Tolz, "The Burden of Imperial Legacy," *RFE/RL Research Report*, 2, no. 20 (14 May 1993), 42.
14. Anatoliy Glivakovskiy, "Russia's National Security and Geopolitics," *Kentavr*, October-December 1991, 50, in Igor Torbakov, "The 'Statists' and the Ideology of Russian Imperial Nationalism," *RFE/RL Research Report*, 1, no. 49 (11 December 1992), 13.
15. For Shafarevich's view that Russia's ills are due to a campaign of russophobic subversion by Western countries and domestic non-Russian minorities, mainly Jews, see *Nash sovremennik*, no. 6 (June 1989), 167-92, and no. 12 (December 1991), 124-39.
16. *Washington Post*, 8 November 1992.
17. Interfax, 3 July 1992, in *FBIS-SOV*, 8 July 1992, 42-3.
18. See ITAR-TASS, 24 October 1992, in *FBIS-SOV*, 26 October 1992, 25; and *RFE/RL Daily Report*, no. 208, 28 October 1992.
19. *RFE/RL Daily Report*, no. 30, 15 February 1993.
20. According to interviews held by Karen Dawisha and Russian Littoral

Project Coordinating Committee member Ilya Prizel in the Russian MFA, 28 October 1992.

21. Interfax, 17 July 1992, cited in Suzanne Crow, "Russia Prepares to Take a Hard Line on 'Near Abroad'," *RFE/RL Research Report*, 1, no. 32 (14 August 1992), 22.

22. *Izvestiya*, 8 July 1992, in *FBIS-SOV*, 10 July 1992, 35.

23. See Crow, "Russia Prepares to Take a Hard Line," 23; *Izvestiya*, 11 July 1992, in *FBIS-SOV*, 13 July 1992, 32-3. The presidential edict establishing the commission was published in *Rossiyskaya gazeta*, 18 December 1992. Permanent members are ex officio the Russian president (who is also ex officio the chairman of the Council); the vice-president; the first deputy chairman of the Supreme Soviet Presidium; the prime minister; and the secretary of the council. Several nonvoting members, including the ministers of internal affairs, defense, and security, also sit on the council. As of June 1993, permanent voting members of the council were Boris Yeltsin, Aleksandr Rutskoy, Viktor Chernomyrdin, and Yuriy Voronin. Sergey Shakhray (who became Yeltsin's adviser on ethnic affairs in November 1992 and was added to the council at the same time) and Yuriy Nazarkin (who was named deputy secretary of the council in January 1993) were also voting members as of this date. For Shakhray, see *RFE/RL Daily Report*, no. 222, 17 November 1992; for Nazarkin, see ibid., no. 10, 18 January 1993. The former secretary of the council, Yuriy Skokov, was fired by Yeltsin in May 1993 (ibid., no. 90, 12 May 1993). On 11 June, Yeltsin nominated CIS commander in chief Yevgeniy Shaposhnikov to replace Skokov, though as of the end of July 1993 Shaposhnikov had not yet received the necessary parliamentary approval for the post. At the end of June, Yeltsin appointed Lieutenant General Valeriy Manilov assistant secretary of the council, and Colonel Vladimir Markin head of its secretariat. See also Moscow Radio Rossii Network in Russian, 10 December 1992, in *FBIS-SOV*, 14 December 1992, 39; ITAR-TASS, 30 June 1993, in *FBIS-SOV*, 30 June 1993, 34.

24. Crow, "Russia Prepares to Take a Hard Line," 24; and *Nezavisimaya gazeta*, 10 July 1992, in *FBIS-SOV*, 13 July 1992, 33.

25. *Moskovskiye novosti*, 15 November 1992, suggested that Shelov-Kovedayev and Starovoytova had lost their positions because they had disagreed with the policies of the government in sending troops to North Ossetia.

26. For example, Interfax reported on 5 November that Russian defense minister Pavel Grachev and internal affairs minister Viktor Barannikov flew to North Ossetia to draw up proposals on management of the conflict for an "upcoming meeting of the Security Council." On the decision to send troops, the presidium of the parliament also met in closed session; and both Yegor Gaidar and Sergey Shakhray went on fact-finding missions. See *RFE/RL Daily Report*, no. 215, 6 November 1992; and ibid., no. 36, 23 February 1993.

27. Interfax, 13 January 1993, in *FBIS-SOV*, 13 January 1993, 28.

28. ITAR-TASS, 17 December 1992, in *RFE/RL Daily Report*, no. 243, 18

December 1992. The edict establishing the Interdepartmental Foreign Policy Commission of the Security Council was carried in *Rossiyskaya gazeta*, 18 December 1992. The functions of the commission were outlined in *Rossiyskaya gazeta*, 3 February 1993.

29. According to unnamed departmental head within the Foreign Ministry, quoted by Interfax, 18 December 1992, in *FBIS-SOV*, 24 December 1992, 11. Also see Suzanne Crow, "Processes and Policies," *RFE/RL Research Report*, 2, no. 20 (14 May 1993), 47-52.
30. Russian Television Network, 25 February 1992, in *FBIS-SOV*, 26 February 1992, 24.
31. Moscow Teleradiokompaniya Ostankino Television, 28 July 1992, in *FBIS-SOV*, 28 July 1992, 42; *Komsomolskaya pravda*, 29 July 1992, in *FBIS-SOV*, 29 July 1992, 28-9.
32. Quoted in Suzanne Crow, "Russia's Response to the Yugoslav Crisis," *RFE/RL Research Report*, 1, no. 30 (24 July 1992), 33; "Weekly Review 5-11 August 1992," *RFE/RL Research Report*, 1, no. 33 (21 August 1992), 73; Suzanne Crow, "Ambartsumov's Influence on Russian Foreign Policy," *RFE/RL Research Report*, 2, no. 19 (7 May 1993), 36-41. For an interesting discussion of the historical background surrounding Russian-Serbian relations, see Sergei Romanenko, "The Yugoslav Question in the Foreign Policy of Russia at the Beginning of the 20th Century," Russian Littoral Project Working Paper No. 2, draft, University of Maryland, College Park, and The Johns Hopkins School of Advanced International Studies (hereafter UMCP/SAIS), May 1993.
33. The decree is contained and discussed in *Izvestiya*, 19 December 1992. For an analysis of this issue, see *Washington Post*, 24 February 1993.
34. Interfax, 18 December 1992, quoting a MFA departmental head, in *FBIS-SOV*, 24 December 1992, 11.
35. *Washington Post*, 19 June 1992. See also Chapter 8.
36. *Nezavisimaya gazeta*, 28 October 1992. "Why are the military," an exasperated Kozyrev had demanded to know in July 1992, "deciding the most important political issues?" *Izvestiya*, evening edition, 30 June 1992.
37. The poll data appear in *New Times* (Moscow), no. 34 (August 1992), 11.
38. Stephen Foye, "The Defense Ministry and the New Military 'Opposition'," *RFE/RL Research Reports*, 2, no. 20 (14 May 1993), 68-73.
39. Vitaliy Portnikov, "Tramplin v Evropu," *Nezavisimaya gazeta*, 1 January 1992.
40. For an analysis of the political positions of the various groups, see Bohdan Harasymiw, "Transition to Democracy in Ukraine," unpublished paper presented at the Annual Convention of the American Association for the Advancement of Slavic Studies, Phoenix, Arizona, November 1992.
41. ITAR-TASS, 14 September 1992, in *FBIS-SOV*, 15 September 1992, 28.
42. Ostankino Television, 15 December 1992 in *RFE/RL News Briefs*, 2, no. 2 (10-23 December 1992), 18.
43. *RFE/RL News Briefs*, 2, no. 3 (28 December 1992-8 January 1993), 19.

Only the representatives of the Socialist Party of Ukraine and the Ukrainian Society of War Veterans came out in favor of signing the draft CIS Charter. See Roman Solchanyk, "Ukraine and the CIS: A Troubled Relationship," *RFE/RL Research Report*, 2, no. 7, (12 February 1993), 25.

44. According to a poll taken by the National Institute of Strategic Research, the Green Party of Ukraine enjoyed the support of 40 percent of the respondents, followed by 25 percent for Rukh. The Democratic Party of the Ukraine came in third. Twenty-five percent expressed no preference, and stated they did not want to participate in the next elections. No further details were provided about the poll. Kiev Ukrainske Telebachennya, 9 January 1993, in *FBIS-SOV*, 12 January 1993, 51.

45. A research poll conducted throughout Ukraine by RFE/RL in mid-1992 found that nearly 50 percent of Ukrainians expressed confidence in Kravchuk personally, making him far and away the most popular political figure in the country. The polling data are reported in Kathleen Mihalisko, "Public Confidence in the Ukrainian Leadership," *RFE/RL Research Report*, 1, no. 43 (30 October 1992), 8-12.

46. Interviews by Karen Dawisha and Russian Littoral Project Coordinating Committee member Ilya Prizel in Kiev, October 1992. See also Alexei Sekarev, "Ukraine's Policy Structure," *RFE/RL Research Report*, 1, no. 32 (14 August 1992), 60–63; and International Monetary Fund, *Economic Review: Ukraine*, Washington, D.C., April 1992, 2.

47. Nikolay A. Kulinich, "Ukraine within the European Security Context," unpublished paper, Kiev Institute of International Relations, October 1992.

48. Speech by Leonid Kravchuk, Interfax, 16 December 1992, in *FBIS-SOV*, 17 December 1992, 41.

49. Interfax, 1 October 1992, in *FBIS-SOV*, 2 October 1992, 23.

50. "Novosti," *Ekho Moskvy*, 15 January 1993, in Roman Solchanyk, "Ukraine and the CIS." 26.

51. For the history of Crimea and an understanding of its centrality in the development of both Russian and Ukrainian identity, see Orest Subtelny, *Ukraine: A History*, Toronto: University of Toronto Press, 1988; Mykhailo Hrushevsky, *A History of Ukraine*, New York: Archon, 1970; and Nicholas Riasanovsky, *A History of Russia*, 5th ed., New York: Oxford University Press, 1993.

52. See ITAR-TASS, 21 May 1992, in *FBIS-SOV*, 22 May 1992, 37; and Roman Solchanyk, "The Crimean Imbroglio: Kiev and Simferopol," *RFE/RL Research Report*, 1, no. 33 (21 August 1992), 13-16.

53. See ITAR-TASS in English, 26 January 1993, in *FBIS-SOV*, 27 January 1993, 42 for an account of the meeting which Russia's ambassador to Ukraine held with Crimean leaders. Also see *RFE/RL News Briefs*, 2, no. 2, (10-23 December 1992), 12, and *RFE/RL Daily Report*, no. 133 (15 July 1993), for conflicting Russian and Ukrainian parliamentary statements on Crimea.

54. ITAR-TASS, 23 September 1992, in *FBIS-SOV*, 1 October 1992, 37.

55. See Kravchuk's comments during a visit to Kiev by German foreign min-

ister Klaus Kinkel in February 1993. ITAR-TASS, 15 February 1993, in *FBIS-SOV*, 16 February 1993, 40.

56. Following a visit from Polish prime minister Hanna Suchocka, Ukrainian prime minister Leonid Kuchma stressed that Poland is a "strategic partner" for Ukraine (Kiev Ukrainske Telebachennya, 12 January 1993, in *FBIS-SOV*, 13 January 1993, 41). The following month Polish defense minister Janusz Onyszkiewicz and Ukrainian defense minister Konstantin Morozov signed a defense cooperation agreement covering disarmament, training, and information exchange. The two ministers referred to their two countries as "strategic partners," but emphasized that the agreement was not directed against any third country. See *RFE/RL Daily Report*, no. 23, 4 February 1993.

57. See Interfax, 22 May 1992, in *FBIS-SOV*, 27 May 1992, 20; and PAP (Warsaw), 22 May 1992, in *FBIS-East Europe*, 26 May 1992, 19.

58. *RFE/RL Daily Report*, no. 97, 24 May 1993.

59. *Komsomolskaya pravda*, 22 January 1992.

60. Interfax, 27 October 1992, in *FBIS-SOV*, 27 October 1992, 54.

61. Minsk's initial foreign policy priority, as Shushkevich perhaps wryly noted, was "pointing out where Belarus is located on the map," *Svenska dagbladet* (Stockholm), 4 October 1992, in *FBIS-SOV*, 7 October 1992, 47.

62. TASS International Service, 13 March 1992, in *FBIS-SOV*, 16 March 1992, 83.

63. Interview with Foreign Minister Krauchanka by Karen Dawisha and Russian Littoral Project Coordinating Committee member Ilya Prizel, Minsk, 26 October 1992; and Interfax, 16 March 1992, in *FBIS-SOV*, 17 March 1992, 62.

64. ITAR-TASS, 19 August 1992, in *FBIS-SOV*, 21 August 1992, 59.

65. Interfax, 10 April 1992, in *FBIS-SOV*, 13 April 1992, 46.

66. Moscow Central Television, 26 July 1992, in *FBIS-SOV*, 27 July 1992, 51.

67. *Rossiyskaya gazeta*, 22 October 1992.

68. Radio Minsk Network, 31 March 1993, in *FBIS-SOV*, 1 April 1993, 59; and Belarusian Radio, 19 March 1993, as quoted in Kathleen Mihalisko, "Belarus: Neutrality Gives Way to 'Collective Security'," *RFE/RL Research Report*, 2, no. 17 (23 April 1993), 26.

69. *RFE/RL Daily Report*, no. 60, 29 March 1993.

70. Mihalisko, "Belarus: Neutrality Gives Way," 31.

71. See Kebich's speech to local Belarusian officials in Interfax, 18 March 1993, in *FBIS-SOV*, 19 March 1993, 48; and Kathleen Mihalisko, "Belarus: Neutrality Gives Way," 27.

72. *Respublika* (Minsk), 19 March 1993, in Mihalisko, "Belarus: Neutrality Gives Way," 26.

73. Mihalisko, "Belarus: Neutrality Gives Way," 31.

74. Interfax, 28 October 1992, in *FBIS-SOV*, 29 October 1992, 54. The source did not provide any information about the age or other socioeconomic characteristics of the respondents.

75. The poll is reported in Mihalisko, "Belarus: Neutrality Gives Way," 24. Additional polls that show a plurality of Belarusians exhibiting similar sentiments are cited in *RFE/RL Daily Report*, no. 100, 27 May 1993.

76. Several of these hardline Communist and Russian supremacist groups joined together in early 1993 to form the reactionary People's Movement of Belarus. See Interfax, 20 March 1993, in *FBIS-SOV*, 22 March 1993, 83.

77. *Narodnaya hazeta* (Minsk), 3 March 1993, as quoted in Mihalisko, "Belarus: Neutrality Gives Way," 28.

78. *7 Dney*, no. 17, 1992, reprinted in *Consensus*, political monthly published by the Center for Political Forecasting, Department of Political Science, Belarusian State University, no. 5 (May 1992), 5.

79. Interfax, 25 September 1992, in *FBIS-SOV*, 28 September 1992, 34.

80. Radio Minsk Network, 31 March 1993, in *FBIS-SOV*, 1 April 1993, 58-60.

81. Interfax, 1 April 1993, in *FBIS-SOV*, 1 April 1993, 60.

82. Belarus, for example, continued to support Russian proposals for greater CIS integration long after the Baltics and Ukraine had announced their opposition. Belarusian relations with Poland, too, have been designed to serve as a bridge between Warsaw and Moscow, with Chairman Shushkevich characterizing Belarus's contribution primarily to be in promoting "the importance and responsibility of the present stage of Russo-Polish relations." ITAR-TASS, 21 January 1993, in *FBIS-SOV*, 22 January 1993, 67.

83. The Baltic Sea States Council was founded in March 1992 by Germany and Denmark to address regional issues not under the purview of other organizations. It brings together Germany, Norway, Denmark, Sweden, Finland, Russia, Estonia, Latvia, Lithuania, and Poland. *RFE/RL Daily Report*, no. 52, 17 March 1993. Estonia was admitted to the Council of Europe despite Russia's objection over the treatment of the Russian community in Estonia. It is expected that all the Baltic states will eventually join all these regional organizations.

84. Russian concerns about second-class citizenship and 'apartheid' policies, so frequently voiced in the central Russian press, have led to charges that U.S. human-rights monitoring has not followed up abuses to the same degree that it did against Russia in decades past. However, a report prepared by the staff of the Commission on Security and Cooperation in Europe indicated that although the waiting period requirement of the citizen laws in Estonia had the effect of excluding 40 percent of the population from September 1992 elections, this effect would be transitory. See the commission's report, *Russians in Estonia: Problems and Prospects*, September 1992.

85. *New York Times*, 30 October 1992.

86. See the critical remarks by Russian defense minister Pavel Grachev, reported in *RFE/RL Daily Report*, no. 61, 30 March 1993.

87. See *RFE/RL Daily Report*, no. 213, 4 November 1992; and ibid., no. 62, 31 March 1993. Troop levels had dropped from approximately 58,000 in

spring 1992 to 30,000 in fall 1992 in Latvia; from 50,000 in August 1991 to 9,000 by the end of 1992 in Estonia, and from 22,000 in September 1992 to 5,500 by the end of December 1992 in Lithuania. (From ITAR-TASS, 14 January 1993, in *FBIS-SOV*, 15 January 1993, 72; Dzintra Bungs, "Latvia: Toward Full Independence," *RFE/RL Research Report*, 2, no. 1 (1 January 1993), 97; and Riina Kionka, "Estonia: A Difficult Transition," *RFE/RL Research Report*, 2, no. 1 (1 January 1993), 91. Total Russian combat troop levels in the Baltics had declined, according to U.S. government figures, to less than 11,000 by summer 1993, as discussed in Chapter 7 (*Washington Post*, 5 August 1993).

88. See Philip Hanson, "Estonia's Narva Problem, Narva's Estonian Problem," *RFE/RL Research Report*, 2, no. 18 (30 April 1993), 17-23; *RFE/RL Daily Report*, no. 140, 26 July 1993.

89. *RFE/RL Daily Report*, no. 51, 16 March 1993; *RFE/RL Daily Report*, no. 52, 17 March 1993; and *Washington Post*, 8 June 1993.

90. For more on the crisis, see Sergiu Verona, "Moldovan Crisis," *CRS Issue Brief*, Washington, D.C.: Congressional Research Service, July 1992.

91. See Vladimir Socor, "Moldova's 'Dniester' Ulcer," *RFE/RL Research Report*, 2, no. 1 (1 January 1993), 12-16.

92. ITAR-TASS, 9 February 1993, in *FBIS-SOV*, 10 February 1993, 9.

93. *Kazakhstanskaya pravda*, 16 May 1992, in *FBIS-SOV*, 4 June 1992, 85.

94. Interfax, 20 July 1992, in *FBIS-SOV*, 21 July 1992, 44-5.

95. *Komsomolskaya pravda*, 17 October 1992. On 19 October, President Akayev did meet King Fahd, which resulted in the expression of Saudi readiness to invest in the Kyrgyz economy. The next day, before returning to Kyrgyzstan, President Akayev found time to visit Islamic shrines in Medina.

96. *Human Rights and Democratization in the Newly Independent States of the Former Soviet Union*, Washington, D.C.: Commission of Security and Cooperation in Europe, January 1993, 198.

97. *Kazakhstanskaya pravda*, 16 May 1992, in *FBIS-SOV*, 4 June 1992, 75.

98. Ibid., 76.

99. Interfax, 23 July 1992, in *FBIS-SOV*, 24 July 1992, 60; *Human Rights and Democratization*, 174-7.

100. *Nezavisimaya gazeta*, 26 May 1992; Interfax, 5 July 1992, in *FBIS-SOV*, 10 July 1992, 86. Pulatov has also stated (in an interview by Russian Littoral Project Coordinating Committee member Martha Brill Olcott on 15 October 1992) that the attack was also meant to disrupt his plans to unify Erk and Birlik.

101. Quoted in *Human Rights and Democratization*, 208.

102. See Christopher J. Panico, "Turkmenistan Unaffected by Winds of Democratic Change," *RFE/RL Research Report*, 2, no. 4 (22 January 1993), 6-10.

103. Ibid., 8.

104. Interfax, 7 August 1992, in *FBIS-SOV*, 10 August 1992, 64.

105. Interfax, 18 June 1992, in *FBIS-SOV*, 19 June 1992, 69.

106. Dushanbe Radio Network, 4 July 1992, in *FBIS-SOV*, 7 July 1992, 59.

107. For a full account of the different factions, and the transition, see Arkadiy

Dobnov, "Despite Armistice Feuding Continues," *New Times* (Moscow), no. 2 (1993), 10-13.

108. *Nezavisimaya gazeta*, 3 September 1992. The brunt of the initiative on Tajikistan fell to Kyrgyz vice-president Feliks Kulov, who during five trips to Tajikistan negotiated an agreement to introduce first Kyrgyz and then Kazakh forces. The accord, however, was rejected by Kyrgyzstan's legislature before the Kazakhs (who were expected to approve it) could vote on it. (Information from Russian Littoral Project Coordinating Committee member Martha Brill Olcott). The final document of the CSCE was signed in 1976 by countries in East and West Europe, the USSR, and North America. It contains a set of principles to which member states agree to adhere covering military security, economic interaction, and human rights. The difficulty of gaining acceptance to build such a community in Central Asia (and indeed elsewhere) has been rooted in governmental resistance to international oversight of human-rights violations.

109. *RFE/RL Daily Report*, no. 92, 14 May 1993.

110. *Komsomolskaya pravda*, 12 January 1993. See also *Krasnaya zvezda*, 30 March 1993; and Interfax, 30 March 1993, in *FBIS-SOV*, 31 March 1993, 74.

111. See Gregory Gleason, "Central Asia: Land Reform and the Ethnic Factor," *RFE/RL Research Report*, 2, no. 3 (15 January 1993), 28-33.

112. Interview with Karimov in *Liberation* (Paris), 8 September 1992, in *FBIS-SOV*, 14 September 1992, 35-6.

113. Galina Kovalskaya, "Now that Mutalibov has gone," *New Times* (Moscow), no. 11 (March 1992), 8.

114. *Bakinskiy rabochiy*, 10 March 1992, cited in Elizabeth Fuller, "Azerbaijan's Relations with Russia and the CIS," *RFE/RL Research Report*, 1, no. 43 (30 October 1992), 52.

115. *Bakinskiy rabochiy*, 17 June 1992, as quoted in Fuller, "Azerbaijan's Relations with Russia and the CIS," 53.

116. See Elizabeth Fuller, "Transcaucasia: Ethnic Strife Threatens Democratization," *RFE/RL Research Report*, 2, no. 1 (1 January 1993), 17-24.

117. Interfax, 12 January 1993, in *FBIS-SOV*, 13 January 1993, 58.

118. The Lezgins were fearful that formalizing the Russian-Azerbaijani frontier would greatly hinder, if not sever, contacts between Lezgin communities in the two states. See Elizabeth Fuller, "Caucasus: The Lezgin Campaign for Autonomy," *RFE/RL Research Report*, 1, no. 41 (16 October 1992), 30-2.

119. Ibid.

120. Interfax, 12 January 1993, in *FBIS-SOV*, 13 January 1993, 58. See also Turan (Baku), 24 February 1993, in *FBIS-SOV*, 25 February 1993, 77.

121. For more on the historic basis of Azerbaijan's foreign policy, see Tadeusz Swietochowski, "Azerbaijan: A Borderland at the Crossroads of History," Russian Littoral Project Working Paper No. 8, draft, UMCP/SAIS, May 1993.

122. Alek Rasizade, "Halfway from Moscow to Ankara," *New Times* (Moscow), no. 8 (February 1993), 7.

123. Interfax, 3 February 1993, in *FBIS-SOV*, 4 February 1993, 55.

124. Turan (Baku), 27 October 1992, in *FBIS-SOV*, 28 October 1992, 61.

125. *Nezavisimaya gazeta*, 16 February 1993.

126. For an assessment of Aliyev's likely anti-Turkish and pro-Russian orientation, see the interview with him in *Milliyet* (Istanbul), 2 July 1993, in *FBIS-SOV*, 6 July 1993, 77.

127. Interfax, 1 February 1993, in *FBIS-SOV*, 2 February 1993, 62; and *Washington Post*, 3 July 1993.

128. Ibid.

129. Shevardnadze interview in *Nepszabadsag* (Budapest), 5 January 1993, in *FBIS-SOV*, 14 January 1993, 72.

130. Mayak Radio Network, 3 February 1993, in *FBIS-SOV*, 4 February 1993, 57; Radio Baku, 3 February 1993, in *FBIS-SOV*, 4 February 1993, 58.

131. Turan (Baku), 3 February 1993, in *FBIS-SOV*, 4 February 1993, 56.

132. *Nezavisimaya gazeta*, 4 March 1993.

133. Snark (Erevan), 24 February 1993, in *FBIS-SOV*, 25 February 1993, 76.

134. Interfax, 1 February 1993, in *FBIS-SOV*, 2 February 1993, 61.

135. Interfax, 12 January 1993, in *FBIS-SOV*, 13 January 1993, 60.

136. The foreign minister named in February 1993, Vahan Papazyan, was a specialist on Armenian-Iranian relations. Snark (Erevan), 26 February 1993, in *FBIS-SOV*, 1 March 1993, 69.

137. See the sections on Armenia, Azerbaijan, and the Nagorno-Karabakh conflict in *Human Rights and Democratization*, for an excellent analysis of the conflict. Also for a detailed analysis of the historical roots of Armenian foreign policy, see Richard G. Hovannisian, "Historical Memory and Foreign Relations: The Armenian Perspective," Russian Littoral Project Working Paper No. 7, draft, UMCP/SAIS, May 1993.

138. Radio Erevan, 26 February 1993, in *FBIS-SOV*, 1 March 1993, 69. A visit by Ter-Petrossyan and other ministers to Moscow in January 1993 had produced a promise of several tons of fuel deliveries and millions of rubles of credit for food purchases. Interfax, 13 January 1993, *FBIS-SOV*, 14 January 1993, 65.

139. For details of Turkish-Armenian relations, see Elizabeth Fuller, "The Thorny Path to an Armenian-Turkish Rapprochement," *RFE/RL Research Report*, 2, no. 12 (19 March 1993), 47-51; and Armenian Radio First Program Network, 3 February 1993, in *FBIS-SOV*, 4 February 1993, 55-6.

140. *New York Times*, 7 March 1992.

141. *RFE/RL Daily Report*, no. 68, 8 April 1993.

142. *New York Times*, 9 March 1992. Uzbek president Islam Karimov has similarly noted that, for his country, "stability in Russia is stability at home." See Interfax, 15 April 1993, in *FBIS-SOV*, 16 April 1993, 39.

143. *Izvestiya*, evening edition, 7 August 1992.

144. Russian Television Network, 28 February 1993, in *FBIS-SOV*, 1 March 1993, 21. Also see Suzanne Crow, "Russia Seeks Leadership in Regional Peacekeeping," *RFE/RL Research Report*, 2, no. 15 (9 April 1993), 28-32.

145. *New York Times*, 9 March 1992.

146. *Washington Post*, 17 March 1993.
147. See *RFE/RL Daily Report*, no. 16, 26 January 1993; and ibid., no. 18, 28 January 1993. This pact apparently bore fruit when two thousand conscripts from trans-Dniester were sent to assist Abkhaz rebels. *Washington Post*, 3 July 1993.
148. Interfax, 27 January 1993, in *FBIS-SOV*, 28 January 1993, 41.
149. In fact, Moldovan officials, who blamed the Dniester–Gagauz–Abkhazian accord on "pro-imperial circles in Moscow," implicitly suggested Chisinau might consider similar pacts with Chechnya or Tatarstan. See *RFE/RL Daily Report*, no. 18, 28 January 1993.

7. Military Issues

1. The figure comes from Russian estimates of the number of Russian military personnel stationed outside Russia eligible to vote in the April 1993 Russian referendum. It therefore makes no distinction between the number of Russians stationed outside the country who are seconded abroad at the request of authorities in other states (as for example in Turkmenistan, Kazakhstan, Belarus, Tajikistan), those that are in the process of being withdrawn (as in Germany), and those whose presence abroad is a subject of dispute between Russia and the foreign state or locality (as in the Baltics and areas of the Caucasus, Moldova, and Ukraine). *RFE/RL Daily Report*, no. 76, 22 April 1993.
2. For a discussion of the special role of the military in Russian imperial life, see C. Bellamy, "Seventy Years On: Similarities Between the Modern Soviet Army and its Tsarist Predecessor." *RUSI Journal*, September 1979, 33–5; and D. R. Jones, "Continuity and Change in the Russian Military Tradition." ibid., June 1979, 30–1. For the same discussion with reference to the Soviet era, see Timothy Colton, *Commissars, Commanders and Civilian Authority: The Structure of Soviet Military Politics*, Cambridge, Mass.: Harvard University Press, 1979; Roman Kolkowicz, *The Soviet Military and the Communist Party*, Princeton, N.J.: Princeton University Press, 1967; Raymond L. Garthoff, *Soviet Military Policy: An Historical Analysis*, New York: Praeger, 1966; and Alvin Z. Rubinstein, *Soviet Foreign Policy Since World War II: Imperial and Global*, New York: HarperCollins, 1992.
3. ITAR–TASS, 22 February 1993, in *FBIS–SOV*, 24 February 1993, 21.
4. Bruce Parrott, "The Soviet System, Military Power, and Diplomacy: From Brezhnev to Gorbachev" and "Conclusion," in Bruce Parrott, ed., *The Dynamics of Soviet Defense Policy*, Washington, D.C.: The Wilson Center Press, 1990, 7–40, 355–72. Elite disagreements over the centrality of the military as an instrument of foreign policy certainly played a role in military support for the use of force in Czechoslovakia and elsewhere. See Karen Dawisha, *The Kremlin and the Prague Spring*, Berkeley and Los Angeles: University of California Press, 1984.
5. "Foreign Policy Concept of the Russian Federation," dated 25 January

1993, submitted by the Russian Foreign Ministry to the Russian Supreme Soviet in March 1993, in *FBIS–USR*, 25 March 1993, 1–5.

6. This statement was attributed to Yeltsin by several participants at a Russian Security Council meeting, and reported in *Kommersant Daily*, 5 March 1993.

7. These differences are outlined in Sergey Rogov, *The Debates on the Future Military Doctrine of Russia*, Occasional Paper, Alexandria, Va.: Center for Naval Analysis, December 1992.

8. For a discussion of the development of Soviet military objectives up to the Gorbachev period, see Michael MccGwire, *Perestroika and Soviet National Security*, Washington, D.C.: Brookings Institution, 1991; and for an alternative view, see Raymond Garthoff, *Deterrence and the Revolution of Soviet Military Doctrine*, Washington, D.C.: Brookings Institution, 1990.

9. CIS Joint Armed Forces Commander in Chief, Marshal Yevgeniy Shaposhnikov, stated that "the United States is stepping up its attempts to design a monopolar system of world administration in which it would have the decisive role.... All this, taken together, has to be borne in mind by ... Russia if, of course, it does have geostrategic interests." Radio Rossii, 11 December 1992, in Suzanne Crow, "Russia Seeks Leadership in Regional Peacekeeping," *RFE/RL Research Report*, 2, no. 15 (9 April 1993), 31.

10. Scott McMichael, "Russia's New Military Doctrine," *RFE/RL Research Report*, 1, no. 40 (9 October 1992), 45–50.

11. *Washington Post*, 11 June 1992.

12. Ibid., 17 June 1992.

13. A poll conducted in January 1993 of Russians in Russia found that 63 percent opposed letting Siberia become an independent state, even if its residents desired it, while fully 20 percent would allow Siberian independence. If 20 percent would consider allowing mineral-rich Siberia to leave Russia, it seems reasonable to conclude that other non-Russian and poorer areas, like the northern Caucasus, would hold even less appeal for Russian respondents, particularly given the negative image that respondents had of the nationalities who reside there. *Opinon Research Memorandum*, Office of Research, U.S. Information Agency, 4 June 1993.

14. *Krasnaya zvezda*, 22 July 1992. Also see Stephen Foye, "Post-Soviet Russia: Politics and the New Russian Army," *RFE/RL Research Report*, 1, no. 33 (21 August 1992), 11.

15. Articles published in October 1992 by Dr. Aleksey Arbatov and (naval) Capt. Boris Makeyev deny the islands' military value. The Makeyev article clearly indicates the diversity of opinion on this issue in the military establishment. See "The Kuril Barrier," *New Times* (Moscow), no. 42 (October 1992), 24–6, and no. 43 (October 1992) 24–5.

16. Polls conducted among Black Sea Fleet officers in January 1993 indicated their deep dissatisfaction with living standards and perceived discriminatory treatment by Ukraine. Forty-five percent of respondents were for Sevastopol's belonging to Russia, 43 percent for the restoration of a single state, and only 7 percent believed Sevastopol must belong to Ukraine.

Eighty–seven percent were for the introduction of dual citizenship in Crimea. ITAR–TASS, 29 January 1993, in *FBIS–SOV*, 2 February 1993, 37.

17. Radio Rossii, 23 February 1993, *FBIS–SOV*, 24 February 1993, 24.
18. I.N. Rodionov, "The Fundamentals of Russia's Military Doctrine," *Voennaya mysl*, Special Edition, July 1992, 6–14. Also see McMichael, "Russia's New Military Doctrine," 6; Mary C. Fitzgerald, "Russia's New Military Doctrine," *RUSI Journal* (October 1992), 46–8; and Sergey Rogov et al., *Commonwealth Defense Arrangements and International Security*, Occasional Paper, Center for Naval Analysis, Alexandria, Virginia, June 1992.
19. Aside from Russia, the other signatories were Kazakhstan, Uzbekistan, Kyrgyzstan, Tajikistan, and Armenia. Belarus declined to sign on the grounds that it is a neutral state; but it did sign a bilateral agreement recognizing Russia's military interests, and later debated the collective security treaty. Ann Sheehy, "The CIS: A Progress Report," *RFE/RL Research Report*, 1, no. 38 (25 September 1992), 3; and *Washington Post*, 16 May 1992.
20. *RFE/RL Daily Report*, no. 92, 14 May 1993.
21. Belarusian parliamentary chairman Stanislau Shushkevich, in arguing against Belarus's accession to the treaty, noted that Armenia had been the only country to lodge the instruments of ratification necessary for the treaty to go into effect; but he was overridden by the parliament. Interfax, 14 April 1993, *FBIS–SOV*, 16 April 1993, 2.
22. Ministers of internal affairs of eleven of the new states met in Erevan in May 1993 to coordinate actions to stem the flow of illicit goods across state borders, thereby showing a greater tendency for cooperation in border security issues than other areas of military cooperation. *RFE/RL Daily Report*, no. 92, 14 May 1993.
23. BBC World Service, in English, 17 March 1993 (as heard).
24. *Washington Post*, 14 May 1993; and *Los Angeles Times*, 1 April 1993.
25. A typical example was the statement in Washington, D.C., by Yevgeniy Ambartsumov, head of the Russian Parliamentary Committee on International Affairs and Foreign Economic Policy, that Russia should seek a border adjustment in eastern Ukraine where, he said, ethnic Russians feel "deceived" by their inclusion within Ukraine's border. *Washington Post*, 3 April 1993.
26. *Post-Soviet/East European Report*, 9, no. 31 (1 August 1992), 3; *New York Times*, 7 August 1992; Russian Television Network, 31 July 1992, in *FBIS–SOV*, 31 July 1992, 9. What remains troubling about these shooting incidents is that in both cases it appeared that the Baltic troops had initiated the incident, suggesting that these states or elements therein are prepared to take matters into their own hands.
27. See Vladimir Socor, "Russia's Fourteenth Army and the Insurgency in Eastern Moldova," *RFE/RL Research Report*, 1, no. 36 (11 September 1992), 41–8.

28. "Weekly Review of Events 1–7 July 1992," *RFE/RL Research Report*, 1, no. 29 (17 July 1992), 73.
29. *Komsomolskaya pravda*, 3 July 1992. The 14th Army consisted of only about six thousand men, including one understrength motorized rifle unit and some support units. Other units, including the 300th Airborne Regiment, were withdrawn.
30. Interview in *Rossiyskiye vesti*, 6 May 1993.
31. *RFE/RL Daily Report*, no. 52, 17 March 1993. These sentiments were clearly supported by other officers under Lebed's command. A poll of officers of the 14th Army conducted in January 1993 indicated that 90 percent believe the Dniester region should be given the right to self-determination. The majority (42 percent) supported its emergence as an independent state, and half of them said that if the 14th Army were withdrawn by Moscow, they would retire from the Russian army and enlist in the armed forces of the Dniester region. ITAR–TASS, 11 January 1993, *FBIS–SOV*, 13 January 1993, 47.
32. *Los Angeles Times*, 1 April 1993.
33. *Washington Post*, 9 September 1992; and *New York Times*, 7 August 1992.
34. ITAR–TASS, 8 July 1992, in *FBIS–SOV*, 9 July 1992, 11.
35. Military concern over troop withdrawals from Moldova, Germany, and the Baltics appears to be predicated not only on the hastiness of the 'retreat' imposed by civilian leaders but on the potential lack of serious analysis by these leaders of whether withdrawal is really in Russia's national security interest. General Lebed, for example, expressed the view that "I am sick of retreating. . . . For seven years the army was torn to shreds, impudently dismissed to barracks." Yeltsin's difficulty in keeping him in line lends some credence to Lebed's statement that "the vast majority of generals and officers feel as I do." Interview in *Sovetskaya Rossiya*, 4 August 1992.
36. The Latvian population includes about fifty thousand veterans of the Second World War and approximately fifty thousand retired Soviet officers, plus their families. Also see Dzintra Bungs, "Soviet Troops in Latvia," *RFE/RL Research Report*, 1, no. 34 (28 August 1992), 20. The Russians' fears of discrimination are fanned by the statements of some fervent Baltic nationalists. For instance, one Estonian political figure recently drew a parallel between the Russian civilians in the Baltics and the German civilians who accompanied the Nazi forces that occupied the countries of Eastern Europe during World War II. Just as the latter had been summarily forced to return to Germany, he said, so could the Russians who had come during the Soviet occupation of the Baltic properly be compelled to return to Russia. Interview on National Public Radio, 16 November 1992.
37. *RFE/RL Daily Report*, no. 92, 14 May 1993 reported that the Russian side in Estonian–Russian talks was still talking in terms of a final date of 1999, while the Estonians sought a speedier pullout.
38. *RFE/RL Daily Report*, no. 210, 30 October 1992. This was down from the 140,000 troops estimated to have been stationed in the Baltics in 1990.

39. *Jane's Defence Weekly*, 13 March 1993, 14.
40. BALTFAX, 15 March 1993, in *FBIS–SOV*, 16 March 1993, 32.
41. They are the Union of Cossack Armies of Russia (UCAR), formed in July 1991; and the rival Union of Cossacks, formed shortly thereafter by Communist opponents of the UCAR.
42. "The Cossacks," *Eastern Europe Newsletter*, 6, no. 15 (20 July 1992), 5–7. If the reports are true that the former chief of the Soviet General Staff, Marshal Nikolay Ogarkov, has been made a Cossack hetman, this would suggest a significant level of top-level support for their reemergence.
43. See Defense Minister Grachev's remarks during his trip to the North Caucasus, where Cossack units have been active, in ITAR–TASS, 25 February 1993, in *FBIS–SOV*, 26 February 1993, 29.
44. According to Defense Minister Grachev, as cited in *RFE/RL Daily Report*, no. 78, 26 April 1993.
45. Ibid., no. 73, 19 April 1993.
46. Article by Lt. Col. Aleksandr Zhilin, chief editor of *Armiya Rossii*, in *Kuranty*, 17 February 1993.
47. Ibid.
48. See Michael Checinski, *Military-Economic Implications of Conversion of the Post-Soviet Arms Industry*, Research Paper No. 75, The Hebrew University of Jerusalem, The Marjorie Mayrock Center for Soviet and East European Research, Winter 1992.
49. "Russia: A Gun For Sale," *Eastern Europe Newsletter*, 6, no. 14 (6 July 1992), 5; Radio Rossii, 16 June 1992, in *FBIS–SOV*, 23 June 1992, 30; Russian Television Network, 22 June 1992, in ibid. The oil and gas industry is the other major industrial sector capable of competing on the world market. Speaking before the Congress of People's Deputies in December 1992, Acting Prime Minister Yegor Gaidar conceded that Russia needed the hard currency derived from arms sales. "Naturally we don't intend to spark international conflicts and deliver weapons to conflict zones," he said, "but we have absolutely no grounds to leave this most important market." See *Washington Post*, 3 December 1992.
50. *New York Times*, 24 September 1992.
51. Interfax, 8 May 1992, in *FBIS–SOV*, 11 May 1992, 16–17.
52. For Sobchak, see *RFE/RL Daily Report*, no. 219, 1992; 12 November 1992; for Rutskoy, see ibid., no. 73, 19 April 1993.
53. *Literaturna Ukraina*, 29 August 1991.
54. See Edward F. Bruner, "Soviet Armed Forces in Transition," *CRS Issue Brief*, Congressional Research Service, 22 March 1993; and Adrian Karatnycky, "The Ukrainian Factor," *Foreign Affairs*, 71, no. 3 (Summer 1992), 93.
55. The Commonwealth of Independent States was founded on 8 December 1991 by Russia, Ukraine, and Belarus. Later in the month, the first full meeting at Minsk also included Central Asian states.
56. In its 1990 declaration of sovereignty, Ukraine had stated its right to establish its own armed forces. This was motivated by a number of factors: popular concerns about deaths of Ukrainian soldiers fighting in support

of the Soviet empire in various non–Slavic 'hot spots'; the suffering of Ukrainian conscripts from intensifying interethnic conflicts and hazing from other members of the Soviet military; and a growing desire to acquire a key institutional symbol of national sovereignty.

57. Estimate, which includes the Black Sea Fleet, provided in Rogov et al., *Commonwealth Defense Arrangements*, 39.
58. Karatnycky, "The Ukrainian Factor," 90. The statement is something of an exaggeration given that the Ukrainian government's real ability to control these forces remains uncertain.
59. According to Viktor Antonov, minister for machine building, the military-industrial complex, and conversion, in *Krasnaya zvezda*, 28 November 1992.
60. See Jan B. de Weydenthal, "Polish–Ukrainian Rapprochement," *RFE/RL Research Report*, 1, no. 9 (28 February 1992), 25–7. The quote comes from then-Ukrainian ambassador to Poland Teodorsky Starak.
61. Ibid., 26.
62. *RFE/RL Daily Report*, no. 208, 28 October 1992.
63. See comments by Moldovan presidential adviser Vadim Malakhov in *RFE/RL Daily Report*, no. 222, 17 November 1992.
64. A military-cooperation agreement, signed between Romania and Moldova in December 1992, was designed to work out a unified defense doctrine. Interfax, 17 December 1992, *FBIS–SOV*, 18 December 1992, 71. Also see Michael Shafir, "Growing Political Extremism in Romania," *RFE/RL Research Report*, 2, no. 14 (2 April 1993), 18–25.
65. "Military and Security Notes," *RFE/RL Research Report*, 1, no. 29 (17 July 1992), 56.
66. Reuters, 9 January 1992, quoted in Roman Solchanyk, "Ukraine," *RFE/RL Research Report*, 1, no. 7 (14 February 1992), 4.
67. See for example, Sergey Rogov, ed., *Conventional Force Deployments within the Commonwealth of Independent States in Compliance with the CFE Treaty and the Republics' Security Requirements*, Occasional Paper, Brookings Institution, Washington, D.C., October 1992.
68. Ukrainian Defense Minister Morozov, quoted on Moscow Russian Television's Vesti program, in *FBIS–SOV*, 12 April 1993, 47.
69. Kiev Ukrainske Telebachennya Network, 25 January 1993, *FBIS–SOV*, 26 January 1993, 55.
70. See Serhii M. Plokhy, "Historical Debates and Territorial Claims: Cossack Mythology in the Russian–Ukrainian Border Dispute," Russian Littoral Project Working Paper No. 10, draft, University of Maryland, College Park, and the Johns Hopkins School of Advanced International Studies (hereafter UMCP/SAIS), May 1993. Ukraine's efforts mirrored Russian Cossack claims that all Cossacks, by definition, were for Russia.
71. *RFE/RL Daily Report*, no. 78, 26 April 1993.
72. It had been under Russian jurisdiction until Soviet leader Nikita Khrushchev in 1954 gave it as a present to Ukraine.
73. *Izvestiya*, evening edition, 22 July 1992; *Izvestiya*, 23 July 1992, in *FBIS–SOV*, 24 July 1992, 11.

74. Ibid.
75. See "Ukraine and Russia agree to joint control of fleet," *Ukrainian Weekly*, no. 32 (6 August 1992), 1, 15; and *New York Times*, 19 August 1992.
76. See, for example, *RFE/RL Daily Report*, no. 225, 23 November 1992.
77. Ibid., no. 218, 11 November 1992.
78. Ibid., no. 223, 19 November 1992.
79. Interfax, 10 April 1993, *FBIS–SOV*, 12 April 1993, 48.
80. The opinion poll was conducted by military sociologists of 187 officers of various ranks and posts. ITAR–TASS, 29 January 1993, *FBIS–SOV*, 2 February 1993, 37. Details were not available about the circumstances under which the poll was taken.
81. Cited in Rogov et al., *Commonwealth Defense Arrangements*, 43.
82. See reports in "Military and Security Notes," *RFE/RL Research Report*, 1, no. 43 (30 October 1992), 61; and ibid., 1, no. 45 (13 November 1992), 59. It is important to note that the *Varyag* could not set sail without Russian equipment located outside Ukraine.
83. See *RFE/RL Daily Report*, no. 198, 14 October 1992.
84. Opinion poll conducted by the Kiev Sociological Center of 1,227 adults in October–November 1992, as reported in *Opinion Research Memorandum*, Office of Research, U.S. Information Agency, 22 February 1993.
85. RID (Minsk), 13 April 1993, *FBIS–SOV*, 14 April 1993, 68.
86. Moscow Radio Mayak, 4 July 1992, in *FBIS–SOV*, 10 July 1992, 70; Radio Rossii, 7 July 1992, in *FBIS–SOV*, 10 July 1992, 70.
87. Shushkevich interview in *Komsomolskaya pravda*, 9 January 1992.
88. "Military and Security Notes," *RFE/RL Research Report*, 1, no. 21 (22 May 1992), 42.
89. *Krasnaya zvezda*, 10 December 1992; and *Vo slavu rodiny* (Minsk), 17 September 1992.
90. "Military and Security Notes," *RFE/RL Research Report*, 1, no. 33 (21 August 1992), 59; ibid., 1, no. 31 (31 July 1992), 61.
91. Ibid., 1, no. 23 (5 June 1992), 56–9.
92. Ibid., 1, no. 30 (24 July 1992), 58.
93. Rogov et al., *Commonwealth Defense Arrangements*, 65.
94. For discussions of various doctrines, the threat "from the East" and relations with the West, see BALTFAX, 12 December 1992, *FBIS–SOV*, 15 December 1993, 51; ADN (Berlin), 31 December 1992, *FBIS–SOV*, 31 December 1992; BALTFAX, 26 January 1993, *FBIS–SOV*, 27 January 1993, 63; and BALTFAX, 10 March 1993, in *FBIS-SOV*, 11 March 1993, 82.
95. See, for example, Adeed Dawisha, *Egypt in the Arab World*, London: Macmillan, 1976; Samuel Finer, *The Man on Horseback: The Role of the Military in Politics*, London: Pall Mall, 1962; James Rosenau, ed., *Domestic Sources of Foreign Policy*, London: Collier–Macmillan, Ltd., 1967.
96. Interfax, 16 July 1992, in *FBIS–SOV*, 17 July 1992, 60.
97. Moscow Ostankino First Program Television Network, 8 June 1992, in *FBIS–SOV*, 9 June 1992, 81; and Interfax, 8 June 1992, in *FBIS–SOV*, 8 June 1992, 58.
98. Interfax, 11 June 1992, in *FBIS–SOV*, 12 June 1992, 82.

99. *Nezavisimaya gazeta*, 16 June 1992.
100. Interfax, 4 August 1992, in *FBIS–SOV*, 5 August 1992, 76.
101. ITAR–TASS, 10 June 1992, in *FBIS–SOV*, 11 June 1992, 17.
102. *Kazakhstanskaya pravda*, 16 May 1992, in *FBIS–SOV*, 4 June 1992, 84.
103. "The Cossacks," *Eastern Europe Newsletter*, 6, no. 15 (20 July 1992), 5.
104. See Gueorgui Otyrba, "War in Abkhazia: The Regional Significance of the Georgian–Abkhazian Conflict," Russian Littoral Project Working Paper No. 19, draft, UMCP/SAIS, June 1993. In addition to Russian mercenaries, Otyrba estimates that more than a thousand Ukrainian mercenaries were helping the Georgians to maintain their occupation of Sukhumi.
105. This concern appeared to be justified, given the unprecedented holding of limited military maneuvers by Uzbekistan in the Osh region of Kyrgyzstan in March 1993. That the maneuvers had been authorized not by Kyrgyz national authorities but rather by local government officials, was the subject of a round of diplomatic exchanges. ITAR–TASS, 5 May 1993, in *RFE/RL News Briefs*, 2, no. 20 (3–7 May 1993), 8.
106. Alma-Ata Radio Network, 9 July 1992, in *FBIS–SOV*, 9 July 1992, 68.
107. Moscow Central Television Network, 15 July 1992, in *FBIS–SOV*, 24 July 1992, 61.
108. See *Eastern Europe Newsletter*, 6, no. 17 (24 August 1992), 7.
109. Radio Rossii, 22 July 1992, in *FBIS–SOV*, 22 July 1992, 72.
110. Kazakhstan's military consists of ground forces, air forces, and nominal air defense troops and naval units. See *Nezavisimaya gazeta*, 19 May 1992. Armenia and Georgia have no navy and Azerbaijan's is small; all three have weak air-defense forces.
111. Moscow Russian Television Network, 28 May 1992, in *FBIS–SOV*, 3 June 1992, 55.
112. Moscow Central Television Network, 15 July 1992, in *FBIS–SOV*, 23 July 1992, 55. This figure corresponds to the one motorized rifle division already stationed there.
113. *Nezavisimaya gazeta*, 16 June 1992.
114. Rogov et al., *Commonwealth Defense Arrangements*, 60–4.
115. Ibid., 58.
116. *Washington Post*, 14 May 1993.
117. Turan (Baku), 7 June 1993, in *FBIS–SOV*, 8 June 1993; *RFE/RL Daily Report*, no. 106, 7 June 1993, and no. 108, 9 June 1993.
118. Robert L. Arnett, "Civil–Military Relations under Yeltsin," Paper presented to the 24th National Convention of the American Association for the Advancement of Slavic Studies, Phoenix Arizona, 19–22 November 1992, 1.
119. Lt. Gen. A. Tyurin and Lt. Col. V. Gavrilov, *Krasnaya zvezda*, 23 January 1992.

8. The Nuclear Factor

1. At its peak in 1986, according to estimates provided by Russian atomic energy minister Viktor Mikhailov, there were 45,000 warheads in the

Soviet arsenal, which had declined by 20 percent in mid-1992. By mid-1993, there were an estimated 15,000 operational warheads remaining, with a further 17,000 in storage that either could be returned to active service or are awaiting disassembly and disposal. The 15,000 figure includes 9,500 strategic offensive weapons (see Table 8.1), 1,450 strategic defensive weapons (antiballistic and surface-to-air missiles), 2,000 warheads on land–based nonstrategic bombers and fighters, and 1,850 warheads on naval nonstrategic weapons systems (attack aircraft, submarine-launched cruise missiles, and antisubmarine aircraft and weapons), according to Robert Norris and William M. Arkin, "Nuclear Notebook," *Bulletin of Atomic Scientists*, July–August 1993, 57. For other analyses of the historic and current nature of the Soviet nuclear threat, see George Quester, "The Changing Nature of the Soviet Threat," in Armand Clesse and Archie Epps, eds., *Present at the Creation*, New York: Harper and Row, 1990; George Quester, "The Soviet Opening to Nonprovocative Defense," in Robert Jervis and Seweryn Bialer, eds., *Soviet-American Relations After the Cold War*, Durham, N.C.: Duke University Press, 1991; Catherine McArdle Kelleher, "Classical Arms Control in a Revolutionary Future: Europe," *Daedalus*, Winter 1991, 111–31; William C. Potter, *Nuclear Profiles of the Soviet Successor States*, Monograph No. 1, Monterey, Calif.: Program for Nonproliferation Studies, Monterey Institute of International Studies, May 1993; Amy F. Woolf, "Nuclear Weapons in the Former Soviet Union: Issues and Prospects," *CRS Issue Brief*, 9 September 1992, 1; T. Cochran and R. Norris, "Soviet Nuclear Warhead Production," Working Paper NWD 90–3 (3d rev.), Washington, D.C.: Natural Resources Defense Council, February 1991; and William Walker, "Nuclear Weapons and the Former Soviet Republics," *International Affairs*, 68, no. 2 (April 1992), 258–60.

2. Through mid-1993, Russia alone has retained the ability to authorize the launching of nuclear weapons outside Russia, although by CIS agreement it must first obtain the permission of the other three states. It appears, however, that neither Ukraine, Belarus, nor Kazakhstan is able to 'block' a launch command emanating from Moscow. Launch preventability is something Ukraine in particular has been adamant about obtaining. President Kravchuk has claimed that Kiev does in fact possess the technical means to block a launch command from Moscow, but U.S. officials have expressed doubts as to Kravchuk's assertion. See *Washington Post*, 6 November 1992. Ukrainian–Russian differences, discussed in greater detail in the sections on Ukraine, are also affected by the issue of ownership of missiles and the loyalty of the troops stationed on Ukrainian soil who are guarding them. See ibid., 11 April 1993.

3. Former Soviet Marshal Yevgeniy Shaposhnikov was named CIS commander in chief in mid-February 1992.

4. Warhead estimates differ slightly from source to source. Also see U.S. Department of Defense, *Military Forces in Transition*, 1991; Carnegie Endowment for International Peace, Nuclear Non–Proliferation Project, *Nonproliferation Project Newsletter*, 28 July 1992; and Ashton B. Carter and

Owen Cote, "Disposition of Nuclear Materials," in Graham Allison, Ashton B. Carter, Steven E. Miller, and Philip Zelikow, eds., *Cooperative Denuclearization: From Pledges to Deeds*, Cambridge, Massachusetts: Harvard University Center for Science and International Affairs, January 1993.

5. Shaposhnikov took over command of the CIS strategic nuclear forces in November 1992, replacing Maksimov, who was removed after stringent protests by Ukraine and others that the CIS had become a tool for Russian control of nuclear weapons. Even Shaposhnikov did little to allay their fears, saying in an *Izvestiya* interview (17 November 1992) that it was "illogical" not to have the Russian minister of defense in the CIS nuclear chain of command, and that nuclear command and control must remain solely with Russia.

6. According to participants in a conference of the radical nationalist Ukrainian National Assembly devoted to the issue of nuclear weapons, as reported in *Narodna armiya*, 25 March 1993, *RFE/RL Daily Report*, no. 63, 1 April 1993.

7. *Washington Post*, 1 November 1992.

8. From an interview broadcast on "Utro," Ostankino Television, 13 January 1993, in Douglas L. Clarke, "The Impact of START–II on the Russian Strategic Forces," *RFE/RL Research Report*, 2, no. 8 (19 February 1993), 70.

9. *New York Times*, 15 October 1992. The timetable is discussed in detail in *Rossiyskaya gazeta*, 3 November 1992. Using Minister Mikhailov's statement (note 1, this chapter) that the Soviet arsenal of 45,000 warheads had been reduced by 20 percent by mid-1992, and accepting that the current dismantlement rate is 2,000 warheads per year, Russia would need much longer than a decade to get down to the 3,000–3,500 warhead range each side is permitted under the terms of START–II, unless additional dismantlement capability is added. See Robert Norris and William M. Arkin, "Nuclear Notebook," *Bulletin of Atomic Scientists*, March 1993, 49.

10. For more discussion of these issues, see Bruce G. Blair, *The Logic of Accidental Nuclear War*, Washington, D.C.: The Brookings Institution, 1993, 261–3.

11. Plutonium is produced during the course of nuclear fuel processing occurring in nuclear reactors, and thus may be extracted from the spent reactor fuel. While plutonium extracted from regular nuclear reactors is fissile, it is also more unreliable and can't easily be used for nuclear-weapons production. Naturally found uranium must be highly enriched to a level of 90 percent or more to be used in nuclear detonations.

12. See William C. Potter, "Proliferation Threats and Nonproliferation Opportunities in a Decentralized Soviet Union," unpublished paper, Carnegie Foundation Project on Nuclear Non-Proliferation, 24 September 1991; and William C. Potter and Eve E. Cohen, *Nuclear Assets of the Former Soviet Union*, Occasional Paper, CIS Nonproliferation Project, Center for Russian and Eurasian Studies, Monterey Institute of International Studies, September 1992. However, it would be technically difficult and both economically and politically costly to attempt to use existing reactors to pro-

duce weapons–grade plutonium, particularly since all these facilities are subject to inspection by the International Atomic Energy Authority.

13. Russian Foreign Intelligence Service, *A New Challenge After the Cold War: The Proliferation of Weapons of Mass Destruction*, translated in *FBIS–JPRS, Proliferation Issues*, February 1993, 11–13.
14. Vsevolod Rybakov, "Great Russia – a Myth or a Reality?" *New Times* (Moscow), no. 30 (August 1992), 4.
15. *Rossiyskaya gazeta*, 21 January 1992.
16. *Washington Post*, 19 June 1992.
17. *Pravda*, 6 January 1993.
18. For a discussion of this issue, see Douglas L. Clarke, "The Impact of START–2 on the Russian Strategic Forces," 65–70.
19. Moscow Ostankino Television, 6 January 1993, in *FBIS–SOV*, 7 January 1993, 1.
20. ITAR–TASS, 28 January 1993, in *FBIS–SOV*, 29 January 1993, 1.
21. *Washington Post*, 11 November 1992.
22. Ibid., 6 November 1992.
23. Ibid., 1 November 1992.
24. Carnegie Endowment, *Nonproliferation Project Newsletter*, 28 July 1992.
25. For a detailed analysis of Russian concerns on this issue, see Oleg Bukharin, *The Threat of Nuclear Terrorism and the Physical Security of Nuclear Installations and Materials in the Former Soviet Union*, Occasional Paper No. 2, Center for Russian and Eurasian Studies, Monterey Institute of International Studies, August 1992.
26. *Washington Post*, 2 April 1993. Many other stories circulated in the Western press in the fall of 1992 about the smuggling of highly enriched uranium into Europe, primarily from Russia, but only this incident was substantiated by the CIA. See also William C. Potter, "Nuclear Exports from the Former Soviet Union: What's New, What's True," *Arms Control Today*, January–February 1993, 3–10.
27. *RFE/RL Daily Report*, no. 201, 19 October 1992.
28. The activities of this service, plus the absolute (if not surprising) denial that any smuggling of fissile material took place, is contained in the Russian Foreign Intelligence Service report, *A New Challenge After the Cold War*.
29. *Izvestiya*, evening edition, 29 October 1992; and *RFE/RL Daily Report*, no. 209, 29 October 1992.
30. A poll conducted by the Kiev Sociological Center of 1,227 adults in October–November 1992, replicating a similar poll conducted in December 1991–January 1992. *Opinion Research Memorandum*, Office of Research, U.S. Information Agency, 22 February 1993.
31. Quoted in *Izvestiya*, evening edition, 26 May 1992.
32. *Washington Post*, 6 November 1992. This statement was made before South Africa, unilaterally and without seeking compensation, renounced its nuclear weapons.
33. Ibid., 3 June 1993.
34. One Ukrainian people's deputy, for example, castigated fellow parliamentarians favoring denuclearization, telling them that "no one [takes] a non-

nuclear country seriously." *Pravda Ukrainy*, 10 April 1992, in Roman Solchanyk, "Ukraine and Russia: The Politics of Independence," *RFE/RL Research Report*, 1, no. 19 (8 May 1992), 16.

35. TASS, 12 March 1992, in *FBIS–SOV*, 13 March 1992, 1; *New York Times*, 13 March 1992.
36. *Washington Post*, 29 April 1992.
37. Ibid., 5 November 1992.
38. *New York Times*, 13 November 1992; *RFE/RL Daily Report*, no. 218, 11 November 1992.
39. Quoted in Roman Solchanyk, "Ukraine's Search for Security," *RFE/RL Research Report*, 2, no. 21 (21 May 1993), 6.
40. *RFE/RL Daily Report*, no. 209, 29 October 1992.
41. *New York Times*, 13 November 1992.
42. *Washington Post*, 6 November 1992.
43. *New York Times*, 13 November 1992.
44. See *RFE/RL Daily Report*, no. 195, 9 October 1992; no. 196, 12 October 1992; and no. 197, 13 October 1992.
45. *Washington Post*, 6 November 1992.
46. Ibid., 11 April 1993.
47. For U.S. and Russian statements concerning Ukrainian efforts to obtain operational control of some nuclear missiles, see *Washington Post*, 3 June 1993; and *Sevodnya*, 8 June 1993, in *Current Digest of the Post–Soviet Press*, 45, no. 23, 14. The Ukrainian ambassador's statement is reported in the *New York Times*, 11 February 1993. Kuchma's statement was reported in the same *Sevodnya* article and in the *Financial Times*, 4 June 1993.
48. As quoted in Bohdan Nahaylo, "The Shaping of Ukrainian Attitudes toward Nuclear Arms," *RFE/RL Research Report*, 2, no. 8 (19 February 1993), 41.
49. *New York Times*, 11 February 1993; *RFE/RL Daily Report*, no. 143, 29 July 1993.
50. *Krasnaya zvezda*, 16 July 1992.
51. "Military and Security Notes," *RFE/RL Research Report*, 1, no. 20 (15 May 1992), 26; *Nuclear Proliferation Status Report*, report published by the Nuclear Non-Proliferation Project, July 1992, 2.
52. *RFE/RL Daily Report*, no. 198, 14 October 1992; no. 207, 27 October 1992.
53. Ibid., no. 196, 12 October 1992; no. 197, 13 October 1992.
54. Cited in John W. R. Lepingwell, "Ukraine, Russia, and the Control of Nuclear Weapons," *RFE/RL Research Report*, 2, no. 8 (19 February 1993), 17.
55. Interfax, 1 July 1992, in *FBIS–SOV*, 2 July 1992, 2; "Military and Security Notes," *RFE/RL Research Report*, 1, no. 23 (5 June 1992), 57.
56. Quoted in Kathleen Mihalisko, "Belarus: Neutrality Gives Way to 'Collective Security'," *RFE/RL Research Report*, 2, no. 17 (23 April 1993), 27.
57. Concerning transfer of nuclear weapons to Russia for destruction, then-

Acting Defense Minister Pyotr Chaus said on 15 March that there was "totally insufficient information about the place and method of destruction" of these arms. See Douglas L. Clarke, "Uproar Over Nuclear Weapons," *RFE/RL Research Report*, 1, no. 13 (27 March 1992), 51.

58. *New York Times*, 5 February 1993.
59. Potter and Cohen, *Nuclear Profiles of the Soviet Successor States*. Also see John W. R. Lepingwell, "Kazakhstan and Nuclear Weapons," *RFE/RL Research Report*, 2, no. 8 (19 February 1993), 59–61.
60. Ibid.
61. See Murray Feshbach and Alfred Friendly, Jr., *Ecocide In the USSR: Health and Nature Under Siege*, New York: Basic, 1992.
62. Interfax, 25 May 1992, in *FBIS–SOV*, 27 May 1992, 2.
63. Woolf, "Nuclear Weapons in the Former Soviet Union," 6.
64. *Washington Post*, 20 May 1992.
65. Ibid., 22 March 1992.
66. Blair, *Logic of Accidental Nuclear War*, 63.
67. ITAR–TASS, 16 July 1992, in *FBIS–SOV*, 17 July 1992, 57.
68. Interfax, 17 July 1992, in *FBIS–SOV*, 20 July 1992, 55.
69. *Washington Post*, 6 May 1992.
70. Ibid., 18 May 1992.
71. Interfax, 25 May 1992, in *FBIS–SOV*, 27 May 1992, 2.
72. In a poll conducted by the Republic Center of Public Opinion and Market Research in Almaty in August 1992, interviewing 1,180 adults, in a nationally representative group: 447 were Kazakh, 450 Russian, 717 urban, 463 rural. The Kazakhs expressed the strongest positive view in favor of retention of nuclear weapons, with 43 percent for, 35 percent against, and 22 percent "don't know." Only 33 percent of the Russians supported nuclear status, 50 percent were opposed, and the remainder were "don't know." *Opinion Research Memorandum*, Office of Research, U.S. Information Agency, December 1992.
73. Moderate Russian officials having voiced Russian territorial claims on northern Kazakhstan include former Moscow mayor Gavriil Popov, St. Petersburg mayor Anatoliy Sobchak, and Aleksey Surkov, a member of the Russian Parliamentary Committee on International Affairs and Foreign Economic Policy. For their statements, see respectively *RFE/RL Daily Report*, no. 163, 28 August 1991; Interfax, 9 April 1992, in *FBIS–SOV*, 10 April 1992, 31; and *Rossiyskaya gazeta*, 12 June 1992.
74. *RFE/RL Daily Report*, no. 162, 27 August 1991; Moscow All-Union Radio-1 Network, 29 August 1991, in *FBIS–SOV*, 30 August 1991, 125.
75. Tokyo NHK Television, 1 May 1992, in *FBIS–SOV*, 4 May 1992, 47; Interfax, 25 May 1992, in *FBIS–SOV*, 27 May 1992, 2.
76. *Washington Post*, 6 May 1992.
77. *RFE/RL Daily Report*, no. 41, 28 February 1992.
78. Edith M. Lederer, Associated Press, 30 April 1992; "West's Recognition of Nuclear Republics Eyed," *Kuranty*, 7 May 1992; "Testimony by Robert Gates, Director of Central Intelligence and Gordon Oehler, Director of Central Intelligence Center for Non-Proliferation," *Non-Proliferation of*

Weapons of Mass Destruction and Regulatory Improvement Act of 1992, Hearings before the House Banking Committee, U.S. House of Representatives, 102d Congress, 2d Sess., 8 May 1992, all cited in Carnegie Endowment for International Peace, *Nonproliferation Project Newsletter*, 28 July 1992, 8.
79. Lepingwell, "Kazakhstan and Nuclear Weapons," 59.
80. Interfax, 25 January 1993, in *FBIS–SOV*, 26 January 1993, 6.
81. Presidential adviser Burkutbay Ayagonov, for example, noted that Kazakhstan's inherited nuclear arsenal had made it "an equal among other sovereign states," *RFE/RL Daily Report*, no. 41, 28 February 1992.
82. *RFE/RL Daily Report*, no. 221, 16 November 1992.
83. Bukharin, *The Threat of Nuclear Terrorism*, 1–2.
84. Ibid., 16.
85. All India Radio Network, 18 March 1992, in *FBIS–Near East and South Asia*, 19 March 1992, 34.
86. Interfax, 6 August 1992, in *FBIS–SOV*, 7 August 1992, 76.
87. Interfax, 18 July 1992, in *FBIS–SOV*, 21 July 1992, 46.
88. ITAR–TASS, 5 April 1993, in *RFE/RL Daily Report*, no. 66, 6 April 1993. The report noted finding 8 million tons of highly radioactive waste and another 225 million tons of less radioactive material. While it is possible that uranium-mining byproducts could produce such large quantities of less radioactive materials, the figure of 8 million tons of highly radioactive waste is probably wrong, not least because all high-level nuclear wastes are in Russia.
89. *The Economist*, 3 April 1993, 52.
90. *Washington Post*, 30 May 1993.
91. One Western argument that a nuclear-armed Ukraine best serves Western security interests by deterring Russian aggression is found in John Mearsheimer, "The Case for a Ukrainian Nuclear Deterrent," *Foreign Affairs*, 72, no. 3 (Summer 1993), 50–66.

Conclusion

1. Theda Skocpol, *States and Social Revolutions: A Comparative Analysis of France, Russia, and China*, Cambridge University Press, 1979; Peter Murrell, *The Nature of Socialist Economies*, Princeton, N.J.: Princeton University Press, 1990.
2. Joseph Rothschild, *East Central Europe Between the Two World Wars*, Seattle: University of Washington Press, 1983, chapter 1; Rupert Emerson, *From Empire to Nation: The Rise to Self-Assertion of Asian and African Peoples*, Boston: Beacon, 1960, chapter 15; Larry Diamond, Juan J. Linz, and Seymour Martin Lipset, eds., *Politics in Developing Countries: Comparing Experiences with Democracy*, Boulder, Colo.: Lynne Rienner, 1990.
3. See Joseph Joffe, "The New Europe: Yesterday's Ghosts," *Foreign Affairs*, 72, no. 1 (1992–3), 28–44.
4. Rajan Menon and Henri J. Barkey, "The Transformation of Central Asia: Implications for Regional and International Security," *Survival*, 34, no. 4

(Winter 1992–3), 81–2. For a discussion of the "great game" in both its original nineteenth-century meaning and its twentieth-century application under Soviet rule, see Alvin Z. Rubinstein, ed., *The Great Game: Rivalry in the Persian Gulf and South Asia*, New York: Praeger, 1983.

5. J. Richard Walsh, "China and the New Geopolitics of Central Asia," *Asian Survey*, 33, no. 3 (March 1993), 272–84.

6. Gerald Segal, "China and the Disintegration of the Soviet Union," *Asian Survey*, 32, no. 9 (September 1992), 864. For an analysis of the limits of this change with respect to potential military conflicts involving North Korea, see Hung P. Nguyen, "Russia and China: The Genesis of an Eastern Rapallo," *Asian Survey*, 33, no. 3 (March 1993), 299–300.

7. Two nuanced expressions of this point of view can be found in Bernard Lewis, "The Return of Islam," in Michael Curtis, ed., *The Middle East Reader*, New Brunswick, N.J.: Transaction, 1986, 82; and Daniel Pipes, "Understanding Islam in Politics," ibid., 88. For a contrary point of view, see Edward Mortimer, *Faith and Power: The Politics of Islam*, New York: Random House, 1982, 396–407.

8. For a provocative example of this approach, see Samuel Huntington, "The Clash of Civilizations?" *Foreign Affairs*, 72, no. 3 (Summer 1993), 29–35, 39–42.

9. This intellectual failing has a close analogue in some Western studies of Soviet politics during the post-Stalin era. During the 1960s and 1970s a fixation on an allegedly immutable Communist ideology prevented some observers from detecting the appearance of new currents of thought within the political elite. These new currents contributed to the rise of a radical reformist wing inside the Communist Party and to the liberalization from above that ultimately led to the USSR's collapse.

10. Thus, for instance, for many years the Roman Catholic hierarchy refused to condemn authoritarian regimes in Spain, Portugal, and Latin America. In the 1960s and 1970s the church's stance underwent a fundamental reversal that contributed substantially to the ensuing wave of democratization in the Latin American countries. (Samuel Huntington, *The Third Wave: Democratization in the Late Twentieth Century*, Norman: University of Oklahoma Press, 1991, 74–84.) For the parallel between the reformist trend in Islam and in the Catholic church, see Robin Wright, "Islam, Democracy and the West," *Foreign Affairs*, 71, no. 3 (Summer 1992), 131–45. As noted in Chapter 4, in present-day Russia adherence to Russian Orthodoxy is correlated with a heightened tendency to favor political authoritarianism.

11. This is the approach applied by Samuel Huntington in *The Third Wave*.

12. As discussed in Anders Aslund, "The Nature of the Transformation Crisis in the Former Soviet Countries," paper presented at the Kiel Institute of World Economies, Germany, April 1993.

13. See the opinion survey result reported by Reuters, 24 August 1993.

14. Geographical contiguity is a key factor in the internal dynamics of empires and in the process of imperial collapse, partly because it allows for the emergence of "interperipheral ties and the potential for solidarity among

the empire's manifold regional elites." (Alexander Motyl, "From Imperial Decay to Imperial Collapse: The Fall of the Soviet Empire in Comparative Perspective," in Richard L. Rudolph and David F. Good, eds., *Nationalism and Empire: The Habsburg Empire and the Soviet Union*, New York: St. Martin's, 1992, 19.)

15. For a comparative historical study of the impact of such competition, see Paul Kennedy, *The Rise and Fall of the Great Powers: Economic Change and Military Conflict from 1500 to 2000*, New York: Random House, 1987. See also the discussion in Motyl, "From Imperial Decay to Imperial Collapse."

16. Bruce Parrott, *Politics and Technology in the Soviet Union*, Cambridge, Mass.: MIT Press, 1983.

17. Kennedy, *The Rise and Fall of the Great Powers*, 215–18; Dankwart Rustow, "The Military: Turkey," and Robert E. Ward and Dankwart A. Rustow, "Conclusion," in Robert E. Ward and Dankwart A. Rustow, eds., *Political Modernization in Japan and Turkey*, Princeton, N.J.: Princeton University Press, 1964, 353–5, 434–58; William McNeill, *The Pursuit of Power: Technology, Armed Force, and Society since A.D. 1000*, Chicago: University of Chicago Press, 1982, 147.

18. Motyl, "From Imperial Decay to Imperial Collapse," 32, suggests that in the collapse of empires, revolutionary social transformations initiated by the imperial state itself are the functional equivalent of war. However, in some cases, the political effects of these two kinds of systemic shock may be quite different.

19. Z. A. B. Zeman, *The Break-Up of the Habsburg Empire, 1914–1918: A Study in National and Social Revolutions*, New York: Oxford University Press, 1961; Bernard Lewis, *The Emergence of Modern Turkey*, New York: Oxford University Press, 1967, 237–8.

20. The Afghanistan conflict did demoralize many people and contribute to the growth of antimilitarism in Soviet society, but its direct effect on society was incomparably smaller than that, say, of World War I, and responsibility for losing the war did not play a central part in subsequent debates over whether to maintain or abolish the Soviet state.

21. John-Paul Himka, "Nationality Problems in the Habsburg Monarchy and the Soviet Union: The Perspective of History," in *Nationalism and Empire*, 89. Also see Hugh Seton-Watson, "Russian Nationalism in Historical Perspective," in Robert Conquest, *The Last Empire: Nationality and the Soviet Future*, Stanford, Calif.: Hoover Institution Press, 1986, 14–30.

22. Although there were those within the Young Turk movement who looked to Ottoman successes in forging a vast empire, the dominant trend, under Mustafa Kemal Ataturk, was thoroughly to reject Ottoman culture and institutions. See James A. Bill and Robert Springborg, *Politics in the Middle East*, New York: HarperCollins, 1990, 181–7.

23. See Arthur Goldschmidt, Jr., *A Concise History of the Middle East*, Boulder, Colo.: Westview, 1991, 198–208.

24. Ibid., 174; and Lewis, *The Emergence of Modern Turkey*, 343–54.
25. We are grateful to Professor Muriel Atkin for bringing these points to our attention.
26. On the background of the development of Hungarian nationalism, see Tofik M. Islamov, "From *Natio Hungarica* to Hungarian Nation," in *Nationalism and Empire*, 159–84.
27. See the section on the influence of the legacy of St. Stephen in Karen Dawisha, *Eastern Europe, Gorbachev and Reform: The Great Challenge*, Cambridge University Press, 1990, 55–9.
28. Fritz Stern, *The Politics of Cultural Despair: A Study in the Rise of the Germanic Ideology*, Berkeley and Los Angeles: University of California Press, 1961.
29. See M. Rainer Lepsius, "From Fragmented Party Democracy to Government by Emergency Decree and National Socialist Takeover: Germany," in Juan J. Linz and Alfred Stepan, eds., *The Breakdown of Democratic Regimes: Europe*, Baltimore, Md.: Johns Hopkins University Press, 1978, 34–79.
30. Giuseppe Di Palma, *To Craft Democracies*, Berkeley and Los Angeles: University of California Press, 1990.
31. Michael Mandelbaum, "Coup de Grace: The End of the Soviet Union," *Foreign Affairs*, 71, no. 1 (1992), 181–3.
32. Thus, for instance, secret voting in legislative elections was not adopted in Britain until 1872, in the United States until 1884, and in France until 1913. Most democratic countries denied women the right to vote in national elections until the second decade of the twentieth century; in France this basic political right was established for women only after World War II, and in Switzerland only in 1971. (Robert Dahl, *Democracy and Its Critics*, New Haven, Conn.: Yale University Press, 1989, 234–5.)
33. Juan Linz, *The Breakdown of Democratic Regimes: Crisis, Breakdown, and Reequilibration*, Baltimore, Md.: Johns Hopkins University Press, 1978, 18. The observation that the positive contemporary view of democracy is currently dominant is not meant to suggest that democratic liberalism has triumphed in the thinking of political and cultural elites throughout the world. Clearly this is not the case. However, the international political appeal of liberal democratic ideas is stronger than it has been at any time since the early twentieth century.

Index

Abdildin, Serikbolsyn, 317
Abdullaev, Mukhtarkhan, 116
Abdullodzhanov, Abdumalik, 306, 308, 325, 326
Abdurazzakov, Ubaydulla, 329
Abisala, Aleksandras, 302, 303, 321
Abiyev, Safar, 313
Abkhazia (Georgia), 67, 87, 88, 153–4, 225, 310, 317
  chronology of events in (Jan. 1992–Oct. 1993), 298–310
  economic toll of, 190–1
  pact with Dniester and Gagauz regions, 230, 406n147
  religion and, 285
  Russian troops and, 170, 239–40, 254
Afghanistan, 45, 47, 100, 101, 117, 197, 223, 228, 239, 253, 254–5, 257, 283, 290, 396n91, 421n20
Agrarian Club (Moldova), 146
Agrarian Democratic Party (Moldova), 322
Agzybirlik (Unity) party (Turkmenistan), 150, 327
Akayev, Askar, 51, 148, 151–2, 219, 253–4, 255, 279, 299, 300, 302, 306, 307, 308, 309, 310, 318, 319, 387n159
  Islam and, 113, 218–19, 375n118, 386–7n135, 403n95
Akhmedov, Rustam, 329
Akhundov, Namik, 312
Aksyuchits, Viktor, 201
Alash party (Kazakhstan), 83, 151, 318, 366n124
Alimov, Rashid, 325
Aliyev, Gaidar, 154, 225, 312, 313, 388n164
Aliyev, Gulam, 329
All-Russia Association of Privatizing and Private Enterprises, 168

Allahverdiyev, Abdullah, 313
Almatov, Zakirzhon, 329
Ambartsumov, Yevgeniy, 79, 200–1, 204, 205, 229, 323, 408n25
Andrejevs, Georgs, 319, 320
Andronov, Iona, 263
Antall, Jozsef (Hungarian president), 306
anti-Semitism
  in Central Asia, 118
  in Russia, 66, 98, 202, 397n15
  in Ukraine, 37, 74
  in USSR, 13, 94
Antoci, Constantin, 321
Antyufeyev, Vladimir, 394n70
Ararktssyan, Babken, 311
Archbishop Mesters, 110
Armenia (see also Nagorno-Karabakh)
  chronology of events in (Jan. 1992–Oct. 1993), 298–310
  civil society in, 147, 154–5, 158
  currency of, 173, 392n36
  disintegration of the USSR and, 347n64
  economic issues for, 189–92, 194, 287, 389n4
  energy resources and, 175, 190
  ethnicity in, 86–8
  foreign policy priorities of, 223–8
  history's legacy and, 53–5
  military issues for, 252, 254
  nationalism in, 86–8
  1989 census data for, 339
  nuclear assets of, 264, 265
  nuclear weapons and, 279
  political culture in, 147, 154–5, 158
  religion and, 118–19, 120, 121, 285
  Russian troops and, 239, 406n1
Armenian Apostolic church, 118–19, 120
Armenian National Movement, 155
Armenian Revolutionary Federation (the Dashnaks), 227, 311

426 *Index*

Yeltsin and, 380n33
Concord for Latvia, 320, 386n123
Confederation of the Mountain Peoples
of the North Caucasus, 67
Conference on Security and Cooperation
in Europe (CSCE), 17, 216, 222,
346n55, 402n84, 404n108
Congress of Civil and Patriotic Forces, 97
Congress of Estonia, 315
Congress of Moldovan Intellectuals, 321
Congress of National Democratic Forces
(CNDF) (Ukraine), 137
Congress of People's Deputies (CPD)
(Russia), 126, 200, 203, 303, 323,
324, 325, 347n60
dissolved by Yeltsin, 325
economy and, 165, 168
party factions in, 130
Sevastopol and, 210
Yeltsin and, 122, 127–8, 130, 134–5,
136, 167, 169, 205, 275, 300, 325,
379n19
Conventional Forces in Europe (CFE)
treaty, 246, 247
Cossacks, 233
Russian, 64–5, 83, 217, 242–3, 254
Ukrainian, 38, 41, 72, 248, 353n71
Council of Baltic Sea States, 299, 306,
307
Council of Brest (1596), 102
Council of Europe, 216, 402n83
Council of the Federation (Russia), 169
Creanga, Pavel, 321, 322
Crimea, 43, 65, 66, 71–2, 73, 98, 108,
136, 138, 203, 209, 237, 248, 271,
273, 351n47, 354n81, 408n16
chronology of events in (Jan. 1992–
Oct. 1993), 298, 299, 300, 301, 302,
306, 310
Khrushchev and, 40, 411n72
Kravchuk and, 42, 210, 249
military in, 238
Rutskoy and, 34, 41
Yeltsin and, 32, 41, 63, 210, 249
Crimean War, 30, 41
Crownlands of St. Stephen, 293
Czech Republic, 211–12, 307
Czechoslovakia, 16, 406n4

Daghestan, 224
1989 census data for, 336
Danayev, Andrey, 379n27
Danilou, Henadz, 275
"Declaration on the Rights of Nationali-
ties of the Ukraine," 72, 74
Demirel, Suleyman, 227

Democratic Bloc coalition (Ukraine), 135
Democratic Center Party (Latvia),
386n123
Democratic Choice (Russia), 131
Democratic Club (Moldova), 146
Democratic Party (Turkmenistan), 150
Democratic Party of Russia, 130
Democratic Party of Tajikistan, 152, 325,
326–7, 387n139
Democratic Party of Turkmenistan, 150,
327
Democratic Party of Ukraine, 138,
400n44
Democratic Russia movement, 130, 131
Democratic Union party (Georgia), 316,
317
Denmark, 184, 402n83
Dniester region (Moldova), 42, 43, 66,
79, 109, 138, 170, 183–4, 203, 211,
217, 247, 321, 322, 386n127,
394n70, 409n31
chronology of events in (Jan. 1992–
Oct. 1993), 299, 300, 301, 302, 304,
305, 307
Cossacks in, 64–5, 217, 243
Lebed and, 146–7, 240–1, 301
pact with Abkhazia and Gagauz re-
gions, 230, 304, 406n147
Dniester Republic, *see* Dniester region
Donbas region (Ukraine), 41, 73, 97,
108, 179, 180, 328
Dostoevsky, Fyodor, 33, 350n27
Drach, Ivan, 353n80, 361n64, 362n74,
383n72
Druc, Mircea, 322
Duma (Russia), plan for 1993 elections
to, 325
Dzemyantsei, Mikalai, 314
Dzhanasayev, Bulat, 317
Dzhekshemkulov, Alikbek, 318

Eastern Europe, 10, 13, 16, 20, 40, 46,
125, 131, 144, 213, 282–3, 287, 294
Economic Cooperation Organization
(ECO), 182, 188, 308, 309
economic issues for new states, 161–3,
192–4
see also under individual country names
Edinstvo (Unity) party (Kazakhstan), 83,
151, 318
Elchibey, Abulfaz, 87, 154, 191, 192,
223, 224–5, 226, 303, 306, 313
energy resources, map of, 164
see also under individual country names
Erk (Will) party (Uzbekistan), 116, 150,
329, 375n128, 403n100
Erkin (Free) Kyrgyzstan party, 319

Sharashenidze, Levon, 317
Sharma, Shankar Dayal (Indian president), 309
Shatokhin, Sergey, 215
Shelov-Kovedayev, Fyodor, 203, 398n25
Sherimkulov, Medetkan, 318
Shevardnadze, Eduard, 20–1, 153, 191, 225–7, 240, 255, 301, 302, 304, 306, 307, 308, 310, 316, 317
Shikhmuradov, Boris, 229, 327
Shirkouskiy, Eduard, 142, 214, 313
Shishlyannikov, Aleksandr, 325, 326
shock therapy, 163, 165–8, 193, 389–90n7
Shumeyko, Vladimir, 390n12
Shumov, Vladimir, 317
Shushkevich, Stanislau, 75, 76, 141, 142, 143, 251, 275, 301, 302, 304, 307, 309, 310, 313, 314–15, 408n21
economy and, 181–2, 183
foreign policy and, 213, 214, 215, 401n61, 402n82
Siberia, 67–8, 69, 100, 407n13
Sidorova, Galina, 201
Sigua, Tengiz, 305, 317
Silas, Ivars, 319
Simac, Anatol, 321
Simonyants, Eduard, 311, 312
Sinkiang province, 12, 45, 47, 283
Siradegyan, Vanik, 311
Skokov, Yuriy, 203, 204, 323, 324, 398n23
Slavic Fund (Kyrgyzstan), 83, 152
Slezevicius, Adolfas, 306, 308, 309, 310, 320, 321
Slovakia, 211–12, 307
Snegur, Mircea, 43, 109, 217, 246, 298, 299, 301, 302, 303, 304, 305, 306, 307, 309, 321, 322, 354n89
Sobchak, Anatoliy, 21, 34, 200, 245, 247, 418n73
Social-Democrat Party (Kyrgyzstan), 152
Social Democratic party (Kazakhstan), 151, 219
Social Democratic Party (Moldova), 322
Socialist Party (Kazakhstan), 151, 219
Socialist Party of Ukraine, 138, 400n43
Soglasiye (Accord) Club (Moldova), 146
Solovyov, Sergey, 350n27
Solzhenitsyn, Aleksandr, 66, 202
South Korea, 187, 193, 197, 283
South Ossetia, *see* Ossetia
Stalin, 11–13, 55, 80, 344n23, n31
collectivization and, 37, 38–9, 40, 48, 356n127

creation of Central Asian republics and, 52–3
historiography and, 32, 33, 36–7, 49
religion and, 94, 99, 104, 111, 368n19
repression of subject populations and, 41, 42, 47, 291
Stankevich, Sergey, 64, 200, 203, 204, 269
Starovoytova, Galina, 203, 398n25
START-I treaty, 260–2, 263, 267–8, 269, 271, 272, 274, 275, 278, 280, 300, 302, 303, 305, 308, 309
START-II treaty, 262–3, 268–9, 301, 304, 415n9
Stepashin, Sergey, 212, 323
Sterligov, Aleksandr, 61, 202
strategic arms reduction treaty, *see* START-I treaty; START-II treaty
Subanov, Myrzakan, 318, 319
Subtelny, Orest, 353n70
Suchocka, Hanna, 401n56
Suleymenov, Nizami, 154
Suleymanov, Olzhas, 50
Suleymanov, Tuleutai, 317
Sultalinov, Abdybek, 318
Supreme Soviet (Belarus), 142
Supreme Soviet (Russia), 126, 135, 179, 204–5, 207, 210, 241, 323, 324, 325, 347n60
Surkov, Aleksey, 49, 418n73
Sweden, 6, 184, 305, 402n83
Symonenko, Valentin, 178, 328
Syria, 112, 283

Taiwan, 197
Tajikistan
chronology of events in (Jan. 1992–Oct. 1993), 299–310
civil society in, 149–53, 155–7
civil war in, 84, 86, 101, 114, 152–3, 187, 221–2, 223
currency of, 174, 188
economic issues for, 181, 186–9, 389n4
energy resources and, 175, 186, 187
ethnicity in, 80–6, 364–5n108
foreign policy priorities of, 218–23
history's legacy and, 45–53
military issues for, 252–5
nationalism and, 80–6, 364n105
1989 census data for, 340
nuclear assets of, 265
political culture in, 147–53, 155–7, 387n139
religion and, 111–18, 121
Russian troops in, 406n1
Takhmazov, Fakhreddin, 313